MOUNTAIN GUIDE

12TH EDITION

**AMC'S QUINTESSENTIAL GUIDE TO
THE HIKING TRAILS OF MAINE**
FEATURING BAXTER STATE PARK AND ACADIA NATIONAL PARK

Compiled and edited by
Carey Michael Kish

Appalachian Mountain Club Books
Boston, Massachusetts

AMC is a nonprofit organization, and sales of AMC Books fund our mission of protecting the Northeast outdoors. If you appreciate our efforts and would like to become a member or make a donation to AMC, visit outdoors.org, call 800-372-1758, or contact us at Appalachian Mountain Club, 10 City Square, Boston, MA 02129.

outdoors.org/books-maps

Distributed by National Book Network

Front cover photograph of a hiker on the Bigelow Range © Scott Disnard

Back cover photograph of a hiker on Katahdin © Chris Shane

Cartography by Larry Garland © Appalachian Mountain Club

Cover design by Katie Metz

Interior design by Abigail Coyle

ISBN 978-1-62842-156-9

ISSN 1544-3604

The paper used in this publication meets the minimum requirements of the American National Standard for Information Sciences-Permanence of Paper for Printed Library Materials, ANSI Z39.48-1984.

Outdoor recreation activities by their very nature are potentially hazardous. This book is not a substitute for good personal judgment and training in outdoor skills. Due to changes in conditions, use of the information in this book is at the sole risk of the user. The authors and the Appalachian Mountain Club assume no liability for accidents happening to, or injuries sustained by, readers who engage in the activities described in this book.

Interior pages and cover are printed on responsibly harvested paper stock certified by The Forest Stewardship Council®, an independent auditor of responsible forestry practices. Printed in the United States of America, using vegetable-based inks.
5 4 3 2 1   23 24 25 26 27 28

EDITIONS OF THE
MAINE MOUNTAIN GUIDE

First Edition	1961	Seventh Edition	1993
Second Edition	1968	Eighth Edition	1999
Third Edition	1971	Ninth Edition	2005
Fourth Edition	1976	Tenth Edition	2012
Fifth Edition	1985	Eleventh Edition	2018
Sixth Edition	1988	Twelfth Edition	2023

KEY TO LOCATOR MAPS

The numbers in the boxes below and on the locator maps at the beginning of each section indicate which pull-out map or maps cover that section. Trail descriptions are listed by the section in which the trailhead is located; parts of a trail may lie in another section or sections.

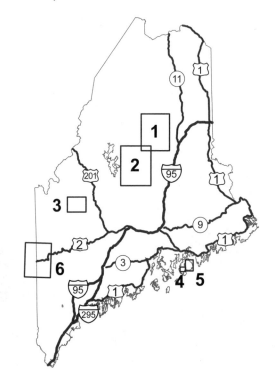

Map 1: Baxter State Park–Katahdin Woods and Waters National Monument

Map 2: 100-Mile Wilderness

Map 3: Bigelow Range

Map 4: Western Mt. Desert Island

Map 5: Eastern Mt. Desert Island

Map 6: Mahoosuc Range–Evans Notch

CONTENTS

MAP INDEX

IN-TEXT MAPS

PULL-OUT MAPS

KEY TO HIKING ICONS

Distance

Elevation gain

Time

Waterfall

Pond, stream, spring, or other water feature

Alpine zone (an ecological zone characterized by the lack of trees; ground cover and plants are typical of arctic environments)

Exposed ledges (trail crosses an exposed ledge—a consideration in severe weather or in wet or icy conditions; hikes that end at a scenic ledge but do not cross an exposed ledge en route are not marked with this icon)

Steep or difficult terrain

Difficult brook crossings

Shelter or hut

Designated tentsite

Wilderness Area (federally designated areas of restricted human activity, with specific rules and regulations)

Kid-friendly

Dog-friendly

Universally accessible (fully or partially)

Snowshoeing

Cross-country skiing

Scenic views

Fire/observation tower (although some are more stable than others, all towers should be considered climb-at-your-own-risk)

Fee

Day use/picnic area

Swimming

Fishing

Visitor center

KEY TO MAP ICONS

Conservation land (fee)

Conservation easement

Entrance or ranger station

Lodge, hut, cabin

Campground

Shelter

Parking

Day use area

Tentsite

Summit

4,000-Footer

Gate

Fire/observation tower

Highway

Improved road

Unimproved road

Trail

Mountain bike trail

Bike path

Appalachian Trail

ABBREVIATIONS AND ACRONYMS

The following abbreviations and acronyms are used in this book.

7LA 7 Lakes Alliance

100MW 100-Mile Wilderness

ALL Attean Lake Lodge

AMC Appalachian Mountain Club

ANP Acadia National Park

AT Appalachian Trail

ATC Appalachian Trail Conservancy

ATV all-terrain vehicle

Ave. Avenue

AWW Allagash Wilderness Waterway

BHHT Blue Hill Heritage Trust

BKP Bingham's Kennebec Purchase

BPP Bingham's Penobscot Purchase

BSP Baxter State Park

CC City of Calais

CCA Clifton Climbers Alliance

CG Campground

CMLT Coastal Mountains Land Trust

CMNEMBA Central Maine New England Mountain Bike Association

CMP Central Maine Power

COB Cobscook Shores

CS campsite

CTA Chatham Trails Association

CV Town of Carrabassett Valley

DBT Debsconeag Backcountry Trail

DCC Downeast Coastal Conservancy

Dept. Department

DIFW Maine Department of Inland Fisheries and Wildlife

DLCF Downeast Lakes Community Forest

DLLT Downeast Lakes Land Trust

DLWA Debsconeag Lakes Wilderness Area

Dr. Drive

ED Eastern Division

FBC Frenchman Bay Conservancy

FOHIS Friends of Holbrook Island Sanctuary

FR Forest Route

FSHT Francis Small Heritage Trust

ft. foot, feet

GCT Great Circle Trail

GHP Georges Highland Path

GIS Geographic Information Systems

GLLT Greater Lovell Land Trust

GLWMA Gene Letourneau (Frye Mtn.) Wildlife Management Area

GPMCT Great Pond Mountain Conservation Trust

GPS Global Positioning System

GRLT Georges River Land Trust

GWRLT Great Works Regional Land Trust

HA Hebron Academy

HMLT Hedgehog Mountain Land Trust

HPA High Peaks Alliance

hr. hour(s)

HST Hills to Sea Trail

HSTC Hills to Sea Trail Coalition

IAT International Appalachian Trail

IHT Island Heritage Trust

IWT Inland Woods + Trails

jct. junction

KAC Katahdin Area Council

KAWW Katahdin Woods and Waters National Monument

KELT Kennebec Estuary Land Trust

KLT Kennebec Land Trust

LELT Loon Echo Land Trust

LGP Land & Garden Preserve

LHFT Libby Hill Forest Trails

Ln. Lane

LP loop
MA Maine Audubon
MACP Mount Agamenticus Conservation Program
MATC Maine Appalachian Trail Club
MATVR Moosehead ATV Riders
MBPL Maine Bureau of Parks and Lands
MCAP Maine Civil Air Patrol
MCC Midcoast Conservancy
MCHT Maine Coast Heritage Trust
MD Middle Division
MDI Mount Desert Island
ME Maine
MECC Maine Conservation Corps
MFS Maine Forest Service
MHT Maine Huts & Trails
mi. mile(s)
min. minute
MLT Mahoosuc Land Trust
MNWR Moosehorn National Wildlife Refuge
MOFGA Maine Organic Farmers and Gardeners Association
MRSC Moosehead Riders Snowmobile Club
Mt. Mount
MTF Maine Trail Finder
Mtn. Mountain
MWI Maine Woods Initiative
ND Northern Division
NEFC New England Forestry Consultants
NFTM no formal trail maintainer
NH New Hampshire
NHVIS Northeast Harbor Village Improvement Society
NMW North Maine Woods
NPS National Park Service
NWP North of Waldo Patent
OW one way
PC Plum Creek
PL Public Land(s)
R Range
Rd. Road

RMT Round the Mountain Trail
RR Railroad
RRCT Royal River Conservation Trust
RT round trip
RWD Rumford Water District
SCT Schoodic Connector Trail
SD Southern Division
SFMA Scientific Forest Management Area
SIA Sentiers International des Appalaches
sq. square
St. Street
T Township
TCH Town of Castle Hill
TMNK trail maintainer not known
TNC The Nature Conservancy
TOF Town of Freeport
TOHCC Town of Hiram Conservation Committee
TOL Town of Leeds
TOS Town of Sebago
TOW Town of Waterford
TRAC Trails for Rangeley Area Coalition
US United States
USFS United States Forest Service
USFWS United States Fish & Wildlife Service
USGS United States Geological Survey
USVLT Upper Saco Valley Land Trust
WBPC West Branch Pond Camps
WCC Woodstock Conservation Commission
WELS West of the Easterly Line of the State
WFLT Western Foothills Land Trust
WKR West of Kennebec River
WMA Wildlife Management Area
WMNF White Mountain National Forest
yd. yard(s)

FOREWORD

This hiker has been tramping the woods and mountains of Maine for going on five decades, since moving to the state in 1971 at the age of 13.

As a kid, I had a curiosity for any patch of woods, whether behind a neighbor's house or beyond the ball field fence. Blazing trails into those dark and mysterious places always meant great adventure, and my friends and I would emerge hours later, dirty from head to toe with cuts and scratches and insect bites and smiles a mile wide. Living in Maine, where big woods were seemingly everywhere, certainly changed the scale of these childhood explorations. When we had thoroughly covered and mentally mapped the forests and trails around Bangor as far as our feet and bikes could take us, my adventurous group of pals moved on to hitchhiking to the hills east of town and then south to the mountains of Acadia. And when my dad finally took me up to Baxter State Park and I climbed Katahdin, I might as well have been standing atop Mt. Everest, such was the elation. I was irrevocably hooked on hiking.

I bought my first *Maine Mountain Guide* in 1976 and, with that, realized the amazing wealth of mountains and trails across the state. I knew I had to hike them all. I was so inspired I decided to hike the entire Appalachian Trail, from Springer Mtn. in Georgia to Katahdin, a life-changing trek I completed in 1977 (and again in 2015). Ever since then, I've been seeking out the forested trails and craggy summits of our beautiful state of Maine, striving to hike all the trails in the guide. Given the explosion of trail building across the state in recent years, that task has certainly gotten a lot tougher. I'm almost there (12 peaks to go), but perhaps your work (fun!) has just begun.

The 12th edition of this book captures and describes a host of these new trails and summits for your hiking pleasure, plus all the old favorites. Open it wide, thumb through the pages, scribble some notes, pore over the maps, dream a little, and plan your next adventure or two. So many wild and scenic natural places in Maine await your footsteps, your eyes and ears, and the company of your family and friends. Start the journey with this guide and then go savor time well spent in the Maine woods. Hope to see you on the trail. And if not, let me know how it goes.

Carey Michael Kish
Mt. Desert Island, Maine
March 1, 2023

ACKNOWLEDGMENTS

The *Maine Mountain Guide* is the product of the hard work and dedication of many people, including those who contributed in so many ways, large and small, to the eleven previous editions of the book since its inception in 1961. You helped build the foundation for this guide, and as editor for the last three editions, I cannot thank you all enough. I am honored to follow in your footsteps and proud to carry on with this important outdoor tradition.

Huge thanks go to my wife and favorite trail companion, Fran Leyman, for accompanying me on many of the hundreds of trails that required hiking over the last several years; for putting up with my incessant note taking, GPS fiddling, and picture taking; for keeping the home fires burning, so to speak, while I traipsed remote trails and roads all over Maine for long weeks at a time; and for kindly ignoring the enormous mess I made of our house during the research and writing of this book. Fran, you're an angel, and I love you.

Sincere thanks are due to the great staff at AMC Books. Tim Mudie, senior books editor, provided a wealth of advice, guidance, and support throughout the lengthy writing and editing process; and Abigail Coyle, senior production manager, shepherded the book through the production process with aplomb. Thanks as well to Lenore Howard for her excellent and thorough copyedit. Serious appreciation is also due to Larry Garland, AMC's cartographer, for the outstanding color and black-and-white maps that accompany this guide; they are not only eminently useful but works of art, in my humble opinion. Rob Burbank, former AMC public affairs director, got me started on this guidebook adventure back in 2010; thanks always, my friend.

A plethora of heartfelt thanks goes out to so many people across Maine, all those dedicated and caring individuals who gave much-needed assistance in the shaping of this guide: carefully reviewing trail descriptions and other sections of the text and offering valuable comment; identifying new trails for inclusion, providing maps, and drafting new trail descriptions; and hitting the trail in earnest and gathering firsthand information in the field. This guide could not have been improved and expanded without your help and encouragement.

Steve Smith and Ken MacGray are the editors extraordinaire of AMC's *White Mountain Guide*. For this edition, Section Five: Mahoosuc Range and Grafton Notch and Section Six: White Mountain National Forest and Evans Notch were adapted from their venerable guidebook. They are also responsible for a sizable chunk of the introductory content, which was first adapted for the 10th edition of this guide during its major reformatting and has since been revised and expanded. Many thanks, Steve and Ken, for your hard work and your sage advice and support.

For the 10th edition of the *Maine Mountain Guide*, the Acadia National Park trail descriptions were adapted from *Discover Acadia National Park* (AMC Books, 2010, now revised as *Outdoor Adventures: Acadia National Park* (AMC Books, 2017) by Jerry and Marcy Monkman. Thank you for that good start! Since that time, I've been able to field-check almost every ANP trail on Mt. Desert Island, Schoodic Peninsula, and Isle au Haut (easy and fun when you live next to the park) to revise and expand the descriptions for this edition of the guide.

The description of the International Appalachian Trail through Katahdin Woods and Waters National Monument and on Mars Hill was first adapted from the great work of the Maine Chapter of the IAT, and I've since had the pleasure to walk those paths myself with field notebook in hand. Thanks, always, to Dick Anderson, Don Hudson, and the many other visionaries of the IAT.

The Kennebec Highlands trail descriptions were first provided by Pete Kalin of the Belgrade Regional Conservation Alliance (now the 7 Lakes Alliance) in 2017. I've since been able to visit most of those trails for a firsthand look around, adapting figures and words as needed. Thanks, Pete, and Laura Rose Day, for your work.

Dan Hester, who almost single-handedly helped preserve Mt. Cutler in Hiram, penned and updated the descriptions for the trails on the mountain for the last two editions of this guide. Dan has once again come through with updated and expanded trail descriptions for the land now preserved as Mt. Cutler Park and Conservation Area. Thank you, my friend.

Steve McPike is one of the big champions behind the trails at Libby Hill Forest Recreation Area in Gray, and has once again crafted a wonderful description for hikers wishing to explore those lovely trails.

So many individuals from Maine's incredible community of conservation organizations, land trusts, environmental groups, trail clubs, trail advocates, outdoor recreation groups, state and federal agencies, and other friends of Maine trails provided invaluable information, advice, support, and encouragement. These include Steve Tatko, Jenny Ward, Phil Coyne, Heather Clish, Eliza Townsend, Sam Jamke, Charlene Fearnley, the Appalachian Mountain Club; Josie Holden, Attean Lake Lodge; Jessie Perkins, Bethel Conservation Commission; Savage Bloomer; George Fields, Blue Hill Heritage Trust; R. "Bud" Hoffses, Boy Scouts of America, Katahdin Area Council; Polly Jones, Coastal Mountains Land Trust; Charlie Howes, Cobscook Shores; Greg Shute and Lynne Flacus, Chewonki Foundation; Larry Stifler, Mary McFadden, Bruce Barrett, Crooked River Headwaters; Cathy

Lookabaugh, Colin Brown, Downeast Coastal Conservancy; David Montague, Susan Bard, Downeast Lakes Land Trust; Kristen Hoffman, Forest Society of Maine; Kayla Small, Ellie Ezekiel, Frenchman Bay Conservancy; Stephanie Clement, Friends of Acadia; Matt Bonner, Laura Miller, Georges River Land Trust; Landon Fake, Carl Derian, Roger Greene, Great Pond Mtn. Conservation Trust; Rhyan Paquereau, Greater Lovell Land Trust; Jill Crosbie, Brenna Crothers, Donovan Spaulding, Tom Gilmore, Great Works Regional Land Trust; Brent West, High Peaks Alliance; Bill Jarvis, Hilton Timberlands; Gabe Perkins; Inland Woods + Trails; Theresa Kerchner, Tyler Kennison, Jean-Luc Theriault, Kennebec Land Trust; Sarah Crawford, LandVest; Chris Stevenson, Land & Garden Preserve; Jon Evans, Loon Echo Land Trust; Barbara Murphy, John Wohley, Lizz Peacock, Bonnie Pooley, Larry Ely, Mahoosuc Land Trust; Ron Tebbetts, Maine Appalachian Trail Club; Simon Rucker, Maine Appalachian Trail Land Trust; Bill Cobb, Maine Chapter, Forest Fire Lookout Association; Jacek Makowski; Kyle Winslow, Jeff Romano, Jane Arbuckle, Maine Coast Heritage Trust; Buck O'Herin, Chris Shorn, Ann Reed, Midcoast Conservancy; Mountain View Campground, Dixfield; Robin Kerr, Mt. Agamenticus Conservation Program; Greg Seamans, New England Forestry Consultants; Tom Pelletier at North Maine Woods and his great staff of gatekeepers: Jodi, Chris, Tina, Jean and Joel Cyr, Katie Shields; Julie Renaud Evans, Isabella Ronson, Northern Forest Center; Chuck Loring, Faye Lawson, Penobscot Nation; David Miller, Shelby Rousseau, Ian Adelman, Rangeley Lakes Heritage Trust; Alan Stearns, Royal River Conservation Trust; Glen Horne, Spencer Pond Camps; Ethan Austin, Sugarloaf; Dan Grenier, Robbie Smith, Nancy Sferra, The Nature Conservancy, Maine Field Office; Dave Cota, Sacha Gillespie, Town of Carrabassett Valley; Burt Adelman, Trails for Rangeley Area Coalition; Abby King, Upper Saco Valley Land Trust; Lee Dassler, Western Foothills Land Trust; Jane Chandler, Marcel Polak, Vern Maxfield, Woodstock Conservation Committee; Rex Turner, Vern Labbe, Jay Hall, Doug Reed, Jim Britt, Maine Bureau of Parks and Lands; Jay Young, Alissa Lutz, Allagash Wilderness Waterway; Charles Cannon, Holbrook Island Sanctuary; Steve Dunham, Maine Dept. of Inland Fisheries and Wildlife. Thanks to Dan Rinard and Brennan Turner from Baxter State Park for all your help and your great trail crews on the Dudley Trail: Brennan and Nathan Cote, Ben Weber, Dawson McKenney, and Zach Bailey. From the US Dept. of the Interior, National Park Service: Charlie Jacobi, Gary Stellpflug, and John Kelly of Acadia National Park; Jeanne Roy, Katahdin Woods and Waters National Monument. Thanks also to Matt Jacobs, American Forest Management; Ruthie Grover, Bethel Village Motel; Lori Boynton Cormier, Big Moose Inn, Cabins & Campground; Carrier Timberlands;

Tom Bell, North Woods Trading Post; the great staff at Northern Outdoors in The Forks; and the friendly folks at Cathedral Pines CG in Eustis.

Sincere thanks to my many fun trail companions, whether for a few minutes or a few days: Dana and Janet Thurston, Bruce Hyman, Carl Eppich, Phil DiPierro, John Wuestneck, Dave Benham, Kathy Kinch, Bonnie Farrand, Donna and Jeff Tippett, Melie Guzek, Gina Grant, Jo Aldrich, Jordan Labbe, Sarah Hunter, Denise Anderson, Dolores Burns, Willow Sherwood, Jenny Ward, Cathy Sweetser, Constance Mensink, William McArtor, Ken Saindon, Kirk Cratty, Alan Look, Tobin Dominick, Tom Tanner, John and Rachel Tanner, Shelley Darling, Rick Bennett, Amy Patenaude, Charlie Gunn, Mel Boucher, Jason Pare, Steve Lyons, Merrie Eley, Bob Laney, Andy and Becky Walsh, Scott and Melissa Wels, Marc Moore, Bob and Joan Westfall, Robin Zinchuk, Matt Zinchuk, Robin Gorrill, Mike Ewing, Michael Starks and Gizmo; Gary and Heidi Noyce, Ron and Meg Logan, Stephen Brezinski, Bennett, Owen, and Katie Kaufman. You were great company; let's go hiking again soon!

Thank you to many other members of Maine's hiking community who made important contributions—from recommendations to boots-on-the-ground trail miles and field notes—for this guide: Bill Spach, Susy Kist, Phil Coyne, Brian Alexander, Greg Westrich, Kathy Littlefield, Sam Lemaire, Missy and Dan Herrick, Aislinn Sarnacki, Betta Stothart, Paul-William Gagnon, Deanna Burtchell, Billy Barker, P. J. Hitchcock, Alain Ouellette, Eric and Elaine Hendrickson, Tim Caverly, Steve Krasinski, Paul Schumacher, Rebecca Goldfine, Jenny Galusha, Ted Eliot, Jody Brinser, Judy Tammaro, Chris Keene, Amy Niemczura-Sowa, Tom Lawton, Ron and Marianne Maliga, Sam Shirley, Samantha Horn, Dan Feldman, Jay Baxter, Allison Beeb Adams, Malcolm Hunter, Scott Walton, Gene Roy, Nicole Belanger, Val Belanger, Mark Leathers, John Gallagher, Earl Brechlin, Shawn Keeley, Paul Sannicandro, Chris Drew, Ashley Pillsbury. Steve Spencer: your name and Maine trails will always appear together in my mind's eye; thank you.

References consulted in preparing and revising the introductory text include *A Geography of Maine* (Eldred Rolfe, University of Maine-Farmington, 1981), *Forest Trees of Maine* (Maine Forest Service, 2008), *Surficial Geologic History of Maine* (Maine Geological Survey, 2005), and *Bedrock Geologic History of Maine* (Maine Geological Survey, Robert G. Marvinney, 2012).

This 12th edition is dedicated to the trail maintainers and trail builders throughout Maine, and in particular to the incredible Baxter State Park trail crews, who over the past 10 years have accomplished three enormous relocation projects, one on Mt. OJI and two on Katahdin—Abol Trail and Dudley Trail. Absolutely amazing work. Thank you!

HOW TO USE THIS BOOK

This book aims to provide complete coverage of hiking trails in Maine's mountains, which are scattered across a large and geographically diverse area, ranging from the rockbound coast to the inland hills to the remote mountains of the northern interior. Trails on 330 mountains and hills are described, from Mt. Agamenticus in the southwestern corner of the state to Deboullie Mtn. and Black Mtn. in northern Aroostook County, and from Aziscohos Mtn. in northwestern Maine near the New Hampshire border to Klondike Mtn. in Lubec, not far from the easternmost point in Maine and the international border with New Brunswick, Canada.

The trails are segmented into 12 geographic regions. Four sections— Southwestern Maine, Midcoast, Acadia National Park, and Downeast— describe mountains near the coast, as well as some of the inland hills. The Southwestern Maine section includes all of York County and Cumberland County and the southern part of Oxford County. The Midcoast section includes the entirety of Waldo County, Knox County, Lincoln County, and Sagadahoc County. The Acadia National Park section covers Mt. Desert Island and Schoodic Peninsula in Hancock County and Isle au Haut in Knox County. The Downeast section covers all of Hancock County (except for Acadia National Park) and Washington County.

In the southern interior of Maine, the Oxford Hills and White Mountain Foothills section stretches westward from the Androscoggin River to the section covering the Maine portion of the White Mountain National Forest near the New Hampshire border, in the vicinity of Evans Notch. To the north, the rugged summits of the Mahoosuc Range encompass the deep glacial valley of Grafton Notch. Northeast from there are the high peaks of the Longfellow Mountains and the Appalachian Trail corridor, which are described in Western Lakes and Mountains, as well as in the section on the 100-Mile Wilderness and Moosehead Lake. This mountainous chain culminates in Katahdin and a jumble of wilderness summits within the boundaries of Baxter State Park. East of the park are the wild and rugged lands of Katahdin Woods and Waters National Monument. North and northeast of the park are the vast forestlands and scattered mountains of Aroostook County. The mountain character of the Kennebec River valley and Moose River valley ranges from scattered low hills in the south to remote high peaks near the Canadian border in the north.

Each section begins with a list of the major mountains in that region, as well as any significant public or private land preserves. Next, an introduction describes the geography of the region, its boundaries, the dominant natural features, and the general location of the mountains covered. An overview of the major roads follows, describing in general terms the access to the various trailheads. Each introduction also includes options for public and private roadside and backcountry camping.

SUGGESTED HIKES

At the beginning of each section is a list of suggested hikes, selected to provide hikers with numerous options for easy, moderate, and strenuous routes within the given region. Criteria can vary from trail to trail, but in general, an easy hike may have little to no elevation gain, covers a relatively short distance, and can be completed in several hours or less. A moderate hike can take as long as half a day and covers a longer distance, often with more elevation gain. A strenuous hike requires a full day of 6 to 8 hours, with significant mileage and/or elevation gain. The icons refer to features of note that hikers will encounter (see Key to Hiking Icons, p. vii). The numbers that follow indicate total distance, elevation gain, and time required. When choosing a trail, hikers should consider mileage, elevation gain, time required, available daylight, and difficulty of the terrain, as well as the experience, physical fitness, goals, and size of the group. For more information on planning a group trip, see *AMC's Mountain Skills Manual* by Christian Bisson and Jamie Hannon (AMC Books, 2017).

TRAIL DESCRIPTIONS

Trail descriptions are segmented by the mountains on which the trails are found, although some trails are not associated with a mountain. Each trail is described individually, in the most commonly traveled direction—usually ascending. When a hike uses a combination of trails, readers may need to consult several descriptions. In the parenthetical next to the trail name, a reference to a map or maps that correspond to the trail is given. This list of maps may name the AMC in-text map or pull-out map, a US Geological Survey quad, *Maine Atlas and Gazetteer* road map(s), Maine Appalachian Trail Club map, a land management agency map available in print or online, or any combination thereof that best covers that particular trail. The acronym for the organization responsible for maintaining the trail is given at the beginning of each description.

A typical trail description first provides an overview of the trail, including its origin and destination and, if notable, its general character (gradient, roughness, etc.), and perhaps the view to be seen from the summit. Driving directions to the trailhead are covered, where appropriate. This is followed by concise, turn-by-turn directions for hiking the trail. The description includes important features, such as trail junctions, stream crossings, viewpoints, summits, and any significant difficulties. *Always check AMC's Books and Maps page online and scroll down to Book Updates for a list of the most recent trail closures, relocations, and other changes before you head out: outdoors.org/resources/books-and-maps.*

DISTANCES, TIMES, AND ELEVATIONS

The summary table above the trail description lists the distances, times, and elevation gains for the trail(s), which are cumulative from the starting point at the head of the table.

Most of the trails in this guide have been measured using GPS. Minor inconsistencies sometimes occur when measured distances are rounded, and the distances given may differ from posted trail signs and land management maps.

Elevations, when they are precisely known, are indicated. Otherwise, elevations are estimated to the nearest 50-ft. contour. In some places, such as where several minor ups and downs occur, these figures are only roughly accurate. USGS maps are the basis for these calculations.

Summit elevations in this edition have been revised based on recently released LiDAR data, as interpreted by AMC cartographer Larry Garland. LiDAR (Light Detection and Ranging) uses laser light pulses from airborne sensors to collect very dense and accurate information about surface characteristics of a regional landscape. Current technology allows LiDAR measurements to be accurate to approximately 4 in. of elevation. With a nominal pulse density of 2 or more laser pulses per square meter, the data are aggregated to produce an assigned elevation for ground areas that are typically less than a square meter in size. Waveform and intensity values of each laser-pulse return can differentiate between vegetation, buildings, cars, water, and bare earth; summit elevations used in this guide are based on bare earth values.

Most of the LiDAR-derived summit elevations are within 20 ft. of pre-LiDAR elevations—a typical contour line on a topographic map. Thus, estimated hiking times and elevation gains are not significantly affected by these revisions. Most trail junctions and non-summit elevations (for example, viewpoints, cols, and other features) have not been reevaluated in this edition. Elevations are estimated as closely as possible when not given precisely by USGS source maps or updated LiDAR data.

No reliable method exists for predicting how much time a particular hiker or group of hikers will take to complete a hike on a specific day, because many factors influence the speed of an individual or group. To give hikers a basis for planning, estimated times have been calculated in this book using the formula of 30 min. for each mile of distance and 30 min. for each 1,000 ft. of climbing. These are known as "book times." These estimated time allowances do not include snack or lunch stops, scenery appreciation, or rest breaks. Some parties may require more time, and others may need less. Special factors, such as stream crossings, steep slopes, rough footing, heavy packs, fatigue, and weather conditions, can affect trail times. For example, a 6-mi. hike on easy terrain will require less effort, though perhaps more time, than a 3-mi. hike over rough ground with 1,500 ft. of elevation gain. The given times have not been adjusted for the difficulties of specific trails, so hikers should plan accordingly, always leaving a good margin for safety. Average descent times can vary even more, based on such factors as agility and the condition of a hiker's knees. In winter, times can be even less predictable; on a snow-packed trail, travel may be faster than in summer, while in deep, untracked snow with heavy backpacks, the time may double or triple the summer estimate.

Time is given as hours and minutes, so 1:30 should be read as "one hour and thirty minutes."

The following examples demonstrate how to read the information in the summary table at the beginning of each trail description.

BURNT MTN. TRAIL (MAP 1: B2)			
From Burnt Mtn. Picnic Area (1,086 ft.) to:			
Burnt Mtn. summit (1,796 ft.)	1.3 mi.	710 ft.	1:00
elevation	*distance*	*elevation gain (reverse elevation gain)*	*time*

For Burnt Mtn. Trail, refer to Map 1 included with this guide. To locate the trail on the map, use the grid references on the left (letters) and top (numbers) edges. This trail is found at the intersection of B and 2. The starting point is Burnt Mtn. Picnic Area at an elevation of 1,086 ft. The distance covered to summit Burnt Mtn. at 1,796 ft. is 1.3 mi., the elevation gain between trailhead and summit is 710 ft., and the hike will take an estimated time of 1 hour.

When no AMC map reference is listed in the table, the trail is not covered by any of the maps provided with this guide. In such cases, please refer to the summary table for the name of the appropriate map(s) for the trail, as in this example:

DANIEL BROWN TRAIL (USGS NORWAY QUAD, MTF MT. TIRE'M MAP, GAZETTEER MAP 10)			
From Plummer Hill Rd. (550 ft.) to:			
Mt. Tire'm summit (1,102 ft.)	0.6 mi.	552 ft.	0:35
elevation	*distance*	*elevation gain (reverse elevation gain)*	*time*

Because there is no AMC map for Daniel Brown Trail, hikers should consult the USGS Norway quad (quadrangle map), the Maine Trail Finder Mt. Tire'm map, and Map 10 of the *Maine Atlas and Gazetteer.*

MAPS AND NAVIGATION

This guide features two folded map sheets that contain 6 full-color maps covering many of Maine's popular hiking areas. The full set of maps consists of Map 1: Baxter State Park–Katahdin Woods and Waters National Monument; Map 2: 100-Mile Wilderness; Map 3: Bigelow Range; Map 4: Western Mt. Desert Island; Map 5: Eastern Mt. Desert Island; and Map 6: Mahoosuc Range–Evans Notch. These high-quality maps, produced using GPS and GIS technology, indicate a range of data useful to the hiker, including trails, trail segment mileage, tentsites, shelters and campsites, campgrounds, public land ownership, parking areas, visitor centers and ranger stations, fire towers, and day-use areas. Each map uses a contour interval of 100 ft. The scales vary from map to map, as does the magnetic declination, which in Maine ranges from 14.25 to 16.5 degrees west of true north. Latitude and longitude coordinates and Universal Transverse Mercator grid coordinates are included on the maps and allow their use with a handheld GPS unit. Contact information pertinent to the maps is also included.

A series of handy black-and-white maps covering a variety of trail networks are also provided within the text of this guide. Please refer to the Map Index on p. vi for a complete list.

Given the geographic distribution of mountains and hiking trails in Maine, not every trail described appears on the maps provided. For the areas not covered, please refer to the USGS 7.5-minute (1:24,000-scale) quadrangle map listed in the trail summary. Although the topographic quality of these maps is excellent, be aware that some trails may not be accurately depicted or may not appear at all. USGS maps are available from local retailers and outdoor shops or directly from USGS (online at store. usgs.gov, where there is also a very helpful map locator tool), 888-ASK-USGS, and usgsstore@usgs.gov. Index maps showing the available USGS quads in any state and the informative pamphlet *Topographic Maps* are available free from USGS upon request. USGS quads for all of New England are also available through various online sources.

Many state parks, land trusts, and other conservation and recreation organizations have useful trail maps available online and/or in print at trailheads. Where such maps are available, they are mentioned in the trail description. Appendix A: Helpful Information and Contacts (p. 600) offers more information on land management and other agencies.

References to the appropriate *Maine Atlas and Gazetteer* map are included with each trail description, except for those trails covered by the maps included in the guide. The atlas is a useful (and sometimes indispensable) tool for trip planning and navigation to the trailhead, indicating back roads, dirt roads, some trails and trailheads, elevation contours, lakes and streams, public lands, land use cover, and boat ramps. Garmin, the Swiss GPS firm, purchased the atlas's Maine publisher, DeLorme, in 2016 and has continued to produce the venerable publication, which is available at many retail and online locations, including garmin.com/en-US/c/delorme-atlas-gazetteer.

This book describes many of the mountain peaks along the AT in Maine, and readers may find *The Official Appalachian Trail Guide to Maine* (Maine Appalachian Trail Club, 2021) to be a helpful companion guide. It contains seven topographic and profile maps that cover the 282-mile trail route from Katahdin to the New Hampshire state line, plus numerous side trails. The guidebook and maps are available at outdoor retailers and many bookstores or from MATC online at matc.org.

For an excellent primer on map and compass use, GPS use, and other navigation skills, consult *AMC's Mountain Skills Manual* by Christian Bisson and Jamie Hannon (AMC Books, 2017).

INTRODUCTION

For this 12th edition of the *Maine Mountain Guide*, we have revised, updated, and expanded many existing trail descriptions, and we have added 90 new trails, thereby increasing the already wide variety of hiking possibilities available for every interest and ability level. In all, more than 700 trails are described on 330 mountains, a hiking bounty totaling more than 1,600 mi. and ranging from easy woodland walks to moderate hill climbs to strenuous mountain traverses. A series of detailed topographic pull-out maps highlighting seven popular hiking destinations as well as 26 topographic in-text maps complement the hike descriptions. We hope that readers will find the guide and maps to be a helpful companion, leading to many days of outdoor pleasure and healthful exercise on the trails through the scenic woods and mountains of Maine.

MAINE'S PUBLIC AND PRIVATE LANDS

The forestland of Maine covers an estimated 17.6 million acres, or about 89.1 percent of the state, making it the most heavily forested state in the United States. Large tracts of undeveloped forestland, much of it commercial timberland, are in northern, western, and eastern Maine. In other parts of the United States, particularly in the west, such large blocks of land are usually publicly owned and managed by the federal government—primarily the USFS or Bureau of Land Management (BLM). In Maine, however, just 9.6 percent of the forestland, or about 1.7 million acres, is publicly owned, while Native American tribes own 1.3 percent, or about 230,000 acres. The remaining bulk of the forestland, about 15.7 million acres, is privately held by large timberland owner groups, which include the forest products industry, corporate investors, families, and other miscellaneous parties.

The state of Maine owns more than 1 million acres of land. This includes 36 state parks totaling 67,000 acres, 156 public lands totaling 630,000 acres, and 15 historical sites totaling 276 acres. These state lands are managed by the Maine Dept. of Agriculture, Conservation, and Forestry, Bureau of Parks and Lands. The 210,000-acre Baxter State Park is administered as a separate entity by the BSP Authority, which consists of the Maine attorney general, the director of the Maine Forest Service, and the commissioner of the Maine Dept. of Inland Fisheries and Wildlife. DIFW manages 100,000 acres of land as wildlife management areas.

The federal government owns about 275,000 acres of land in Maine. This includes a 50,000-acre section of the White Mountain National Forest in and around Evans Notch in western Maine; 37,700 acres in Acadia National Park on Mt. Desert Island, Schoodic Peninsula, Isle au Haut, and 18 other islands; 10 national wildlife refuges totaling 64,600 acres, including Moosehorn, the largest in the state; 87,500 acres in Katahdin Woods and Waters National Monument; and the 31,800-acre Appalachian Trail corridor administered by the Appalachian Trail Conservancy under the guidance of the National Park Service. Land preserved through easements brings the total of all government lands in Maine to 1,746,000 acres.

Maine has a robust network of more than 80 land trusts and conservation organizations, including the Appalachian Mountain Club, the Maine Chapter of The Nature Conservancy, and the Maine Coast Heritage Trust. Altogether, Maine land trusts have protected 2,685,000 acres of land through fee ownership and conservation easements.

Public and private conservation land in Maine, in fee ownership and conservation easements, now totals 4,431,000 million acres, or a little more than 25 percent of the state's land area.

The Land for Maine's Future (LMF) program is an important source of conservation funding in the state. LMF was established in 1987 when Maine citizens voted to fund $35 million to purchase lands of statewide importance. Voters approved five additional bond issues between 1999 and 2012. In three decades, the program has conserved more than 600,000 acres of land in Maine, including Mt. Kineo, Mt. Agamenticus, Mt. Abraham, Tumbledown Mtn., the Camden Hills, Cutler Coast, Rumford Whitecap, Sawyer Mtn. Highlands, Amherst Mountains, Gulf Hagas–White Cap Range, and Eagle Bluff. In 2021, LMF received an appropriation of $40 million to be distributed over four years and will issue annual calls for proposals.

TRAIL ETIQUETTE

The many hundreds of miles of trails on Maine's public and private lands exist due to the generosity of landowners and the stewardship of many organizations and individuals. On all public lands and some private lands, agreements—some formal and some not—exist to allow for foot trails and their public use. Some trails cross private land with no formal permission from the landowner. In such cases, these trails exist by virtue of a long tradition of public use.

Regardless of whether a trail is on public or private land, hikers should exercise care to observe all regulations that have been designed to protect the land itself and the rights of the landowners. Despite a history of public use and enjoyment, trails—especially those on private land—are subject to closure at the will of the landowner. Therefore, it is imperative that hikers treat all trails and property with great respect, as if the land were their own. This might require cleaning up after others less mindful.

Hikers should be aware they will sometimes share designated trails with other users, such as ATV riders, mountain bikers, and horseback riders. The Maine outdoors has room for all to enjoy, so please be courteous.

Dog owners should have their pets under control at all times, whether by leash or voice command. Dogs are not allowed in BSP and on some land trust properties. In ANP, dogs are allowed on leash. Please check with the land management agency in advance for particular rules regarding dogs.

APPALACHIAN TRAIL

With the passage of the National Trails System Act (NTSA) by Congress in 1968, the AT became the first federally protected footpath in the United States and was officially designated the Appalachian National Scenic Trail. In 1978, amendments to the NTSA authorized funds and directed NPS and USFS to acquire lands to protect the AT corridor. In 1984, the Dept. of the Interior delegated the bulk of the responsibilities for managing the trail to the Appalachian Trail Conference, which changed its name to the Appalachian Trail Conservancy in 2005 to better reflect its role. Today, ATC works to maintain and protect the AT in conjunction with a host of organizations—including the Maine Appalachian Trail Club—in the 14 states through which the trail passes.

The AT enters Maine at the Maine–New Hampshire border in the Mahoosuc Range, negotiates the difficult mile-long stretch of Mahoosuc Notch, and proceeds to climb over a long series of high peaks—many exceeding 4,000 ft.—that make up the Longfellow Mountains. After traversing Bigelow Range, the AT crosses the wide and swift Kennebec River at Caratunk on its way to Monson, the last outpost of civilization before the 100-Mile Wilderness. Rugged mountains, lakes, ponds, waterfalls, and deep forests characterize this final leg of the trail to BSP. The northern terminus of the 2,192-mi. AT is atop the lofty alpine summit of Katahdin, the highest mountain in the state. Most of the mountains along the 282 mi.-route of the AT in Maine are described in this guide.

INTERNATIONAL APPALACHIAN TRAIL

The brainchild of Dick Anderson of Freeport, Maine, the International Appalachian Trail was first proposed to the public in 1994. Anderson "visualized a trail that would connect two countries and cultures, link a state and two provinces and traverse two major watersheds—the Gulf of

Maine and the Gulf of St. Lawrence." Today, the IAT extends across northern Maine, from just east of Katahdin and BSP in the Katahdin Woods and Waters National Monument, through New Brunswick and Quebec, to Crow Head on the northernmost tip of Newfoundland (also the northernmost point of the Appalachian Mountains in the Western Hemisphere), a distance of more than 1,900 mi. Parts of the IAT route in North America have been extended to Prince Edward Island and Nova Scotia.

In Maine, the IAT crosses the summits of Deasey Mtn. and Lunksoos Mtn. Just west of the Canadian border, it climbs Mars Hill for a final view across Aroostook County before entering New Brunswick. This guide describes each of these three peaks.

NORTH MAINE WOODS

North Maine Woods is a nonprofit corporation composed of a variety of public and private landowners. The consortium manages recreational access to 3.5 million acres of working forestland in northern Maine, ranging roughly from the Canadian border east to BSP and north through Aroostook County, including all of Allagash Wilderness Waterway and the upper reaches of the St. John River. NMW also manages access to the 175,000-acre KI Jo-Mary Multiple Use Forest between Millinocket, Greenville, and Brownville, which includes Gulf Hagas and a portion of the 100-Mile Wilderness.

Hikers entering NMW-managed lands must pass through a checkpoint and pay a fee for day use and camping. These fees help maintain hundreds of miles of roads and more than 560 campsites. (*Note*: Fees are payable by cash or check only, no credit cards accepted.) Travel through NMW lands is on active industrial logging roads. For safety, visitors should always yield the right of way to trucks (best practice is to pull over and stop); avoid stopping on bridges, curves, and main roads; and drive attentively and prudently.

NMW gatekeepers are knowledgeable about the terrain you are about to enter and happy to answer questions about directions, road conditions, campsites, and the like. The magazine *North Maine Woods*, which includes the *Map of North Maine Woods*, is free and available at all NMW gates. The free pamphlet *KI Jo-Mary Guide Map and Information* is also available.

NMW lands are very remote. Services are few and far between and should not be counted on. Carry a cell phone, but be aware that service may be spotty or nonexistent in many places. Be sure to leave a trip plan with family or friends at home. In your vehicle, carry extra fuel, spare tire and jack, winch or come-along, fire-making materials, shovel, and extra food and water in case of delay or the unexpected need to spend the night out.

SKI AREAS

Although not described in this guide, the ski trails at Maine's downhill skiing areas and resorts offer hiking routes that, due to their width and zigzag course over steep slopes, often make for pleasant summer climbing. In the skiing off-season, factors to consider include lack of shade, rough footing, and wet areas. In winter, ski mountains and their ready-made packed trails allow for straightforward snow travel, and wide-open ascent routes offer continuous views. Ski areas are private property and, summer or winter, hikers should ask about the uphill access policy and request permission.

FIRE TOWERS

In 1905, Maine erected its first fire lookout on Big Moose Mtn. near Moosehead Lake. The tower proved the effectiveness of mountaintop fire detection, so the Maine Forestry Dept. (the historical name of MFS) began a program to erect as many such towers as possible in the coming years. By 1950, MFS was staffing more than 100 fire towers statewide. By the beginning of the 1960s, however, use of fire towers began to decline as the use of aircraft for fire detection grew in popularity and was ultimately found to be more economical. The decline continued, with only critical fire towers being staffed, until 1991, when the state closed the remaining towers. This ended an era of fire detection history that included the building of 144 fire towers overall.

Aside from fire protection, the era of fire towers opened many remote mountains to hiking opportunities. Fire warden's trails and related phone line trails provided maintained systems for hikers, and many were also incorporated into trails such as the AT. With the abandonment, degradation, and removal of fire towers over the years, many of these trails have been lost. But through the determined efforts of some volunteer groups, including the Maine Chapter of the Forest Fire Lookout Association, some fire towers are being maintained, restored, and even staffed. Given Maine's rich history of working forests and lumbering, the historical value of fire towers is recognized, and the towers continue to be a well-known symbol of fire detection. More than 60 fire tower trails are described in this guide.

GEOGRAPHY

Maine is the easternmost state in the United States. It is bordered by New Hampshire, the Canadian provinces of Quebec and New Brunswick, and the Atlantic Ocean. At more than 35,000 sq. mi., Maine is nearly as large as the other five New England states combined. It is 39th in size among all states and roughly 320 mi. long from south to north and 210 mi. wide from west to east at its greatest extents. Maine's latitude ranges from 43° 4' N to

47° 28' N, and its longitude ranges from 66° 57' W to 71° 7' W. The geographic center of Maine is in Piscataquis County, 18 mi. north of Dover-Foxcroft.

Maine's mountains extend from the coast to the northern interior and feature more than 100 summits greater than 3,000 ft. in elevation, with the highest peak on Katahdin at 5,267 ft., the northern terminus of the AT. The expansive landscape is home to 6,000 lakes and ponds, 32,000 mi. of rivers and streams, more than 17 million acres of forestland, and an abundance of wildlife. The state's coastline covers a geographic expanse of 230 mi. as the crow flies, but 3,500 mi. when every nook and cranny and some 3,000 islands are measured on the undulating margin from Kittery to Lubec.

To the south, Maine is bounded by the Atlantic Ocean from the Piscataqua River at Kittery to Passamaquoddy Bay at Lubec. The eastern boundary is a meridian line between Canada to the east and the United States to the west and extends from Hamlin to Pole Hill east of North Amity. The international boundary then follows Mountain Brook to North Lake, Grand Lake, and Spednik Lake. The St. Croix River forms the state boundary from Vanceboro to Passamaquoddy Bay. To the west, a meridian line separates Maine and New Hampshire from the junction of the Maine, New Hampshire, and Quebec borders west of Bowman Hill south to Grand East Lake in Acton. From that point to Portsmouth Harbor and the Atlantic Ocean, the Salmon Falls River and then the Piscataqua River are the boundaries. The northern boundary is the most complex. From Bowman Hill in Bowmantown Township, the boundary follows the mountainous height-of-land separating the St. Lawrence River watershed from the Kennebec and Penobscot river watersheds. From Little St. John Lake, the Southwest Branch of the St. John River is the border as far as a point just west of Hardwood Mtn. in the unorganized township of T9 R18 WELS. From there, a straight line runs to Lac Frontiere; then another line angles northeast to the Crown Monument at Estcourt. The St. Francis River flows east from there to empty into the St. John River near the village of St. Francis. The St. John River is the border as far as Hamlin just west of Grand Falls, Canada.

REGIONS

Maine can be divided into four distinct physical regions based on the general landforms found therein: the coastal lowlands, the hilly interior belt, the western mountains, and the dissected uplands.

The coastal lowlands include the sandy beaches from Kittery to Casco Bay. Between Casco Bay and Penobscot Bay is the peninsula coast, characterized by long arms of land reaching out into the ocean. Farther north between Rockland and Schoodic Point is a region of big bays, wide peninsulas, and large islands, including Penobscot Bay, Blue Hill Bay, and Frenchman Bay. The area between Frenchman Bay and Passamaquoddy Bay is known as Downeast, where the bays are more exposed to the ocean and where the peninsulas are broader, with fewer and smaller islands. The coastal lowlands are interrupted by a stretch of interior hills that extends from Unity to the Camden Hills on the coast. The mountains of Mt. Desert Island and ANP are also part of the hilly interior that reaches south to the ocean. This physical region includes some of the mountains in the Southwestern Maine, Midcoast, and Downeast sections, and all the ANP section.

Inland from the coast is the hilly interior belt, a swath of rolling hills, woods, farmland, lakes, ponds, and rivers that ranges from the New Hampshire border to Bangor and on to the New Brunswick border. The hills are mostly scattered and range from a few hundred feet to about 2,000 ft. in elevation. Included are the mountains in the White Mountain National Forest and Evans Notch section, as well as the Oxford Hills and White Mountain Foothills section; many of the trails in the Southwestern Maine, Midcoast, and Downeast sections; and some of the trails in the Kennebec and Moose River Valleys section.

The western mountains extend from the White Mountains east along the New Hampshire border and north across the state to Katahdin and the cluster of mountains nearby. This heavily forested region is characterized by the chain of high peaks known as the Longfellow Mountains—more than 75 peaks exceed 3,000 ft. and a handful exceed 4,000 ft.—and a series of large lakes, from Umbagog and Flagstaff to Moosehead and Grand Lake Seboeis. The western mountains encompass the entire Maine portion of the AT, BSP, and a variety of large conservation lands, including the AMC's Maine Woods recreation and conservation area. This expanse covers the following sections: Mahoosuc Range and Grafton Notch, Western Lakes and Mountains, 100-Mile Wilderness and Moosehead Lake, and Baxter State Park and Katahdin Woods and Waters National Monument. It is also part of the northernmost mountains in the Kennebec and Moose River Valleys section.

The dissected uplands in northern Maine comprise all of Aroostook County and the far northern parts of Somerset, Piscataquis, and Penobscot counties. Forestland and farmland, scattered low mountains as high as 2,000 ft. in elevation, the Allagash Wilderness Waterway, and the valley of the St. John River characterize this region, which includes all the mountains in the Aroostook County section.

GEOLOGY

The bedrock geology of Maine is the result of a series of complex natural forces—primarily sedimentation and volcanic and mountain-building activities—from as early as the Late Proterozoic era, about 650 million years ago, to the Mesozoic era, about 66 million years ago. The continental rift between the combined European and African plates and the North American plate in the Late Mesozoic era led to continued uplift, erosion, faulting, and fracturing of the bedrock of the Appalachian Mountains of western Maine during the Tertiary period of the Cenozoic era about 1.6 million years ago.

Glaciation events of the Pleistocene epoch shaped much of the natural landscape we see today in Maine. Starting about 35,000 years ago, the Laurentide Ice Sheet spread across what is now southern Quebec and New England. The ice sheet was as thick as 10,000 ft. and covered the highest mountains, including Katahdin. The sheer mass of the ice sheet depressed the land many hundreds of feet. The movement of the glacial ice scoured the mountains and valleys, eroding the rock and carving enormous basins out of the mountainsides, moving great quantities of sand and gravel southward.

Due to climatic warming, the glaciers began to retreat about 21,000 years ago. The melting waters flooded as far as 75 mi. inland, creating the long peninsulas and islands that exist today. The retreating ice sheet dramatically changed the coastline, shaped the mountain landscape, left behind more than 6,000 lakes and ponds, and altered the courses of the major rivers. The glaciers disappeared altogether about 11,000 years ago.

CLIMATE AND VEGETATION

Given Maine's geographic location on the eastern edge of the North American continent, its climate is influenced primarily by continental air masses flowing across the land on the westerly winds. This can be cold, dry air from Canada or warm, moist air from the Gulf of Mexico. The climate is affected to a lesser degree by cool, moist air from the Atlantic Ocean, which moderates the temperatures along the coast. Maine's location between the latitudes 43 degrees north and 47.5 degrees north reduces the sun's influence, making for generally mild summers and cold winters. The higher elevations in the mountains are usually cooler in summer and much colder in winter. The mean January temperature ranges from 20 degrees Fahrenheit along the coast to 15 degrees inland to 10 degrees in the far north. The mean July temperature ranges from 65 degrees along the coast and in the far north to 67 degrees inland. Annual rainfall ranges from around 50 in. along the coast to 36 in. in the north, although the western mountains receive significant precipitation due to the effect of the cooler air at higher elevations. Snowfall totals range from as much as 80 in. along the coast to 81 to 100 in. inland to more than 110 in. in the western mountains and northern interior.

Maine occupies a transition zone between predominantly deciduous forests to the south and predominantly coniferous forests to the north. Within this zone, the broad mix of forest cover types is influenced to some degree by latitude, although soil variation and local climate also play a role. Along the coast from Casco Bay east to Passamaquoddy Bay, and in the western mountains and into the dissected uplands, the dominant tree species are spruce, fir, cedar, and larch. In southwestern Maine and in the western section of the hilly interior belt, the dominant species are oak, white pine, and hemlock. The northern hardwood mix of beech, maple, and birch dominates in a band stretching east from the western mountains to Washington County in the hilly interior and north in a band east of BSP to Canada and down along the St. John Valley of eastern Aroostook County.

TRIP PLANNING, WEATHER, AND SAFETY

The traditional hiking season in Maine extends from Memorial Day to Indigenous Peoples' Day, although an increasing number of hikers have come to know the joy of empty trails in the shoulder months of early spring and late fall. Trail conditions in Maine vary by geography. Coastal trails and those just inland will be snow-free much earlier than those farther north, along the mountains of the AT corridor, and will remain so longer, into fall and possibly even early winter. In some years, ice or snow drifts can linger at higher elevations into late May or early June, possibly later in some major cirques and bowls on north-facing slopes and high ridges, as well as in some sheltered areas, such as Mahoosuc Notch. Such conditions vary greatly from year to year and place to place. When snow or ice is present, trails may be more difficult to follow and more hazardous. If icy trail conditions are expected, it is prudent to bring some type of traction footgear.

Even if it feels like summer in the lower elevations, it can be like winter on the high ridges and summits. In fact, winter conditions can occur in the higher mountains in any month of the year. Keep in mind that air temperatures will drop 3 to 5 degrees Fahrenheit with each 1,000 ft. of elevation gain, without factoring in the impact of windchill. As a result, even on sunny days in midsummer, hikers venturing to the exposed summits should always be prepared for cold weather with a minimum of a synthetic fleece jacket or wool sweater, hat, gloves, and a wind parka, all of which will provide comfort and protection against sudden storms. The often windy, wet, and foggy conditions along the Maine coast demand similar precautions.

Plan your trip with safety in mind. Consider the skill and experience of your party and the strenuousness of the hike: the overall distance, the amount of climbing, and the roughness of the terrain. Get a weather report, but be aware that a forecast may not apply to the mountain regions.

The National Weather Service provides detailed local weather forecasts on its website at weather.gov and on NOAA Weather Radio; check the website for a list of broadcast stations serving Maine. You can also get a recorded forecast by calling 207-688-3210 (Portland area) or 207-492-0170 (northern Aroostook County, Caribou, Presque Isle, Bangor, southern Penobscot County). Frequent weather updates are also available on weather.com and smartphone weather apps.

Plan to finish your hike with daylight to spare, and remember that days grow shorter rapidly in late summer and fall. Hiking after dark, even with flashlights or headlamps (which frequently fail), makes finding trails more difficult and crossing streams hazardous. Let someone know where you will be hiking, and don't allow people to become separated from the group, especially those who are inexperienced.

Many unpaved roads may not be passable until Memorial Day or after. Take extra precautions to ensure your vehicle has a full gas tank and a usable spare tire and that you have extra food, water, and clothing before driving into Maine's remote regions. Please check with the specific land management agency for road conditions and closures before you go.

Consider bringing your children or those of friends on appropriate hikes, as introducing young people to the outdoors has many benefits. Kids who are exposed to frequent, unstructured outdoor play are healthier, do better in school, have higher self-esteem, feel more connected to nature, and are more likely to be tomorrow's conservation leaders. AMC is committed to helping kids build strong connections to the outdoor world, including protection of the environment. Bringing children into the outdoors teaches them the need to take care of the world around them.

HIKESAFE HIKER RESPONSIBILITY CODE

The Hiker Responsibility Code was developed and is endorsed by the WMNF and New Hampshire Fish and Game, and is supported by BSP. For more information, visit hikesafe.com.

You are responsible for yourself, so be prepared:

1. **With knowledge and gear.** Become self-reliant by learning about the terrain, conditions, local weather, and your equipment before you start.

2. **To leave your plans.** Tell someone where you are going, the trails you are hiking, when you will return, and your emergency plans.

3. **To stay together.** When you start as a group, hike as a group and end as a group. Pace your hike to the slowest person.

4. **To turn back.** Weather changes quickly in the mountains. Fatigue and unexpected conditions can also affect your hike. Know your limitations and when to postpone your hike. The mountains will be there another day.

5. **For emergencies.** Even if you are headed out for just an hour, an injury, severe weather, or a wrong turn could become life threatening. Don't assume you will be rescued; know how to rescue yourself.

6. **To share the hiker code with others.** HikeSafe: It's Your Responsibility.

FOLLOWING TRAILS

In general, trails are maintained to provide a clear pathway while protecting the environment by minimizing erosion and other damage. Some may offer rough and difficult passage. Many hiking trails are marked with paint blazes on trees or rocks, with signs marking the trailhead and intermediate points en route. The AT in Maine is marked with white 2-by-6-in. vertical paint blazes. Side trails off the AT are usually marked with blue paint blazes. Trails may be marked in a variety of colors, and some exhibit colored flagging (plastic tape) along the way. Some trails lack any signs or markers. Above treeline, on open ridges and ledge areas, cairns (piles of rocks) usually mark the trails.

Below treeline, the treadway is usually visible except when covered by snow or fallen leaves. In winter, snow often covers signs at trailheads and intersections and blazes. Trails following or crossing woods roads require taking special care at intersections to distinguish the trail from diverging roads, particularly because blazing may be sporadic or nonexistent while the trail follows the road. Around shelters or campsites, beaten paths may lead in all directions, so look for signs and paint blazes.

Hikers should be aware that some trails in this book (as noted in descriptions) are less easy to follow than others. The presence of signs and blazes varies, and some trails are too new to have a well-defined treadway; others have received very little use and are overgrown and becoming obscure. Trails may not be cleared of fallen trees and brush until late summer, and not all trails are cleared every year. Inexperienced hikers should avoid trails described as being difficult to follow, and all trail users should observe and follow trail markings carefully.

Although trails vary greatly in the amount of use they receive and the ease with which they can usually be followed, almost any trail might close unexpectedly or suddenly become obscure or hazardous under certain conditions. Landowners can reroute, abandon, or close trails. Trail signs are stolen or fall from their posts. Storms may cause blowdowns or landslides, which can close a trail for an entire hiking season or longer. Logging operations can cover trails with debris and add a bewildering network of new roads. Development and road construction can obliterate trails.

Momentary inattention to trail markers—particularly arrows at sharp turns or signs at junctions—or misinterpretation of signs or guidebook descriptions can cause hikers to become separated from all but the most heavily traveled paths. At a minimum, it can lead them into what may be a much longer or more difficult route. Please remember that this book is an aid to planning, not a substitute for observation and judgment. All the trail-maintaining organizations, including AMC, reserve the right to discontinue any trail without notice and expressly disclaim any legal responsibility for the condition of any trail.

A number of online sites post hiker reports on trails and mountain peaks in Maine and around New England, and when available for your particular hike, this information can help you better plan and prepare. *Always check AMC's books updates page online for the most recent trail closures, reroutings, and other changes before you head out: outdoors.org/books-maps.*

IF YOU'RE LOST

Keeping track of where you are at all times and how long ago you observed the last trail marker is the best way to avoid becoming lost. In the event you wander off the trail and are no longer sure where you are, stop and briefly assess the situation. Often just by looking side to side, you can find the trail. If not, try backtracking a short distance to the last known trail marker.

If you are not with your hiking companions, yell or blow a whistle. They or others are likely nearby. If you still cannot find the trail and no one answers your calls, try to remain calm. Many situations in which a person has become lost for any length of time involve panic and aimless wandering, so it is important to stop and take a break, make an inventory of useful information, decide on a course of action, and stick to it. (The caution against allowing inexperienced persons to become separated from a group should be emphasized here, as they are most likely to panic and wander. Also make sure all group members are familiar with the route of the trip and the names of the trails so that if they do become separated, they will have some prospect of rejoining the group.)

Even when you cannot immediately find the trail, the situation is not necessarily serious. If you have kept track of your location on the map, some careful forays from your current position should help you relocate the trail. Should this effort fail, you can usually find a nearby stream, trail, or road to which you can set a compass course to follow. In many areas, distances are short enough (except in North Maine Woods region in Aroostook County, the northern reaches of Somerset County and Piscataquis County, and along the Canadian border) that it is possible, in the absence of alternatives, to reach a road in half a day, or at most in a whole day, simply by hiking downhill until you come upon a river or brook. Follow the watercourse downstream, and it should lead to civilization.

BUSHWHACKING

This guide deals mostly with mountains in Maine that have recognized foot trails, with a few exceptions. Mt. Redington is one of Maine's 14 4,000-ft. peaks, and the unofficial herd path from the top of South Crocker Mtn. that has been used by bushwhackers for years is included, as is a longer unmarked route via Caribou Valley Rd. Some of the remote peaks on NMW-regulated lands in Aroostook County have obscure treadways, blowdowns, and few if any trail markers, which can make navigation difficult. All other trailless peaks in Maine are excluded. In general, bushwhacking is not recommended because it poses a threat to plant and animal life and can hasten erosion.

WHAT TO CARRY AND WEAR

Adequate equipment for a hike in the mountains of Maine varies greatly according to the time of year, the geographic location, the length of the trip, the potential terrain hazards, and the difficulty of getting to the nearest trailhead if a problem arises. For even short day hikes, AMC advocates preparedness. If your hike plan includes remote backcountry woods or above treeline or other exposed terrain and you and your group are not inclined to turn back at the first sign of questionable weather, you will need a pack outfitted with plenty of warm clothing, plus food and water for emergency use, along with the usual gear.

AMC recommends always carrying the Ten Essentials:

- guidebook (or pages of it or photographs of pages) and maps
- waterproof matches/fire starter
- compass
- first-aid and repair kits
- warm clothing, including hat and gloves
- whistle
- rain and wind gear
- extra food (high-energy snacks) and water (minimum 2 liters per hiker, per day; always treat water sourced in the woods before drinking)
- pocketknife or multitool
- headlamp or flashlight, with extra batteries and a spare bulb

You might also bring:

- watch
- bandanna or buff
- extra shirt(s)
- personal medications
- nylon cord and safety pins
- trash bag
- toilet paper (and plastic bag to pack out used TP)
- wet wipes and hand sanitizer
- sunscreen and sunglasses or brimmed hat
- insect repellent
- cell phone
- GPS/satellite communicator
- space blanket or bivouac sack
- lighter or waterproof matches
- notebook and pen or pencil

Wear comfortable, broken-in hiking boots. Lightweight to medium-weight boots provide the needed ankle support on rough and rocky trails. Two pairs of socks are recommended: a lightweight inner pair and a heavier outer pair that are both at least partly wool. Adjustable trekking poles offer many advantages to hikers, especially on descents, traverses, and stream crossings.

Blue jeans, sweatshirts, and other cotton clothing are not recommended because once they become wet, they dry very slowly. In adverse weather conditions, they can quickly drain a cold and tired hiker's heat reserves; thus, the hiker maxim: "cotton kills." Synthetics and wool are superior materials for outdoor apparel, especially for hikers intending to travel in adverse conditions, to remote places, or above treeline. Modern synthetics and wool retain much of their insulating value even when wet and are indispensable for hikers wanting to explore areas from which return to the trailhead might require substantial time and effort if conditions turn bad. Multiple layers of clothing are best, from wicking undergarments to insulating down and/or fleece to a wind and rain shell. Additional clothing is always a smart choice: hats, gloves, and other similar gear provide an extra margin of safety in adverse conditions, and they allow hikers to enjoy the summits in comfort on those crisp, clear days when the views are particularly fine. A camera, binoculars, nature identification guides, altimeter, book for leisure reading, and GPS unit are extras to consider. For more on essential clothing and gear, refer to *AMC's Mountain Skills Manual* (AMC Books, 2017).

HIKING WITH KIDS

Many trails in this book are suitable for hiking with children. It is important to choose a hike that suits the age, fitness, and agility of the child and to bring adequate gear, food, and water. A wealth of additional information on family hiking is available at outdoors.org.

HIKING WITH DOGS

Many hikers enjoy the companionship of their dogs on the trail. Out of consideration for other hikers, please keep your dog under voice control at all times and on a leash, if necessary. Some areas require dogs to be leashed at all times, so check with local trail managers beforehand. Due to the fragile vegetation, dogs should always be leashed in the alpine zone. Carry out or bury dog waste, and do not leave waste bags on the trail or at the trailhead. Choose a hike that matches your dog's fitness, age, and agility. Some trails—such as those with ladders or difficult boulder or ledge scrambling—are not suitable for dogs. The sharp rocks above treeline on Katahdin, for example, are extremely rough on a dog's paws. Be sure your dog has adequate water to drink, especially on hot summer days. For more advice on hiking with kids and with dogs, see *AMC's Mountain Skills Manual*.

BACKCOUNTRY CAMPING

Trailside camping is available on a first-come-first-serve basis at established lean-tos and tentsites along the AT corridor. Where caretakers (AMC or MATC) are in place, a fee may be charged. Backcountry campsites are also available at a number of Maine's public lands units. MBPL allows dispersed camping on most public lands, provided backpackers practice Leave No Trace principles (see p. xlviii). Lean-tos and tentsites in remote areas of BSP are available with advanced reservations only. Five lean-tos along the IAT, four in KAWW, and one on Mars Hill near the Canadian border are available. Overnight camping is permitted in nearly all the WMNF backcountry in Maine, although campers should check with USFS on the latest forest protection area rules, if any, for the areas they wish to visit. ANP has five remote shelters on Isle au Haut.

Backcountry campers tend to have more of an impact on the land than do day-hikers. Backpackers should take great care to minimize their effect on the mountains by practicing low-impact camping. If available on your chosen trip route, the best alternative is to use formally designated campsites to concentrate impact and minimize damage to vegetation. Many popular campsites and shelters have caretakers. In other areas, choose previously established campsites to minimize the impact caused by the creation and proliferation of new campsites. When selecting an established campsite, choose one that is farther from surface water to protect the water quality for future and downstream users.

If you camp away from established sites, look for a spot more than 200 ft. from the trail and from any surface water, and observe any specific camping regulations for the area. Bring all needed shelter, including whatever poles, stakes, ground insulation, and cords are required. Do not cut boughs or branches for bedding or firewood or young trees for poles. Avoid clearing vegetation, and never make a ditch around the tent. Wash your dishes and yourself 200 ft. away from streams, ponds, and springs. Bury human waste at least 200 ft. from the trail, the campsite, and any water sources. Heed the rules of neatness, sanitation, and fire prevention, and carry out everything that you carry in. Do not keep food in your tent; hang food from a tree (use a high, sturdy branch at least 10 ft. off the ground and 4 ft. from the tree trunk) or store it in a bear canister to protect it from raccoons and bears.

In some popular camping areas, a "human browse line," where people have gathered firewood over the years, is quite evident: limbs are gone from trees, the ground is devoid of dead wood, and vegetation has been trampled. Please refrain from exacerbating this problem. The use of portable stoves is often mandatory in popular areas and is encouraged everywhere to prevent damage to vegetation. Do not make wood campfires unless ample dead and downed wood is available near your site and you are certain that fires are legal in the area. Where fires are allowed, clear a space at least 5 ft. in radius of all flammable material, down to the mineral soil, before you begin to build your fire. Under no circumstances should you leave a fire unattended. All fires must be completely extinguished with earth or water before you leave a campsite, even temporarily. Restore the campfire site to as natural an appearance as possible (unless using a preexisting fire ring) when you are ready to move on.

ROADSIDE CAMPING

Drive-in camping is available at a variety of public campgrounds, in ANP, BSP, and at the WMNF campgrounds in the Evans Notch area, and at 11 state parks. More than 500 primitive roadside campsites are available within the boundaries of NMW, and some 60 campsites are within the KI Jo-Mary Multiple Use Forest. Close to 200 privately owned and operated campgrounds throughout Maine offer a wide variety of facilities and amenities. See Appendix A: Helpful Information and Contacts (p. 600) for information on campground locations and reservations.

FIRE REGULATIONS

Campfire permits are required for some remote campsites in the unorganized townships. Permits are site specific and valid only for a short time period. In organized towns, landowner permission must be obtained and a permit issued by the town forest fire warden. Most Maine maps, including the *Maine Atlas and Gazetteer*, distinguish between campsites that require a permit (permit sites) and those that do not (authorized sites). If unsure, contact the nearest MFS office; see Appendix A: Helpful Information and Contacts (p. 600). Campfire permits are not required when the ground is covered by snow. Permits are free.

In BSP, ANP, and Maine public lands and state parks, fires are allowed only at designated sites. Along the AT, fires are allowed only at designated shelters and tentsites. Use of backpacker stoves is strongly encouraged on the AT and elsewhere to help minimize environmental impact and campsite degradation. Fires are allowed in the backcountry of the WMNF in Maine except where prohibited by the specific rules of Forest Protection Areas.

The Maine legislature has banned the transport of all firewood from outside the state to help control the spread of potentially devastating insect pests, such as the emerald ash borer and Asian long-horned beetle. If firewood is transported, it must be completely burned within 24 hours. Campers are urged to leave all firewood at home and buy it locally where it will be used.

WINTER CONSIDERATIONS

This book describes trails in the snowless season, which can vary considerably from year to year. Higher elevations have much shorter snow-free seasons. Because snowshoeing and winter hiking in the woods and mountains of Maine have steadily become more popular, a few general considerations are provided here.

Road access and parking are, in general, much more limited in winter. Many access roads are unplowed, necessitating long walks to reach trailheads that one can drive to in summer. Many parking areas along major roads are generally plowed within a day or two after a storm, but some are not plowed at all, and roadside parking is limited by snowbanks. To avoid ticketing or towing, all wheels of a parked vehicle must be outside the travel corridor. If no safe parking is available, consider an alternative trip. Hikers should make sure their vehicle is winter ready and should always have a shovel.

Advances in clothing and equipment have made it possible for experienced winter travelers to enjoy greater levels of comfort and safety. Although hiking on lower elevation trails in average conditions can be relatively safe, much more experience is required to recognize and avoid dangerous situations in winter than in summer. Summer hiking boots are inadequate; regular headlamp batteries fail quickly; and drinking water freezes unless carried in an insulated container. The winter hiker should be in good physical condition and should dress carefully to avoid overheating and excessive perspiration, which soaks clothing and soon leads to chilling. Hikers should avoid cotton clothes in general, but especially in winter. Dress in multiple layers: a moisture-wicking base layer of synthetic or wool, a middle layer of fleece, an insulating layer of down or synthetic fill, and then a wind or rain shell garment. Extra clothing is always a smart choice. Hikers should increase fluid intake, as dehydration can be a serious problem in the cold and dry winter air. Larger packs are necessary to carry the additional clothing and gear required in winter.

Snow, ice, and weather conditions are constantly changing, and a relatively minor error in judgment may have serious, even lethal, consequences. Conditions can vary greatly from day to day and from trail to trail. Days are very short, particularly in early winter when darkness falls around 4 P.M. Trails are frequently difficult or impossible to follow in deep snow, and navigation skills may be hard to apply in adverse weather conditions. (Thus, out-and-back hikes—where one retraces one's tracks—are often preferable to loop hikes, where unknown conditions ahead could make completing the trip much more difficult than anticipated.) Brook crossings can be difficult and potentially dangerous if the water is not adequately frozen.

Deep snow requires snowshoes or skis and the skill to use them efficiently (although some popular trails may be packed out through most of winter). Breaking trail on snowshoes through new snow can be strenuous and exhausting. Trail courtesy suggests that winter hikers wear snowshoes when trails are not solidly packed out. Post-holing, or plunging one's legs into and out of deep snow, is unnecessarily tiring and creates unpleasant and potentially hazardous trail conditions for those who follow.

When ice is present on trails, as it often is in late fall, early spring, and after winter freeze-thaw cycles, mountains with steep, open slopes or ledges are particularly dangerous. If you expect icy trail conditions, bring traction footgear (devices include spikes, hiking crampons, and steel crampons). In spring, deep snowdrifts may remain on northern slopes and wooded ridgelines, even at lower elevations, after snow has melted on southern exposures.

It is important to note that some trails, such as those on Katahdin, pass through areas that may pose a danger of avalanches. Basin walls, ravines, and open slopes are especially prone to avalanches, though slides can also occur below treeline. These areas should be regarded as technical terrain and strictly avoided unless party members have been trained in avalanche safety.

Above treeline, hiking often requires specialized equipment and skills, as well as experience of a different magnitude. The conditions on Katahdin, the Bigelows, Saddleback, Abraham, and other high and exposed alpine summits can be severe, and only the most experienced and well-equipped climbers should attempt hikes. Severe storms can develop suddenly, but perhaps the most dangerous aspect of winter in the higher elevations of the Maine mountains is the variability of the weather. It is not unusual for a chilly, penetrating, wind-driven rain to be followed within a few hours by a cold front that brings below-zero temperatures and high winds.

No book can begin to impart all the knowledge necessary to cope safely with the potential for such serious conditions, but those interested in learning more about winter hiking should consult the *Essential Guide to Winter Recreation* by Andrew Vietze (AMC Books, 2019). Hikers who are interested in extending their activities into the winter season, especially at higher elevations, are strongly advised to seek out organized parties with leaders who have extensive winter experience. AMC's Maine Chapter sponsors numerous evening and weekend workshops, in addition to introductory winter hikes and regular winter treks on which participants can gain experience. Information on these activities can be found at amcmaine.org and activities.outdoors.org.

No attempt is made to cover any kind of skiing in this guide, although several of the hiking trails described are well suited to cross-country and backcountry skiing. For more on these activities, see *Best Backcountry Skiing in the Northeast* by David Goodman (AMC Books, 2020).

BACKCOUNTRY HAZARDS

Safe hiking means knowing how to avoid potentially dangerous situations and being prepared to deal with problems when they do occur. AMC and many other outdoor organizations offer courses that teach the principles of backcountry safety, wilderness first aid, and incident management. Dozens of helpful books are available on these subjects. Some of the common hazards encountered in the Maine outdoors and how to approach them are outlined here.

Falls and Injuries

Injuries on the trail are always a serious matter, but more so with increasing distance from the trailhead. Be alert for places where the footing may be poor, especially in rainy weather and on steep, rough, or wet sections of trail. In fall, wet leaves and hidden ice are particular hazards. Remember that carrying a heavy pack can affect your balance. Another potential cause of injury in mountainous areas is rockfall from ledges that rise above the trail.

In case of serious injury, apply first aid and keep the injured person warm and comfortable. Then take a minute to assess the situation before going or calling for help. Backcountry evacuation can take many hours, so don't rush. Write down your location, the condition of the injured person, and any other pertinent facts. If cell phone service is not available, at least one person should stay with the injured hiker while two others go for help. (Hence the maxim that it is safest to hike in the backcountry in groups of four or more.)

Hypothermia

Hypothermia, the most serious danger to hikers in the Maine woods and mountains, is the loss of ability to preserve body heat and may be caused by injury, exhaustion, lack of sufficient food, and inadequate or wet clothing. This often occurs on wet, windy days at between 32 and 50 degrees Fahrenheit.

Symptoms of moderate hypothermia include uncontrolled shivering, impaired speech and movement, lowered body temperature, and drowsiness. Be on the lookout for what current hypothermia education programs refer to as the "umbles"—stumbles, mumbles, and bumbles—which amount to a loss of agility, an inability to speak clearly, difficulty with knots and zippers, and similar issues that indicate loss of normal muscular and mental functions. An affected hiker should be put in dry clothing and a sleeping bag, if available, and then given quick-energy food to eat and something warm (not hot) to drink.

In cases of severe hypothermia, which occurs when a body's temperature has reached a point below 90 degrees Fahrenheit, shivering ceases, but the person suffers an obvious lack of coordination to the point that walking becomes impossible. Sure indicators are slurred speech, mental confusion, irrational behavior, disorientation, and unconsciousness. Only prompt evacuation to a hospital offers reasonable hope for recovery. Extreme care must be used in attempting to transport such a person to a trailhead, because even a slight jar can bring on heart failure. The victim should be protected from further heat loss as much as possible and handled very gently. Call trained rescue personnel for immediate assistance.

Successful rescue of a profoundly hypothermic person from the backcountry is difficult, so the need for prevention or early detection is essential. The advent of hypothermia is usually fairly slow, and in cold or wet weather all members of a hiking group must be aware of the signs of developing hypothermia and pay constant attention to the first appearance of such signs—which may be fairly subtle—in all fellow group members.

Heat Exhaustion

Excessive heat can also be a serious problem in the mountains, particularly in midsummer on hot, humid days. Heat exhaustion, usually in a mild form, is quite common. The hiker feels tired, perhaps light-headed or nauseous, and may have cramps in large muscles. The principal cause is dehydration and loss of electrolytes (mostly salt) through perspiration, often combined with overexertion. On a hot day, a hiker can be well on the way to serious dehydration before feeling any thirst. To prevent heat exhaustion, hikers should carry plenty of water (and the means to treat or filter it) and drink copiously before thirst is evident. Wearing a hat to block the sun is another preventive measure.

The treatment for heat exhaustion is to provide adequate water and possibly salt (salt without adequate water will make the situation worse), to help victims cool down (especially the head and torso) by moving them into the shade, and to minimize further physical exertion. Heat exhaustion must be taken seriously because it can progress to life-threatening cardiac problems or to heatstroke, a medical emergency in which irreversible damage to the brain and other vital organs can quickly occur. This condition requires immediate cooling of the victim.

Lightning

Lightning is another serious hazard on any open ridge or summit; avoid these dangerous places when thunderstorms are likely. Look for shelter in thick woods as quickly as possible if an unexpected "thumper" is detected. Most thunderstorms occur when a cold front moves through or on very warm days. Storms produced by cold fronts are typically more sudden and violent. Weather forecasts that mention cold fronts or predict temperatures much above 80 degrees Fahrenheit in the lowlands and valleys should arouse concern.

Wildlife

In recent years, there have been hundreds of collisions between automobiles and moose, most occurring in spring and early summer, although the hazard exists year-round. Motorists need to be aware of the seriousness of the problem, particularly at night when these large, dark-colored animals are both active and very difficult to see. Instinct often causes moose to face an auto rather than to run from it, and they are apt to cross the road unpredictably as a car approaches. Be aware that where one moose crosses, there may well be another coming right behind it. Moose typically constitute little threat to hikers on foot, although it would be wise to give a wide berth to a cow with young or to a bull during the fall mating season.

Bears are common but tend to keep well out of sight. The black bear is a large and unpredictable animal that must be treated with respect. Deliberately feeding bears or allowing a dog to harass them may unnecessarily provoke an attack. No animal in the wild should be approached, startled, or fed. Bears are omnivorous opportunists, especially fond of nuts and berries, and sometimes hikers' food bags. They have become a nuisance and even a hazard at some popular campsites, because any bear that has lost its natural fear of humans—and has gotten used to living off hiker leftovers—is potentially very dangerous. Hikers confronted by a bear should attempt to appear neither threatened nor frightened and should back off slowly. Never run. Food should not be abandoned unless the bear appears overly aggressive. A loud noise, such as that made by a whistle or by banging metal pots, is often useful.

Careful protection of food and scented items, such as toothpaste, at campsites is essential. Food bags should never be kept overnight in a tent but rather hung between trees and well off the ground—at least 10 ft. high and 4 ft. away from the tree trunk. This helps keep other curious critters out of the larder as well. Bear canisters are effective and less work and thereby increasingly popular. Where there is a metal bear box, please use it.

No known poisonous snakes live in Maine.

Insect Pests

Mosquitoes and blackflies are the woodland residents that hikers most frequently encounter in Maine. Mosquitoes are worst throughout summer in low, wet areas, and blackflies are most bloodthirsty in late May, June, and early July. Head nets of fine nylon mesh can be useful. The most effective repellents for mosquitoes and blackflies, as well as gnats, no-see-ums, deerflies, and chiggers, are based on the active chemical ingredient N,N-diethyl-meta-toluamide, commonly known as DEET. These repellents are available in a variety of forms, including aerosols, pump sprays, lotions, and wipes and in different concentrations, from 100 percent DEET to lesser mixtures with more inert ingredients. Some questions exist about the safety of using DEET, so hikers should apply such repellents to clothing, rather than directly on the skin, where possible; avoid use on small children. Alternatives to DEET include picaridin, which is odor-free and not oily like DEET, and repellents using natural or synthesized plant oils.

Ticks are most common along the coast and in the woods and fields of southern and central Maine, but are spreading to other areas of the state. More than a dozen species of ticks reside in the Maine woods, but the deer tick, *Ixodes scapularis*, is the most troublesome. This tick can transmit the bacterium that causes Lyme disease. In the early stages, flu-like symptoms may appear, as well as an expanding or bull's-eye-shaped rash around the site of the tick bite. Detected early, Lyme disease can be treated with antibiotics. Left untreated, this serious illness can spread to joints, the heart, and the nervous system, leading to chronic health issues.

Countermeasures against ticks include using insect repellent on shoes, socks, and pant legs; wearing light-colored long pants tucked into socks; and frequently checking clothing and skin. Ticks wander for several hours before settling on a spot to bite, so they can be removed easily if found promptly. Once a tick is embedded, take care to remove it in its entirety, as the head detaches easily and may remain in the skin, possibly producing infection. Use tweezers or a special notched spoon or remover.

Bee stings may be painful, and for some individuals with allergies, they can cause potentially deadly anaphylactic reactions. Hikers with known allergies should carry Benadryl tablets and a prescription epinephrine pen.

Poison Ivy

Two types of poisonous plants are common in Maine: poison ivy and poison sumac. Poison ivy is found throughout the state, but poison sumac is much less common, found mostly in the southern part. Poison ivy generally has three dark green leaves that shine in the sun but are dull in the shade.

Direct contact with the oil (urushiol, an allergen) from the leaves, roots, stems, flowers, or fruit of these plants, or indirect contact with an object that has touched the plant, may result in an allergic skin rash. Symptoms include itchy skin and a red area or red streaks where the oil or contaminated object touched the skin, small bumps or larger raised areas, and blisters with fluid that may leak out and cause the rash to spread. The rash usually appears between 8 and 48 hours after contact. Early treatment involves thoroughly washing the contact area with soap and water. The next step is the use of a topical cortisone cream. In severe cases, antibiotics or even steroids may be necessary.

Stream Crossings

Hikers often cross streams, brooks, and rivers without bridges, stepping from rock to rock. Trekking poles, a hiking staff, or a stout stick can be a great aid to balance in these cases. Use caution, however, because serious injuries or worse can result from a fall on slippery rocks, especially in the middle of a stream. If you need to wade across a stream, it is recommended that you wear your boots (but not necessarily socks). If you know in advance that wading may be required, a good option is to carry lightweight sandals or other water footwear and change into them before crossing, keeping your boots dry. Unbuckle backpack straps so you can shrug out of the pack if necessary in a fall.

Many water crossings that may be only a nuisance in summer can be a serious obstacle in cold weather, when feet and boots must be kept dry. Another type of hazard can occur in late fall, when cold nights may cause exposed rocks to be coated with a treacherous thin layer of ice. Higher waters can turn innocuous brooks into raging torrents in spring, as snow melts, or after heavy rainstorms, particularly in fall when trees drop their leaves and take up less water. Avoid trails with potentially dangerous stream crossings during these high-water periods. If you are cut off from roads by swollen streams, it is better to make a long detour, even if you need to wait and spend a night in the woods. Rushing currents can make wading extremely hazardous and not worth the risk. Floodwaters may subside within a few hours, especially in small brooks. It is particularly important not to camp on the far side of a brook en route to your exit point if the crossing is difficult and heavy rain is predicted.

Hunting Seasons

Deer-hunting season (with firearms) in Maine generally starts on the Monday of the first week of November and lasts through the Saturday after Thanksgiving. A youth deer-hunting day is usually held the third Saturday in October, and a Maine resident day is held the fourth Saturday in October. Archery season is generally from late September through late October, and muzzleloader season is usually late November through early to mid-December. The start and duration of moose-hunting season varies by region, generally from late September to late November. The start and duration of wild turkey hunting in spring varies by region but is usually from late April to early June; in fall, the season is generally from early to late October.

Most hunters stay fairly close to roads, so, in general, the harder it would be to haul a deer out of a given area, the lower the probability a hiker will encounter hunters there. In any case, avoid wearing brown or anything that might give a hunter the impression of the white flash of a white-tailed deer running away. Wearing at least two pieces of bright orange clothing, the same as required of hunters, is strongly recommended. For the specific dates of Maine hunting seasons, visit maine.gov/ifw or call 207-287-8000. Hunting is not allowed on Sundays in Maine.

Drinking Water

The presence of microscopic cysts of the intestinal parasite *Giardia lamblia* in water sources in Maine is thought to be common, if difficult to prove. *Cryptosporidium* is another similar parasite of concern. It is impossible to be sure whether a given source is safe, no matter how clear the water seems or how remote the location. The safest course is for hikers to carry their own water from home. For those who source water in the woods, always purify the water before drinking it.

Water purification methods include boiling, chemical treatment (tablets or drops), ultraviolet treatment, and water filters. When boiling water, bring it to a rolling boil and boil for at least 5 minutes. The downside to boiling is the increased consumption of fuel. Water can be treated with an iodine-based disinfectant. Allow extra contact time and use twice as many tablets if the water is very cold. Chlorine-based products are ineffective in water that contains organic impurities, and all water-purification chemicals tend to deteriorate quickly. Sterilizer pens using ultraviolet light are relatively new and apparently very effective. Inserting the pen into the water for a few minutes kills viruses, bacteria, and protozoa. The water must be filtered before sterilizing, and hikers will need to carry extra batteries. Various types of pump filters remove impurities, often making the water look and taste better; several new gravity filters eliminate hand pumping and allow for water storage.

The symptoms of giardiasis and cryptosporidiosis are similar and include severe intestinal distress and diarrhea. But such discomforts can have many other causes, making the diseases difficult to diagnose accurately. The principal cause of the spread of these noxious ailments in the woods is probably careless disposal of human waste (see "Sanitation," below).

Sanitation

Keep human waste at least 200 ft. away from water sources. Use a toilet where one is available. If no toilets are nearby, dig a hole 6 to 8 in. deep (but not below the organic layer of the soil) for a latrine and cover the hole completely after use. The bacteria in the organic layer of the soil will decompose the waste naturally. Be scrupulous about washing hands or using a hand sanitizer after answering calls of nature. Put used toilet tissue and wet wipes in a plastic bag and pack it out to minimize impact.

Theft

Cars parked at trailheads are frequently targets of break-ins, so never leave valuables or expensive equipment inside your vehicle while you are hiking, particularly overnight.

Search and Rescue

In emergencies, call 911 or any of the Maine State Police 24-hr. regional communications centers:

Augusta	207-624-7076
Bangor	207-973-3700
Houlton	207-532-5400

Hikers should be aware that cell phone coverage in Maine's backcountry, both along the coast and in the mountains, can be very unreliable, particularly in deep valleys and under thick foliage, but also on some summits, and there is absolutely no assurance that a cell phone call will get through to authorities in an emergency. Both phones and their batteries can fail, often at inconvenient times. Sometimes a text message will get through when a call will not, but hikers should not rely on cell reception.

By state law, the Maine Warden Service of DIFW is responsible for search-and-rescue operations in the Maine outdoors. Whenever the commissioner receives notification that any person has gone into the woodlands or onto the inland waters of the state and has become lost or stranded, the commissioner will take reasonable steps to ensure the safe and timely recovery of that person. The commissioner reserves the right to end a search-and-rescue operation by members of the department when all reasonable efforts have been exhausted. The person for whom the search and rescue was conducted may be responsible for all directly related costs.

Search-and-rescue operations are serious matters. Time is required to organize rescue parties, which typically require a minimum of 18 people for litter carries and can endanger the rescuers. In addition, an unnecessary rescue mission may leave no resources if a real emergency occurs. Please make sure there really is an emergency before you call or go for help.

STEWARDSHIP AND CONSERVATION

Trails don't just happen. The trails we use and enjoy are the product of the dedication and hard work of local, state, and federal agencies; many public and private nonprofit organizations; and a host of volunteers. A significant number of trails in Maine are on private property and are open for public use through the generosity of the various landowners. Many trails, particularly on private property, are cared for by one dedicated person or a small group. Funds for trail work are scarce, and unless hikers contribute both time and money to maintenance, the diversity of trails available to the public may be threatened. Every hiker can make some contribution to trail improvement, if nothing more than pushing a blowdown off the path rather than walking around it. But a more formal commitment, even if it is just one day or one weekend each year, is welcomed. Many hands do make light work, and working together for the betterment of our trails is a fun and satisfying way to give something back.

Volunteer trail maintenance opportunities abound in Maine through public and private agencies such as AMC, MATC, BSP, MBPL, ANP, and the WMNF. The primary mission of MATC is to oversee the 282 mi. of the AT, its many shelters and campsites, and miles of side trails. AMC's Maine Chapter is active in building and maintaining trails. In addition, dozens of local and regional land trusts, conservation commissions, outdoor clubs, and recreation departments welcome assistance. Many of these organizations are listed in Appendix A: Helpful Information and Contacts (p. 600).

LEAVE NO TRACE

AMC is a national educational partner of Leave No Trace, a nonprofit organization dedicated to promoting and inspiring responsible outdoor recreation through education, research, and partnerships. The Leave No Trace program seeks to develop wild land ethics: ways in which people think and act in the outdoors to minimize their impact on the areas they visit and to protect natural resources for future enjoyment. Leave No Trace unites four federal land management agencies—USFS, NPS, Bureau of Land Management, and USFWS—with manufacturers, outdoor retailers, user groups, educators, organizations such as AMC, and individuals.

The Leave No Trace ethic is guided by these seven principles:

- Plan ahead and prepare.
- Travel and camp on durable surfaces.
- Dispose of waste properly.
- Leave what you find.
- Minimize campfire impacts.
- Respect wildlife.
- Be considerate of other visitors.

AMC is a national provider of the Leave No Trace Master Educator course. AMC offers this five-day course, designed especially for outdoor professionals and land managers, as well as the shorter two-day Leave No Trace Trainer course, at locations throughout the Northeast.

For Leave No Trace information and materials, contact the Leave No Trace Center for Outdoor Ethics, P.O. Box 997, Boulder, CO 80306; 800-332-4100 or 303-442-8222; or lnt.org. For a schedule of AMC Leave No Trace courses, see activities.outdoors.org.

SECTION ONE

BAXTER STATE PARK AND KATAHDIN WOODS AND WATERS NATIONAL MONUMENT

Pull-Out Map
Map 1: Baxter State Park–Katahdin Woods and Waters National Monument

SEC 1

INTRODUCTION

This section on Baxter State Park and the Katahdin region describes 93 trails on 36 mountains. Featured are trails to the high mountain peaks, as well as a wide variety of hikes along streams and rivers and to remote ponds and lakes. This section provides comprehensive coverage of the hiking trails in BSP and describes trails in the neighboring and relatively new Katahdin Woods and Waters National Monument, which abuts the park to the east. At present, only those mountains along or near the route of the IAT through KAWW are included; more trails will be added as they are developed over time. In the outlying areas around BSP and KAWW, hikers will find additional mountains and trails. To the south is Trout Mtn. on land owned by TNC; to the east are Sugarloaf Mtn., Mt. Chase, and Bald Mtn. on private timberlands; and to the north is Owl's Head at Scraggly Lake PL.

BAXTER STATE PARK

BSP was created as a gift from the former governor Percival P. Baxter in 1931 when he donated Katahdin and 5,960 surrounding acres to the state of Maine to be kept forever wild. Baxter's deed of gift for this original parcel made his intentions clear, stipulating that the land "shall forever be used for public park and recreational purposes, shall forever be left in the natural wild state, shall forever be kept as a sanctuary for wild beasts and birds…" Over the next three decades, Governor Baxter continued to purchase additional lands and add them to the park in deeds of trust, a total of 28 donations in all; his last, in 1962, brought the extent of BSP to more than 200,000 acres. Governor Baxter died in 1969. BSP has continued to expand in recent years, adding more than 8,000 acres through purchase or gift, including 4,100 acres around iconic Katahdin Lake in 2006. The park is now 209,644 deeded acres and features more than 220 mi. of hiking trails and more than 300 campsites.

About 75 percent of BSP is managed as a wildlife sanctuary, while 14 percent of the park (in its northwest corner) is managed as the Scientific Forest Management Area, where timber harvesting is allowed. About 25 percent of the park is open to hunting (though not for moose) and trapping. BSP is not part of Maine's state park system; the park is operated through user fees, income from trust funds provided by Governor Baxter, and revenue from timber sales. Governance of the park is the sole responsibility of the BSP Authority, which consists of Maine's attorney general, the commissioner of the DIFW, and the director of MFS.

Hiking Considerations

The trails on many BSP routes are among the steepest and most difficult in New England. Hikers planning to go to higher and more distant elevations should take plenty of food, water, and warm clothing and should be in good physical condition. Others may want to limit their activities accordingly. Hikers should not leave the trails, particularly on Katahdin or during inclement weather or times of limited visibility.

Severe injuries and deaths have occurred in the park over the years. Visitors must be responsible for their own safety and that of their group. The upper summits are very rugged and exposed above treeline. Weather and trail conditions can change quickly, even in summer. The weather on Katahdin is similar to that of Mt. Washington, but longer access routes can make conditions even more dangerous.

The alpine environment above treeline on Katahdin is home to many rare and unusual plants and animals. Please help care for these fragile ecosystems by staying on marked trails. Observe all wildlife from a safe distance.

The staff of BSP and volunteers maintain all the park's trails. All trails are blazed with blue paint; the only exception is the white-blazed AT.

Regulations

Persons planning to camp, hike, and use the facilities in the park should be familiar with the rules and regulations, which are revised periodically. A complete list can be found at baxterstatepark.org. The salient points for hikers and campers are summarized as follows:

- Camping is permitted by reservation only, and only at authorized campgrounds and campsites, between May 15 and October 15 (except for Kidney Pond, Daicey Pond, and Katahdin Stream campgrounds, which are open until October 22) and from December 1 through March 31.
- All persons entering the park by road or trail must register at the first opportunity at a staffed gatehouse or a self-registration station. Prior registration is required for groups of 12 or more.
- Hiking or mountain climbing may be restricted at the discretion of the park director.
- Hunting and trapping are prohibited, except in specifically designated areas. Maine fishing laws apply within the park.
- Pets and other domestic animals are not allowed in the park. Do not bait, feed, or disturb any animal in the park.
- Fires and cooking or heating devices are permitted only at designated campsites or picnic areas.
- Anything carried into the park must be carried out; for example, trash and gear.
- No person may use electronic devices in any way that impairs others' enjoyment of the park.
- No person may disturb or remove natural objects, plants, or animals.
- Single vehicles more than 9 ft. high, 7 ft. wide, or 22 ft. long—or 44 ft. long for combined units—are prohibited. Motorcycles, ATVs, and motorized trail bikes are prohibited. Bicycles are allowed only on park roads.
- Aircraft are generally prohibited in the park. The possession of a drone on any trail or waterway is prohibited.
- All groups of 5 or more persons younger than age 16 must be accompanied by an adult.

GEOGRAPHY

BSP is a vast wilderness area in the northern reaches of Piscataquis County. A portion of the park near Grand Lake Matagamon and around Katahdin Lake spills over into neighboring Penobscot County. Katahdin is the predominant natural feature of BSP and is Maine's highest mountain, an irregular-shaped mass of rock that rises abruptly from comparatively flat terrain to a gently sloping plateau above treeline. The massif culminates on its southeastern margin in a series of low summits, of which the southern two are the highest. These peaks are 0.3 mi. apart, and

Baxter Peak (5,267 ft.) to the northwest is the higher of the two. From southeastern South Peak (5,251 ft.), a serrated ridge of vertically fractured granite known as Knife Edge curves away to the east and northeast, culminating in a rock spire called Chimney Peak (4,888 ft.). Immediately beyond Chimney Peak, separated from it by a sharp cleft, is the broader summit of Pamola (4,904 ft.), named for the spirit that inhabits the mountain, according to Penobscot mythology. West and north of Baxter Peak is the Tableland, a broad, open plateau of alpine terrain ranging from Baxter Peak to Thoreau Spring and the Gateway north to the Saddle. North of the Saddle, the wide mass of Hamlin Peak (4,752 ft.) rises above the Tableland, which extends to Howe Peak (4,745 ft.), the highest of the North Peaks, and the Northwest Plateau.

The Tableland is nearly 4 mi. long and drops away abruptly by 1,000 to 2,000 ft. on all sides. After that, the slope becomes gentler. Large ridges extend out and around to encompass a series of glacial cirques, or basins. Great Basin and its branch, North Basin, are the best known. At the bottom of Great Basin, at an elevation of 2,914 ft., lies Chimney Pond, flanked by impressive cliffs and bordered by dense spruce and fir forest. The pond is about 8 acres in size and serves as a base for many varied mountain climbs. The compact basin immediately beyond (southwest of) Chimney Pond is known as South Basin. North of Great Basin, but still on the eastern side of the mountain, is North Basin, at an elevation of 3,100 ft., where high mountain walls surround a barren, boulder-strewn floor. Nearby Little North Basin is trailless and sees few visitors. On the western side of the Tableland, remote Northwest Basin lies at about 2,800 ft., and farther south is a broad valley known as the Klondike. Klondike Pond rests in a small glacial arm of this valley, just below the plateau, at 3,435 ft. The pond is 0.3 mi. long, deep, narrow, and remarkably beautiful. From the peaks at its northern and southern ends, the Tableland slopes gradually toward the center, known as the Saddle. The land falls off gently from the eastern escarpment of the Saddle toward the dense scrub that carpets the northwestern edge. Many avalanches have scored the walls of the Tableland, but only one of these scorings is still a trail: Saddle Slide at the western end of Great Basin. Abol Trail on Abol Slide, on the southwestern flank of the mountain, was rerouted in 2014–15 after significant landslides made the trail too dangerous.

The isolated location of Katahdin allows for exceptional views that take in dozens of lakes and ponds, including Moosehead Lake, the winding Penobscot River, and, to the south, the peaks of Mt. Desert Island and the Camden Hills on the coast. To the southwest is the 100MW and the mountains along the AT corridor. White Cap, the Bigelows, and Mt.

SEC 1

Abraham are among the peaks visible. Katahdin is the northern terminus of the 2,192-mi. AT, which follows Hunt Trail on Katahdin itself.

The Owl (3,695 ft.) lies west of Katahdin, across the Klondike, where trailless Barren Mtn. (3,701 ft.), Mt. OJI (3,427 ft.), West Peak (2,492 ft.), Mt. Coe (3,784 ft.), South Brother (3,960 ft.), North Brother (4,143 ft.), and Fort Mtn. (3,860 ft.) are also located. On the west side of Nesowadnehunk Stream is twin-peaked Doubletop Mtn. (north summit 3,482 ft.; south summit 3,455 ft.). Sentinel Mtn. (1,863 ft.) is in close proximity to a host of wild and beautiful ponds in the park's southwestern corner. Trailless Mullen Mtn. (3,459 ft.) and Wassataquoik Mtn. (2,981 ft.) lie in the remote area between Fort Mtn. and Wassataquoik Lake. To the east are Wassataquoik Stream and Russell Pond, in the heart of the park's interior. Wadleigh Mtn. (1,261 ft.) sits alone amid the sprawling woods of the Scientific Forest Management Area on the park's northern edge. Northwest of Nesowadnehunk Lake between the North Branch and South Branch of Trout Brook is Burnt Mtn. (1,796 ft.). Trout Brook Mtn. (1,781 ft.) and Horse Mtn. (1,592 ft.) are south of Grand Lake Matagamon in the Fowler Ponds area. Traveler Mtn., the principal mountain in the northern section of the park, is crowned by four high summits: Center Ridge (3,264 ft.), The Traveler (3,543 ft.), Traveler Ridge (2,976 ft.), and North Traveler (3,149ft.). The upper and lower sections of South Branch lie at the western base of Traveler Mtn. Rising steeply west of South Branch Pond are South Branch Mtn. (2,627 ft.) and Black Cat Mtn. (2,613 ft.). Barrel Ridge (2,090 ft.) is between South Branch Pond and the Five Ponds area. South Turner Mtn. (3,126 ft.) is just northeast of Katahdin and offers fantastic views; trailless North Turner Mtn. (3,326 ft.) is nearby. The magnificent Katahdin Lake sprawls at the base of the Katahdin massif a few miles to the east.

BSP ROAD ACCESS

The south entrance of BSP at Togue Pond Gate is reached by traveling on I-95 to Exit 244 at Medway. From there, travel west on ME 157 and then ME 157/11 through East Millinocket to Millinocket and finally on Baxter Park Rd. to reach the park. It is about 18 mi. from Millinocket to the gate. The north entrance of the park at Matagamon Gate is reached by traveling on I-95 to Exit 264 at Sherman. Proceed north on ME 11 to Patten and then northwest on ME 159 to Shin Pond. From there, take Grand Lake Rd. west to the park. It is about 26 mi. from Patten to the gate. Togue Pond Gate and Matagamon Gate are open for vehicular traffic from May 15 to at least October 22. The actual end of the season varies and is determined by weather conditions.

All park visitors must stop at the entrance gate to register and obtain a park pass. Rangers can also assist with directions and information about hiking trails and camping. Hikers entering the park via the AT must register at the trail kiosk at the park boundary near Abol Bridge. Most visitors enter the park at Togue Pond Gate. An entrance fee is charged for vehicles bearing out-of-state license plates. Just beyond the gate, the road forks. The right fork is Roaring Brook Rd., which leads 8.1 mi. to Roaring Brook CG. To the left is Park Tote Rd., leading 41.1 mi. to the north entrance at Matagamon Gate.

In accordance with the terms of Governor Baxter's deeds of trust, park roads are unpaved and relatively unimproved. Park Tote Rd. and Roaring Brook Rd. are very narrow, winding dirt and gravel roads. Dense foliage restricts views to the immediate corridor for much of the way, but there are occasional outlooks. From Togue Pond Gate, Park Tote Rd. first leads northwest and then generally north, skirting the southern and western flanks of Katahdin. During the first 5 or so miles of the drive, the mountain is briefly visible a few times. After passing Abol and Katahdin Stream campgrounds, the road reaches Foster Field, where you can see Doubletop Mtn., Mt. OJI, and other mountains in the range west of Katahdin. After that, the views are very restricted much of the way to Matagamon Gate. Most of Park Tote Rd. follows the routes of old logging roads.

Park Tote Rd. from Togue Pond Gate to:

Roaring Brook Rd.	100 ft.
Abol CG	5.7 mi.
Katahdin Stream CG	7.7 mi.
Daicey Pond access road (1.1 mi. to Daicey Pond from Park Tote Rd.)	10.0 mi.
Kidney Pond access road (1.4 mi. to Kidney Pond from Park Tote Rd.)	10.3 mi.
Foster Field	10.3 mi.
Nesowadnehunk CG	16.8 mi.
Trout Brook Crossing	33.8 mi.
South Branch Pond CG via access road from Trout Brook Crossing	36.1 mi.
Trout Brook CG	38.5 mi.
Matagamon Gate	41.1 mi.

Roaring Brook Rd. diverges right from Park Tote Rd. 100 ft. beyond Togue Pond Gate. Katahdin is immediately visible on the left across Helon Taylor and Rum ponds. Roaring Brook Rd. then proceeds through the woods, following the base of the mountain to the east, passing Rum Brook Day Use Site, Bear Brook Group Site, and Avalanche Field before reaching its terminus at Roaring Brook CG.

Roaring Brook Rd. from Togue Pond Gate to:

Rum Brook Day Use Site	1.3 mi.
Bear Brook Group Site	5.2 mi.
Avalanche Field	6.6 mi.
Roaring Brook CG	8.1 mi.

The park is open to the public 12 months a year, although access is often limited during spring thaw, from April to mid-May. Roads are unplowed during winter and are available for cross-country skiing; snowmobiling is allowed on Park Tote Rd.

BSP headquarters is at 64 Balsam Dr. in Millinocket. The park operates a seasonal visitor center at Togue Pond, a short distance before Togue Pond Gate.

Day-Use Parking

From June to October, day-use visitors desiring to climb Katahdin are strongly urged to use the Day Use Parking Reservation (DUPR) system. This service is available for a small fee ($5 in 2022) for hikers wanting to climb Katahdin from Roaring Brook, Abol, or Katahdin Stream campgrounds. DUPRs can be reserved online at reservation.baxterstatepark.org or by calling the reservation office at 207-723-5140.

CAMPING

The park offers a wide variety of camping opportunities at 10 campgrounds, from drive-in campsites, walk-in tentsites, cabins, and bunkhouses to remote backcountry lean-tos and tentsites. Camping is permitted by reservation only, and only at authorized campgrounds and campsites, between May 15 and October 15 (Kidney Pond, Daicey Pond, and Katahdin Stream campgrounds are open until October 22), and from December 1 through March 31.

Reservations

Camping reservations are mandatory and can be made through a rolling reservation system. Reservations may be made online, by mail (check), or in person (cash or check) at park headquarters in Millinocket up to 4 months in advance of the desired trip date. Reservations are limited to 7 days at any single site and 14 days total for any single visit to the park.

Last-minute reservations may be made by phone 14 days or less before the desired arrival date. Reservations made by phone must be paid by credit card. To get a printable camping reservation form, to view campsite availability, or to make a reservation, go to reservation.baxterstatepark.org or call the reservation office at 207-723-5140. Mailing address is 64 Balsam Dr., Millinocket, ME 04462; physical address for in-person reservations is the same.

Camping Availability

Seven drive-in campgrounds are along Park Tote Rd.: Abol, Katahdin Stream, Nesowadnehunk, Kidney Pond, Daicey Pond, South Branch Pond, and Trout Brook. Group camping sites are also available at Foster Field, Nesowadnehunk, and Trout Brook. Roaring Brook CG and Bear Brook Group Site are on Roaring Brook Rd. Backcountry campgrounds, with access only on foot, are at Chimney Pond and Russell Pond. Gain access to Chimney Pond by trail from Roaring Brook CG. Trails from Roaring Brook, Nesowadnehunk, and South Branch Pond campgrounds lead to Russell Pond. In all, 24 primitive backcountry campsites (which may be lean-tos or tentsites) are reachable on foot.

All campgrounds have lean-tos (except Daicey Pond and Kidney Pond) and tentsites (except Chimney Pond, Daicey Pond, and Kidney Pond). Daicey Pond and Kidney Pond have cabins only. Bunkhouses are at Roaring Brook, Nesowadnehunk, South Branch Pond, Russell Pond, Chimney Pond, and Trout Brook. All these sites offer only the most basic facilities. No hot showers, grocery stores, or gas stations are available in the park. Water is available but is untreated throughout the park, so some method for purifying is essential. Campers and visitors must supply their own camping gear, food, and cooking utensils. Fires are permitted only at designated sites. Firewood is available for purchase.

Canoes, paddles, and personal flotation devices are available for rent at many campgrounds and select backcountry sites. Check with a ranger for more information.

Abol CG

This campground is on Abol Stream, at the foot of Abol Slide on the southwestern flank of Katahdin, 5.7 mi. north of Togue Pond Gate. Visitor facilities include a day-use area with picnic tables and toilet and camping at twelve lean-tos and nine tentsites. Abol Trail (see p. 19) leaves from the campground and climbs more than 3,300 ft. to reach a vast alpine plateau called the Tableland below the summit of Katahdin, merging with Hunt

Trail at Thoreau Spring for the final ascent to Baxter Peak. A side trail to Little Abol Falls from the campground offers a pleasant short walk.

Katahdin Stream CG

This campground is on Katahdin Stream, at the base of Katahdin's southwestern flank, 7.7 mi. from Togue Pond Gate. Facilities include picnic shelters and toilets, plus twelve lean-tos and ten tentsites. Nearby Foster Field Group Area (2.6 mi. north) has a capacity of 50 people. The AT enters Katahdin Stream CG and merges with Hunt Trail on its way to the summit of Katahdin. A variety of other day hikes are possible from this location: to Katahdin Stream Falls; the Owl; Tracy, Elbow, Daicey, and Grassy ponds; and Blueberry Ledges.

Roaring Brook CG

This campground is on the southern bank of Roaring Brook at the terminus of Roaring Brook Rd., 8.1 mi. from Togue Pond Gate. Facilities include nine lean-tos, ten tentsites, and a ten-person bunkhouse. Nearby Bear Brook Group Area has three group campsites with a capacity of 42 persons. Roaring Brook CG is the base for ascending Katahdin from the east and for backpacking into the southern interior of the park. Trails to Pamola, Chimney Pond, and Russell Pond start here. Close by is Sandy Stream Pond, where hikers can often see moose and other wildlife, and South Turner Mtn.

Chimney Pond CG

This campground, the oldest in the park, is in a spectacular setting near the north shore of Chimney Pond in Katahdin's Great Basin, where the walls of the mountain rise more than 2,000 ft. to the high summits of Baxter Peak and Pamola. The campground is reachable only via a 3.3-mi. hike from Roaring Brook CG. Facilities include nine lean-tos and a ten-person bunkhouse. Open fires are not allowed at Chimney Pond, so campers must bring a lightweight backpacking stove for cooking. Saddle, Cathedral, and Dudley trails leave from Chimney Pond and ascend to the high summits and ridges of Katahdin: Baxter Peak, Knife Edge, South Peak, and Pamola. Nearby Hamlin Ridge Trail leads to Hamlin Peak and Howe Peak, and North Basin Trail leads to North Basin and Blueberry Knoll.

Russell Pond CG

Along the western shore of Russell Pond, in the heart of the wilderness north of Katahdin, this hike-in-only campground makes a convenient base for exploring the central interior of the park. Wildlife watching in this remote area is especially intriguing. Facilities include three tentsites, five lean-tos, and an eight-person bunkhouse. Little Wassataquoik CS, Island CS on Wassataquoik Lake, and Wassataquoik Stream and Pogy Pond campsites are easily reached from Russell Pond. Short trails nearby lead to Caverly Lookout, Grand Falls, Six Ponds, and Wassataquoik Lake.

Daicey Pond CG

This campground is on Daicey Pond, 11.1 mi. north of Togue Pond Gate via Park Tote Rd. and the Daicey Pond access road. Established as a sporting camp in the early 1900s and operated as York's Twin Pine Camps until 1971, the scenic Daicey Pond CG offers outstanding views of the west side of Katahdin and, from a canoe on the pond, fine views of Doubletop Mtn. and other nearby peaks. The campground features ten self-service cabins, a library, canoe and kayak rentals, and trailhead parking. Day-use parking is available in a clearing on the Daicey Pond access road, 1.0 mi. south of Park Tote Rd. and 0.1 mi. north of Daicey Pond CG. The AT passes close to the campground and follows the north shore of the pond for 0.4 mi. South of the pond, the AT passes Toll Dam on Nesowadnehunk Stream, Little Niagara Falls, and then Big Niagara Falls. All are worth seeing and within an easy walk of the campground. Daicey Pond is also a good alternate starting point for access to Sentinel Mtn. and Kidney Pond, although Sentinel Mtn. Trail from this direction does require fording Nesowadnehunk Stream. Beautiful Tracy, Elbow, and Grassy ponds are also within easy reach. Inquire at the Daicey Pond ranger cabin about other short pond hikes not described here.

Kidney Pond CG

This campground is on Kidney Pond, 11.8 mi. north of Togue Pond Gate via Park Tote Rd. and the Kidney Pond access road. The cabins at Kidney Pond were established as a sporting camp in 1899 and operated as a private camp until 1988. Kidney Pond CG now serves as a central hub for hiking, as well as for fishing and canoeing on Kidney Pond and the surrounding ponds, including Rocky, Celia, Jackson, and Lily Pad. The campground features twelve self-service cabins, a library, canoe and kayak rentals, and trailhead parking. Kidney Pond is a convenient base for hikes to Sentinel and Doubletop mountains, as well as to many pretty outlying ponds.

Nesowadnehunk CG

This attractive campground, 16.8 mi. north of Togue Pond Gate via Park Loop Rd., is along the eastern bank of Nesowadnehunk Stream. Nesow-adnehunk is the base for the approach to Doubletop Mtn. from the north and for trails to Center Pond, Wassataquoik Lake, and Russell Pond to the

SEC
1

northeast. The campground features nine tentsites, eleven lean-tos, a four-person bunkhouse, and two group areas.

South Branch Pond CG

South Branch Pond, consisting of an upper section and a lower section in a deep valley between Traveler Mtn. to the east and South Branch and Black Cat mountains to the west, has one of the most spectacular surroundings anywhere in Maine. The campground, at the north end of Lower South Branch Pond, is a base for hiking the peaks of Traveler Mtn. From the water, visitors are rewarded with choice views of the peaks and ridges of Traveler Mtn., rising south and east, and of the bulk of South Branch Mtn., rising to the south and west. The campground features 21 tentsites, 12 lean-tos, an 8-person bunkhouse, 2 walk-in/canoe-in sites on Lower South Branch Pond, 1 walk-in/canoe-in site on Upper South Branch Pond, a picnic area, canoe and kayak rentals, and trailhead parking.

Trout Brook CG

Trout Brook CG is on the site of a farm dating to 1837 that once supported logging operations. The campground is on the north side of Park Tote Rd., about 27 mi. west of Patten, 2.6 mi. west of Matagamon Gate, and 4.7 mi. east of Trout Brook Crossing Day Use Site, where the road to South Branch Pond CG leads south. The campground features fourteen tentsites, one walk-in lean-to along Trout Brook, four group sites, canoe rentals, and trailhead parking. The campground is a convenient starting point for a variety of explorations in this region of the park, including hikes on Freezeout Trail to the north and the network of trails in the Fowler Ponds area to the south. The trail to Trout Brook Mtn. leaves just across the road from the campground. Trout Brook CG is also a useful base for canoe trips on the brook and nearby Grand Lake Matagamon.

KATAHDIN WOODS AND WATERS NATIONAL MONUMENT

Katahdin Woods and Waters National Monument preserves 87,500 acres of craggy mountain peaks, deep woods, and free-flowing rivers and streams in the Maine woods east of BSP, an area long recognized for its ecological, recreational, and cultural importance. Using the authority granted by the Antiquities Act of 1906, President Barack Obama established the monument with a proclamation on August 24, 2016. Protected are scenic stretches of the East Branch of the Penobscot River, Wassataquoik Stream, and the Seboeis River, as well as a rugged ridgeline of peaks, including the historical fire tower atop Deasey Mtn. The views of Katahdin to the west from many points in KAWW are particularly striking.

KAWW is the latest addition to a diverse matrix of public and private conservation lands that range southwest across the 100MW to Moosehead Lake and then west to the Canadian border. The lands that compose the new monument were assembled by the privately held Elliotsville Plantation Inc. between 2001 and 2014 and then donated to the federal government. Along with the land, the foundation donated $20 million to establish an endowment for the monument and pledged to raise an additional $20 million in the future.

NPS manages the monument and, with the support of Friends of Katahdin Woods & Waters, is working through a multiyear strategic management plan to develop and improve access and infrastructure for the recreating public.

KAWW is open year-round for a variety of recreational activities, including hiking, backpacking, canoeing, kayaking, mountain biking, fishing, bird and wildlife watching, cross-country skiing, and horseback riding. Drive-in camping is available but limited. Katahdin Loop Rd. is a gravel road that traces a 17-mi. route through the southern section of KAWW, offering visitors a good introduction by touching on popular short hikes and walks and viewpoints. The road is rough in places and a high-clearance vehicle is recommended.

From late May to mid-October, NPS staff are available to provide information and trip-planning assistance from a desk inside the Patten Lumbermen's Museum on ME 159 in Patten. Maps and brochures are also available.

GEOGRAPHY

Bordering BSP to the east, the main section of KAWW has as its eastern boundary a wild and beautiful stretch of the East Branch of the Penobscot River. Wassataquoik Stream slices through the southern half of the heavily forested monument to empty into the East Branch near Lunksoos. Seven mountains ranging between 1,000 and 2,000 ft. in elevation dot the landscape; three have trails that lead to spectacular views of Katahdin and the mountainous skyline of Baxter. Barnard Mtn. (1,628 ft.) has the easiest access; it looks out over Katahdin Lake. North of Wassataquoik Stream are Lunksoos Mtn. (1,796 ft.) and Deasey Mtn. (1,951 ft.), the latter with a fire tower cab. Straddling the BSP–KAWW boundary just north of Wassataquoik Stream is Lookout Mtn. (1,953 ft.) and its south-facing summit ledges.

SEC 1

ROAD ACCESS

Two main access routes exist for KAWW.

To reach the southern section: From I-95, Exit 264 at Sherman, drive west on ME 158 for 0.6 mi. to the jct. of ME 11, turn south on ME 11 (ME 11 bears sharply left), and drive 5.0 mi. to Swift Brook Rd. For an alternate route from I-95, take Exit 244 at Medway, drive west on ME 157 for 0.75 mi., turn north on ME 11, and proceed 20.0 mi. to Swift Brook Rd. on the left.

From either of the options above, turn onto Swift Brook Rd., which quickly becomes a gravel road. (*Note*: Active logging traffic uses this road; please yield to trucks.) At a jct. 5.2 mi. from ME 11, turn left for Katahdin Loop Rd. and in another 1.7 mi. reach Whetstone Bridge over the East Branch of the Penobscot River. Pass Roberts Rd. on the left and then Stacyville Rd. on the left on the way to Sandbank Stream CS, which is 2.9 mi. from Whetstone Bridge. At this old gravel pit are an information kiosk and three car-camping sites with picnic tables, firepits, and a vault toilet. This is the official start of Katahdin Loop Rd. The main jct. of the road is 2.2 mi. ahead; visitors desiring to drive the entire loop should turn left at that point to travel in the recommended clockwise direction (several steep, narrow sections after Mile 7 are one-way). Visitors planning to hike Barnard Mtn. and the IAT should proceed right from the main jct. A high-clearance vehicle is recommended for travel on Katahdin Loop Rd.

To reach the northern entrance: From I-95, take Exit 264 at Sherman and drive west on ME 158 for 0.6 mi. to the jct. of ME 11. Bear right on ME 11 for 9.3 mi. to the northerly jct. of ME 159 and ME 11 in Patten. Turn left on ME 159 and drive 24.2 mi. (ME 159 becomes Grand Lake Rd. after Shin Pond) to Messer Pond Rd., which is on the left, just after the bridge over the East Branch of the Penobscot River and Matagamon Wilderness CG. Matagamon Gate is 0.7 mi. south on Messer Pond Rd.

KAWW CAMPING AND HUTS

Find drive-in primitive camping at Sandbank Stream CS, which provides three first-come-first serve sites. Four backcountry lean-tos—at Katahdin Brook, Wassataquoik, Lunksoos, and Grand Pitch—plus Haskell Hut, are along the IAT as it threads through Katahdin Woods and Waters National Monument. West of the IAT corridor, Big Spring Brook Hut lies along old tote roads. Except for Sandbank Stream CS, all KAWW campsites and huts must be reserved by visiting recreation.gov. A fire permit from MFS is required for all campsites.

OUTLYING AREAS

East of the bulk of KAWW, between Shin Pond and the Seboeis River, is the steep and shapely peak of Sugarloaf Mtn. (1,868 ft.); farther east and just north of Patten, Mt. Chase (2,440 ft.) rises prominently from a low range of summits; its neighbor to the east, Bald Mtn. (1,685 ft.), also has trails. Northeast of BSP, the wooded bump of Owl's Head (930 ft.) looks out over Scraggly Lake. Bordering BSP in the south near Togue Pond looms Trout Mtn. (1,408 ft.) and its observation tower.

Access to Mt. Chase and Bald Mtn. is via ME 11. Owl's Head in Scraggly Lake PL is reached by ME 159 and Grand Lake Rd. Access to Trout Mtn. is by ME 157 and Baxter Park Rd.

At least seven privately operated campgrounds are in the Katahdin region.

SUGGESTED HIKES

■ Easy

KATAHDIN STREAM FALLS

RT via Hunt Trail	2.4 mi.	500 ft.	1:25

From Katahdin Stream CG, hike to pretty Katahdin Stream Falls, an 80-ft. series of cascades in a mossy canyon. See Hunt Trail, p. 20.

BIG AND LITTLE NIAGARA FALLS

RT via AT Southbound	2.2 mi.	110 ft.	1:10

This easy jaunt from Daicey Pond leads to three thundering waterfalls: Toll Dam, Little Niagara Falls, and Big Niagara Falls. See AT Southbound from Daicey Pond trailhead, p. 33.

DAICEY, GRASSY, AND ELBOW PONDS

LP via AT Northbound, Elbow Pond Connector, and Tracy and Elbow Ponds Trail	3.0 mi.	300 ft.	1:35

Enjoy grand Katahdin views and watch for moose and other wildlife on this lovely loop through spruce woods in the vicinity of three idyllic ponds. To begin, see AT Northbound from Daicey Pond trailhead, p. 33.

LEDGES NORTH OF SOUTH BRANCH POND

LP via Ledges Trail	1.3 mi.	150 ft.	0:45

This short loop hike leads to open ledges with views south across the steep-walled valley that contains Lower and Upper South Branch ponds. See Ledges Trail, p. 53.

OWL'S HEAD

RT via Owl's Head Trail	3.4 mi.	285 ft.	1:50

The long drive to get here is worth it when you hike to the ledges on Owl's Head. Enjoy the fine view over pristine Scraggly Lake to high summits of BSP and many other peaks. See Owl's Head Trail, p. 68.

■ Moderate

CHIMNEY POND

RT via Chimney Pond Trail	6.6 mi.	1,425 ft.	4:00

Hike from Roaring Brook CG to Chimney Pond, dramatically located at the base of the towering walls of South Basin. Baxter Peak, Knife Edge, and Pamola loom high above. See Chimney Pond Trail, p. 21.

KATAHDIN LAKE

LP via Katahdin Lake Trail and Martin Ponds Trail	7.4 mi.	470 ft.	4:00

Hike to iconic Katahdin Lake for lunch and return by way of Martin Ponds Trail to get a brilliant sighting of Katahdin from the campsite there. To begin, see Katahdin Lake Trail, p. 29.

FIVE PONDS LOOP

LP via Five Ponds Trail	6.0 mi.	500 ft.	3:30

This loop around the base of Trout Brook Mtn. passes five scenic ponds: Littlefield, Billfish, Round, High, and Long. See Five Ponds Trail, p. 54.

BARNARD MTN.

RT via IAT and Barnard Mtn. Trail	4.4 mi.	758 ft.	2:35

From Katahdin Loop Rd. at Mile 12, hike the IAT and Barnard Mtn. Trail to the large ledge atop Barnard for grand vistas of Katahdin Lake and majestic Katahdin. To begin, see Barnard Mtn. Trail, p. 63.

TROUT MTN.

RT via Trout Mtn. Trail	5.2 mi.	808 ft.	3:00

On the observation deck atop the 80-ft. steel tower on Trout Mtn., hikers will enjoy an outstanding 360-degree panorama from Katahdin to the 100MW. See Trout Mtn. Trail, p. 64.

■ Strenuous
KATAHDIN GRAND CIRCUIT

LP via Chimney Pond, Dudley, and Saddle trails	11.8 mi.	4,079 ft.	8:00

This exciting lollipop loop hike starts and ends at Roaring Brook. Climb Pamola via Dudley Trail, traverse the airy crest of Knife Edge to Baxter Peak, and descend by way of Saddle Trail. To begin, see Chimney Pond Trail, p. 21.

DOUBLETOP MTN.

OW via Doubletop Mtn. Trail	8.2 mi.	2,497 ft.	5:20

This outstanding hike from Kidney Pond to Nesowadnehunk Field climbs the craggy twin summits of Doubletop Mtn. for impressive views of Katahdin, South Brother, Mt. Coe, Mt. OJI, and Barren Mtn. A vehicle spot is required. See Doubletop Mtn. Trail, p. 38.

MT. OJI AND WEST PEAK

RT via Mt. OJI Trail and West Peak Overlook Spur	8.4 mi.	2,555 ft.	5:30

Climb to lookouts on West Peak and at Old Jay Eye Rock; then follow an airy ridgeline for expansive sights of Mt. Coe, South Brother, and Katahdin. To begin, see Mt. OJI Trail, p. 40.

SEC 1

TRAVELER MTN. CIRCUIT

◐ ❀ 🐾 🏃 ⛺   �??   ↗   ○

| LP via Pogy Notch, Center Ridge, Traveler Mtn., and North Traveler Mtn. trails | 11.1 mi. | 3,795 ft. | 7:30 |

This demanding loop hike over the summits of Center Ridge, Traveler, Traveler Ridge, and North Traveler Mtn. rewards hikers with outstanding vistas from the high and craggy alpine ridges and summits en route. To begin, see Pogy Notch Trail, p. 47.

DEASEY MTN.

◐ 🐾 ◣ ▲ ⛺ 🗼   ↕   ↗   ○

| RT via Orin Falls Trail and IAT Northbound | 9.2 mi. | 1,570 ft. | 6:05 |

From the end of Orin Falls Rd. in KAWW, hike to the IAT and follow it north across Wassataquoik Stream (ford) to bag the rocky summit of Deasey Mtn., which features a historical ground house fire tower and excellent views west to the BSP mountain skyline. To begin, see Orin Falls Trail, p. 62.

TRAIL DESCRIPTIONS
KATAHDIN
KATAHDIN: BAXTER PEAK (5,267 FT.), PAMOLA (4,904 FT.), SOUTH PEAK (5,251 FT.), AND CHIMNEY PEAK (4,888 FT.)

At 5,267 ft., Katahdin is Maine's highest mountain and as wild and alluring as any mountain in the eastern United States. Rising majestically from the Maine woods just north of the West Branch of the Penobscot River, about 80 mi. north of Bangor, Katahdin is BSP's crown jewel. Its first recorded ascent was via the southwest ridge (once known as the Southwest Spur, now Hunt Spur) in 1804 by a party of 11, including Charles Turner Jr., who wrote an account of the trip. Unrecorded ascents may have occurred during the next 15 years, but we do know that people climbed the mountain again in 1819 and 1820. After this date, ascents became more regular. Henry David Thoreau scaled the mountain in 1846 but did not reach the top. Katahdin has six major summits—Baxter Peak, Pamola, South Peak, Chimney Peak, Hamlin Peak, and Howe Peak—and features a network of trails (all blazed blue except for Hunt Trail [the AT]) that ascend the mountain from every major compass direction.

ABOL TRAIL (MAP 1: E3)
Cumulative from Abol CG (1,300 ft.) to:

SEC 1

Thoreau Spring and Hunt Trail (4,636 ft.)	3.4 mi.	3,336 ft.	3:30
Baxter Peak (5,267 ft.) via Hunt Trail	4.4 mi.	3,967 ft.	4:10

BSP Abol Trail is the shortest route to Baxter Peak from a park road, and as such, it is the mountain's most popular ascent route. A huge avalanche created the obvious Abol Slide in 1816, and it has been a prominent landmark for Katahdin climbers ever since. The first recorded ascent of Abol Slide was in 1819 by a party of British surveyors led by Colin Campbell. The famous slide was an integral part of Abol Trail until 2013, when significant landslide activity moved untold tons of rocks, gravel, and other debris, leaving the unstable slope too dangerous for hiking and forcing its closure. Crews routed the trail away from Abol Slide to the slope immediately west over the next two summers; the trail reopened in summer 2016.

The route leaves Park Tote Rd. at Abol CG, passes through the campground and, at 0.2 mi. between lean-tos 11 and 12, enters an old tote road to reach the southern bank of a tributary of Abol Stream. Abol Trail continues along the water for 0.6 mi. before bearing sharply right (northeast), away from the brook. The trail reaches a gravel wash from Abol Slide and begins to steepen. Just above, in sight of Abol Slide, the trail diverges left onto the new treadway. After a long, rising traverse and multiple sets of rock steps, the trail switchbacks east and continues to climb steeply.

At treeline, enjoy a fine panoramic vista over the 100MW and a pleasant view west to Hunt Spur and the AT. Here, Abol Trail turns east again to reach the top of Abol Slide and offers a sweeping look down the former route. From here to the Tableland, the original rock scramble—600 ft. of strenuous climbing—remains. Upon reaching the Tableland, the trail leads 0.1 mi. to Thoreau Spring (unreliable water source) and the jct. with Hunt Trail at 3.4 mi. For Baxter Peak, turn right on Hunt Trail and continue northeast up gentler slopes for 1.0 mi. to the summit.

LITTLE ABOL FALLS TRAIL (MAP 1: E3)
From Abol CG (1,300 ft.) to:

Little Abol Falls (1,550 ft.)	0.8 mi.	250 ft.	0:30

BSP This short, scenic trail leads easily from Abol CG to a series of falls on a branch of Abol Stream. Katahdin is visible along the route.

HUNT TRAIL (MAP 1: E2–E3)

Cumulative from Katahdin Stream CG (1,099 ft.) to:

Owl Trail (1,590 ft.)	1.1 mi.	491 ft.	0:45
Katahdin Stream Falls (1,690 ft.)	1.2 mi.	591 ft.	0:50
The Gateway (4,537 ft.)	3.6 mi.	3,438 ft.	3:30
Thoreau Spring (4,627 ft.) at Abol Trail and Baxter Peak Cutoff	4.4 mi.	3,528 ft.	4:00
Baxter Peak (5,267 ft.)	5.4 mi.	4,168 ft.	4:50

BSP White-blazed Hunt Trail is the route of the AT up Katahdin and climbs the mountain from the southwest. The first recorded ascent of Katahdin was in 1804 by a surveyor named Charles Turner Jr., who is believed to have climbed the peak via the Southwest Spur, later renamed Hunt Spur and the route of Hunt Trail. Hunt Trail was first cut in 1900 by Irving O. Hunt, who operated a sporting camp on Nesowadnehunk Stream. Hunt Trail requires 4,168 ft. of elevation gain, the most of any route to Baxter Peak; from treeline to the Tableland, the trail is long, steep, and rough.

From the day-use parking lot, follow Hunt Trail north through the campground. Just past tentsite 16, the trail enters the woods to closely follow the northern side of Katahdin Stream. At 1.1 mi. from the campground, Hunt Trail passes the trail to the Owl on the left and then crosses Katahdin Stream. Soon after, a short spur path leads left to Katahdin Stream Falls, an 80-ft. cascade in a mossy canyon. Hunt Trail steepens through the spruce and fir forest, ascending via rock staircases in places. The trail crosses O-Joy Brook, the last sure water, at 2.0 mi. At 2.8 mi., Hunt Trail reaches two large rocks that form a cave.

The trail passes through a growth of small spruce and fir and, in another 0.2 mi., emerges on Hunt Spur, a bare, steep crest on the southwest shoulder of the mountain. Here, cairns mark the route, which winds among huge boulders. Steel rungs aid the ascent in places. The trail then traverses a broad shelf and climbs steeply for 0.5 mi. over broken rock to the Tableland at 3.6 mi., where two slabs of rock mark the "Gateway."

The trail continues east, following a worn path and paint blazes, until it reaches Thoreau Spring, an unreliable water source, at 4.2 mi. At the spring, Baxter Peak Cutoff Trail goes left and reaches Saddle Trail in 0.9 mi. To the right, Abol Trail descends 3.4 mi. to Abol CG. From the spring, Hunt Trail climbs moderately northeast for 1.0 mi. to the summit of Baxter Peak, with its commanding panoramas and outstanding vistas of Great Basin, Chimney Pond, and Knife Edge.

HELON TAYLOR TRAIL (MAP 1: E4)
Cumulative from Roaring Brook CG (1,489 ft.) to:

Start of Helon Taylor Trail (1,550 ft.) via Chimney Pond Trail	0.1 mi.	60 ft.	0:05
Pamola summit (4,904 ft.) and jct. Dudley Trail and Knife Edge	3.6 mi.	3,415 ft.	3:20
Baxter Peak (5,267 ft.) via Knife Edge	4.7 mi.	3,989 ft.	4:20

BSP This direct route from Roaring Brook CG to Pamola follows the exposed Keep Ridge. It provides the most sustained views of any trail on Katahdin, but hikers are exposed to the elements for most of the climb. Consider avoiding this trail in bad weather, particularly if plans include Baxter Peak via Knife Edge.

The route leaves left (south) from Chimney Pond Trail 0.1 mi. northwest of the ranger cabin at Roaring Brook CG. Helon Taylor Trail climbs 0.5 mi. through mixed growth to a ridge crest and then levels off for a short period, passing through scrub and a boulder field. After that, the trail climbs steeply through small birch, enters an old flat burn, and drops to the small Bear Brook (unreliable), one of the branches of Avalanche Brook and the only water on the trail.

Beyond, Helon Taylor Trail ascends steeply through scrub, a fine stand of conifers, and a boulder field with wide views in all directions. It then climbs over and between boulders to Keep Ridge and runs along the open ridge with spectacular views ahead to Knife Edge, north to the Basin ponds and South Turner Mtn., and east to Katahdin Lake. The trail reaches the summit of Pamola at 3.6 mi., where there are excellent sights of Baxter Peak, Great Basin, Chimney Pond, and the high peaks of the Katahdin massif. From Pamola, it is 1.1 mi. to Baxter Peak via Knife Edge.

CHIMNEY POND TRAIL (MAP 1: D4–E4)
Cumulative from Roaring Brook CG (1,489 ft.) to:

Brook crossing (1,870 ft.)	1.0 mi.	381 ft.	0:40
North Basin Cutoff (2,500 ft.)	2.3 mi.	1,010 ft.	1:40
North Basin Trail (2,830 ft.)	3.0 mi.	1,341 ft.	2:10
Chimney Pond CG (2,914 ft.)	3.3 mi.	1,425 ft.	2:15

BSP This trail begins at the ranger cabin at Roaring Brook CG. Just ahead, Russell Pond Trail (p. 43) leaves right (leads 6.6 mi. to Russell Pond), and at 0.1 mi., Helon Taylor Trail leaves left (leads 3.6 mi. to Pamola). Continuing on, Chimney Pond Trail climbs west along the south bank of Roaring Brook. After 0.6 mi., the trail bears gradually away from the brook and climbs more steeply. At 1.0 mi., it crosses a brook, the outlet of Pamola Pond.

Chimney Pond Trail reaches Lower Basin Pond at 1.9 mi., and a short side trail on the right leads to the pond, where there are excellent views of the northern summits, cirques, and ridges of Katahdin. At 2.3 mi., North Basin Cutoff leaves to the right (leads 0.7 mi. to North Basin Trail). Beyond this jct., pass a depression known as Dry Pond, which holds water in spring and after heavy rains. At 3.0 mi., North Basin Trail to Hamlin Ridge and North Basin leaves to the right. At 3.3 mi., North Basin Trail enters a small clearing that sports a covered day shelter with benches on the left. Beyond, the trail proceeds gently down through Chimney Pond CG to the ranger cabin and, just ahead, Chimney Pond. From this vantage point are magnificent vistas of Great Basin, formed by the sweeping rock walls of Katahdin, from Pamola and Chimney Peak to South Peak and Baxter Peak. (*Note*: No swimming, washing, or wading is allowed in Chimney Pond.)

DUDLEY TRAIL (MAP 1: E4)
Cumulative from Chimney Pond CG (2,914 ft.) to:

Pamola summit (4,904 ft.) and Helon Taylor Trail and Knife Edge	1.7 mi.	1,990 ft.	1:50
Baxter Peak (5,267 ft.) via Knife Edge	2.8 mi.	2,564 ft.	2:40

BSP This trail ascends from Chimney Pond to Pamola via its north ridge, also known as Dudley Ridge. In 2016, a rock slide on the lower portion of Dudley Trail at the jct. of the Pamola Caves side trail permanently interrupted the route, resulting in the trail's closure. Crews worked on rerouting the trail across difficult terrain for four summers; the trail finally reopened along this new route in late summer 2020.

Dudley Trail starts from the ranger cabin at Chimney Pond and heads east for 0.1 mi. before turning sharply left onto the new section of trail and heading northeast. For the next 0.5 mi., the trail weaves in and out of the woods as it crosses talus slopes along the base of Pamola. Some scrambling is required to negotiate the route as it winds between large boulders. After passing between two large "gateway" boulders, Dudley Trail reaches a side trail that leads right 0.25 mi. (and gains about 150 ft. of elevation) to Pamola Caves, an interesting series of passages through the rocks. Soon after the Pamola Caves jct., Dudley Trail begins a steep ascent of a forested ridge punctuated by mossy boulders. Portions of the treadway have been hardened with rock and wood steps and water bars, but more work will be done over the next few years. After a series of short switchbacks and rising contours, Dudley Trail reaches the upper jct. with the old route and turns sharply left, ascends, and soon emerges from the trees. For much of the next 0.4 mi., the trail is a scramble through a jumble of large boulders. After passing a slab cave, the trail reaches Index Rock, a prominent finger of granite jutting out from the ridge. From here, Dudley Trail continues in the open at a more gradual angle to the top of Pamola and the jct. with Helon Taylor Trail and Knife Edge. It is 1.1 mi. to Baxter Peak via Knife Edge and 3.6 mi. down to Roaring Brook CG via Helon Taylor Trail.

KNIFE EDGE (MAP 1: E3–E4)
From Pamola summit (4,904 ft.) to:

Baxter Peak (5,267 ft.)	1.1 mi.	434 ft.	1:45

BSP This long, narrow, serrated ridge tops the southern wall of Great Basin and connects South Peak with Pamola. Steep cliffs plummet more than 2,000 ft. into Great Basin to the north, and in places, the ridge is only 2 or 3 ft. in width. The dizzying height, sheer cliffs, and extreme exposure combine to make this one of the most spectacular mountain trails in the eastern United States. (*Note*: Knife Edge can be hazardous in bad weather. Under no circumstances should hikers leave the trail, as there are no safe alternate routes. Over the years, a number of attempts at shortcuts down to Chimney Pond have had tragic results. Knife Edge is not recommended for persons with a fear of heights.)

From the summit of Pamola, the trail leads southwest (follow the cairns) before dropping abruptly into the sharp cleft at the top of the Chimney. It then climbs the equally steep rock tower of Chimney Peak (4,900 ft.), a short but strenuous scramble. Beyond, the trail takes an undulating route over a series of rocky knobs before descending to a low point on the ridge. It then climbs steeply to South Peak (5,240 ft.) and continues along the spine of the summit ridge to Baxter Peak, joining Hunt Trail and Saddle Trail.

CATHEDRAL TRAIL (MAP 1: E3–E4)
Cumulative from Chimney Pond CG (2,914 ft.) to:

Cathedral Cutoff (4,700 ft.)	1.2 mi.	1,786 ft.	1:30
Saddle Trail (5,150 ft.)	1.5 mi.	2,236 ft.	1:55
Baxter Peak (5,267 ft.) via Saddle Trail	1.7 mi.	2,353 ft.	2:05

BSP This is the shortest route to Baxter Peak from Chimney Pond, climbing past the three immense, columnar Cathedral Rocks on its way to the summit. From the ranger cabin at Chimney Pond, follow Saddle Trail for 100 ft. and then turn left on Cathedral Trail and ascend through thick forest to reach Cathedral Pool on the right at 0.3 mi. At 0.4 mi., by a large cairn, the trail turns right toward the Cathedrals, crosses a bridge of rock covered with low growth, climbs steeply through boulders to a high point, and continues upward through low trees.

Blazes mark the way around to the right and then up the steep side of the first Cathedral at 0.8 mi. The second Cathedral offers spectacular views of the Chimney and Knife Edge. The route continues to the top of the third Cathedral. At 1.2 mi., the trail forks: to the right (west) is Cathedral Cutoff, which leads 0.3 mi. to Saddle Trail and Baxter Peak Cutoff. Cathedral Trail bears left (south) and climbs over large boulders to join Saddle Trail, which leads a gradual 0.2 mi. left to Baxter Peak.

SADDLE TRAIL (MAP 1: E3–E4)
Cumulative from Chimney Pond CG (2,914 ft.) to:

Saddle and Northwest Basin Trail (4,300 ft.)	1.4 mi.	1,340 ft.	1:25
Cathedral Cutoff and Baxter Peak Cutoff (4,700 ft.)	1.9 mi.	1,790 ft.	1:55
Cathedral Trail (5,150 ft.)	2.2 mi.	2,240 ft.	2:15
Baxter Peak (5,267 ft.)	2.4 mi.	2,353 ft.	2:25

BSP Climbers have taken this general route out of Great Basin via Saddle Slide since an avalanche in winter 1898–99 enlarged an existing but smaller slide. Saddle Trail offers the most moderate route up Katahdin from Chimney Pond.

From the ranger cabin near the pond, the worn trail climbs a rocky path through dense softwoods. Beyond, the trail swings to the right (north) and becomes easier underfoot and more gradual. It crosses Saddle Brook at 0.8 mi. and then climbs steeply over large boulders. At 0.9 mi., the route bears left up Saddle Slide and passes through stunted birches. At 1.0 mi., Saddle Trail emerges into the open and climbs for 0.2 mi. up the loose rocks and gravel of the slide.

The trail reaches the top of the slide at 1.4 mi. and gains the level, open ground of the Tableland in the Saddle between Baxter and Hamlin peaks and a trail jct. To the right (north), Northwest Basin Trail leads to Hamlin Ridge Trail, North Peaks Trail, Northwest Basin, and eventually to Russell Pond. Go left (south) and continue south on Saddle Trail over moderate slopes, with cairns marking the well-worn path. At 1.9 mi., the trail passes a large boulder and a jct. To the left (east), Cathedral Cutoff connects to Cathedral Trail in 0.3 mi. To the right (west), Baxter Peak Cutoff contours southwest along the base of the summit cone for 0.9 mi. to connect with Abol Trail and Hunt Trail at Thoreau Spring, while

Saddle Trail continues straight. Cathedral Trail from Chimney Pond enters on the left at 2.3 mi. Ahead, Saddle Trail climbs easily to Baxter Peak at 2.5 mi.

BAXTER PEAK CUTOFF (MAP 1: E3)
Cumulative from Chimney Pond CG (2,914 ft.) to:

Start of Baxter Peak Cutoff (4,700 ft.) via Saddle Trail	1.9 mi.	1,790 ft.	1:55
Thoreau Spring (4,636 ft.) and jct. Hunt Trail and Abol Trail	2.8 mi.	1,840 ft.	2:25

BSP This 0.9-mi. trail leaves the jct. of Saddle Trail and Cathedral Cutoff 1.9 mi. from Chimney Pond via Saddle Trail. Baxter Peak Cutoff contours southwest over the Tableland along the base of Baxter Peak, ending at Thoreau Spring and the jct. of Hunt Trail and Abol Trail, making it possible to hike a loop over Baxter Peak. In addition, the cutoff provides an alternate path to a safer descent in case of bad weather.

KATAHDIN: HAMLIN PEAK (4,752 FT.) AND HOWE PEAK (4,745 FT.)

Hamlin Peak is the second-highest summit in Maine. Rising prominently north of Baxter Peak and the Saddle, Hamlin is part of the extensive alpine area on Katahdin that includes the Tableland and six high peaks. Five trails cross the flanks of this mountain. Immediately north of Hamlin Peak is Howe Peak, the southernmost and highest summit of the North Peaks.

NORTH BASIN TRAIL (MAP 1: D4)
Cumulative from Chimney Pond CG (2,914 ft.) to:

North Basin Trail (2,830 ft.) via Chimney Pond Trail	0.3 mi.	–84 ft.	0:10
Hamlin Ridge Trail (2,993 ft.)	0.7 mi.	163 ft.	0:25
North Basin Cutoff (2,990 ft.)	0.9 mi.	183 ft.	0:35
Blueberry Knoll (3,073 ft.)	1.1 mi.	243 ft.	0:40

BSP From Chimney Pond, Chimney Pond Trail leads northeast toward the Basin ponds. At 0.2 mi., North Basin Trail starts on the left (north) and runs through spruce-fir forest to a jct. with Hamlin Ridge Trail on the left (west). It then passes across the foot of Hamlin Ridge to a jct. (signs, large cairn) with North Basin Cutoff. Ahead, North Basin Trail continues to the lip of North Basin and then reaches Blueberry Knoll and a sweeping view of both North Basin and Great Basin, as well as the landscape to the east, including South Turner Mtn., Katahdin Lake, and the forestland of KAWW.

NORTH BASIN CUTOFF (MAP 1: D4)
Cumulative from Roaring Brook CG (1,489 ft.) to:

North Basin Cutoff via Chimney Pond Trail (2,500 ft.)	2.3 mi.	1,010 ft.	1:40
North Basin Trail (2,990 ft.)	3.0 mi.	1,500 ft.	2:15

BSP This 0.7-mi. trail from the Basin ponds to the base of Hamlin Ridge and North Basin forks right (sign) at a point 2.1 mi. from Roaring Brook CG via Chimney Pond Trail. The cutoff traverses an area of second-growth softwoods, passes several active beaver ponds, and then climbs steeply through old growth to a jct. with North Basin Trail at 0.7 mi.; to reach Hamlin Ridge, turn left (southwest). To reach Blueberry Knoll and North Basin, turn right (northeast).

HAMLIN RIDGE TRAIL (MAP 1: D3–D4)
Cumulative from Chimney Pond CG (2,914 ft.) to:

Hamlin Ridge Trail (2,993 ft.) via Chimney Pond Trail and North Basin Trail	0.7 mi.	163 ft.	0:25
Hamlin Peak (4,752 ft.) and North Peaks Trail	2.2 mi.	1,922 ft.	2:05
Caribou Spring (4,630 ft.)	2.4 mi.	1,922 ft.	2:10

BSP This trail climbs largely in the open up Hamlin Ridge, which separates North Basin and Great Basin. The scenery is superb in every direction.

From Chimney Pond CG, follow Chimney Pond Trail 0.3 mi. north to North Basin Trail. Follow this for 0.4 mi. to the start of Hamlin Ridge Trail. Hamlin Ridge Trail reaches treeline after about 20 min. of climbing. After a short stretch of boulder-strewn slope, the trail rises to the ridge proper and then ascends moderately, following the open ridge to Hamlin Peak (4,752 ft.) and the jct. with North Peaks Trail at 2.1 mi. (North Peaks Trail leads right [north] for 0.5 mi. to Howe Peak [4,745 ft.], the southernmost and highest summit of the North Peaks, and then on to Russell Pond in another 5.8 mi.)

Beyond Hamlin Peak, Hamlin Ridge Trail descends gradually 0.2 mi. west across the Tableland and through a boulder field to Caribou Spring (unreliable) and another trail jct. at 2.4 mi. Bearing sharply right, Hamlin Peak Cutoff leads 0.2 mi. to North Peaks Trail, which travels along the headwall of North Basin to Howe Peak in another 0.3 mi. To the left (south), Northwest Basin Trail meets Saddle Trail in 0.9 mi.; to the right, Northwest Basin Trail leads to Russell Pond in 7.5 mi.

HAMLIN PEAK CUTOFF (MAP 1: D3)

BSP Following a path along a contour at about 4,650 ft., this 0.2-mi. connector trail links North Peaks Trail with Northwest Basin Trail at Caribou Spring, gaining 30 ft. of elevation en route.

SEC 1

NORTH PEAKS TRAIL (MAP 1: D3)
Cumulative from Hamlin Peak (4,752 ft.) to:

Hamlin Peak Cutoff (4,650 ft.)	0.3 mi.	-102 ft.	0:06
Howe Peak (4,750 ft.)	0.6 mi.	100 ft.	0:15
Northwest Basin Trail (1,431 ft.)	5.2 mi.	112 ft.	2:40
Russell Pond CG via Northwest Basin Trail (1,333 ft.)	6.4 mi.	112 ft.	3:15

BSP This trail extends from the summit of Hamlin Peak to Howe Peak and then north to Russell Pond. From the jct. of Hamlin Ridge Trail atop Hamlin Peak, North Peaks Trail descends gradually northwest along the edge of North Basin to a shallow col, where Hamlin Peak Cutoff enters from the left. North Peaks Trail then climbs over broken rocks to reach Howe Peak at 0.5 mi. Hike over a knob on the ridge beyond to reach the northernmost of the North Peaks at 1.0 mi. and then descend gradually, crossing two knobs. On the ridge beyond are views north to the valley of Wassataquoik Stream and the peaks of Traveler Mtn. Scramble over the last rocky knob on the long and exposed ridge and make a steady descent to treeline and then a moderate descent into the trees below. Ahead, the trail drops steeply into the deep valley between Russell Mtn. to the east and a shoulder of Tip-Top Mtn. to the west. It reaches Tracy Brook and continues down through the narrow ravine along the cascading brook. In another 0.1 mi., the trail crosses Tracy Brook and continues along its bank at an easier grade. Following the ridge of an esker, the trail descends to the confluence of Tracy Brook and Wassataquoik Stream and then fords the latter. (*Caution*: This ford can be hazardous in high water.) Bearing away from the stream, the trail ends at the jct. with Northwest Basin Trail. Russell Pond CG is 1.2 mi. to the right via Northwest Basin Trail.

NORTHWEST BASIN TRAIL (MAP 1: E3–D4)
Cumulative from Saddle Trail (4,300 ft.) to:

Caribou Spring (4,630 ft.) and Hamlin Ridge Trail and Hamlin Peak Cutoff	0.9 mi.	330 ft.	0:40
Davis Pond Lean-to (2,940 ft.)	3.3 mi.	350 ft.	1:50
Russell Pond CG (1,333 ft.) via Russell Pond Trail	8.4 mi.	350 ft.	4:10

BSP This trail extends from the Saddle between Baxter Peak and Hamlin Peak to Russell Pond, taking in the extensive alpine terrain on the west side of Hamlin Peak and the Northwest Plateau, secluded Davis Pond and Lake Cowles high in rugged Northwest Basin, and a stretch of Wassataquoik Stream en route.

The route starts at the jct. with Saddle Trail, 1.4 mi. above Chimney Pond and 1.0 mi. below the summit of Katahdin at Baxter Peak. Northwest Basin Trail descends gradually before steadily ascending Hamlin Peak. At 0.9 mi., the trail reaches Caribou Spring and a jct. Here, Hamlin Ridge Trail leads 0.2 mi. east to the summit of Hamlin Peak, while Hamlin Peak Cutoff leads 0.2 mi. northeast to North Peaks Trail.

From Caribou Spring, Northwest Basin Trail bears left and descends gradually north and then west to reach a large cairn on a high knob at 2.0 mi. on the western end of the Northwest Plateau, a level extension of the northern Tableland that separates Northwest Basin from the Klondike Pond ravine. From this point, the trail bears north and begins a steep descent. At treeline, it enters scrub growth. Farther below, the descent turns very steep for 0.3 mi. At the base, the trail soon reaches Davis Pond and then Davis Pond Lean-to at the pond's northwest corner at 3.3 mi. Beyond, the trail climbs a heath-covered glacial sheepback rock, which provides excellent views of the entire Northwest Basin. Descending the far side of the sheepback, the trail reaches Lake Cowles and soon crosses its outlet. A knoll just beyond the lake offers some attractive views. From the large pile of stones nearby, the trail turns right and begins a steep descent out of Northwest Basin. After the polished rock of a streambed, the angle eases and the trail joins the route of an old tote road that parallels Northwest Basin Brook. At 4.8 mi., ford Wassataquoik Stream and then continue north on old Wassataquoik Tote Rd. At 5.9 mi., the trail crosses Annis Brook. It eventually trends away from Wassataquoik Stream to cross the relatively level terrain in the area southwest of Russell Pond. At 7.2 mi., North Peaks Trail enters from the right. Continuing straight, Northwest Basin Trail descends gradually on old tote roads to reach Turner Deadwater. Cross the outlet and soon reach the jct. with Russell Pond Trail at 8.3 mi. Russell Pond Trail leads 0.1 mi. to the southern end of Russell Pond CG.

KATAHDIN LAKE—ROARING BROOK

In 2006, 4,119 acres to the east of Katahdin were gifted to BSP. The predominant feature of this parcel of land is the iconic 640-acre Katahdin Lake, which offers outstanding vistas of Katahdin, including Baxter Peak, Knife Edge, Pamola, Hamlin Peak, and Howe Peak. Soon after, a network of trails was developed for hikers, including three backcountry campsites.

Trailhead access to the trails around Katahdin Lake is from Avalanche Field on Roaring Brook Rd., 6.6 mi. north of Togue Pond Gate and 1.5 mi. south of Roaring Brook CG. Rising prominently west of Katahdin Lake are South Turner Mtn. and trailless North Turner Mtn.

KATAHDIN LAKE TRAIL (MAP 1: E4–E5)
Cumulative from Avalanche Field at Roaring Brook Rd. (1,254 ft.) to:

Martin Ponds Trail, upper jct. (1,150 ft.)	1.7 mi.	110 ft.	0:55
Martin Ponds Trail (1,025 ft.), lower jct.	2.9 mi.	140 ft.	1:30
Katahdin Lake CS (1,025 ft.)	3.0 mi.	140 ft.	1:35

BSP This trail leaves Roaring Brook Rd. at Avalanche Field (parking, toilet, register box) and heads east on an old woods road (the former Katahdin Lake Tote Rd.), which it follows for much of its route to Katahdin Lake. The trail crosses a small stream at 0.1 mi. At 0.5 mi., it crosses Sandy Stream near the ruins of Hersey Dam, an old logging structure once used by river drivers. Beyond, the trail ascends gently to crest a low ridge before descending to cross the former park boundary. At 1.7 mi., Martin Ponds Trail diverges left (northwest); it leads 0.6 mi. to Martin Ponds and Martin Ponds CS (lean-to).

Continuing on, Katahdin Lake Trail crosses a wet area and then ascends gradually to reach the lower jct. of Martin Ponds Trail on the left. Ahead, it is 100 yd. to South Katahdin Lake CS (lean-to), 0.1 mi. to the Day Use Picnic Site, and 0.2 mi. to Katahdin Lake and a supply of rental canoes.

MARTIN PONDS TRAIL (MAP 1: D5–E5)
Cumulative from Avalanche Field at Roaring Brook Rd. (1,254 ft.) to:

Start of trail (1,150 ft.) via Katahdin Lake Trail	1.7 mi.	110 ft.	0:55
Martin Ponds CS (1,230 ft.)	2.3 mi.	190 ft.	1:10
North Katahdin Lake Trail (1,240 ft.)	2.6 mi.	190 ft.	1:25
Katahdin Lake Trail (1,025 ft.) near South Katahdin Lake CS	4.4 mi.	190 ft.	2:20

BSP This trail diverges left (northwest) from Katahdin Lake Trail 1.7 mi. east of Avalanche Field. Martin Ponds Trail traverses a low ridge before skirting a beaver flowage and crossing the outlet of the southerly of the two Martin ponds. At 2.3 mi., it reaches a jct. with a short side trail to Martin Ponds CS, where there is an excellent view of Katahdin. Ahead, the trail passes to the west and north of the northerly of the two Martin ponds before descending to an outlook to South Turner and East Turner mountains. The trail reaches a jct. with North Katahdin Lake Trail at 2.6 mi. Beyond, Martin Ponds Trail descends gradually to reach Katahdin Lake, traversing several streams en route. From there, the trail follows the west shore to an inlet and an old beaver dam. Cross the dam and bear left along the sandy beach of the lake to reach the jct. with Katahdin Lake Trail at 4.4 mi. South Katahdin Lake CS is 100 yd. to the east.

NORTH KATAHDIN LAKE TRAIL (MAP 1: D5)
Cumulative from Avalanche Field at Roaring Brook Rd. (1,254 ft.) to:

North Katahdin Lake Trail (1,240 ft.) via Katahdin Lake Trail and Martin Ponds Trail	2.6 mi.	40 ft.	1:20
North Katahdin Lake CS (1,022 ft.)	4.5 mi.	40 ft.	2:15

BSP This route leaves from Martin Ponds Trail at a point 0.9 mi. from Katahdin Lake Trail and 2.6 mi. from Avalanche Field. North Katahdin Lake Trail traverses a ridge to the north before descending toward Katahdin Lake, crossing several streams along the way. The trail reaches North Katahdin Lake CS (lean-to) at 1.8 mi. Clear views of the Katahdin massif are possible from the lakeshore.

TWIN PONDS TRAIL (MAP 1: D5)
From North Katahdin Lake CS (1,022 ft.) to:

End of trail at Upper Twin Pond (1,840 ft.)	3.9 mi.	820 ft.	2:20

BSP This trail leaves the lean-to on the north shore of Katahdin Lake and heads north to the BSP boundary. Twin Ponds Trail crosses into KAWW and then swings west around the lower slopes of East Turner Mtn. to enter Katahdin Lake PL. The trail crosses several brooks before climbing to Lower Twin Pond. Skirting the pond's eastern shore, the trail continues west into the basin and ends on the north side of Upper Twin Pond in the cirque below North Turner Mtn.

SOUTH TURNER MTN. (3,126 FT.)
This mountain northeast of Katahdin offers magnificent vistas of Katahdin's massif and sheer-walled basins. The approach is from Roaring Brook CG and involves a moderate climb up the mountain's south side.

SOUTH TURNER MTN. TRAIL (MAP 1: D4)
Cumulative from Roaring Brook CG (1,489 ft.) to:

South Turner Mtn. Trail (1,500 ft.) via Russell Pond Trail and Sandy Stream Pond Trail	0.7 mi.	20 ft.	0:20
South Turner Mtn. summit (3,126 ft.)	2.2 mi.	1,646 ft.	1:55

BSP This route leaves from Sandy Stream Pond Trail at a point 0.7 mi. from Roaring Brook CG. South Turner Mtn. Trail proceeds easily at first and then rises gradually as it weaves over rocks and boulders. Beyond, the trail climbs the south slope of the mountain at a steady, moderate grade. A series of rock staircases aid in the ascent. At 0.2 mi. past a side trail to a spring, the angle eases and the trail soon reaches treeline and a large cairn at the base of a rock slide. Climb in the open over the gravelly slide of loose rocks and then scramble up a steep slope of rocks to the sign atop the summit. The fine panorama encompasses Katahdin and its neighboring high peaks and ridges to the west, sparkling Katahdin Lake and the low mountains of KAWW to the east, and the forests and hills of Aroostook County to the north.

SANDY STREAM POND LOOP
(MAP 1: KATAHDIN AND ROARING BROOK INSET)
Cumulative from Roaring Brook CG (1,489 ft.) to:

South Turner Mtn. Trail (1,500 ft.)	0.7 mi.	20 ft.	0:20
Russell Pond Trail (1,592 ft.)	1.3 mi.	112 ft.	0:40
Complete loop	2.5 mi.	180 ft.	1:20

BSP This hike combines Sandy Stream Pond Trail and segments of Russell Pond Trail for a pleasant and popular circuit. From the ranger cabin, follow the path north and quickly arrive at a jct. with Russell Pond Trail (p. 43). Follow Russell Pond Trail and cross the bridge over Roaring Brook. At 0.1 mi., where Russell Pond Trail bears left, continue straight on Sandy Stream Pond Trail around the south shore of the pond. On the way, three side trails offer outstanding views of the Katahdin massif: the first is a loop along the pond, the second heads to the pond at Big Rock, and the third goes to the pond's outlet (Sandy Stream). At 0.7 mi., the trail reaches a jct. with South Turner Mtn. Trail, which leads straight ahead. Sandy Stream Pond Trail continues to the left toward Whidden Ponds and crosses a brook. At the jct. with Russell Pond Trail, turn left (south) on that trail. Russell Pond Trail crosses two inlet brooks to Sandy Stream Pond on its way south back to Roaring Brook CG.

ABOL POND–TOGUE POND
CRANBERRY POND TRAIL (MAP 1: E4–F4)
From Togue Pond Day Use Site (623 ft.) to:

Park Tote Rd., upper jct. (639 ft.)	1.4 mi.	50 ft.	0:45

BSP This trail departs from Togue Pond Day Use Site, just beyond the BSP Visitor Information Center on the access road into Togue Pond Gate. The trail ambles southwest of the road past Upper Togue Pond, Cranberry Pond, and Rocky Pond, ending at Park Tote Rd. at 1.4 mi., just across from Kettle Pond Trail.

KETTLE POND TRAIL (MAP 1: E3–E4)
Cumulative from Park Tote Rd. (639 ft.) to:

Park Tote Rd., north jct. (650 ft.)	1.4 mi.	40 ft.	0:40
Abol Beach Day Use Site access road (601 ft.)	1.7 mi.	40 ft.	0:50

BSP The southern trailhead for this short but scenic route is on the right (north) side of Park Tote Rd., 1.0 mi. from Togue Pond Gate. In 200 yd., a short side trail leads right to Caverly Pond. At 0.1 mi., the trail forks. To the right, Rum Pond Trail leads 2.0 mi. past Rum Pond to Roaring Brook Rd. south of Rum Brook Day Use Site. Follow the left fork past several kettles (small ponds) to the intersection with Park Tote Rd. at 1.4 mi. Cross the road and hike an additional 0.3 mi. to the access road for Abol Pond. The beach at Abol Pond and a day-use area are 50 yd. south.

RUM POND TRAIL (MAP 1: E4)
Cumulative from Park Tote Rd. (639 ft.) to:

Rum Pond Trail (650 ft.) via Kettle Pond Trail	0.1 mi.	0 ft.	0:05
Roaring Brook Rd. (650 ft.)	2.1 mi.	120 ft.	1:05

BSP Rum Pond Trail forks right from Kettle Pond Trail, 0.1 mi. from that trail's southern trailhead. Rum Pond Trail winds east around Caverly Pond and Rum Pond to meet Roaring Brook Rd. at a point about 0.1 mi. south of Rum Brook Day Use Site. Togue Pond Gate is 1.0 mi. from either end of this trail.

ABOL STREAM TRAIL (MAP 1: E3)
From AT jct. (570 ft.) to:

Abol Beach Day Use Site (592 ft.)	1.2 mi.	50 ft.	0:35

BSP To reach this trail, start from Golden Rd. 0.2 mi. east of Abol Bridge and hike north on the AT. In 0.4 mi., Abol Stream Trail departs right and follows an old tote road. Cross a bridge over an unnamed stream and then continue along Abol Stream. Ahead, leave Abol Stream and climb over a low ridge. At the outlet of Abol Pond, cross a bridge to reach Abol Beach Day Use Site.

ABOL POND TRAIL (MAP 1: E3)
From Blueberry Ledges Trail (630 ft.) to:

Abol Beach Day Use Site access road (601 ft.)	1.7 mi.	110 ft.	0:55

BSP To reach this trail, start from Golden Rd. 0.2 mi. east of Abol Bridge and hike north on the AT. In 0.4 mi., Abol Stream Trail departs right. Ahead on the AT, at 0.6 mi., there is a jct. with Blueberry Ledges Trail at a BSP information kiosk. Turn north here to follow Blueberry Ledges Trail. In another 0.2 mi., Abol Pond Trail departs to the right.

Abol Pond Trail proceeds over mild terrain. After several beaver ponds, the trail intersects with several old woods roads. Bear left at the first and then sharply right at the second. Beyond, make a steep descent to Abol Stream. At a wide pathway (old road), bear left to end at the access road to Abol Beach Day Use Site, which is 50 yd. south.

DAICEY POND–KIDNEY POND

AT SOUTHBOUND (MAP 1: E2–E3)
Cumulative from Daicey Pond day-use parking (1,050 ft.) to:

Side trails to Toll Dam and Little Niagara Falls (1,040 ft.)	0.9 mi.	–10 ft.	0:25
Side trail to Big Niagara Falls (940 ft.)	1.1 mi.	–110 ft.	0:35
Alternate high-water trail (780 ft.)	1.8 mi.	–270 ft.	0:55
Abol Bridge (588 ft.)	7.2 mi.	–462 ft.	3:15

BSP From the Daicey Pond day-use parking area 0.1 mi. northwest of Daicey Pond CG, follow the AT south. At 0.1 mi., Nature Trail leaves left to circumnavigate Daicey Pond. Continue on the AT. A side trail on the right leads to Toll Dam on Nesowadnehunk Stream at 0.9 mi. About 100 yd. ahead, another side trail goes right to Little Niagara Falls. At 1.1 mi., a side trail travels 200 ft. to Big Niagara Falls. At 1.8 mi., an alternate high-water trail leads left; this trail avoids two possibly difficult high-water crossings of a branch of Nesowadnehunk Stream. It rejoins the AT 0.8 mi. south.

Continuing south on the AT, cross the stream branch, and in another 1.0 mi., cross back again. Reach the jct. of Foss and Knowlton Pond Trail at 6.1 mi. (returns to Daicey Pond in 5.4 mi. via Lost Pond Trail and Nature Trail). Just ahead, at 6.4 mi., Blueberry Ledges Trail departs left (leads 4.2 mi. to Katahdin Stream CG). Abol Stream Trail is at 6.6 mi.; it reaches Abol Pond in 1.2 mi.

Continuing south, the AT reaches Golden Rd. at 7.0 mi.; turn right (west) here. A store and campground are just ahead; walk past them to reach the West Branch of the Penobscot River at Abol Bridge at 7.2 mi.

AT NORTHBOUND (MAP 1: E2–E3)
Cumulative from Daicey Pond day-use parking (1,050 ft.) to:

Tracy and Elbow Ponds Trail (1,092 ft.)	0.4 mi.	80 ft.	0:15
Elbow Pond Connector (1,150 ft.)	1.1 mi.	150 ft.	0:40
Park Tote Rd. at Katahdin Stream CG (1,099 ft.)	2.1 mi.	160 ft.	1:10

BSP From the Daicey Pond day-use parking area, follow the AT north. Climb over a knoll and then descend to the shore of Daicey Pond and follow the AT to a jct. Here, Tracy and Elbow Ponds Trail leaves left, heading 1.0 mi. to Park Tote Rd. Continue north on the AT along the pond to a jct. with Nature Trail at 0.6 mi. (leads 0.8 mi. along the south shore of the pond to the campground). The AT (also called Grassy Pond Trail from here to Park Tote Rd.) turns left and makes its way through a pleasant mix of forest to a jct. with Elbow Pond Connector at 1.1 mi. (connects with Tracy and Elbow Ponds Trail in 0.8 mi.). Beyond, the AT skirts the south end of Grassy Pond, crosses the outlet (Katahdin Stream), and ends at Park Tote Rd. across from the entrance road to Katahdin Stream CG at 2.1 mi.

TRACY AND ELBOW PONDS TRAIL (MAP 1: E2)
Cumulative from Daicey Pond day-use parking area (1,050 ft.) to:

Tracy and Elbow Ponds Trail (1,092 ft.) via AT Northbound	0.4 mi.	80 ft.	0:15
Elbow Ponds Connector (1,050 ft.)	1.0 mi.	100 ft.	0:30
Park Tote Rd. (1,060 ft.)	1.4 mi.	120 ft.	0:45

BSP This trail departs left (north) from the AT 0.4 mi. from the Daicey Pond CG access road. The trail climbs over a low ridge before descending to follow the southeast shore of Elbow Pond. After a gradual ascent, Grassy Pond Trail enters from the right. Ahead, Tracy and Elbow Ponds Trail crosses a bridge over the outlet of Elbow Pond, climbs a knoll, and then descends to cross a bridge over the outlet of Tracy Pond. Beyond, the trail follows an esker (a ridge of gravel or sediment deposited by the meltwater of a retreating glacier) to end at Park Loop Rd., 0.6 mi. northwest of Katahdin Stream CG. Enjoy attractive views of Doubletop Mtn. and Mt. OJI along this trail.

ELBOW POND CONNECTOR (MAP 1: E2)
BSP This short 0.8-mi. trail connects Tracy and Elbow Ponds Trail and the AT and makes an interesting loop hike from Daicey Pond, climbing over a low ridge between the two ponds. Excellent Katahdin views are possible along the way.

NATURE TRAIL (MAP 1: E2)
From Daicey Pond ranger cabin (1,087 ft.) to:

Lost Pond Trail (1,090 ft.)	0.6 mi.	20 ft.	0:20
Grassy Pond Trail (1,090 ft.)	0.8 mi.	20 ft.	0:25
Complete loop via AT Southbound	1.5 mi.	60 ft.	0:45

BSP This pleasant route explores the south and east sides of Daicey Pond; combine it with the AT for a loop hike. From the ranger cabin at Daicey Pond CG, follow a wide path south. Soon, the AT enters from the right and heads south. Turn left here onto a foot trail to reach the shore of Daicey Pond. Near the southeast corner of the pond, pass Lost Pond Trail on the right. Ahead, Nature Trail merges with the AT. Continue west on the AT Southbound to complete the loop on the Daicey Pond CG access road opposite the day-use parking area. Turn left on the access road to reach the campground.

LOST POND TRAIL (MAP 1: E2)
From Daicey Pond ranger cabin (1,087 ft.) to:

Lost Pond Trail (1,090 ft.)	0.6 mi.	20 ft.	0:20
Foss and Knowlton Pond Trail (1,150 ft.)	1.5 mi.	90 ft.	0:45
Lost Pond via spur path (1,118 ft.)	1.55 mi.	90 ft.	0:50

BSP The route leaves from the south shore of Daicey Pond, 0.6 mi. from Daicey Pond CG via Nature Trail. Lost Pond Trail heads southeast over easy terrain to reach the jct. with Foss and Knowlton Pond Trail in another 0.9 mi. A short spur path leads to the north shore of Lost Pond.

FOSS AND KNOWLTON POND TRAIL (MAP 1: E2–E3)
Cumulative from Daicey Pond CG (1,087 ft.) to:

Foss and Knowlton Pond Trail via Nature Trail and Lost Pond Trail (1,150 ft.)	1.4 mi.	70 ft.	0:40
Foss and Knowlton Pond side trail (1,050 ft.)	2.3 mi.	75 ft.	1:10
AT (580 ft.)	5.3 mi.	75 ft.	2:40
Abol Bridge (588 ft.)	6.4 mi.	75 ft.	3:10

BSP This trail heads south from Lost Pond at a point 1.4 mi. south of Daicey Pond via Nature Trail and Lost Pond Trail. Foss and Knowlton Pond Trail uses fire roads built to fight the BSP fire of 1977 and traverses the burned area that is still being reclaimed by the forest. After a side path (leads 0.3 mi. to Foss and Knowlton Pond's north shore), the trail closely follows the pond's west shore (Katahdin views) before trending southeast to meet the AT. From this jct., the AT passes Blueberry Ledges Trail, Abol Pond Trail, and Abol Stream Trail to reach Golden Rd. and Abol Bridge in another 1.1 mi.

BLUEBERRY LEDGES TRAIL (MAP 1: E2–E3)
Cumulative from Park Tote Rd. east of Katahdin Stream CG (1,050 ft.) to:

Abol Pond Trail (630 ft.)	4.2 mi.	230 ft.	2:15
AT (570 ft.)	4.4 mi.	230 ft.	2:20
Golden Rd. east of Abol Bridge (600 ft.)	5.0 mi.	230 ft.	2:35

BSP From Katahdin Stream CG, this trail travels through a variety of forest types and offers many interesting landscapes before meeting up with the AT near Abol Bridge on the West Branch of the Penobscot River. Much of the route goes through the area burned in the BSP fire of 1977. The trail's namesake ledges are about midway through the hike, along the tumbling waters of Katahdin Stream. The location includes large expanses of exposed bedrock with views of Katahdin and other geological features.

Ahead, descend off the ridge into the valley proper, emerging into an extensive area of open ledges of smooth granite. Follow these ledges for the next 0.5 mi. To the right, several side paths lead to Katahdin Stream and a series of cascades, sluice drops, and pools. Swimming holes abound, as do blueberries in high summer. Descending over ledges, the trail reaches an old woods road and follows it to meet Abol Pond Trail, which merges from the left at 4.0 mi. Blueberry Ledges Trail ends just ahead at 4.2 mi. at the jct. with the AT. Follow the AT south to reach Golden Rd. in 0.6 mi. and Abol Bridge in 0.8 mi.

SENTINEL MTN. (1,863 FT.)

This low mountain in the southwest corner of BSP rises just north of the West Branch of the Penobscot River and offers fine views of the west side of Katahdin and its neighboring high peaks. Direct access to the mountain is from Kidney Pond CG via Sentinel Link Trail and Sentinel Mtn. Trail. Access to the mountain is also possible from the east at Daicey Pond via Kidney Pond Trail, although hiking from this direction requires fording Nesowadnehunk Stream.

SENTINEL LINK TRAIL AND SENTINEL MTN. TRAIL (MAP 1: E2)
Cumulative from Kidney Pond CG (1,051 ft.) to:

Sentinel Landing (1,051 ft.) via Sentinel Link Trail	0.5 mi.	0 ft.	0:15
Sentinel Mtn. summit (1,800 ft.) loop	2.6 mi.	749 ft.	1:40
Loop over Sentinel Mtn. summit (1,863 ft.)	3.1 mi.	821 ft.	1:55

BSP From the trailhead parking area at Kidney Pond CG at the end of the access road, follow Sentinel Link Trail and skirt the west side of Kidney Pond. Pass Celia and Jackson Ponds Trail and reach Sentinel Landing, a canoe landing on Kidney Pond, in 0.5 mi. From the landing, the Daicey–Kidney Link Trail enters from the east. Here, turn right (south) on Sentinel Mtn. Trail.

In 0.8 mi. from Sentinel Landing, Sentinel Mtn. Trail crosses a small stream near a beaver pond. At 1.2 mi., it crosses Beaver Brook on stepping-stones. The trail climbs the northeast side of the mountain along a brook, which crosses the route at 1.6 mi. The trail reaches a wooded saddle at 2.0 mi. On the left, a short spur leads to an outstanding view over the West Branch of the Penobscot River. Return to Sentinel Mtn. Trail and climb to a fork at 2.1 mi. on the summit ledges. This is the start of a 0.5-mi. loop trail. Follow the ledges to the right (north) to reach the true summit and excellent views of Katahdin.

KIDNEY POND TRAIL (MAP 1: E2)
Cumulative from Daicey Pond day-use parking (1,050 ft.) to:

Sentinel Landing (1,051 ft.), Sentinel Link Trail, and Sentinel Mtn. Trail	1.0 mi.	0 ft.	0:30
Sentinel Mtn. summit ledges (1,863 ft.) and loop	3.6 mi.	786 ft.	2:10

BSP Kidney Pond Trail leaves from the Daicey Pond access road at a small parking pullout next to Nesowadnehunk Stream, 0.9 mi. from Park Tote Rd. and 0.2 mi. from Daicey Pond CG. The trail immediately crosses Nesowadnehunk Stream (this is a ford and should not be attempted in high water) and enters an alder swamp. A side trail to Kidney Pond is on the right, and then Lily Pad Pond Trail appears on the left. At 1.0 mi. from Nesowadnehunk Stream, Kidney Pond Trail ends at its jct. with Sentinel Link and Sentinel Mtn. trails. Turn left to climb Sentinel Mtn. in 2.6 mi., or continue ahead to reach Kidney Pond in 0.5 mi.

ROCKY POND TRAIL (MAP 1: E1–E2)
From Kidney Pond CG (1,050 ft.) to:

Rocky Pond (1,090 ft.)	0.7 mi.	50 ft.	0:20
Little Rocky Pond (1,090 ft.)	1.2 mi.	100 ft.	0:35

BSP This trail leads from Kidney Pond CG to the south shore of Rocky Pond and ends at Little Rocky Pond.

CELIA AND JACKSON PONDS TRAIL (MAP 1: E1–E2)
Cumulative from Kidney Pond CG (1,050 ft.) to:

Celia and Jackson Ponds Trail via Sentinel Link Trail (1,050 ft.)	0.3 mi.	0 ft.	0:10
Celia Pond (1,220 ft.)	1.2 mi.	200 ft.	0:40
Jackson Pond (1,225 ft.)	1.6 mi.	250 ft.	0:55

BSP From Kidney Pond CG, Sentinel Link Trail leads south around the pond to the jct. with Celia and Jackson Ponds Trail. Turn right (west) on

Celia and Jackson Ponds Trail to reach the north shore of Celia Pond. The south shore of Jackson Pond is 0.4 mi. farther west.

LILY PAD POND TRAIL (MAP 1: E2)
Cumulative from Kidney Pond CG (1,050 ft.) to:

Lily Pad Pond Trail (1,050 ft.) via Sentinel Link Trail and Kidney Pond Trail	0.9 mi.	30 ft.	0:25
Beaver Brook (1,050 ft.)	1.2 mi.	80 ft.	0:40

BSP Reach the start of this route via Sentinel Link Trail and Kidney Pond Trail from Kidney Pond CG. Lily Pad Pond Trail heads south to its end at Beaver Brook.

SLAUGHTER POND TRAIL (MAP 1: E1–E2)
Cumulative from Kidney Pond access road (1,050 ft.) to:

Doubletop Mtn. Trail, first jct. (1,080 ft.)	0.7 mi.	60 ft.	0:20
Doubletop Mtn. Trail, second jct. (1,110 ft.)	1.3 mi.	80 ft.	0:40
Slaughter Pond (1,113 ft.)	2.3 mi.	100 ft.	1:15

BSP Slaughter Pond Trail begins on the Kidney Pond access road immediately beyond the bridge over Nesowadnehunk Stream 0.4 mi. west of Park Tote Rd. The route follows an old tote road to meet Doubletop Mtn. Trail, which enters from the left. The two trails coincide for the next 0.6 mi., then Doubletop Mtn. Trail departs right, and Slaughter Pond Trail continues ahead to end at Slaughter Pond, just outside the BSP boundary.

DOUBLETOP MTN.—SOUTH PEAK (3,455 FT.) AND NORTH PEAK (3,482 FT.)

The steep, slide-scarred eastern slopes of Doubletop Mtn. make it easy to identify from many points in the Katahdin region. Both peaks offer impressive views of Katahdin, South Brother Mtn., Mt. Coe, Mt. OJI, and Barren Mtn. Doubletop can be climbed from Kidney Pond in the south or from Nesowadnehunk CG in the north. The most popular route is from Kidney Pond, and as such, Doubletop Mtn. Trail is described in that direction.

DOUBLETOP MTN. TRAIL (MAP 1: D2–E2)
Cumulative from Kidney Pond CG (1,051 ft.) to:

Slaughter Pond Trail, second jct. (1,110 ft.)	1.9 mi.	50 ft.	1:00
Doubletop Mtn., South Peak (3,455 ft.)	4.6 mi.	2,404 ft.	3:30
Doubletop Mtn., North Peak (3,482 ft.)	4.8 mi.	2,457 ft.	3:40
Nesowadnehunk CG (1,300 ft.)	8.2 mi.	2,497 ft.	5:20

DOUBLETOP MTN. TRAIL, IN REVERSE (MAP 1: D2–E2)
Cumulative from Nesowadnehunk CG (1,300 ft.) to:

Stream crossing (1,700 ft.)	1.4 mi.	400 ft.	0:55
Doubletop Mtn., North Peak (3,482 ft.)	3.4 mi.	2,182 ft.	2:50
Doubletop Mtn., South Peak (3,455 ft.)	3.6 mi.	2,207 ft.	3:00
Kidney Pond CG (1,051 ft.)	8.2 mi.	2,207 ft.	5:10

BSP Doubletop Mtn. Trail starts at Kidney Pond CG. At 0.3 mi., a side trail leads 0.1 mi. to Draper Pond. Ahead, cross Slaughter Brook and skirt the south shore of Deer Pond. At 1.3 mi., Slaughter Pond Trail enters from the right. The two trails coincide for the next 0.6 mi. along an old woods road (the former Slaughter Pond Tote Rd.). At a jct. at 1.9 mi., Doubletop Mtn. Trail forks right (north), leaving the old Camp 3 clearing near its northwest corner. Straight ahead (west), Slaughter Pond Trail continues 1.0 mi. to Slaughter Pond. (Watch carefully: this jct. can be easy to miss.)

Doubletop Mtn. Trail follows an old woods road northwest up a valley, traversing a stream four times. The stream and trail run together for a while, which often makes the route wet and muddy. The trail passes close under the cliffs on Moose's Bosom, the peak west of Doubletop Mtn. Just after crossing a small stream, the trail reaches a thick stand of spruce and fir and passes a spring. Turning north again, it climbs to a saddle between Moose's Bosom and Doubletop.

Beyond, the trail angles up a very steep and rocky timbered slope on the west side of the mountain to reach the open summit of the South Peak at 4.6 mi. Spectacular scenic panoramas abound from this vantage point, one of the finest in BSP, which includes the Katahdin massif and the high peaks to its west and north, plus the vast 100MW to the south.

Doubletop Mtn. Trail continues on to reach the North Peak at 4.8 mi. and a section of steel ladder from the former fire tower (the 1918 tower was removed in 2000). From here, the trail descends steadily (steeply at times) to the north, eventually reaching a brook at 6.8 mi. Beyond the brook, the descent becomes more gradual. The last mile is fairly level and reaches Nesowadnehunk CG at 7.9 mi. At the picnic area, bear right to cross a bridge over Nesowadnehunk Stream. The ranger cabin and day-use parking is a short distance ahead on the left at 8.2 mi.

WEST OF KATAHDIN
THE OWL (3,695 FT.)
This is the first summit in the long, high range that runs west and north from Katahdin around the Klondike. The distinctive cliffs on its southern face overlooking the valley of Katahdin Stream are especially steep and impressive.

OWL TRAIL (MAP 1: E3)
Cumulative from Katahdin Stream CG (1,099 ft.) to:

Owl Trail (1,590 ft.) via Hunt Trail	1.1 mi.	490 ft.	0:45
The Owl summit (3,695 ft.)	3.5 mi.	2,596 ft.	3:00

BSP From Katahdin Stream CG, follow Hunt Trail for 1.1 mi. to a jct. Here, Owl Trail diverges left just before Katahdin Stream. The trail then follows the north bank of a tributary before turning sharply right (southeast) and crossing the tributary at 1.6 mi. (last source of water). The trail climbs gradually through dense spruce and fir and follows the western spur toward the summit. At 2.9 mi., the trail rises steeply through a ravine and then across the upper part of the Owl's prominent cliffs. At 3.4 mi., the trail reaches the first outlook. After a more gradual climb, it reaches the summit at 3.5 mi. Views in all directions are outstanding, especially those into the Klondike and Witherle Ravine.

MT. OJI (3,427 FT.) AND WEST PEAK (2,492 FT.)
Mt. OJI got its name from three slides on its southwestern slope that at one point in time formed the shapes of the three letters. After a major storm in 1932, however, the slides began to enlarge, and the letter shapes became distorted. A fourth large slide came down in 1954.

MT. OJI TRAIL (MAP 1: D2–E2)
Cumulative from Park Tote Rd. at Foster Field Picnic Area (1,090 ft.) to:

West Peak Overlook Spur (2,330 ft.)	2.7 mi.	1,240 ft.	2:00
West Peak (2,492 ft.) via spur path	2.9 mi.	1,402 ft.	2:10
Old Jay Eye Rock (3,000 ft.)	3.5 mi.	1,940 ft.	2:45
Mt. OJI summit (3,427 ft.)	4.0 mi.	2,390 ft.	3:15
OJI Link Trail (3,200 ft.)	4.2 mi.	2,390 ft.	3:20

BSP The route leaves Park Tote Rd. just north of Foster Field Picnic Area and 200 ft. south of the road into Kidney Pond, 10.3 mi. north of Togue Pond Gate. Mt. OJI Trail passes a brook to the left and then goes through a cedar swamp. After a blowdown area and a grove of mature beech, the trail begins to climb at a moderate grade. (*Note*: Park crews have been working to replace old bog bridging over the first 1.5 mi. of trail, and as of 2022, there was more work to be done.) Turning northwest, Mt. OJI Trail crosses a stream and then climbs via switchbacks. Soon after passing a cave in an overhanging cliff wall, the trail reaches the saddle separating West Peak and OJI Ridge and a jct. at 2.7 mi.

West Peak Overlook Spur. From the jct., the spur path leads left (southwest), climbing gradually for 0.2 mi. to a fine viewpoint that includes the valley of Nesowadnehunk Stream, the slides and summit on Mt. OJI, Barren Mtn. and Hunt Ridge, the Tableland, and the summit of Katahdin.

Mt. OJI Trail continues easily across the saddle and passes a seep spring. It then follows a rising contour north and proceeds up several switchbacks to a rock on the left and a view of Doubletop. Crest the ridge after weaving through thick firs and boulders. Turn southeast and ascend steadily and steeply up the ridge, passing through a narrow cleft in a rock outcropping (requires some squeezing and scrambling to get through). At Old Jay Eye Rock, admire excellent views over West Peak to Doubletop Mtn. and beyond, to the Whitecap Range and the distinctive profiles of Big and Little Spencer. The trail drops into a rugged notch and then climbs left and up rocks to the open, airy ridge above. The vistas from the vantage point are spectacular, displaying the shapely summit cone of Mt. OJI as well as Katahdin, Mt. Coe, and South Brother Mtn. From here, reenter thick growth and arrive at the wooded summit of Mt. OJI. The trail then descends 0.2 mi. to meet OJI Link Trail, which leads 0.5 mi. to Mt. Coe Trail southwest of the summit.

Another approach to Mt. OJI is hiking via Marston Trail and Mt. Coe Trail to OJI Link Trail (a combined distance of 1.7 mi.), following OJI Link Trail, and finally ascending Mt. OJI Trail northbound for 0.2 mi.

NORTH BROTHER MTN. (4,143 FT.) AND
SOUTH BROTHER MTN. (3,960 FT.)

North and South Brother are open peaks that offer splendid views in all directions, especially of the Katahdin massif. (*Caution*: Early in the hiking season, sometimes through mid-June, hikers should expect to find deep snow at the higher elevations on these peaks, often starting about 1.5 mi. from the trailhead.)

MARSTON TRAIL (MAP 1: D2–D3)
Cumulative from Park Tote Rd. south of Slide Dam Picnic Area (1,190 ft.) to:

Mt. Coe Trail, lower jct. (2,140 ft.)	1.3 mi.	950 ft.	1:10
Mt. Coe Trail, upper jct. (3,430 ft.)	3.7 mi.	2,240 ft.	3:00
North Brother summit (4,143 ft.)	4.6 mi.	2,953 ft.	3:45
Cumulative from Park Tote Rd. south of Slide Dam Picnic Area (1,190 ft.) to:			
South Brother Trail (3,600 ft.)	4.3 mi.	2,410 ft.	3:20
South Brother summit (3,960 ft.) via Mt. Coe Trail	4.6 mi.	2,770 ft.	3:40

BSP This route is the best approach for exploring the Brothers area. Trailhead parking is on the east side of Park Tote Rd. 0.2 mi. south of Slide Dam Picnic Area, 5.7 mi. north of Katahdin Stream CG, and about 3.5 mi. south of Nesowadnehunk CG.

At 0.2 mi., the trail crosses a brook; it then bears left and climbs over a slight rise into the drainage of a second brook. Ascending steadily, the trail follows this brook closely. At 0.8 mi., it crosses the brook. Several more crossings appear in the next 0.4 mi. before the trail reaches a jct. with Mt. Coe Trail at 1.3 mi. Here, Marston Trail leads to the left and climbs gradually through extensive blowdowns, reaching Teardrop Pond at 2.2 mi. Beyond the pond's outlet, the trail climbs steeply, passing several viewpoints. After leveling off, Marston Trail reaches the upper jct. with Mt. Coe Trail at 3.7 mi. To the right, Mt. Coe Trail leads 0.9 mi. to South Brother via South Brother Trail. To the left, it is 0.9 mi. to North Brother via Marston Trail.

Continuing on Marston Trail after crossing a fairly level area, pass a spring and then climb steeply. Ahead, the trail leaves the scrub and travels among open boulders, reaching the summit of North Brother at 4.6 mi. Here are fine views of the western slopes of Katahdin and, in the opposite direction, of Nesowadnehunk Lake and Little Nesowadnehunk Stream. The long, flat ridgeline of trailless Fort Mtn. is immediately northeast.

MT. COE (3,784 FT.)

This peak, just north of Mt. OJI, has excellent views into the Klondike and is well worth the challenge of the climb. Mt. Coe's high summit ridge provides access to both Mt. OJI and South Brother Mtn.

MT. COE TRAIL (MAP 1: D2–D3)
Cumulative from Park Tote Rd. south of Slide Dam Picnic Area (1,190 ft.) to:

Mt. Coe Trail (2,140 ft.) via Marston Trail	1.3 mi.	950 ft.	1:10
OJI Link Trail (3,040 ft.)	2.7 mi.	1,850 ft.	2:15
Mt. Coe summit (3,784 ft.)	3.4 mi.	2,594 ft.	3:00
South Brother Trail to South Brother summit (3,600 ft.)	4.5 mi.	2,704 ft.	3:35
South Brother summit (3,960 ft.) via South Brother Trail	4.8 mi.	3,061 ft.	4:00
Marston Trail (3,430 ft.)	5.1 mi.	3,061 ft.	4:10

Cumulative from Park Tote Rd. south of Slide Dam Picnic Area (1,190 ft.) to:

Mt. Coe Trail (2,140 ft.) via Marston Trail	1.3 mi.	950 ft.	1:10
OJI Link Trail (3,040 ft.)	2.7 mi.	1,850 ft.	2:15
Mt. OJI (3,427 ft.) via OJI Link Trail and Mt. OJI Trail	3.4 mi.	2,237 ft.	2:50

BSP Follow Marston Trail to a sign 1.3 mi. from Park Tote Rd. Turn right on Mt. Coe Trail to reach the bottom of the Mt. Coe slide (it follows a stream) at 1.5 mi. Beyond, the steady climb is moderate at first and then steep. At 2.5 mi., the trail bears left and climbs the left center of a wide slide area on granite slabs and loose gravel. At 2.7 mi., Mt. Coe Trail reaches the jct. with OJI Link Trail (leads right 0.5 mi. to Mt. OJI Trail and 0.2 mi. farther to the summit of OJI).

At 3.1 mi., Mt. Coe Trail enters scrub growth; it reaches the summit at 3.4 mi. Continuing on, the trail descends the eastern ridge of Mt. Coe and proceeds toward South Brother. At 4.3 mi., it passes two clearings with fine views of Mt. Coe. At 4.5 mi., South Brother Trail leads right 0.3 mi. steeply up to the summit of South Brother. At 5.1 mi., Mt. Coe Trail reaches the jct. with Marston Trail. Ahead, it is 0.9 mi. to the summit of North Brother via Marston Trail. To the left, Marston Trail leads 3.7 mi. to Park Tote Rd. just south of Slide Dam.

RUSSELL POND

Three long trails lead deep into the heart of BSP: Russell Pond Trail from the south, Wassataquoik Lake Trail from the west, and Pogy Notch Trail from the north. These trails converge at Russell Pond, where a number of shorter trails lead to local sights in the pond's vicinity.

RUSSELL POND TRAIL (MAP 1: D4)
Cumulative from Roaring Brook CG (1,489 ft.) to:

Sandy Stream Pond Trail, upper jct. (1,592 ft.)	1.1 mi.	105 ft.	0:35
Wassataquoik Stream Trail (1,500 ft.)	3.1 mi.	135 ft.	1:40
Wassataquoik Tote Rd. (1,350 ft.)	6.3 mi.	375 ft.	3:20
Northwest Basin Trail (1,350 ft.)	6.6 mi.	375 ft.	3:30
Russell Pond CG (1,333 ft.)	6.7 mi.	375 ft.	3:35

BSP This trail extends from Roaring Brook CG northward to Russell Pond CG through the valley of Wassataquoik Stream between Katahdin and Turner Mtn. It is the principal approach to the Russell Pond area deep in the park's interior.

Leaving from the ranger cabin at Roaring Brook CG, where Chimney Pond Trail turns left (west), Russell Pond Trail crosses a bridge over Roaring Brook. At 0.1 mi., the trail turns left (northwest). (To the right, Sandy Stream Pond Trail leads to Sandy Stream Pond and on to South Turner Mtn. via South Turner Trail.) In the next 0.5 mi., Russell Pond Trail traverses several brooks while gradually climbing to the low height-of-land between Sandy Stream Pond and Whidden Pond. It then descends and passes east (right) of Whidden Pond, where there is an extensive view of the basins and peaks on the east side of Katahdin.

At 1.1 mi., Sandy Stream Pond Trail joins from the right. Ahead, an open area yields pleasant scenery. Beyond, Russell Pond Trail moves into denser forest and crosses several brooks, and at 3.1 mi., the trail reaches a jct. on the right with Wassataquoik Stream Trail (leads 2.3 mi. to Wassataquoik Stream CS and rejoins Russell Pond Trail in 3.6 mi.). Ahead, Russell Pond Trail traverses the South Branch of Wassataquoik Stream and soon crosses an unnamed brook. (*Note*: No bridges are available. The crossing is knee-deep in dry weather, and in wet weather, it can be hazardous.)

The trail, now on the west side of the valley, passes under an overhanging glacial erratic (a rock that has been transported and deposited by a glacier). Moving away from Wassataquoik Stream, the trail passes several brooks and springs and climbs gently for about 2 mi. before descending gradually to cross the main branch of Wassataquoik Stream at 6.3 mi. At 6.5 mi., Russell Pond Trail crosses the old Wassataquoik Tote Rd. and passes a clearing on the right. At a jct., Wassataquoik Stream Trail leads right (east) 1.3 mi. to Wassataquoik Stream CS. Immediately beyond the tote road, Russell Pond Trail crosses Turner Brook. At 6.6 mi., Northwest Basin Trail to the Saddle leaves to the left (west). Soon after, Russell Pond Trail reaches Russell Pond and Russell Pond CG and the jct. with Pogy Notch Trail.

WASSATAQUOIK STREAM TRAIL (MAP 1: D4–D3)
Cumulative from Roaring Brook CG (1,489 ft.) to:

Wassataquoik Stream Trail (1,500 ft.) via Russell Pond Trail	3.1 mi.	135 ft.	1:35
Wassataquoik Stream CS (1,255 ft.)	5.4 mi.	135 ft.	2:45
Russell Pond CG (1,333 ft.) via Russell Pond Trail	7.1 mi.	210 ft.	3:40

BSP Formerly known as Tracy Horse Trail or Wassataquoik South Branch Trail, this trail extends from Russell Pond Trail along the South Branch of Wassataquoik Stream to the main branch of the stream.

Wassataquoik Stream Trail leaves on the right (east) side of Russell Pond Trail 3.1 mi. north of Roaring Brook CG, just before that trail crosses the

South Branch (*Caution*: hazardous during high water). Wassataquoik Stream Trail then leads 2.3 mi. to the jct. with a side trail leading to Wassataquoik Stream CS (two lean-tos). Turn left to cross a tributary stream, and then continue along the southern bank of the main branch of Wassataquoik Stream for about 100 yd.

Cross to the north side of Wassataquoik Stream (no bridge; fording may be difficult in high water) and merge with old Wassataquoik Tote Rd. at the jct. with Grand Falls Trail (leads 1.6 mi. to Inscription Rock, 2.0 mi. to Grand Falls, and 3.8 mi. to the north side of Russell Pond). Beyond this point, Wassataquoik Stream Trail reaches a jct. with Russell Pond Trail. Turn right on Russell Pond Trail and cross Turner Brook to reach Northwest Basin Trail and then the south end of Russell Pond and Russell Pond CG.

GRAND FALLS TRAIL (MAP 1: C4–D4)
Cumulative from Russell Pond CG (1,333 ft.) to:

Caverly Lookout Trail (1,360 ft.) via Pogy Notch Trail	0.4 mi.	0 ft.	0:10
Side trails to Grand Falls and Inscription Rock (1,150 ft.)	2.2 mi.	70 ft.	1:05
Wassataquoik Stream Trail (1,250 ft.)	3.8 mi.	170 ft.	2:00

BSP This trail leads east from the north end of Russell Pond CG to several interesting locations in Wassataquoik Valley and then returns west to near the south end of Russell Pond.

From the campground, follow Pogy Notch Trail around the west shore of the pond. Wassataquoik Lake Trail leaves to the left soon after the start of the route. At a jct. at 0.2 mi., Pogy Notch Trail continues north (left). Head right on Grand Falls Trail, pass the ranger station, and continue to the next jct. at 0.4 mi. Here, Caverly Lookout Trail leaves to the left (north) and leads 0.9 mi. to a viewpoint. Stay right to continue on Grand Falls Trail, which climbs easily over a low ridge, passes Bell Pond, and crosses a wet area.

At a jct. close to Wassataquoik Stream at 2.2 mi., a side trail leaves to the left (north) and follows the north side of the stream downstream 0.4 mi. to Grand Falls, which drops steeply between high granite walls. The ruins of a logging dam lie just upstream. From this same jct., another side trail to the right leads 50 ft. to the bank of Wassataquoik Stream and Inscription Rock, a huge boulder inscribed with a historical 1883 notice about logging in the area.

Continuing to the right, Grand Falls Trail follows the west bank of Wassataquoik Stream, passing Ledge Falls to meet Wassataquoik Stream Trail at the South Branch of Wassataquoik Stream at 3.8 mi. To the right, it is 0.4 mi. west to a crossing of Turner Brook and then another 1.3 mi. to Russell Pond via Russell Pond Trail (a second crossing of Turner Brook is required).

CAVERLY LOOKOUT TRAIL (MAP 1: C4–D4)
Cumulative from Russell Pond CG (1,333 ft.) to:

Caverly Lookout Trail (1,360 ft.) via Grand Falls Trail	0.2 mi.	30 ft.	0:10
Caverly Lookout ledges (1,730 ft.)	1.3 mi.	370 ft.	0:50

BSP This high outlook (1,730 ft.) offers views ranging from Traveler Mtn. to Katahdin and is easy to reach from the north end of Russell Pond CG. From the jct. of Pogy Notch Trail, follow Grand Falls Trail for 0.4 mi. and turn left at a jct. Caverly Lookout Trail climbs moderately and steadily to reach open ledges and fine views southeast to North Turner and South Turner mountains, and Knife Edge from Pamola to Baxter Peak.

WASSATAQUOIK LAKE TRAIL (MAP 1: D1, C3, D3)
Cumulative from Park Tote Rd. near Nesowadnehunk CG (1,300 ft.) to:

Center Pond Lean-to (1,700 ft.)	4.8 mi.	400 ft.	2:35
Little Wassataquoik Lake CS (1,630 ft.)	9.4 mi.	450 ft.	4:55
Side trail to Wassataquoik Lookout (1,600 ft.)	9.5 mi.	450 ft.	5:00
Wassataquoik Lake Lean-to (1,380 ft.)	10.4 mi.	450 ft.	5:25
Side trail to Green Falls (1,380 ft.)	11.2 mi.	475 ft.	5:50
Side trail to Wassataquoik Lake (1,350 ft.) and launch to Island Lean-to	12.1 mi.	475 ft.	6:15
Six Ponds (1,340 ft.)	12.8 mi.	475 ft.	6:40
Deep Pond (1,340 ft.)	13.8 mi.	475 ft.	7:10
Russell Pond CG (1,333 ft.)	14.3 mi.	475 ft.	7:25

BSP This trail, one of the longest in BSP, extends east from Nesowadnehunk CG to Center Pond and then Wassataquoik Lake to reach Russell Pond in the central interior of the park. The trail begins on Park Tote Rd. about 200 ft. south of the bridge over Little Nesowadnehunk Stream and 300 ft. south of the entrance road to Nesowadnehunk CG.

The route follows the southern bank of Little Nesowadnehunk Stream, crosses the stream at 1.0 mi., and then follows the north bank for a distance before trending away. At 4.7 mi., it reaches Center Pond and follows its westerly shore to a jct. 0.1 mi. ahead. Here, a side trail leads 0.1 mi. to Center Pond Lean-to. Well beyond Center Pond, Wassataquoik Lake Trail descends into the Trout Brook drainage, crosses the South Branch of Trout Brook, and then gradually bears away to join an old tote road.

At 8.0 mi., the trail turns sharply right onto another old tote road and, after a gradual ascent, reaches an old field and ascends to a gap. Beyond the gap, the trail is a footpath and soon reaches a side trail leading left 175 yd. to Little Wassataquoik CS next to a small stream. A short distance beyond this jct., a side trail leads 0.3 mi. and about 200 ft. up to a viewpoint over Wassataquoik Lake and the Wassataquoik Valley.

SEC 1

Ahead, the trail reaches Little Wassataquoik Lake and follows its western shore. After the lake, the trail skirts a beaver flowage and makes a moderate descent along the lake's outlet to the west end of Wassataquoik Lake. The route closely follows the lakeshore and soon reaches a short side trail on the left leading to Wassataquoik Lake Lean-to. Farther down the lake, a side trail on the right leads 0.1 mi. to the base of pretty Green Falls. Near the south end of Wassataquoik Lake, a path on the left leads 0.1 mi. to the lakeshore and the canoe landing for reaching Wassataquoik Island Lean-to, which is 50 yd. across the lake on a small island. Continuing on, Wassataquoik Lake Trail crosses a brook and soon passes between two of the Six Ponds on a narrow esker. It then passes a boggy flowage, crosses a grassy flowage with a small stream, and passes a side trail leading left to Deep Pond. At 14.3 mi., enter a cleared area near the west shore of Russell Pond and the jct. with Pogy Notch Trail. Russell Pond CG is along the pond to the left and right.

POGY NOTCH TRAIL (MAP 1: B4, C4, D4)
Cumulative from South Branch Pond CG (1,000 ft.) to:

North Traveler Trail (1,000 ft.)	0.1 mi.	0 ft.	0:05
Howe Brook Trail (1,000 ft.)	0.9 mi.	30 ft.	0:30
Center Ridge Trail (1,050 ft.)	1.4 mi.	80 ft.	0:45
South Branch Mtn. Trail (1,006 ft.)	1.9 mi.	120 ft.	1:00
Pogy Pond (1,150 ft.) and side trail to lean-to	5.6 mi.	350 ft.	3:00
Russell Pond CG, north end (1,333 ft.)	8.8 mi.	400 ft.	4:35
Russell Pond CG, south end (1,133 ft.) and jct. Russell Pond Trail	9.0 mi.	400 ft.	4:40

BSP This trail connects South Branch Pond CG with the trails on Traveler Mtn. and then continues through Pogy Notch to Pogy Pond and finally to Russell Pond CG in the central backcountry of BSP.

From the east end of South Branch Pond CG, opposite campsite 19, enter the woods on Pogy Notch Trail toward the eastern shore of the pond. North Traveler Trail diverges left at 0.1 mi. Passing between the pond on the right and cliffs on the left, Pogy Notch Trail reaches Howe Brook and Howe Brook Trail, which leaves to the left (east) to visit Howe Brook Falls in 0.9 mi. Ahead, Pogy Notch Trail climbs over the end of the cliff between Lower and Upper South Branch ponds. Center Ridge Trail diverges left at 1.4 mi. Pogy Notch Trail descends, follows the east shore of Upper South Branch Pond, and reaches a jct. with South Branch Mtn. Trail at 1.9 mi. Upper South Branch Pond CS is 0.2 mi. west on this trail.

Pogy Notch Trail continues south, passing through an alder swamp and beaver works. The route traverses several brooks and rises and falls moderately for the next 0.5 mi. At a fork, turn and climb gradually to pass through Pogy Notch. Beyond, bear left into a sparsely grown old burn. The trail then crosses a beaver canal and descends into the Pogy Pond watershed. It crosses a brook several times while passing out of the notch area and then crosses several other brooks before reaching the head of Pogy Pond, where there are views of Traveler Mtn. and North Turner Mtn., as well as Katahdin, from the shore of the pond. The trail then bears right, uphill, and at 5.6 mi., a side trail on the left leads 0.2 mi. to Pogy Pond CS (lean-to).

Pogy Notch Trail descends nearly to the pond and then bears right, away from the water. It rises gradually and then descends through an old burn, traverses a series of shallow rises, and bears right. Beyond, the trail drops into the gully of the western tributary of Pogy Brook, crosses it, and climbs the opposite slope. Then Pogy Notch Trail runs through a swampy hollow, climbs a rocky rise, and descends gradually to cross another brook. Immediately after this second brook, the trail bears right and climbs gradually through sparse mixed growth. It traverses a beaver meadow, reaches a rough boulder field, and descends through it and toward Russell Pond. Just before the pond, the trail to Grand Falls and Caverly Lookout leaves to the left; a short distance ahead, Wassataquoik Lake Trail leaves to the right. Pogy Notch Trail reaches Russell Pond CG at 8.8 mi. It ends 0.2 mi. ahead near the southwest corner of Russell Pond CG at the jct. with Russell Pond Trail (p. 43).

NORTHEAST OF NESOWADNEHUNK LAKE
BURNT MTN. (1,796 FT.)

The trail to Burnt Mtn. begins at Burnt Mtn. Picnic Area on Park Tote Rd., 6.4 mi. west of the access road to South Branch CG. The summit, the site of a former fire tower, is wooded, but the ledges just beyond the tower provide surprising views south to Katahdin and many more peaks.

BURNT MTN. TRAIL (MAP 1: B2)
From Burnt Mtn. Picnic Area (1,086 ft.) to:

Burnt Mtn. summit (1,796 ft.)	1.3 mi.	710 ft.	1:00

BSP Starting to the right of the picnic area pit toilet, the wide trail proceeds gradually over the north slope of the mountain, passing through mature woods. The easy ascent becomes moderate through parklike woods before reaching a grassy clearing. Here are the concrete stanchions of the old fire tower; the 40-ft. structure was erected in 1924 and removed in 2005. Continue on for 250 ft. to the viewpoint, which looks to Katahdin and Knife Edge, the Howe (North) Peaks, North and South Brother, Fort Mtn., Center Mtn., Mt. Coe, and Doubletop.

DWELLEY POND TRAIL (MAP 1: B2–C2)
Cumulative from Park Tote Rd. (1,500 ft.)

Dwelley Pond (1,400 ft.)	1.6 mi.	65 ft.	0:50
Park Tote Rd. south of Burnt Mtn. Day Use Site (1,320 ft.)	5.4 mi.	235 ft.	2:50

BSP This easy hike starts from an old turnout on Park Tote Rd. at a point 5.7 mi. north of Nesowadnehunk CG. It follows the overgrown route of a former park road for its 5.4-mi. length, reaching Dwelley Pond and Dwelley Pond Day Use Site. Beyond, the trail continues east and turns north along the base of McCarty Mtn. It follows the South Branch of Trout Brook and passes through McCarty Field before finally crossing the brook. The trail then bears northwest around Burnt Mtn. to end at Park Loop Rd.

SOUTH BRANCH PONDS
SOUTH BRANCH MTN. (2,627 FT.)
AND BLACK CAT MTN. (2,613 FT.)
South Branch Mtn. and Black Cat Mtn. rise steeply above the western shores of Lower and Upper South Branch ponds and offer commanding views of Traveler Mtn. The summits and ridges of Katahdin are fully visible to the south.

SOUTH BRANCH MTN. TRAIL (MAP 1: B4–C4)
Cumulative from South Branch Pond CG (981 ft.) to:

South Branch Mtn. summit (2,627 ft.)	2.2 mi.	1,646 ft.	1:55
Black Cat Mtn. summit (2,613 ft.)	2.6 mi.	1,800 ft.	2:10
Pogy Notch Trail (950 ft.)	4.7 mi.	1,800 ft.	3:35
South Branch Pond CG (981 ft.) via Pogy Notch Trail	6.6 mi.	1,800 ft.	4:10

BSP This route extends from South Branch Pond CG over both summits and down to Pogy Notch Trail, joining it at the southeastern corner of Upper South Branch Pond.

South Branch Mtn. Trail starts at the northwest corner of Lower South Branch Pond, just south of the ranger cabin and adjacent to the picnic and dock area. Head west to cross the outlet brook, and then pass a side trail to several walk-in campsites. The trail parallels the brook for a distance before climbing a ridge to lookouts with vistas of the ponds and the peaks of Traveler Mtn. After a gradual ascent, South Branch Mtn. Trail turns abruptly to the left and climbs more steeply to ledges, a rocky knob, and then more open ledges, with excellent views of the pond below and the mountain peaks to the east. The trail reaches the partially wooded summit of South Branch Mtn. at 2.2 mi.

Beyond the summit, the trail makes a brief descent into a saddle and then climbs to the top of Black Cat Mtn., at 2.6 mi., where the reward is a panoramic vista. Continuing on, South Branch Mtn. Trail descends through meadows and rocky fields to open ledges on the southern side of Black Cat Mtn. and then swings eastward and descends through mixed forests. After a brief climb, the trail continues down toward Upper South Branch Pond. A side trail on the left leads to Upper South Branch CS, and beyond it crosses a brook with beaver works before joining Pogy Notch Trail at 4.7 mi. Turn left (north) here for South Branch Pond CG (in 1.9 mi.) or right (south) for Pogy Notch and Russell Pond CG (in 7.1 mi.).

TRAVELER MTN.: CENTER RIDGE (3,264 FT.), THE TRAVELER (3,543 FT.), TRAVELER RIDGE (2,976 FT.), AND NORTH TRAVELER MTN. (3,149 FT.)

This starfish-shaped mountain mass has four high ridges that sprawl to the south, west, northwest, and north, with four shorter spurs between them. Fires have ravaged the mountain, the last one in 1902, so although its lower slopes support trees of some size, its upper reaches are mostly bare. This is the highest volcanic mountain in New England and possibly the highest on the East Coast. It was formed by a volcanic eruption similar in nature to the violent explosion at Mt. Saint Helens in Oregon in 1980.

Combining Pogy Notch, Center Ridge, Traveler Mtn., and North Traveler trails creates an excellent, if long and strenuous, hike known as Traveler Loop. (*Note*: It is recommended that hikers attempting this circuit ascend via Center Ridge Trail and descend by way of North Traveler Trail.)

NORTH TRAVELER TRAIL (MAP 1: B4)
Cumulative from South Branch Pond CG (1,000 ft.) to:

North Traveler Trail (1,000 ft.) via Pogy Notch Trail	0.1 mi.	0 ft.	0:05
North Traveler summit (3,149 ft.) and Traveler Mtn. Trail	2.9 mi.	2,149 ft.	2:30

BSP From the east end of South Branch Pond CG, across from campsite 19, follow Pogy Notch Trail (p. 47) for 0.1 mi. to North Traveler Trail, which diverges left. North Traveler Trail climbs through semi-open woods to the crest of the north ridge, which it follows over bare rhyolite (a type of extrusive igneous rock high in silica content) ledges and crags in places, with spectacular views of the valley ponds and the peaks to the west. Note the interesting columnar formations of rhyolite as you ascend, but watch your footing—the trail is often steep and its treadway is a mix of loose gravel and scree. After a wooded stretch, the trail passes through pretty alpine meadows and fine old woods that alternate with steep ledges. At about 1.7 mi., in one of the wooded sections, a side trail leaves left to a spring. After emerging from the last section of woods, North Traveler Trail continues in the open up the ridge to the broad alpine summit of North Traveler Mtn. at 2.9 mi. and the jct. with Traveler Mtn. Trail.

HOWE BROOK TRAIL (MAP 1: B4)
Cumulative from South Branch Pond CG (1,000 ft.) to:

Howe Brook Trail (1,050 ft.) via Pogy Notch Trail	0.9 mi.	30 ft.	0:30
End of trail (1,660 ft.)	2.9 mi.	690 ft.	1:50

BSP Howe Brook Trail begins at the southeastern corner of Lower South Branch Pond, where the rocky, fanlike delta of Howe Brook merges with the pond. This inlet is 0.9 mi. south along Pogy Notch Trail (p. 47) from South Branch Pond CG. Leaving left (east), Howe Brook Trail follows the route of the brook to the first chutes and potholes. Howe Brook is noted for its many pools, potholes, slides, and chutes, which continue for quite a distance up the valley. The trail crosses the brook numerous times before ending at a beautiful waterfall.

CENTER RIDGE TRAIL (MAP 1: B4–C4)
Cumulative from South Branch Pond CG (1,000 ft.) to:

Center Ridge Trail (1,050 ft.) via Pogy Notch Trail	1.4 mi.	50 ft.	0:45
Center Ridge (3,264 ft.)	3.7 mi.	2,314 ft.	3:00

BSP This route starts at the foot of Center Ridge near the northeastern corner of Upper South Branch Pond, at a point 1.4 mi. south on Pogy Notch Trail (p. 47) from South Branch Pond CG. Diverging left (east) from Pogy Notch Trail, Center Ridge Trail climbs steadily and steeply through woods before breaking into the open on the ridge above, which reveals excellent views of the South Branch ponds, Howe Brook valley, and North Traveler Mtn. Follow the open ridge over ledges and slabs, boulders and scree, and numerous false summits to reach the narrow crest known as

Little Knife Edge. Turn left to quickly reach the summit of Center Ridge, also called Peak of the Ridges, at 3.7 mi., and a jct. with Traveler Mtn. Trail. From this vantage point, the summit of Traveler looms ahead in the distance, and Katahdin rises above the Wassataquoik Valley to the south.

TRAVELER MTN. TRAIL (MAP 1: B4–C4)
Cumulative from South Branch Pond CG (1,000 ft.) to:

Center Ridge Trail (1,050 ft.) via Pogy Notch Trail	1.4 mi.	50 ft.	0:45
Center Ridge (3,264 ft.) and Traveler Mtn. Trail	3.7 mi	2,314 ft.	2:55
The Traveler summit (3,543 ft.)	5.2 mi.	2,960 ft.	4:05
Traveler Ridge (2,976 ft.)	7.0 mi.	3,195 ft.	5:05
North Traveler Mtn. summit (3,149 ft.)	8.2 mi.	3,795 ft.	6:00
South Branch Pond CG (981 ft.) via North Traveler Trail and Pogy Notch Trail	11.1 mi.	3,795 ft.	7:30

BSP Traveler Mtn. Trail starts from the Center Ridge summit; this point is reached via Pogy Notch Trail and Center Ridge Trail. Traveler Mtn. Trail traverses across and down Little Knife Edge, a vertical spine of columnar rhyolite rock. Cairns, broken rock, rough footing, and some scrambling mark this rugged stretch. Steep switchbacks lead over a talus slope before the trail enters the thick spruce and fir of the saddle between Center Ridge and Traveler. Cross an alpine meadow and climb through stunted coniferous forest and over several scree walls of rock to reach a huge talus field. Cairns lead diagonally up the mass of loose rock. At a large cairn, angle left and up across the scree slope and then proceed through thick growth to reach a good treadway on the ridge. Break out of the trees, make one last rocky scramble, and arrive at the summit of Traveler. Enjoy excellent panoramic views from this fine vantage point.

Beyond, Traveler Mtn. Trail traverses a long stretch of open terrain. (*Caution*: In bad weather, watch carefully for blazes and cairn route markers.) Cross more talus fields and then pass to the right around a large rock outcropping. Soon after, reenter the trees. After dipping into a ravine, continue the ascent on the narrow trail through thick conifers. Break out into the open again and traverse the open rocks of the ridge spine. After another brief dip, climb again into the open to reach the crest of Traveler Ridge, where there are views of Bald Mtn., Billfish Mtn., Trout Brook Mtn., Horse Mtn., and of course, Traveler and Center Ridge.

From Traveler Ridge, descend into a notch between it and North Traveler Mtn. Easily cross the saddle and then follow cairns over mostly open ledges on the ridge. After scaling a rock rib, traverse a small scree slope to the top of North Traveler Mtn. and the jct. with North Traveler Trail.

From here it is 2.9 mi. over the north ridge of North Traveler down to Lower South Branch Pond.

BARREL RIDGE (2,090 FT.)

The long ridgeline of Barrel Ridge rises in the midst of the wild country between the South Branch ponds and Five Ponds. Open ledges atop its craggy southeastern summit afford excellent views to the south, east, and north. The approach to Barrel Mtn. Trail is by way of Ledges Trail and Middle Fowler Pond Trail from the access road into South Branch Pond CG.

LEDGES TRAIL (MAP 1: B4)
Cumulative from South Branch Pond CG (981 ft.) to:

Ledges Trail (990 ft.)	0.1 mi.	10 ft.	0:03
Middle Fowler Pond Trail (1,060 ft.)	0.3 mi.	80 ft.	0:10
South Branch Pond access road (1,100 ft.) via Ledges Trail	0.7 mi.	240 ft.	0:30
Complete lollipop loop	1.3 mi.	240 ft.	0:45

BSP From South Branch Pond CG, walk north on the access road for 0.1 mi. and then turn right on Ledges Trail. At the jct. with Middle Fowler Pond Trail, turn left to continue on Ledges Trail, which climbs to and traverses open ledges with views south over the steep-walled valley that contains Lower and Upper South Branch ponds. Beyond, the trail descends to end at the access road. Turn left and hike back to the campground.

MIDDLE FOWLER POND TRAIL (MAP 1: B4)
Cumulative from South Branch Pond CG (981 ft.) to:

Middle Fowler Pond Trail via Ledges Trail (1,060 ft.)	0.3 mi.	80 ft.	0:10
Barrel Ridge Trail (1,800 ft.)	2.7 mi.	1,117 ft.	1:55
Middle Fowler Pond (990 ft.) and campsite side trail	3.6 mi.	1,117 ft.	2:10
Middle Fowler Pond, north end (990 ft.) and campsite side trail	4.1 mi.	1,167 ft.	2:45
Lower Fowler Pond Trail (1,000 ft.)	5.2 mi.	1,267 ft.	3:15
Park Tote Rd. (650 ft.) via Lower Fowler Pond Trail and Fowler Brook Trail	6.9 mi.	1,267 ft.	4:05

BSP From South Branch Pond CG, walk north on the access road for 0.1 mi. Here, Ledges Trail departs left. At a jct. at 0.3 mi., Middle Fowler Pond Trail continues, climbing gradually and following a small brook to open ledges. From there, the trail proceeds through the gap between Big Peaked Mtn. and Little Peaked Mtn. It then traverses the north slope of

Traveler Mtn., providing occasional views of the crags on Barrel Ridge. The mildly undulating route crosses Dry Brook and, at 2.7 mi., reaches Barrel Ridge Trail on the left.

Barrel Ridge Trail. From Middle Fowler Pond Trail, Barrel Ridge Trail proceeds through woods to climb a series of open ledges. Note the interesting columnar rhyolite rock as you ascend. After a sharp right, scramble up the final ledges to the sign and cairn atop Barrel Ridge. The fine 180-degree vista includes North Traveler Mtn., Bald Mtn., Billfish Mtn., Trout Brook Mtn., and Deasey and Lunksoos mountains in KAWW. Barrel Ridge Trail gains 290 ft. in 0.3 mi.

From the Barrel Ridge Trail jct., Middle Fowler Pond Trail descends and reaches Middle Fowler Pond and a jct., where a side path to the right leads to Middle Fowler South CS. The main trail continues to the left along the west shore of the pond to its outlet, where a side path leads 0.1 mi. right to Middle Fowler North CS. Beyond, the trail proceeds to a jct. with Lower Fowler Pond Trail, which leads left to Lower Fowler Pond and on to Park Tote Rd. (in 1.7 mi.), while Middle Fowler Pond Trail joins Five Ponds Trail to reach Trout Brook CG (in 2.4 mi.).

FIVE PONDS

The scenic Five Ponds area (despite the name, there are seven in all) is west of Horse Mtn., south of Trout Brook Mtn., and northeast of South Branch Pond CG in the northeast corner of BSP south of Park Tote Rd. From west to east are Lower and Middle Fowler ponds, High and Long ponds, Round and Billfish ponds, and Littlefield Pond. A system of trails connects the ponds and seven backcountry campsites, providing fine day and overnight hiking. Hikers can gain access to trails from Park Tote Rd. at several points and from South Branch CG.

FIVE PONDS TRAIL (MAP 1: B4–B5)
Cumulative from Park Tote Rd. (689 ft.) to:

Trout Brook Mtn. Trail, upper jct. (790 ft.)	0.15 mi.	100 ft.	0:10
Trout Brook Mtn. Trail, lower jct. (898 ft.)	1.0 mi.	209 ft.	0:35
Horse Mtn. Trail (930 ft.)	2.5 mi.	250 ft.	1:20
Lower Fowler Pond Trail (848 ft.)	4.0 mi.	275 ft.	2:10
Complete loop	6.0 mi.	460 ft.	3:15

BSP This trail makes a loop around the base of Trout Brook Mtn. and passes seven scenic ponds. It is described in a clockwise direction from the trailhead on Park Tote Rd., across from Trout Brook Farm CG. Begin from the left or eastern corner of the parking lot.

SEC
1

In a few minutes, the trail to Trout Brook Mtn. diverges to the right. Continue on a contour to the east. Near Littlefield Brook, Five Ponds Trail turns south and climbs gradually to meet the other end of Trout Brook Mtn. Trail. Then it climbs into the valley of Littlefield Brook, meets the brook, and follows it to Littlefield Pond; a spur path leads 200 ft. to the pond's north shore. Circling around above the west side of the pond, Five Ponds Trail descends to meet Horse Mtn. Trail, which enters from the left. A short distance ahead, a side trail leads right to Billfish Pond CS. For much of the next 1.5 mi., Five Ponds Trail follows an esker as it weaves between ponds.

Passing above Round Pond, the trail reaches High Pond (on the right). Ahead, with High Pond below on the right, a side trail on the left that leads 0.15 mi. to Long Pond Pines CS. Along the esker between High Pond and Long Pond, a spur on the left leads to a BSP canoe rental area. Soon after, another spur path on the left travels 0.1 mi. to Long Pond Outlet CS. Continue on the course of the esker and then descend to a T jct., where Lower Fowler Pond Trail departs to the left. Turn right to stay on Five Ponds Trail. Cross the outlet of High Pond and then climb gradually over the lower west shoulder of Trout Brook Mtn. Five Ponds Trail trends easily north down to the trailhead and the conclusion of the loop.

FOWLER BROOK TRAIL (MAP 1: B4)
From Park Tote Rd. (695 ft.) to:

Lower Fowler Pond (870 ft.)	1.2 mi.	195 ft.	0:40

BSP Fowler Brook Trail leads south from Park Tote Rd. 2.0 mi. west of Trout Brook Farm CG. It generally follows the course of Fowler Brook, climbing over a low ridge, regaining the brook, and passing a pretty flume. The trail then leads to the north shore of Lower Fowler Pond, Lower Fowler Outlet CS, and the jct. with Lower Fowler Pond Trail.

LOWER FOWLER POND TRAIL (MAP 1: B4)
From Lower Fowler Pond Trail (848 ft.) to:

Middle Fowler Pond Trail (1,000 ft.)	0.4 mi.	150 ft.	0:15
Fowler Brook Trail (870 ft.)	0.9 mi.	150 ft.	0:30

BSP This route connects Five Ponds Trail with Lower Fowler Pond, Middle Fowler Pond, and Fowler Brook trails. Lower Fowler Pond Trail diverges south from Five Ponds Trail at a point 2.0 mi. from Park Tote Rd. across from Trout Brook CG. After crossing the outlet of Long Pond, the trail climbs gradually south to the jct. of Middle Fowler Pond Trail, which continues straight ahead. Lower Fowler Pond Trail descends to the right to reach Lower Fowler Pond and eventually Fowler Brook Trail at the jct. with the side trail to Lower Fowler Outlet CS.

SEC 1

TROUT BROOK MTN. (1,781 FT.)

This low mountain rises to the south of Trout Brook CG and offers fine views of the Traveler Mtn. massif and more from its summit ledges.

TROUT BROOK MTN. TRAIL (MAP 1: B4)
Cumulative from Park Tote Rd. (689 ft.) to:

Trout Brook Mtn. Trail (790 ft.)	0.15 mi.	100 ft.	0:10
Trout Brook Mtn. summit (1,781 ft.)	1.3 mi.	1,092 ft.	1:05
Five Ponds Trail	2.5 mi.	1,092 ft.	1:50

BSP This hike starts from Park Tote Rd. directly opposite Trout Brook CG. Begin from the left or eastern corner of the parking lot and follow Five Ponds Trail for 0.15 mi. Then turn right on Trout Brook Mtn. Trail. In 500 ft., turn sharply left and climb gradually. Pass right around a mossy boulder. The ascent is steady but moderate on a rising contour up to the right. Turning left, the trail climbs steeply over exposed bedrock, passing an outlook to the north. Ledges of pine and spruce lead to a level stretch, interrupted by a single ledge step. After several shallow dips, the gradual climbing becomes steeper over mossy ledges. After the next outlook to the north, reach the summit of Trout Brook Mtn. in a gravelly opening in the trees. The wooded summit yields no views, but walk a short distance farther to find great views from ledges about 100 ft. to the right of the trail. The panorama takes in Long Pond, Bald Mtn., North Traveler Mtn. and The Traveler, Black Cat Mtn., South Branch Mtn., and Barrel Ridge. Continuing along, the trail reaches a view of Billfish Pond and Horse Mtn., as well as Deasey and Lunksoos mountains in KAWW. From here, descend the steep edge of Trout Brook Mtn. past another lookout. Reentering the woods, the trail angles more gradually down the slope to pass a grassy meadow. After a short, steep pitch, follow a falling contour, cross a small stream, and soon reach the T jct. with Five Ponds Trail. Turn left to follow Five Ponds Trail north 1.0 mi. back to Park Tote Rd.

HORSE MTN. (1,592 FT.)

This mountain rises steeply above the west shore of Grand Lake Matagamon in BSP's northwest corner and features sheer cliffs on its east face. An old fire tower on top, erected in 1913, was removed in 1999.

HORSE MTN. TRAIL (MAP 1: B5)
Cumulative from Park Tote Rd. (794 ft.) to:

East Spur Trail to East Spur Overlook (1,470 ft.)	1.2 mi.	676 ft.	0:55
Horse Mtn. summit side trail (1,470 ft.)	1.25 mi.	676 ft.	1:00

| Spur to Billfish Gorge (1,050 ft.) | 2.2 mi. | 676 ft. | 1:30 |
| Five Ponds Trail (930 ft.) | 3.0 mi. | 676 ft. | 1:50 |

BSP Horse Mtn. Trail leaves the south side of Park Tote Rd. 0.6 mi. west of Matagamon Gate. It rises gradually over the mountain's north flank to a shallow saddle and the jct. with East Spur Overlook Trail on the left.

East Spur Overlook Trail. This 0.4-mi. trail climbs gradually through mossy woods and boulders to a crest, descends slightly, rises to a bedrock knob, and finishes across open ledges. The view valley of the East Branch of the Penobscot River is excellent, taking in Grand Lake Matagamon, Sugarloaf Mtn., and Mt. Chase. To the south, Traveler Mtn., Bald Mtn., Billfish Mtn., and Deasey and Lunksoos mountains are all visible.

Just ahead on Horse Mtn. Trail, a side trail leaves right and climbs gradually 0.2 mi. and 122 ft. up to a small clearing on the wooded summit of Horse Mtn.

Ahead, Horse Mtn. Trail proceeds easily over the east side of the mountain, descends, and swings west to cross the head of a ravine. At a jct., a side trail leads straight ahead and steeply down 0.1 mi. to Billfish Gorge on Billfish Brook. Continuing to the right on Horse Mtn. Trail, follow a contour and then drop down to Billfish Pond. Soon after, reach a T jct. with Five Ponds Trail. To the left, Billfish Pond CS is 0.1 mi., and the west leg of Five Ponds Trail leads 3.5 mi. to the trailhead on Park Tote Rd. To the right, the east leg of Five Ponds Trail also leads to the same trailhead on Park Tote Rd., but in 2.5 mi.

NORTHERN BAXTER STATE PARK

Partially bounded to the south by Park Tote Rd., the northern tier of BSP ranges from Grand Lake Matagamon in the east to Webster Lake in the west. A 29,537-acre chunk of this vast, remote forestland is known as the Scientific Forest Management Area. This is the only location in the park where timber harvesting is allowed, thanks to Governor Baxter, who believed having such an area set aside was in the interest of good forestry science. The SFMA was established in the mid-1950s. Its mandate, as Baxter wrote in 1955, was to serve as "a show place for those interested in forestry, a place where a continuing timber crop can be cultivated, harvested, and sold—an example and inspiration to others." Hikers may pass through sections of active or recent timber harvesting, and at times may hear harvesting equipment, but most often will experience a true sense of remoteness in this wild northern part of the park. Hunting is also allowed in the northern section of BSP. Freezeout Trail, Wadleigh Brook Trail, and Frost Pond Trail wind through the SFMA.

FREEZEOUT TRAIL (MAP 1: A2–A4, B2)

Cumulative from Trout Brook CG (665 ft.) to:

Frost Pond Trail (658 ft.)	4.0 mi.	160 ft.	2:05
Northwest Cove CS (654 ft.)	5.0 mi.	220 ft.	2:35
Little East CS (654 ft.)	5.4 mi.	240 ft.	2:50
Grand Pitch side trail (718 ft.)	5.8 mi.	300 ft.	3:00
Wadleigh Brook Trail (820 ft.)	11.7 mi.	440 ft.	6:05
Webster Lake CS (911 ft.)	14.1 mi.	560 ft.	7:20

BSP This trail starts from Trout Brook CG, at the end of the campground road that leads to Trout Brook, where there is parking. Immediately cross Trout Brook on a footbridge, and soon pass several backcountry campsites and a walk-in lean-to site. Continue on the wide, graded trail, formerly a woods road (Freezeout Rd.). Traverse two branches of Boody Brook and then pass over several low ridges. Cross Frost Pond Brook, and at about 3.5 mi., reach a large sawdust pile (the remains of an old mill site) on the right on the shore of Grand Lake Matagamon. At 4.0 mi., Frost Pond Trail diverges left (south).

Ahead, cross Hinckley Brook and continue to parallel the lake. Pass Northwest Cove CS at 5.0 mi. (campsite to right, spring to left), and soon reach a sharp left turn at 5.4 mi. Little East CS (lean-to) is a short walk straight ahead, at the confluence of the East Branch of the Penobscot River and Webster Stream.

From this point west to Webster Lake, Freezeout Trail follows the south bank of Webster Stream. At 5.8 mi., a side trail leads 0.2 mi. to Grand Pitch, a thunderous 35-ft. waterfall on Webster Stream that drops into a narrow slate canyon. The side path rejoins Freezeout Trail in 0.3 mi.

Continue easily on Freezeout Trail for a long 5-mi. stretch, with minor changes in elevation and scenery. Soon after passing over Pine Knoll, the trail reaches the jct. with Wadleigh Brook Trail, which enters from the left at 11.7 mi. Cross Wadleigh Brook and then follow sections of old corduroy road and traverse Ice Wagon Field, an old log yard. With Webster Lake in sight, pass a privy on the left. A side trail on the right leads to Webster Lake CS (lean-to and tentsite) on the east end of the lake at 14.1 mi.

WADLEIGH MTN. (1,261 FT.)

This low mountain, the only one in the vast SFMA, is traversed by Frost Pond Trail. Freezeout Trail provides access to Frost Pond Trail from the east, while Wadleigh Brook Trail offers access from the west.

FROST POND TRAIL (MAP 1: A4–B3)
Cumulative from Trout Brook CG (665 ft.) to:

Frost Pond Trail (658 ft.)	4.0 mi.	160 ft.	2:05
Frost Pond CS (880 ft.)	5.5 mi.	215 ft.	2:50
Wadleigh Mtn. west summit (1,261 ft.)	9.3 mi.	796 ft.	5:05
Wadleigh Brook Trail (820 ft.)	10.3 mi.	796 ft.	5:35

BSP This route leaves left (west) from Freezeout Trail at a point 4.0 mi. from Trout Brook CG. Frost Pond Trail ascends gradually southwest for 1.5 mi. to reach Frost Pond CS (lean-to) at 5.5 mi. It continues south over a low ridge and then descends to cross Boody Brook and reach a wet area. Winding up the north slope of Wadleigh Mtn., the trail turns west below the mountain's east peak, gains the ridge, and continues to the western-most and highest summit. Here are views of Traveler Mtn. and South Branch Mtn. to the south. Descending to the west, Frost Pond Trail crosses a gravel road and soon meets Wadleigh Brook Trail 1.4 mi. north of Park Tote Rd.

WADLEIGH BROOK TRAIL (MAP 1: A2–B3)
Cumulative from Park Tote Rd. (800 ft.) to:

Frost Pond Trail (850 ft.)	1.4 mi.	50 ft.	0:40
Hudson Pond CS (900 ft.)	7.9 mi.	260 ft.	4:05
Freezeout Trail (850 ft.)	9.9 mi.	380 ft.	5:10

BSP Wadleigh Brook Trail leaves Park Tote Rd. 1.0 mi. west of the bridge over Trout Brook at Trout Brook Crossing Day Use Site. The trail follows Wadleigh Brook west for a short distance and then turns north to meet Frost Pond Trail, which enters from the right. Wadleigh Brook Trail returns to Wadleigh Brook, tracing a route along its eastern bank. The trail wends around the upper side of Wadleigh Bog and crosses a brook draining Blunder Pond. At 6.8 mi., Wadleigh Brook Trail crosses a gravel road at Blunder Pond Day Use Site. It traverses the inlet of Hudson Pond and soon reaches the pond proper. Here, a short side trail leads uphill to Hudson Pond CS (lean-to). Wadleigh Brook Trail follows the north shore of the pond before turning northeast and climbing over a low ridge to reach Hudson Brook and, soon after, Freezeout Trail near Pine Knoll.

Via Freezeout Trail, to the left it is 2.4 mi. to Webster Lake and its campsite; to the right, it is 11.7 mi. to Trout Brook CG, passing two campsites on the way.

KATAHDIN WOODS AND WATERS NATIONAL MONUMENT

The 1,900-mi. IAT officially begins near Mile 12 on Katahdin Loop Rd. and heads northeast to the Canadian border just east of Mars Hill. From there, the IAT crosses New Brunswick and Quebec to its current North American terminus in Newfoundland at Belle Isle. Within KAWW's boundaries, 30 mi. of the IAT threads south to north. Marked with 2-by-6-in. blue and white plastic blazes, the IAT crosses two scenic mountains, Deasey and Lunksoos, which offer outstanding views of Katahdin from their open summits. The side trail to Barnard Mtn. comes early on in the IAT route; the mountain's summit ledges offer additional fine views of Katahdin.

DEASEY MTN. (1,951 FT.) AND LUNKSOOS MTN. (1,796 FT.)

The craggy summits of these two mountains reward hikers with excellent views west to Katahdin, including Baxter Peak, South Peak, Knife Edge, and Pamola, plus Hamlin Peak, South Turner and North Turner, the peaks of Traveler Mtn., and many more mountaintops on the eastern side of BSP. The IAT crosses both Deasey Mtn. and Lunksoos Mtn.

IAT NORTHBOUND (MAP 1: C6, D5–D7, AND E5)
Cumulative from Katahdin Loop Rd. at Mile 12 (1,050 ft.) to:

Katahdin Brook Lean-to (960 ft.)	0.3 mi.	−90 ft.	0:10
Barnard Mtn. Trail (1,070 ft.)	1.4 mi.	110 ft.	0:45
Wassataquoik Lean-to (600 ft.)	4.1 mi.	110 ft.	2:10
Orin Falls Trail (650 ft.)	4.6 mi.	160 ft.	2:25
Wassataquoik Stream ford (590 ft.)	4.8 mi.	160 ft.	2:35
Deasey Mtn. summit (1,951 ft.)	9.5 mi.	1,675 ft.	5:40
Lunksoos Mtn. summit (1,796 ft.)	10.8 mi.	1,975 ft.	6:30
Lunksoos Lean-to (1,250 ft.)	11.8 mi.	1,975 ft.	7:00
Grand Pitch Lean-to (517 ft.)	22.4 mi.	2,281 ft.	12:25
Matagamon Gate (647 ft.)	29.3 mi.	2,520 ft.	16:00
Grand Lake Rd. (645 ft.)	30.0 mi.	2,520 ft.	16:10

IAT From the main jct. of Katahdin Loop Rd., 2.2 mi. west of Sandbank Stream CS, proceed to the right (north). At 1.3 mi., pass Orin Falls Rd. on the right and stay left on Katahdin Loop Rd. (Orin Falls Rd. leads 2.5 mi. to a barrier and parking area not far from Wassataquoik Stream and the start of Orin Falls Trail. That trail is a shorter alternative for hikers wanting to make a day trip to Deasey and Lunksoos mountains.) At 4.9 mi., turn right at a T intersection near Mile 12 on Katahdin Loop Rd. and in 100 ft. reach the trailhead for the IAT and Barnard Mtn. Trail. Parking for several cars is on the right.

To begin, hike north on old Gardner Rd. (the IAT) past a gate, then head downhill to cross a bridge over Katahdin Brook. Just past the bridge on the left is Katahdin Brook Lean-to. Beyond, climb a long grade to a jct. with an old logging road. Turn right (east) on this road and reach the jct. of Barnard Mtn. Trail on the right at 1.4 mi. (leads 0.8 mi. to the top of Barnard Mtn., see p. 63).

Continue to follow the IAT around the north side of Barnard Mtn. to a jct. with Old Wassataquoik Tote Rd. Keep right (south) to reach Wassataquoik Lean-to. Beyond the campsite, continue on the tote road, cross Katahdin Brook, and follow an esker south. At 4.8 mi., at a jct., the IAT departs left (east) down to Wassataquoik Stream, while Orin Falls Trail continues straight ahead (leads 0.5 mi. to parking near the end of Orin Falls Rd.). Staying on the IAT, ford Wassataquoik Stream (*Caution*: difficult crossing in high water) and walk along the east bank. The IAT turns left, crosses a tributary stream with sandy banks, and follows a blue-flagged trail west to a beaver dam. Cross on logs just below the dam, turn right, and gradually climb a bank before turning left to join the route of Old Keep Path. The IAT nears Wassataquoik Stream once more, crosses another small tributary, and then turns northeast.

At 6.1 mi., the IAT leaves Old Keep Path, turns northeast, and ascends to the col between Deasey Mtn. and a small hill to the south. The trail skirts the nose of Deasey Mtn., passes the house-sized boulder dubbed Earl's Erratic at 6.3 mi., and then crosses Owen Brook at 7.0 mi. Beyond a mature forest of spruce, hemlock, pine, and birch, the IAT turns north and climbs the east ridge of Deasey Mtn. At 8.0 mi., a spur path leads 50 ft. right to a view of the East Branch of the Penobscot River. The trail descends gradually to cross a stream and then reaches the old Deasey Mtn. fire warden's cabin at 8.5 mi., now in ruins. It passes in front of the cabin, turns left, and steeply climbs northwest. Just below the summit of Deasey Mtn. at 9.5 mi., the IAT turns sharply right (north). Here, a spur path leads left 100 ft. to the summit of Deasey, where the restored historical cabin sits directly on the ground (as it has since 1929), and hikers can enjoy panoramic vistas. Continuing north, the IAT drops into the col between Deasey Mtn. and Lunksoos Mtn. and traverses a wet area and brook. A steep, winding climb then leads to a series of open ledges on the ridge summit of Lunksoos Mtn. Cairns mark the route across the ledges. At 10.8 mi., reach the top of Lunksoos Mtn. and enjoy fine views of Sugarloaf Mtn., Mt. Chase, and the valley of the East Branch of the Penobscot River. The IAT descends to reach Lunksoos Lean-to at 11.8 mi.

From Lunksoos Lean-to, the IAT skirts the west side of Hathorn Mtn. and swings east across the north slopes of Little Spring Brook Mtn. to reach the East Branch of the Penobscot River and old Telos Tote Rd. The trail more or less follows this road north along the river corridor to Grand Pitch Lean-to, Haskell Rock, and Haskell Deadwater before turning west to join Messer Pond Rd. The IAT follows Messer Pond Rd. north out of KAWW to Grand Lake Rd., which it reaches at 30.0 mi. from its southern terminus at Mile 12.

A useful companion for hiking this and other sections of the IAT in Maine is the *Maine IAT Guide and Maps*, a free publication available at maineiat.org.

ORIN FALLS TRAIL (NPS; MAP 1: D6)
Cumulative from trailhead on Orin Falls Rd. (690 ft.) to:

IAT near Wassataquoik Stream ford (650 ft.)	0.5 mi.	–40 ft.	0:15
Wassataquoik Lean-to (600 ft.)	1.0 mi.	–90 ft.	0:30
Orin Falls (690 ft.)	3.5 mi.	90 ft.	1:45

NPS This route offers a shorter approach for hikers looking to make a day trip to Deasey and Lunksoos mountains. On its own, Orin Falls Trail (also known as Old Wassataquoik Tote Rd. and Wassataquoik Stream Rd.) is a pleasant trip along Wassataquoik Stream to a series of cascades over boulders. Driving from the main jct. of Katahdin Loop Rd., 2.2 mi. west of Sandbank Stream CS, proceed to the right. At 1.3 mi., reach Orin Falls Rd. on the right. Turn right and drive 2.5 mi. to a barrier and parking.

Orin Falls Trail follows an old road north to an esker on the south side of Wassataquoik Stream and turns left to follow Old Wassataquoik Tote Rd. In 0.5 mi., Orin Falls Trail joins the IAT just west of Wassataquoik Stream. Continue north, cross Katahdin Brook on a bridge, and reach Wassataquoik Lean-to. Where the IAT turns left, continue straight ahead on Orin Falls Trail, still following the old tote road. Nearing the cascades, Orin Falls Trail leaves the old road and follows a narrow path to the water.

BARNARD MTN. (1,628 FT.)
This mountain rises just east of BSP and Katahdin Lake. A large ledge on the summit rewards hikers with excellent views west to the high peaks of

Katahdin and southwest across the 100MW to Jo-Mary Mtn., the White Cap Range, and Baker Mtn.

BARNARD MTN. TRAIL (MAP 1: D5–D6)
Cumulative from Katahdin Loop Rd. at Mile 12 (1,050 ft.) to:

Katahdin Brook Lean-to (960 ft.)	0.3 mi.	–90 ft.	0:10
Barnard Mtn. Trail (1,070 ft.)	1.4 mi.	110 ft.	0:45
Barnard Mtn. summit and ledge view (1,628 ft.)	2.2 mi.	668 ft.	1:30

NPS Barnard Mtn. Trail begins from the IAT 1.4 mi. north of the start of that trail near Mile 12 on Katahdin Loop Rd. From the IAT, Barnard Mtn. Trail ascends the southeast ridge of the mountain via switchbacks to a huge erratic. The trail swings around the glacial boulder and passes through a large crevice in the rock. It contours past mossy boulders and then climbs moderately via more switchbacks. The angle eases, and the trail passes a cairn, soon emerging on a large slab of granite on the west side of the summit, where there is a picnic table and a fine vista of Katahdin Lake and the Katahdin massif.

LOOKOUT MTN. (1,953 FT.)
While this peak on the BSP–KAWW boundary requires considerable effort to attain, its summit ledges afford outstanding views of the Katahdin massif to the west. From Matagamon Gate at the north entrance of KAWW, drive south on Messer Pond Rd. for 2.5 mi. to Haskell Gate and park in the small lot. This is as far as vehicular traffic is allowed during the traditional hiking season of late spring into early fall.

LOOKOUT TRAIL (MAP 1: A5–C5)
Cumulative from Haskell Gate (670 ft.) to:

Haskell Hut side trail (591 ft.)	1.4 mi.	0 ft.	0:40
Little Messer Pond Road and IAT jct. (595 ft.)	2.6 mi.	25 ft.	1:20
K-Comp Road (660 ft.)	2.9 mi.	90 ft.	1:30
Big Spring Brook Hut side trail (830 ft.)	5.3 mi.	345 ft.	2:50
Lookout Trail (900 ft.)	5.6 mi.	415 ft.	3:00
Lookout Mtn. summit (1,953 ft.)	8.0 mi.	1,468 ft.	4:45

NPS From Haskell Gate, follow the IAT south. Soon after a side trail to Stair Falls, another side trail on the right leads a short distance to Haskell Hut. Farther south along the IAT, reach Haskell Rock, a 20-ft. conglomerate pillar that protrudes out of the East Branch of the Penobscot River. At the next fork, where the IAT continues south toward Grand Pitch, turn right on Little Messer Pond Road. The route is well marked up to this point but less so from here to the Lookout; a map and moderate navigation skills are required.

Following Little Messer Pond Road, in another 0.3 mi., pass K-Comp Road on the left. Pass a short side trail on the left that leads to Messer Pond. At 5.3 mi. from Haskell Gate, a side trail on the left leads 0.3 mi. to Big Spring Brook Hut. Beyond this jct., cross a bridge over Big Spring Brook to reach Lookout Trail. Turn right onto Lookout Trail and begin ascending the Lookout. In another 1.0 mi., turn left off the old tote road onto a narrower trail and climb southwesterly to the summit ledges atop the Lookout. The views south over the Wassataquoik Stream valley are excellent, as is the look southwest toward Katahdin in BSP.

SOUTH, EAST, AND NORTH OF BAXTER STATE PARK
TROUT MTN. (1,408 FT.)

The forested dome of Trout Mtn. rises to 1,408 ft. in the unorganized township of T2 R9 WELS, just south of the southern boundary of BSP. An observation deck atop an 80-ft. steel tower affords an outstanding panoramic vista from Katahdin across the 100MW to the peaks around Moosehead Lake. Trout Mtn. is part of 3,598-acre Trout Mtn. Preserve, which is owned and managed by TNC.

From the jct. of ME 11 (south) and the end of ME 157, 0.2 mi. west of downtown Millinocket, bear right and follow signs for BSP. The road has several names along its length, including Millinocket Lake Rd., Lake Rd., and Baxter Park Rd. At 8.6 mi., pass North Woods Trading Post and Big Moose Inn, Cabins & Campground on the right. Pass the colorful Pockwockamus Rock ("Maine is Beautiful") at 14.5 mi. Just shy of the BSP boundary at 16.0 mi., turn right into an old gravel pit and proceed a short distance to the trailhead parking area.

TROUT MTN. TRAIL (TNC; MAP 1: F4)
Cumulative from Baxter Park Rd. trailhead (600 ft.) to:

Trout Mtn. observation tower (1,408 ft.)	2.6 mi.	808 ft.	1:45

TNC The blue-blazed trail leaves the left edge of the parking area and follows a rutted skidder track for 0.1 mi. It then threads between the BSP boundary on the left and an old cut area on the right. At 0.4 mi., enter Trout Mtn. Preserve. The trail climbs gradually in an easterly direction before turning to the southeast up a drainage. At 1.8 mi., the trail tops out in the broad western shoulder of Trout Mtn. Soon after, the moderate climb resumes to the summit of the mountain. Pass a privy in the woods

50 ft. right of the trail and then turn left on a skidder road and walk past two picnic tables to the base of the observation tower. TNC erected the new tower in 2020, a welcome replacement for the old 1931 fire tower, which was burned and toppled by BSP in 1977. Climb the tower at your own risk to enjoy the extraordinary vista. The remains of the fire tower, in the woods a short distance beyond the new tower, are worth exploring.

MT. CHASE (2,450 FT.)

This mountain in the Penobscot County town of Mt. Chase is the highest among a cluster of seven peaks between Shin Pond to the west and the Aroostook County line to the east.

From the northernmost jct. of ME 11 and ME 159 in Patten, drive north on ME 11 for 6.4 mi. Turn left (west) on the gravel-surfaced Mountain Rd. Reach a gravel pit on the right and a grassy parking area on the left at 1.1 mi. Beyond this point, Mountain Rd. is rocky and rough and a high-clearance vehicle is recommended. At 1.8 mi., a side road leaves to the left; continue straight ahead on Mountain Rd. At 2.2 mi. from ME 11, Mountain Rd. turns sharply left; continue straight into a grassy clearing, where there is a picnic table and parking on the left and right.

MT. CHASE TRAIL (USGS MT. CHASE QUAD, GAZETTEER MAP 52)
Cumulative from Mountain Rd. parking (1,010 ft.) to:

Waterfall Trail (1,670 ft.)	0.9 mi.	660 ft.	0:45
Old fire warden's cabin (1,750 ft.)	1.1 mi.	740 ft.	0:55
Eagle Rock side trail (2,150 ft.)	1.5 mi.	1,140 ft.	1:20
Mt. Chase summit (2,450 ft.)	1.8 mi.	1,440 ft.	1:40

TMNK To find the start of the trail, do not follow the grassy jeep road that heads north from the parking area and picnic table (this is the start of Waterfall Trail to Bald Mtn.). Go left (west) from the parking area, following the old tote road for 100 ft. Here, a jeep track leaves to the right into the woods. Watch for a sun-bleached wooden sign with spray-painted orange letters ("Trail") to the left of the old tote road.

Turn onto the jeep track, a rocky old woods road that leads easily uphill. At 0.35 mi., continue straight through a 4-way jct. Soon after, at a fork, bear right and up. Pass a rock wall, and a short distance beyond, reach a jct. Old and faded signs on trees point right ("Waterfall") and ahead and up ("Mountain Trail"). To the right, Waterfall Trail descends 0.5 mi. to a beautiful cascade at the jct. of Bald Mtn. Trail.

From the Waterfall Trail jct., continue straight ahead on Mt. Chase Trail. After cresting, the trail descends slightly and levels off. The summit ridge of Mt. Chase is in view ahead. Enter a grassy clearing with the ruins of an old fire warden's cabin to the right. From the cabin site, ascend more steeply on eroded trail. Climb a slippery rock slab (rope), and then continue the moderate-to-steep ascent.

At 1.5 mi., a side trail on the left leads 500 ft. to a cairn atop the airy pinnacle of Eagle Rock, a worthwhile detour. From the jct., wind up the southwest ridge, where attractive views west to shapely Sugarloaf Mtn. and the Shin ponds (upper and lower) come into sight. Emerge into the semi-open and continue on the rocky ridge to the summit of Mt. Chase and a small communications tower. The footings of an old (1917) fire tower are here (the tower was moved to the Patten Lumbermen's Museum in 2001). Views from this vantage point are grand: Katahdin and Traveler Mtn. to the west, the Rocky Brook Range to the north-northeast, Peaked Mtn. to the north, and Haystack Mtn. and Mars Hill to the northeast.

BALD MTN. (1,685 FT.)

This mountain to the southeast of Mt. Chase features a series of cascading waterfalls and, from its summit ledges, excellent views south to Katahdin and its neighboring peaks. Waterfall Trail connects to Mt. Chase Trail and Bald Mtn. Trail; the latter climbs to the top of Bald Mtn.

WATERFALL TRAIL (USGS MT. CHASE QUAD, GAZETTEER MAP 52)
Cumulative from Mountain Rd. parking and picnic table (1,010 ft.) to:

Bald Mtn. Trail (1,300 ft.)	0.35 mi.	290 ft.	0:20
Mt. Chase Trail (1,670 ft.)	0.8 mi.	660 ft.	0:45

TMNK From the parking area picnic table, walk north into the woods on the grassy old tote road. At 0.2 mi., where the tote road turns left uphill, proceed straight and up along a brook on a footpath. At the base of a series of stepped waterfalls, cross the brook and climb along its east side. The trail veers away from the brook and then back to it at a mossy falls. Walk between the falls and a lichen-covered erratic. Pass more mossy waterfalls on the way to a jct. at 0.35 mi. and a beautiful 20-ft. cascade. Here, Bald Mtn. Trail leaves to the right, leading 0.5 mi. to the summit of Bald Mtn. To continue on Waterfall Trail, cross the brook below the cascade and climb the other side of the falls, going up along a brook and past another series of falls. At 0.55 mi., the trail joins a wide old road; turn right here and continue climbing. At 0.8 mi., reach a T jct. at Mt. Chase Trail, which leads right and up to the summit of Mt. Chase in 0.9 mi., or left and down to the Mt. Chase/Waterfall trailhead in 0.9 mi.

BALD MTN. TRAIL (USGS MT. CHASE QUAD, GAZETTEER MAP 52)
From Waterfall Trail jct. (1,300 ft.) to:

Bald Mtn. summit (1,685 ft.)	0.5 mi.	425 ft.	0:25

TMNK From the jct. of Waterfall Trail and a 20-ft. cascade at a point 0.35 mi. from the parking area picnic table, turn right on Bald Mtn. Trail, which angles up the slopes and then contours past a mossy ledge outcropping. Descend to cross a small brook below a pretty cascade and then continue on a contour. Turn left and head up an old tote road; soon leave the tote road for a path on the right (small cairn and colored flagging tape). Follow a contour to a mossy outcropping in a small opening (cairn); here, turn left and go up to weave between rocks at a moderate grade. At 0.4 mi., scramble up an outcropping wall to a view south to Katahdin. Continue to the next mossy ledge wall and then up over semi-open ledges where there's a view northwest to Mt. Chase. The unmarked summit of Bald Mtn. is just beyond. The view south from Bald Mtn. is outstanding. (*Note*: An obscure trail continues east along the Bald Mtn. summit ridge, but its condition and destination were unknown as of 2022.)

SUGARLOAF MTN. (1,876 FT.)
The mountain is in the unorganized township T5 R7 WELS, west of Shin Pond village and east of the Seboeis River. Panoramic views from its bare summit ledges include the peaks of the Katahdin massif north to Traveler Mtn. and beyond, as well as the summits and forestland of KAWW, Mt. Chase, Mars Hill, and many others.

From the jct. of ME 159 and ME 11 in Patten, drive northwest on ME 159 for 5.7 mi. Turn left (west) on Grondin Rd. and reset your mileage counter. At 2.7 mi. from ME 159, pass Sucker Brook Rd. on the right. At 3.0 mi., pass American Thread Rd. on the left. Cross a bridge at 3.9 mi. At 5.8 mi., bear left at a fork (orange and black sign for Sugarloaf Trail, the snowmobile trail). At 6.6 mi., cross an old bridge. Immediately beyond the bridge is a small clearing and a 4-way intersection; stay straight (sign: "64 Sugarloaf Trail"). At the next 4-way intersection, at 7.2 mi., turn left and proceed 150 yd. to a small parking area on the right. Look toward the trees for a wooden sign with "Sugarloaf Mtn" in red letters.

SUGARLOAF MTN. TRAIL
(USGS SHIN POND QUAD, GAZETTEER MAP 51)
From parking area (940 ft.) to:

Sugarloaf Mtn. summit (1,876 ft.)	0.95 mi.	936 ft.	1:00

NFTM Follow the wide, grassy trail into the woods. In 400 ft., climb a steep pitch. Strips of flagging tape mark the distinct trail corridor. Continue up the south ridge at a moderate but steady grade. At 0.55 mi., reach the base of the summit cone. The ridge narrows and the grade becomes moderate to steep. Pass a boulder with a small cave at its base at 0.65 mi. Reach a level shelf and continue easily for a short distance. The final stretch to the peak involves multiple pitches of steep scrambling over ledges. Reach the top of Sugarloaf at 0.95 mi. The 360-degree vistas from the summit include Katahdin and the peaks of BSP, White Cap Mtn., the Barren–Chairback Range, Norway Bluff, Round Mtn., Haystack Mtn., and Mars Hill. Grand Pitch on the Seboeis River is visible in the valley below to the west.

OWL'S HEAD (964 FT.)

Scraggly Lake PL, a 9,000-acre preserve just northeast of BSP, features a climb to Owl's Head, a prominent rocky knob overlooking Scraggly Lake and the forestland north of the park. From the northern jct. of ME 11 and ME 159 in Patten, drive west on ME 159 for 10.1 mi. to the village of Shin Pond. Soon after Shin Pond, ME 159 becomes Grand Lake Rd. At 6.0 mi. beyond Shin Pond, cross the Seboeis River and 0.7 mi. ahead reach Scraggly Lake Rd. on the right. Turn right on Scraggly Lake Rd. and follow it 9.3 mi. to signed trailhead parking on the right just before Scraggly Brook.

OWL'S HEAD TRAIL (USGS HAY LAKE QUAD, SCRAGGLY LAKE PUBLIC LAND, MAINE; GAZETTEER MAP 57)

Cumulative from parking near Scraggly Lake outlet (725 ft.) to:

Loop jct.	1.4 mi.	20 ft.	0:40
Owl's Head summit (964 ft.)	1.6 mi.	260 ft.	0:50
Complete lollipop loop	3.4 mi.	285 ft.	1:50

MBPL The blue-blazed trail enters the woods on the left side of the small parking area, meandering north over a knoll through spruce and cedar woods. At 0.45 mi., reach the outlet arm of Scraggly Lake. Bear right along the shore. At 0.65 mi., views open up to a boat launch across the lake to the left and to the distinctive bump of Owl's Head to the right. At 1.1 mi., a 20-ft. spur on the left offers another look at Owl's Head. Cross the steep slope between the lake and hill on a narrow path. An outcropping provides pleasant scenery. At 1.3 mi., a spur on the left leads 50 ft. down to the lake; this is the old water-access trailhead. The loop jct. is ahead at 1.35 mi. Bear right to ascend to Owl's Head. Climb a short, steep, rocky pitch; level off, traverse left, and then head right and up a moderate-to-steep section. A spur to the left leads to a ledge and wonderful views over Scraggly Lake.

The vista takes in the Traveler summits and other peaks in the northern reaches of BSP, the high summits of Katahdin, the craggy ridgelines of Deasey Mtn. and Lunksoos Mtn., and shapely Sugarloaf Mtn. Climb the rocks of the final ledges. Atop Owl's Head, a spur leads left over a narrow, rocky ridge to more views.

Descend steeply down the back side of Owl's Head on switchbacks and several sets of rock steps. Pass through an impressive grove of mature hemlock and reach the shore of Scraggly Lake. Traverse the slope above the lake, passing through more mature spruce, hemlock, red pine, and cedar woods. Reach the lakeshore again and then climb left and up to the loop jct. Bear right to return to the trailhead.

SECTION TWO

100-MILE WILDERNESS AND MOOSEHEAD LAKE

SEC 2

INTRODUCTION

This section describes 80 trails on 39 mountains in the 100-Mile Wilderness and Moosehead Lake region, which includes the southern half of sprawling Piscataquis County in north-central Maine, roughly 1.4 million acres. The second largest but least populous county in Maine, Piscataquis gets its name from the Abenaki word meaning "branch of the river" or "at the river branch." Five major rivers cross the county. The northern half of Piscataquis County features the wilds of BSP, a portion of the Allagash Wilderness Waterway, and an abundance of other lakes, rivers, hills, and mountains but only Allagash Mtn. has a trail (see p. 596 in Section Twelve: Aroostook County). The southern half of Piscataquis County is bounded on the north by BSP, the West Branch of the Penobscot River, and Golden Rd. To the east, the section is more or less bounded by ME 11. To the south, ME 16/6 and ME 6 form an approximate boundary, while Moosehead Lake and ME 6/15 form the western boundary.

The 100MW is the name given to the next-to-last section of the AT on its 2,192-mi. route from Springer Mtn. in Georgia to Katahdin in Baxter State Park. The name is credited to Stephen Clark, editor of the *Official Appalachian Guide to Maine* from 1964 to 1982, who created the colorful label to alert AT thru-hikers that no resupply points existed along this remote 100-mi. stretch of trail, and that is still largely the case today. The moniker has long since come to refer to the entire 750,000-acre expanse of forests, mountains, lakes, ponds, rivers, and streams between the village of Monson, just south of Moosehead Lake, and Abol Bridge, which is on the West Branch of the Penobscot River on Golden Rd., at the doorstep of BSP. Greenville in the west and Brownville Junction and Millinocket in the east further define the bounds of the 100MW.

Moosehead Lake is the largest lake in Maine; at 35 mi. long with an area of 120 sq. mi., it is the predominant natural feature in this region. The Moose River feeds into Moosehead Lake from the west, and the Roach River empties into the lake from the east. The Kennebec River flows from two outlets on the west side of the lake, emptying into the Atlantic Ocean 170 mi. downriver near Popham Beach. In the center of the region, the East Branch and West Branch of the Pleasant River flow eastward and join at Brownville Junction. From its source near the southwest corner of Moosehead Lake, the Piscataquis River flows south and then east across the county to merge with the Penobscot River at Howland. The Sebec River flows east from Sebec Lake to empty into the Piscataquis River at Milo.

Conservation lands abound in the 100MW, and when combined with the protected lands around Moosehead Lake, the total exceeds 2,000,000 acres of nearly contiguous conservation lands ranging west to the Canadian border and north into the watersheds of the St. John and Allagash rivers, thanks to the determined efforts of a host of public agencies and private conservation groups.

AMC established a presence in the 100MW in 2003 with the purchase of the Katahdin Iron Works Tract. AMC has since acquired four additional parcels: the Roach Pond Tract, Baker Mtn., Silver Lake, and the Pleasant River Headwaters, bringing its total holdings—known as AMC's Maine Woods Initiative Recreation and Conservation Area—to 100,000 acres.

The 43,000-acre Nahmakanta PL is one the largest in Maine's public lands system managed by MBPL. Nahmakanta Lake is the predominant natural feature among the 24 lakes and ponds that lie amid mountain peaks and ridges ranging as high as 2,524 ft. Nearly one-quarter of the preserve, or 11,802 acres, is designated as an ecological reserve to ensure that environmentally sensitive plant life will remain in its natural condition and be periodically monitored. This includes the 9,200-acre roadless area known as the Debsconeag Backcountry.

Debsconeag Lakes Wilderness Area (DLWA) is a 46,271-acre tract of mature forests and pristine lakes and ponds rich with wildlife, situated at the far northern end of the 100MW, just south of the West Branch of the Penobscot River. Acquired by TNC in 2002, DLWA is an ecological reserve that protects the highest concentration of remote ponds in New England as well as undisturbed stands of 300-year-old trees.

The Moosehead Region Conservation Easement (MRCE) was established in 2012, the result of a state-approved concept plan for lands owned by Plum Creek Timber Company (now Weyerhaeuser). The 363,000-acre easement around Moosehead Lake is one of the largest working forest conservation easements in the United States. The project was a partnership between Plum Creek, the Forest Society of Maine, TNC, and AMC. MRCE permanently restricts development while allowing commercial forest management and similar land uses, and allows for the development of a variety of nonmotorized and motorized recreational opportunities.

East of Greenville and Moosehead Lake is Little Moose PL. The predominant natural feature of the 15,000-acre parcel is Big Moose Mtn., a sprawling mountain peak with a narrow summit that provides outstanding views of the Moosehead Lake region.

AMC'S MAINE WOODS INITIATIVE (MWI)

AMC's Maine Woods Initiative is one of the most important multiuse recreation and land conservation projects in the United States today, a landscape-scale project to conserve and protect land in a corridor of more than 1 million acres in the 100MW between Monson and BSP. This working model uses an innovative and thoughtful approach to conservation that combines recreation, natural resource protection, overnight lodging, responsible forest management, education, and local community partnerships to protect this beautiful region and preserve it for future generations.

AMC has permanently conserved 100,000 acres of forestland in the 100MW, including 27,000 acres of ecological reserve. AMC's Maine Woods Initiative Recreation and Conservation Area includes more than 157 sq. mi. of the 100MW, including 36 lakes and ponds, more than 20 mi. of the West Branch of the Pleasant River, countless miles of streams, 3,521-ft. Baker Mtn., Caribou Bog, Silver Lake, and multiple stands of late-successional forest, wetlands, and other critical wildlife habitats. To date, AMC has completed 80 fish passage projects and reopened 82 mi. of stream habitat with a goal of removing all barriers to fish passage on these lands by 2026.

In 2021, AMC's Maine Woods Initiative property was designated an International Dark Sky Park by the International Dark-Sky Association. This certification, the first in New England, is given to land possessing an exceptional quality of starry nights and a nocturnal environment that is specifically protected for its scientific, natural, educational, and cultural heritage, as well as for public enjoyment. Because most of the eastern United States has light pollution that prevents pristine views of the night sky, there are only a few International Dark Sky Parks in the region.

AMC has been conserving land and building recreation infrastructure in the 100MW since 2003, when the club purchased the 37,000-acre Katahdin Iron Works Tract. In 2009, AMC added the abutting 29,500-acre Roach Ponds Tract. In 2015, AMC purchased 4,300 acres on wild and trailless Baker Mtn., the largest chunk of subalpine terrain outside Katahdin. And in 2016, AMC gained 4,000 acres around Silver Lake. Boosting AMC's MWI project to 100,000 acres, the organization purchased the 27,000-acre Pleasant River Headwaters Forest in 2022, which encompasses some of the richest Atlantic salmon spawning and rearing habitat in the Piscataquis River watershed.

AMC's property is the southern anchor of a 63-mi. corridor of conserved land encompassing more than 500,000 acres, which includes properties owned by TNC, MBPL, NPS, and Elliotsville Plantation Inc. When adjacent working forest easement lands are included, the extent of conservation lands from Moosehead Lake to the northern end of BSP and east to the new Katahdin Woods and Waters National Monument exceeds 800,000 acres.

MWI has created a world-class destination for backcountry outdoor recreation. Three sporting camps in the Maine tradition have been opened to the public. These Maine Wilderness Lodges—Little Lyford near the Little Lyford Ponds, Gorman Chairback on Long Pond, and Medawisla on Second Roach Pond—offer visitors rustic charm, creature comforts, tasty food, and camaraderie amid spectacular natural surroundings. AMC has constructed more than 100 mi. of new trails, as well as more than a dozen backcountry campsites, and today maintains more than 200 mi. of trails on the property for hiking, paddling, mountain biking, cross-country skiing, snowshoeing, fishing, wildlife watching, and camping.

For more information on MWI, visit outdoors.org/resources/amc -outdoors/tag/maine-woods-initiative.

GEOGRAPHY

In the heart of the 100MW, trails from AMC's Little Lyford Lodge connect to a host of pristine ponds, to the West Branch of the Pleasant River and the spectacular slate canyon of Gulf Hagas, to craggy lookouts on Indian Mtn. (2,341 ft.), and to the AT. From Gorman Chairback Lodge on Long Pond, trails lead to Gulf Hagas and to the peaks on the eastern reaches of the Barren–Chairback Range via the AT, including Fourth Mtn. (2,376 ft.), Third Mtn. (2,082 ft.), Columbus Mtn. (2,338 ft.), and Chairback Mtn. (2,199 ft.). Barren Mtn. (2,648 ft.)—the site of an old fire tower, ledges, and rock slides—anchors the range on the western end. Near Medawisla Lodge, paths explore the area around Second Roach Pond. South of the pond are Shaw Mtn. (the north peak is 2,492 ft., the middle peak is 2,633 ft.) and Hedgehog Mtn. (2,128 ft.).

East of AMC's land are the four high peaks of the White Cap Range, beginning with Gulf Hagas Mtn., which rises to 2,688 ft. east of the West Branch of the Pleasant River. From there, elevations increase along the AT across the range, with West Peak at 3,179 ft. and Hay Mtn. at 3,242 ft. The range culminates atop White Cap Mtn. (3,650 ft.). Topped with gnarled tree growth and scree fields, the White Cap summit provides panoramic views that are among the best in the state. Northeast of White Cap Mtn., along the AT west of Crawford Pond, is Little Boardman Mtn. (2,020 ft.). South of Barren Mtn., on the opposite side of Lake Onawa, is twin-peaked Borestone Mtn. Its east peak is 1,948 ft., and its west peak is 1,938 ft. A subsidiary peak, Peregrine Ridge (1,644 ft.), is just west of the main Borestone peaks. Three pretty tarns are tucked into the high slopes of Borestone, which is distinctly visible from the sandy beach on Sebec Lake farther south. Here, a loop trail winds over the ledges on the northeast side of Birch Mtn. (1,090 ft.).

Popularly known as the Grand Canyon of Maine, Gulf Hagas is just west of the AT and the White Cap Range. This scenic area consists of a deep, narrow slate canyon on the West Branch of the Pleasant River. The river drops about 400 ft. in about 4 mi., and in many places, the vertical walls of the canyon force the river into very narrow channels that form a series of waterfalls, rapids, chutes, and pools.

North of the Mt. Kineo peninsula and east of North Bay on Moosehead Lake is shapely Little Kineo Mtn. (1,934 ft.). Between Spencer Pond and Ragged Lake, the long ridgelines of Big Spencer Mtn. (3,227 ft.) and Little Spencer Mtn. (3,064 ft.) dominate the landscape for miles around; on Little Spencer, hikers must negotiate a narrow rock chimney to gain the summit. Lobster Mtn. (2,336 ft.) rises south of Lobster Lake and is reachable only by water.

The state of Maine owns the 43,000-acre Nahmakanta PL unit in the north-central section of the 100MW. Rugged Turtle Ridge (1,643 ft.) and the ponds and ledges of the Debsconeag Backcountry are here. Rising steeply over the northern end of Nahmakanta Lake is Nesuntabunt Mtn. (1,551 ft.), where visitors have fine views of Katahdin. Southwest of Nesuntabunt is Wadleigh Mtn. (1,862 ft.); a former fire tower site, the mountain is traversed by a section of the new Great Circle Trail.

Immediately to the east is a portion of the 210,000-acre Katahdin Forest Easement, which protects many miles of shoreline on Pemadumcook Lake, Jo-Mary Lake, the West Branch of the Penobscot River, and several other water bodies. Sprawling Potaywadjo Ridge (1,273 ft.) rises just west of Pemadumcook Lake and Lower Jo-Mary Lake. Abutting Nahmakanta PL to the north is Debsconeag Lakes Wilderness Area, which contains the highest concentration of pristine lakes and ponds in New England, including Rainbow Lake. The AT threads a sinuous route through this area and leads to Rainbow Ledges (1,517 ft.) and Rainbow Mtn. (1,663 ft.). The craggy ridgeline of Rainbow Summit (1,630 ft.) rises north of Rainbow Lake.

Just west of Greenville, rising from the southwest shore of Moosehead Lake, are the rugged mountain peaks encompassed by the 15,000-acre Little Moose PL. Big Moose Mtn., the site of Maine's first fire tower, erected in 1905, reigns supreme at 3,194 ft. At the far end of the mountain's northwestern ridge is the airy pinnacle of Eagle Rock (2,378 ft.), which affords far-reaching views over Moosehead Lake to the east and the upper Kennebec River valley to the west. The long and bumpy ridgeline of Little Moose Mtn. has a 2,225-ft. highpoint near its western end.

Midway up Moosehead Lake on a peninsula across from Rockwood is the iconic Mt. Kineo (1,788 ft.); the impressive 700-ft. wall of its southeast face is unmistakable from many vantage points in the region. On a peninsula on the eastern side of Moosehead Lake just north of Greenville is the wooded Burnt Jacket Mtn. (1,691 ft.). A few miles east, the remains of a crashed B-52 bomber lie scattered on the lower slopes of Elephant Mtn. (2,644 ft.). East of Lily Bay on Moosehead Lake and south of First Roach Pond is Number Four Mtn. (2,893 ft.). Number Four Mtn. and the neighboring and formerly trailless Baker Mtn. (3,528 ft.) are sites of ambitious trail-building efforts by AMC and MBPL crews, as is neighboring Blue Ridge (2,356 ft.)

Northeast of Moosehead Lake, in the remote timberlands between Seboomook Lake and the Canadian border, is Green Mtn. (2,397 ft.) with its summit fire tower.

ROAD ACCESS

Running the length of the east side of the 100MW is ME 11, which connects Milo to Millinocket. Along the west side of the 100MW, east of Moosehead Lake, are Lily Bay Rd. and Greenville Rd. To the south, ME 6/16 connects Milo to Dover-Foxcroft. To the west, ME 6/15 connects Dover-Foxcroft to Monson, Greenville, and then along the west side of Moosehead Lake to Rockwood. From Millinocket on the northern end of the 100MW, Millinocket Lake Rd., Baxter Park Rd., and Golden Rd. offer access to trails.

Once off these main roads and into the 100MW, visitors must travel on gravel logging roads. In the southern portion of the 100MW, KI Rd. is the major route from the east at Brownville Junction; Greenville Rd. is the major road in from the west. From Kokadjo on Lily Bay Rd., Frenchtown Rd. provides access. From ME 11 between Brownville Junction and Millinocket, Jo-Mary Rd. is the route into the northeastern interior of the 100MW. Lily Bay Rd. and Greenville Rd. connect Greenville to Golden Rd. near Caribou Lake, and these roads offer access to the peaks northeast of Moosehead Lake.

Some of the mountains and trails in this section lie within the boundaries of North Maine Woods and KI Jo-Mary Multiple Use Forest, two large blocks of forestland, most of which is privately owned and cooperatively managed for renewable resources while providing outdoor recreational opportunities for the public. Visitors must register at a checkpoint and pay camping and day-use fees (cash or check only) to enter these areas. The *Map of North Maine Woods* is a useful publication for navigating NMW property; ask for your free copy at any NMW checkpoint. The *Katahdin Iron Works Guide Map and Information* pamphlet is useful for navigating the roads in the KI Jo-Mary Forest; it, too, is available for free at KI Jo-Mary checkpoints. See p. xxv for information about access to the lands managed by NMW.

CAMPING AND LODGING

Numerous primitive campsites reachable by vehicles throughout Nahmakanta PL allow for extended visits. Several primitive sites on Nahmakanta Lake can be reached by canoe or boat. Along the route of Great Circle Trail, Debsconeag Backcountry Trail, and Turtle Ridge Loop Trail are seven primitive backcountry campsites. A number of pondside primitive backcountry campsites are in Little Moose PL.

Lily Bay State Park on Moosehead Lake north of Greenville features 90 drive-in campsites, with hot showers, restrooms, and other amenities,

SEC 2

while Peaks–Kenny State Park on Sebec Lake in Dover-Foxcroft has 56 campsites and similar amenities.

Numerous primitive roadside campsites are within the boundaries of NMW, and 60 drive-in campsites are available within the KI Jo-Mary Multiple Use Forest. At least eleven privately operated campgrounds throughout this region offer a variety of camping and lodging choices with amenities.

AMC's MWI Recreation and Conservation Area features three wilderness lodges with private cabins and shared bunkhouses, plus a growing number of drive-in, paddle-in, and walk-in campsites.

Gorman Chairback Lodge & Cabins

Built as a private camp in 1867, Gorman Chairback Lodge & Cabins is at the eastern end of beautiful Long Pond at the base of the rugged Barren–Chairback Range. The lodge can be reached by vehicle during summer and fall, and by ski, snowshoe, and dogsled in winter (though dogs are not allowed overnight).

Accommodations include four private deluxe cabins, eight private shoreline cabins, and a shared bunkhouse. The central bathhouse in the main lodge has composting toilets and hot showers. It also has a wood-heated sauna in winter. Meals are provided in the main lodge, which has—in addition to the dining area—a fireplace, sitting area, library, cubbies for gear storage, game room, and a small store.

A network of trails extends out from the lodge to reach Third Mtn., Indian Pond, Chairback Mtn., Gulf Hagas, and the AT. Even more trails are open in winter for cross-country skiing and snowshoeing. Several backcountry campsites are available.

Little Lyford Lodge & Cabins

The first of AMC's lodges in the 100MW, Little Lyford is adjacent to the Little Lyford Ponds on the site of a sporting camp that has been serving guests for more than 140 years. The lodge can be reached by vehicle during summer and fall, and by ski, snowshoe, and dogsled in winter. Little Lyford Lodge & Cabins is the only AMC-run property that allows dogs.

Accommodations include nine private log cabins and a shared bunkhouse. Each cabin features a porch, a woodstove, gas lamps, and cold running water. A central bathhouse near the main lodge has composting toilets and hot showers, and a wood-heated sauna is available in winter. Meals are provided in the main lodge, which, in addition to the dining area, houses a fireplace, a sitting area, a library, and a small store.

A network of summer trails in the vicinity leads to the nearby Little Lyford Ponds, the West Branch of the Pleasant River, Gulf Hagas, the AT, a host of pristine ponds to the west, and outlooks high on Indian Mtn. In winter, even more trails are open for cross-country skiing and snowshoeing. A number of frontcountry and backcountry campsites are available.

Medawisla Lodge & Cabins

Rebuilt from the ground up and reopened in summer 2017, Medawisla Lodge (*Medawisla* is the Abenaki word for loon) is the newest of AMC's Maine Wilderness Lodges. At the confluence of Second Roach Pond and the Roach River, the area boasts a growing multiuse trail network for hikers and mountain bikers, plus bountiful opportunities for paddling, fishing, and camping. The lodge can be reached by vehicle year-round.

Accommodations include five private hilltop cabins with bath and shower, four waterfront cabins with bath and shower (these cabins also have a kitchenette), and two shared bunkhouses (hilltop and waterfront). Each cabin and bunkhouse has LED lighting and a woodstove. Meals for guests staying in the full-service cabins are provided in the main lodge, which, in addition to the dining area, has a fireplace, sitting area, game room, conference space, library, and a small store.

For information and reservations for AMC's Maine Wilderness Lodges, as well as outdoor recreation opportunities near each, visit outdoors.org /destinations/maine.

SUGGESTED HIKES

■ Easy
LITTLE LYFORD PONDS

LP via Pond Loop Trail	1.9 mi.	230 ft.	1:05

Make a circuit around two ponds, where moose sightings are possible. See Pond Loop Trail, p. 88.

BIG MOOSE POND AND LITTLE MOOSE POND

LP via Loop Trail	3.7 mi.	695 ft.	2:10

Wander through the wilds around these two scenic ponds and then climb to the ridge beyond for a clear look over the waters to Big Moose Mtn. See Loop Trail, p. 128.

SEC 2

DEBSCONEAG ICE CAVES

		〽	⟳
RT via Ice Caves Trail	2.2 mi.	250 ft.	1:15

Hike to a cavernous hole beneath a jumble of boulders that often retains ice well into summer. See Ice Caves Trail, p. 118.

ELEPHANT MTN.

		〽	⟳
RT via B-52 Memorial Crash Site Trail	0.5 mi.	100 ft.	0:20

Take a short hike on the lower slopes of Elephant Mtn. to a somber memorial at the 1963 crash site of a B-52 bomber. See B-52 Memorial Crash Site Trail, p. 137.

BURNT JACKET MTN.

		〽	⟳
LP via Green Trail, Blue Trail, and Allagash Rd.	1.3 mi.	500 ft.	0:55

Enjoy this fun little mountain hike for views of Moosehead Lake, Mt. Kineo, and Big and Little Moose mountains. To begin, see Green Mtn. Trail on p. 147.

■ Moderate
GORMAN LOOP

		〽	⟳
LP via Gorman Loop Trail, Third Mtn. Trail, and Chairback Mtn. Rd.	5.4 mi.	720 ft.	3:05

Hike over the northern slopes of Columbus Mtn. and Third Mtn., crossing a number of streams and wetlands to get to views higher up. To begin, see Gorman Loop Trail, p. 92.

GULF HAGAS

		〽	⟳
LP via AT, Rim Trail, and Pleasant River Tote Rd.	8.0 mi.	850 ft.	4:25

Get a good look at every waterfall in the spectacular slate canyon of Gulf Hagas on this scenic loop hike. Visit the stately pines of the Hermitage on the West Branch of the Pleasant River, too. To begin, see Gulf Hagas Loop, p. 97.

DEBSCONEAG WILDERNESS–RAINBOW LOOP

LP via Horserace Brook Trail, Blue Trail, and Rainbow Loop Trail	6.3 mi.	1,040 ft.	3:40

Combine these trails for a wonderful circuit through wild and scenic Debsconeag Lakes Wilderness Area. To begin, see Horserace Brook Trail, p. 119.

BIG MOOSE MTN.

RT via Big Moose Mtn. Trail	4.2 mi.	1,834 ft.	3:00

Climb to the site of Maine's first fire tower (erected in 1905, removed in 2011) for panoramic views over Moosehead Lake to the jumble of peaks ranging as far north as Katahdin. See Big Moose Mtn. Trail, p. 125.

MT. KINEO

LP via Carriage Trail, Indian Trail, and Bridle Trail	3.4 mi.	818 ft.	2:05

Take a scenic ferry ride on Moosehead Lake to the Mt. Kineo peninsula; then tackle a great loop hike to the top of the 700-ft. cliffs on Mt. Kineo and its summit observation tower. To begin, see Carriage Trail, p. 133.

■ Strenuous
BARREN–CHAIRBACK RANGE

OW via AT Northbound	15.4 mi.	4,005 ft.	10:00

Hike across the rugged Barren–Chairback Range from the Otter Pond AT trailhead, tackling Barren Mtn., Fourth Mtn., Third Mtn., Columbus Mtn., and Chairback Mtn. Three lean-tos en route make this a good two- to three-day backpacking trip. See AT Northbound, Monson Approach, p. 99.

WHITE CAP RANGE

OW via AT Northbound	14.7 mi.	3,965 ft.	9:20

Trek across all four peaks of the White Cap Range, from Gulf Hagas Mtn. and West Peak to Hay Mtn. and White Cap Mtn. via the AT in one long day or make it a multiday backpack. Three campsites offer overnight options. See AT Northbound, p. 106.

WHITE CAP MTN.

RT via AT Southbound	6.4 mi.	2,063 ft.	4:15

Climb the north side of White Cap Mtn. for outstanding vistas far and wide over the 100MW, from Katahdin and Big Spencer Mtn. to the peaks of the Barren–Chairback Range. See AT Southbound, p. 104.

GREAT CIRCLE TRAIL

LP via Great Circle Trail	27.3 mi.	2,660 ft.	15:00

Hike this new 27.3-mi. backpacking circuit through the backcountry of Nahmakanta PL, which combines sections of Debsconeag Backcountry Trail, the AT, and Turtle Ridge Trails, plus 14 mi. of newly constructed trail. See Great Circle Trail, p. 114.

LITTLE SPENCER MTN.

RT via The Ram Trail	2.2 mi.	1,880 ft.	2:05

This short but very challenging hike climbs through a narrow chimney and over steep terrain to the summit ledges of Little Spencer Mtn., with excellent views ranging from Katahdin to Moosehead Lake. See The Ram Trail, p. 142.

TRAIL DESCRIPTIONS
AMC'S MAINE WOODS INITIATIVE

AMC's MWI Recreation and Conservation Area is in the heart of the 100MW east of Greenville and west of ME 11 at Brownville Junction. A KI Jo-Mary Multiple Use Forest gate fee is charged (cash or check only) from May through October for vehicle access to the southern half of AMC's lands (waived for overnight guests staying at the AMC lodges). Please note that the access roads are not paved, and conditions can vary. Limit speed to 25 miles per hour and yield to logging trucks. No fuel is available after leaving the state highways. Contact AMC in advance for road conditions during spring and fall or when storms are expected.

To Gorman Chairback and Little Lyford from Greenville in the west: From the blinking traffic light in the center of Greenville on ME 6/15, proceed

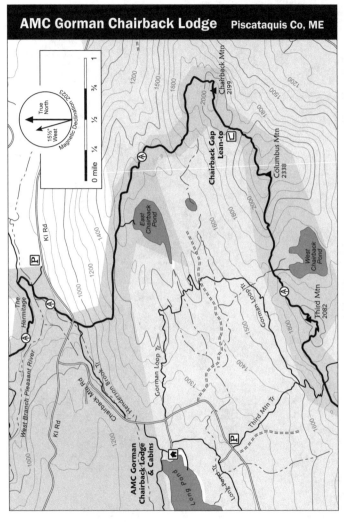

AMC Gorman Chairback Lodge   Piscataquis Co, ME

north 1 block and turn right onto Pleasant St. (immediately after North-
woods Outfitters). Make a jog around Greenville Municipal Airport. In
2.1 mi., the road becomes gravel. At 3.7 mi., cross a bridge over Big Wilson
Stream. Beyond this point, the road is called KI Rd. At 10.4 mi., reach a

SEC
2

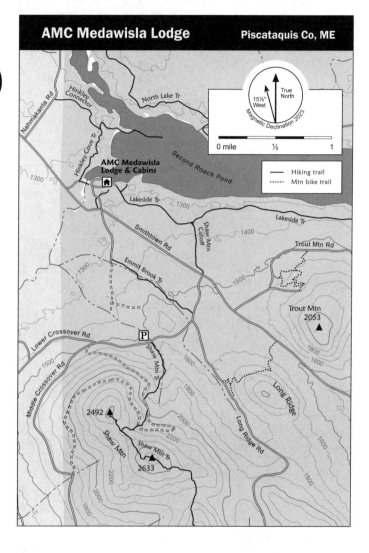

AMC Medawisla Lodge   Piscataquis Co, ME

large clearing with parking; this is the winter trailhead and as far as you can drive in winter. Reach Hedgehog Checkpoint at 12.1 (register and pay fee). At 1.8 mi. beyond the checkpoint, reach the jct. of KI Rd. and Upper Valley Rd. For Gorman Chairback Lodge & Cabins, turn right and drive 3.3 mi. to Chairback Mtn. Rd. on the right. Turn right on this road and proceed 1.3 mi. to the entrance drive for Gorman Chairback, which leads directly to the facility. For Little Lyford Lodge, from the checkpoint on KI Rd., turn left on Upper Valley Rd. and proceed 2.2 mi. to the entrance drive for Little Lyford Lodge & Cabins. Follow the blue squares with reflective arrows to the guest parking area a short distance from the lodge.

To Gorman Chairback and Little Lyford from the east at ME 11: KI Rd. is on ME 11 at a point 26.0 mi. south of Millinocket and 5.5 mi. north of Brownville Junction. Look for signs for Katahdin Iron Works Historic Site (these may be missing, so check your mileage). From ME 11, turn west onto KI Rd. Katahdin Ironworks Checkpoint at the entrance to KI Jo-Mary Forest is 6.3 mi. from ME 11. Stop and register (day-use fee is charged, cash or check only). At 7.3 mi. from the gate, Chairback Mtn. Rd. is on the left; the entrance drive for Gorman Chairback Lodge & Cabins is 1.3 mi. west on this road. For Little Lyford Lodge, continue on KI Rd. for 3.3 mi. to the jct. of KI Rd. and Upper Valley Rd. Proceed straight ahead (north) on Upper Valley Rd. for 2.2 mi. to the entrance drive for Little Lyford Lodge & Cabins on the right. Follow the blue squares with reflective arrows to the guest parking area a short distance from the lodge.

To Medawisla Lodge from Greenville: From the blinking traffic light in the center of Greenville on ME 6/15, drive north on Lily Bay Rd. for 18.8 mi. to the village of Kokadjo and Kokadjo Trading Post at the west end of First Roach Pond. Reset trip mileage. At 0.3 mi. beyond Kokadjo Trading Post, the pavement ends at a fork. Bear left to continue on Greenville Rd. At 1.5 mi., pass Spencer Bay Rd. on the left. Reach Smithtown Rd. on the right at 1.9 mi.; turn right here. At 6.7 mi., pass Penobscot Pond Rd. on the left, and at 7.6 mi., turn left onto the entrance road for Medawisla Lodge & Cabins.

INDIAN MTN. (2,341 FT.)

Indian Mtn. rises prominently from the valley west of the West Branch of the Pleasant River. Its open summit ledges are reached via Laurie's Ledge Trail, which provides hikers with excellent views over AMC's MWI property lands to the many peaks and valleys beyond.

LAURIE'S LEDGE TRAIL (MAP 2: E2)
Cumulative from Upper Valley Rd. parking lot (1,300 ft.) to:

Indian Mtn. Circuit, east jct. (1,510 ft.)	0.4 mi.	210 ft.	0:15
Indian Mtn. Circuit, west jct. (1,590 ft.)	0.7 mi.	290 ft.	0:30
Laurie's Ledge, westerly overlook (2,300 ft.)	1.6 mi.	1,000 ft.	1:20

SEC 2

AMC Named for Laurie Burt, a former president of AMC's Board of Directors, the trail offers fine views to the north from its easterly overlook high on Indian Mtn. The summits of the White Cap Range are visible, and on a clear day, visitors can see Katahdin. From the westerly outlook, there are views of Elephant Mtn., Prong Pond Mtn., and many of the area's ponds, including Horseshoe, Pearl, Mountain Brook, and Grassy. Parking for the trail is on the left side of Upper Valley Rd., 2.3 mi. north of the jct. of Greenville Rd. and KI Rd. (0.1 mi. after the entrance drive to Little Lyford Lodge & Cabins).

Follow Laurie's Ledge Trail up the roadside bank and then head left across a log bridge. The trail leads along the edge of a large boulder, where there is a view of the Little Lyford Ponds, Elephant Mtn., and part of Baker Mtn. The trail then switchbacks to the left. After a gradual but steady ascent, it reaches a jct. with Indian Mtn. Circuit at 0.4 mi. The two trails share the same route, a grassy old logging road, for the next 0.3 mi. At 0.7 mi., where Indian Mtn. Circuit continues straight, Laurie's Ledge Trail turns left.

The trail ascends moderately, passing to the left of four huge boulders. Beyond, the trail climbs to the base of a large cliff band and runs along the lower part for 100 yd. It then turns right and climbs steeply to a narrow ledge with a fine view to the east and south. Ahead, a side trail on the right leads 50 yd. to the easterly overlook and views to Barren Mtn. and the other summits of that range. Laurie's Ledge Trail continues to climb steadily, steeply at times, for 0.4 mi. The angle finally eases as the trail leads over the upper slopes to reach the westerly overlook below the true summit of Indian Mtn.

INDIAN MTN. CIRCUIT (MAP 2: E2)
Cumulative from Upper Valley Rd. (1,300 ft.) to:

Laurie's Ledge Trail, east jct. (1,510 ft.)	0.4 mi.	210 ft.	0:20
Laurie's Ledge Trail, west jct. (1,590 ft.)	0.7 mi.	290 ft.	0:30
Gravel road (1,550 ft.)	1.7 mi.	400 ft.	1:05
Pearl Ponds Trail (1,500 ft.)	2.0 mi.	400 ft.	1:15
Horseshoe Pond (1,480 ft.) side trail	2.6 mi.	400 ft.	1:30
End of trail on gravel road (1,650 ft.)	3.1 mi.	570 ft.	1:45

**SEC
2**

AMC This multiuse trail shared with mountain bikers extends across the northern flank of Indian Mtn., just west of the Little Lyford Ponds. The trail starts on Upper Valley Rd., diagonally across from the entrance to Little Lyford Lodge & Cabins, at a point 2.2 mi. north of the jct. of Greenville Rd. and KI Rd. Parking is in a small lot at the trailhead.

Indian Mtn. Circuit ascends gradually through the forest to the jct. with Laurie's Ledge Trail (sign) at 0.4 mi. The two trails share the same route for the next 0.3 mi. Where Laurie's Ledge Trail leaves to the left (south), Indian Mtn. Circuit continues its westerly course around the mountain, generally on a contour. At 1.7 mi., the trail crosses a logging road 100 yd. south of Baker Pond Rd. and continues directly across the road.

The wide, grassy forest path traverses four log bridges through a wet area to reach the jct. with Pearl Ponds Trail on the right at 2.0 mi. Continuing ahead on Indian Mtn. Circuit, the route follows a contour around the base of Indian Mtn. on an increasingly rough foot trail, crossing 29 bog bridges. Heading gradually downhill, the trail crosses a small stream just before a large wooden bridge. A view of Pearl Ponds lies to the right. The wide path climbs a small rise and then descends to a jct. just above the pond at 2.6 mi. A spur path to the right leads 50 yd. to Horseshoe Pond CS and the pond, where a grassy clearing offers a beautiful view across the water to Elephant Mtn.

Continuing on, the path leads northeast, away from the pond, climbing gradually to its end on a gravel logging road at 3.1 mi. To the left (north), this road may be followed for 0.8 mi. to intersect the trail just south of Baker Pond Rd., thus making a lollipop loop hike possible.

NATION'S NATURE TRAIL (MAP 2: E2)
Cumulative from Upper Valley Rd. parking lot (1,300 ft.) to:

Start of trail (1,300 ft.)	0.2 mi.	–40 ft.	0:05
Complete loop	1.2 mi.	100 ft.	0:40
Complete loop from Upper Valley Rd.	1.4 mi.	150 ft.	0:45

AMC Named for longtime AMC member and volunteer Peg Nation, this yellow-blazed loop trail circles the area around Little Lyford Lodge & Cabins, passing through woodlands and wetlands and reaching the Pinnacle and the West Branch of the Pleasant River. Park at the Laurie's Ledge Trail parking lot on Upper Valley Rd. 0.1 mi. north of the driveway into Little Lyford Pond Lodge & Cabins.

Cross Upper Valley Rd. to gain access to a spur path leading 0.2 mi. east to Nation's Nature Trail. The trail is over mostly easy ground except for one short, moderately steep climb to the Pinnacle. Along the river, the trail coincides with Pleasant River Trail. Each area that the route passes through has its own distinct ecological communities. Twelve interpretive stations along the way offer more information, and a detailed brochure is available at Little Lyford Lodge & Cabins.

PLEASANT RIVER TRAIL (MAP 2: E2–F2)
From Little Lyford Lodge & Cabins (1,216 ft.) to:

End of trail at woods road and bridge over West Branch of Pleasant River (1,155 ft.)	1.1 mi.	-60 ft.	0:30

AMC This trail, an old logging tote road, extends along the West Branch of the Pleasant River. A portion of the trail—from Little Lyford Lodge & Cabins south along the west bank of the river to a bridge crossing the river—is also referred to as Lodge-to-Lodge Trail because it is a part of the winter ski route between Little Lyford and Gorman Chairback lodges.

Pleasant River Trail leaves from behind Mountain View Cabin at the Little Lyford Lodge & Cabins site. Start by crossing a wet area on bog bridges before reaching a jct. with a spur path (leads to the Pleasant River at the site of an old dam). Just ahead, at 0.15 mi., Nation's Nature Trail diverges to the right.

Pleasant River Trail continues at a moderate grade, following a ridge parallel to the river. Dropping down, it crosses a spot next to the river and then climbs gradually, traversing a minor drainage. The trail then continues south, bearing away from the river. Forrest's Folly, a winter ski trail, is on the right at 0.8 mi. Reach a woods road at 1.1 mi. A bridge over the West Branch of the Pleasant River is visible on the left. Cross the bridge to connect with Head of the Gulf Trail, which provides access to Gulf Hagas, or cross the woods road to continue on Head of the Gulf Trail to parking on Upper Valley Rd., in 0.5 mi.

POND LOOP TRAIL (AMC; MAP 2: E2)
Cumulative from Upper Valley Rd. (1,350 ft.) to:

Pond Loop Trail (1,200 ft.)	0.2 mi.	–150 ft.	0:05
Pleasant River Trail, south jct. (1,200 ft.)	0.9 mi.	40 ft.	0:25
Pleasant River Trail, north jct. (1,250 ft.)	1.4 mi.	80 ft.	0:45
Complete loop (via spur path and Pleasant River Trail)	1.9 mi.	230 ft.	1:05

Using a portion of Pleasant River Trail, Pond Loop Trail circles the upper pond of the Little Lyford Ponds. Numerous side trails provide opportunities for wildlife watching from vantage points along the shores of the upper and lower ponds. Trailhead parking is on Upper Valley Rd. at a point about 2.6 mi. north of the jct. of Greenville Rd. and KI Rd.

To reach Pond Loop Trail, walk across Upper Valley Rd. to the start of a spur path and follow it east for 0.2 mi. to a jct. Turn right on Pond Loop Trail to circle the upper pond in a counterclockwise direction. Views of the upper pond appear through the trees as the path winds over a few small rises. Shortly the trail crosses the upper pond's inlet on bog bridges. Climbing gradually uphill, it bears away from the pond to reach an old grassy road, which it follows through a clearing. Soon, the lower pond is visible through the trees on the right. Pass a large old stone chimney marked Gerry's Gazebo. Pryor's Path crosses the trail, leading left to a dock on the upper pond and right to a dock on the lower pond.

SEC
2

Pond Loop Trail continues to a jct. with Pleasant River Trail at 0.9 mi. The two trails share the route for the next 0.5 mi. Turn left and climb gradually. Follow a small brook before dropping down to the upper pond and views of Baker Mtn. through the trees. The route descends the ridge and traverses a large wooden bridge, known as Kendall's Crossing, over the outlet of the upper pond. Beyond the bridge, the combined trails climb again, bearing away from the pond. At a jct. at 1.4 mi., bear left off Pleasant River Trail to continue on Pond Loop Trail. After a quick downhill, the trail levels off and winds through the forest, passing a side trail on the left to the upper pond. Traverse a dozen bog bridges to reach a jct. at 1.7 mi. On the left is a clearing on the shore of the upper pond, where canoes are available for use by AMC guests. Turn right (west) to return to the trailhead parking lot at 1.9 mi.

MOUNTAIN BROOK POND TRAIL (MAP 2: E2)
From parking lot on Upper Valley Rd. (1,550 ft.) to:

Mountain Brook Pond (1,530 ft.)	0.2 mi.	−20 ft.	0:50

AMC This short walk leads to the south shore of pretty Mountain Brook Pond. It begins in a small parking lot on the left side of Baker Pond Rd., 1.2 mi. west of Upper Valley Rd. and 4.5 mi. north of the jct. of Greenville Rd. and KI Rd. (*Note*: From the same parking lot, Pearl Ponds Trail heads south.)

The trail to the pond (sign) leaves the road to the north about 20 ft. east of the lot. Cross the road and head north on a wooded path, which leads to a small clearing just short of Mountain Brook Pond. Log bridges lead down to the shore. Canoes are available for use by AMC guests.

PEARL PONDS TRAIL (MAP 2: E2)
Cumulative from parking lot on Baker Pond Rd. (1,550 ft.) to:

Side trail to Pearl Ponds (1,500 ft.)	0.3 mi.	25 ft.	0:10
End of trail at Baker Pond Rd. near Grassy Pond (1,500 ft.)	0.6 mi.	25 ft.	0:20

SEC 2

AMC Parking for this trail is the same as for Mountain Brook Trail. From the parking lot, Pearl Ponds Trail leads 0.2 mi. south to a jct. Here, a spur path goes left (east) to join Indian Mtn. Circuit in 0.3 mi. Turn right (west) to continue on Pearl Ponds Trail. After traversing two small wooden bridges, the trail soon intersects with a short side trail on the left, which leads to Pearl Ponds. Continuing straight on wide and grassy Pearl Ponds Trail, bear left over a bridge to reach a wooden bench with a view of the water. The trail continues left and uphill to another jct. To the right, a side trail leads to several Pearl Ponds roadside campsites. Straight ahead on the main trail is a jct. with Baker Pond Rd. Grassy Pond Trail starts just across the road.

BAKER POND TRAIL (MAP 2: A1 AND E2)
Cumulative from parking lot on Baker Pond Rd. (1,550 ft.) to:

Start of trail via Baker Pond Rd. (1,560 ft.)	0.5 mi.	10 ft.	0:15
Baker Pond Trail and Mountain Brook Pond Trail extension (1,620 ft.)	1.7 mi.	90 ft.	0:50
Baker Pond CS (1,650 ft.)	2.2 mi.	130 ft.	1:05
From parking lot on Baker Pond Rd. (1,550 ft.) to:			
Mountain Brook Pond (1,530 ft.) via Baker Pond Rd. and Mountain Brook Trail Extension	2.5 mi.	160 ft.	1:15

AMC Parking for this trail is the same as for Mountain Brook Trail and Pearl Ponds Trail. From the parking lot, walk 0.5 mi. west along Baker Pond Rd. Turn right and walk around a yellow gate and then up an old, rocky roadbed. Where an older overgrown roadbed branches to the left, Baker Pond Trail heads right; it crests over three small hills and then straightens out. It then crosses a brook and bears right. The trail reaches a jct. where a sign indicates that Baker Pond is 0.5 mi. to the left and Mountain Brook Pond is straight ahead. Follow Baker Pond Trail north on a graded path, which soon bears left and crosses a wooden bridge. (*Note*: This lowland trail can often be wet and muddy.) As the path narrows, look for bog bridges around the pond. The trail ends at Baker Pond CS. Just below the campsite is a pleasant view across the water.

Mountain Brook Pond Trail Extension. From the jct., the trail to Mountain Brook Pond, an extension of Mountain Brook Pond Trail, continues along the rocky roadbed. It quickly reaches a jct. with an old logging road. Here, the trail turns right (sign). It becomes overgrown and passes through a small clearing with views of Baker Mtn. The trail turns into a grassy path as it heads down into the woods, descending to Mountain Brook Pond and a small clearing with pond views. Mountain Brook Pond Trail Extension is 0.8 mi. and gains 100 ft. of elevation.

GRASSY POND TRAIL (MAP 2: A1 AND E2)
Cumulative from parking lot on Baker Pond Rd. (1,550 ft.) to:

Start of trail (1,500 ft.) via Baker Pond Rd. or Pearl Ponds Trail	0.6 mi.	25 ft.	0:20
Grassy Pond (1,550 ft.)	0.8 mi.	25 ft.	0:25

SEC 2

AMC Parking for this trail is the same as for the previous three trails. From the parking lot, walk 0.6 mi. west along Baker Pond Rd., past the start of Baker Pond Trail, to a grassy trail entrance on the right, immediately opposite the west end of Pearl Ponds Trail. A pleasant alternative is to follow Pearl Ponds Trail to Grassy Pond Trail.

Pass between three large boulders, following a wide path. The trail goes uphill briefly and then descends a set of log stairs to the east shore of Grassy Pond.

HORSESHOE POND TRAIL (MAP 2: E2)
From parking lot at end of Baker Pond Rd. (1,490 ft.) to:

Horseshoe Pond (1,465 ft.)	0.3 mi.	–25 ft.	0:20

AMC From the jct. of Greenville Rd. and KI Rd., drive 2.1 mi. north on Upper Valley Rd. to the jct. with Baker Pond Rd. Turn left onto Baker Pond Rd. and follow it to its end at a parking lot (sign) and the Pearl Ponds campsite. From the lot, follow the wide, graded trail. The flat, winding route leads gradually uphill and then down. The trail ends at a tiny inlet on the north shore of Horseshoe Pond, where the Norkin Shelter is located (erected in 2021, the shelter honors Andrew Norkin, AMC's longtime trails director, who passed away earlier that year). Wooden stairs lead down to the water.

HENDERSON BROOK TRAIL
(MAP 2: F3, AMC GORMAN CHAIRBACK LODGE MAP)
From parking lot on Chairback Mtn. Rd. (1,100 ft.) to:

AT and KI Rd. (776 ft.)	1.1 mi.	–325 ft.	0:35

AMC This trail winds along the banks and through the gorge of Henderson Brook just east of Long Pond. To reach the trailhead, drive south from the jct. of Greenville Rd. and KI Rd. for 3.4 mi. Turn right (south) onto Chairback Mtn. Rd. and follow it for 0.9 mi. to a small parking lot on the right.

The trail starts across the road, heads northeast, and descends to the edge of Henderson Brook, which it follows down the valley past a series of pretty waterfalls and pools. The trail crosses and recrosses the brook several times. (*Note*: A rope strung across the brook in two places offers some assistance.) At 1.1 mi., the trail merges with the AT, which enters from the right. KI Rd. is 50 ft. beyond the jct.

GORMAN LOOP TRAIL (MAP 2: F3, AMC GORMAN CHAIRBACK LODGE MAP)
Cumulative from Chairback Mtn. Rd. (1,210 ft.) to:

Third Mtn. Trail (1,500 ft.)	3.6 mi.	720 ft.	2:15
Chairback Mtn. Rd. (1,200 ft.) via Third Mtn. Trail	4.6 mi.	720 ft.	2:40

AMC This route makes a circuit from the Gorman Chairback Lodge area, reaching a high point on the northern slopes of Columbus Mtn. and Third Mtn. Several outlooks offer views along the Barren–Chairback Range and to Blue Ridge, Elephant Mtn., Baker Mtn., Indian Mtn., and Long Pond. The trail roams through a variety of ecological habitats, from northern hardwood ridges to montane spruce-fir forest, forested wetlands, and non-forested kettle bogs.

Gorman Loop Trail starts from Chairback Mtn. Rd., nearly opposite the entrance drive for Gorman Chairback Lodge. It climbs at a mostly moderate grade to a ridge, levels off, and passes through several bogs, one of which features a 250-ft. boardwalk and a bench—a convenient spot for a break. The trail then drops into a drainage, leads up and over the next low ridge, and crosses the outlet of East Chairback Pond. It switchbacks up the slope beyond to a narrow ridge and then winds down to cross a brook draining the west basin of Chairback Mtn. The route continues south and then turns west to traverse the outlet stream of West Chairback Pond. Scramble up rocks to a high point beyond, where there is a viewpoint north, and then follow a contour for a stretch before angling across and down to meet Third Mtn. Trail on the north slope of Third Mtn., passing several more viewpoints en route. Turn left here to climb to the AT on the ridgeline above and then go on to Monument Cliff atop Third Mtn. (reached in 1.8 mi.) or descend to the right on Third Mtn. Trail to return to Chairback Mtn. Rd. at a point 0.8 mi. west of the Gorman Loop Trail trailhead.

THIRD MTN. TRAIL (MAP 2: F3, AMC GORMAN CHAIRBACK LODGE MAP)
Cumulative from Chairback Mtn. Rd. (1,200 ft.) to:

Gorman Loop Trail (1,500 ft.)	1.0 mi.	300 ft.	0:40
AT jct. west of Third Mtn. summit (1,860 ft.)	1.5 mi.	660 ft.	1:05
Indian Pond and campsites (1,060 ft.)	4.0 mi.	660 ft.	2:20
From Chairback Mtn. Rd. (1,200 ft.) to:			
Monument Cliff atop Third Mtn. (2,082 ft.) via AT	2.3 mi.	880 ft.	1:35

AMC This trail climbs the north slope of Third Mtn. from the Gorman Chairback Lodge area to reach the AT (which provides access to the Third

Mtn. summit); it then descends to the south and ends at a remote campsite on the north shore of Indian Pond. Park in the lot (on the left) just past the trailhead (sign) on Chairback Mtn. Rd. at a point 2.2 mi. from its jct. with KI Rd. and 0.8 mi. beyond the entrance drive for Gorman Chairback Lodge.

Leaving Chairback Mtn. Rd., Third Mtn. Trail makes a short, steep ascent through a stand of birch. Follow the blue blazes as the route winds through the hardwood forest over the lower slopes of Third Mtn. Traverse several small streams on wooden bridges and a wet area on bog bridges. The trail begins to climb steadily on a number of long switchbacks, heading toward several large boulders before climbing several steep rock staircases and then a wooden ladder. Views begin to open up through the trees, and soon the angle eases and the trail reaches a jct. with the AT at 1.9 mi. at a height-of-land on the ridgeline. To the left (east), it is 0.5 mi. via the AT to grand vistas atop Monument Cliff on Third Mtn.

Beyond the AT jct., Third Mtn. Trail crosses the wide saddle between the peaks before making a mostly moderate descent. After crossing a stream, the trail levels out and joins the route of an old woods road. At 3.5 mi., Third Mtn. Trail leaves the old road and turns sharply left. It ends at the pond, which has an earthen tent pad, a fire ring, and a privy.

SHAW MTN. (NORTH PEAK, 2,492 FT.; MIDDLE PEAK, 2,663 FT.)

The twin summits of Shaw Mtn. rise east of First Roach Pond and south of Second Roach Pond, offering views over the 100MW as far north as Katahdin. To reach the trailhead, from the entrance road to Medawisla Lodge, continue east on Smithtown Rd. for 1.1 mi. Turn right on Lower Crossover Rd. In another 0.4 mi., where Long Ridge Rd. forks left toward West Branch Pond Camps, stay right. Trailhead parking for Shaw Mtn. Trail is 0.4 mi. ahead on the right.

SHAW MTN. TRAIL (MAP 2: D3, AMC MEDAWISLA LODGE MAP)
Cumulative from Lower Crossover Rd. (1,520 ft.) to:

Trail jct. in sag between north and south summits (2,410 ft.)	1.4 mi.	890 ft.	1:10
Shaw Mtn., north peak (2,492 ft.)	1.7 mi.	972 ft.	1:20
Shaw Mtn., middle peak (2,663 ft.)	1.8 mi.	1,225 ft.	1:30

AMC Shaw Mtn. Trail climbs alongside a brook into the drainage between the north and south peaks of Shaw Mtn. and then joins an old woods road and continues uphill to the left. The track narrows to a foot trail and crosses an old skidder trail. At 0.7 mi., it joins an old haul road and turns sharply left; this road is part of the new Skyline Trail, a multiuse trail. Shaw Mtn. Trail crosses Skyline Trail again 0.3 mi. ahead.

Beyond, with a view of the summit ridge in sight, bear right off the haul road onto a foot trail. Ascend steadily on a moderate grade to reach a bench on the right. Soon after the bench, bear right and climb steeply. Cross a grassy skidder trail and then climb a rock staircase. Reach a sag between the peaks and a jct.

To reach the north summit of Shaw Mtn., turn right. Easy walking on this 0.3-mi. spur path along the ridge leads to a short climb to the flat, wooded summit. To reach the south summit of Shaw Mtn., turn left, pass a view northeast to Second Roach Pond, and continue to the top in 0.4 mi. AMC trail crews will be working over the next several years to extend Shaw Mtn. Trail south to connect with Hedgehog Mtn.

EMMIT BROOK TRAIL (MAP 2: D3, AMC MEDAWISLA LODGE MAP)
From Smithtown Rd. (1,283 ft.) to:

Lower Crossover Rd. (1,520 ft.)	1.3 mi.	240 ft.	0:45

AMC This trail provides a convenient link between Medawisla Lodge and Shaw Mtn. Trail. From the Medawisla Lodge guest parking lot, walk the entrance road out to Smithtown Rd. Emmit Brook Trail begins immediately across the road from this jct.

Emmit Brook Trail follows the route of a 1950s logging road and has been graveled and graded for family biking and easy hiking. It heads southeast along the course of Emmit Brook, reaching Lower Crossover Rd. 0.5 mi. north of the start of Shaw Mtn. Trail.

HINCKLEY COVE TRAIL (MAP 2: D3, AMC MEDAWISLA LODGE MAP)
From Medawisla Lodge guest parking lot (1,275 ft.) to:

Point on Second Roach Pond (1,280 ft.)	1.3 mi.	40 ft.	0:40

AMC Hinckley Cove Trail traces a route used by river drivers in the late 1800s to gain access to the cove from the Second Roach Pond outlet dam. Hinckley Cove was the site of many logjams due to slow-moving water and foul winds.

Hinckley Cove Trail leaves the Medawisla Lodge guest parking lot and leads west to a snowmobile trail bridge across the Roach River just west of Second Roach Pond. Beyond, the wide gravel trail travels through the woods around Hinkley Cove and passes the jct. with Hinkley Connector Trail at 0.6 mi. (The connector leads 0.6 mi. west to Nahmakanta Rd. at a point 0.4 mi. north of its jct. with Smithtown Rd.) Hinckley Cove Trail arrives at the start of a long point that reaches east into Second Roach Pond. Here is a small sand and gravel beach. Just north is a large gravel esker offering great views of the Hinckley Cove wetlands complex, one of the most significant inland waterfowl wading environments in the Moosehead region.

NORTH LAKE TRAIL (MAP 2: C3)
From Penobscot Pond Rd. (1,300 ft.) to:

Remote campsite on north shore of Second Roach Pond (1,270 ft.)	4.3 mi.	170 ft.	2:15

AMC This route through the woods on the north side of Second Roach Pond was built for mountain biking and cross-country skiing, but it is equally suited for summer hiking. North Lake Trail starts on Penobscot Pond Rd. From the jct. of Smithtown Rd. and the entrance drive to Medawisla Lodge, proceed west on Smithtown Rd. for 1.0 mi. Turn right (north) on Nahmakanta Rd. and travel 1.2 mi. Park on the side of the road by a gate at the start of the trail.

North Lake Trail meanders east through mildly rolling terrain. On the stretch along the lakeshore are fine views south to Shaw Mtn. and Trout Mtn. At 3.7 mi., at a barrier at Penobscot Pond Rd., the trail turns sharply south to end at a remote campsite on Second Roach Pond. The campsite can also be reached by canoe or kayak.

LAKESIDE TRAIL (MAP 2: C3, AMC MEDAWISLA LODGE MAP)
From Medawisla Lodge guest parking lot (1,275 ft.) to:

Shaw Mtn. Cutoff (1,360 ft.)	0.8 mi.	85 ft.	0:25
Campsite and boat launch on Second Roach Pond at end of Trout Pond Rd. (1,280 ft.)	2.7 mi.	145 ft.	1:25

AMC This trail follows the route of the earliest road in Shawtown Township, Yoke Pond Rd., which dates to the 1840s. The wide gravel trail is designed for mountain biking and cross-country skiing, but it is equally suited for hiking. From the Medawisla Lodge guest parking lot, stroll to the main lodge and then walk east on Lakeside Trail. The trail rises gradually up the slope south of Second Roach Pond and reaches a jct. with Shaw Mtn. Cutoff on the right; this spur leads 0.5 mi. south to Smithtown Rd. at its jct. with Lower Crossover Rd.

Lakeside Trail continues east, more or less on a contour, to end at the boat launch and campsite on the pond at the end of Trout Pond Rd.

HEDGEHOG MTN. (2,128 FT.)
Hedgehog Mtn. is north of First West Branch Pond and Second West Branch Pond and south of Shaw Mtn. and Medawisla Lodge. The trail starts from Frenchtown Rd.

Directions from Greenville: From the blinking traffic light in the center of Greenville on ME 6/15, follow Lily Bay Rd. north 17.6 mi. to Frenchtown Rd., a wide dirt road on the right marked by a street sign and a long row of mailboxes. Turn right onto Frenchtown Rd. and drive 9.9 mi. to the trailhead on the left. Parking is along the road. (*Note*: If you reach the driveway for West Branch Pond Camps, you've gone 0.2 mi. too far.)

Directions from Medawisla Lodge: From the jct. of the entrance road to the lodge and Smithtown Rd., drive southwest on Smithtown Rd. for 1.1 mi. Turn right (south) on Lower Crossover Rd. and drive for 5.5 mi.; then turn left on Frenchtown Rd. and proceed another 2.5 mi. to the trailhead on the left.

HEDGEHOG MTN. TRAIL (MAP 2: D3)
From Frenchtown Rd. (1,550 ft.) to:

Hedgehog Mtn. summit (2,128 ft.)	1.8 mi.	580 ft.	1:10

AMC This route dates back to the 1880s when West Branch Pond Camps was first founded as a sporting camp. The old trail was reclaimed and improved by AMC crews in 2017. From the road, Hedgehog Mtn. Trail (marked by red diamonds) travels north through mixed hardwood and softwood forests. After crossing a small stream, the trail dips slightly and then follows a contour before climbing again. A moderate pitch leads to the level summit ridge, where a cairn marks the flat, wooded top, which offers no views. The plan is for AMC crews to continue the trail northward in the future, eventually connecting with Shaw Mtn.

GULF HAGAS

Gulf Hagas was designated a National Natural Landmark in 1968, and 500 acres—including the entire canyon—were set aside for public enjoyment. In 1986, NPS obtained nearly 2,000 acres, including the Gulf and the corridor along Gulf Hagas Brook, to permanently protect the natural beauty of this area. (*Note*: Camping and campfires are prohibited in Gulf Hagas.) Much of the Gulf Hagas trail system runs near the rim of the canyon, with frequent side trails to viewpoints and falls. By using the old Pleasant River Tote Rd. on the return trip, a loop hike is possible.

To reach the main trailhead parking for Gulf Hagas (and the AT Southbound to Chairback Mtn. and Northbound to Gulf Hagas Mtn.), drive north on ME 11 from Brownville Junction for 5.5 mi. Turn left (west) on Katahdin Iron Works Rd. and drive 6.5 mi. to Katahdin Ironworks Checkpoint at KI Jo-Mary Multiple Use Forest (register and pay fee; cash or check only). Beyond the gate, cross the bridge over the West Branch of the

Pleasant River, and at the fork beyond, bear right to continue on KI Rd. At a fork at 3.5 mi., bear left (signs for Gulf Hagas, Horseshoe, Greenville, and Long Pond to the left) and in another 0.2 mi., cross another bridge over the West Branch of the Pleasant River. KI Rd. reaches the AT and Gulf Hagas parking area on the right at 6.7 mi. from the gatehouse.

SEC 2

In times of high water when it may be dangerous to ford the West Branch of the Pleasant River, or simply to avoid the ford at any time, use the Head of the Gulf Trail route (see p. 98).

GULF HAGAS LOOP (MAP 2: F2–F3)
Cumulative from KI Rd. parking area (670 ft.) to:

AT (660 ft.)	0.2 mi.	–10 ft.	0:06
Rim Trail and Pleasant River Tote Rd. (900 ft.)	1.5 mi.	260 ft.	0:55
Gulf Hagas Cutoff via Rim Trail (1,030 ft.)	3.2 mi.	660 ft.	1:55
Head of the Gulf at Pleasant River Tote Rd. via Rim Trail (1,150 ft.)	4.3 mi.	760 ft.	2:35
AT via Pleasant River Tote Rd.	6.5 mi.	840 ft.	3:35
Complete Gulf Hagas Loop	8.0 mi.	850 ft.	4:25

MATC This hike combines a section of the AT, Rim Trail, and Pleasant River Tote Rd. for a complete circuit through Gulf Hagas. From the KI Rd. parking area, follow the spur path downhill to a jct. with the AT at 0.2 mi. Turn right onto the AT, and quickly reach the south bank of the West Branch of the Pleasant River. Ford the river (knee-deep in normal water conditions) to reach a jct. with Pleasant River Tote Rd. at 0.4 mi. Turn left (west) and walk through the Hermitage, a 35-acre preserve of old-growth white pines that is a National Natural Landmark protected by the Maine chapter of TNC. At 1.5 mi., the AT bears sharply right (north). To enter the Gulf Hagas area proper, proceed straight ahead on Pleasant River Tote Rd. and ford Gulf Hagas Brook (no bridge; use caution in high water).

Immediately after the crossing, the trail reaches a jct. Pleasant River Tote Rd. continues straight ahead for 2.2 mi. to the rocky island called Head of the Gulf. Most hikers use this trail for the return trip. Rim Trail leaves left and then drops steeply along Gulf Hagas Brook past Screw Auger Falls to the rim of the canyon. Continue west to a side trail leading left to Hammond Street Pitch, a point high above the canyon that offers a fine view of the gorge. Return to Rim Trail, turn left, and soon pass a short connector trail on the right that leads back to Pleasant River Tote Rd.

Continuing along Rim Trail, several side paths lead to views of the Jaws, where the river squeezes around a slate spur and narrows in many places.

In another 0.5 mi., Gulf Hagas Cutoff diverges right, crosses Pleasant River Tote Rd. in 0.2 mi., and meets the AT in 1.2 mi. To the left, a spur path leads to a viewpoint below Buttermilk Falls.

Beyond the spur jct., the canyon gradually becomes shallower, and at times, Rim Trail approaches the banks of the West Branch of the Pleasant River. At 2.5 mi. from Pleasant River Tote Rd., pass Billings Falls. In another 0.1 mi., reach the ledge above Stair Falls, where the narrow river drops into a large pool. Just 0.1 mi. ahead, Rim Trail bears sharply away from the river (at this point, a short side trail leads left to the edge of the river near Head of the Gulf, where you can see some interesting logging artifacts) and soon reaches a jct. To the right (east), Pleasant River Tote Rd. proceeds on a contour high above Gulf Hagas back to the jct. with the AT in 2.2 mi. Although it is often very marshy and wet, the road offers a quicker return than Rim Trail. To the left, Head of the Gulf Trail leads 1.2 mi. to a bridge over the West Branch of the Pleasant River (an alternate route to Gulf Hagas during high-water conditions).

HEAD OF THE GULF TRAIL (MAP 2: F3–E2)
Cumulative from Upper Valley Rd. trailhead (1,150 ft.) to:

Bridge over West Branch of Pleasant River (1,150 ft.) via Lodge-to-Lodge Trail	0.5 mi.	0 ft.	0:15
Rim Trail and Pleasant River Tote Rd. (1,150 ft.)	1.7 mi.	0 ft.	0:50

AMC Lodge-to-Lodge Trail and Head of the Gulf Trail provide access to the Gulf Hagas area without requiring a ford of the West Branch of the Pleasant River. In high-water conditions or with small children or if you simply want to avoid fording a river, this route is a smart choice. Lodge-to-Lodge Trail leaves the east side of Upper Valley Rd. at an information kiosk. This point is 0.9 mi. north of the jct. of KI Rd. and Greenville Rd. Trailhead parking is 50 ft. past the trailhead on the left (north).

Lodge-to-Lodge Trail starts out wide and flat. In 200 ft., it bears left at a jct.; at 0.2 mi., it crosses a bridge over a small brook; in another 0.2 mi., it traverses a grassy floodplain on bog bridges. At 0.5 mi., the trail joins a gravel road and turns right to cross a bridge over the West Branch of the Pleasant River. Here, Head of the Gulf Trail leaves the road to the right at 0.6 mi. and continues as a wide treadway. An unmarked angler's path leaves left to Lloyd Pond at 0.9 mi., and just ahead, the trail crosses the rocky outlet of that pond. Following a stretch of rocky footing, Head of the Gulf Trail enters a balsam fir stand at 1.4 mi. After the trail crosses a brook and ascends briefly, a short spur to the right leads to views of the West Branch of the Pleasant River. Head of the Gulf Trail makes a short descent before it takes a sharp right turn and enters NPS land (yellow sign), where it narrows and crosses a split-log bridge over a brook. At 1.7 mi., it reaches a jct. To the right, Rim Trail leads along the rim of Gulf Hagas canyon for 2.8 mi. to a jct. with the AT near Screw Auger Falls. Straight ahead, Pleasant River Tote Rd. follows an easier route high above the river canyon, reaching a jct. with the AT in 2.2 mi.

SEC 2

PLEASANT RIVER TOTE RD. ACCESS TO
AT AND GULF HAGAS (MAP 2: F3)

AMC Another alternative for reaching both Gulf Hagas and the AT Northbound to Gulf Hagas Mtn. is to hike in from Hay Brook via Pleasant River Tote Rd. To reach this trailhead, follow driving directions for White Brook Trail on p. 105. A high-clearance vehicle is recommended beyond this point. From the jct. 0.2 mi. beyond High Bridge, turn left on the side road and drive up and over a hill. In 0.5 mi., turn sharply left (sign for campsites). The road ends 1.4 mi. ahead at Hay Brook, where there are campsites and a privy.

To reach the AT on foot, walk past the boulder barriers, ford Hay Brook, and follow Pleasant River Tote Rd. easily 0.7 mi. west, passing Pugwash Pond.

APPALACHIAN TRAIL CORRIDOR
BARREN MTN. (2,648 FT.)

The AT traverses Barren Mtn. in Elliotsville Township, the highest of the five mountain peaks of the rugged Barren–Chairback Range. Barren Slide and Barren Ledges on the south side of the mountain offer excellent lookouts over Bodfish Intervale and Lake Onawa to Borestone Mtn. The abandoned fire tower (on the summit since 1951) is in disrepair. The AT on the west side of Barren Mtn. can be reached from Monson or Greenville.

AT NORTHBOUND, MONSON APPROACH
(MAP 2: G1–G2 AND F1–F2)

Cumulative from parking area north of Otter Pond (620 ft.) to:

AT jct. (1,020 ft.)	0.7 mi.	400 ft.	0:30
Barren Slide (1,980 ft.)	1.7 mi.	1,360 ft.	1:30
Barren Ledges (2,010 ft.)	1.9 mi.	1,390 ft.	1:40
Barren Mtn. summit (2,648 ft.)	3.7 mi.	2,080 ft.	2:55

MATC From ME 15 in Monson, drive north 0.5 mi. to Elliotsville Rd. Turn right and drive 7.7 mi. to a bridge over Big Wilson Stream. Cross the bridge and immediately turn left. Follow Bodfish Valley Rd. across the Central Maine & Quebec Railway tracks at 8.4 mi. Pass the trailhead for Borestone Mtn. Sanctuary at 8.5 mi. Just beyond, the road turns to gravel, levels off on the west shoulder of Borestone Mtn., and descends. At 10.5 mi., the road narrows and enters the site of the former Bodfish Farm. At 10.7 mi., bear left and cross a bridge over Long Pond Stream. Turn left onto a dirt road at 11.3 mi. to reach a small cul-de-sac parking area at 12.0 mi.

An informal side trail leaves the rear of the parking area and goes north and then east for 0.7 mi. to a jct. with the AT just east of Long Pond Stream Lean-to. The side trail is flagged with surveyor's tape most of the way and is easy to follow. Nearing the AT, the flagged trail veers right to avoid a muddy stretch. At the AT jct., bear right (east) to continue to Barren Mtn.

The white-blazed AT climbs the northwestern slope of Barren Mtn., gradually at first, crossing an old woods road. It steepens and becomes rockier through spruce and fir. Beyond a small clearing, the trail bears left and becomes easier. On the crest of the ridge, the AT rises to a jct. on the right at 1.8 mi. Here, a blue-blazed side trail leads 250 ft. down to the head of Barren Slide, an interesting mass of boulders with a southerly vista. At 2.0 mi., the AT reaches the open Barren Ledges and another striking view. The old tower atop wooded Barren Mtn. is visible to the east. The route bears left and winds along the northern slope of the range over rough terrain to the base of the summit cone at 3.0 mi. It then climbs steeply through boulders for a short distance to the summit at 3.8 mi.

The AT continues about 12 mi. northeast over the remaining peaks of the range—Fourth Mtn., Third Mtn., Columbus Mtn., and Chairback Mtn.—to KI Rd. in the valley of the West Branch of the Pleasant River. This full hike is a backpacking trip of several days over rugged terrain.

AT NORTHBOUND, GREENVILLE APPROACH
(MAP 2: G1–G2 AND F1–F2)
Cumulative from old road at AT crossing (630 ft.) to:

Long Pond Stream (600 ft.)	150 yd.	−30 ft.	0:03
Side trail to Long Pond Stream Lean-to (900 ft.)	0.9 mi.	270 ft.	0:35
Spur path from parking area near Otter Pond (1,020 ft.)	1.0 mi.	390 ft.	0:40
Barren Slide (1,980 ft.)	2.0 mi.	1,350 ft.	1:40
Barren Ledges (2,010 ft.)	2.2 mi.	1,380 ft.	1:50
Barren Mtn. summit (2,648 ft.)	4.0 mi.	2,070 ft.	3:00

MATC From the blinking yellow light in downtown Greenville, drive north on Lily Bay Rd. for 100 ft. and then turn right on Pleasant St. and drive east. Pleasant St. becomes East Rd. as it heads to Greenville Municipal Airport. Continue past the airport as the road becomes gravel surfaced. At 3.7 mi., after the road crosses Wilson Stream, it becomes KI

Rd. Pass Rum Pond Rd. on the left at 7.1 mi. At 7.4 mi., turn right on Barren Mtn. Rd. (*Note*: This road is rough and rocky in spots and is best suited to a high-clearance vehicle. The last 0.3 mi. to the AT crossing is extremely rough and difficult to negotiate even with four-wheel drive.) Reset trip mileage.

At 0.2 mi., cross a bridge and bear left. Crest a hill (view of Barren Mtn.), cross a bridge, and reach a T jct. at 3.9 mi. Turn right, and ahead at 4.8 mi., turn sharply right. Around the 5.4-mi. mark, consider parking along the side of the road (never block this or any other forest road) and walking the final 0.3 mi. to the AT crossing on the heavily eroded, rocky surface.

Turn left (northbound) on the AT and descend 150 yd. to Long Pond Stream. Cross at the ford (usually knee-deep). A fixed guide rope is available for assistance during high-water conditions. The trail turns east, passes Slugundy Gorge, and at 0.9 mi. reaches a blue-blazed side trail leading 150 yd. to Long Pond Stream Lean-to. Just ahead, the unmarked spur from the parking area north of Otter Pond joins from the right. See the prior Monson Approach description (p. 99) for the AT route to the summit of Barren Mtn. from this point.

FOURTH MTN. (2,376 FT.), THIRD MTN. (2,082 FT.), AND COLUMBUS MTN. (2,338 FT.)

These three peaks, bookended by Barren Mtn. to the west and Chairback Mtn. to the east, form the heart of the Barren–Chairback Range. The AT connects the craggy summits and passes a number of fine viewpoints and a couple of high ponds. The route is described northbound from the summit of Barren Mtn. See AT Northbound, Monson Approach on p. 99 for hiking directions to the top of Barren Mtn.

AT NORTHBOUND (MAP 2: F2–F3)
Cumulative from Barren Mtn. summit (2,650 ft.) to:

Cloud Pond side trail to Cloud Pond Lean-to (2,480 ft.)	0.9 mi.	60 ft.	0:25
Fourth Mtn. high point (2,300 ft.)	3.0 mi.	620 ft.	1:50
Third Mtn. Trail (1,860 ft.)	5.0 mi.	780 ft.	2:55
Monument Cliff on Third Mtn. (2,068 ft.)	5.5 mi.	985 ft.	3:15
West Chairback Pond outlet (1,760 ft.)	6.1 mi.	985 ft.	3:35
Columbus Mtn. high point (2,326 ft.)	7.4 mi.	1,575 ft.	4:30
Chairback Gap Lean-to (1,930 ft.)	7.8 mi.	1,575 ft.	4:45
Chairback Mtn. summit (2,199 ft.)	8.3 mi.	1,845 ft.	5:05
KI Rd. (776 ft.)	11.7 mi.	1,925 ft.	6:55

MATC From the fire tower on the summit of Barren Mtn., the AT heads east along the high ridgeline through thick spruce and fir, trending easily down to the jct. with a side trail on the right that leads 0.3 mi. to Cloud Pond Lean-to on the pretty tarn, Cloud Pond. The trail is reasonably level for the next 0.5 mi. but then drops abruptly and steeply, using rock stairs to reach the sag below. Cross a brook on the floor of the sag and then hike easily to Fourth Mtn. Bog and traverse it on a long string of bog bridges. The hump of Fourth Mtn. can be seen ahead, and soon enough, the trail begins to steadily ascend the steep slope to reach a relocation completed in 2022. The AT now veers left and quickly reaches the site of a small plane crash that occurred in the early 2000s. From the crash site, the AT climbs to a high point on the north slope of Fourth Mtn. and skirts the summit before following switchbacks to rejoin the old trail route on the northeast side of the mountain. It continues down to a low point between Fourth Mtn. and Third Mtn., and the next stretch is a strenuous one, leading into several gullies and climbing up and out to open ledges. After climbing over a knob, the AT descends, and Third Mtn. Trail crosses it at 5.0 mi.

The AT soon reaches the base of the Third Mtn. summit cone and begins to climb. The steep ascent arrives at an open slab on top of Third Mtn. and then continues along the craggy ridge to the long, flat ledge called Monument Cliff, where the wide-open vista to the north, west, and east is a pleasure to behold. The scene includes all the White Cap Range peaks, Baker Mtn., Elephant Mtn., Indian Mtn., Long Pond, and the valley of the West Branch of the Pleasant River. From the cliff, the AT continues along the ridge before descending into the sag at the base of Columbus Mtn., where it crosses the outlet stream of West Chairback Pond. (The pond is a short distance uphill to the right and well worth a visit.) The trail rises moderately and then more steeply. The angle eases at a viewpoint, and the going is more gradual to the open ledge on top of Columbus Mtn. at 7.4 mi. From the summit, the AT drops steeply to Chairback Gap Lean-to. Another drop next to the shelter leads to the gap itself, which is often wet and muddy. The trail bears right along a small stream and then begins to climb again, finally arriving at the open ledges on Chairback Mtn. at 8.3 mi. From there, it is 3.4 mi. down to KI Rd.

CHAIRBACK MTN. (2,199 FT.)

This craggy peak in Bowdoin College East Grant Township rises south of the West Branch of the Pleasant River and forms the eastern end of the Barren–Chairback Range, which the AT traverses. To reach the trailhead parking, follow the driving directions for Gulf Hagas (p. 96), which lead to the AT parking area on KI Rd.

CHAIRBACK MTN. VIA AT SOUTHBOUND (MAP 2: F3)
Cumulative from KI Rd. parking (670 ft.) to:

AT (660 ft.)	0.2 mi.	–10 ft.	0:06
KI Rd. (776 ft.)	0.7 mi.	115 ft.	0:25
Side trail to East Chairback Pond (1,680 ft.)	1.9 mi.	1,020 ft.	1:30
Chairback Mtn. summit (2,199 ft.)	4.1 mi.	1,540 ft.	2:50

SEC 2

MATC From the parking area, follow the spur path downhill (north) to a jct. with the AT. Turn left (west) and hike uphill to cross KI Rd. Just beyond, Henderson Brook Trail leaves to the right. Continue straight on the AT as it climbs moderately up the mountainside, passing a spring at 1.4 mi. At 1.9 mi., a side trail leads downhill off the ridge 0.2 mi. to East Chairback Pond. Continuing south on the AT, climb at a moderate grade over several knobs to reach the base of the summit cone of Chairback Mtn. Finish the ascent over steeper open ledges and a talus slope, which leads to the top of Chairback Mtn. at 4.1 mi. The summit offers outstanding views of the White Cap Range, Baker Mtn., and Elephant Mtn.

Farther south on the AT, it is 0.5 mi. to Chairback Gap Lean-to, 0.9 mi. to a high point on Columbus Mtn., 2.2 mi. to a short side trail leading to West Chairback Pond, 2.8 mi. to Monument Cliff on Third Mtn., and 3.3 mi. to the jct. with Third Mtn. Trail, which leads off the mountain and 1.4 mi. down to Chairback Mtn. Rd.

WHITE CAP MTN. (3,650 FT.)
White Cap Mtn. in Bowdoin College Grant East Township is the highest point on the AT between Katahdin and the Bigelow Range and is the highest peak in the east–west range of mountains that includes Hay Mtn., West Peak, and Gulf Hagas Mtn. Rising north of the West Branch of the Pleasant River in the heart of the 100MW, White Cap Mtn. offers outstanding views from its high ridges and alpine summit.

Three trail approaches lead to White Cap Mtn.: from the north via the AT from Logan Brook Rd.; from the south via White Brook Trail and the AT; and from the south and west via the AT across the peaks of the White Cap Range.

Driving directions from Greenville: From the blinking traffic light in the center of Greenville on ME 6/15, follow Lily Bay Rd. north for 17.6 mi. to Frenchtown Rd., a wide dirt road on the right marked by a street sign and a long row of mailboxes. Turn right onto Frenchtown Rd. and drive 10.3 mi. to the driveway of West Branch Pond Camps on the right. At 0.8 mi. beyond WBPC, Long Ridge Rd. leaves to the left; bear right here. Bear right at a fork at 1.6 mi. beyond WBPC. In another 1.2 mi., the road, now called Logan Brook Rd., has a large yellow gate. Park on either side of the road before the gate, but do not block the gate. Walk east along Logan Brook Rd. for 0.4 mi. to its intersection with the AT (sign). A spring is on the right 100 yd. farther east along Logan Brook Rd.

Driving directions from ME 11 at Jo-Mary Rd.: From ME 11 in T4 R9 NWP, just south of the Piscataquis–Penobscot county line and about half-way between Brownville Junction and Millinocket, drive north on Jo-Mary Rd. In 0.2 mi., hikers must stop and register at Jo-Mary Checkpoint, where a fee is charged for day use and camping (cash or check only). At a major fork in another 5.9 mi., bear left on Johnson Pond Rd. Drive 2.7 mi. and turn left on B Pond Rd. (old V plow blade at jct. is landmark). Reset trip mileage. Pass several minor roads: to the left at 2.9 mi.; to the right at 4.4 mi.; and left at 4.9 mi. Reach the AT crossing at 5.6 mi. from the B Pond Rd. jct. Roadside parking is available before and after the AT.

AT SOUTHBOUND (MAP 2: E4)
Cumulative from AT crossing on Logan Brook Rd. (1,587 ft.) to:

Logan Brook Lean-to (2,400 ft.)	1.8 mi.	813 ft.	1:20
White Cap Mtn. summit (3,650 ft.)	3.0 mi.	2,063 ft.	2:40

MATC From Logan Brook Rd., hike southbound on the AT, which rises steadily up the north side of White Cap at a mostly moderate grade. At 0.8 mi. from Logan Brook Rd., cross a dry creek bed and join the route of an old tote road, which ascends gradually up the ravine of Logan Brook. Reach Logan Brook Lean-to at 1.8 mi. The trail climbs at a moderate-to-steep grade on rough terrain to reach a contour and, soon after, turns sharply right on the ridge. After several more stepped rises, the AT arrives at a viewpoint on the right at 2.0 mi., where the northeast ridge of White Cap is fully visible, plus Big Spencer Mtn. and Katahdin. The moderate ascent continues, and 0.3 mi. beyond the viewpoint, a long series of rock steps (dubbed the "stairway to heaven" by MATC maintainers) begins. At treeline at 2.6 mi., the views north over the 100MW are unobstructed and grand, and now include Big and Little Boardman mountains and Jo-Mary Mtn. The AT rounds the ridge to the south side and continues to climb in the open. The scree fields of the exposed summit area soon lead to the top of White Cap at 3.0 mi.

Panoramic vistas from the summit include the long ridge of Saddleback to the east, Little Spruce Mtn. and Big Spruce Mtn. just to the southeast, Baker Mtn. and the other summits of the White Cap Range to the west, Big Moose Mtn. to the southwest, the rugged summits of the Barren–Chairback Range to the south, Big Spencer Mtn. to the northwest, and the vast lake country to the north, ranging all the way to Katahdin. The scene is arguably one of the finest in the state.

WHITE BROOK TRAIL (MAP 2: E3–E4)
Cumulative from old tote road parking near fork of new logging road (1,950 ft.) to:

Trail sign and start of White Brook Trail (2,260 ft.)	1.1 mi.	310 ft.	0:40
Fire Warden's Trail (closed) (2,626 ft.)	1.5 mi.	676 ft.	1:25
AT (2,990 ft.)	1.9 mi.	1,040 ft.	1:30
White Cap Mtn. summit (3,650 ft.) via AT	3.0 mi.	1,700 ft.	2:20

MATC To reach White Brook Trail (the former route of the AT, still maintained by MATC), turn left (northwest) off ME 11 5.5 mi. north of Brownville Junction. The sign for Katahdin Iron Works at the turnoff marks the start of a 6.5-mi. drive on KI Rd. from ME 11 to a gate at Katahdin Iron Works, an interesting state historical site with a blast furnace and a beehive charcoal burner. Stop and register at the gatehouse, where a fee is charged for day use and camping (cash or check only) in the KI Jo-Mary Multiple Use Forest, a 175,000-acre block of privately owned commercial forestland between Greenville and Brownville. A camping fee, if applicable, is also charged. (*Note*: All payments are by cash or check only.)

Beyond the gate, cross the bridge over the West Branch of the Pleasant River, and at the fork beyond, bear right to continue on KI Rd. At a fork at 3.5 mi., bear right (signs for Greenwood, Hay Brook, and High Bridge to the right). Reset mileage. At 2.2 mi., reach a fork; bear left here and cross a high, narrow bridge over White Brook dubbed "High Bridge." At 2.4 mi., a road on the left leads uphill toward Hay Brook; continue straight. At 5.9 mi., pass through a long, large log yard. At its far end, where a new logging road bears left uphill, continue straight on a barely discernable old tote road. Proceed 100 ft. and park on the left. This is the trailhead for White Brook Trail.

From the mossy parking area, walk north along the narrow, shrubby corridor of the old tote road. Cross two brooks in the first 0.25 mi. In 0.5 mi., White Cap Mtn. comes into view ahead. The ascent is gradual, and even though the corridor is growing in, there is still a discernable path from regular use. Occasional cairns mark the route, as does one blue blaze on a rock at 0.7 mi. At 1.1 mi. enter a large clearing—an old log yard. At the far end of the clearing, just before reentering the woods at its upper left corner, look for a large, low cairn to the right of the trail. Also, look left for a trail sign on a tree that marks the official start of blue-blazed White Brook Trail.

Climbing steadily up toward the sag between Hay Mtn. and White Cap, White Brook Trail crosses White Brook near the site of the old fire warden's cabin. Just beyond on the right is Fire Warden's Trail (closed). To the left, White Brook Trail climbs more steeply and reaches a jct. with the AT in another 0.5 mi. From this point, it is a 1.1-mi. hike northbound (right) on the AT along a high ridge to the open summit of White Cap Mtn.

GULF HAGAS MTN. (2,688 FT.), WEST PEAK (3,179 FT.), AND HAY MTN. (3,242 FT.)

In addition to White Cap Mtn., three other high peaks make up the White Cap Range: Gulf Hagas Mtn., West Peak, and Hay Mtn. The AT traverses the range and offers some of the finest ridge walking in the state. Visitors can explore the peaks in a long day via a loop hike with considerable elevation gain and loss, ascending via the AT from the Pleasant River and returning via White Brook Trail and logging roads, but the trek is perhaps better done as a multiday backpacking trip. Several campsites are available along the AT.

To reach trailhead parking for the AT Northbound, see driving directions for Gulf Hagas on p. 96.

AT NORTHBOUND (MAP 2: F3 AND E3–E4)
Cumulative from KI Rd. parking area (670 ft.) to:

AT (660 ft.)	0.2 mi.	−10 ft.	0:06
Rim Trail and Pleasant River Tote Rd. (900 ft.)	1.5 mi.	260 ft.	0:55
Gulf Hagas Cutoff (1,030 ft.)	2.2 mi.	420 ft.	1:40
Carl Newhall Lean-to (1,900 ft.)	5.7 mi.	1,290 ft.	3:30
Gulf Hagas Mtn. summit (2,688 ft.)	6.6 mi.	2,080 ft.	4:20
Sidney Tappan CS (2,430 ft.)	7.5 mi.	2,080 ft.	4:50
West Peak summit (3,179 ft.)	8.2 mi.	2,830 ft.	5:30
Hay Mtn. summit (3,242 ft.)	9.8 mi.	3,295 ft.	6:35
White Brook Trail (2,990 ft.)	10.4 mi.	3,295 ft.	6:50
White Cap Mtn. summit (3,650 ft.)	11.5 mi.	3,965 ft.	7:45
Logan Brook Rd. (1,587 ft.)	14.7 mi.	3,965 ft.	9:20

MATC From the KI Rd. parking area, follow the spur path downhill to a jct. with the AT. Turn right, and quickly reach the south bank of the West Branch of the Pleasant River. Ford the river (knee-deep in normal water conditions) to reach a jct. with Pleasant River Tote Rd. Turn left (west) here and walk through the Hermitage, a 35-acre preserve of old-growth white pines that is a National Natural Landmark protected by the Maine Chapter of TNC. At a jct. at 1.5 mi., the AT bears sharply right (north). Straight ahead, Pleasant River Tote Rd. leads to Rim Trail and Gulf Hagas.

The AT climbs steadily up the valley of Gulf Hagas Brook, passing Gulf Hagas Cutoff on the left. Nearing Gulf Hagas Mtn., the AT crosses Gulf Hagas Brook and reaches Carl Newhall Lean-to on the left. Soon after the shelter, the trail begins to climb Gulf Hagas Mtn., moderately at first and then more steeply on switchbacks through the thick spruce and fir forest. Finally, the angle eases and the trail proceeds along the summit ridge (6.6 mi.) through several semi-open clearings. With West Peak in view just ahead, the AT drops down into the gap between the peaks and arrives at a small clearing, Sidney Tappan CS.

SEC
2

The AT continues north on the course of an old skidder road, rising up the side of West Peak. It leaves the wide track to the right and ascends steeply and steadily through the dense woods on switchbacks and occasional rock staircases to the wooded summit of West Peak. Descending steeply off the northeast side of the mountain, the AT reaches the saddle below Hay Mtn. It climbs up and out to the west shoulder of Hay Mtn. and, after a brief easy stretch, ascends steadily to the broad summit plateau of Hay Mtn.

Below, in the next saddle, White Brook Trail enters from the right. This old AT route descends the south side of the range to an old logging road, which then goes to the base of the mountains and the West Branch of the Pleasant River. Continuing the ascent, the AT reaches the White Cap summit ridge, where the angle eases briefly before the steady ascent resumes. The AT finally breaks out of the trees on the summit of White Cap Mtn., where there is an extensive talus field and outstanding views south and east. A spur path from the summit leads a few yards north for a vista over the 100MW to Katahdin. Big Spencer Mtn. dominates the scene to the west.

The AT continues north from this point toward Logan Brook. It's worth the effort to follow the trail a short distance ahead over the rocky terrain for more excellent views to the north.

LITTLE BOARDMAN MTN. (2,020 FT.)

Little Boardman Mtn. is on the AT just west of Crawford Pond. Its summit is wooded, but ledges a short distance beyond offer views of the peaks along the White Cap Range plus Elephant Mtn. and Baker Mtn.

From ME 11 in T4 R9 NWP, just south of the Piscataquis–Penobscot county line and about halfway between Brownville Junction and Millinocket, drive north on Jo-Mary Rd. In 0.2 mi., hikers must stop and register at Jo-Mary Checkpoint, where a fee is charged for day use and camping (cash or check only). Drive another 5.9 mi. to a fork and bear left on Johnson Pond Rd. Reset trip mileage. Pass B Pond Rd. on the left at 2.7 mi. (old V-plow blade at fork). Reach the AT crossing at 8.3 mi. Park alongside the road either before or after the trail.

SEC 2

AT SOUTHBOUND (MAP 2: D5)
Cumulative from Johnson Pond Rd. (1,254 ft.) to:

Little Boardman Mtn. summit and viewpoint (2,020 ft.)	1.3 mi.	766 ft.	1:00

MATC Hike southbound on the AT, gradually ascending Little Boardman Mtn. At 1.0 mi. into the walk, after a brief dip, climb at a moderate grade to a bedrock outcropping, and then continue easily along the summit ridge. Reach a T jct., where a spur path on the right leads 75 ft. (not 300 ft. as the sign reads) to the summit.

For views, continue south and slightly down from the jct. on the AT for 200 ft. to the ledges on the left.

POTAYWADJO RIDGE (1,273 FT.)

The open ledges atop this pretty ridgeline in T1 R10 WELS offer excellent views northeast over Pemadumcook Lake and Katahdin, east to Lower Jo-Mary Lake, and south to Jo-Mary Mtn. Potaywadjo Ridge is reached from the AT via a side trail. Make the trek as a long day hike or as a pleasant overnight trip. Two campsite options are possible.

From ME 11 in T4 R9 NWP, just south of the Piscataquis–Penobscot county line and about halfway between Brownville Junction and Millinocket, drive north on Jo-Mary Rd. In 0.2 mi., hikers must stop and register at Jo-Mary Checkpoint, where a fee is charged for day use and camping (cash or check only). At a major fork in another 5.9 mi. (Johnson Pond Rd. to left), bear right and continue on Jo-Mary Rd. At 11.6 mi. from ME 11, reach the AT crossing just after the bridge over Cooper Brook. Parking is available just before the bridge on the right and left.

AT NORTHBOUND (MAP 2: D6—C6)
Cumulative from Jo-Mary Rd. (608 ft.) to:

Antler's CS (500 ft.)	4.2 mi.	90 ft.	2:10
Potaywadjo Ridge Trail at Lower Jo-Mary Lake (520 ft.)	5.7 mi.	90 ft.	2:55

MATC From Jo-Mary Rd., follow the AT north along attractive Cooper Brook. At 2.7 mi., cross an old woods road next to a snowmobile bridge (on the right) over Cooper Brook. Ahead, the AT soon traverses several flows on high bog bridges. At 3.2 mi., rock-hop or ford Mud Brook (rope line 25 ft. upstream for assistance in high water). In 0.1 mi., cross another outlet of Mud Pond by rock-hopping or fording. Mud Pond is to the left as the trail climbs a low rise. Beyond, the AT wends west through the woods south of Lower Jo-Mary Lake. At 4.2 mi., a side trail leads 100 yd. to Antler's CS on a point cloaked in red pines near the west end of Lower Jo-Mary Lake.

Ahead on the AT in 150 ft. is a privy on the left; on the right is another side trail to the campsite. In 1.0 mi., the trail reaches the lakeshore and winds around its far western side to a small beach before crossing an inlet. Potaywadjo Ridge Trail begins 1.5 mi. from Antler's CS. The jct. is marked by several cut logs and a sign that faces northbound (easy to miss).

POTAYWADJO RIDGE TRAIL (MAP 2: C6)
From AT on Lower Jo-Mary Lake (520 ft.) to:

Potaywadjo Ridge (1,200 ft.) at trail's end	0.8 mi.	610 ft.	0:35

MATC From the AT, ascend blue-blazed Potaywadjo Ridge Trail. In 350 ft., pass through a gully of boulders. The trail is lightly used, so the treadway is not always well defined, and the blazes in the woods are faded (as of 2022), so pay close attention as you climb. The steady, rising contour reaches the sheer face of a large erratic on the right, and then the trail angles northwest to cross mossy slabs. Follow the route, marked by occasional cairns, in and out of the patchy woods. Blazes are sparse for the last several hundred feet across the upper ledges. Keep trending left across the slope to find the trail's end marked with blue capital letters on the rock at ground level: "END." Nearby is a rock that is convenient for sitting and enjoying the vista of Jo-Mary Mtn., Lower Jo-Mary Lake, and the peaks of the White Cap Range.

NAHMAKANTA PUBLIC LANDS
More than 30 mi. of hiking trails are in Nahmakanta PL, including Turtle Ridge Loop, Tumbledown Dick Trail, Debsconeag Backcountry Trail, and Great Circle Trail. A roughly 9-mi. stretch of the AT travels the preserve.

TURTLE RIDGE (1,643 FT.)
A scenic figure-8 loop hike on the southern boundary of the public lands traverses the many rugged bumps of Turtle Ridge and passes a series of remote mountain ponds. Hikers can enjoy beautiful views over this wild region in the heart of the 100MW from various outlooks. Blue-blazed Turtle Ridge Loop Trail can be hiked from either its eastern or western trailhead; this guide describes it from the western trailhead.

TURTLE RIDGE LOOP TRAIL (MAP 2: C5)
Cumulative from western trailhead (1,260 ft.) to:

Sing Sing Pond outlet (1,250 ft.)	1.1 mi.	80 ft.	0:35
Turtle Ridge high point (1,635 ft.)	2.3 mi.	470 ft.	1:25
Loop jct. east of Hedgehog Pond loop (1,340 ft.)	3.1 mi.	465 ft.	1:45
Eastern trailhead Rabbit Pond (1,089 ft.)	4.2 mi.	465 ft.	2:20
Henderson Pond lookout (1,520 ft.)	5.0 mi.	595 ft.	2:50
Complete Turtle Ridge Loop via Henderson Pond	8.2 mi.	885 ft.	4:35

MBPL From ME 11 in T4 R9 NWP, just south of the Piscataquis–Penobscot county line and about halfway between Brownville Junction and Millinocket, drive north on Jo-Mary Rd. In 0.2 mi., hikers must stop and register at Jo-Mary Checkpoint, where a fee is charged for day use and camping (cash or check only). At a major fork in another 5.9 mi. (Johnson Pond Rd. to left), bear right and continue on Jo-Mary Rd. At 11.6 mi. from ME 11, reach the AT crossing just after the bridge over Cooper Brook. At 14.3 mi., pass through unstaffed Henderson Checkpoint, and 0.3 mi. beyond, enter Nahmakanta PL. At 16.0 mi., Turtle Ridge Trail starts on the west (left) side of Jo-Mary Rd. Cross the bridge over Rabbit Brook to reach the trailhead parking lot on the left in 0.1 mi.

To reach the western trailhead for the Turtle Ridge loop hike, continue north on Jo-Mary Rd. for another 3.9 mi. to a 3-way jct. Turn left on Penobscot Pond Rd. In 0.9 mi., trailhead parking for Great Circle Trail is on the right (view of Katahdin from this lot). Continue another 0.4 mi. and then turn left on Penobscot Brook Rd. Parking for the western trailhead for Turtle Ridge is 1.0 mi. down this road on the right, 100 ft. before a bridge over Penobscot Stream.

(The western trailhead for Turtle Ridge Loop Trail—and the other trailheads in Nahmakanta PL—can also be reached from the west at Greenville via Lily Bay Rd., Greenville Rd., and Smithtown Rd. Refer to the driving directions for Medawisla Lodge on p. 85. At the jct. of Smithtown Rd. and Nahmakanta Rd., turn north on Nahmakanta Rd. and drive 10.4 mi. to Penobscot Brook Rd. Continuing east on Penobscot Pond Rd., it is 0.4 mi. farther to Great Circle Trail and a total of 1.3 mi. to the jct. of Penobscot Pond Rd., Jo-Mary Rd., and Wadleigh Pond Rd.)

To reach the start of Turtle Ridge Loop Trail, walk south over the bridge. Blue-blazed Turtle Ridge Loop Trail enters the woods on the left soon after. Proceed 1.1 mi. east to a jct. near the southwest corner of Sing Sing Pond. Turn left (north) and cross a footbridge over the outlet of the pond.

After a short climb, the trail emerges at the west end of the Turtle Ridge cliffs to meet Great Circle Trail at 1.6 mi. Turtle Ridge Loop Trail continues up and then east through semi-open spruce forest and across ledges to a cliff-top viewpoint overlooking the pond. The trail then descends to a jct. at the northeast corner of Hedgehog Pond. The path to the right connects to the loop on the opposite side of the pond. Proceed straight ahead on Turtle Ridge Loop Trail, which reaches a jct. with the eastern half of the loop. Continue straight and then down to the outlet of Rabbit Pond and its large granite slabs. Cross the outlet and continue over open granite ledges and through some woods to the next jct. in an open ledge area. From there, it is 0.5 mi. to the eastern trailhead on Jo-Mary Rd.

Continuing to the right, the trail climbs the spine of a ridge to reach a series of cliffs with views to Katahdin and the many lakes to the north and east. The loop follows the ridgeline to a side trail leading to a lookout over Henderson Pond. Then it descends to the north shore of Henderson Pond before turning west and rising easily through semi-open forest to a height-of-land. The route then drops down through mature forest to return to the loop jct. Turn left (west) to reach Hedgehog Pond, and then continue along the south shore of Sing Sing Pond (campsite) and farther on to the western trailhead and the completion of the loop.

TUMBLEDOWN DICK TRAIL (MAP 2: C5–C6)
Cumulative from Jo-Mary Rd. (1,089 ft.) to:

Tumbledown Dick Falls side trail (800 ft.)	3.5 mi.	120 ft.	1:50
AT (600 ft.)	4.4 mi.	150 ft.	2:15
Nahmakanta Stream Rd. (640 ft.) via AT	5.0 mi.	190 ft.	2:35

MBPL Blue-blazed Tumbledown Dick Trail links Turtle Ridge Loop Trail to the AT and Debsconeag Backcountry Trail and makes possible several overnight backpacking possibilities. The route leaves Jo-Mary Rd. at a point 250 ft. north of the eastern trailhead for Turtle Ridge Loop Trail on that road.

Traveling east, Leavitt Pond is soon visible through the trees. A side trail leads to a viewpoint on its northwest shore. Ahead, Tumbledown Dick Trail follows the edge of the pond before bearing away to reach a jct. Here, a side trail leads right 175 yd. to a campsite and another view across the pond. Continuing through mostly cutover forest, the main trail arrives at Tumbledown Dick Pond and a campsite set in the pines. It follows the west shore and, after crossing the pond's outlet, contours above Tumbledown Dick Stream through a pleasant forest.

Where the trail touches a logging road and bridge, it crosses the stream and immediately turns north to continue down the other side of the stream and soon reaches Tumbledown Dick Falls. From an open spot immediately northeast of the falls is a view of Katahdin. The falls is a wonderful narrow drop worthy of exploration. Just ahead, a side trail right leads 0.1 mi. to a pool at the base of the falls. Beyond the jct., Tumbledown Dick Trail is a gentle downhill walk to a jct. with the AT near a swimming hole on a sharp 90-degree bend in Nahmakanta Stream, 100 yd. above the stream's second dead water. To the left (upstream), it is 0.6 mi. to Nahmakanta Stream Rd., and another 0.2 mi. via the AT to a hand-carry boat launch and beach on the south shore of Nahmakanta Lake.

DEBSCONEAG BACKCOUNTRY TRAIL (MAP 2: B5)
Cumulative from parking area on Fourth Debsconeag Rd. (722 ft.) to:

Loop jct. at Fifth Debsconeag Pond (800 ft.)	0.8 mi.	80 ft.	0:25
Connector trail to Sixth Debsconeag Pond (1,250 ft.)	4.3 mi.	960 ft.	2:40
Spur path to northern trailhead (800 ft.)	6.8 mi.	1,160 ft.	4:00
Sixth Debsconeag Pond via loop (950 ft.)	9.5 mi.	1,475 ft.	5:30
Loop jct. at Fifth Debsconeag Pond (800 ft.)	11.5 mi.	1,600 ft.	6:35
Complete Debsconeag Backcountry Trail loop	12.3 mi.	1,600 ft.	6:55

MBPL The outstanding Debsconeag Backcountry Trail covers more than a dozen scenic miles over a series of hills and ridges that hide at least a dozen pleasant little ponds in the wild country east of Nahmakanta Lake. The trail rambles through a large chunk of ecological reserve and roadless area. Primitive campsites lie along the trail at Sixth Debsconeag Pond and Fifth Debsconeag Lake. The loop can also be hiked over the course of a long day.

To reach the southern trailhead: Follow driving directions for Turtle Ridge Loop Trail (p. 110). From the Turtle Ridge trailhead on Jo-Mary Rd. 16.1 mi. from ME 11, continue north on Jo-Mary Rd. for 3.9 mi. to a 3-way jct. Reset trip mileage. Continue straight ahead on Wadleigh Pond Rd. At a fork at 0.6 mi., where Deadwater Rd. goes right, bear left. Reach Nahmakanta Stream Rd. at 0.9 mi. and turn right onto it. At 1.8 mi., turn right (sign for "hiking trails" and "DLWC"). At 3.9 mi., pass a road on the left that leads to the boat landing on Nahmakanta Lake. Just 0.1 mi. beyond, there is parking on the right at the AT crossing. Cross the bridge over Nahmakanta Stream; from here, the road continues as Fourth Debsconeag Rd. At 0.9 mi. beyond the bridge, reach a parking area on the left and the southern trailhead (kiosk) for Debsconeag Backcountry Trail.

To reach the northern trailhead: From the jct. of Nahmakanta Stream Rd. and Wadleigh Pond Rd., drive north on Wadleigh Pond Rd. In 4.1 mi., pass Pollywog Pond Rd. on the left. In 0.2 mi., the AT crosses Wadleigh Pond Rd. (a few parking spaces on the left). Drive 1.3 mi. farther to a bridge over Pollywog Stream. Some parking is available on the right 200 ft. before the bridge. On the other side of the bridge, Debsconeag Backcountry Trail, Great Circle Trail, and the AT all meet. Turn right on the access road for Nahmakanta Lake Camps and drive 0.3 mi. to trailhead parking for all three trails.

Blue-blazed Debsconeag Backcountry Trail is described from the southern trailhead. DBT heads north through mixed woods and occasional sandy-soiled openings to a jct. just south of Fifth Debsconeag Lake. To the right, it is 0.5 mi. along a stream to Fourth Debsconeag Rd. and a parking area near a boat landing on Fourth Debsconeag Lake. To the left, it is 2.0 mi. to the west side of Sixth Debsconeag Pond. Go straight ahead to begin the loop.

Cross the outlet stream and continue along the east shore of Fifth Debsconeag Lake. Bear away from the lake, cross a stream, and climb alongside it to reach Stink Pond. Bear west and climb to the open granite ledges above the pond, where there are fine views of White Cap Mtn., before dropping into a shallow valley. DBT ascends to the extensive open ledges above Seventh Debsconeag Pond, with views of Nesuntabunt Mtn., White Cap Mtn., Fifth Debsconeag Lake, and Pemadumcook Lake. Descending the ledges, arrive at a jct. To the left, a section of the loop trail leads 1.0 mi. past Sixth Debsconeag Pond. Straight ahead from the jct., DBT crosses a stream and, on ledges, passes south of an unnamed pond and soon reaches Eighth Debsconeag Pond. Swinging west away from the pond, the trail descends moderately to reach Gould Brook and a jct. To the right, a spur path leads 0.9 mi. to the northern trailhead. Straight ahead, DBT follows Gould Brook downhill to reach a small sand beach near the north end of Nahmakanta Lake. Nahmakanta Lake Camps can be seen a short distance west along the lake. The trail then parallels the shore for nearly half the length of the lake, until finally bearing east away from the water and rising through a small ravine to reach a jct. at Sixth Debsconeag Pond. Straight ahead, the trail connects in 1.0 mi. to the loop above Seventh Debsconeag Pond. To the right, the trail follows the south side of Sixth Debsconeag Pond, climbs over a hillside, and then reaches Fifth Debsconeag Pond, which it follows to the original loop jct. Straight ahead, it is a direct 0.8 mi. back to the trailhead parking area. To the left, the route leads to Fourth Debsconeag Pond, where there is parking and a boat landing.

WADLEIGH MTN. (1,862 FT.)

Wadleigh Mtn. rises west of Wadleigh Pond. A 36-ft. fire tower stood on the mountain's summit from 1927 until 2017. Several outlooks offer excellent views over the 100MW to Katahdin.

GREAT CIRCLE TRAIL (MAP 2: B4–C5)
Cumulative from Jo-Mary Rd. at Turtle Ridge Loop Trail (1,089 ft.) to:

Tumbledown Dick Falls side trail (800 ft.)	3.5 mi.	120 ft.	1:50
AT (600 ft.)	4.4 mi.	150 ft.	2:15
Nahmakanta Stream Rd. (640 ft.) via AT	5.0 mi.	190 ft.	2:35
Fourth Debsconeag Rd. trailhead parking (722 ft.)	6.0 mi.	270 ft.	3:10
Fifth Debsconeag Pond (800 ft.)	6.8 mi.	350 ft.	3:35
Sixth Debsconeag Pond (950 ft.)	8.8 mi.	650 ft.	4:45
Gould Brook trail jct. (800 ft.)	11.5 mi.	800 ft.	6:10
Trailhead parking on Nahmakanta Lake Camps access road (671 ft.)	12.1 mi.	800 ft.	6:25
AT jct. at Pollywog Stream bridge (682 ft.)	12.4 mi.	910 ft.	6:35
Crescent Pond and AT jct. (970 ft.)	13.7 mi.	1,200 ft.	7:25
Pollywog Pond Rd. (920 ft.)	14.4 mi.	1,360 ft.	7:55
Wadleigh Outlet Rd. (915 ft.)	15.9 mi.	1,400 ft.	8:40
Wadleigh Pond shelter site (920 ft.)	16.3 mi.	1,400 ft.	8:55
Katahdin view spur path (1,800 ft.)	18.7 mi.	2,280 ft.	10:30
Wadleigh Mtn. summit (1,862 ft.)	19.1 mi.	2,350 ft.	10:45
Third Musquash Pond (1,240 ft.)	20.4 mi.	2,350 ft.	11:25
Penobscot Pond Rd. trailhead parking (1,170 ft.)	22.8 mi.	2,350 ft.	12:35
Turtle Ridge Loop Trail (1,420 ft.)	24.4 mi.	2,640 ft.	13:30
Hedgehog Pond, east end (1,332 ft.)	26.1 mi.	2,660 ft.	14:25
Turtle Ridge Loop Trail, eastern trailhead at Jo-Mary Rd. (1,089 ft.)	27.3 mi.	2,660 ft.	15:00

MBPL Great Circle Trail is a new, roughly 28-mi. backpacking circuit through the backcountry of Nahmakanta PL. The route combines sections of Tumbledown Dick Trail, DBT, the AT, and Turtle Ridge Loop Trail, plus 14 mi. of newly constructed trail. Conceived by Jay Hall, a longtime MBPL Nahmakanta Unit forester, the work was completed between 2006 and 2021 by trail crews from MECC, AMC, Caribou Parks and Recreation Dept., and Unity College. GCT, opened to the public in October 2021, is a significant addition to the state's inventory of multiday backpacking opportunities. Along the GCT are six primitive tentsites, each with a picnic table and box privy. Wadleigh Pond offers two lean-tos, a tent pad, and a regular privy.

GCT is described from the popular starting point at the Turtle Ridge Loop Trail eastern trailhead on Jo-Mary Rd. (see driving directions on p. 110) and follows the route counterclockwise. Access also exists from DBT's southern and northern trailheads (see driving directions on pp. 112 and 113), from Penobscot Pond Rd., and from the Turtle Ridge Loop Trail western trailhead (see driving directions on p. 110).

Tumbledown Dick Trail (GCT) leaves Jo-Mary Rd. at a point 250 ft. north of the Turtle Ridge Loop eastern trailhead.

In 0.25 mi., reach Leavitt Pond, where a side trail leads to a viewpoint on its northwest shore. Ahead, GCT follows the edge of the pond before bearing away to reach a jct., where a side trail leads right 175 yd. to a campsite. Traversing a low ridge, the trail arrives at Tumbledown Dick Pond and a campsite. GCT follows the west shore and, after crossing the pond's outlet, contours above Tumbledown Dick Stream.

Where the trail touches a logging road and bridge, it crosses the stream and immediately turns north to continue down the other side of the stream and soon reaches Tumbledown Dick Falls. Just ahead, a side trail right leads 0.1 mi. to a pool at the base of the narrow slot falls. Beyond the jct., GCT is a gentle downhill walk to a jct. with the AT near a swimming hole on a sharp 90-degree bend in Nahmakanta Stream, 100 yd. above the stream's second dead water. To the left (upstream), it is 0.6 mi. to Nahmakanta Stream Rd. via the AT. At Nahmakanta Stream Rd. at 5.0 mi., turn right on the road, cross a bridge over Nahmakanta Stream, and proceed 1.0 mi. on Fourth Debsconeag Rd. to trailhead parking on the left.

GCT heads north through mixed woods and occasional sandy openings to a jct. just south of Fifth Debsconeag Pond. Turn left to follow the pond's west shore (pass campsite), and then climb over a low ridge to reach Sixth Debsconeag Pond (campsite) and a jct. at its west end; turn left and descend toward Nahmakanta Lake. Cross a stream and hike through the woods along the lakeshore to its north end. Leave the lake and follow Gould Brook uphill to a jct. Cross a footbridge over the brook and descend to Rainbow Stream. Ford the stream to reach the access road into Nahmakanta Lake Camps (to the left), and turn right to reach trailhead parking. Follow the road out to Wadleigh Pond Rd., which is reached at 12.4 mi. Here, the AT enters from the right and merges with GCT. Turn right and cross the bridge over Pollywog Stream. Immediately after the bridge, turn right off the road and follow the AT along Pollywog Stream. In 0.5 mi., leave the stream and climb to the rim of the gorge above and follow along it. A short spur path offers an attractive view over Pollywog Gorge.

Continue up the hillside to Crescent Pond and a jct. The AT continues straight along the north side of the pond; turn right here to stay on GCT and cross the pond's outlet. Climb over a ridge, drop down to Pollywog Pond Rd., and hike along the west side of the pond past two campsites. Reach Wadleigh Outlet Rd. at 15.9 mi. Cross the pond's outlet on a stone causeway and then follow the shore of Wadleigh Pond to a beautiful meadow, where there are two shelters next to an old stone fireplace, all that remains of the former Wadleigh Pond Camps. A tent pad is near the pond's shore.

From the shelter site, walk west and then bear left to follow an old tote road. Leave the road on the left and cross a bridge over Female Brook. Climb the slope beyond and turn south to begin the ascent of Wadleigh Mtn., following a stream valley much of the way. High on the mountain's east side, a spur path leads to a fine view of Katahdin. Continue to the wooded summit at 19.1 mi., where only the concrete stanchions of the former fire tower remain. South of the summit are two outlooks with views to the White Cap Range. Descend the mountain along a stream valley to reach the boggy east shore of Third Musquash Pond. Pass several side trails to the pond and one leading to a campsite. Continue the descent along the pond's outlet, traverse the stream, contour along the side of a ridge, cross a small brook, and reach a trailhead parking lot on Penobscot Pond Rd. at 22.8 mi. An outlook at the cleared lot reveals a grand view of Katahdin.

Cross the road and continue into the woods to an obscure jct., where a trail on the left makes a loop to and along cascades on Musquash Stream. This loop rejoins GCT from the left in another 0.2 mi. Ascend through the valley of Musquash Stream, cross an old logging road bridge over the stream, and begin the ascent of Turtle Ridge. Meet Turtle Ridge Loop Trail and descend to Sing Sing Pond. Bear west around the pond's inlet and soon meet the section of Turtle Ridge Loop Trail that joins from 1.1 mi. west at Penobscot Brook Rd. Turn left and hike along the route of an old tote road, passing a campsite on Sing Sing Pond. Continue to Hedgehog Pond and then to a 4-way jct. with segments of Turtle Ridge Loop Trail to the left and right. Proceed straight ahead to Rabbit Pond, cross the pretty granite slabs at its outlet, and head downhill to trail's end at Jo-Mary Rd. at 27.3 mi.

NESUNTABUNT MTN. (1,551 FT.)

This rugged mountain, part of the NPS corridor, rises prominently to the west of Nahmakanta Lake. Its summit offers excellent looks at Katahdin as well as views over the wilderness terrain around Nahmakanta Lake. The AT traverses the mountain, and access is described via the AT Southbound.

The AT trailhead for Nesuntabunt Mtn. is on Wadleigh Pond Rd. near the northwest corner of Nahmakanta PL. To get there, follow driving directions for the northern trailhead of DBT on p. 113. The AT crosses Wadleigh Pond Rd. on the way, and there is trailhead parking for the AT on the left just before the crossing.

SEC 2

AT SOUTHBOUND (MATC; MAP 2: B4)
From AT crossing on Wadleigh Pond Rd. (1,010 ft.) to:

Nesuntabunt Mtn., high point (1,520 ft.)	1.2 mi.	510 ft.	0:50
Ledges on east side of summit (1,500 ft.)	1.25 mi.	510 ft.	0:55

MATC Follow the AT southbound. The climbing is gradual as the trail trends east and then south on a rising contour. The grade becomes moderate as the AT ascends the east side of the peak to reach a large open ledge with a great view over Nahmakanta Lake to Katahdin. Several short, steep pitches punctuate the rising contour. Climb a rock staircase and then switchback to the right below a mossy ledge wall. Go down a rock staircase and swing around the north side of the peak below huge cliffs. At a jct. at the peak, a spur path leads left 200 ft. to a vista over Nahmakanta Lake and Debsconeag Lakes Wilderness Area to Katahdin and its neighboring peaks.

DEBSCONEAG LAKES WILDERNESS AREA

The AT meanders through DLWA for about 15 mi., entering near Murphy Ponds and exiting on Golden Rd., just west of Abol Bridge. Along the way, the AT hugs the entire south shore of Rainbow Lake, the largest lake in the DLWA. A side trail climbs Rainbow Mtn. near the eastern end of the lake. Beyond, the AT climbs over Rainbow Ledges for outstanding views of Katahdin. Around 8 mi. of trails lead into the northern section of the DLWA from Golden Rd., including Horserace Brook, Blue, Rainbow Loop, and Ice Caves trails. (*Note*: Dogs are not allowed in DLWA. Backcountry camping is permitted at designated sites only.)

Driving directions to DLWA: From I-95, Exit 244 in Medway, drive west on ME 157 through Medway and East Millinocket to downtown Millinocket at 11.6 mi. At the jct. of ME 11 (south) and the end of ME 157 just past downtown at 11.8 mi., bear right and follow signs for BSP. The road has several names, including Millinocket Lake Rd., Baxter State Park Rd., and simply Lake Rd. Drive 8.6 mi. to North Woods Trading Post and Big Moose Inn, Cabins & Campground on the right. Bear left onto the parallel Golden Rd. and drive another 10.1 mi. to Abol Bridge Campground and Store on the right. Just beyond, cross Abol

Bridge over the West Branch of the Penobscot River (excellent view of Katahdin to the north).

To Ice Caves Trail trailhead: Immediately beyond Abol Bridge, turn left onto a gravel road and soon pass a DLWA information kiosk. At 3.1 mi., reach a fork. To the right is the Hurd Pond boater's access. For Ice Caves Trail, continue straight ahead for another 0.7 mi. to parking on the right (kiosk and red gate).

To Horserace Brook Trail, Rainbow Loop Trail, and Blue Trail trailhead: From Abol Bridge, continue west on Golden Rd. for 5.4 mi. to a narrow road on the left (this left turn is at the top of a hill just past the state campsite at Rainbow Deadwater; there's a small sign, but it's easy to miss). Turn here and follow this partially paved road to its end in another 0.3 mi., where there is parking and a kiosk (please parallel park along the side of the road, not in the turnaround area by the kiosk).

ICE CAVES TRAIL (MAP 2: B7)
Cumulative from parking area at end of road near Hurd Pond Stream (564 ft.) to:

Ice Caves (650 ft.)	1.1 mi.	170 ft.	0:40
First Debsconeag Lake (501 ft.)	1.5 mi.	170 ft.	0:50

TNC Go around the red gate and cross the bridge over Hurd Pond Stream. Just ahead, turn left into the woods on a footpath. Following light-blue blazes, weave through boulders covered with ferns and mosses and then climb the hillside. Pass through two more huge rocks and then slab across the hillside. At 0.7 mi., Ice Caves Trail goes left on an old forest road and quickly turns right off that road into the woods. Follow an undulating route to a jct. at 0.9 mi. To the right, a spur path leads 0.1 mi. to a cliff-top view over First Debsconeag Lake to Jo-Mary Mtn.

For the Ice Caves and First Debsconeag Lake, continue left from the jct. Make a moderate descent to the next jct., where a spur to the right leads 0.2 mi. to a handrail and rungs leading down to the rocks below; these are the Ice Caves. Return to the jct. and make a moderate to steep descent. The trail passes under a rock roof and then drops down to the rocks along the north shore of First Debsconeag Lake, where it ends. (*Note*: Due to heavy use and to protect this sensitive area, it is important that visitors stay on the trail, especially at the Ice Caves entrance.)

RAINBOW SUMMIT (1,630 FT.)
This craggy outlook along Rainbow Loop Trail provides panoramic views ranging from Katahdin to the 100MW. The summit can be reached via Blue Trail or Horserace Brook Trail.

HORSERACE BROOK TRAIL (MAP 2: A5–A6)
Cumulative from Horserace Brook trailhead (620 ft.) to:

Blue Trail (690 ft.)	0.5 mi.	70 ft.	0:20
Horserace Pond (1,056 ft.) and Rainbow Loop Trail	2.0 mi.	436 ft.	1:10

SEC 2

TNC Start to the left of the kiosk and cross a footbridge over Horserace Brook. The yellow-blazed trail soon joins the route of an old forest road. Cross another footbridge and soon arrive at a jct., where Blue Trail departs to the left. Bear right to stay on Horserace Brook Trail, which continues on a slippery treadway of rocks and roots to meet Horserace Brook. The trail turns left to follow the brook, climbing gently west up the valley. Cross a small brook and pass a huge boulder (with fading graffiti on it) on the left, make a quick up and down, and then walk between more huge boulders to reach a small day-use area with a firepit. Here, a side trail on the right leads 0.1 mi. to a campsite on the east side of Horserace Pond. The main trail continues to an overlook on the edge of Horserace Pond and reaches the pond and a campsite at 2.0 mi.; a third campsite is nearby. Rainbow Loop Trail begins and ends here.

BLUE TRAIL (MAP 2: A5–A6)
Cumulative from Horserace Brook Trail (690 ft.) to:

Rainbow Loop Trail (1,350 ft.)	1.6 mi.	660 ft.	1:10
Rainbow Lake (1,050 ft.)	2.8 mi.	710 ft.	1:45

TNC From its jct. with Horserace Brook Trail, blue-blazed Blue Trail climbs a slope of mature forest growth, ascends along the right side of a ravine, and heads up along the right side of a mossy cliff. The trail reaches a small saddle and then switchbacks up the slope beyond. It levels off, contours on the hillside, and then ascends easily. After a stretch of mostly level terrain, it reaches the jct. with Rainbow Loop Trail on the right at 1.6 mi. Blue Trail then gradually descends to Clifford Pond, reaching a side trail to the pond on the right. In the next 0.25 mi., there are two more side trails to the pond. Ahead, Woodman Pond appears on the right. Beyond the pond, Blue Trail passes to the right of a huge, prow-like boulder and then makes a gradual to moderate descent to end at the north shore of Rainbow Lake. Across the lake is private Rainbow Lake Camps; Rainbow Mtn. rises beyond.

RAINBOW LOOP TRAIL (MAP 2: A5–A6)
From Blue Trail (1,350 ft.) to:

Large cairn and vista (1,505 ft.)	0.8 mi.	275 ft.	0:35
Rainbow Summit (1,630 ft.)	1.3 mi.	515 ft.	0:55
Horserace Pond (1,056 ft.)	2.0 mi.	515 ft.	1:15

**SEC
2**

TNC This orange-blazed trail leaves Blue Trail at a point 1.6 mi. from the Horserace Brook trailhead via Horserace Brook Trail. Rainbow Loop Trail follows an undulating route through majestic stands of pine and spruce before climbing steadily to the first outlook, where there is a view over Clifford Pond. Minor ups and downs continue until the trail finally ascends a steep slope to a small beaver pond at the head of an outlet stream. After a sharp left uphill over some steep sections, the trail emerges on a flat area of open bedrock marked by a large cairn, where there is an expansive vista south over Rainbow Lake far into the 100MW to Jo-Mary Mtn., the White Cap Range, Baker Mtn., and Boardman Mtn.

Several hundred feet beyond, turn sharply downhill into the woods and reach a side trail to a pond on the right. Beyond, Rainbow Loop Trail turns sharply left around an erratic and continues along the west side of the pond before climbing to a long, narrow rock outcropping and a fine view of Katahdin. Continue up to the second outlook and then the third (Rainbow Summit) to enjoy vistas ranging from Katahdin to Rainbow Lake and farther south. From the last outlook, hike through a level area of scrubby trees before descending through the mature forest above Horserace Pond. Glimpses of the pond are possible as the trail descends a short rock staircase to the water's edge. After a viewpoint west down to the pond, follow the shoreline to a campsite and then to the jct. with Horserace Brook Trail, which leads to the trailhead in 2.0 mi.

RAINBOW LEDGES (1,517 FT.) AND RAINBOW MTN. (1,663 FT.)

The extensive Rainbow Ledges are found east of Rainbow Lake and west of Hurd Pond in the northeastern section of DLWA. From numerous points atop the ledges, outstanding views are possible north to Katahdin and south over the vast 100MW as far as the White Cap Range and Baker Range. Farther west, Rainbow Mtn. rises above the east end of Rainbow Lake. Rainbow Ledges and Rainbow Mtn. are most easily reached via the AT Southbound from Abol Bridge. (*Note*: A round trip to Rainbow Mtn. is a considerable distance and may be best done as an overnight with a camping stay at Hurd Brook Lean-to.)

For driving directions to the AT and Abol Bridge, refer to the introductory text for DLWA (p. 117). Just beyond the bridge, there is an AT/DLWA trailhead parking area on the left, off Golden Rd.

AT SOUTHBOUND (MAP 2: A7–B5)
Cumulative from parking area west of Abol Bridge (590 ft.) to:

Hurd Pond Lean-to (700 ft.)	3.3 mi.	440 ft.	1:50
Rainbow Ledges (1,510 ft.) at Katahdin view	5.9 mi.	1,350 ft.	3:40

Rainbow Ledges summit (1,517 ft.)	6.0 mi.	1,350 ft.	3:45
Rainbow Lake (1,050 ft.)	7.7 mi.	1,350 ft.	4:30
Rainbow Mtn. Trail (1,120 ft.)	9.5 mi.	1,480 ft.	5:30

SEC
2

MATC From the parking area, walk west on Golden Rd. for 0.1 mi. and then turn south into the woods on the AT. This is the start of the 100MW. The rolling route climbs to a ridge, descends, climbs again, and then drops down to cross a stream just south of Pitman Pond. Then the AT climbs over a ridge, passes a spring, and descends to Hurd Brook Lean-to, which is to the right of the trail at 3.5 mi.

Just beyond, ford both branches of Hurd Brook (may be difficult in high water). The AT ascends west, crosses a stream, climbs built steps, and reaches the wooded eastern top of Rainbow Ledges. It descends into a sag between the peaks and then ascends to open ledges on the western top of Rainbow Ledges, where there is a very fine view of Katahdin. Weaving across semi-open ledges (the area burned in a large forest fire in 1923) and crossing the true summit of Rainbow Ledges, the trail reaches a signpost and a view southwest over the northern reaches of the 100MW to Jo-Mary Mtn. and the White Cap Range. Leaving the ledges, the AT descends steadily and then turns sharply right to cross a stream. Climbing over a low ridge, the AT arrives at a side trail on the right that leads to Big Beaver Pond in 0.7 mi. Just ahead, cross the outlet of Little Beaver Pond at the far eastern end of Rainbow Lake. Follow a mildly undulating route along the south shore of the lake, and at 9.5 mi., reach the signed jct. with Rainbow Mtn. Trail on the left.

RAINBOW MTN. TRAIL (MAP 2: B5–B6)
From AT on Rainbow Lake (1,120 ft.) to:

Rainbow Mtn. high point (1,570 ft.)	0.75 mi.	450 ft.	0:35

MATC From the AT, the blue-blazed Rainbow Mtn. Trail ascends steadily. After a double blaze, the grade moderates as the trail climbs moss-and-lichen-covered slabs. Pass a view to Rainbow Ledges and Katahdin and continue easily along the ridge. Soon after passing a squarish boulder with a blaze on it, begin a short, moderate-to-steep climb through mossy slab walls. Across lichen beds on exposed granite, the trail climbs a knob, turns sharply right, turns sharply left, and reaches its end at a wide-open viewpoint amid huckleberry bushes. The scene of Katahdin and its neighboring peaks from this wild vantage point is outstanding.

BORESTONE MTN. AUDUBON SANCTUARY
BORESTONE MTN.: EAST PEAK (1,948 FT.)
AND WEST PEAK (1,938 FT.)

SEC 2

This rugged mountain in Elliotsville Township is the central natural feature of Borestone Mtn. Audubon Sanctuary, a 1,693-acre wildlife preserve owned and managed by Maine Audubon. Rising steeply above Lake Onawa, Borestone offers 360-degree views from both its craggy peaks. Three small ponds are high on its southwestern slopes. Two trails, Base and Summit, combine to reach the top of the mountain, and the access road can be used to form a loop hike.

To reach the sanctuary, drive 0.5 mi. north on ME 15 from the center of Monson. Turn right on Elliotsville Rd. and drive 7.7 mi. to Big Wilson Stream. Cross the bridge and immediately turn left on Bodfish Valley Rd. and drive 0.6 mi. up the hill. Cross the tracks of the Central Maine & Quebec Railway and proceed another 0.1 mi. to the trailhead (sign) on the right. A parking area is on the left side of the road.

BASE TRAIL (USGS BARREN MTN. WEST
AND MONSON EAST QUADS, MA BORESTONE MTN.
AUDUBON SANCTUARY MAP, GAZETTEER MAP 41)
From Bodfish Valley Rd. (850 ft.) to:

Sunrise Pond and visitor center (1,332 ft.)	1.0 mi.	590 ft.	0:45
Summit Trail and Fox Pen Trail jct. (1,340 ft.)	1.1 mi.	600 ft.	0:50

MA Follow the access road through a gate. Just beyond is an information kiosk on the left and the start of Base Trail. A toilet is to the right. (*Note*: A small day-use fee is charged, and no dogs are allowed.) The trail, marked with green triangles, quickly reaches a rock staircase and continues upward through the forest at a moderate grade. In 0.5 mi., the angle eases, and soon Base Trail reaches the jct. with a side trail on the right, which leads 0.1 mi. to a pleasant viewpoint overlooking Little Greenwood Pond and Big Greenwood Pond. Base Trail continues easily ahead and then descends gradually to the access road at 0.9 mi. Turn left on the road and soon pass two privy stalls on the right. The road then winds around a corner to reach Sunrise Pond and the Robert T. Moore Visitor Center at 1.0 mi. The center features wildlife displays and information about the interesting history of the mountain. A bench and picnic table make for a convenient place to relax and enjoy the view of the upper reaches of Borestone Mtn., which rises steeply above the far shore of the pond. Peregrine Trail leaves opposite the visitor center. Summit Trail continues across the pond's outlet (*caution*:

poison ivy) to the jct. with Summit Trail (to the left) and Fox Pen Trail (to the right) at 1.1 mi.

**SUMMIT TRAIL (USGS BARREN MTN. WEST
AND MONSON EAST QUADS, MA BORESTONE MTN.
AUDUBON SANCTUARY MAP, GAZETTEER MAP 41)**
Cumulative from Base Trail and Fox Pen Trail jct. (1,340 ft.) to:

Borestone Mtn., west peak (1,938 ft.)	0.8 mi.	600 ft.	0:40
Borestone Mtn., east peak (1,948 ft.)	1.0 mi.	660 ft.	0:50

MA From the jct. of Base Trail and Fox Pen Trail, bear left on Summit Trail, which swings around the north shore of the pond. (Fox Pen Trail makes a 0.4-mi. loop to some of the old pens of the former fox ranch that Robert T. Moore operated on the mountain in the early 1900s.) At 0.3 mi., begin a steep ascent away from the pond on a series of rock steps to attain the ridge proper. After a short level stretch, make a steep climb on rocks and roots. Ahead, the angle eases briefly before more rocks and roots. Scramble over a steep bulge to emerge from the trees. Two iron rungs and a handrail assist with the climb through the ledges beyond. More scrambling leads to a second handrail. At 0.8 mi., one more rung step and a low handrail lead up to the western summit of Borestone, a wide-open crag with outstanding views of Onawa Lake, the rugged ridgeline of Barren Mtn., Baker Mtn., Big Moose Mtn., Big Greenwood Pond, Sebec Lake, and more. Drop into a notch between the peaks, and then make a brief climb to the eastern and highest summit of Borestone at 1.0 mi. The iron bolts that secured the former fire tower (erected in 1913, removed in 1950) remain. The scenery is spectacular in all directions.

PEREGRINE RIDGE (1,644 FT.)

This craggy ridge rises steeply to the southwest of Midday Pond and Sunset Pond high on the western slope of Borestone Mtn.

**PEREGRINE TRAIL (USGS BARREN MTN. WEST
AND MONSON EAST QUADS, MA BORESTONE MTN.
AUDUBON SANCTUARY MAP, GAZETTEER MAP 41)**
From visitor center at Sunrise Pond (1,332 ft.) to:

Viewpoint overlooking Sunset Pond (1,580 ft.)	0.5 mi.	250 ft.	0:25

MA Peregrine Trail, marked with orange triangles, leaves from Base Trail at Sunrise Pond opposite the visitor center. Climb easily above Sunrise Pond and Midday Pond to a fork. Here, Talus Trail (sanctuary staff only) bears right; continue to the left on Peregrine Trail, which veers away from the pond and climbs the ridge through spruce woods. A short moderate-to-steep pitch leads to an open ledge at trail's end, with an excellent view over the three ponds to the twin peaks of Borestone.

PEAKS–KENNY STATE PARK

BIRCH MTN. (1,090 FT.)

Much of the northeastern quadrant of Birch Mtn. lies within Peaks–Kenny State Park in Dover-Foxcroft. The 839-acre park features more than 1 mi. of shoreline on Sebec Lake and has a 56-site campground and a sandy beach that offers great swimming, as well as fine views north to Borestone Mtn. and Barren Mtn. A trail makes a pleasant loop over the wooded eastern slopes of Birch Mtn. but does not reach its summit.

From downtown Dover-Foxcroft at the jct. of ME 16/6 and ME 153, drive north on ME 153 for 4.6 mi. Turn left on State Park Rd. (sign) and drive 1.1 mi. to the park entrance station (fee). Reach the large beach parking lot in another 0.5 mi. The grassy promenade and beach on Sebec Lake are just beyond. Restrooms are to the east of the parking lot (right, if you are looking at the lake).

BIRCH MTN. LEDGE TRAIL (USGS SEBEC LAKE, MBPL PEAKS–KENNY STATE PARK MAP, GAZETTEER MAP 32)
Cumulative from beach parking lot (330 ft.) to:

Picnic table sculpture at high point (650 ft.)	1.0 mi.	350 ft.	0:40
Complete loop	2.6 mi.	350 ft.	1:30

MBPL The trail starts at the south end of the parking lot (away from the lake). Follow blue blazes through the hemlock woods in a shallow ravine. The lower end of Loop Trail (no sign) leaves to the left. Stay straight to reach the upper end of Loop Trail (sign). Birch Mtn. Ledge Trail continues easily ahead and soon crosses a footbridge over a brook. Walk across a gravel park road (to the right, it leads to the campground) at 0.4 mi. The trail climbs gently into softwood forest with mossy ledges. At 0.8 mi., pass to the right of a large boulder. In 0.1 mi., a mossy erratic is to the left. Follow the right side of a depression to a clearing and a large cairn-and-picnic-table combination, one of twelve picnic table sculptures placed throughout the park that were created by artist Wade Kavanaugh through Maine's Per Cent for Art Act.

Beyond the sculpture, descend gradually through an impressive stand of white pines and hemlocks. Cross a brook and tread through sections of hemlock woods and mossy boulders. Birch Mtn. Ledge Trail then weaves through parklike groves of mature hardwood and softwood trees, some measuring more than 3 ft. in diameter. At 2.1 mi., reach a clearing and an old road, with a pumphouse to the left. Bear right on the grassy gravel road. At a 4-way jct. at 2.4 mi., go left to reach the beach. Pass through the picnic area, enter the grassy promenade, and cross a footbridge to the beach. At the lifeguard tower, turn right and follow the paved walkway to the parking lot.

SEC 2

LITTLE MOOSE PUBLIC LAND

Nestled into the long, undulating ridgeline of Little Moose Mtn., the namesake peak of 15,000-acre Little Moose PL, are five scenic ponds. A wonderful system of blue-blazed trails wends through the preserve, connecting the ponds and leading to numerous outlooks, as well as climbing to the peak of Big Moose Mtn., the site of the first fire tower in Maine. One trail leads north through the preserve to the pinnacle of Eagle Rock.

BIG MOOSE MTN. (3,194 FT.)

Big Moose Mtn. dominates the landscape southwest of the lower section of Moosehead Lake. The mountain, in Big Moose Township west of Greenville, is well known for its exceptional views of the Moosehead Lake region, Big Spencer Mtn., Little Spencer Mtn., and Katahdin.

The 1919 steel fire tower that marked the site of Maine's first fire lookout (the original structure, made of logs, was erected in 1905 and replaced 14 years later with the steel tower) was removed from the summit and reassembled next to the Moosehead Lake Region Visitor Center on ME 15 on the way into Greenville from the south. A replica of the fire warden's cabin was later built next to the restored tower.

From the blinking traffic light in the center of Greenville, drive north on ME 6/15 for 5.0 mi. Turn left (west) on North Rd. and enter Little Moose PL (sign). Proceed 1.5 mi. to trailhead parking on the right.

BIG MOOSE MTN. TRAIL
(AMC LITTLE MOOSE PUBLIC LAND MAP)
Cumulative from North Rd. trailhead (1,360 ft.) to:

Old fire warden's cabin ruins (2,260 ft.)	1.4 mi.	900 ft.	1:10
Big Moose Mtn. summit (3,194 ft.)	2.1 mi.	1,834 ft.	2:00

MBPL The blue-blazed trail leaves the rear of the parking lot to the right of a kiosk. In 750 ft., the trail joins an old forest road and turns left to make a long, rising traverse to the west. It passes a spring at 0.9 mi. and climbs moderately. At 1.1 mi., the trail bears right and climbs parallel to a brook. Just ahead, it crosses a footbridge over a small brook and continues to parallel the larger brook to the left. The ruins of the old fire warden's cabin are on the right at 1.4 mi. Go 100 ft. beyond, meet the brook, turn right, and shortly after, cross the brook. Beyond this crossing, Big Moose Mtn. Trail begins a steady ascent via rock stairs and log stairs, climbing at a moderate-to-steep grade. Reach a level shelf on the south ridge of the mountain at 1.6 mi., where a spur on the left leads 0.1 mi. to several scenic overlooks. The first one on the right looks west to the Bigelow Range and the ski slopes of Sugarloaf; the second looks north to the upper reaches of Big Moose Mtn. and east over Big Moose Pond and Little Moose Pond to a whole host of peaks beyond Moosehead Lake in the 100MW.

Continuing the steady ascent, the trail reaches the narrow crest of the high ridgeline and climbs the final distance to the open summit ledges at 2.1 mi., where there is a small communications tower and the footings of the old fire tower. The incredible vista now spans north all the way to Katahdin and the jumble of high mountains around it in BSP.

From the summit, a short trail leads north around a tower and solar array to a helipad and a ledge with a view down over Mirror Lake, an isolated pond on the northeastern spur of the mountain. Another trail continues north to the top of the Squaw Mtn. ski area.

MTN. LINK TRAIL (AMC LITTLE MOOSE PUBLIC LAND MAP)
From North Rd. trailhead (1,350 ft.) to:

Loop Trail (1,540 ft.)	1.5 mi.	220 ft.	0:50

MBPL This trail connects the Big Moose Mtn. trailhead with Loop Trail near Big Moose Pond. From the parking area, walk left (north) on North Rd. for 300 ft. to the start of Mtn. Link Trail on the right. In 350 ft., the trail crosses a brook. After cresting a low rise, reach Intake Pond and turn south along Moose Brook. Climb gradually at first and then moderately to intersect Loop Trail 0.2 mi. east of that trail's start on Mountain Rd.

LITTLE MOOSE MTN. (2,225 FT.)
Little Moose Mtn. is a long and hilly ridgeline extending for more than 5 mi. from the northeast to the southwest, just west of the southern end of Moosehead Lake. This wooded, multisummited mountain (the highest peak reaches 2,225 ft. at its western end) offers a surprising number of fine viewpoints, and primitive camping is available at four ponds along the mountain's length. The trail system on Little Moose Mtn. can be reached from ME 6/15 in the east; from a trailhead on North Rd. to the north; and from two trailheads on Mountain Rd., one near Big Moose Pond and another near the two Notch ponds, in the west.

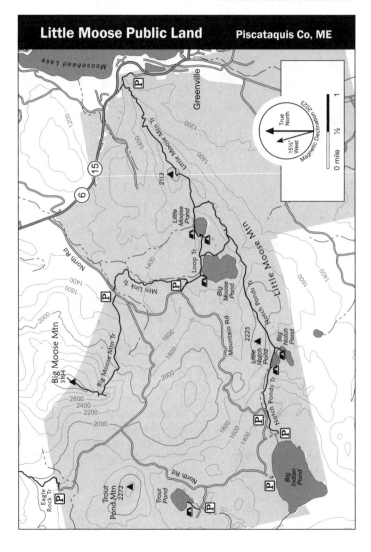

Little Moose Public Land
Piscataquis Co, ME

LOOP TRAIL (AMC LITTLE MOOSE PUBLIC LAND MAP)
Cumulative from Mountain Rd. trailhead (1,660 ft.) to:

Mtn. Link Trail (1,540 ft.)	0.2 mi.	−140 ft.	0:05
Little Moose Mtn. Trail (1,620 ft.)	1.5 mi.	140 ft.	0:50
Notch Ponds Trail (1,770 ft.)	2.4 mi.	530 ft.	1:25
Close loop at Big Moose Pond	3.0 mi.	530 ft.	1:45
Complete loop	3.7 mi.	695 ft.	2:10

MBPL This trail leads to Big Moose Pond and Little Moose Pond and then makes a circuit over the central section of Little Moose Mtn. before returning to Big Moose Pond.

From the blinking traffic light in the center of Greenville, drive north on ME 6/15 for 5.0 mi. Turn left (west) on North Rd. and enter Little Moose PL (sign). Pass the trailhead for Big Moose Mtn. and Mtn. Link Trail on the right at 1.5 mi. and then reach a fork at 1.7 mi. Turn left at the fork and follow Mountain Rd. for 1.0 mi. to the Big Moose Pond trailhead pullout on the left (kiosk).

At 0.2 mi., Loop Trail descends a winding set of slate steps to meet Mtn. Link Trail, which joins from the left. Loop Trail then crosses a curving footbridge over a small brook. A bog is on the left just beyond. At a jct. at 0.4 mi., a side trail goes south over a low hump to several campsites on Big Moose Pond. Continue to the left on Loop Trail. A short distance ahead, cross a footbridge on the old concrete dam at the outlet (Moose Brook) of Big Moose Pond. At 0.7 mi., Loop Trail splits; go left to follow the circuit in a clockwise direction. Ahead, the easy trail goes over a low rise and then trends down to Little Moose Pond at 1.0 mi. A campsite and toilet are immediately to the right. Loop Trail soon bears away from the pond, passing a pit toilet on the left and a spur path to a campsite on the right. The narrow and sometimes rough route continues along the pond's margin to reach a clearing with a campsite and toilet. The pond's outlet (Little Moose Brook) is just beyond. Leave the pond and climb a rise, pass to the right of a cliff wall, and cross the outlet of Papoose Pond before reaching the jct. of Little Moose Mtn. Trail at 1.5 mi.

Loop Trail bears right and climbs to the ridgeline of Little Moose Mtn. and a scenic outlook, where there is an attractive view over the pond below. The trail continues southwest on the rugged, craggy ridge, crossing two knobs en route to the next outlook at a large outcropping (reached by a short spur path), which provides a fine view over Big Moose Pond to Big Moose Mtn. Soon after, at 2.6 mi., Loop Trail meets Notch Ponds Trail. Loop Trail heads right and descends to Big Moose Pond. Following the pond's west shore, the trail closes the loop near the northeast corner of the pond at 3.0 mi. Big Moose Pond trailhead on Mountain Rd. is 0.7 mi. to the left.

NOTCH PONDS TRAIL (AMC LITTLE MOOSE PUBLIC LAND MAP)
Cumulative from Notch Ponds lower trailhead parking lot (1,230 ft.) to:

Notch Ponds upper trailhead parking lot (1,400 ft.)	0.5 mi.	170 ft.	0:20
Little Notch Pond campsite spur path (1,590 ft.)	1.2 mi.	260 ft.	0:45
Big Notch Pond campsite spur path (1,620 ft.)	1.5 mi.	290 ft.	0:55
Loop Trail (1,770 ft.)	3.4 mi.	990 ft.	2:15

SEC 2

MBPL Notch Ponds Trail connects to Little Notch Pond and Big Notch Pond before climbing to the western ridgeline on Little Moose Mtn. to meet Loop Trail.

To reach the trailheads for Notch Ponds Trail, follow the driving directions for Loop Trail. From the Big Moose Pond trailhead, continue on Mountain Rd. In 2.8 mi., the upper trailhead parking lot for Notch Ponds Trail is on the right. The trail leaves immediately across the road. To reach the lower trailhead parking lot for Notch Ponds Trail, continue downhill on Mountain Rd. to a T intersection. Turn left to reach parking on the right at the end of the road. The trail starts just ahead at a kiosk and large boulder.

Notch Ponds Trail is described from the lower trailhead parking lot. From the kiosk and large boulder, proceed east to cross the footbridge over Notch Ponds Brook, the outlet of the two Notch ponds. At 40 ft. beyond the crossing, leave the wide, grassy woods road and enter the woods on the left (sign). Follow the brook uphill, eventually crossing it on a mossy footbridge. The trail emerges at an overflow parking spot on Mountain Rd. at 0.4 mi. Turn right and walk up Mountain Rd. Pass the upper trailhead parking area on the left and, just beyond, duck into the woods on the right. A kiosk is ahead.

On Notch Ponds Trail, cross a footbridge over Notch Ponds Brook and follow the course of the brook eastward. Well beyond, the trail climbs a short, moderate pitch and soon reaches a jct. at 1.2 mi. Straight ahead, a spur leads 200 ft. to a campsite at Little Notch Pond. Turn left here and cross a bridge over the outlet brook. The trail follows an undulating route across a slope on the north side of the pond to reach a jct. at 1.5 mi. To the right, a spur leads 0.15 mi. to several campsites on Big Notch Pond.

From the jct., Notch Ponds Trail rises steadily and then steeply to a saddle high on the western ridgeline of Little Moose Mtn. It follows the rugged heights across and then down to a notch south of Big Moose Pond. Notch Ponds Trail then climbs steeply out to end at the jct. with Loop Trail at 3.4 mi.

LITTLE MOOSE MTN. TRAIL
(AMC LITTLE MOOSE PUBLIC LAND MAP)
From trailhead parking near ME 6/15 (1,100 ft.) to:

Loop Trail near Little Moose Pond (1,620 ft.)	2.4 mi.	950 ft.	1:55

SEC 2

MBPL The route starts at the northeastern base of Little Moose Mtn. and traverses a portion of the ridge to connect with Loop Trail near Little Moose Pond. From the blinking traffic light in the center of Greenville, drive north on ME 6/15 for 2.0 mi. Turn left (sign) and follow a gravel drive for 0.3 mi. to the trailhead parking lot at the end of the road.

Little Moose Mtn. briefly follows the old roadbed (the former ME 15) for 200 ft., then turns left onto a foot trail, which soon reaches a vista and picnic table. The old trail from Moose Mountain Inn on ME 15 enters here. From this point, Little Moose Mtn. Trail ascends moderately to the southwest along the ridgeline of Little Moose Mtn. Frequent outlooks provide views eastward to Borestone Mtn., the peaks of the Barren–Chairback Range, and Baker Mtn. to the north across Moosehead Lake, as well as wide views of Big Spencer Mtn., Little Spencer Mtn., and Mt. Kineo. Crest the eastern ridge of Little Moose Mtn. and then descend steeply to Papoose Pond, where Big Moose Mtn. can be seen rising impressively in the distance. At 2.4 mi., reach the jct. with Loop Trail. To the right via Loop Trail, it is 1.5 mi. to the Mountain Rd. trailhead past Little Moose Pond and Big Moose Pond. To the left, Notch Ponds Trail leads over the west ridge of Little Moose Mtn. to Big Notch Pond and Little Notch Pond and on the lower Notch Ponds trailhead on Mountain Rd. in 3.4 mi.

EAGLE ROCK (2,378 FT.)

The long ridgeline of Big Moose Mtn. extends northwest several miles toward Indian Pond and the Kennebec River, where it culminates at a large, bald outcropping known as Eagle Rock, which offers a spectacular 360-degree vista. To the north, across the length and breadth of Moosehead Lake, are the peaks of Mt. Kineo, Little Kineo Mtn., Big Spencer Mtn., Little Spencer Mtn., Number Four Mtn., Lily Bay Mtn., and Baker Mtn. The sights range as far as Katahdin and the jumbled peaks of BSP, a distance of more than 50 mi. as the crow flies. To the west are the rugged and remote mountains reaching to Jackman and the Canadian border. To the south are the summits of the Bigelow Range and the many peaks and ridges along the AT corridor. The mass of Big Moose Mtn. dominates to the east.

A portion of Eagle Rock lies within the Moosehead Region Conservation Easement. In 2015, MBPL completed Eagle Rock Trail to the peak from the south in Little Moose PL. An informal trail, referred to as Old Eagle Rock Trail, reaches Eagle Rock from the north.

EAGLE ROCK TRAIL (AMC LITTLE MOOSE PUBLIC LAND MAP, MBPL LITTLE MOOSE PUBLIC LAND, GAZETTEER MAP 40)
Cumulative from Moore Bog Rd. (1,778 ft.) to:

SEC 2

Raven Ledge (2,460 ft.)	2.5 mi.	925 ft.	1:45
Eagle Rock (2,378 ft.)	3.7 mi.	1,246 ft.	2:25

MBPL To reach the southern trailhead for Eagle Rock, follow the driving directions for Big Moose Mtn. From the Big Moose Mtn. trailhead, continue west on North Rd. for 0.2 mi. to a fork. To the left, Mountain Rd. continues to trailheads for Big Moose Pond and the two Notch ponds. Proceed straight (right) on Moore Bog Rd. and drive 1.4 mi. to the end of the road (boulders and ditch) and trailhead parking on the right.

Eagle Rock Trail starts from the rear of the lot and heads east at first, following blue blazes. In 0.25 mi., it crosses an old gravel logging road and then runs along a contour. Cross a small brook at 0.45 mi. and begin to climb out of the ravine along the brook's route. Above, cross the brook again, go up a rock staircase, cross the brook one more time, and climb to the northwest. Hike around a knob and then trend gradually down across a steep slope to reach the floor of a saddle. Climb up and around the next knob on a path that is moderate to steep. At 2.5 mi., a side trail on the left leads 0.1 mi. to a fine lookout at Raven Ledge.

From the side trail jct., descend to a saddle and wind around the south side of the next knob to another saddle. Climb a moderate grade to a crest and drop down over the next knob to a saddle at 3.5 mi. A small notch at 3.6 mi. marks the end of the official MBPL trail at the unmarked boundary of the conservation easement. Old Eagle Rock Trail from the north side enters here; follow it left for a steep climb up the final slabs to the airy and spectacular pinnacle of Eagle Rock at 3.7 mi. with far-reaching views in every direction.

OLD EAGLE ROCK TRAIL (USGS INDIAN POND NORTH QUAD, GAZETTEER MAP 40)
From Burnham Pond Rd. (1,063 ft.) to:

Eagle Rock (2,378 ft.)	1.3 mi.	1,315 ft.	1:20

NFTM From the blinking traffic light in the center of Greenville, drive north on ME 6/15 for 8.5 mi. Turn left (west) on Burnham Pond Rd. and go 3.7 mi. to a fork. Bear left at the fork and drive 1.2 mi. to the trailhead on the left (marked by pink flagging and a handmade sign). Park just ahead along the road on the right.

The trail proceeds east for a distance at an easy grade before starting to climb in switchbacks. This is a well-used and well-marked path but has occasional blowdowns. A wooden ladder and a rope aid in scrambling up a steep section. After leveling off for a time, the trail ascends steeply again, dips briefly, and then gains the huge open ledge at Eagle Rock with its panoramic views. Just before the final steep slabs to the pinnacle of Eagle Rock, Eagle Rock Trail enters from the left.

MT. KINEO STATE PARK

Mt. Kineo rises dramatically from a peninsula jutting from the eastern shore of Moosehead Lake in Kineo Township, just north of Rockwood. The sheer 700-ft. southeastern face of this iconic mountain is visible from points throughout the region. In 1990, the state of Maine purchased 800 acres from the cliff face north to form Mt. Kineo State Park (the remainder

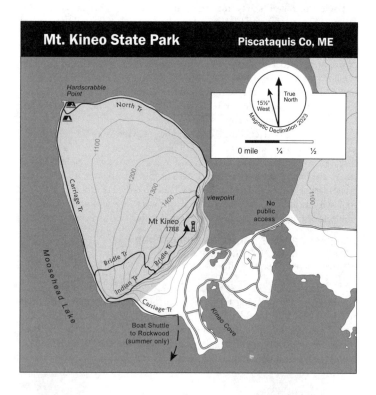

of the peninsula is privately owned). Hikers to the summit ridge and fire tower are rewarded with remarkable views of the remote and beautiful woods and mountains around Moosehead Lake and far beyond. No road offers access to Mt. Kineo. The most convenient—and scenic—way to reach it is by ferry from Rockwood.

MT. KINEO (1,788 FT.)

Carriage Trail, North Trail, Bridle Trail, and Indian Trail can be used to climb Mt. Kineo and to form loop hikes of varying lengths.

From the blinking yellow traffic light in the center of Greenville, travel north on ME 6/15 for 19.0 mi. to the village of Rockwood. Turn right onto Village Rd., which is marked with signs for Rockwood Public Landing. In 0.3 mi., turn right onto Kineo Dock Rd. and then left into the parking area. From the landing, it is about a 10-min. boat ride to the base of Mt. Kineo. The Kineo Shuttle is the sole provider of ferry services to Mt. Kineo for hikers, sightseers, and golfers. The shuttle operates from late May through early October. A per-person fee for the round trip is cash only and paid on the boat to the captain. From Memorial Day weekend through June, the shuttle leaves Rockwood at 9 A.M., 11 A.M., 1 P.M., and 3 P.M.; in July and August, the shuttle runs hourly from 8 A.M. to 6 P.M.; in September and October (through Indigenous Peoples' Day), it runs hourly from 9 A.M. to 4 P.M. Call the Mt. Kineo Golf Course at 207-534-9012 for the latest information on rates and schedules.

CARRIAGE TRAIL (AMC MT. KINEO MAP)
Cumulative from Kineo public boat landing (1,029 ft.) to:

Indian Trail (1,029 ft.)	0.6 mi.	0 ft.	0:20
Bridle Trail (1,029 ft.)	0.8 mi.	0 ft.	0:25
North Trail (1,029 ft.)	2.0 mi.	0 ft.	1:00
Hardscrabble Point (1,029 ft.)	2.1 mi.	0 ft.	1:05

MBPL From the dock and bench, turn left and proceed 100 ft. to the kiosk (day-use fee). To the right is Mt. Kineo Golf Course and its clubhouse, where sandwiches, snacks, and beverages are available to the public. Follow Carriage Trail north along the shore of Moosehead Lake, with great views of the Kineo cliff face. Pass a talus slope with views across the lake to Rockwood, the Moose River, Misery Ridge, and Big Moose Mtn. At the base of the cliff, the path narrows and reaches the jct. with Indian Trail at 0.6 mi. Just ahead, Carriage Trail passes a burned cabin on the right and a dock on the left. The trail continues easily along the west shore of the Mt. Kineo peninsula to a jct. with North Trail on the right at 1.8 mi. Carriage

Trail continues ahead another 0.1 mi. to its end at Hardscrabble Point, which has a gravel beach and picnic tables. Two designated campsites (picnic table, fire ring, privy) are near the North Trail jct. and two more designated campsites are at Hardscrabble Point.

SEC 2

INDIAN TRAIL (AMC MT. KINEO MAP)
Cumulative from Kineo public boat landing (1,029 ft.) to:

Indian Trail (1,029 ft.) via Carriage Trail	0.6 mi.	0 ft.	0:20
Bridle Trail, upper jct. (1,670 ft.)	1.1 mi.	641 ft.	0:50
Mt. Kineo summit (1,788 ft.) via Bridle Trail	1.5 mi.	818 ft.	1:10

MBPL Indian Trail is the shortest route to the summit and its observation tower and provides the most views. Indian Trail diverges right from Carriage Trail at 0.6 mi. from the public boat landing. A steep scramble over rocks and roots leads to ledges with vistas to the southeast and southwest. After a level stretch and another outlook, the trail turns left and climbs through the woods on the margin of the cliff face. The views over the golf course below and to the lake and the mountains beyond get bigger and better the higher you climb. Indian Trail ends at the jct. with Bridle Trail at 0.5 mi. Continue northeast on Bridle Trail to reach the top of the mountain and the observation tower, a former fire tower (erected in 1917).

BRIDLE TRAIL (AMC MT. KINEO MAP)
Cumulative from Kineo public boat landing (1,029 ft.) to:

Indian Trail, lower jct. (1,029 ft.)	0.6 mi.	0 ft.	0:20
Start of Bridle Trail (1,029 ft.)	0.8 mi.	0 ft.	0:25
Indian Trail, upper jct. (1,680 ft.)	1.5 mi.	641 ft.	1:05
Mt. Kineo summit (1,788 ft.) via Bridle Trail	1.9 mi.	818 ft.	1:30

MBPL Bridle Trail is the original fire warden's trail to the summit. It begins 0.2 mi. north of Indian Trail, or 0.8 mi. along Carriage Trail from the public boat landing. Bridle Trail is slightly longer than Indian Trail and has fewer views, but it does offer more moderate grades. Bridle Trail follows a wide, rocky, and eroded track at first before making a moderate climb and then easing off to meet Indian Trail. Here is an expansive view over Mt. Kineo Golf Course and Kineo House, and far across Moosehead Lake to Lily Bay Mtn., Number Four Mtn., Baker Mtn., and many other peaks. Bridle Trail continues northeast up the mountain, crests a knob, and makes a short, steep drop. It continues to the tower on the wooded summit, which is 1.9 mi. from the landing. Climb the tower for an outstanding scenic panorama, one of the finest in Maine.

NORTH TRAIL (AMC MT. KINEO MAP)
From Mt. Kineo summit (1,788 ft.) to:

Carriage Trail near Hardscrabble Point (1,029 ft.)	2.0 mi.	50 ft.	1:00

MBPL North Trail connects the summit of Mt. Kineo with Hardscrabble Point at the northwest corner of the Mt. Kineo peninsula. From the summit observation tower, North Trail descends the north side of the mountain, following a narrow corridor through the spruce woods. The going is steep at first, levels off, and then drops steeply again. After a short side trail to a viewpoint on the right, the trail descends very steeply. It levels off on a shelf and continues down at a more moderate grade until it reaches the shore of Moosehead Lake at 0.7 mi. Shaw Mtn. is visible across the lake. Rough and wet in spots, North Trail heads northwest along a steep slope above the lake. It bears away from the lake at 1.8 mi. and soon bears sharply right (old trail to left). North Trail ends at the jct. with Carriage Trail at 2.0 mi., 0.1 mi. south of Hardscrabble Point and 2.0 mi. north of the public boat landing via Carriage Trail.

EAST OF MOOSEHEAD LAKE
BURNT JACKET MTN. (1,691 FT.)
This little mountain in Beaver Cove rises in the center of a peninsula on the southeastern side of Moosehead Lake, on private land amid a development named Burnt Jacket, which is owned by McPherson Timberlands. Hikers have access to Burnt Jacket Mtn. between June 1 and October 31. Three color-coded trails ascend the south and west slopes of the mountain.

From the blinking traffic light in the center of Greenville on ME 6/15, drive north on Lily Bay Rd. for 5.6 mi. Turn left on Burnt Jacket Rd. and proceed west on a good gravel road (passing Otter Slide Ln. and Pine Marten Run on the right). At 1.8 mi. from Lily Bay Rd., turn left on a lesser gravel road (small sign for Burnt Jacket Mtn. Trail). At the next sign in another 0.2 mi., turn right and drive 0.3 mi. to a gravel pit (this steep, rough stretch may not be suitable for passenger cars). Proceed past the pit to a parking area (watch for the sign) in the grassy meadow.

BURNT JACKET MTN. (RED) TRAIL
(USGS LILY BAY QUAD, GAZETTEER MAP 41)
From grassy meadow parking (1,240 ft.) to:

Burnt Jacket Mtn. summit (1,691 ft.)	0.7 mi.	451 ft.	0:35

TMNK From the parking sign in the gravel pit, walk past the next trail sign and follow the continuation of the old and narrow woods road. The road leads along the base of the mountain, and in 0.15 mi., look for the start of

SEC 2

Burnt Jacket Mtn. Trail on the right. Leave the road and enter the woods (there is a sign just into the woods nailed to a spruce tree). Burnt Jacket Mtn. Trail (also referred to as Red Trail) is somewhat overgrown for much of its lower section but is well marked with red paint splotches, and the treadway is well defined. After traversing several small clearings (old skidder trails), the trail climbs a moderate pitch, levels off, and parallels an old, grassy skidder trail. Reenter the woods at a large sugar maple with a red paint dot on it. Ascend easily to an obvious rectangular rock in the path; at the rock, bear right and up, again paralleling the old skidder trail. At 0.65 mi., Blue Trail enters from the left and coincides with Burnt Jacket Mtn. Trail. In another 100 ft., the combined Burnt Jacket Mtn. and Blue trails merge with Green Trail, which leads to the ledges and cairn on top of the mountain. A plastic jar in the cairn contains a hiker logbook. Views are limited but worth seeing, especially from the ledges just below the top. Moosehead Lake, Big Moose Mtn., Little Moose Mtn., and even the cliff face of Mt. Kineo are all part of the scene.

GREEN TRAIL (USGS LILY BAY QUAD, GAZETTEER MAP 41)
From Allagash Rd. (1,200 ft.) to:

Burnt Jacket Mtn. summit (1,691 ft.)	0.6 mi.	491 ft.	0:35

TMNK Green Trail ascends Burnt Jacket Mtn. from the southwest. From Burnt Jacket Rd. at the turnoff to the Burnt Jacket Mtn. Trail trailhead, continue west on Burnt Jacket Rd. At a fork in 1.7 mi., bear left and up on Allagash Rd. Just 0.3 mi. beyond, at the crest of the hill, reach a small parking turnout on the left at the start of Green Trail (green blazes). A faded color-coded trail map is posted here.

Green Trail enters the woods just left of the power pole and rises to reach a large ledge and a view of Moosehead Lake. Climb past a boulder, making sure to look behind to see Big Moose Mtn. Just above, look for round, white plastic trail markers on the right. Follow these down the slope to the right and then resume climbing. Ascend steadily on the well-defined treadway. After the angle eases, enter an open meadow-like area and turn sharply right (cairn and blazes on the rock). Proceed easily and then bear right along the base of lichen-covered ledges. After a sharp left, switchback up through the conifers to reach the small summit sign on the left nailed to a thin spruce. A narrow, cleared corridor yields a view of the cliffs on Mt. Kineo. A few steps ahead, arrive at the ledges on the mostly wooded summit.

BLUE TRAIL (USGS LILY BAY QUAD, GAZETTEER MAP 41)
From Burnt Jacket Mtn. summit (1,691 ft.) to:

Allagash Rd. (1,199 ft.)	0.4 mi.	−492 ft.	0:15

TMNK No parking is available at the base of Blue Trail on Allagash Rd., so this trail is best used to make a loop hike along with Burnt Jacket Mtn. (Red) Trail or Green Trail. From the summit of Burnt Jacket Mtn., walk east on Green Trail for 100 ft. and then continue on the coinciding Burnt Jacket Mtn. Trail and Blue Trail. In another 100 ft., turn right and down on Blue Trail (blue blazes). Descend steadily to reach Allagash Rd. To the right, it is 0.3 mi. to the start of Green Trail; to the left, it is 0.4 mi. to the start of Burnt Jacket Mtn. Trail and 0.55 mi. to that trail's gravel pit parking area.

SEC 2

ELEPHANT MTN. (2,644 FT.)

Unlike other mountains of the same name in Maine, this Elephant Mtn. actually does resemble an elephant's head, minus the tusks. The sloping southern face and the small ledge that appears as an eye are recognizable from many surrounding peaks. Although no foot trail reaches its summit, a short trail on its lower western slope leads hikers to the crash site of a B-52 bomber. On January 24, 1963, a US Air Force Stratofortress bomber ran into severe turbulence and mechanical problems and crashed into the mountainside in subzero temperatures and blizzard conditions. Of the nine crew members, only the pilot and the navigator survived.

The site is maintained by Weyerhaeuser, Moosehead Riders Snowmobile Club, Maine Civil Air Patrol, and Moosehead ATV Riders.

From the blinking traffic light in the center of Greenville on ME 6/15, drive north on Lily Bay Rd. for 7.0 mi. Turn right (east) onto Prong Pond Rd. At 10.7 mi., bear left at a fork. At 12.4 mi., cross a wooden bridge and then take the next left at 12.5 mi. Continue to the parking area and trailhead at 14.3 mi.

B-52 MEMORIAL CRASH SITE TRAIL
(USGS NUMBER FOUR MTN. QUAD, GAZETTEER MAP 41)
From trailhead parking (1,670 ft.) to:

Memorial site (1,770 ft.)	0.25 mi.	100 ft.	0:10

PC, MRSC, MCAP, MATVR The trail begins opposite the parking area. The walk to the crash site is an easy 0.25 mi. Pieces of the wreckage line both sides of the route, which culminates at an information kiosk and a large slate memorial leaning against a big section of the cabin of the downed plane. Visitors have left a variety of flags and wreaths over time. It is a moving experience and a different kind of hike.

BLUE RIDGE (2,356 FT.)

This mountain ridgeline, between Greenville and AMC's MWI Recreation and Conservation Area, extends about 5 mi. in an east–west direction.

Two small ponds, Cranberry and Notch, are on the ridge; Rum Pond is at its western base and Hedgehog Pond near its eastern edge.

Blue Ridge is the focus of recent trail-building efforts by MBPL using Maine Conservation Corps trail crews to construct the roughly 9-mi. Blue Ridge Trail system between Rum Pond and AMC's property line northeast of Hedgehog Pond. AMC trail crews have been working in concert with MBPL on this effort to connect the trail with AMC's existing trail system west of Indian Mtn. MBPL has recently completed a trail connection between Rum Pond and the AT on the west end of Barren Mtn.; the Headwaters Trail and the Vaughan Stream Trail. These projects are all part of the Moosehead Lake Region Concept Plan, a cooperative initiative to expand local backcountry multiuse recreation opportunities for hikers, backpackers, trail runners, and mountain bikers. Check with MBPL for updated information and trail maps pertaining to these new trail projects.

RUM–CRANBERRY LOOP (MAP 2: F1–F2)
Cumulative from Rum Pond parking area (1,310 ft.) to:

High point on Blue Ridge (1,720 ft.)	1.4 mi.	487 ft.	1:00
Cranberry Pond (1,596 ft.)	1.9 mi.	487 ft.	1:15
Complete loop	3.4 mi.	487 ft.	2:00

MBPL The Blue Ridge Trail system is a work in progress, but a short hiking circuit at the west end of the ridge—the Rum–Cranberry Loop—is open to the public. This trip uses a portion of two trails: Blue Ridge Trail and Rum Brook Trail.

From the blinking yellow light in downtown Greenville, drive north on Lily Bay Rd. for 100 ft. and then turn right onto Pleasant St. and drive east. Pleasant St. becomes East Rd. as it heads to Greenville Municipal Airport. Continue past the airport as the road becomes gravel surfaced. At 3.7 mi., after the road crosses Wilson Stream, it becomes KI Rd. In another 3.3 mi., turn left onto Rum Pond Rd. (sign) and continue 1.0 mi. to the trailhead parking area on the right. The start of Blue Ridge Trail is 100 ft. ahead on the road.

Walk 250 ft. to a jct. Straight ahead, the spur path leads 250 ft. to the east shore of Rum Pond. Blue Ridge Trail (blue markers) continues to the right, passes a posted trail map, reaches a grassy road, and turns left to cross a woods road bridge over Rum Brook. Turning left, reach the jct. with Rum Brook Trail (yellow markers; your return route if doing the loop), which leaves to the right. Bear left to stay on Blue Ridge Trail. Climb the hillside above Rum Pond and then descend to its north shore. Just beyond, a spur path leads to a proposed campsite. Continue ahead to cross a grassy road, pass a large mossy boulder, and climb gradually. After leveling off, pass a large rock face on the left and angle up the slope to reach the western crest of Blue Ridge at 1.4 mi. Slab down the far side to pass a view window to Little Kineo Mtn., Moosehead Lake, and Upper and Lower Wilson Pond. Cross an old logging road to reach a spur path on the left leading to a proposed campsite.

Blue Ridge Trail continues to pretty Cranberry Pond and along its south shore. Bear away from the pond and soon reach a jct. Here, Blue Ridge Trail—still incomplete—proceeds across the ridge crest for about 6 mi. to its current end at a logging road (date for completion is TBD). Hikers desiring to explore this section of Blue Ridge will have to double back as the route is not yet a thru-trail.

From the Blue Ridge Trail jct., turn right on Rum Brook Trail (yellow markers) and drop down gradually from the ridge. Level off and meet Headwaters Trail (red markers), which leaves to the left (Headwaters Trail leads 2.1 mi. to a yet-to-be-developed trailhead on KI Rd. next to Vaughn Stream). Turn right to continue on Rum Brook Trail. Over the next 1.5 mi., the trail crosses recently logged areas and woods roads that are growing back in, passes slate outcroppings, and offers a few limited views to the southwest. At 3.3 mi., join Blue Ridge Trail and turn left to return to the trailhead and complete the loop.

HEADWATERS TRAIL (MAP 2: F1)
Cumulative from Rum Pond parking area (1,310 ft.) to:

Headwaters Trail via Blue Ridge Trail and Rum Brook Trail (1,445 ft.)	0.9 mi.	135 ft.	0:30
Vaughn Stream at KI Rd. (1,200 ft.)	3.0 mi.	135 ft.	1:35

MBPL Headwaters Trail connects Rum Brook Trail to KI Rd. and Vaughn Stream Trail. Begin from the Rum Pond parking area and follow Blue Ridge Trail (blue markers). In 250 ft., reach a jct. Straight ahead, the spur path leads 250 ft. to the east shore of Rum Pond. Blue Ridge Trail continues to the right, passes a posted trail map, reaches a grassy road, and turns left to cross a woods road bridge over Rum Brook. Turn left to reach the jct. with Rum Brook Trail (yellow markers). Turn right and follow Rum Brook Trail, which ascends easily to the start of Headwaters Trail on the right.

Headwaters Trail descends to cross a brook and then skirts a boggy area before reaching the valley of Vaughn Stream. Following a contour for much of its length, Headwaters Trail ends at KI Rd. where the road crosses Vaughn Stream.

VAUGHN STREAM TRAIL (MAP 2: F1—G1)
Cumulative from KI Rd. (1,200 ft.) to:

Barren Mtn. Rd. (1,000 ft.)	1.6 mi.	–200 ft.	0:50
AT near Wilbur Brook (650 ft.)	3.7 mi.	–550 ft.	1:50

MBPL This trail connects KI Rd. to the AT near Wilbur Brook at a point 0.7 mi. west of Long Pond Stream. As its name implies, the trail follows Vaughn Stream for most of its distance. From KI Rd., Vaughan Stream Trail descends gradually along the east side of the stream. At Barren Mtn. Rd., turn right to cross a bridge over the stream, and then turn left to continue south along the west side of the tumbling waters. At about 3.2 mi. into the hike, the trail leaves the stream and bears west to reach an old woods road. From this unmarked jct., turn left and proceed about 100 yd. to the white-blazed AT. If desired, turn right on the AT and walk 0.7 mi. to reach the old tote road at the end of the Greenville approach to the AT on Barren Mtn. (see p. 100). Long Pond Stream is just beyond. To return to KI Rd., retrace your steps on Vaughn Stream Trail.

NUMBER FOUR MTN. (2,893 FT.)

Rising south of First Roach Pond in Frenchtown Township, Number Four Mtn. offers excellent views from the open ledges and the abandoned fire tower on its summit. The route to the top of the mountain is part of an ambitious trail-building effort undertaken by MBPL through the Moosehead Lake Region Concept Plan, on lands owned by Weyerhaeuser that are under the Moosehead Region Conservation Easement.

From the blinking traffic light in the center of Greenville on ME 6/15, drive north on Lily Bay Rd. for 17.6 mi. to Frenchtown Rd. (*Note*: At 13.4 mi. from Greenville, blue-and-white directional signs for Number Four Mtn. tell you to turn right onto the unsigned Meadow Brook Rd. and take that to the Number Four Mtn. trailhead. As of 2022, Meadow Brook Rd. was not friendly to passenger cars, so this road should be avoided.) Turn right onto Frenchtown Rd. and follow it for 2.2 mi. Turn right onto Lagoon Brook Rd., proceed 1.3 mi., and turn left onto Meadow Brook Rd. Follow this road south for 0.9 mi. to the signed trailhead on the left. The road passes over Lagoon Brook about 500 ft. before reaching the trailhead. Ample parking is available along the road.

NUMBER FOUR MTN. TRAIL (MAP 2: D1)
From Meadow Brook Rd. (1,420 ft.) to:

Number Four Mtn. summit (2,893 ft.)	1.8 mi.	1,473 ft.	1:40

MBPL The start of the blue-blazed trail is an old woods road. In 0.25 mi., bear right onto a footpath. Just ahead on the right are cabin ruins. Beyond, the trail picks up the route of another old road and climbs gently. For the next 0.5 mi., the hike alternates between sections of old and eroded trail and switchbacks on a recently built treadway. The steady grade turns from moderate to steep as the path follows an old fire warden's trail. Rock steps, log steps, and more switchbacks aid in the ascent. At 1.6 mi., the angle decreases, and the going is easier on the narrowing ridgeline. At 1.8 mi., look for a viewpoint 50 ft. to the left. After a level stretch, a quick climb leads to the old fire tower (built in 1925), which no longer has a cab. The trail continues north a short distance to a lookout and bench, where the sights include Baker Mtn., Lily Bay Mtn., Big Moose Mtn., Little Moose Mtn., Moosehead Lake, Columbus Mtn., Chairback Mtn., and the White Cap Range. The new Baker Mtn. Trail proceeds south from this point (see Baker Mtn. Trail below).

BAKER MTN. (3,528 FT.)

This high and wild peak on the eastern side of the town of Beaver Cove is south of Number Four Mtn. and southeast of Lily Bay Mtn. In 2015, AMC purchased 4,311 acres on Baker Mtn., which was surrounded by conservation lands but was unprotected until AMC's ownership. A new trail from the summit of Number Four Mtn., constructed by crews from the Maine Conservation Corps and AMC, now extends south to the summit of Baker Mtn. AMC plans to connect the trail to its existing system farther south.

BAKER MTN. TRAIL (MAP 2: D1–E1)
Cumulative from Number Four Mtn. summit (2,894 ft.) to:

Snowmobile trail and planned campsite (2,710 ft.)	2.3 mi.	265 ft.	1:15
Baker Mtn. summit (3,528 ft.)	4.6 mi.	1,222 ft.	2:55

AMC, MBPL Heading southwest from the top of Number Four Mtn., Baker Mtn. Trail winds along a mildly undulating ridge through fairly open forest, eventually entering thicker spruce and fir stands near the notch where the ridges of Number Four Mtn., Baker Mtn., and adjacent Lily Bay Mtn. come together. At this point, about 2.3 mi. from the Number Four summit area, the route crosses a snowmobile trail before beginning the moderate climb up Baker Mtn. After a modest ascent, the trail reaches a small false summit before dropping back down. It then slowly rises on its way toward the true summit of Baker Mtn. Nearer the summit, open stands with low regrowth provide attractive views of the mountains and lakes ranging from Katahdin all the way to Moosehead Lake. From the snowmobile trail crossing to the summit area on Baker Mtn. is about 2.3 mi. (*Note*: A designated campsite is planned for a location north of the snowmobile trail crossing, but until that time, no camping is allowed on Baker Mtn. Trail.)

LITTLE SPENCER MTN. (3,064 FT.)

The elongated mass of Little Spencer Mtn. in East Middlesex Canal Township, with its steep flanks and rock faces, is a distinctive landmark in the Moosehead Lake region. The Little Spencer summit and the open ledges on its upper south face offer outstanding views.

From the blinking traffic light in the center of Greenville on ME 6/15, drive north on Lily Bay Rd. for 18.8 mi. to the village of Kokadjo and Kokadjo Trading Post at the west end of First Roach Pond. Reset trip mileage. At 0.3 mi. beyond Kokadjo, the pavement ends at a fork. Bear left to continue on Greenville Rd. At 1.5 mi., turn left on Spencer Bay Rd. Follow it for another 7.4 mi. to an offset 4-way intersection. Turn right here (sign for Spencer Pond Camps) and drive another 2.2 mi. to the trailhead on the right (marked by a small cairn and blue flagging on a stick). Parking is on either side of the road.

THE RAM TRAIL (USGS LOBSTER MTN. QUAD, GAZETTEER MAP 49)
From Spencer Bay Rd. trailhead (1,184 ft.) to:

Fixed ropes and narrow chimney (2,100 ft.)	0.6 mi.	916 ft.	0:45
Little Spencer Mtn., west summit (3,064 ft.)	1.1 mi.	1,880 ft.	1:30

NFTM A short distance into the woods is a commemorative plaque for "The RAM Trail." This is in honor of Richard Manson, who in the 1960s explored various routes to the summit from Spencer Pond Camps. The well-trodden trail is marked with flagging tape and sporadic old blazes. (Occasional trail maintenance [although not of the ropes above!] is done by the proprietors of Spencer Pond Camps.) The Ram Trail rises gently for 0.3 mi. and then ascends steeply, at first on a rising contour to the left and then straight up. Traverse a boulder slide at 0.5 mi. and then angle up the mountainside on rocky terrain. A few cairns mark the route. The next semi-open slide offers a view south over Spencer Pond to Mt. Kineo in Moosehead Lake. Cross the slide, continue to angle up the slope, and cross the next slide (be alert for markers, as the path can be difficult to follow). Climb through rocks and around trees to the next slide of smaller rocks. Here, turn sharply left and ascend at a moderate-to-steep grade. At the next scree field, go left and up again. Reach a fixed rope line in a gully at 0.6 mi. Climb the gully to reach the next fixed rope line at the base of a steep, narrow chimney. Negotiate the strenuous passage up through the slot, and where the rope line ends, scramble out of the chimney to a lookout on a large, open talus slope.

**SEC
2**

(*Caution*: Any fixed ropes found in the chimney for assistance have been placed there by anonymous members of the public. The reliability of these ropes cannot be guaranteed, so use at your own risk. Further, due to the difficulty of the chimney, this hike may not be a wise choice when the rocks are wet, or at any time with young children or dogs.)

From the lookout at the top of the chimney, the grand vista takes in Big Moose Mtn., Coburn Mtn., Mt. Kineo, Little Kineo Mtn., Boundary Bald Mtn., and much more. Climb to the left into the woods and proceed steeply up through the rocks and ledges. At 0.8 mi., out on the edge of the rock face, scramble on rocks and roots over the steep, angled slope to reach the top of the south face of the mountain. Leave the face and hike through thick conifers at an easy angle. More moderate scrambling over rocks and through thick woods leads to a spur path on the right and another panoramic vista. Beyond the spur path jct. is the summit cairn, and 50 ft. beyond that is a fine view to the north. The breathtaking sights include Katahdin, Big Spencer Mtn., Lobster Mtn., Lobster Lake, Moosehead Lake, Lily Bay Mtn., Number Four Mtn., First Roach Pond, White Cap Mtn., Big Moose Mtn., and much more of the impressive North Maine Woods landscape.

LITTLE KINEO MTN. (1,934 FT.)

Rising prominently east of North Bay on Moosehead Lake and northeast of Mt. Kineo, Little Kineo Mtn., in Days Academy Grant Township, is part of Days Academy PL. The mountain is remote and takes some work to get to but rewards hikers with lovely views from its summit ledges.

From the blinking traffic light in the center of Greenville on ME 6/15, drive north on Lily Bay Rd. for 18.8 mi. to the village of Kokadjo and Kokadjo Trading Post at the west end of First Roach Pond. Reset trip mileage. At 0.3 mi. beyond Kokadjo, the pavement ends at a fork. Bear left to continue on Greenville Rd. At 1.5 mi., turn left on Spencer Bay Rd. Reset trip mileage.

In 7.4 mi., reach an offset 4-way intersection. On the right is the road to Spencer Pond Camps; continue straight through this jct. At a fork, proceed straight (left leads to Spencer Bay). At 8.6 mi., cross a bridge over the outlet of Spencer Pond at Spencer Pond Dam. Immediately after a small pond on the right at 10.5 mi., bear right at a fork. Cross a short bridge over Lucky

Brook at 12.4 mi. Just after the mile 14 marker at 14.1 mi., cross a short bridge over Cowan Brook. At 14.2 mi., reach a T intersection.

At the T intersection, turn left toward Cowan Cove and Kelly Wharf CS. At 15.0 mi., cross a short bridge over Cowan Brook. Avoid the road to the left at 15.3 mi. Reach a jct. at 15.7 mi.; here, turn sharply right toward Little Kineo Mtn. and Kelly Wharf (left goes to Cowan Cove). At a T jct. at 17.0 mi., turn left toward Kelly Wharf and Little Kineo Mtn. (signs). At 18.0 mi., arrive at trailhead parking on the right for Little Kineo Mtn.

LITTLE KINEO MTN. TRAIL (USGS MT. KINEO QUAD, MTF LITTLE KINEO MAP, MBPL MOOSEHEAD SHORELINE PUBLIC LANDS MAP, GAZETTEER MAP 41)
From trailhead parking (1,420 ft.) to:

Little Kineo Mtn. summit (1,934 ft.)	0.7 mi.	514 ft.	0:35
Trail's end (1,880 ft.)	1.0 mi.	564 ft.	0:50

MBPL Blue-blazed Little Kineo Mtn. Trail leaves the north side of the road and proceeds easily through a low area of mixed woods. In 0.2 mi., begin climbing steeply. Pass between a spruce tree and a rock, and then switchback right. Moderate climbing gains the ridge, where the trail contours right and up along the base of some rocks. Scramble up natural rock steps and ledges to an open view to the southwest that reveals Mt. Kineo, Boundary Bald Mtn., Coburn Mtn., and the Bigelow Range. Continuing the rocky ascent, pass a series of cairns in the semi-open woods of spruce and fir. Reach the summit, a yellow-hued, rocky knob topped with a large cairn on the right (no views).

Continue left toward a scenic overlook (sign). Proceed easily along the ridgetop, descend slightly, and then scramble up a rocky knob. Reach the end of the trail at a cairn with a blue X painted on top. Trees partially obscure the views, but visitors can still enjoy a 90-degree window that takes in Spencer Pond, Little Spencer Mtn., Big Spencer Mtn., Katahdin, Lobster Mtn., and Moosehead Lake.

BIG SPENCER MTN. (3,227 FT.)

Rising sharply from the countryside north of Kokadjo and First Roach Pond, Big Spencer Mtn., in the unorganized townships of T2 R13 WELS and TX R14 WELS, is a prominent landmark in the area northeast of Moosehead Lake. The remains of the 1927 fire tower sit on the northeastern end of its long summit ridge. The true summit is 0.3 mi. southwest of the tower. Panoramic views are possible from both points. The mountain lies within the 4,244-acre Big Spencer Ecological Reserve managed by MBPL.

From the blinking traffic light in the center of Greenville on ME 6/15, drive north on Lily Bay Rd. for 18.8 mi. to the village of Kokadjo and Kokadjo Trading Post at the west end of First Roach Pond. Reset trip mileage. At 0.3 mi. beyond Kokadjo, the pavement ends at a fork. Bear left to continue on Greenville Rd. At 1.5 mi., pass Spencer Bay Rd. on the left. Pass Smithtown Rd. on the right at 1.9 mi. At a fork at 4.4 mi., bear left. At 8.6 mi., cross a narrow one-lane bridge over Bear Pond Brook. In 0.1 mi., turn left onto Spencer Mtn. Rd. (sign for Big Spencer Mtn.) and proceed 6.1 mi. to the trailhead parking lot (blue sign) on the left.

**SEC
2**

BIG SPENCER MTN. TRAIL (USGS BIG SPENCER MTN. QUAD, MTF BIG SPENCER PUBLIC LANDS MAP GAZETTEER MAP 49)
From Spencer Mtn. Rd. trailhead (1,356 ft.) to:

Big Spencer Mtn. (3,210 ft.)	1.8 mi.	1,850 ft.	1:50

MBPL Pass big rocks to start south up blue-blazed Big Spencer Mtn. Trail, which is on an old tote road that rises gradually at first. In 0.5 mi., the grade turns to moderate. Cross a small brook at 0.7 mi. Beyond an eroded section of road, proceed on a contour and then cross a footbridge over a brook. Arrive at a small meadow and the site of the old fire warden's cabin at 1.0 mi., which provides a picnic table, a privy, and a wonderful view north to Katahdin and the many summits in BSP. The bulk of Big Spencer Mtn. rises precipitously south of the clearing.

Beyond the old cabin site, cross a footbridge over another brook and circle around a beaver pond. Just beyond, the trail gains more than 1,000 ft. of elevation over the final 0.7 mi. to the summit ridgeline of Big Spencer. Steep rock staircases and the first of several wooden ladders aid in the ascent at 1.25 mi. The eroded trail above is a steep scramble on rocks and roots. Scale a second wooden ladder at 1.35 mi. and a third at 1.45 mi. Climb several short rock walls, level off, and then move up to scale a fourth and a fifth ladder. Treeline is just ahead at 1.7 mi. In another 0.1 mi., reach the old fire tower base, a helipad, and a small communications building on the northernmost peak on the long Big Spencer Mtn. summit ridge. Hikers are asked to respect the privately owned communications infrastructure in view just ahead on the next summit, now the site of a large solar array and a complex of communications towers, and to conclude their hike here.

LOBSTER MTN. (2,336 FT.)
This mountain in Lobster Township rises in a long, curving ridge south of Lobster Lake and east of the northern end of Moosehead Lake. Lobster Mtn. and Lobster Lake are central features in the wildest part of the

Penobscot River Corridor, a vast assemblage of properties and easements between BSP and Seboomook Lake and Moosehead Lake, all managed by MBPL.

The trail to Lobster Mtn. can only be reached by canoe or kayak. The adventure starts at a put-in on Lobster Stream just south of the West Branch of the Penobscot River. To reach this access point requires considerable driving over active gravel logging roads, which visitors must share with heavy truck traffic (go slow and always yield). From the launch site, paddle downstream on Lobster Stream and then cross Lobster Lake to reach the trailhead. Due to the time and distances involved, this trip is best planned as an overnight journey. Numerous primitive campsites on Lobster Lake (picnic table, fire ring, privy) are available on a first-come-first-serve basis. The boat launch on Lobster Stream may be reached from the south at Greenville or from the east at Millinocket.

Directions from Greenville: Drive north on Lily Bay Rd. to Kokadjo. Continue north, and in 0.3 mi., reach a fork where the pavement ends. Bear left on Greenville Rd. and follow it to Golden Rd. at the south end of Caribou Lake, a distance of 15.0 mi. The directions from Millinocket join the route here.

Directions from Millinocket: At the jct. of ME 11 (south) and the end of ME 157 just past downtown, bear right and follow signs for BSP. The road has several names along the way, including Millinocket Lake Rd., Baxter State Park Rd., and simply Lake Rd. Drive 8.6 mi. to North Woods Trading Post and Big Moose Inn, Cabins & Campground on the right. Bear left onto the parallel Golden Rd. and drive 10.1 mi. to Abol Bridge Campground and Store on the right. Just beyond, cross Abol Bridge over the West Branch of the Penobscot River. Continue on Golden Rd. for about 19 mi. to the jct. of Greenville Rd.

Directions from the jct. of Greenville Rd. and Golden Rd. from Millinocket: Drive west on Golden Rd. for 6.0 mi. to NMW's Caribou Checkpoint, where visitors must pay day-use and camping fees (cash or check only). From the gatehouse, continue west on Golden Rd. for 9.2 mi. to an unmarked road on the left (Lobster Trip Rd.; signs for Raymond's Country Store and Northeast Carry). Turn here, and in another 3.4 mi., cross a bridge over Lobster Stream and reach the boat launch parking lot on the left (kiosk, toilet).

From the launch, paddle south on Lobster Stream for 1.8 mi. to Lobster Lake. Bear southeast across the lake to Ogden Point, a distance of 1.2 mi. Lobster Mtn. rises beyond, while the sprawling flat-topped bulk of Big Spencer Mtn. dominates to the left. Paddle east around Ogden Point and then south into Jackson Cove to the Jackson Cove campsite on the south shore, about 0.8 mi. from Ogden Point. To the left of the campsite, at a gap in the thick, shrubby shoreline growth, is a brown sign: "Lobster Mtn. 2 mi."

LOBSTER MTN. TRAIL (USGS LOBSTER MTN. QUAD, MBPL PENOBSCOT RIVER CORRIDOR & SEBOOMOOK PUBLIC LANDS MAP, GAZETTEER MAP 49)
From Jackson Cove trailhead on Lobster Lake (965 ft.) to:

Outlook at trail's end (1,982 ft.)	1.3 mi.	1,017 ft.	1:10

MBPL Blue-blazed Lobster Mtn. Trail strikes off to the south through mixed forest. A portion of the route is eroded, and there are several steep sections of rocky terrain. After leading through woods of spruce and fir, the trail ends at an overlook high on the north side of the mountain's northernmost summit, where there is a bench built by a Boy Scout troop from Connecticut. The view over Lobster Lake is lovely and well worth the significant effort.

NORTHWEST OF MOOSEHEAD LAKE
GREEN MTN. (2,397 FT.)

An old fire tower (erected in 1920, no cab) stands atop the southerly and highest summit of Green Mtn., which straddles the town lines of Hammond Township, Dole Brook Township, and Comstock Township in a remote area northwest of Seboomook Lake and Pittston Farm and northeast of Boundary Bald Mtn.

From ME 6/15, just west of the village of Rockwood, turn north on Northern Rd., immediately crossing a bridge over Moose River. Turn right after the bridge and follow Northern Rd. for 19.8 mi. to the jct. with Seboomook Rd. Bear left here, and in 0.5 mi., pass Pittston Farm and cross the South Branch of the Penobscot River to reach NMW's Twenty-Mile Checkpoint, where visitors must register and pay a day-use fee (and camping fee, if applicable) to enter (cash or check only).

From the checkpoint gate, drive 1.9 mi. to a fork. Bear left onto Cutoff Rd. (no sign) and drive 1.5 mi. to the jct. with South Branch Access Rd. Turn left and follow South Branch Access Rd. west for 2.2 mi. Turn right (north) on Old Boundary Rd. and drive 3.2 mi. (passing two campsites on the left) to a small trailhead parking area on the right. A sign nailed to a tree here reads "GREEN" in green ink.

GREEN MTN. TRAIL
(USGS FOLEY POND QUAD, GAZETTEER MAP 48)
From Old Boundary Rd. trailhead (1,769 ft.) to:

Green Mtn. summit (2,397 ft.)	1.6 mi.	628 ft.	1:15

NFTM Green Mtn. Trail starts immediately uphill on an old jeep track; it then levels off and soon reaches a small clearing, the former site of a fire warden's cabin. Proceed straight ahead through the brush to pick up the foot trail beyond, which is liberally marked with orange and pink flagging tape (and occasionally other colors). The treadway can be obscure in places, so go slow and follow the flagging closely. Ahead, the trail contours across the side of the mountain until it reaches a brook. Then it turns uphill and crosses a wooded ridge before dropping into a slight depression and then rising again across the contours. The trail climbs the mountain in steps, following a series of old logging haul roads that are now heavily grown into corridors of brush and weeds and barely recognizable as any kind of roads.

At 1.2 mi., bear sharply left and push through a short section of spruce blowdowns. Beyond, the path is again distinct. Cross a small brook and reach a small, disintegrating cabin (the old fire warden's lightning shelter) on the left at 1.5 mi. Continue an additional 0.1 mi. to the wooded summit and the tower standing in a small clearing. Climb the tower ladder to enjoy 360-degree views.

SECTION THREE

KENNEBEC AND MOOSE RIVER VALLEYS

In-Text Map
Kennebec Highlands Public Lands   156

SEC 3

INTRODUCTION

This section describes 42 trails on 25 mountains in the Kennebec River and Moose River valleys, which includes all of Kennebec County, most of Somerset County, and the town of Leeds in Androscoggin County. The region encompasses an area ranging roughly from the capital city of Augusta and neighboring Gardiner west to the lower Androscoggin River and north along the valley of the Kennebec River to the headwater of the South Branch of the Penobscot River east of the Canadian border. The region is bordered by the coastal lowlands in the south and roughly by Seboomook Lake and the Penobscot River's South Branch in the north. Along the eastern boundary with Piscataquis County are the interior hills and mountains, Moosehead Lake, and the forestland between the Allagash River and St. John River watersheds. A portion of the Penobscot and Waldo county lines form the southern part of the eastern boundary. To the west are the high peaks along the border with Quebec, Canada. From its source at Moosehead Lake, the Kennebec River flows south through the center of the region for 170 mi., emptying into the Gulf of Maine east of Popham Beach. The Moose River originates near the Canadian border and flows generally east to empty into Moosehead Lake at Rockwood.

GEOGRAPHY

In the southern reaches of the Kennebec River valley are numerous low hills, including Howard Hill (484 ft.) in Augusta not far from the Kennebec River. West of Maine's capital city is Monks Hill (680 ft.) near Shed Pond, and farther west, amid a series of large lakes, are a variety of mountains less than 1,000 ft. in elevation, from Mt. Pisgah (812 ft.) and its tall fire tower to Monument Hill (670 ft.) and its summit granite obelisk. To the north in the beautiful Belgrade Lakes area are the Kennebec

Highlands, where a small cluster of peaks dot the landscape of the 6,800-acre preserve. McGaffey Mtn. is the highest of these peaks at 1,289 ft. Nearby are Round Top Mtn. (1,137 ft.) and Sanders Hill (853 ft.). French Mtn. (745 ft.), Mt. Phillip (760 ft.), and auspiciously named The Mountain (664 ft.) are in the same neighborhood and sport loop trails. West of McGaffey Mtn. is the Pinnacle, which rises to 716 ft. in the Vienna Woods. East of Skowhegan is pretty Lake George, which has a regional park on its southern end that protects both sides of the lake, including a wooded slope known as the Pinnacle (655 ft.).

SEC
3

Farther north along the Kennebec River valley, east of Bingham, Kelly Mtn. rises to 1,676 ft. From Bingham north to The Forks, the mountains on both sides of the Kennebec River valley begin to exceed 2,000 ft. At Caratunk, the AT crosses the Kennebec River and leads to the craggy summits of Pleasant Pond Mtn. (2,477 ft.), Moxie Bald Mtn. (2,632 ft.), and Moxie Bald's North Peak (2,379 ft.). Moxie Pond sits between these peaks, and at its northwestern end is the impressive hump of Mosquito Mtn. (2,226 ft.). The wild, rocky heights of Moxie Mtn. (2,933 ft.) are also found in Caratunk southwest of Moxie Pond; miles of gravel logging roads provide access.

Northwest of the upper Kennebec River are the jumbled high peaks of the remote border region, many of which are more than 3,500 ft. in elevation. Lengthy travel over sometimes rough gravel roads is often required to reach these trailheads. Coburn Mtn., southwest of Parlin Pond, is the highest at 3,720 ft. Boundary Bald Mtn., near the Canadian border, reaches 3,641 ft. In the wildlands of the Moose River valley west of Jackman are Sally Mtn. (2,227 ft.) and multisummited Burnt Jacket Mtn. (its easternmost peak is 2,113 ft.). Number Five Mtn. tops out at 3,183 ft. The ridgeline of Williams Mtn. (2,409 ft.) is east of US 201 and south of Long Pond and the Moose River.

The AT traverses this section, extending roughly 42 mi. from Flagstaff Lake at the foot of the Bigelow Range north to Bald Mtn. Pond just beyond Moxie Bald Mtn.

ROAD ACCESS

US 201 bisects the Kennebec River and Moose River valleys south to north, from Gardiner to Sandy Bay Township on the Canadian border; this highway is the primary travel route through the Kennebec River valley. US 202/ME 11/ME 100 provide access to trails between Newport, Skowhegan, and New Sharon; ME 17 offers access between Augusta and

Readfield. ME 6/15 heads east from Jackman and follows the Moose River to Moosehead Lake at Rockwood. ME 27 leads to the heart of the Kennebec Highlands in the Belgrade Lakes region. Significant travel on gravel logging roads is required to reach some of the more remote trailheads.

CAMPING

Thirteen lean-tos and campsites along the AT in this region are available for trailside camping. No state parks or public lands are available for either remote or drive-in camping. At least 13 privately operated campgrounds, as well as some run by whitewater rafting outfitters along the Kennebec River from Bingham to West Forks, offer a variety of camping and lodging choices with amenities.

SEC 3

SUGGESTED HIKES

■ Easy

MT. PHILLIP

LP via Mt. Phillip Trail	1.4 mi.	364 ft.	0:55

Admire views over Great Pond and the Kennebec Highlands to the west on this pleasant loop hike. See Mt. Phillip Trail, p. 159.

HOWARD HILL

LP via Howard Hill Trails	2.6 mi.	374 ft.	1:40

Enjoy sights of the Maine State House, the capital city of Augusta, and the Kennebec River valley on this in-town loop hike. See Howard Hill Trails, p. 162.

MT. PISGAH

LP via Tower Trail and Blueberry Trail	2.4 mi.	537 ft.	1:30

Combine these trails for a wonderful loop that leads over Mt. Pisgah, which is topped by a 60-ft. fire tower that offers outstanding panoramic views. To begin, see Tower Trail, p. 164.

MONUMENT HILL

LP via Red Trail and Orange Trail   1.0 mi.   230 ft.   0:35

A fun circuit to a Civil War monument and ledges offers pleasant views of the hills and farmlands of the Androscoggin River valley to the west. To begin, see Red Trail, p. 166.

SEC 3

■ Moderate
ROUND TOP MTN.

LP via Round Top Trail, Round Top Spur Trail, and Kennebec Highlands Trail   4.5 mi.   775 ft.   2:40

Follow this route for attractive views of the Kennebec Highlands and the beautiful Belgrade Lakes region. To begin, see Round Top Trail, p. 155.

MOSQUITO MTN.

RT via Mosquito Mtn. Trail   3.0 mi.   1,242 ft.   2:10

Enjoy panoramic vistas from the summit ledges of Mosquito Mtn., featuring Moxie Pond and the peaks ringing Moosehead Lake, Katahdin, and the Bigelow Range. See Mosquito Mtn. Trail, p. 168.

PLEASANT POND MTN.

RT via AT Northbound   3.2 mi.   1,175 ft.   2:10

Hike to the craggy summit ledges of Pleasant Pond Mtn. for excellent views. A post-hike swim at Pleasant Pond is a bonus. See AT Northbound, p. 169.

COBURN MTN.

LP via Coburn Mtn. Trail and Snowmobile Trail   3.0 mi.   1,296 ft.   2:10

Climb the highest peak in the region, with spectacular views from the summit observation tower among the best in Maine. To begin, see Coburn Mtn. Trail, p. 176.

NUMBER FIVE MTN.

	⤵	↗	⟳
RT via Number Five Mtn. Trail	5.8 mi.	1,163 ft.	3:30

This long, gradual trek leads to a rocky summit topped with an old fire tower, where the reward is a scenic panorama of mountains and ponds. See Number Five Mtn. Trail, p. 177.

SEC 3

■ Strenuous
MOXIE BALD MTN.

	⤵	↗	⟳
RT via AT Northbound and Summit Bypass Trail	9.5 mi.	1,720 ft.	5:35

Follow the AT to the summit ledges on Moxie Bald Mtn., where extensive views include the peaks of Katahdin, Bigelow, Sugarloaf, Abraham, Coburn, and Boundary Bald. To begin, see AT Northbound, p. 169.

MOXIE MTN.

	⤵	↗	⟳
RT via Moxie Mtn. West Trail and Moxie Mtn. South Trail	3.0 mi.	1,700 ft.	2:20

Travel from the remote Deer Bog trailhead to the sprawling cliffs on the mountain's south face for outstanding views of Maine's High Peaks, including those around Sugarloaf Mtn. and the Bigelow Range. To begin, see Moxie Mtn. West Trail, p. 174.

SALLY MTN.

	⤵	↗	⟳
RT via Sally Mtn. Trail and Sally Mtn. Trail Extension	10.2 mi.	1,135 ft.	5:40

Hike to the long, eastern ridgeline of Sally Mtn. for excellent views over the wild country of the upper Moose River valley. Along the way, visit an old fire tower site and enjoy a swim in Attean Pond. To begin, see Sally Mtn. Trail, p. 178.

BOUNDARY BALD MTN.

	⤵	↗	⟳
RT via Boundary Bald Mtn. Trail	4.4 mi.	1,591 ft.	3:00

Enjoy 360-degree vistas from the long, open summit ridge of Boundary Bald Mtn., including the lake country of northern Somerset County, the Moosehead Lake region, and southern Canada. See Boundary Bald Mtn. Trail, p. 181.

TRAIL DESCRIPTIONS
KENNEBEC HIGHLANDS

At 6,800 acres, the Kennebec Highlands constitute the largest contiguous block of conservation land in central Maine, encompassing the highest mountains in Kennebec County, miles of streams, several wetlands, and five undeveloped ponds. The 7 Lakes Alliance, in partnership with MBPL, is working to protect the Kennebec Highlands, which range across the towns of Rome, Mt. Vernon, and Vienna in Kennebec County and New Sharon in Franklin County. 7LA manages an additional 3,000 acres of conserved land near the Kennebec Highlands. 7LA trails lead to Round Top Mtn., Sanders Hill, French Mtn., Mt. Phillip, and The Mountain; most are blazed blue. The route for The "A" Trail on McGaffey Mtn. is not blazed.

SEC 3

ROUND TOP MTN. (1,137 FT.)

This mountain provides wonderful views over Long Pond and Great Pond, the village of Belgrade Lakes, and the surrounding hills.

From the jct. of ME 27 and Watson Pond Rd., 4.4 mi. north of the village of Belgrade Lakes, turn left on Watson Pond Rd. and drive 4.0 mi. south to a parking lot at the corner of Wildflower Estates and Watson Pond Rd. Ascend Round Top Mtn. by combining Round Top Trail and Round Top Spur Trail.

ROUND TOP TRAIL (AMC KENNEBEC HIGHLANDS MAP)
Cumulative from Watson Pond Rd. trailhead (494 ft.) to:

Round Top Spur Trail (1,100 ft.)	1.8 mi.	606 ft.	1:15
Complete loop via Kennebec Highlands Trail	3.9 mi.	738 ft.	2:20

7LA Round Top Trail leaves the parking lot in a westerly direction, crossing The "A" Trail at 0.2 mi. After an initial rise, the trail briefly opens up for a view of Round Top Mtn. just before dropping to a well-signed jct. with Kennebec Highlands Trail at 1.0 mi. After crossing Kennebec Highlands Trail, Round Top Trail climbs steadily to the northwest. As the trail approaches the summit of Round Top Mtn., views open up to the east and south. Near the summit, at 1.8 mi., Round Top Spur Trail departs to the left (see p. 157).

Round Top Trail continues northeast, passing an overlook with views of Long Pond, the village of Belgrade Lakes, and Great Pond. The trail descends steeply to merge with Kennebec Highlands Trail at 2.2 mi. Turn right (south) onto this broad gravel treadway. At 2.9 mi., bear right onto a

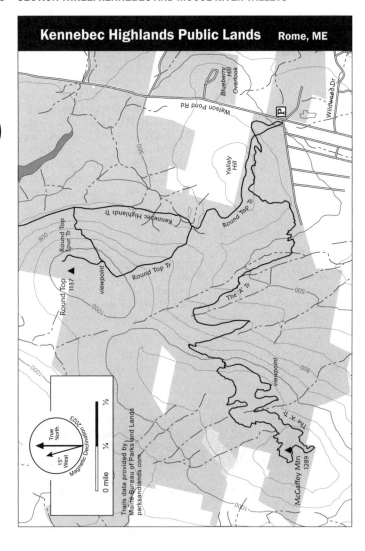

SEC
3

narrower section. At 3.0 mi., coinciding trails join a snowmobile trail and soon reach the signpost marking the initial jct. of Round Top Trail and Kennebec Highlands Trail. Turn left (east) and follow Round Top Trail back to the parking lot.

Round Top Spur Trail. This 0.3-mi. spur leads from Round Top Trail to the north end of Round Top Mtn. (but does not go to the summit), gaining 37 ft. of elevation. The first view looks north and east to Round Pond below and to French Mtn., Mt. Phillip, and Great Pond. The spur path ends at a second overlook, with views of Watson Pond, Sanders Hill, and Vienna Mtn. (northwest through the trees).

SEC 3

McGAFFEY MTN. (1,289 FT.)

This twin-peaked mountain, immediately southwest of Round Top Mtn., is the tallest in the Kennebec Highlands. The "A" Trail, designed as a multiuse route to be shared by both hikers and mountain bikers, leads to the summit of McGaffey Mtn.

THE "A" TRAIL (AMC KENNEBEC HIGHLANDS MAP)
Cumulative from Watson Pond Rd. trailhead (490 ft.) to:

Scenic lookout (1,125 ft.)	3.3 mi.	650 ft.	2:00
McGaffey Mtn. summit (1,289 ft.)	4.5 mi.	1,050 ft.	2:50

CMNEMBA The "A" Trail, unblazed but signed, starts at the northeast corner of the same parking lot as Round Top Trail (see directions on p. 155). The "A" Trail climbs to cross Round Top Trail at 0.3 mi. and continues west over the south slope of Yallaly Hill. It turns south and descends to Goat Path at 1.0 mi. The "A" Trail continues down to intersect an old woods road at 1.3 mi. and then follows the woods road to the right (northwest), crossing a brook at 1.5 mi. At 1.8 mi., the trail leaves the old road for a footpath on the left, and over the course of the next 0.5 mi., it alternates between footpath and old woods road. At 2.3 mi., the old road descends gradually, makes a hairpin turn to the right, and then resumes climbing. At 3.0 mi., switchback left and up off the old road and onto a footpath. Follow a long, rising contour and a series of tight switchbacks to a lookout on the left at 3.8 mi. with a view over Long Pond.

From the lookout, The "A" Trail climbs over bedrock outcroppings and descends to cross a shallow ravine. At 4.7 mi., pass two large boulders, traverse a small open area of exposed bedrock, and then descend slightly into a ravine. Climb up and out into another open area of exposed bedrock at 5.0 mi. To the left is an alternate descent trail; straight ahead is the summit of McGaffey Mtn., marked by a cairn with a length of plastic pipe stuck in it.

Alternate Descent Route. An alternate descent trail leaves the top of McGaffey Mtn. on the left just before the summit and follows a circuitous course for 1.6 mi. to meet The "A" Trail at that trail's 2.3 mi. mark on the ascent (this jct. is unmarked and not easily visible; it is not mentioned in the ascent description for these reasons). The trail is lightly used and its treadway is indistinct in many places, so it should be attempted only by experienced hikers well versed in route-finding and navigating with map and compass and/or GPS.

SEC 3

SANDERS HILL (853 FT.)

This hill in Rome rises just west of Watson Pond in the scenic northern part of the Kennebec Highlands. From the jct. of ME 27 and Watson Pond Rd., 4.4 mi. north of the village of Belgrade Lakes, turn left onto Watson Pond Rd. and drive south 1.3 mi. to a small parking area on the right. Sanders Hill Trail, which makes a loop hike, is described counterclockwise.

SANDERS HILL TRAIL (USGS BELGRADE LAKES QUAD, 7LA TRAIL MAP AND GUIDE TO THE KENNEBEC HIGHLANDS AND NEARBY AREAS, GAZETTEER MAP 20)
Cumulative from Watson Pond Rd. (450 ft.) to:

High point on Sanders Hill (840 ft.)	1.2 mi.	390 ft.	0:50
Complete loop	2.9 mi.	430 ft.	1:40

7LA Sanders Hill Trail leaves from the north side of the parking area to the right of the trailhead kiosk and soon reaches a large, flat rock affording views across Watson Pond. The trail bears right onto an old logging road and after several hundred feet turns left off the road, narrowing and climbing moderately to the west. It eventually turns right (north) and traverses a rock field, where there are partial views to the east of Watson Pond, Mt. Phillip, and French Mtn. The trail cuts directly over and through some large granite slabs at 0.9 mi.; it then turns left (west) and climbs to the sparsely wooded summit area, which offers partial views to the east and south through the trees at 1.1 mi.

The trail continues northwest over Sanders Hill and then descends to cross Kennebec Highlands Trail at 1.3 mi. After reentering the woods, Sanders Hill Trail turns south and rambles along the bank of Beaver Brook. At 2.0 mi., it again crosses Kennebec Highlands Trail. Sanders Hill Trail swings east and then north, briefly following an old logging road before bearing left and descending to a large boulder at 2.3 mi., where it crosses that same logging road. The trail continues east and then north over gently rolling terrain. At 2.8 mi., it intersects an old logging road at a wide, grassy jct. Turning right (east) onto the logging road, Sanders Hill Trail leads back to the parking lot.

FRENCH MTN. (745 FT.)

This summit in Rome boasts attractive views of the Belgrade Lakes area, including Whittier Pond to the east, Mt. Phillip to the northeast, and Long Pond to the southeast. From the jct. of ME 27 and Watson Pond Rd., proceed south on Watson Pond Rd. for 0.7 mi. to a paved parking area on the east side of the road.

FRENCH MTN. TRAIL (USGS BELGRADE LAKES QUAD, 7LA TRAIL MAP AND GUIDE TO KENNEBEC HIGHLANDS AND NEARBY AREAS, GAZETTEER MAP 20)

SEC 3

Cumulative from Watson Pond Rd. (500 ft.) to:

French Mtn. summit (745 ft.)	0.4 mi.	245 ft.	0:20
Complete loop	0.8 mi.	245 ft.	0:30

7LA French Mtn. Trail is a loop that can be followed in either direction; clockwise is described here. The trail leaves from the southeast corner of the parking lot, enters the woods, and heads east. It soon splits at a large signboard. Stay left for the most direct path to the summit. The trail climbs to the east and then swings south, following the ridge of French Mtn. (716 ft.) to reach a rocky precipice with views of Whittier Pond to the east and Long Pond to the south. The trail continues along the open rocks, above steep cliffs overlooking the northern end of Long Pond. From here hikers can also see Great Pond, The Mountain, and the village of Belgrade Lakes. Just south of the summit, French Mtn. Trail turns west into the woods and descends several switchbacks before turning north and gradually descending back to the jct. and the parking lot.

MT. PHILLIP (760 FT.)

This summit overlooking Great Pond in Rome provides views of the Kennebec Highlands to the west. From the jct. of ME 27 and ME 225 at Rome Corner, travel east on ME 225 for 1.5 mi. to a parking lot on the north side of the road, directly across from Starbird Ln.

MT. PHILLIP TRAIL (USGS BELGRADE LAKES QUAD, 7LA TRAIL MAP AND GUIDE TO KENNEBEC HIGHLANDS AND NEARBY AREAS, GAZETTEER MAP 20)

Cumulative from ME 225 (396 ft.) to:

Mt. Phillip summit (760 ft.)	0.7 mi.	364 ft.	0:30
Complete loop	1.4 mi.	364 ft.	0:55

7LA This loop trail can be followed in either direction; counterclockwise is described here. Mt. Phillip Trail leaves from the northeast corner of the parking lot and heads east. In less than 0.1 mi., the trail splits; bear right to follow it counterclockwise. The trail heads northwest up the eastern slope of

Mt. Phillip, continues to a rocky ledge on the mountain's eastern side at 0.6 mi., and crosses a ledge westward to a partial summit clearing (755 ft.) with views of Great Pond to the south and the Kennebec Highlands to the west. To continue the loop, descend to the west, make a sharp turn in a southerly direction, and follow Mt. Phillip Trail back to the jct. and the parking lot.

THE MOUNTAIN (664 FT.)

The Mountain in Rome sits amid 207 acres owned and managed by 7LA and Belgrade Lakes Association. It rises between Long Pond and Great Pond, offering fine views of the Kennebec Highlands and the surrounding lakes and woods. From the village of Belgrade Lakes, drive 1.0 mi. north on ME 27. Turn right (east) onto Mountain Dr. and proceed 0.3 mi. to a parking area on the left (north) side of the road. The trail network on The Mountain consists of Main Trail (0.8 mi. long) and three side trails that can be combined for loop hikes of up to 2.5 mi. The side trails can be hiked in either direction but are described here from south to north.

MAIN TRAIL (USGS BELGRADE LAKES QUAD, 7LA TRAIL MAP AND GUIDE TO KENNEBEC HIGHLANDS AND NEARBY AREAS, GAZETTEER MAP 20)
From Mountain Dr. parking area (375 ft.) to:

Great Pond Loop, lower jct. (545 ft.)	0.4 mi.	170 ft.	0:15
Long Pond Loop, lower jct. (565 ft.)	0.5 mi.	190 ft.	0:20
Long Pond Loop and Great Pond Loop, upper jct. (630 ft.)	0.8 mi.	255 ft.	0:30

7LA Main Trail, an old logging road, heads north from the parking area. Great Pond Loop (marked by green arrows) leaves to the right (east) 0.4 mi. up Main Trail. Long Pond Loop (white arrows) leaves Main Trail on the left (west) at 0.5 mi. Main Trail continues straight ahead and up, ending at a high point on the south ridge of The Mountain and a jct. with Great Pond Loop (joins from the right) and Long Pond Loop (joins from the left).

Great Pond Loop. This loop, marked with green arrows, is 0.35 mi. long. From the parking area, follow Main Trail. At 0.15 mi., Outer Loop (described on p. 161) leaves to the right. Ahead on Main Trail, at 0.4 mi., Great Pond Loop departs to the right. Great Pond Loop climbs west to a small open area high on The Mountain and turns north. Outer Loop rejoins from the right at 0.3 mi. Keeping left, Great Pond Loop descends steeply to its terminus at the jct. with Main Trail and Long Pond Loop.

Long Pond Loop. This loop, 0.4 mi. long and marked with white arrows, leaves Main Trail on the left (west), 0.5 mi. from the parking area. Long Pond Loop descends from Main Trail, passing over a cliff with steep dropoffs and views of Long Pond and the Kennebec Highlands. The trail soon turns east and climbs to reach the jct. with Main Trail and Great Pond Loop.

OUTER LOOP (USGS BELGRADE LAKES QUAD, 7LA TRAIL MAP AND GUIDE TO KENNEBEC HIGHLANDS AND NEARBY AREAS, GAZETTEER MAP 20)
From Great Pond Loop, lower jct. (570 ft.) to:

The Mountain summit (664 ft.)	1.0 mi.	120 ft.	0:30
Great Pond Loop, upper jct. (650 ft.)	1.1 mi.	120 ft.	0:35

7LA Outer Loop is a 1.1-mile, blue-blazed trail that begins and ends on Great Pond Loop (described on p. 160). Outer Loop leaves to the right (north), 0.15 mi. from Great Pond Loop's lower jct. with Main Trail, climbing through a rocky area before leveling out and proceeding northward. At 0.4 mi., Outer Loop passes two overlooks with views to Great Pond, both marked by "Steep Drop-Off" signs. Outer Loop then descends and turns west, crossing a snowmobile trail at 0.6 mi. It soon turns south through open woods, climbs several steps, crosses the snowmobile trail again at 1.0 mi., and ends at 1.1 mi. Here, Outer Loop rejoins Great Pond Loop just southeast of its upper jct. with The Mountain Trail.

KENNEBEC LAND TRUST
HOWARD HILL (484 FT.)
The 164-acre Howard Hill Historical Park, a property of the Kennebec Land Trust, is an urban oasis on the west side of Augusta that features a network of trails on namesake Howard Hill. The upper, eastern slopes of the hill provide views to the capitol dome, downtown Augusta, and the Kennebec River. Several access points exist for Howard Hill; the most popular and the one recommended by KLT is the trailhead on Sewall St. directly across from Brooklawn Ave.

From I-95, Exit 109 in Augusta, drive east on Western Ave. (US 202 and ME 11/17/100) for 0.6 mi. Turn right onto Armory St. In 0.2 mi., bear left onto Capitol St. and follow it for 0.6 mi. Turn right onto Sewall St., and in 0.1 mi., turn left to enter the Burton Cross Building parking lot, where public parking is available.

HOWARD HILL TRAILS (USGS AUGUSTA QUAD, KLT HOWARD HILL HISTORICAL PARK MAP, GAZETTEER MAP 12)

Cumulative from Sewall St. parking lot (110 ft.) to:

Start of trail (110 ft.) via Sewall St.	0.1 mi.	0 ft.	0:03
Capitol Overlook (325 ft.)	0.7 mi.	215 ft.	0:25
Capitol Vista (375 ft.)	0.9 mi.	265 ft.	0:35
Howard Hill summit (484 ft.)	1.2 mi.	374 ft.	0:45
Complete lollipop loop	2.6 mi.	374 ft.	1:40

SEC 3

KLT Walk south on Sewall St. for 0.1 mi. to a paved drive on the right opposite Brooklawn Ave. Walk up the paved drive for 75 ft. and turn left onto the blue-blazed trail. Climb the slope on a wide path. A ravine is below on the right. Pass two benches and reach a spur path on the left leading to Reflection Point. Ahead, pass two more benches before reaching a jct. where the trail from Blaisdell St. enters from the left (bench on right). Continue to the right, pass another bench, and soon after, turn sharply left toward the Capitol Overlook and to reach another bench and a view east. At the next jct., continue straight ahead to a spur leading left to a bronze marker for "Howard Hill" at the Capitol Overlook and a view of the Maine State House and the capital city of Augusta (three granite benches here). Return to the jct. and walk straight ahead on the wide path, an old forest road. Pass a bench on the left and then reach a jct. where Harrington Trail goes left; stay right toward Ganneston Rd. and soon arrive at a T jct. and two benches in a small clearing. Turn left (sign: "Hallowell") and reach the wooded top of Howard Hill and a bench.

From the summit, continue south to a bench and jct. Here, Harrington Trail goes left while Parkwood Trail goes right; turn left toward Hallowell (sign). At the next jct. (bench), continue straight toward a sign that reads "vista." Beyond, turn left off the old forest road onto a trail (sign: "vista") and follow a contour to the Capitol Overlook. From the vista spur, go left to the next jct. to close the loop and then turn right to retrace your footsteps to the Sewall St. trailhead.

MONKS HILL (680 FT.)

Rising above undeveloped Shed Pond, this hill is part of Gannett Woods and Wyman Memorial Forest, a combined 160-acre tract owned and managed by KLT that straddles the Readfield–Manchester town line.

From I-95, Exit 109 in Augusta, travel west on US 202/ME 17 for 2.6 mi. to Manchester. Turn right on ME 17. In another 3.2 mi., at the jct. of ME 17 and ME 135, turn right onto ME 135. At a point 1.3 mi. ahead, turn right onto Scribner Hill Rd.; in 1.0 mi., watch for a pullout on the right for parking (small KLT sign in woods).

MONKS HILL TRAIL (USGS WINTHROP QUAD, KLT GANNETT WOODS AND WYMAN MEMORIAL FOREST MAP, GAZETTEER MAP 12)
Cumulative from Scribner Hill Rd. (410 ft.) to:

Shed Pond Trail (410 ft.)	375 ft.	15 ft.	0:02
Monks Hill summit (680 ft.)	0.9 mi.	285 ft.	0:35

SEC 3

KLT From the road, walk 100 ft. into the woods to a trail register. Cross a brook on stone slabs and at the fork beyond, bear right to continue on blue-blazed Monks Hill Trail, which follows an old woods road. (To the left is Shed Pond Trail, worth checking out upon returning from Monks Hill.) Soon, turn left off the old woods road and follow a rising contour. Cross several rock walls and then turn left onto an old woods road. Pass a sharp-angled rock sticking out to the left of the trail. Soon after, turn right off the old road, reach a boundary marker with a smiley face on it, and proceed through a pine grove to the wooded top of Monks Hill. The trail continues south for about 0.5 mi. to ME 17, but there is no parking there and the route is not described. Instead, retrace your steps to Scribner Hill Rd.

THE PINNACLE (IN VIENNA) (716 FT.)
Just west of the village of Vienna and Flying Pond is the Vienna Woods Conservation Area, a 60-acre property managed by KLT. The Pinnacle is the high point, and its summit ledges offer a view eastward to McGaffey Mtn. in the Kennebec Highlands.

From the jct. of ME 41 and Kimball Pond Rd. in the village of Vienna, travel north on ME 41 for 1.4 mi. Turn left on Trask Rd. and drive 0.4 mi. to trailhead parking on the right.

VIENNA WOODS TRAIL (USGS FARMINGTON FALLS QUAD, KLT VIENNA WOODS CONSERVATION AREA MAP, GAZETTEER MAP 20)
Cumulative from Trask Rd. (630 ft.) to:

The Pinnacle lookout and bench (700 ft.)	0.4 mi.	88 ft.	0:15

KLT Arrive at a trail register in about 75 ft. and climb gently, following blue blazes (yellow and orange blazes mark the property boundary). Rock steps lead to the spine of the narrow ridge known as Devil's Backbone. After leveling off, a spur path on the left leads 100 ft. to a bench and viewpoint.

From the lookout jct., Vienna Woods Trail continues southeast to connect with other trails in the Vienna Woods (not described here). Consult the KLT trail map for additional hiking options.

ANDROSCOGGIN LAKE AREA
MT. PISGAH (812 FT.)

The 950-acre Mt. Pisgah Community Conservation Area in Wayne and Winthrop is co-owned and co-managed by KLT, the town of Winthrop, and a private landowner. Mt. Pisgah is the central feature. A 60-ft. summit fire tower, in place since 1949, affords 360-degree views ranging from Mt. Washington and the Presidential Range in the west to the Camden Hills on the east.

From the jct. of US 202/ME 11/ME 100 and ME 132 in Monmouth, proceed east on US 202/ME 11/ME 100 for 0.5 mi. Turn left (north) onto North Main St. and drive 0.8 mi. to the crossroads in North Monmouth. Turn right onto Wilson Pond Rd. and go 0.2 mi. to Mt. Pisgah Rd. Turn left and drive 1.6 mi. to the trailhead on the right. Tower Trail and Blueberry Trail diverge from this common trailhead and combine for a hiking loop. Ledges Trail offers a pleasant option around the summit.

TOWER TRAIL (USGS WAYNE QUAD, KLT MT. PISGAH COMMUNITY CONSERVATION AREA MAP, GAZETTEER MAP 12)
Cumulative from Mt. Pisgah Rd. (470 ft.) to:

Ledges Trail (785 ft.)	0.8 mi.	325 ft.	0:35
Mt. Pisgah summit (812 ft.)	1.0 mi.	342 ft.	0:45

KLT Proceed left of the kiosk on the gravel tower access road, passing Blueberry Trail on the right, to a gate. Here, blue-blazed Tower Trail departs left, up stone steps. The trail climbs gradually through a forest of pines and hardwoods. Beyond a series of bog bridges and a jct. of stone walls, pass a large rock cairn to the left. Ledges Trail departs to the left at 0.8 mi. Staying on Tower Trail, climb the summit ledges to reach the fire tower in a small meadow on top of Mt. Pisgah. A cell tower and the gravel tower access road are just beyond.

BLUEBERRY TRAIL (USGS WAYNE QUAD, KLT MT. PISGAH COMMUNITY CONSERVATION AREA MAP, GAZETTEER MAP 12)
Cumulative from Mt. Pisgah summit (812 ft.) to:

Ledges Trail (665 ft.)	0.3 mi.	0 ft.	0:10
Mt. Pisgah Rd. (470 ft.)	1.4 mi.	195 ft.	0:45

KLT Blueberry Trail is commonly used as a descent route and thus is described from the summit of Mt. Pisgah to the trailhead. From the fire tower, cross the gravel tower access road and head downhill. A sign indicates that highbush blueberry restoration is in progress. Blueberry Trail passes through a forest of large white pines, maples, and oaks as it descends the mountain's south slope. At the 550-ft. contour, the trail heads west, climbing to a knoll and crossing three small streams, the first and second via footbridges and the third via rocks. After cresting the knoll, Blueberry Trail descends along a stone wall, follows a contour, and then weaves through several stone walls to join an old woods road. Ahead, leave the old road to the right and follow a stone wall to the base of the mountain. Turn left on the gravel tower access road to return to the trailhead.

LEDGES TRAIL (USGS WAYNE QUAD, KLT MT. PISGAH COMMUNITY CONSERVATION AREA MAP, GAZETTEER MAP 12)
From Tower Trail (785 ft.) to:

Blueberry Trail (665 ft.)	1.4 mi.	170 ft.	0:45

KLT Ledges Trail allows for a longer loop hike that connects Tower Trail with Blueberry Trail on a ridgeline north of the Mt. Pisgah summit. The trail is described clockwise from Tower Trail to Blueberry Trail.

Ledges Trail leaves Tower Trail 0.8 mi. from the trailhead and heads north. Ledges Trail winds through a dense forest of hemlock and mixed hardwoods as it descends gradually and turns east to cross the north ridge of Mt. Pisgah. Reach a posted trail map at 0.6 mi. and follow a contour south. After crossing a stone wall, climb gradually along a mossy ledge face, ascend a ravine on switchbacks, and traverse sloping, mossy slabs. Ahead, the trail follows a contour around the east side of Mt. Pisgah (pass several impressive old-growth sugar maples) before descending easily to join Blueberry Trail. Turn left to return to the trailhead in 1.1 mi. following Blueberry Trail, or turn right on Blueberry Trail to reach the summit of Mt. Pisgah and to return to the parking area via Tower Trail in 1.3 mi.

TOWER ROAD (USGS WAYNE QUAD, KLT MT. PISGAH COMMUNITY CONSERVATION AREA MAP, GAZETTEER MAP 12)
From Mt. Pisgah Rd. (470 ft.) to:

Mt. Pisgah summit tower (812 ft.)	1.0 mi.	342 ft.	0:40

KLT Gravel-surfaced Tower Road connects the trailhead to the summit tower; it is often used by hikers on the ascent or descent as part of a loop hike on Mt. Pisgah.

SEC 3

MONUMENT HILL (670 FT.)

Monument Hill, just west of Androscoggin Lake in Leeds, offers attractive views of the hills and farmlands of the Androscoggin River valley to the west. A granite obelisk on the summit is dedicated to Leeds soldiers and sailors of the Civil War. The monument is inscribed "Peace was sure 1865." Community members of the town of Leeds maintain the trails. Red Trail and Orange Trail combine to make a pleasant loop over the mountain.

SEC 3

To reach the trailhead from US 202 between Lewiston and Augusta, take ME 106 north for 6.2 mi. to Leeds. Take Church Hill Rd. left (west) for 0.9 mi. to North Rd. on the right. Proceed 0.9 mi. to the trailhead on the right (sign) and roadside parking.

RED TRAIL (USGS TURNER CENTER QUAD, MTF MONUMENT HILL, GAZETTEER MAP 12)
From North Rd. (440 ft.) to:

Monument Hill summit (670 ft.)	0.45 mi.	230 ft.	0:20

TOL From the trailhead kiosk (posted map), follow a wide, unmarked path 200 ft. to the jct. of Orange Trail and Red Trail. Bear right on Red Trail (red blazes) to gently ascend the mountain in a counterclockwise direction. Pass a picnic area on the right and then Blue Trail (a 235-ft. shortcut to Orange Trail) on the left. On the summit, the obelisk is 50 ft. beyond a flagpole and picnic table. The open ledge below on the right offers a broad vista to the west that includes Pleasant Mtn., Streaked Mtn., and Mt. Washington.

ORANGE TRAIL (USGS TURNER CENTER QUAD, MTF MONUMENT HILL, GAZETTEER MAP 12)
From Monument Hill summit (670 ft.) to:

North Rd. (440 ft.)	0.5 mi.	−230 ft.	0:15

TOL Orange Trail (orange blazes) leaves the Monument Hill summit to the left of the obelisk. Ahead at 0.25 mi., bear left at a fork and, soon after, reach the jct. with Blue Trail (a 235-ft. link between Red Trail and Orange Trail) on the left. Beyond the jct., Orange Trail trends easily down the slope to the loop jct. and on to North Rd.

LAKE GEORGE REGIONAL PARK
THE PINNACLE (IN CANAAN) (655 FT.)

This wooded hill rises above the east, or Canaan, side of Lake George in Lake George Regional Park, which lies astride the Skowhegan–Canaan town line. The park features 320 acres of hilly terrain and 8,000 ft. of shoreline on pretty Lake George. In this pleasant network of trails, one climbs the Pinnacle (also shown as Jewell Hill on USGS topographic maps).

From US 2 in Canaan, 7.0 mi. east of downtown Skowhegan and 1.3 mi. west of the jct. of ME 23 and US 2 in Canaan, turn north into Lake George Regional Park East and drive 500 ft. to trailhead parking for the Pinnacle on the right. Look for a trail sign, a posted map, and an iron ranger for depositing the day-use fee.

SEC 3

PINNACLE TRAIL (USGS CANAAN QUAD, LAKE GEORGE REGIONAL PARK MAP, GAZETTEER MAP 21)
From trailhead parking (250 ft.) to:

The Pinnacle summit (655 ft.)	1.4 mi.	405 ft.	0:55

TOL The well-worn path leaves from the corner of the lot and proceeds through mature woods of pine, hemlock, and maple. Old paint blazes and arrows mark the way. A number of stone walls are along the route. Look for signs marked "PINN" at multiple jcts. At the first jct., stay straight. At the next two 4-way jcts., continue straight. At a T jct. at 0.4 mi., turn left. At a 4-way jct. with a snowmobile trail at 0.5 mi., turn left and quickly turn left again. Soon, merge with another snowmobile trail and bear left. At the next fork, bear right. In another 100 ft., bear left off the snowmobile trail. Traverse the gentle slope, and at the next 4-way jct., proceed straight ahead. At a T jct., turn sharply left. At the 4-way jct. with an old tote road, the trail to the left leads to East Branch (sign); stay straight on the trail to the Pinnacle (sign). The trail, now an old jeep road, climbs gradually to a high point on the Pinnacle's north slope and then drops slightly to an open spot on some ledges. The lake below is not visible, but some hills can be seen to the north.

MOXIE POND AREA
MOSQUITO MTN. (2,226 FT.)
Rising just west of Moxie Pond in The Forks, this mountain offers excellent views in all directions from its summit ledges, from the many peaks ringing Moosehead Lake to Katahdin and the Bigelow Range.

From US 201 in The Forks, just before the highway crosses the Kennebec River, turn right onto Lake Moxie Rd. and immediately pass The Forks rest area on the left. Pass the trailhead for Moxie Falls (worth a look post-hike) at 1.9 mi. and reach a T jct. at Lake Moxie Station at 5.3 mi. Here, paved Indian Pond Rd. continues to the left; turn right on gravel Troutdale Rd. and follow the former railroad bed south along Moxie

Pond. The road is narrow and can be rough in places, and many camps are along it, so please drive slowly and carefully. At 1.9 mi. on Troutdale Rd., just beyond where the road bears left away from the power line and enters the woods, there is a small parking area on the right, across from two camps. The space is just large enough for two to three vehicles. A faded red bear paw is painted on a rock at the trailhead. (*Note*: Please do not park along Troutdale Rd. or in any of the camp owners' driveways. If the small lot is full, please return at another time.)

SEC 3

MOSQUITO MTN. TRAIL
(USGS MOXIE POND QUAD, GAZETTEER MAP 30)
Cumulative from Troutdale Rd. (984 ft.) to:

Spur path to overlook (2,050 ft.)	1.2 mi.	1,066 ft.	1:10
Mosquito Mtn. summit (2,226 ft.)	1.5 mi.	1,242 ft.	1:25

TMNK Mosquito Mtn. Trail begins from the rear of the parking area. The wide path, marked with occasional red paw prints, soon narrows and crosses a CMP power-line corridor. At 0.3 mi., turn left on a grassy old road and then quickly turn right back into the woods. At 0.4 mi., turn left onto a gravelly, shrubby old road corridor and then quickly turn right back into the woods. At 0.7 mi., the gradual grade becomes more moderate. The trail contours to the right and proceeds steadily up past a huge overhanging boulder. At 1.2 mi., negotiate a steep, rugged passage beneath the impressive cliff walls. Above, walk along a mossy cliff wall to reach a jct. where a spur path leads left 200 ft. to open ledges. Look for a register box and an American flag on a pole. From this airy vantage point, the view over Moxie Pond is breathtaking. Big Moose Mtn. is in sight to the northeast, Moxie Bald Mtn. to the southeast, and Pleasant Pond Mtn. and Moxie Mtn. to the south.

Return to Mosquito Mtn. Trail and climb the steep, rocky treadway, which becomes more moderate upon reaching the upper east ridge. Several herd paths diverge here and there along this upper section; follow the cairns and bits of flagging to stay on track. Cross the craggy summit area and look right for a small sign on a little spruce tree: "Mosquito Mtn. 2115 ft." The true summit is atop the outcropping directly behind the sign. The scenic panorama includes Coburn Mtn., Sugarloaf Mtn., Katahdin, and many others.

MOXIE BALD MTN. (2,632 FT.)

This mountain in Bald Mtn. Township features a long ridge extending north and south for about 4 mi. Its summit is alpine in nature, owing to the extensive area of open ledges. The views from the summit are excellent and include

Katahdin to the northeast; Bigelow, Sugarloaf, and Abraham mountains to the west; and Coburn and Boundary Bald mountains to the north. Moxie Bald Mtn. is reached via the AT, which leaves from a point on Troutdale Rd. just south of Joe's Hole, the southernmost point on Moxie Pond.

The Moxie Bald Mtn.–AT trailhead can be reached from US 201 in The Forks to the north and east or from US 201 in Bingham in the south.

Directions from US 201 in The Forks: Just before US 201 crosses the Kennebec River, at a point roughly 23 mi. north of Bingham, turn right onto Lake Moxie Rd. Follow this paved road for 5.2 mi. to Lake Moxie Station and a T intersection. Turn right onto Troutdale Rd., a former railroad grade, and follow it along Moxie Pond. (*Note*: This road can be rough and narrow in places, and many camps are on this shore of the pond, so please drive carefully.) At 13.0 mi., reach a small parking area on the right side of the road. The sign for the AT and Moxie Bald Mtn. is on the left.

Directions from US 201 in Bingham: Follow directions for reaching the southern trailhead on Moxie Mtn. on p. 174. From the jct. of Deadwater Rd. and Heald Pond Rd. at 5.0 mi., continue north on Deadwater Rd. (reset mileage before continuing). In 1.9 mi., Bald Mtn. Rd. diverges to the right; continue straight ahead as Deadwater Rd. now becomes Troutdale Rd. Pass a road on the left at 2.2 mi. and reach an offset 4-way jct. at 4.7 mi. Here, Baker Dimmock Rd. departs left and crosses a bridge, while AT Rd. leaves to the right. To intersect the AT just north of Bald Mtn. Brook Lean-to and make a shorter hike to the Moxie Bald Mtn. summit, turn right to follow AT Rd. (For a longer hike, continue north from this point on Troutdale Rd. for an additional 2.0 mi. to the AT crossing at Baker Stream at the south end of Moxie Pond.) Reset trip mileage. At 0.3 mi. from Troutdale Rd., pass under power lines. At 0.8 mi., turn left to stay on AT Rd. Stay right at a fork at 1.7 mi. Cross a bridge over Bald Mtn. Brook at 3.8 mi. Park on the right at a small pullout. The AT crosses the gravel road just ahead.

AT NORTHBOUND (USGS MOXIE POND AND DIMMICK MTN. QUADS, MTF APPALACHIAN TRAIL – MOXIE BALD, GAZETTEER MAP 30)
Cumulative from Troutdale Rd. (977 ft.) to:

Bald Mtn. Brook Lean-to (1,310 ft.)	2.5 mi.	400 ft.	1:30
AT Rd. (1,330 ft.)	2.7 mi.	420 ft.	1:35
Summit bypass trail, south jct. (2,150 ft.)	4.0 mi.	1,240 ft.	2:35
Moxie Bald Mtn. summit (2,632 ft.)	4.6 mi.	1,720 ft.	3:10
Summit bypass trail, north jct. (2,410 ft.)	5.0 mi.	1,720 ft.	3:20

MATC The white-blazed AT to Moxie Bald Mtn. leaves the east side of Troutdale Rd. and immediately crosses Baker Brook near the inlet to Moxie Pond. (*Note*: Even in times of moderate water levels, this crossing may be difficult.) At 0.3 mi., the trail travels under a power line, and at 1.1 mi., it crosses a rocky brook. The AT crosses Bald Mtn. Brook at 2.5 mi., where there is a campsite and privy. Soon after, reach a side trail leading 500 ft. to Bald Mtn. Brook Lean-to. Just beyond a second side trail (leads 200 ft. to the shelter) at 2.7 mi., cross a multiuse gravel road (AT Rd).

Continue climbing at a gradual-to-moderate grade to a fork at 4.0 mi., where Summit Bypass Trail leads left to connect to the AT again 0.4 mi. north of the summit. Bear right to continue on the AT. Follow a rising contour, walk along a mossy ledge wall, and climb again. Pass through a slab cave, under a slab roof, and through a passageway in the rock. Beyond, follow switchbacks up the west slope. Views begin to open to the west as you gain elevation: Moxie Pond, Pleasant Pond Mtn., Moxie Mtn., the Bigelow Range, and Mt. Abraham. Emerge onto open granite slabs and climb steadily, following cairns. Number Five Mtn. and Coburn Mtn. are in sight now. Reach a spur path on the left that leads 100 ft. to the top of Moxie Bald Mtn., site of a fire tower from 1910 until 1994 (the iron rungs and old footings can still be seen). The view to the north includes Big Moose Mtn., Little Spencer Mtn., Big Spencer Mtn., Lily Bay Mtn., Number Four Mtn., Baker Mtn., the peaks of the White Cap Range, and Katahdin.

To make a loop around the top of Moxie Bald Mtn., continue north on the AT across the granite ledges of the open summit and then turn left and descend. Enjoy a pleasant view over Bald Mtn. Pond just before the trail turns to follow a sidewalk ledge. The AT meets the north end of Summit Bypass Trail 0.4 mi. from the summit of Moxie Bald Mtn. Turn left (south) here to rejoin the AT in 0.5 mi. To the right, the AT and then a side trail lead to the beautiful North Peak of Moxie Bald Mtn. in 1.4 mi.

Summit Bypass Trail. This 0.5-mi. blue-blazed side trail avoids the open ledges on top of Moxie Bald Mtn., a wise choice in inclement weather. The route can also be used to make a pleasant loop around the mountain's summit. From its south jct., the bypass trail gains 260 ft. of elevation.

MOXIE BALD MTN., NORTH PEAK (2,379 FT.)

The extensive open ledges, abundant blueberries in high summer, and extraordinary panoramic views make this subsidiary peak north of the main summit of Moxie Bald Mtn. a worthwhile side trip if time and weather allow.

**AT NORTHBOUND AND NORTH PEAK TRAIL
(USGS MOXIE POND AND DIMMICK MTN. QUADS,
MTF APPALACHIAN TRAIL – MOXIE BALD, GAZETTEER MAP 30)**
Summit Bypass Trail, north jct. with AT (2,410 ft.) to:

North Peak Trail (2,210 ft.)	0.6 mi.	–200 ft.	0:20
Moxie Bald Mtn., North Peak (2,379 ft.)	1.4 mi.	230 ft.	0:45

MATC From the north jct. of Summit Bypass Trail, head north on the AT, which descends gradually through semi-open terrain. Cairns mark the route in places. After a moderate drop, the AT reaches North Peak Trail on the left. Turn here and follow this side trail across semi-open ledges marked with cairns. Continue easily down to a wide saddle. Leave the brief tree cover and climb on bedrock to a false summit; then move across the ridge. Finally, weave steeply up through ledges to end at the summit sign, where there is an extraordinary 360-degree panorama.

SEC
3

PLEASANT POND MTN. (2,477 FT.)
Situated between Moxie Pond and the Kennebec River in The Forks, the long ridgeline of Pleasant Pond Mtn. has extensive open ledges that offer fine views in all directions. Hikers can reach the mountain via the AT from either the south or the north. The long and hilly north ridge of Pleasant Pond Mtn. features impressive forests of mature spruce and fir. A fire tower stood on the summit of Pleasant Mtn. from 1910 until 1951, when it was moved to Barren Mtn. in Elliotsville.

**AT SOUTHBOUND (USGS THE FORKS AND
MOXIE POND QUADS, MATC MAP 4, GAZETTEER MAP 30)**
Cumulative from Troutdale Rd. (975 ft.) via AT Southbound to:

Power line (1,000 ft.)	0.1 mi.	25 ft.	0:05
Brook crossing (1,050 ft.)	0.5 mi.	75 ft.	0:15
Pleasant Pond Mtn. summit (2,477 ft.)	4.9 mi.	1,500 ft.	3:15

MATC To hike Pleasant Pond Mtn. from its north side, use the same approach by road as for Moxie Bald Mtn. (see p. 169).

Walk north along Troutdale Rd. from the parking area for 0.2 mi. to where the AT heads west up the mountain from a spot near Joe's Hole at the southern end of Moxie Pond. At 0.1 mi., the trail travels under a power line and then passes through a low area of beaver bogs. It crosses a brook at 0.5 mi. Beyond, the trail ascends to the long southerly ridge of the mountain and follows it over the middle summit until finally reaching the craggy ledges on the main summit at 4.9 mi.

**AT NORTHBOUND (USGS FORKS AND
MOXIE POND QUADS, MATC MAP 4, GAZETTEER MAP 30)**
Cumulative from parking area (1,420 ft.) via AT Northbound to:

Side trail to Pleasant Pond Lean-to and beach (1,300 ft.)	0.3 mi.	–80 ft.	0:10
Pleasant Pond Mtn. summit (2,477 ft.)	1.6 mi.	1,175 ft.	1:25

MATC The road approach for the hike from the south side of Pleasant Pond Mtn. starts at US 201 in the village of Caratunk about 14 mi. north of the jct. of US 201 and ME 16 in Bingham. Leave US 201 to the right at a sign for Caratunk and Pleasant Pond. Proceed 0.8 mi. to Caratunk, and then turn right and head uphill on Pleasant Pond Rd. At 3.9 mi., take the left fork onto North Shore Rd. At 4.2 mi. the pavement ends. At 5.3 mi., bear right where Boise Crossover Rd. bears left, and proceed straight into the woods on the parking lot driveway. Trailhead parking signs soon become evident as you approach a grassy opening and the AT at 5.5 mi.

The AT leaves the parking area and heads north toward Pleasant Pond Mtn. At 0.3 mi., reach a side trail leading 0.1 mi. to Pleasant Pond Lean-to. From the lean-to, a side trail leads an additional 0.2 mi. to a small sand beach on Pleasant Pond. Ahead on the AT, at 0.5 mi., another side trail leads 0.2 mi. to the same beach. Beyond, the rocky trail rises steeply through dense woods. At 1.5 mi., the trail climbs over rock ledges and, at 1.6 mi., breaks out onto open ledges at the summit and the site of the former fire tower.

US 201 CORRIDOR
KELLY MTN. (1,676 FT.)

This low mountain rises east of Bingham and the Kennebec River in Brighton Plantation. On the summit, the 1925 fire tower still stands, and the observation platform atop the tower offers excellent views of the surrounding countryside. The fire warden's trail once used to reach the tower has become overgrown and more recently has been obliterated by logging. The current trail follows an ATV route from the southwest.

To reach the trail from US 201 in Bingham, turn east on ME 16 and drive 10.3 mi. to the jct. of ME 151 at Mayfield Corner. Proceed south on ME 151 (Athens Rd.) for 4.2 mi. to the jct. of ME 151 and ME 154. From this jct., shown as Brighton on *Gazetteer* map 31, drive south on ME 151 for an additional 0.1 mi. Here, turn right (west) onto Stagecoach Rd. Reset mileage counter. Pass the Brighton Fires Shed and enter Weyerhaeuser Timberlands property. Go up and over a hill. At 0.9 mi., the road veers sharply left; at 1.3 mi., it curves sharply right. At 2.3 mi., the road turns sharply right again and crosses a bridge. At 3.1 mi., a road enters from the right; continue straight and cross a bridge. Arrive at an offset 4-way jct. at 3.4 mi.; turn sharply right here. At the fork 0.1 mi. ahead, bear right onto a lesser gravel road. Wind turbines come into view at 3.9 mi. Enter a grassy old log yard at 5.3 mi. and park on the left.

KELLY MTN. TRAIL
(USGS KINGSBURY QUAD, GAZETTEER MAP 31)
From trailhead at old log yard (1,240 ft.) to:

Kelly Mtn. summit (1,676 ft.)	0.6 mi.	436 ft.	0:30

NFTM The trail, an unmarked double-track old jeep road, exits the log yard to the north. Pass through a ditch and then turn sharply right on the obvious ATV track and begin climbing. The track is alternately muddy and rutted and rocky and eroded. At 0.4 mi., a grassy track, the old fire warden's trail, enters from the right. Stay on the grassy trail. Ahead, after entering thicker woods, the trail crests and easily crosses the summit ridge to the tower in a small clearing on top. The 360-degree vista from the platform includes Mt. Blue, Jackson Mtn., the Bigelow Range, Moxie Mtn., Moxie Bald Mtn., Big Moose Mtn., and much more.

MOXIE MTN. (2,933 FT.)
This exceptional mountain peak in Caratunk is east of the Kennebec River and US 201 and west of the north–south series of logging roads that connect ME 16 and Moxie Pond. Moxie Mtn. is often confused with Moxie Bald Mtn. on the AT some 8 mi. northeast. The huge open ledges on the mountain's south face several hundred feet below the summit offer stunning views of the High Peaks in and around Carrabassett Valley, including Mt. Abraham, Sugarloaf Mtn., and Bigelow Mtn., as well as some interesting rock formations.

Moxie Mtn. can be climbed from the west and from the south.

To reach the western trailhead: At a point 8.4 mi. north of the jct. of US 201 and ME 16 in Bingham, US 201 crosses Carney Brook (sign) as it curves to the left. Just 0.2 mi. beyond (and 0.25 mi. south of the Wyman Lake rest area), turn right onto Cates Hill Rd. and enter a large gravel lot. Reset mileage counter. Cates Hill Rd. continues to the left; bear right to follow Carney Brook Rd. (sign) out of the lot and into the woods and soon enter Weyerhaeuser Timberlands property. At a fork at 1.9 mi., stay straight. At 4.2 mi., where Chase Pond Rd. leaves to the right, continue straight. Soon after, Moxie Mtn. comes into view ahead. Around 4.4 mi., be watchful for a rough culvert; in 2022, it was quite passable, but unseen it can provide quite a jolt and perhaps do damage. Pass a road on the right at 5.1 mi. At a fork at 6.2 mi., turn right (sign: "Moxie Mtn. Hiking .4 mi."). As of 2022, a bridge 0.1

mi. farther along this road was impassable due to its poor condition, so hikers should park in the area near the sign, making sure not to block the road.

To reach the southern trailhead: From the jct. of US 201 and ME 16 in Bingham, travel east on ME 16 for 5.5 mi. Reset mileage counter. Turn left (north) on JW Pinkerton Rd. and enter Weyerhaeuser Timberlands property. Pass an information kiosk for Bald Mtn. Pond on the right at 0.2 mi. At a fork at 0.7 mi., stay right. Merge with Deadwater Rd. at 2.7 mi. and bear right to continue north. At a fork at 2.9 mi., where Palmer Rd. goes right, bear left. Cross an iron bridge over Austin Stream at 4.4 mi., and 0.1 mi. beyond, where Ripple Rd. bears left, stay straight. At 5.0 mi., bear right onto Heald Rd. (sign for Moxie Mtn. Cabins) and drive under power lines. A primitive campsite is on the right at 6.2 mi. Bear left at a fork at 7.5 mi. At a fork at 8.3 mi., bear right (sign for Moxie Mtn. Cabins) and soon pass another primitive campsite on the right. Reach signed parking on the right for Moxie Mtn. Cabins, and 200 ft. ahead is a small grassy parking spot on the right for Moxie Mtn. hikers.

MOXIE MTN. WEST TRAIL (USGS CARATUNK QUAD, GAZETTEER MAP 30)

Cumulative from Deer Bog trailhead (1,260 ft.) to:

Start of Moxie Mtn. West Trail via tote road (1,450 ft.)	0.4 mi.	190 ft.	0:18
Spur path to outlook (2,580 ft.)	1.0 mi.	1,320 ft.	1:10
Moxie Mtn. South Trail (2,640 ft.)	1.2 mi.	1,380 ft.	1:20
Moxie Mtn. summit (2,933 ft.) via Moxie Mtn. South Trail	1.5 mi.	1,700 ft.	1:40

TMNK Follow the old tote road for 0.4 mi., climbing past the deteriorating bridge at 0.1 mi. Where the road begins to level off just before a log yard, look for a sign on the right and the start of Moxie Mtn. West Trail. Following red markers and occasional flagging, the trail climbs at a steady, moderate grade. The angle eases as the trail reaches a narrow portion of the ridge. Soon after, the trail levels off and reveals views to Sugarloaf and neighboring peaks. Continue easily along, following cairns through thin forest cover and several rocky clearings. Reach a signed spur on the right that leads about 300 ft. to a huge open clifftop on the south face of the mountain, which yields a 270-degree viewing arc. The extraordinary vista features Number Five Mtn., Snow Mtn., the Bigelow Range, the Crockers, Mt. Redington, Mt. Abraham, and Jackson Mtn., to name just a few. The extensive sand and gravel shelf is worth some extra time exploring. Return to Moxie Mtn. West Trail, turn right, and continue across the ridgeline. Cross an open slope to a cairn with a pole in it; reenter the woods to its left, then drop down to the T jct. with Moxie Mtn. South Trail. Turn left to follow Moxie Mtn. South Trail 0.3 mi. to the summit of Moxie Mtn.

MOXIE MTN. SOUTH TRAIL (USGS CARATUNK QUAD, GAZETTEER MAP 30)
Cumulative from Heald Pond Rd. (1,530 ft.) to:

Spur path to outlook (2,600 ft.)	1.15 mi.	1,070 ft.	1:05
Moxie Mtn. West Trail (2,640 ft.)	1.2 mi.	1,110 ft.	1:10
Moxie Mtn. summit (2,933 ft.)	1.5 mi.	1,430 ft.	1:30

TMNK Walk north on Heald Pond Rd. for 75 ft. to the start of the trail on the right (sign). Follow blue markers and occasional flagging along the grassy old tote road through a red pine plantation. At 0.75 mi., turn sharply right onto a narrower grassy track (arrow, cairn, flagging) and proceed through a corridor of thick spruce and fir. As the grade steepens, the trail climbs steadily past a rock wall. Scramble left and up to the top of an outcropping and cross a slope of sand and gravel. Pass a ledge wall, drop down slightly, and then resume the ascent. Reach a signed spur on the left that leads 100 ft. to the top of a large outcropping that offers views west and south, including Bigelow Mtn. and Mt. Blue. Several hundred feet beyond the outlook jct., the trail meets Moxie Mtn. West Trail, which enters from the left. Continuing on Moxie Mtn. South Trail, drop into and climb out of a steep, narrow ravine, and then angle right over a slab to reach the base of a cliff wall. Turn left along it and scramble up to a lookout on the right. Soon, the towers on the summit come into view. Pass a helipad on the left and then step right a few feet to the USGS marker on top of Moxie Mtn., where there is a solar array and an outbuilding. Return to the helipad to enjoy a terrific view of Moxie Pond and Moxie Bald Mtn., Big Moose Mtn., Big Spencer Mtn., Baker Mtn., White Cap Mtn., and Katahdin.

COBURN MTN. (3,720 FT.)
This mountain, west of US 201 between the towns of The Forks and Jackman, straddles the Upper Enchanted Township and Johnson Mtn. Township boundaries. Coburn Mtn. is the highest peak in the region, with spectacular views, among the best in Maine. The top of the old fire tower (1938) has been replaced with an observation deck. MBPL owns 200 acres on the mountain, including the summit and southeastern slopes.

At a point 10.6 mi. north of the bridge over the Kennebec River in The Forks and 14.3 mi. south of the jct. of US 201 and ME 6/15 in Jackman, turn west off US 201 onto Enchanted Mtn. Rd. Follow this gravel road for

2.3 mi. to a 4-way jct. in a large clearing; this is the base area of the former Enchanted Mountain ski area (1966–1974). An old ski trail and lift line are visible on the mountainside above. Turn right and follow the road another 0.2 mi. to a sharp right turn where a snowmobile trail on the left leads uphill (sign: "No ATVs"); this is the starting point. Park here off the road.

COBURN MTN. TRAIL (USGS ENCHANTED POND AND JOHNSON MTN. QUADS, GAZETTEER MAP 40)
Cumulative from trailhead (2,424 ft.) to:

First (lower) radio repeater station (3,252 ft.)	0.9 mi.	828 ft.	0:32
Summit footpath (3,290 ft.)	0.92 mi.	866 ft.	0:35
Coburn Mtn. summit (3,720 ft.)	1.2 mi.	1,296 ft.	1:15

NFTM Follow the unmarked but obvious snowmobile trail (a former ski trail) uphill, climbing at a steady moderate-to-steep grade. In a clearing at a jct. of old ski trails, bear right and up past the first radio repeater station. Continue on the snowmobile trail around a rusted gate for 100 ft. to a cairn on the right and a footpath leading into the thick woods. Turn right onto this unmarked trail, which soon turns sharply right and begins climbing steeply. Pass several small cairns along the way. Reach the ridge and level off at a second radio repeater station with a solar array and an outbuilding. Turn right to reach the observation tower on the summit of Coburn Mtn. Climb the tower to take in the astounding vista: to the west, Number Five and Kibby mountains; to the north, Sally and Boundary Bald mountains; to the south, the Bigelow Range; and to the east, Big Moose and Little Moose mountains. These are just a few of the jumble of peaks in the panorama, which extends into Canada.

SNOWMOBILE TRAIL (USGS ENCHANTED POND AND JOHNSON MTN. QUADS, GAZETTEER MAP 40)
Cumulative from Coburn Mtn. summit (3,720 ft.) to:

Summit footpath (3,290 ft.)	0.9 mi.	–428 ft.	0:25
First (lower) radio repeater station (3,252 ft.)	0.92 mi.	–468 ft.	0:27

NFTM This unmarked trail connects the top of Coburn Mtn. to the first (lower) radio repeater station below and offers a more gradual descent than the steep summit footpath. From the observation tower, return to the solar array. Where the summit footpath descends to the left, continue straight ahead along and down the southwest ridge, following the wide swath of the snowmobile trail. At a jct. at 0.3 mi., bear right to avoid the steeper path on the left. Below, the trail swings back around to head northeast on a contour along the base of the upper mountain. Reach the jct. and cairn marking the summit footpath on the left, and then pass the rusted gate to reach the lower radio repeater station. Bear left to continue down the mountain on the snowmobile (Coburn Mtn.) trail to the trailhead in 0.9 mi.

NUMBER FIVE MTN. (3,183 FT.)

This remote mountain west of US 201 at Parlin Pond is bisected by the town lines of T5 R7 BKP WKR and Appleton Township. An old fire tower (1933) still stands on the craggy ledges of the open summit. Number Five Mtn. is in the heart of Leuthold Forest Preserve, 16,934 acres of forestland owned by TNC just south of the Moose River. The preserve abuts a vast swath of other conservation lands. An old trail (reached by a roughly 17-mi. drive on gravel logging roads) on the south side of the mountain, significantly improved by TNC trail crews, offers access to the peak.

From the jct. of US 201 and ME 6/15 in Jackman, drive south on US 201 for 11.5 mi. Opposite the boat launch on Parlin Pond, turn west on Spencer Rd. (a.k.a. Hardscrabble Rd. on the *Gazetteer* map). Reset trip mileage. At 5.3 mi. from US 201, bear right at a fork (street signs here are confusing). Reach the Spencer POW Camp Memorial on the left at 11.8 mi. At 14.4 mi., bear right at a fork. At 16.6 mi., at a small roadside cairn (may be missing) on the right, turn right on a minor double-track road and follow it to its end in a grassy meadow (an old woodyard) in 0.5 mi. Preserve guidelines and a map are posted on a signboard.

NUMBER FIVE MTN. TRAIL (USGS SPENCER LAKE, ATTEAN POND, HOLEB, AND TUMBLEDOWN MTN. QUADS, TNC LEUTHOLD FOREST PRESERVE MAP, GAZETTEER MAP 39)
From trailhead at end of gravel side road (2,020 ft.) to:

Number Five Mtn. summit (3,183 ft.)	2.9 mi.	1,163 ft.	2:00

TNC The trail starts up the grassy road left of the kiosk and soon climbs in and out of a gully. Continue on the grassy road, and at a fork just ahead (marked with a TNC yellow-and-green diamond), stay right. At 0.4 mi., cross onto TNC land (marked with red paint blazes), and in 100 ft., bear right onto a foot trail and follow light-blue paint blazes. For the next 1.75 mi., the trail rises at a pleasant grade, alternating between foot trail and old woods road corridors. The well-constructed treadway features switchbacks, rock steps, stone water bars, wooden bog bridging, turnpikes, and contouring.

At 2.25 mi., traverse a grassy, wet meadow on large log bog bridge sections. Beyond, the trail begins a moderate ascent through dense forest, past mossy boulders. Cross a small stream and pass remnants of an old telephone line. Climb a short, steep, rocky pitch and then a more moderate stretch to open ledges, where the summit tower comes into view. Break into the open at 2.8 mi., with impressive views south, east, and west, especially to Number Six Mtn. next door. Reach the fire tower at 2.9 mi. Views from the summit ledges are excellent in every direction.

SALLY MTN., EAST PEAK (2,227 FT.)

SEC 3

Sally Mtn., in Attean Township between Wood Pond and Attean Pond, features a long, multisummited ridgeline that extends nearly 4 mi. in a semi-circle from east to west. A trail ascends to the eastern summit; the western-most peak is the highest (2,236 ft.), but it is trailless. The mountain offers excellent views of the wild country of the upper Moose River valley. Attean Lake Lodge, on Birch Island in Attean Pond, maintains Sally Mtn. Trail.

From US 201 in Jackman, 100 ft. south of its jct. with ME 6/15, turn west onto Attean Rd., which soon turns to gravel. Drive 1.4 mi. to a dirt parking area on the right.

SALLY MTN. TRAIL (USGS ATTEAN POND QUAD, ALL ATTEAN TRAILS, GAZETTEER MAP 39)
Cumulative from Attean Rd. (1,190 ft.) to:

Start of trail (1,190 ft.) via railroad tracks	1.9 mi.	20 ft.	0:55
Sally Mtn., east summit (2,227 ft.)	3.4 mi.	1,060 ft.	2:15

ALL Walk back along Attean Rd. for 250 ft., then turn left (north) on a gated camp road. At 0.2 mi., pass through a rusted gate, turn left along the railroad tracks of the Central Maine & Quebec Railway and cross the Moose River on a trestle. Follow the tracks west for 1.6 mi., passing rail-road mile markers 76 and 77. Just 0.1 mi. after marker 77, reach Sally Mtn. Trail on the right (a trail on the opposite side of the tracks leads 300 ft. to an MBPL campsite at Sally Beach on Attean Pond).

From the tracks, the blue-blazed trail ascends gradually to cross a grassy old forest road. The climbing is moderate to a spring box on the right at 2.9 mi. and then the grade steepens. Reach a boulder with a blue arrow and then climb a ledge with a blue arrow. Arrive at an open ledge with a view ranging from Katahdin to Coburn Mtn. and the Bigelow Range. Big Wood Pond and Attean Pond are visible below. Several more open ledges along the ridgetop offer more views. On the summit are the rusted legs of the old fire tower (erected in 1908 and abandoned in 1933) and an excellent look north to Boundary Bald Mtn. and the peaks along the Canadian bor-der, and south to Number Five Mtn.

A pleasant alternative to the start of the hike along the railroad tracks is to approach the trail by canoe. Drive to the end of Attean Pond Rd. and a boat launch on Attean Pond. (*Note*: This is the start of the Moose River Bow Trip.) Paddle along the north shore of the pond to reach the second established campsite (Sally Beach) in a small cove directly opposite Birch Island and Attean Lake Lodge. A trail leads 300 ft. to the railroad tracks and the start of the trail as described above.

SALLY MTN. TRAIL EXTENSION (USGS ATTEAN POND QUAD, ALL ATTEAN TRAILS, GAZETTEER MAP 39)

SEC 3

Cumulative from fire tower site atop Sally Mtn. (2,227 ft.) to:

Railroad tracks (1,210 ft.)	2.1 mi.	50 ft.	1:35
Start of Sally Mtn. Trail (1,190 ft.)	4.9 mi.	60 ft.	2:30
Attean Rd. parking (1,190 ft.)	6.8 mi.	75 ft.	3:25

ALL This trail, also maintained by Attean Lake Lodge, descends from the fire tower site on Sally Mtn. It roams west over the ridge and down to the railroad tracks near the north shore of Attean Pond at a point 2.8 mi. from the start of Sally Mtn. Trail and 6.8 mi. from the trailhead on Attean Rd. via the railroad tracks. This trail is well marked with blue blazes but is not well used, so the treadway can be indistinct in places.

From the fire tower site atop Sally Mtn., continue west along the ridge to a subpeak and then to huge open ledges with extensive views to the west, south, and north. The trail drops steeply down over open ledges to enter the trees and then climbs a series of knobs and ledges with views of Number Five Mtn., the Bigelow Range, Attean Pond, and Moose Bog. Continue the descent with views of the western summit of Sally Mtn. At 0.8 mi., reach a saddle and traverse along the base of a mossy cliff face. Climb to a knoll, cross a ridge, and pass beneath more mossy cliff faces. Follow a contour before descending into a prominent saddle at 1.4 mi. The trail turns south through the saddle and begins a steady descent to a grassy old forest road. Reach the railroad tracks at 2.1 mi. Across the tracks, a trail leads 300 ft. to a sandy beach on Attean Pond.

At the railroad tracks, turn east to walk back to the start of Sally Mtn. Trail, which is reached at 4.9 mi. Pass railroad mile markers 79 and 78 en route. From here, retrace your steps back to the Attean Rd. parking area.

BURNT JACKET MTN., EAST PEAK (2,113 FT.)

This sprawling, multisummited peak in Forsyth Township rises south and west of Little Big Wood Pond a few miles west of Jackman.

From the jct. of US 201 and ME 6/15 in Jackman, drive north on US 201. In 2.5 mi., turn left onto Sandy Stream Rd. Ahead, where the pavement ends at a fork, bear left. Reach a 4-way intersection at 6.0 mi. and bear left again. In 0.9 mi., arrive at a gravel parking area on the right (a yellow gate and bridge are just ahead).

BURNT JACKET MTN. TRAIL (USGS JACKMAN, ATTEAN POND, AND STONY BROOK QUADS, GAZETTEER MAP 39)

From bridge over Wood Stream (1,252 ft.) to:

SEC
3

Ledges on Burnt Jacket Mtn., east shoulder of east peak (1,930 ft.)	0.9 mi.	678 ft.	0:50

NFTM Walk across the bridge, and in 200 ft., turn right and follow the grassy logging road about 100 yd., nearly to the top of the first rise. Look for a beaten path and flagging tape on the left. Bits of colored flagging tape and faded blue blazes intermittently mark the trail, which is rocky, rooty, and eroded. At 0.4 mi., bear right at the base of a mossy cliff and climb through the rocks on steep trail. Switchbacks lead over a short, steep pitch to the ridge crest. Bear right, go down slightly, and then begin a steady, moderate climb. After the angle eases, reach a rocky subpeak on the east shoulder of Burnt Jacket Mtn. The view north from here takes in Boundary Bald Mtn., Sandy Stream Mtn., and Big Wood Pond. To the southwest, look for Attean Mtn., Number Five Mtn., Number Six Mtn., Kibby Mtn., and Peaked Mtn. (in Canada).

From this point to the east peak of Burnt Jacket Mtn., a distance of about 0.5 mi., the trail is overgrown with brush, blocked by blowdowns, difficult to follow, and not recommended.

BOUNDARY BALD MTN. (3,641 FT.)

This mountain's high, multisummited ridgeline extends for approximately 4 miles across the remote commercial timberlands in Bald Mountain Township between Jackman and the Canadian border. Boundary Bald Mtn. offers remarkable views: the many trailless mountains on both sides of the international boundary and well into Canada; the high peaks in the Rangeley, Stratton, and Carrabassett Valley areas; and the mountains ringing Moosehead Lake.

From the jct. of US 201 and ME 6/15 in Jackman, drive north on US 201 for 9.4 mi. to Bald Mtn. Rd. on the right (0.5 mi. north of the Falls rest area). Turn onto Bald Mtn. Rd. Bald Mtn. is on land owned by Hilton Timberlands; please observe the rules posted at this jct. At 2.4 mi. from US 201, cross a bridge over Heald Stream (campsite and short trail to Heald

Stream Falls on right after bridge). At 2.9 mi., where Mud Pond Rd. goes right, bear left to stay on Bald Mtn. Rd. At 4.2 mi., turn left on Notch Rd., and in another 0.2 mi., turn right on Trail Rd. Trailhead parking for Boundary Bald Mtn. is 0.4 mi. ahead on the right in an old log yard.

BOUNDARY BALD MTN. TRAIL (USGS BOUNDARY BALD MTN. QUAD, GAZETTEER MAP 47)

Cumulative from Trail Rd. parking area (2,050 ft.) to:

Start of Boundary Bald Mtn. Trail (2,550 ft.) via old road	1.0 mi.	500 ft.	0:45
Boundary Bald Mtn. summit (3,641 ft.)	2.2 mi.	1,591 ft.	1:55

SEC 3

NFTM From the parking area, hike up Trail Rd. for 1.0 mi. to the start of Boundary Bald Mtn. Trail on the left (sign and cairn). Faded blue blazes and occasional colored flagging tape mark the route. The rocky, eroded treadway climbs steadily up the south slope of the mountain. At 1.4 mi., the trail contours to the east across a wet area, ascends moderately, and contours to the west to reach the coniferous zone. Strands of old telephone line appear along the trail, which gets steeper. Climb to the right of a rock crevice, cross a wet area, and scramble over boulders to reach a little ledge with a great view to the south. Amid the krummholz at 1.9 mi., reach a sign at a jct. that indicates the summit is to the right, Notch Rd. is to the left, and Trail Rd. is behind. Follow cairns and blazes through the subalpine terrain of the beautiful summit ridge. After a last dip into thick trees, emerge into the open, cross the helipad, and reach a solar array and a wooden cabin built on the pads of the old (1937) fire tower. Parts of the ruined tower lie on the ground around the summit. Just ahead along the ridge is a wind sock, another tower and outbuilding, and a solar array.

WILLIAMS MTN. (2,409 FT.)

The long ridgeline of Williams Mtn. straddles the town lines of Misery Township and Parlin Pond Township amid the vast commercial timberland west of Moosehead Lake. The mountain lies on the western edge of the 363,000-acre Moosehead Region Conservation Easement, which is held by Forest Society of Maine. Weyerhaeuser owns the land. A steel fire tower, erected in 1914, still stands on the summit of Williams Mtn.

From the blinking light in downtown Greenville at the jct. of ME 6/15 and Lily Bay Rd., drive north on ME 6/15 for 34.1 mi., passing through Rockwood. With Demo Rd. to the right, turn left off the highway onto gravel-surfaced Williams Mtn. Rd. In 0.9 mi., pass Smith Rd. on the right. At 3.6 mi. from ME 6/15, turn right on a minor double-track road and drive uphill for 0.4 mi. to where Williams Mtn. Trail crosses the road. Proceed ahead 100 yd. to a wide, grassy area to turn around and park. (*Note*: The driving directions above lead to temporary parking and a temporary trail start. MBPL is working to acquire land at the base of the mountain for a trailhead parking lot, plus acreage on the summit to preserve both the fire tower and a warden's cabin there.)

SEC 3

WILLIAMS MTN. TRAIL (USGS MISERY KNOB AND LONG POND QUADS, MTF WILLIAMS MOUNTAIN MAP, GAZETTEER MAP 40)
From gravel road (1,800 ft.) to:

Williams Mtn. summit (2,409 ft.)	1.5 mi.	644 ft.	1:15

MBPL From the grassy parking area, walk 100 yd. downhill to the blue-blazed trail. Turn left to begin the hike to Williams Mtn. (*Note*: To the right, a trail leads downhill about 0.25 mi. to the area where MBPL intends to secure property from Weyerhaeuser, the landowner, to construct a permanent trailhead parking lot. This lot would be about 0.5 mi. south along Williams Mtn. Rd. from the current gravel road turnoff.) Williams Mtn. Trail climbs easily west to reach the lower part of the northeast ridge of the mountain and a low granite knob just left of the trail at 0.3 mi. At 0.5 mi., the trail switchbacks left along the fairly narrow ridgeline and reaches an old clear-cut clearing. Proceed along the now-wide ridge through semi-open forest, the remains of heavy timber harvesting. At 0.7 mi., reach the easternmost summit on the Williams Mtn. ridge, with a view ahead to the fire tower on top. Continue easily on the ridge to another clearing, where the summit cone and tower are clearly visible.

At 1.2 mi., the old fire warden's trail enters from the right. From this point on, the new and old trails coincide, the route flagged with yellow tape. Cross a low, wet area, and then climb a moderate pitch up the summit cone and soon reach the old fire warden's cabin, still in surprisingly good condition. The fire tower is a short distance beyond. Here, a 0.1-mi. loop leads right to several viewpoints before returning to the tower.

SECTION FOUR

WESTERN LAKES AND MOUNTAINS

INTRODUCTION

This section describes 64 trails on 39 mountains in the Western Lakes and Mountains region, which includes, from west to east, all the northern and most of the central areas of Oxford County, all of Franklin County, and the western part of Somerset County, roughly south of Flagstaff Lake and the Dead River. The relatively compact Mahoosuc Range, which spans east from the New Hampshire border to Andover, is described in Section Five. The international border with Quebec, Canada, forms the northern boundary of all three counties, and the New Hampshire border forms the western boundary of Oxford County. To the south, the region is bounded by the

Androscoggin River and US 2 as far east as Sandy Stream, which forms much of the eastern boundary.

The region west of Rangeley features numerous large lakes, including Rangeley Lake, Cupsuptic Lake, Mooselookmeguntic Lake, Upper and Lower Richardson lakes, Umbagog Lake, and Aziscohos Lake. Much of this area is drained by the Ellis River, Swift River, and Sandy River, all of which empty into the Androscoggin River. To the northeast is Flagstaff Lake and its feeder, the Dead River. The Carrabassett River and Sandy Stream drain this area and flow south into the Kennebec River.

A nearly continuous chain of mountains extends from East B Hill Rd. at the eastern margin of the Mahoosuc Range northeast to Long Falls Dam Rd. east of Flagstaff Lake. The AT traverses this stretch for 88 mi., and along here are ten of Maine's fourteen 4,000-ft. peaks. Many of the trails are on large swaths of public land, including Grafton Notch State Park, Mahoosuc PL, Tumbledown PL, Mt. Blue State Park, and Bigelow Preserve. Maine Huts & Trails has four backcountry lodges on 80 mi. of multiuse trails in and around Bigelow Preserve. Outside these areas, the trails are mostly on private property and are open for public use through the generosity of various landowners.

SEC 4

GEOGRAPHY

Rumford Whitecap Mtn. (2,201 ft.) is a local favorite that rises just north of the Androscoggin River valley in the area east of Bethel and west of Rumford. Trails connect to neighboring Black Mtn. (2,291 ft.), which is home to a ski area. The ledges on Glassface Mtn. (1,916 ft.) and Mystery Mtn. (1,212 ft.) overlook the wide and winding Androscoggin River. To the east along the river are the craggy bumps of Sugarloaf (1,503 ft.) in Dixfield. North of rugged Black Brook Notch along the AT is Old Blue Mtn. (3,604 ft.) and the five summits on the long ridge of Bemis Mtn. (the highest is 3,579 ft.). A few miles southeast, concentrated in a semicircular ring around the village of Weld, are the high peaks and great cliffs of Tumbledown Mtn. (3,069 ft.); the summits of Little Jackson Mtn. (3,454 ft.), Jackson Mtn. (3,555 ft.), and Blueberry Mtn. (2,958 ft.); and the conical form of Mt. Blue (3,195 ft.). Nearby Center Hill (1,657 ft.) has a picnic area with a fine view of Tumbledown. Just southwest is the rocky ridgeline of Bald Mtn. (2,372 ft.).

West of Rangeley Lake are the lightly traveled summits of Aziscohos Mtn. (3,203 ft.) and West Kennebago Mtn. (its south peak is 3,730 ft.), both former fire tower sites. The popular Bald Mtn. (2,438 ft.) in Oquossoc occupies a commanding location between Mooselookmeguntic Lake and Rangeley Lake, with views of both.

In the 30-mi. stretch of the AT between ME 17 and ME 4 north of Rangeley and south of Stratton is a string of 4,000-ft. summits: Saddleback Mtn. (4,122 ft.), The Horn (4,024 ft.), Spaulding Mtn. (4,011 ft.), Mt. Abraham (4,050 ft.), Sugarloaf (4,238 ft.), North Crocker Mtn. (4,228 ft.), and South Crocker Mtn. (4,048 ft.). Neighboring Mt. Redington (4,002 ft.) is a formerly trailless summit that can now be reached by a rough herd path and old access road turned treadway. Third in line on the alpine Saddleback ridgeline is Saddleback Junior (3,655 ft.). The open summit of Burnt Hill (3,609 ft.), a neighbor of Sugarloaf, is part of the Sugarloaf ski area's backcountry trail system. North of ME 27 is the Bigelow Range and the craggy 4,000-ft. summits of Avery Peak (4,082 ft.) and West Peak (4,134 ft.), along with the shapely subsidiary peaks of North Horn (3,792 ft.) and South Horn (3,812 ft.). Cranberry Peak (3,199 ft.) and Little Bigelow Mtn. (3,041 ft.) bookend the range, which overlooks Flagstaff Lake and Carrabassett Valley.

Amid the extensive timberlands and jumble of trailless mountains in far northern Franklin County northwest of Flagstaff Lake between Stratton and the Canadian border rise lofty Snow Mtn. (3,967 ft.), home to an old fire tower, and Kibby Mtn. (3,656 ft.). Kibby, also sporting an old fire tower, sits on the edge of a huge windpower project.

SEC 4

ROAD ACCESS

US 2 travels the region's southern margin from Gilead on the New Hampshire border east to Farmington. ME 16 slices through the northern tier of lakes and mountains from west to east between Lincoln Plantation and Kingfield. A number of major south–north roads and highways crisscross the high mountains traversed by the AT. From west to east, these are ME 5 and South Arm Rd. between Rumford and South Arm on Lower Richardson Lake; ME 17 between Mexico and Oquossoc; ME 4 between Farmington and Rangeley; and ME 27 from Kingfield to Coburn Gore. Long Falls Dam Rd. bookends the section east of Flagstaff Lake. ME 142 connects Kingfield to Phillips to Dixfield in a generally north to south direction. ME 156 from Wilton connects to ME 142 in Weld near Tumbledown Mtn. and Mt. Blue.

CAMPING AND LODGING

Nineteen lean-tos and campsites along the AT provide for trailside camping. Public campgrounds are at Mt. Blue State Park in Weld and at Rangeley Lake State Park in Rangeley Plantation. At least ten privately operated campgrounds are found throughout this region. Three backcountry huts operated by Maine Huts & Trails around the south and east margins of the Bigelow Range offer self-service lodging and cooking facilities.

SUGGESTED HIKES

■ Easy

BALD MTN. (IN OQUOSSOC)

RT via Bald Mtn. Trail	2.6 mi.	920 ft.	1:35

Enjoy grand lake and mountain views of the Rangeley Lakes region from an observation tower atop Bald Mtn. See Bald Mtn. Trail, p. 219.

CENTER HILL

LP via Center Hill Nature Trail	0.6 mi.	125 ft.	0:25

A self-guided nature trail loop offers outstanding looks at Tumbledown Mtn., Jackson Mtn., and Little Jackson Mtn. from hilltop ledges. See Center Hill Nature Trail, p. 223.

BALD MTN. (IN WASHINGTON TOWNSHIP)

RT via Bald Mtn. Trail	2.2 mi.	1,322 ft.	1:45

Hike a long and beautiful ridge to the open ledges on the summit of Bald Mtn. See Bald Mtn. Trail, p. 219.

GLASSFACE LEDGES

RT via Glassface Ledges Trail	1.6 mi.	670 ft.	1:20

Enjoy fabulous vistas over the bucolic Androscoggin River valley from the craggy outlook at trail's end. See Glassface Ledges Trail, p. 236.

MYSTERY MTN.

RT via Mystery Mtn. Trail	1.4 mi.	510 ft.	1:00

Ledges on this little hill's western edge offer pleasant scenes along the Androscoggin River valley to the mountains around Bethel and beyond. See Mystery Mtn. Trail, p. 236.

■ Moderate

BURNT HILL

RT via Burnt Mtn. Trail | 5.8 mi. | 1,859 ft. | 3:50

Head to the alpine terrain on Burnt Hill for sights of the Sugarloaf ski slopes, North and South Crocker mountains, and the Bigelow Range. See Burnt Mtn. Trail, p. 196.

STRATTON BROOK HUT

RT via Narrow Gauge Pathway, Maine Hut Trail, and Oak Knoll Trail | 8.2 mi. | 670 ft. | 4:25

Hike to this Maine Huts & Trails backcountry hut for impressive views of the Bigelow Range and Sugarloaf. To begin, see Narrow Gauge Pathway, p. 197.

AZISCOHOS MTN.

RT via Aziscohos Mtn. Trail | 3.4 mi. | 1,463 ft. | 2:25

Enjoy one of Maine's finest mountaintop panoramas: from Katahdin to Saddleback to Mt. Washington, plus a handful of large lakes. See Aziscohos Mtn. Trail, p. 221.

MT. BLUE

RT via Mt. Blue Trail | 3.0 mi. | 1,786 ft. | 2:25

The summit of this conical peak features an observation platform and spectacular scenery across the High Peaks region. See Mt. Blue Trail, p. 222.

RUMFORD WHITECAP

LP via Iles Trail and Starr Trail | 4.9 mi. | 1,580 ft. | 3:15

Follow Iles Trail to the long, bald summit ridge of Rumford Whitecap and descend via the ledges on Starr Trail for grand 360-degree vistas. To begin, see Iles Trail, p. 231.

■ Strenuous
BIGELOW HIGH PEAKS

LP via Fire Warden's Trail, AT, and Horns Pond Trail	14.5 mi.	3,750 ft.	9:10

Tag Avery Peak and West Peak (both 4,000-footers), plus South Horn and North Horn on this super circuit in the Bigelow Range. To begin, see Fire Warden's Trail, p. 190.

THE CROCKERS AND MT. REDINGTON

RT via AT Northbound and herd path	9.8 mi.	3,920 ft.	6:55

Bag North Crocker Mtn. and South Crocker Mtn.—both 4,000-footers— via the AT and then go for a third 4,000-footer, Mt. Redington, via an informal herd path. To begin, see AT Northbound, p. 192.

MT. ABRAHAM

RT via Fire Warden's Trail	8.0 mi.	2,887 ft.	5:30

Hike to the summit of Mt. Abraham for a scenic panorama from the second-largest alpine zone in Maine. See Fire Warden's Trail, p. 190.

SADDLEBACK MTN.

RT via Berry Picker's Trail and AT Southbound	7.6 mi.	2,240 ft.	5:00

Hike a historical route used by local residents to harvest berries, and then bag the alpine summit of Saddleback Mtn. via the AT. To begin, see Berry Picker's Trail, p. 213.

LITTLE JACKSON MTN.

RT via Little Jackson Connector and Little Jackson Trail	7.4 mi.	2,655 ft.	5:00

From the extensive alpine area atop this peak, enjoy expansive 360-degree mountain vistas, plus Tumbledown Pond and Webb Lake. To begin, see Little Jackson Connector, p. 227.

SEC 4

TRAIL DESCRIPTIONS

BIGELOW PRESERVE

Bigelow Preserve was established by public referendum in 1976, the first time in Maine a statewide vote was held to create a public parkland. Since then, a series of land donations and purchases have brought the preserve to its present size of 36,000 acres. MBPL manages Bigelow Preserve. The scenic Bigelow Range sprawls about 12 mi. from west to east, encompassing a vast swath of forestland, six high peaks, more than 30 mi. of hiking trails, and miles of pristine lakefront. An approximately 18-mi. section of the AT crosses the preserve, and Maine Hut Trail cuts across the southwest corner.

AVERY PEAK (4,082 FT.), WEST PEAK (4,134 FT.), SOUTH HORN (3,812 FT.), AND NORTH HORN (3,792 FT.)

The predominant natural features of Bigelow Preserve are the alpine summits of Avery Peak and West Peak, both exceeding 4,000 ft. in elevation, and the symmetrical twin peaks of North Horn and South Horn, which rise just shy of the 4,000-ft. mark. These high points offer spectacular vistas over the rugged forested wilderness of hills and mountains, lakes, ponds, rivers, and streams ranging north to Katahdin and the jumble of mountains in the southern part of BSP and south to Sugarloaf, the Crockers, the summits of Mt. Abraham, and far beyond. Horns Pond is tucked into the ridge crest at the base of the Horns. Artificially constructed Flagstaff Lake, Maine's fourth-largest body of water, lies just north of the Bigelow Range. The lake stretches east to west, from one end of the Bigelows to the other.

Three trails approach the range from the south. Fire Warden's Trail is the most direct, albeit steep, route to the main peaks, while Horns Pond Trail provides quick access to Horns Pond, where the trail joins the AT to follow the ridge between the Horns, over South Horn (and past the side trail to North Horn) and West Peak, and on to Avery Peak. A third approach is via the AT, which extends from ME 27 to the ridge west of Horns Pond. A fourth and longer approach is by way of Bigelow Range Trail, which leads east from Stratton to join the AT east of Cranberry Pond. Finally, from East Flagstaff Rd. at Flagstaff Lake, gain access to the high peaks via Safford Brook Trail and the AT.

FIRE WARDEN'S TRAIL (MAP 3: B2–B3)
Cumulative from Stratton Brook Pond Rd. (1,253 ft.) to:

Horns Pond Trail (1,780 ft.)	2.1 mi.	500 ft.	1:20
Moose Falls CS (2,300 ft.)	3.5 mi.	1,050 ft.	2:25
Bigelow Col, Myron Avery CS, AT (3,800 ft.)	4.7 mi.	2,550 ft.	3:40

MATC This trail provides direct and steep access to Avery Peak and West Peak from the south.

From ME 27/16, at a point 3.2 mi. north of the blinking light at its jct. with Sugarloaf Access Rd., and 18.5 mi. north of the jct. of ME 27 and ME 16 in Kingfield, turn right (north) onto Stratton Brook Pond Rd. (small sign for Bigelow Preserve). Ahead on this dirt road at 0.9 mi., cross the AT (limited parking). At 1.6 mi. from ME 27/16, arrive at the trailhead parking area for Fire Warden's Trail and Horns Pond Trail (kiosk).

From the parking area, follow the old woods road east, going slightly up and then down to cross a footbridge over Stratton Brook. The old woods road continues along the north shore of Stratton Brook Pond. Beyond the pond, the trail reaches a fork near a campsite. Bear left and soon arrive at the posted start of blue-blazed Fire Warden's Trail in a clearing. (Esker Trail, a bike and ski trail, continues straight ahead.)

Fire Warden's Trail ascends gradually and then narrows and steepens to climb rocky slopes and rock slabs. After a level stretch, the trail crosses a section of bog bridge and then a small stream to meet the jct. of Horns Pond Trail on the left at 2.1 mi. Ascend a rising traverse, climb occasional rock steps, and cross a rocky brook. After a steep rock staircase, reach the spur to Moose Falls CS on the left at 3.5 mi. Over the next 1.2 mi. to Bigelow Col, Fire Warden's Trail gains more than 1,300 ft. A long series of rock staircases leads directly up the increasingly steep mountainside. Eventually, the angle eases and the trail soon passes through Myron H. Avery CS to end at 4.7 mi. at the jct. with the AT.

From this jct. in Bigelow Col, the AT goes right (north) to Avery Peak or left (south) to West Peak.

For Avery Peak: Go right on the AT and follow a rocky path up and out of the trees and onto the peak's alpine summit at 0.4 mi. Just beyond the summit along the open ridge is the old fire tower (1961) base and a plaque honoring Myron Avery, one of the most prominent forces behind the creation of the AT. The view is magnificent in every direction: north over Flagstaff Lake all the way to White Cap Mtn. and beyond to Katahdin; northwest over a rugged landscape to Canada; and southward to the ski slopes of shapely Sugarloaf, the Crockers, Spaulding Mtn., Mt. Abraham, and more.

For West Peak: Go left on the AT and climb through the trees before breaking out onto the craggy summit at 0.3 mi. The spectacular view takes in the Bigelow Range east to Avery Peak and the long ridge of Little Bigelow; to the west, the pyramidal peaks of South Horn and North Horn; and in every direction, for many miles, a panorama of mountains and lakes.

SEC 4

HORNS POND TRAIL AND AT (MAP 3: B2–B3)
Cumulative from Stratton Brook Pond Rd. (1,253 ft.) to:

Horns Pond Trail (1,780 ft.) via Fire Warden's Trail	2.1 mi.	527 ft.	1:20
AT (3,150 ft.)	4.6 mi.	1,897 ft.	3:20
Horns Pond Lean-tos (3,150 ft.) via AT	4.8 mi.	1,897 ft.	3:25
North Horn side trail (3,685 ft.) via AT	5.2 mi.	2,432 ft.	3:50
South Horn summit (3,812 ft.) via AT	5.3 mi.	2,559 ft.	3:55

MATC Horns Pond Trail provides the most direct access to Horns Pond, a scenic tarn high on the ridgeline of the Bigelow Range at the western base of the Horns. From Horns Pond, the AT leads north to South Horn and North Horn (via short side trail).

The blue-blazed route starts from Fire Warden's Trail, diverging left at a point 2.1 mi. from the parking area west of Stratton Brook Pond. Horns Pond Trail heads northwest, climbing gradually, sometimes on rocky terrain, and paralleling a brook for a stretch. On a shelf above, the trail skirts the southern edge of a grassy meadow (an old bog) with a view of South Horn. Beyond, Horns Pond Trail continues to rise gradually and then gets increasingly steeper, climbing over boulders and up rock staircases. At 4.6 mi., the trail intersects the AT. Bear right on the AT for 0.2 mi. to reach Horns Pond and Horns Pond Lean-tos at the old AT lean-to turned day-use shelter. From this jct., the pond is to the left and the two shelters and tentsites are to the right.

Continue north on the AT, passing the caretaker's tent platform and then a spring. Beyond, climb steadily up the west side of South Horn to a jct., where a 0.2-mi. side trail leads to the 3,792-ft. summit of North Horn (the mostly wooded summit has outlooks and is well worth the effort). Continue the steep climb to reach the ledges atop South Horn at 5.3 mi.

AT NORTHBOUND (MAP 3: B2–B3)
Cumulative from ME 27 (1,390 ft.) to:

Stratton Brook Pond Rd. (1,261 ft.)	0.8 mi.	−80 ft.	0:25
Cranberry Stream CS (1,370 ft.)	1.9 mi.	60 ft.	1:00
Bigelow Range Trail (2,410 ft.)	3.4 mi.	1,020 ft.	2:10
Horns Pond Trail (3,150 ft.)	5.2 mi.	2,170 ft.	3:40
Horns Pond Lean-tos (3,150 ft.)	5.4 mi.	2,170 ft.	3:45
North Horn side trail (3,685 ft.)	5.8 mi.	2,705 ft.	4:15
South Horn (3,812 ft.)	5.9 mi.	2,860 ft.	4:20
West Peak (4,134 ft.)	8.2 mi.	3,760 ft.	6:00

Bigelow Col, Fire Warden's Trail (3,810 ft.)	8.5 mi.	3,760 ft.	6:10
Avery Peak (4,082 ft.)	8.9 mi.	4,035 ft.	6:30
Safford Brook Trail (2,250 ft.)	11.1 mi.	4,035 ft.	7:30

MATC The AT crosses ME 27/16 in Wyman Township at a point 2.6 mi. north of the blinking light at the jct. of Sugarloaf Access Rd. and 17.8 mi. north of the jct. of ME 27 and ME 16 in Kingfield. Ample AT trailhead parking is available on the left (south) side of ME 27.

The trail descends gradually, crosses a brook, and reaches Stratton Brook Rd. at 0.9 mi. Shortly after, it travels across Jones Pond Rd. and then descends to cross a footbridge over Stratton Brook. Beyond, the AT joins an old tote road, turns left, and soon crosses a stream. At 1.9 mi., turn right off the road and soon reach Cranberry Stream CS. Cross a tote road at 2.5 mi., pass an old beaver pond, and then climb gradually but steadily into the basin of Cranberry Pond. Pass a spring (last reliable water before Horns Pond). At 3.2 mi., the AT reaches a jct. and turns sharply right (north). Bigelow Range Trail (sign) continues straight ahead (west) to reach the east end of pretty Cranberry Pond in 0.2 mi., the summit of Cranberry Peak in 1.8 mi., and the trailhead at the end of Currie St. in Stratton at 5.0 mi.

Ahead on the AT, climb steeply on a rough route through rocks and boulders, and at 4.0 mi., arrive at the crest of the ridge. The trail turns right (east) and follows the ridge crest, traversing a minor summit. Where the AT turns sharply left, watch for a lookout a few yards to the right over Horns Pond to the Horns. The trail descends steeply, and at 5.2 mi., Horns Pond Trail enters from the right. The AT continues through the woods, paralleling the south shore of Horns Pond, passing a side trail to Horns Pond Lean-tos at 5.4 mi.

From Horns Pond, the AT continues east, climbing South Horn. At 5.8 mi., blue-blazed North Horn Trail leads 0.2 mi. left to North Horn. Ahead, the AT crosses the peak of South Horn (5.9 mi.) and continues along the undulating crest of the range, reaching West Peak at 8.2 mi. The trail then descends to Bigelow Col and Myron H. Avery CS at 8.5 mi. Here, Fire Warden's Trail enters from the right. The AT continues east, climbing to the summit of Avery Peak at 8.9 mi. From Avery Peak, the AT descends east 2.2 mi. to its jct. with Safford Brook Trail in rugged Safford Notch.

CRANBERRY PEAK (3,199 FT.)

This craggy summit is the westernmost of the six Bigelow Range peaks. Cranberry Pond is a scenic tarn high on the Bigelow Range crest at the eastern base of the peak. Bigelow Range Trail traverses Cranberry Peak from the village of Stratton to the AT, which offers access from the south at ME 27/16.

SEC
4

BIGELOW RANGE TRAIL (MAP 3: B1–B2)
Cumulative from Currie St. (1,180 ft.) to:

Cranberry Peak (3,199 ft.)	2.9 mi.	2,019 ft.	2:30
AT (2,410 ft.)	5.0 mi.	2,019 ft.	3:30

MATC This blue-blazed trail starts from the east side of the village of Stratton at the western end of the Bigelow Range, climbs to Cranberry Peak, and continues east to meet the AT just beyond Cranberry Pond.

From the jct. of ME 27 and ME 16 in Stratton, drive 0.8 mi. south on ME 27/16 to Currie St. (next to the Coplin Plantation municipal office). Currie St. is a paved lane for 0.1 mi. and then becomes a narrow double-track road. Trailhead parking is at the end of the road at 0.4 mi. from ME 27.

Bigelow Range Trail proceeds easily through the woods and then climbs gradually on an old woods road. After crossing a brook at about 1.0 mi., the trail rises steeply to reach Arnold's Well (a deep cleft in the rocks named for Benedict Arnold; no drinking water) at about 1.5 mi. Beyond, the trail reaches semi-open ledges with partial views to the west and north. Pass a short side trail leading 200 ft. to a huge overhanging slab of rock known as "the Cave."

Bigelow Range Trail gradually ascends an undulating route along the wooded north side of the ridge. At 2.9 mi., reach the open summit of Cranberry Peak, which rewards with excellent views of Flagstaff Lake and the major summits along the Bigelow Range. The trail then descends steeply and then more gradually into a narrow valley, where it reaches the north shore of Cranberry Pond. The trail follows a scenic route along the pond before ending at 5.0 mi. at a jct. with the AT.

LITTLE BIGELOW MTN. (3,041 FT.)

Little Bigelow Mtn. is the easternmost peak of the Bigelow Range, separated from Avery Peak by a deep, rugged notch known as Safford Notch. The mountain's ridgeline is long and narrow, with steep cliffs along its southwestern slope. The northeastern face of the mountain slopes steadily to the south shore of Flagstaff Lake. Access to the Little Bigelow summit is via the AT Southbound from East Flagstaff Rd. or via Safford Brook Trail and the AT Northbound.

AT SOUTHBOUND (MAP 3: B3–B4)
Cumulative from East Flagstaff Rd. (1,170 ft.) to:

Little Bigelow Lean-to (1,780 ft.)	1.4 mi.	610 ft.	1:00
Little Bigelow Mtn. summit (3,041 ft.)	3.5 mi.	1,900 ft.	2:40
Safford Brook Trail (2,250 ft.)	6.7 mi.	2,000 ft.	4:20
Avery Peak (4,082 ft.)	8.9 mi.	3,840 ft.	6:20

MATC The AT traverses the long and craggy ridgeline of Little Bigelow Mtn., connecting East Flagstaff Rd. with Safford Notch Trail in Safford Notch.

From the jct. of ME 16 and Long Falls Dam Rd. in New Portland, drive 17.3 mi. north on Long Falls Dam Rd. to Bog Brook Rd., on the left. Bear left onto gravel-surfaced Bog Brook Rd., drive 0.8 mi., and bear left onto East Flagstaff Rd. Reach the AT crossing in another 0.2 mi. Parking is on the right in an old gravel pit.

The AT continues north along the road from the parking area for a short distance before it bears left into the woods and climbs through hardwoods alongside a brook. At 1.4 mi., a blue-blazed side trail leads right across the brook to reach Little Bigelow Lean-to in 0.1 mi. Beyond the jct., the AT continues through the woods, leaves the brook, and climbs a series of open ledges. At 3.0 mi., the trail reaches a viewpoint at the southeastern end of the summit ridge. The true summit is about 0.5 mi. farther. Multiple outlooks offer fine views west along the Bigelow Range and southwest to the ski slopes of Sugarloaf. The AT continues to the jct. with Safford Brook Trail in rugged Safford Notch at 6.7 mi. Safford Notch CS is 0.3 mi. to the left (south).

Continuing southbound, the AT rises steeply west toward Avery Peak, with excellent scenery en route. At 7.6 mi., the AT reaches the ridge crest. Here, a side trail leads left 0.1 mi. to the top of Old Man's Head, a huge cliff on the south side of the mountain. From this jct., the AT continues to climb steeply, reaching timberline and, shortly thereafter, the alpine summit of Avery Peak and the concrete and stone base of the old fire tower (1961). Outstanding vistas are visible in all directions.

SAFFORD BROOK TRAIL (MAP 3: A4, B3–B4)
From East Flagstaff Rd. (1,222 ft.) to:

AT (2,250 ft.) in Safford Notch	2.3 mi.	1,028 ft.	1:40

MATC This trail affords access to Little Bigelow Mtn. and Avery Peak from the north at Flagstaff Lake.

To reach the start of blue-blazed Safford Notch Trail, follow the driving directions for the AT to Little Bigelow Mtn. as described on p. 194. From the AT crossing, continue northwest on East Flagstaff Rd. In 4.1 mi., the road crosses Safford Brook and, just ahead, reaches the trailhead parking area on the right (kiosk). (*Note*: Safford Notch Trail officially starts 0.25 mi. north at Round Barn CS on the shore of Flagstaff Lake, but most hikers headed for Bigelow skip this short stretch and start from the parking lot on East Flagstaff Rd.)

From the road, Safford Brook Trail ascends gradually along Safford Brook and crosses the brook at 0.7 mi. It climbs steeply to a side trail on the

SEC 4

left leading to Safford Overlook and filtered views north to Flagstaff Lake. Continuing on, the main trail steeply ascends into the wild and rugged environs of Safford Notch, with its jumble of house-sized boulders. At 2.3 mi. is the jct. with the AT, which leads north to Little Bigelow Mtn. in 3.2 mi. and south to Avery Peak in 2.2 mi. About 50 yd. east (left) on the AT is a blue-blazed trail that leads south (right) 0.3 mi. to Safford Notch CS.

BURNT HILL (3,609 FT.)

This popular peak in Carrabassett Valley, also known as Burnt Mtn., lies just east of Sugarloaf Mtn. and south of ME 27 and Bigelow Preserve. A forest fire in the early 1900s burned 5,500 acres on the mountain (hence its name) as well as a portion of neighboring Sugarloaf. Burnt Hill offers extensive views from its open alpine summit, including Sugarloaf and its ski slopes, Spaulding Mtn., the long alpine ridge of Mt. Abraham, the Crockers, and the Bigelow Range.

From the jct. of ME 16 and ME 27 in Kingfield, drive north on ME 27/16 for 15.2 mi. Turn left (south) onto the access road to the Sugarloaf ski resort. Continue 1.8 mi. to the base area, where parking is available in Lot C.

BURNT MTN. TRAIL (MAP 3: C3)
From parking at Lot C (1,748 ft.) to:

Start of Burnt. Mtn. Trail (1,750 ft.)	0.4 mi.	0 ft.	0:12
Burnt Mtn. summit (3,609 ft.)	2.9 mi.	1,859 ft.	2:25

Sugarloaf From Lot C, walk to the Sugarloaf Mtn. Hotel and take the steps up through the breezeway to the plaza beyond. Turn left and walk past the base lodge. Pass under the Snubber Chairlift, follow the wide path over a brook, and go behind Gondola Village to reach Adams Mtn. Rd. Continue along Adams Mtn. Rd., cross Mountainside Rd., and proceed along dirt Bigelow Mtn. Rd. to its end. Follow a narrower dirt road to a fork and then bear left down to a bridge. Cross the bridge and, 50 ft. ahead, look for a blue-and-white sign on the right marking the start of Burnt Mtn. Trail.

The blue-blazed trail soon turns sharply right and runs along the West Branch of Brackett Brook. Ahead, rock-hop across the brook, and 200 ft. beyond, recross the brook. (*Note:* If the water is too high, look for the narrow high-water path that avoids the crossings.) The trail soon merges with a grassy ski trail and in 100 ft. reenters the woods.

Burnt Mtn. Trail eventually veers away from the brook, climbs gradually and then at a moderate grade, and travels through several marked ski glades. Pass several cairns before reaching the open col between Burnt Hill and

Sugarloaf. The remainder of the hike is above treeline through alpine terrain. Follow faded blazes and cairns across the col, and then work left and up over rocks and ledges. The route is indistinct in places; pay attention to the cairns. After a false summit, reach the large summit cairn atop Burnt Hill. The views are spectacular in every direction and include the Bigelow Range, the Crockers, Sugarloaf, Mt. Abraham, and Saddleback, to name just a few.

MAINE HUTS & TRAILS

Maine Huts & Trails operates year-round, off-the-grid backcountry huts along more than 80 mi. of people-powered trails through the foothills, rivers, and valleys of the western mountains, between ME 27/16 in Carrabassett Valley and US 201 in West Forks. Three self-service huts—Stratton Brook, Poplar, and Flagstaff—sit amid the spectacular terrain of the Bigelow Range, Poplar Stream Falls, and Flagstaff Lake, respectively (a fourth hut at Grand Falls is temporarily closed). The extensive trails built and maintained by MHT accommodate nonmotorized use, from hiking, mountain biking, and paddling in summer to cross-country skiing, fat biking, and snowshoeing in winter. Trail access is free.

STRATTON BROOK HUT

Stratton Brook Hut features panoramic views of the Bigelow Range, Carrabassett Valley, and Sugarloaf Mtn. To reach Stratton Brook Trailhead from the jct. of ME 27 and ME 16 in Kingfield, drive north on ME 27/16 for 14.8 mi. to the MHT-signed trailhead parking lot on the right (less than 0.1 mi. beyond Sugarloaf Access Rd.). From the trailhead, follow Narrow Gauge Pathway and Maine Hut Trail, and take either Oak Knoll Trail or Newton's Revenge to reach the hut.

NARROW GAUGE PATHWAY, MAINE HUT TRAIL, AND OAK KNOLL TRAIL (MAP 3: B3)
Cumulative from Stratton Brook Trailhead (1,290 ft.) to:

Maine Hut Trail (1,250 ft.) via Narrow Gauge Pathway	0.9 mi.	−50 ft.	0:25
Oak Knoll Trail (1,280 ft.)	1.3 mi.	30 ft.	0:40
Newton's Revenge (1,850 ft.)	3.8 mi.	600 ft.	2:15
Stratton Brook Hut (1,920 ft.)	4.1 mi.	670 ft.	2:25

CV, MHT From the parking lot kiosk, follow the trailhead spur path 0.1 mi. to connect with Narrow Gauge Pathway. Turn left, cross a bridge over the Carrabassett River, and at 0.3 mi., turn right to stay on Narrow Gauge Pathway. Continue down the old graveled rail corridor, gently losing elevation. At 0.9 mi., turn left onto Maine Hut Trail (also signed for Newton's

Revenge). At 1.3 mi., reach the blue-blazed Oak Knoll Trail on the left (sign), a single-track trail with well-crafted stone switchbacks that climb the south side of the hill. Near Stratton Brook Hut, Oak Knoll Trail crosses the hut service road twice. Beyond the first service road crossing, at a T jct. with Newton's Revenge, turn right and in 80 yd. cross the service road for the second time (the hut is 100 yd. up the service road to the left). Ahead, the single-track trail winds through the woods to a great view of the Bigelow Range before reaching Stratton Brook Hut at 4.1 mi.

NARROW GAUGE PATHWAY, MAINE HUT TRAIL, AND NEWTON'S REVENGE (MAP 3: B3)

Cumulative from Stratton Brook Trailhead (1,290 ft.) to:

Maine Hut Trail (1,260 ft.) via Narrow Gauge Pathway	0.9 mi.	–30 ft.	0:25
Oak Knoll Trail (1,280 ft.)	1.3 mi.	30 ft.	0:40
Newton's Revenge (1,540 ft.)	2.5 mi.	290 ft.	1:25
Stratton Brook Hut (1,920 ft.) via Newton's Revenge	3.2 mi.	630 ft.	1:55

CV, MHT From the parking lot kiosk, follow the trailhead spur path 0.1 mi. to connect with Narrow Gauge Pathway. Turn left, cross a bridge over the Carrabassett River, and at 0.3 mi., turn right to stay on Narrow Gauge Pathway. Continue down the old narrow-gauge rail corridor, gently losing elevation. At 0.9 mi., turn left on Maine Hut Trail (also signed for Newton's Revenge). At 1.3 mi., reach blue-blazed Oak Knoll Trail on the left (sign). Continue ahead on Maine Hut Trail, which winds up the south slope of the knoll to a jct. at 2.5 mi. with Newton's Revenge, Maine Hut Trail to Poplar Hut, and a single-track bike trail. Here, Maine Hut Trail turns right and downhill toward Poplar Hut or continues straight and uphill as Newton's Revenge to Stratton Brook Hut. The single-track trail on the left at this intersection braids on and off Newton's Revenge, ending at Oak Knoll Trail. Stay straight on Newton's Revenge, climbing the east ridge to the jct. with Oak Knoll Trail at 3.0 mi. In another 80 yd., Newton's Revenge comes to a T intersection with the hut service road; turn left to follow the road, arriving at Stratton Brook Hut at 3.2 mi.

NEWTON'S REVENGE, APPROACH TRAIL, ESKER TRAIL, FIRE WARDEN'S TRAIL, DEAD MOOSE TRAIL, AND MOUNTAIN TRAIL (MAP 3: B3)

Cumulative from Stratton Brook Hut (1,920 ft.) to:

Newton's Revenge (1,850 ft.)	100 yd.	–30 ft.	0:02
Oak Knoll Trail (1,820 ft.)	180 yd.	–50 ft.	0:04
Approach Trail (1,685 ft.)	0.4 mi.	–195 ft.	0:25

Esker Trail (1,270 ft.)	2.1 mi.	–610 ft.	1:05
Fire Warden's Trailhead, Dead Moose Trail (1,250 ft.)	4.0 mi.	20 ft.	2:00
Mountain Trail (1,370 ft.)	4.7 mi.	140 ft.	2:25
Stratton Brook Hut service road (1,600 ft.)	5.7 mi.	370 ft.	3:00
Stratton Brook Hut (1,920 ft.)	6.3 mi.	690 ft.	3:30

CV, MHT From Stratton Brook Hut, follow the hut service road to its intersection with Newton's Revenge and turn right at 100 yd. Stay straight past Oak Knoll Trail, which turns downhill to the left in about 80 yd. (sign). Continue the steep descent along Newton's Revenge, blazed with MHT white diamond markers. At 0.4 mi., at a large hairpin right-hand corner, Approach Trail turns left from Newton's Revenge. This sustainable hiking, snowshoeing, and backcountry-skiing trail follows the knoll's north-facing contours downhill, eventually crossing (motorized) Mountain Trail, a power-line corridor, and a footbridge over Stratton Brook to a T intersection with Esker Trail.

SEC 4

To loop around Stratton Brook Pond back to Stratton Brook Hut, turn left on Esker Trail from Approach Trail and proceed 1.2 mi. Stay straight past the Fire Warden's Trail intersection on the right and continue for another 0.7 mi. to Fire Warden's Trailhead. At 3.9 mi., turn left at Fire Warden's Trailhead onto the double-tracked, locally named Dead Moose Trail (when facing the trailhead kiosk, the trail is to the right and makes a Y with Fire Warden's Trail and Stratton Brook Pond Rd.). Dead Moose Trail, marked with MHT blue diamond blazes, leads back to Mountain Trail (ATVs and snowmobiles have right of way) at 4.7 mi. Follow MHT cedar-and-blue-diamond signs on Mountain Trail, braiding along a power-line corridor. At 5.7 mi., turn right at a directional cedar-diamond trail sign with a blue blaze, and travel 0.3 mi. to the Stratton Brook Hut service road at 6.0 mi. (going straight leads back to Mountain Trail's crossing of Approach Trail, 0.4 mi. farther up Mountain Trail). At the wide landing area, turn left onto the Stratton Brook Hut service road, climb steeply uphill, pass the Oak Knoll Trail crossings, and arrive at Stratton Brook Hut at 6.3 mi.

POPLAR HUT

The very first hut of the MHT system is southeast of Little Bigelow Mtn., a short distance from pretty Poplar Falls. Poplar Hut can be reached from Airport Trailhead on ME 27/16 in Carrabassett Valley by way of Maine Hut Trail, Larry's Trail, or Warren's Trail. From the jct. of ME 27 and ME 16 in Kingfield, drive north on ME 27/16 for 8.9 mi. to the signed trailhead parking lot on the right.

MAINE HUT TRAIL (MHT; MAP 3: C4—B4)
Cumulative from Airport Trailhead (883 ft.) to:

Carriage Rd. X-ing 1, Warren's Trail (900 ft.)	1.3 mi.	20 ft.	0:40
Larry's Trail (1,050 ft.)	1.8 mi.	170 ft.	1:00
Poplar Hut (1,306 ft.)	3.3 mi.	430 ft.	1:50

MHT From the parking lot kiosk, follow multiuse Maine Hut Trail north to a bridge over the Carrabassett River at 0.2 mi. Cross the bridge to reach a large 5-way intersection. Turn right on Huston Brook Rd. and immediately bear left to follow Maine Hut Trail uphill. The route parallels the Carrabassett River and Huston Brook Rd. before trending away and going around the base of a ridge to meet Carriage Rd. at Carriage Rd. X-ing 1 at 1.3 mi. Here, a bridge crosses Poplar Stream. Warren's Trail departs north to follow the west side of Poplar Stream toward Poplar Hut. To continue on Maine Hut Trail, cross the bridge over Poplar Stream and keep left. The trail starts out flat and then rises to the jct. with Larry's Trail on the left at 1.8 mi. Beyond Larry's Trail, Maine Hut Trail climbs moderately through the valley of Poplar Stream before leveling off for the final stretch to a bridge over Poplar Hut's modest hydropower reservoir at 3.2 mi. Cross the bridge and follow the reservoir before turning right at a signed intersection to reach Poplar Hut at 3.3 mi.

LARRY'S TRAIL (MAP 3: C4—B4)
Cumulative from Airport Trailhead (883 ft.) to:

Warren's Trail (900 ft.)	1.3 mi.	20 ft.	0:40
Larry's Trail (1,050 ft.)	1.8 mi.	170 ft.	1:00
Poplar Hut (1,306 ft.)	3.1 mi.	430 ft.	2:00

MHT Larry's Trail departs left from Maine Hut Trail 1.8 mi. from Airport Trailhead and follows the east side of Poplar Stream, winding through the forest over rolling terrain. Cross a native timber footbridge over the South Branch of Poplar Stream at 2.6 mi. The cascades of Poplar Falls are on the right; Larry's Trail climbs a steep stone staircase straight ahead. At the top of the staircase, Warren's Trail intersects on the left, creating a loop back toward Airport Trailhead. Continue straight for 0.1 mi. and turn right at the T intersection with Maine Hut Trail. Climb uphill beside South Brook (which feeds Poplar Falls and Poplar Hut's hydropower) for 0.3 mi. before reaching a left-hand jct. that leads to Poplar Hut at 3.1 mi.

WARREN'S TRAIL (MAP 3: C4—B4)
Cumulative from Airport Trailhead (883 ft.) to:

Warren's Trail (900 ft.)	1.3 mi.	20 ft.	0:40
Poplar Hut service road (1,150 ft.)	2.8 mi.	250 ft.	1:50

Larry's Trail (1,170 ft.)	3.0 mi.	270 ft.	1:55
Maine Hut Trail (1,190 ft.)	3.1 mi.	290 ft.	2:00
Poplar Hut (1,314 ft.)	3.5 mi.	430 ft.	2:15

MHT Warren's Trail departs left from Maine Hut Trail at 1.3 mi. from Airport Trailhead. After crossing Carriage Rd. at Carriage Rd. X-ing 1, but before crossing the bridge over Poplar Stream, turn left onto Warren's Trail. This primitive path along the west side of Poplar Stream passes through mature tree growth and makes for a great hike to see waterfalls and wildlife. At 2.8 mi., reach the Poplar Hut service road. Turn right on the service road and cross the bridge over Poplar Stream. Immediately after the bridge, at an MHT cedar trail sign, head back into the forest to continue on Warren's Trail, following the boulder-strewn path for 0.1 mi. to the jct. with Larry's Trail. To continue to Poplar Hut, turn left onto Larry's Trail and gradually ascend to Maine Hut Trail at 3.1 mi. Turn right onto Maine Hut Trail. Climb uphill beside South Brook (which feeds Poplar Falls and Poplar Hut's hydropower) for 0.3 mi. before reaching a left-hand jct. that leads to Poplar Hut at 3.5 mi.

SEC 4

FLAGSTAFF HUT

Flagstaff Hut is the most approachable hut in the MHT system due to its gentle lakeside terrain. The hut is on the sandy eastern shore of Flagstaff Lake and features wonderful views across the lake to the north side of the Bigelow Range. Flagstaff Hut can be reached from Long Falls Dam/Flagstaff Trailhead on Long Falls Dam Rd. in Carrying Place Township. From the jct. of ME 27 and ME 16 in Kingfield, travel east on ME 16 for 7.5 mi. to New Portland. Turn left (north) on Long Falls Dam Rd. and drive 22.8 mi. to the signed trailhead parking lot on the left.

MAINE HUT TRAIL (MAP 3: A4)
From Long Falls Dam/Flagstaff Trailhead (1,200 ft.) to:

Flagstaff Hut (1,164 ft.)	2.1 mi.	50 ft.	1:10

MHT Hike south on the trailhead spur of Maine Hut Trail (white diamond trail markers) for 0.2 mi. to a 4-way jct. with Maine Hut Trail (goes left and right, south and north) and Shore Trail, which goes straight to reach Flagstaff Lake. Turn right on Maine Hut Trail, which travels northwest over rolling terrain through cedar, fir, and broadleaf forest. At 1.6 mi., a spur leads to Shore Trail. Turn sharply right to stay on Maine Hut Trail. Proceed 0.3 mi., and bear left on the hut service road. In another 0.1 mi., continue straight along the service road past the intersection of the Grand Falls–bound Maine Hut Trail for an additional 0.2 mi. to reach Flagstaff Hut.

SHORE TRAIL (MAP 3: A4)
Cumulative from Long Falls Dam/Flagstaff Trailhead (1,200 ft.) to:

Shore Trail (1,180 ft.)	0.2 mi.	–20 ft.	0:05
Flagstaff Hut (1,164 ft.)	2.1 mi.	50 ft.	1:05

MHT Hike south on the trailhead spur of Maine Hut Trail (white diamond trail markers) for 0.2 mi. to a 4-way jct. with Maine Hut Trail (goes left and right, south and north) and Shore Trail, which goes straight to reach Flagstaff Lake. Continue ahead on Shore Trail. At Flagstaff Lake, Shore Trail turns northwest to follow the shoreline for more than 1 mi. At 1.6 mi., a spur turns right to Maine Hut Trail; bear left to continue on Shore Trail. At 1.9 mi., Beaver Trail leads right to a dam and beaver lodge viewpoint. A spur on the left at 2.0 mi. leads to a fantastic vista of Flagstaff Lake. Bear right to arrive at Flagstaff Hut at 2.1 mi.

GRAND FALLS HUT
Grand Falls Hut is closed until further notice.

APPALACHIAN TRAIL CORRIDOR
NORTH CROCKER MTN. (4,228 FT.) AND
SOUTH CROCKER MTN. (4,048 FT.)
North Crocker Mtn. and South Crocker Mtn. are just west of Sugarloaf Mtn. in Carrabassett Valley. They are separated from Sugarloaf by Caribou Valley and the South Branch of the Carrabassett River. The peaks and a portion of nearby Mt. Redington are part of the 12,000-acre Crocker Mtn. PL. The AT extends across the Crockers for 8.8 mi. North Crocker Mtn., despite its height, is heavily wooded to the top and has few views. South Crocker Mtn., although also wooded, offers fine views on the ascent from Caribou Valley as well as from a ledge outcropping on its summit. Hikers can approach North Crocker Mtn. from the north via the AT from ME 27, and South Crocker Mtn. from the east at Caribou Valley Rd.

AT SOUTHBOUND (MAP 3: B2—C2)
Cumulative from ME 27 (1,390 ft.) to:

North Crocker Mtn. (4,228 ft.)	5.2 mi.	2,838 ft.	4:00
South Crocker Mtn. (4,048 ft.)	6.2 mi.	3,200 ft.	4:40
Side trail to Crocker Cirque CS (2,720 ft.)	7.3 mi.	3,200 ft.	5:15
Caribou Valley Rd. (2,220 ft.)	8.3 mi.	3,200 ft.	5:45
Parking area and yellow gate (2,130 ft.)	8.8 mi.	3,200 ft.	6:00

MATC In Carrabassett Valley, from the jct. of ME 27 and the blinking light at the jct. of Sugarloaf Access Rd., drive north on ME 27 for 2.6 mi. to the AT crossing, where there is a trailhead parking lot on the left (south) side of the highway.

Follow the AT Southbound, climbing steadily through woods for 1.4 mi. to reach a knoll on the north ridge of Crocker Mtn. Beyond, pass through a long section of coniferous forest before angling up the western side of the ridge through hardwood forest. The AT continues up the ridge, reenters softwoods at about 3.5 mi., and crosses a small stream at 4.2 mi. (usually reliable; last water until Crocker Cirque CS). The trail rises more steeply to the crest just north of Stoney Brook Mtn. and continues climbing to reach the north peak of Crocker Mtn. at 5.2 mi. The descent into the col begins immediately. The AT drops to the low point of the col and soon begins to climb toward rocky South Crocker Mtn. At 6.2 mi., at a signed jct. on top of South Crocker Mtn., where the AT makes a sharp left turn for the descent to Caribou Valley Rd., bear right and hike up 50 yd. to the true summit, where an open ledge offers fine views to Sugarloaf, Spaulding Mtn., and Mt. Abraham. The herd path to Mt. Redington leaves to the right, just before the ledge opening.

SEC 4

AT NORTHBOUND (MAP 3: C2–B2)
Cumulative from Caribou Valley Rd. parking and yellow gate (2,132 ft.) to:

AT crossing (2,220 ft.)	0.5 mi.	88 ft.	0:15
Side trail to Crocker Cirque CS (2,710 ft.)	1.5 mi.	578 ft.	1:00
South Crocker Mtn. (4,048 ft.)	2.6 mi.	1,916 ft.	2:15
North Crocker Mtn. (4,228 ft.)	3.6 mi.	2,460 ft.	3:00
ME 27 (1,390 ft.)	8.8 mi.	2,460 ft.	5:40

MATC From the jct. of ME 27 and Caribou Valley Rd. (no sign), at a point 1.0 mi. north of the blinking light at the jct. of the Sugarloaf Access Rd., turn left (south) on Caribou Valley Rd. and drive 3.8 mi. to the end of the maintained road (blocked by a yellow gate) and a parking area.

To reach the AT, pass around the yellow gate and walk north on Caribou Valley Rd. for 0.5 mi., crossing three bridges (the first is metal, the second and third are wooden). A small cairn on the right marks where the AT enters the woods on the right (west) side of the old road. The AT climbs steadily to a jct. and brook on the right at 1.5 mi., where a 0.2-mi. side trail leads to Crocker Cirque CS. Beyond the jct., the AT climbs steeply via switchbacks and then crosses a talus field with views ahead to North

Crocker and behind to Sugarloaf Mtn. Continuing up the west ridge of the mountain, watch for views of Crocker Cirque below and the Bigelow Range to the north. The moderate climb along the ridge ends at a signed jct. atop South Crocker. Here, the AT bears right and down, while a side trail bears left and up 50 yd. to the true summit and a pleasant ledge viewpoint. Just before the view opening, the herd path to Mt. Redington leaves to the right.

MT. REDINGTON (4,002 FT.)

Mt. Redington straddles the town lines of Redington Township and Carrabassett Valley in the wild region of high peaks southwest of South Crocker Mtn. and North Crocker Mtn. and east of Sugarloaf Mtn. and Spaulding Mtn. The eastern half of Mt. Redington, nearly to the summit, is on conservation land owned by the state of Maine, while the western half is privately owned. Redington is the highest of the two peaks in the Redington Pond Range.

The mountain is the only "trailless" 4,000-footer in Maine and the only bushwhack described in this guide. A herd path, not officially marked or maintained, connects the summit of South Crocker Mtn. with the top of Mt. Redington. Once a fierce bushwhack, this path has become increasingly popular with peak baggers and, as such, is beaten down and pretty obvious the entire way, with bits of colored surveyor's tape marking the route. (*Note*: Even with the herd path, an attempt on Mt. Redington should not be underestimated and should be treated as a bushwhack. Hikers should be prepared for travel into remote terrain with proper gear and the requisite navigational skills.) Alternate access is via the old Caribou Valley Rd. to Caribou Pond and then by old logging roads and a foot path; although also unmaintained, this is a moderate and surprisingly straightforward route.

Redington's summit was once the site of an experimental wind gauge tower, but the windpower project proposal was withdrawn, and the tower removed. The summit is now being reclaimed by forest, but pleasant views remain. A register canister attached to a tree in the thick fir growth adjacent to the summit clearing still bears the old (pre-1989 USGS survey) elevation of 3,984 ft.

MT. REDINGTON HERD PATH (USGS BLACK NUBBLE QUAD, MAP 3: C2, GAZETTEER MAP 29)

Cumulative from South Crocker Mtn. summit (4,048 ft.) to:

Low point between the peaks (3,470 ft.)	0.6 mi.	−578 ft.	0:20
Mt. Redington summit (4,002 ft.)	1.3 mi.	535 ft.	1:00

NFTM To reach the start of the Mt. Redington Herd Path, follow the previous driving directions and trail description for South Crocker Mtn.

and the AT Northbound from Caribou Valley Rd. (p. 203) At the signed jct. atop South Crocker, the AT Northbound bears right and down, while a side trail bears left and up 50 yd. to the true summit and a ledge viewpoint. Just before the view opening, the herd path to Mt. Redington leaves to the right. A small tentsite is visible to the right of the trail at the herd path start.

Follow the flagged path along the ridge and over a low knoll. Descend to a yellow-blazed boundary line (the NPS-owned AT corridor) at 0.1 mi. Turn west along the boundary line, follow it around a corner, and reach a jct. at 0.15 mi., with a low cairn on the left and a low brush pile blocking the boundary corridor ahead. Leave the boundary line by turning left onto a narrow trail. As the trail descends southwest through thick woods, views of Mt. Redington ahead appear through the trees. The descent is mostly moderate with a few steep sections. At 0.4 mi., there's an awkward step off a boulder. At 0.6 mi., the trail bears south along a contour. Reach a small clearing, the low point between South Crocker and Mt. Redington, where there is a view to the northwest. Just ahead, in a semi-open stretch of fir, the dome of Mt. Redington is visible, while behind is a look to North Crocker and the shoulder of South Crocker. Climb, follow a contour, and climb again to reach an old skidder road at 0.7 mi. (cairn on left, small log barrier across road to right).

Turn left up the road, and in another 0.1 mi., reach the saddle between South Crocker Mtn. and Mt. Redington. Here, turn right off the skidder road and follow the trail southwest up the ridge. At a well-flagged jct. at 1.1 mi., the trail route from Caribou Valley enters from the left. Ahead, climb easily, and soon cross a faint yellow-blazed boundary line at 1.3 mi. Just beyond, an old trail (likely the work road built to service the former wind gauge tower) enters from the left. Here, bear right into the summit clearing, and in 50 ft., reach the summit. A log bench is to the left, and a small summit sign is tucked into the woods on the right. Ahead, through a row of firs, is a view north to North Crocker, South Crocker, and the Bigelow Range. From the summit sign, follow a narrow path around to the right to find the register canister attached to a tree.

MT. REDINGTON CARIBOU VALLEY ACCESS ROUTE
(USGS BLACK NUBBLE QUAD, MAP 3: C2, GAZETTEER MAP 29)
Cumulative from Caribou Valley Rd. parking and yellow gate (2,132 ft.) to:

AT crossing (2,220 ft.)	0.5 mi.	88 ft.	0:15
Jct. near Caribou Pond (2,732 ft.)	2.9 mi.	600 ft.	1:45
Herd Path jct. (3,800 ft.)	5.3 mi.	1,680 ft.	3:30
Mt. Redington summit (4,002 ft.)	5.5 mi.	1,880 ft.	3:45

NFTM To reach the start of the Mt. Redington Caribou Valley Access Route, follow the driving directions and trail description for South Crocker Mtn. and the AT Northbound from Caribou Valley Rd. (p. 203). At the AT crossing 0.5 mi. from the start, continue straight ahead on the old Caribou Valley Rd., which leads south through the deep valley of the South Branch of the Carrabassett River.

In a gravelly clearing at 1.5 mi., with a trace of an old road to the right, continue straight and cross a bridge over a brook. At 2.8 mi., look for a falls and pool in the river below to the left. In a large clearing at 2.9 mi., bear right toward Mt. Redington (to the left, the old Caribou Valley Rd. crosses a bridge and reaches the northern end of Caribou Pond in 0.1 mi.; this short detour is worthwhile).

The well-traveled trail is narrow at first but then widens, wending easily through a thick forest of spruce and fir. Views of Redington open up ahead, while behind, Spaulding Mtn. is visible. After cresting, the trail dips slightly. Beyond the dip, in a large, grassy clearing at 3.7 mi., look for a small cairn low on the right; turn right here. Ascend easily over the grassy and then rocky corridor through the thick spruce and fir woods. At 4.2 mi., pass the remains of an old quarry on the right. In 0.1 mi., turn left off the wide track onto a narrower track (this turn is marked by a large cairn on the left). Follow easily along a contour, and at a fork at 4.6 mi., continue straight ahead on the obvious footpath. In a small, mossy clearing at 5.2 mi., turn sharply right and climb at a moderate grade. Intersect the herd path from South Crocker Mtn. at 5.3 mi. Turn left and finish the climb of Mt. Redington via the herd path, reaching the top at 5.5 mi.

SUGARLOAF MTN. (4,238 FT.)

Sugarloaf Mtn. in Carrabassett Valley is the second-highest mountain in Maine. It is best known and most frequented for the ski resort on its northern slopes. For hikers, the view from the symmetrical, bare summit cone is well worth the climb. The number of peaks visible may be unequaled in the state, except perhaps from Katahdin. Spaulding Mtn. is south of Sugarloaf and is connected to it by a high ridge; North Crocker and South Crocker mountains are to the west, across a branch of the Carrabassett River in Caribou Valley.

The approach to Sugarloaf is via the AT Southbound. From the jct. of ME 27 and Caribou Valley Rd. (no sign), at a point 1.0 mi. north of the blinking light at the jct. of Sugarloaf Access Rd., turn left (south) on Caribou Valley Rd. and drive 3.8 mi. to the end of the maintained road (blocked by a yellow gate) and a parking area.

AT AND SUGARLOAF MTN. TRAIL (MAP 3: C2–C3)

Cumulative from Caribou Valley Rd. parking area and yellow gate (2,132 ft.) to:

AT crossing (2,220 ft.)	0.5 mi.	88 ft.	0:15
Sugarloaf Mtn. Trail (3,630 ft.)	2.8 mi.	1,500 ft.	2:10
Sugarloaf Mtn. summit (4,238 ft.) via Sugarloaf Mtn. Trail	3.4 mi.	2,100 ft.	2:45

MATC To reach the AT, go around the yellow gate and walk north on Caribou Valley Rd. for 0.5 mi., crossing three bridges (the first is metal, the second and third are wooden). A small cairn on the right marks where the AT (northbound) enters the woods on the right (west) side of the old road. Just ahead, look left into the thick brush to find the AT going southbound; turn here.

The AT soon crosses the South Branch of the Carrabassett River (no bridge; can be difficult, if not impossible, in high water). It follows the river for a time and then begins to climb, at first gradually and then more steeply (some sections are very rough, steep, and difficult). The route crosses open ledges and skirts the top of a huge cirque on the western side of Sugarloaf. (The last water is a stream at 1.8 mi.) At a jct. at 2.3 mi., the AT turns right toward Spaulding Mtn. and Sugarloaf. Blue-blazed Sugarloaf Mtn. Trail leaves to the left, climbing steadily up the southwest flank of Sugarloaf for 0.6 mi. The trail emerges into the open, and one last rocky scramble is required to reach the summit amid a cluster of towers. The Octagon, the old building that once housed the Sugarloaf gondola, is below to the left, as is the upper station of the Timberline chairlift.

SPAULDING MTN. (4,011 FT.)
AT SOUTHBOUND (MAP 3: C3,
AMC SPAULDING MTN. AND MT. ABRAHAM)

Cumulative from Caribou Valley Rd. parking area and yellow gate (2,132 ft.) to:

AT crossing (2,220 ft.)	0.5 mi.	88 ft.	0:15
Sugarloaf Mtn. Trail (3,630 ft.)	2.8 mi.	1,500 ft.	2:10
Spaulding side trail (3,890 ft.)	4.9 mi.	2,100 ft.	3:30
Spaulding Mtn. summit (4,011 ft.) via side trail	5.0 mi.	2,220 ft.	3:35
Spaulding Mtn. Lean-to (3,110 ft.)	5.7 mi.	2,220 ft.	4:00
Mt. Abraham Trail (3,270 ft.)	6.8 mi.	2,380 ft.	4:35

MATC Spaulding Mtn. in Mt. Abram Township rises high above the long, undulating ridgeline extending southwest from Sugarloaf Mtn. toward the north ridge of Mt. Abraham. The final 2 mi. of the entire 2,190-mi. AT to be completed were cut and blazed along this stretch in 1937.

SEC 4

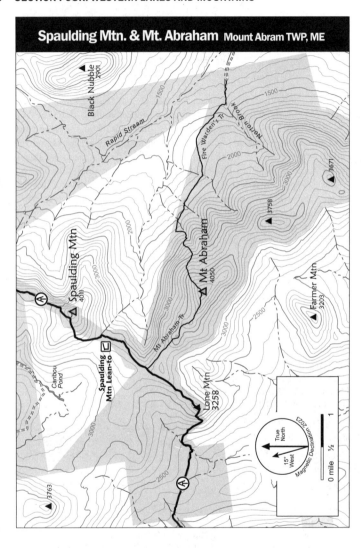

Spaulding Mtn. & Mt. Abraham Mount Abram TWP, ME

SEC
4

Black Nubble
2901

Rapid Stream

Fire Warden's Tr

Norton Brook

1500

1500

2000

2000

3000

3758

3671

Spaulding Mtn
4010

Mt Abraham
4050

Farmer Mtn
3203

3000

3000

3000

Mt Abraham Tr

2500

Caribou Pond

Spaulding Mtn Lean-to

Lone Mtn
3258

2500

3000

3763

2500

True North

15° West

Magnetic Declination 2023

0 mile   ½   1

From its jct. with Sugarloaf Mtn. Trail, 2.3 mi. from Caribou Valley Rd., the AT continues south, traversing the crest of the rugged ridge between Sugarloaf Mtn. and Spaulding Mtn., with views and steep cliffs on the left. Along the route, a large bronze plaque on the north side of the trail honors the members of Maine's Civilian Conservation Corps, who completed the AT near this spot in 1937. Beyond, the AT descends steeply to a deep notch in the ridge, and the ascent of Spaulding Mtn. begins—steeply at first and then more gradually. At 4.9 mi., a side trail leads left 0.1 mi. to the wooded summit. Limited views exist at the summit sign, but a cleared narrow corridor leads north 200 ft. to fine sights of Sugarloaf and the Bigelow Range. Continuing south, the AT descends to Spaulding Mtn. Lean-to (reached via a 150-ft. side trail) at 5.7 mi. It follows an easy route along the wide, mostly level ridge, reaching the jct. of Mt. Abraham Trail at 6.8 mi. (this spur leads 1.7 mi. south to the open 4,050-ft. summit of Mt. Abraham).

SEC 4

MT. ABRAHAM (4,050 FT.)

Mt. Abraham (or "Abram") in Mt. Abram Township and Salem Township lies to the south of Sugarloaf Mtn. and Spaulding Mtn. in the 6,200-acre Mt. Abraham PL, most of which is an ecological reserve. Mt. Abraham has an impressive ridgeline that extends for about 4.5 mi. in a northwest to southeast direction and consists of eight peaks ranging from 3,400 ft. to more than 4,000 ft. Mt. Abraham is home to the second-largest alpine zone in Maine (behind Katahdin), some 350 acres in size. Two trails ascend to the summit: Fire Warden's Trail climbs the mountain from the Kingfield side in the east, and Mt. Abraham Trail approaches from the north via the AT just south of Spaulding Mtn.

From the jct. of ME 27 and ME 16 in Kingfield, drive north on ME 27 for 0.5 mi., crossing a bridge over the Carrabassett River. Turn left (west) onto West Kingfield Rd. At 3.3 mi. from ME 27, the road becomes gravel. At a crossroads at 3.5 mi., proceed straight ahead on Rapid Stream Rd. At a fork at 6.0 mi., bear left, and in about 100 yd., turn left to cross the first of two bridges over Rapid Stream. After the second bridge, the road immediately forks again. Follow the right fork for 0.5 mi. to a T intersection. Parking is to the left; the trail starts straight ahead.

FIRE WARDEN'S TRAIL
(AMC SPAULDING MTN. AND MT. ABRAHAM)
From trailhead parking at T jct. (1,163 ft.) to:

Mt. Abraham summit (4,050 ft.)	4.0 mi.	2,887 ft.	3:35

MATC Fire Warden's Trail climbs west along the south side of Norton Brook. At 0.2 mi., cross to the north side of the brook and continue the gentle ascent. At 0.5 mi., leave the brook, angle up to the right, descend slightly to an old woods road, and then go left. At 1.3 mi., cross an old gravel logging road and in 0.5 mi. descend slightly to cross a brook. Beyond, the trail follows a contour across the mountainside and then drops to cross another brook. The climbing is mostly moderate as the forest transitions from hardwoods to conifers. At 2.6 mi., cross a brook and, 0.1 mi. beyond, reach a privy and campsite on the right. Immediately after, the trail ascends at a steady moderate-to-steep grade. Reach a spring at 3.5 mi. and soon break out of the trees onto a huge talus slope, where there are views of Spaulding, Sugarloaf, Burnt Hill, South Crocker, and Redington, as well as Avery Peak in the Bigelow Range. Fire Warden's Trail soon leaves the talus field and enters thick krummholz, gnarled and stunted trees shaped by exposure to harsh conditions. Bits of old telephone line (used by the fire warden when the tower was in operation) are evident along the trail. At 3.7 mi., leave the gnarled trees and follow cairns over the wide-open slope to the summit of Mt. Abraham, marked by a large cairn and sign. The roof of the ruined cab of the fire tower is to the left, while the rusted remains of the old fire tower (1924) lie just beyond the cairn. The 360-degree panorama from the Mt. Abraham summit is extraordinary. From the top, Mt. Abraham Trail leads 1.7 mi. north to connect with the AT 1.1 mi. south of Spaulding Mtn. Lean-to.

MT. ABRAHAM TRAIL
(AMC SPAULDING MTN. AND MT. ABRAHAM)
Cumulative from AT 1.1 mi. south of Spaulding Mtn. Lean-to (3,270 ft.) to:

Mt. Abraham summit (4,050 ft.)	1.7 mi.	830 ft.	1:15

MATC This trail leaves from the AT south of Spaulding Mtn. at a point 6.8 mi. south of the Caribou Valley Rd. parking area and yellow gate. Refer to the trail description for Spaulding Mtn. to reach the start (p. 207).

From the AT, blue-blazed Mt. Abraham Trail leads southeast along the route of a very old tote road at first, climbing gradually and then steeply up the densely forested northern ridge of the mountain. The trail emerges from the trees and traverses a talus field at 1.1 mi.; it reaches treeline at 1.3 mi. The wide-open alpine summit of Mt. Abraham and the site of the former fire tower are at 1.7 mi.

SADDLEBACK MTN. (4,122 FT.), THE HORN (4,024 FT.), AND SADDLEBACK JUNIOR (3,655 FT.)
Saddleback Mtn. sprawls across Sandy River Plantation, Madrid Township, and Redington Township southeast of Rangeley. The long ridge's undulating crest extends in a northeast to southwest direction for more

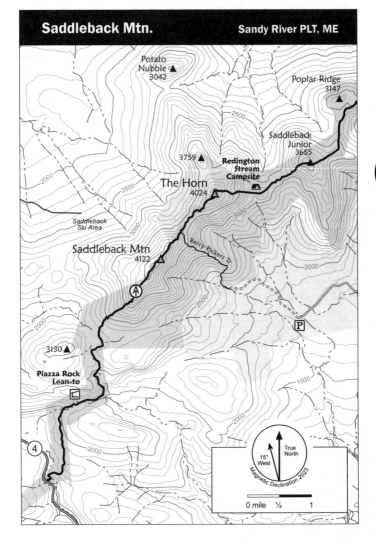

Saddleback Mtn.

Sandy River PLT, ME

Potato Nubble ▲ 3042

Poplar Ridge 3147 ▲

Saddleback Junior 3655

3759 ▲

Redington Stream Campsite

The Horn 4024

Berry Pickers Tr

Saddleback Ski Area

Saddleback Mtn 4122

Ⓐ

Ⓟ

3130 ▲

Piazza Rock Lean-to

Ⓒ

④

SEC 4

True North

15° West

Magnetic Declination 2023

0 mile   ½   1

than 3 mi., with pronounced saddles separating its high peaks. Two of the summits, Saddleback and the Horn, exceed 4,000 ft. Saddleback Junior is only slightly lower at 3,655 ft. The Saddleback Mtn. ski area is on the northwestern slope of the mountain. The bare summits of these peaks have extensive areas above treeline and thereby offer expansive views in all directions. Because of this exposure, however, hikers should proceed with caution during periods of high winds and low visibility. Further, due to the fragile ecology of the alpine terrain on Saddleback, hikers must exercise care to stay on the trail and avoid stepping on plants or disturbing shallow soils. Pets should be leashed.

The AT traverses the four high peaks of Saddleback; Berry Picker's Trail climbs to the high col between Saddleback Mtn. and The Horn. Fly Rod Crosby Trail connects the village of Madrid with the base of the Saddleback ski area on a route over the west shoulder of the mountain.

AT NORTHBOUND (AMC SADDLEBACK MTN.)
Cumulative from ME 4 (1,630 ft.) to:

Piazza Rock Lean-to (2,080 ft.)	1.8 mi.	480 ft.	1:10
Fly Rod Crosby Trail (2,650 ft.)	3.9 mi.	1,050 ft.	2:25
Saddleback Mtn. summit (4,122 ft.)	5.7 mi.	2,520 ft.	4:05
Berry Picker's Trail (3,650 ft.)	6.5 mi.	2,520 ft.	4:30
The Horn summit (4,024 ft.)	7.3 mi.	3,055 ft.	5:10
Saddleback Junior (3,655 ft.)	9.3 mi.	3,750 ft.	6:30
Poplar Ridge Lean-to (2,940 ft.)	10.7 mi.	3,810 ft.	7:15
Orbeton Stream (1,550 ft.)	13.4 mi.	3,960 ft.	8:40
Mt. Abraham Trail (3,270 ft.)	17.6 mi.	5,810 ft.	11:55

MATC To approach Saddleback Mtn. from the south, follow ME 4 for 32.0 mi. north from the jct. of ME 4 and US 2 in Farmington. From the north, at the jct. of ME 4 and ME 16 in Rangeley, the trailhead is 9.9 mi. south on ME 4. The AT crosses ME 4 at a steep, winding section of the road. A large trailhead parking lot is on the west side of the highway.

From ME 4, the AT descends and crosses a bridge over the Sandy River at 0.1 mi. The trail climbs out of the valley, crossing a gravel logging road at 1.1 mi. At 1.8 mi., the trail passes Piazza Rock Lean-to. A side trail leads left 200 yd. to the top of Piazza Rock, a large granite slab protruding from the cliff. Just ahead along the side trail are the Caves, a series of boulder caves with narrow passages.

The AT then climbs steeply, skirting the west shore of Ethel Pond. Turning sharply left at the end of the pond, the trail climbs to pass Mud Pond and then descends slightly to reach Eddy Pond (last reliable water). Watch for a point near the east shore of Eddy Pond about 3.7 mi. from ME 4 where the trail, after turning left onto a gravel road for a few feet, turns sharply right off the road and continues (this gravel road is Fly Rod Crosby Trail). Beyond, the AT rises steeply through conifers, emerging on a scrub-covered slope.

The long, exposed open crest of Saddleback is a particularly scenic hike on a good day but can be difficult in bad weather. Use care to follow the rock cairns and white blazes marking the route. After a lengthy stretch over rocky slopes and heath, the trail descends slightly into a sag and then climbs to reach the summit of Saddleback at 5.7 mi.

SEC 4

The AT continues over the open alpine slopes, descending steeply into the col between Saddleback and the Horn. At 6.5 mi., blue-blazed Berry Picker's Trail enters from the south. Ahead, the AT crosses the wide col and then climbs slabs and ledges to reach the summit of the Horn at 7.3 mi. Continuing north, the AT descends steeply off the peak, reaches treeline, and arrives at a side trail to Redington Stream CS on the left at 8.0 mi. The descent continues, reaching a low point on the west side of Saddleback Junior at 8.8 mi. A steep climb leads to the open summit of Saddleback Junior at 9.3 mi., which has 360-degree views. Poplar Ridge, the canyon of Orbeton Stream, Lone Mtn., Mt. Abraham, Mt. Redington, Black Nubble, Spaulding Mtn., and more fill the scene.

The AT carries on northward, descending steeply off Saddleback Junior to reach a brook and continuing to Poplar Ridge Lean-to at 10.7 mi. Beyond the shelter, the AT climbs to the ledges on Poplar Ridge and then drops steeply into the deep canyon that holds Orbeton Stream, climbs up and out to Lone Mtn., and reaches the jct. of Mt. Abraham Trail at 17.6 mi. Refer to the trail descriptions for Spaulding Mtn. and Mt. Abraham Trail (p. 207) for details beyond this point.

BERRY PICKER'S TRAIL (AMC SADDLEBACK MTN.)
Cumulative from ATV gate (1,810 ft.) to:

Fly Rod Crosby Trail (2,110 ft.)	1.0 mi.	300 ft.	0:35
Start of Berry Picker's Trail (2,260 ft.)	1.5 mi.	480 ft.	1:00
South side of col between Saddleback and the Horn (3,650 ft.)	3.0 mi.	1,870 ft.	2:20
Saddleback Mtn. summit (4,122 ft.) via AT Southbound	3.8 mi.	2,420 ft.	3:10

Cumulative from ATV gate (1,810 ft.) to:

Fly Rod Crosby Trail (2,110 ft.)	1.0 mi.	300 ft.	0:35
Start of Berry Picker's Trail (2,260 ft.)	1.5 mi.	480 ft.	1:00
South side of col between Saddleback and the Horn (3,650 ft.)	3.0 mi.	1,870 ft.	2:20
The Horn summit (4,024 ft.) via AT Northbound	4.2 mi.	2,325 ft.	3:15

MATC Berry Picker's Trail is a side trail between multiuse Fly Rod Crosby Trail and the AT. It follows, in part, a route used by local residents for more than 150 years to harvest mountain blueberries and cranberries on Saddleback Mtn. This was also the route originally planned for the AT in 1933. The trail crosses the Orbeton Stream conservation easement, land owned by ATC, and land owned by the Maine Appalachian Trail Land Trust before finally entering the AT corridor, owned by NPS. Except for occasional double blazes that indicate sharp or unexpected turns, the trail is marked by single, rectangular blue blazes and rock cairns. The route features open ledges with outstanding views.

To reach the trailhead, from the jct. of ME 4 and ME 142 in Phillips, turn north on ME 142. In 2.5 mi., turn left onto East Madrid Rd. (the street sign is often missing, but a large sign reads "Pike Industries" at the turn). Proceed on East Madrid Rd., which becomes a gravel road and passes over Perham Stream in the hamlet of East Madrid. After 5.3 mi., turn left on Potato Hill Rd. This road is also used by ATVs, so please be alert for traffic. After 1.0 mi., the road reaches a wide intersection with Railroad Rd.; stay to the left and proceed on the main road. In 0.8 mi., reach another fork; stay to the left. Continue for 1.8 mi. and stay left. Proceed an additional 0.7 mi. over a wet, low-lying section of road and park at the jct. with an ATV trail.

From the ATV trail gate, walk up the ATV trail for 1.0 mi. and turn left onto multiuse Fly Rod Crosby Trail (marked by white diamonds) at a group of signs on two wooden posts. At 1.5 mi., reach the start of blue-blazed Berry Picker's Trail on the right just before a bridge over Winship Stream. Berry Picker's Trail ascends through mixed hardwood and softwood forest along the stream, which has beautiful cascades. The trail becomes steeper, bears away from the stream, and at 2.0 mi. turns northwest to climb the ridgeline toward Saddleback (in view up to the left). On the right, the former route of the historical Berry Picker's Trail is visible on the slope. The trail transitions to open ledges dominated by dwarf spruce, alpine blueberry, and mountain cranberry. At 2.1 mi., it reaches Boundary Ledge, which is marked with yellow blazes to denote the boundary line between the landowners. At 2.7 mi., Berry Picker's Trail reaches the Erratic (a large boulder).

After following a contour, the trail joins the AT on the south side of the col between Saddleback and the Horn at 3.0 mi. From here, it is 0.8 mi. south to the summit of Saddleback and 1.2 mi. north to the summit of the Horn.

FLY ROD CROSBY TRAIL (USGS SADDLEBACK MTN. AND REDINGTON QUADS, HPA FLY ROD CROSBY TRAIL MAP, GAZETTEER MAPS 19, 29)

Cumulative from Reeds Mill Rd. trailhead (950 ft.) to:

Berry Picker's Trail, lower jct. (2,110 ft.)	7.2 mi.	1,150 ft.	4:10
Berry Picker's Trail, upper jct. (2,260 ft.)	7.8 mi.	1,300 ft.	4:35
AT crossing near Eddy Pond (2,650 ft.)	10.2 mi.	1,800 ft.	6:00
Saddleback ski area base lodge and parking (2,450 ft.)	12.3 mi.	1,800 ft.	7:05

SEC 4

HPA Fly Rod Crosby Trail is a proposed 45-mi. heritage hiking trail that, when completed, will extend from Strong to Oquossoc along the Sandy River, Orbeton Stream, and Hardy Stream, across the AT, and on to Rangeley Lake and the Outdoor Sporting Heritage Museum in Oquossoc. Cornelia "Fly Rod" Crosby (1854–1946), a journalist, fly-fisher extraordinaire, hunter, early conservationist, and outdoor enthusiast, was Maine's first registered guide. Crosby grew up in Phillips, guided in Rangeley, worked for the Maine Central Railroad and Sandy River & Rangeley Lakes Railroad, and is buried in Strong. The trail named for Crosby is closely linked to the landscape of her life. The blue-and-white trail signs sport the drawing of a fishing fly.

Fly Rod Crosby Trail links existing motorized trails, woods roads, and streets and creates some new trails for nonmotorized recreation only. The motorized trails open to foot traffic are referred to as "multiuse" trails. Most of Fly Rod Crosby Trail is on privately owned land; please respect this land and practice Leave No Trace (p. xlviii). The trail is under the care of High Peaks Alliance in partnership with local recreational trail groups.

Currently two sections are open, which total about 19 mi. of continuous trail. A lower elevation section of the trail (approximately 7 mi.) begins in Phillips, crosses the Sandy River, and follows abandoned railroad beds and an existing multiuse trail along the river to Orbeton Stream in Madrid. The roughly 12-mi. section immediately to the north extends through moderate-to-strenuous mountain terrain between Madrid and Saddleback Mtn.; this section is described here.

Trailhead parking for the Madrid to Saddleback section (described in that direction) is at Star Barn Yoga on Reeds Mill Rd. From the jct. of ME 4 and ME 142 in Phillips, drive 4.9 mi. north on ME 4. Turn right on Toothaker Pond Rd. and proceed 2.25 mi. Turn left on dirt Fish Hatchery Rd. and continue for 2.0 mi. to the kiosk and parking lot at the top of the hill on the right, immediately after crossing Orbeton Stream. Check in at the trailhead kiosk to pick up a map and to find out current trail conditions.

From the kiosk, follow the blue-blazed footpath into the woods. This section of the trail exists on private land actively managed as a working forest. The route, while well marked, can vary according to timber-harvesting activities. For about 3 mi., the trail goes north through a mixed forest and runs parallel to Orbeton Stream on the western bank. The next 4.0 mi. of trail closely follow Hardy Stream (along the southern and then western bank), with great views to the north of some of the neighboring high peaks, including Saddleback Mtn., Mt. Abraham, and Spaulding Mtn. The footpath passes the "Horse Hobble," remains of an old horse logging camp, before joining up with a 3.5-mi. stretch of multiuse trail that passes Moose Pond and Deer Pond and meets the AT on the western shoulder of Saddleback Mtn. near Eddy Pond. At the start of this multiuse stretch, Berry Picker's Trail enters from the left. At a point 0.6 mi. ahead, Berry Picker's Trail, which leads to the AT high on the ridgeline of Saddleback Mtn., departs to the right, just before a stream crossing. About 1 mi. beyond the AT crossing near Eddy Pond, the route joins with Rock Pond Trail, a 2-mi. section that passes Midway Pond and Rock Pond before ending at an emergency vehicle turnaround a short distance from the Saddleback ski area base lodge.

To reach the Saddleback base lodge trailhead: From ME 4 just south of Rangeley, turn east on Dallas Hill Rd., drive 2.5 mi., and bear right onto Saddleback Mtn. Rd. In another 4.5 mi., the road enters the Saddleback ski area, with the base lodge on the left and three large parking lots to the right. Park in any of the lots and walk up the main road (first left) as it turns away from the lodge and winds up the mountain through condos. Signs for Rock Pond and Fly Rod Crosby trails are at the end of the road.

BEMIS MTN.: WEST PEAK (3,575 FT.), EAST PEAK (3,532 FT.), THIRD PEAK (3,115 FT.), SECOND PEAK (2,915 FT.), AND FIRST PEAK (2,604 FT.)

Bemis Mtn. in Township D rises south of Mooselookmeguntic Lake, and its long ridge crest extends in a northeast to southwest direction. The AT traverses the range and offers outstanding views from the five peaks en route. West Peak is the highest. Bemis Stream Trail is an alternate route for ascent or descent and, combined with the AT, makes a loop hike over the range possible, with an overnight option at Bemis Mtn. Lean-to. Views from the Bemis summits are excellent in all directions.

Due to logging, Bemis Stream Trail from ME 17 to Bemis Rd. is permanently closed. Parking is very limited on ME 17 near the AT crossing (the Height of Land lot is not meant for hiker parking), so MATC recommends that hikers desiring to walk the Bemis section of the AT and/or Bemis Stream Trail gain access via Bemis Rd., an old railroad grade that is now a gravel road. At a point on ME 17 (noted as "Houghton" on *Gazetteer* map 19) 17.4 mi. north of the jct. of US 2 and ME 17 in Mexico and 18.0 mi. south of the jct. of ME 4 and ME 17 in Oquossuc, turn west on Houghton Rd. and immediately cross a bridge over the Swift River. In 0.25 mi., turn right on Bemis Rd. and follow it for 6.0 mi. to the Bemis Stream Trail crossing. The trail to the right (north) is posted as closed. Park at a pullout here. The new start for Bemis Stream Trail begins on the left (south) side of the road. To reach the AT crossing, continue north on Bemis Rd. for an additional 1.2 mi. and park at a pullout.

SEC 4

AT SOUTHBOUND (USGS HOUGHTON AND METALLAK MTN. QUADS, MATC MAP 7, MTF AT—BEMIS MTN. AND BEMIS STREAM LOOP MAP, GAZETTEER MAP 18)
Cumulative from Bemis Rd. at AT crossing (1,550 ft.) to:

Bemis Mtn., First Peak (2,610 ft.)	1.2 mi.	1,060 ft.	1:10
Bemis Mtn., Second Peak (2,915 ft.)	2.1 mi.	1,410 ft.	1:45
Bemis Mtn. Lean-to (2,820 ft.)	3.6 mi.	1,535 ft.	2:35
Bemis Mtn., Third Peak (3,115 ft.)	4.0 mi.	1,830 ft.	2:55
Bemis Mtn., East Peak (3,532 ft.)	5.2 mi.	2,390 ft.	3:45
Bemis Mtn., West Peak (3,575 ft.)	5.3 mi.	2,455 ft.	3:50
Bemis Stream Trail (3,300 ft.)	6.3 mi.	2,455 ft.	4:20
Complete horseshoe loop via AT and Bemis Stream Trail	11.6 mi.	2,455 ft.	7:00

MATC Soon after leaving Bemis Rd., pass a small spring, the last water source southbound for 3.5 mi. Ahead, climb steeply through woods to emerge on open ledges at 1.5 mi., and then cross a series of rocky knobs, the first at 0.7 mi. Beyond, the trail is marked by cairns and white blazes and follows the ridge crest to reach First Peak at 1.2 mi. and Second Peak at 2.1 mi.

Reach Bemis Mtn. Lean-to at 3.6 mi.; Third Peak is at 4.0 mi. Cross East Peak at 5.2 mi. and West Peak at 5.3 mi. Arrive at the jct. with Bemis Stream Trail at 6.3 mi. Ahead on the AT, it is 3.2 mi. to the summit of Old Blue Mtn. and 6.0 mi. to South Arm Rd. By way of Bemis Stream Trail, it is 5.3 mi. back to Bemis Rd.

BEMIS STREAM TRAIL (USGS HOUGHTON AND METALLAK MTN. QUADS, MATC MAP 7, MTF AT—BEMIS MTN. AND BEMIS STREAM LOOP, GAZETTEER MAP 18)

Cumulative from Bemis Rd. at Bemis Stream Trail (1,692 ft.) to:

Gravel road and bridge over Bemis Stream (2,450 ft.)	3.2 mi.	760 ft.	2:00
AT (3,300 ft.)	5.3 mi.	1,600 ft.	3:30

MATC This trail, formerly part of the AT, provides an alternate route to the Bemis Mtn. peaks and, using the AT, makes a loop hike possible. Follow previous driving directions for the AT Southbound crossing of Bemis Rd. to reach the new Bemis Stream Trail start.

From Bemis Rd., blue-blazed Bemis Stream Trail follows a wide track past a pool in Bemis Stream at 0.3 mi. and then climbs, finally crossing Bemis Stream (may be difficult in high water) at 1.2 mi. Continue to climb, with the stream on the left, and traverse several side streams. At 3.2 mi., reach a gravel logging road. Turn left to cross a bridge; reenter the woods on the right immediately after. Follow Bemis Stream and cross it again at 4.2 mi. Ascend steadily through a mature spruce forest and pass several glacial erratics. At 5.3 mi., reach the jct. with the AT. To the north, it is 1.0 mi. to the summit of West Peak of Bemis Mtn., 2.7 mi. to Bemis Mtn. Lean-to, and 6.3 mi. to Bemis Rd. via the AT. To the south, it is 3.2 mi. to the summit of Old Blue Mtn. and 6.0 mi. to South Arm Rd.

OLD BLUE MTN. (3,604 FT.)

This mountain in Township D rises steeply above Black Brook, south of Elephant Mtn. and west of Lower Richardson Lake. Gain access from the south or north via the AT. To reach the AT from ME 5 in Andover, drive 0.6 mi. east on ME 120 to South Arm Rd. Turn left onto South Arm Rd., and drive north for 7.7 mi. to the AT crossing at Black Brook Notch. Limited parking is available on the right side of the road.

AT NORTHBOUND (USGS EAST ANDOVER QUAD, MATC MAP 7, GAZETTEER MAP 18)

From South Arm Rd. (1,430 ft.) to:

Old Blue Mtn. summit (3,604 ft.)	2.8 mi.	2,170 ft.	2:25

MATC Leaving South Arm Rd., the AT climbs very steeply up the north wall of Black Brook Notch, gaining 900 ft. in 0.6 mi. The climb includes a bare section of rock that must be ascended with the aid of iron rungs and handrails. At the top of the climb is an overlook with views south to Black Brook Notch and the peaks beyond. Ahead, the trail ascends gradually to the base of the upper south slope of Old Blue Mtn., reaching it at 2.3 mi., and making the final ascent to the summit at 2.8 mi. Enjoy outstanding 360-degree views over the tops of the stunted spruce and fir growth. From the summit, the AT descends north into the high valley between Old Blue Mtn. and Elephant Mtn. At 4.3 mi., it reaches a col and an impressive stand of old-growth spruce. Bemis Stream Trail enters from the right at 6.0 mi. (leads to ME 17 in 6.1 mi). Ahead on the AT, it is 7.3 mi. to ME 17.

RANGELEY LAKES AREA
BALD MTN. (IN OQUOSSOC; 2,438 FT.)

This mountain in the village of Oquossoc occupies a scenic location between Mooselookmeguntic Lake and Rangeley Lake and is the central natural feature of 1,923-acre Bald Mtn. PL. The mountain was the site of the short-lived Bald Mountain Skiway, which operated from 1960 into the early 1970s. Views from the summit observation tower range from the surrounding lakes of Mooselookmeguntic, Rangeley, and Cupsuptic to the peaks of Saddleback Mtn., the Bemis Range, Elephant Mtn., and on to Mt. Washington and the Presidential Range. Two trails ascend the peak, from the west and from the north.

SEC 4

BALD MTN. TRAIL (USGS OQUOSSOC QUAD, MTF BALD MTN. TRAIL–OQUOSSOC MAP, GAZETTEER MAP 28)
Cumulative from Bald Mtn. Rd. (1,520 ft.) to:

Bald Mtn. Link (1,640 ft.)	0.3 mi.	120 ft.	0:10
Bald Mtn. summit (2,438 ft.)	1.3 mi.	920 ft.	1:10

MBPL From the jct. of ME 4 and ME 17 in Oquossoc, drive west on ME 4 (also called Dam Rd.) for 1.2 mi. toward its terminus at Haines Landing. Before the landing, turn left (south) onto Bald Mtn. Rd. and follow this road for 0.8 mi. to the trailhead parking area for Bald Mtn. on the left (sign).

Bald Mtn. Trail leaves the lot left of the kiosk and climbs gradually east on a wide gravel path marked with blue blazes. After crossing a footbridge, reach a jct., where Bald Mtn. Link enters from the left. Continue straight ahead on Bald Mtn. Trail, a wide, well-used treadway of rocks and roots. At 0.8 mi., the angle increases as the ascent becomes moderate to steep on eroded trail. Climb sections of bedrock and ledges. The angle finally eases, and the trail crosses bog bridges over a wet section. Climb a slab beyond, dip down, and then continue to the observation tower on top of the summit ledges. A picnic area sits in the small clearing below the tower, but views are limited at ground level. Ascend the 30-foot tower for a scenic panorama that takes in Mooselookmeguntic Lake, Cupsuptic Lake, Rangeley Lake, and a long chain of mountains, from Katahdin to Bigelow to Saddleback and all the way to Mt. Washington.

BALD MTN. LINK (USGS OQUOSSOC QUAD, MTF BALD MTN. TRAIL–OQUOSSOC MAP, GAZETTEER MAP 28)

Cumulative from boat launch parking lot on ME 4 (a.k.a. Dam Rd.) (1,490 ft.) to:

Bald Mtn. Trail (1,640 ft.)	1.0 mi.	150 ft.	0:30
Bald Mtn. summit (2,438 ft.)	2.0 mi.	950 ft.	1:30

MBPL This longer alternate route on Bald Mtn. leaves from the boat launch parking lot on ME 4, just east of Haines Landing. From the jct. of ME 4 and ME 17 in Oquossoc, drive west on ME 4 (also called Dam Rd.) for 1.0 mi. to the large boat launch parking lot on the left. The trail (not signed as Bald Mtn. Link) leaves the far end (south) of the lot at the kiosk. The well-trodden route reaches a jct. at 0.2 mi. Turn left, and at the grassy meadow ahead, turn sharply right. The old tote road crosses bog bridges over a wet area and then begins a gentle ascent. It proceeds on a contour and crosses a footbridge, an old skidder road, and a second footbridge. Immediately after, reach the jct. with Bald Mtn. Trail at 1.0 mi. Turn left to continue toward the summit, which is another 1.0 mi. ahead.

WEST KENNEBAGO MTN. (3,730 FT.)

This isolated peak in Upper Cupsuptic Township, north of Cupsuptic Lake and west of Kennebago Lake, features five summits on the north–south ridge that forms the mountain. Local volunteers from the Trails for Rangeley Area Coalition maintain West Kennebago Mtn. Trail.

To reach the start of the trail, turn right (north) from ME 16 onto Morton Cutoff Rd., 4.8 mi. west of the ME 4 and ME 16 jct. in Oquossoc and 0.3 mi. west of the Maine Forest Service buildings at Cupsuptic Lake. Drive 3.2 mi. from ME 16 to a jct. with Lincoln Pond Rd. Turn right (east), and in 5.5 mi., reach a parking area on the left. The trail begins at the right end of the parking area.

WEST KENNEBAGO MTN. TRAIL (USGS KENNEBAGO QUAD, GAZETTEER MAP 28)

Cumulative from Lincoln Pond Rd. (2,007 ft.) to:

Site of old fire warden's camp (3,050 ft.)	1.2 mi.	1,043 ft.	1:10
West Kennebago Mtn., south summit (3,702 ft.)	1.9 mi.	1,695 ft.	1:50

TRAC The red-blazed trail starts as an old woods road. It soon narrows to a footpath and climbs rather steeply. At 0.9 mi., the trail levels out among conifers and bears left. It begins to climb again, crosses a small stream, and turns sharply right, becoming heavily eroded. At 1.2 mi., the trail reaches a small clearing, the site of an old fire warden's camp. A spring is 100 yd. into the woods to the left of the clearing via a faint path.

West Kennebago Mtn. Trail leaves the site of the old camp from the upper right (northwest) corner of the clearing. At 1.5 mi., it reaches the ridge, where it turns left (south) and follows the ridge nearly to the south summit. The old fire tower, erected in 1914, was removed in 2012 to make way for a radio tower (fenced off, trespassing prohibited). Just before the tower, a wooden platform (used as a helipad) in a clearing offers a convenient place to rest and views of Kennebago Lake to the east, Cupsuptic Lake and Mooselookmeguntic Lake to the south, and the skyline of summits on Saddleback Mtn. (*Note*: West Kennebago Mtn. Trail is on private land and is open to the public through the generosity of the landowner. Please respect the trail and the land to ensure future access.)

AZISCOHOS MTN. (3,203 FT.)

This mountain in Lincoln Plantation, shown as Low Aziscohos Mtn. on some USGS maps, is just south of Aziscohos Lake and offers excellent views over the Rangeley Lakes region and far beyond. The abandoned fire tower (1929) on the summit was removed in 2004. Local volunteers from TRAC maintain Aziscohos Mtn. Trail.

From the jct. of ME 4 and ME 16 in Oquossoc, drive west for 17.8 mi. The trail starts on the south side of ME 16, 100 ft. east of a gravel road leading left (south) into an old woodyard. Park along the shoulder on the south side of the road. No sign exists, and the entrance into the woods is obscure. (As a check, the trailhead is 1.2 mi. east of the bridge over Magalloway River at Aziscohos Lake Dam.)

AZISCOHOS MTN. TRAIL (USGS RICHARDSON POND AND WILSONS MILLS QUADS, GAZETTEER MAP 28)
From ME 16 (1,740 ft.) to:

Aziscohos Mtn. summit (3,203 ft.)	1.7 mi.	1,463 ft.	1:35

TRAC Once in the woods, the trail follows red paint blazes. In 100 yd., pass a trail sign (Aziscohos). The trail leads gradually uphill on an old tote road (can be quite wet at times) through open hardwood and mixed forest. It turns sharply left and soon passes through several old cutover areas, with occasional views north to the hamlet of Wilsons Mills. Beyond, the trail enters conifers and crosses a small brook. It then continues more steeply, becoming quite rough as it leads over boulders and exposed roots. The angle finally eases, and Aziscohos Mtn. Trail reaches abandoned Tower Man's Trail, entering from the right (northwest) at 1.6 mi. Turn left here and

SEC 4

climb on bedrock trail through low spruce growth to the open summit ledges and the concrete footings of the old fire tower.

The mountaintop offers a 360-degree vista that is one of the finest in Maine and includes Katahdin, Big Moose, Big Spencer, Saddleback, Bald, Tumbledown, Mt. Blue, Bemis, Elephant, Old Blue, the Baldpates, Old Speck, the Carter–Moriah Range, the Presidential Range, and many lakes around the Rangeley area, including Rangeley, Mooselookmeguntic, Cupsuptic, and Richardson. (*Note*: Aziscohos Mtn. Trail is on private land and is open to the public through the generosity of the landowner. Please respect the trail and the land to ensure future access.)

SEC 4

MT. BLUE STATE PARK

Mt. Blue State Park is Maine's largest state park, encompassing about 8,000 acres, the bulk of it in the town of Weld, with small portions in Temple and Avon. The largest section of the park lies east of Webb Lake and includes the iconic peak of Mt. Blue and a picnic area on Center Hill. A 136-site campground, beach, picnic area, and nature center are on the southwest shore of Webb Lake. Adjoining the park are the mountainous 22,000 acres of Tumbledown PL, making this location one of Maine's premier outdoor recreation destinations.

MT. BLUE (3,195 FT.)

Rising steeply east of Webb Lake in Weld, Mt. Blue is known for its conical profile, which is unmistakable when seen from surrounding summits. The former fire tower (1932) on the summit was removed in 2011 and replaced with a combination radio tower/observation tower that offers outstanding panoramic views.

From the jct. of ME 156 and ME 142 in the village of Weld, drive east on Church St. In 0.4 mi., bear left on Center Hill Rd. At 2.6 mi., pass the road to Center Hill on the right (this winding 0.4-mi. drive leads to a picnic area and Center Hill Nature Trail). At 3.4 mi., where Center Hill Rd. bears left, continue straight ahead on Mt. Blue Rd. Follow this narrow gravel road for 2.6 mi. to its end at the trailhead parking lot (sign and kiosk). The trail leaves from the northeast end of the lot.

MT. BLUE TRAIL (USGS WELD QUAD, MBPL MT. BLUE STATE PARK AND TUMBLEDOWN PUBLIC LANDS MAP, GAZETTEER MAP 19)
From Mt. Blue Rd. (1,409 ft.) to:

Mt. Blue summit (3,195 ft.)	1.5 mi.	1,786 ft.	1:40

MBPL Well-worn Mt. Blue Trail ascends steadily up the west slope of the mountain at moderate-to-sometimes-steep grades, traveling through thick woods. At 0.5 mi., pass an unmarked trail on the left that leads 50 ft. to a small stream (water). In another 0.1 mi., the remains of the ruined fire warden's cabin are to the left down a short side trail. A small stream runs behind the old cabin. High on the west shoulder of the mountain, the trail swings east and continues with rockier footing. At a level spot, the trail turns south, and after a final steep, rocky pitch, it reaches a spur path on the right that leads 40 ft. to an outlook, where Webb Lake, Tumbledown, Little Jackson, and Jackson mountains are visible. Just ahead, pass a slab cave on the left and enter the summit clearing. Walk past the gravel helipad to reach the tower steps. An outbuilding and solar array are to the right of the tower. The open ledges in front of the tower offer views, but the best sights are from the observation deck halfway up the tower (the locked cab is off-limits). Spectacular in all directions, the vista includes Saddleback Mtn., the Horn, Mt. Abraham, Spaulding Mtn., Sugarloaf Mtn., the Presidential Range, the Carter–Moriah Range, peaks of the Mahoosuc Range, and nearby Bald Mtn.

SEC 4

CENTER HILL (1,657 FT.)

A short circuit around this hill on the way to Mt. Blue yields maximum views for minimal effort. Follow the driving directions for the Mt. Blue trailhead; pass the side road to Center Hill en route. Park in the large lot at the end of the drive.

CENTER HILL NATURE TRAIL
(USGS WELD QUAD, MBPL MT. BLUE STATE PARK AND
TUMBLEDOWN PUBLIC LANDS MAP, GAZETTEER MAP 19)
From Center Hill picnic area (1,570 ft.) to:

Complete loop	0.6 mi.	125 ft.	0:25

MBPL This interesting and scenic self-guided nature loop hike leaves from the lower right edge of the parking lot at the map box and sign (Scenic Trail). Climb the rock steps and walk past the picnic shelter to enter the woods. At 0.15 mi., a side trail to the right leads 150 ft. to Overlook Ledges, with a view west over Webb Lake and to the peaks around Tumbledown Mtn. At 0.25 mi., there are two picnic tables on the left and a bench on the right with a view to Bald Mtn. Not far ahead is another scenic vista on the right and, soon after, a bench with a view of Mt. Blue. At 0.5 mi., descend along ledges and walk through the picnic area and meadow to finish at the parking lot.

BALD MTN. (IN WASHINGTON TOWNSHIP; 2,372 FT.)

Bald Mtn. straddles the town lines of Washington Township and Perkins Township a few miles south of Mt. Blue State Park. Featuring a long and narrow northeast to southwest ridgeline, the peak has been a local favorite for many years. The state of Maine owns a portion of the mountaintop in Perkins Township. The craggy summit of Bald Mtn. yields fine views in every direction.

The trailhead for Bald Mtn. is on the west side of ME 156 9.0 mi. northwest of the jct. of ME 4 and ME 156 in Wilton and 5.3 mi. southeast of the jct. of ME 142 and ME 156 in Weld. Parking is on the broad shoulder on the south side of the road, where there is a trailhead kiosk. Bald Mtn. Trail is on private property and open to the public through the generosity of Carrier Timberlands, the landowner. Please respect the land, stay on the trail, and follow all posted rules.

BALD MTN. TRAIL (USGS MT. BLUE QUAD, MTF BALD MOUNTAIN, GAZETTEER MAP 19)
From ME 156 (1,050 ft.) to:

Bald Mtn. summit (2,372 ft.)	1.1 mi.	1,322 ft.	1:15

TMNK Immediately cross Wilson Stream. In 250 ft., cross a side stream and reach a trail register on the right. Ascend the south side of the stream at a steady, moderate grade, following blue blazes. At 0.6 mi., reach Step I. Climb straight up the rock crevice, or take an easier alternative to the left. After ascending a slab of wavy granite, reach open ledges with a look due north over Kinneys Head to Mt. Blue. Continue over bedrock outcroppings, angling to the right and up to Step II. Scramble up the narrow, rocky passage, or take the easier alternate route to the right. Above, the 180-degree view includes Mt. Blue, Lake Webb, Tumbledown, Little Jackson, Jackson, and the peaks of Saddleback, to name a few. The trail reaches open ledges and climbs the bare slabs to the unsigned outcropping that is the summit.

SADDLEBACK MTN. (A.K.A. SADDLEBACK WIND; 2,590 FT.)
The trail to Saddleback Wind has been permanently closed per request of the private landowner. Hikers may not proceed any farther than 0.5 mi. beyond the summit of Bald Mtn.

TUMBLEDOWN PUBLIC LANDS
This large swath of public land encompasses the Tumbledown Mtn. Range in Township 6 north of Weld. MBPL owns 10,000 acres and holds easements on an additional 12,000 acres in the vicinity, bringing the total of this extraordinary conservation property to 22,000 acres. Tumbledown PL include Tumbledown Mtn., Tumbledown Pond, Little Jackson Mtn., Jackson Mtn., Jackson Pond, and the top of Blueberry Mtn. Seven trails (most

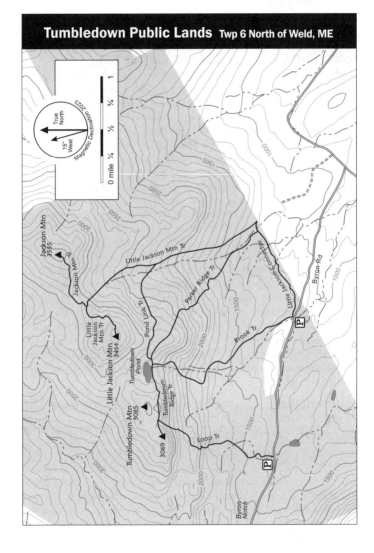

Tumbledown Public Lands Twp 6 North of Weld, ME

True North

15° West

Magnetic Declination 2023

0 mile ¼ ½ ¾ 1

Jackson Mtn 3555

Jackson Mtn Tr

Little Jackson Mtn Tr

Little Jackson Mtn Tr

Little Jackson Mtn 3454

Little Jackson Connector

Pond Link Tr

Parker Ridge Tr

Brook Tr

Byron Rd

Tumbledown Pond

Tumbledown Mtn 3085

Tumbledown Ridge Tr

3069

Loop Tr

Byron Notch

SEC 4

blue blazed) provide miles of hiking opportunities in this scenic and rugged region.

TUMBLEDOWN MTN., WEST PEAK (3,069 FT.)

Tumbledown Mtn. features an extensive alpine area on its high ridges and an impressive 700-ft. cliff on its south face, which has attracted rock climbers for years. Another natural feature is Tumbledown Pond, a pretty tarn tucked into a bowl beneath the peaks of Tumbledown Mtn. and Little Jackson Mtn. The views from the open summit ridges are exceptional. Loop Trail, Brook Trail, Parker Ridge Trail, and Pond Link Trail reach the high terrain on Tumbledown, while Tumbledown Mtn. Trail connects Tumbledown Pond with the west peak of the mountain. (*Note*: By order of MBPL in 2021, all of Tumbledown Mtn. was closed to dispersed camping due to overuse and misuse.)

Directions to Loop Trail and Brook Trail trailheads: From the west, leave ME 17 in Byron at a point 22 mi. south of Oquossoc and 13 mi. north of Mexico (distances are approximate). Travel east on Dingle Hill Rd. to cross over Coos Canyon and the Swift River. Stay on this road for 4.5 mi. (the name changes to Weld Rd. en route) to trailhead parking on the left for Loop Trail. To reach Brook Trail, continue east on the road for another 1.3 mi., where trailhead parking is on the right.

From the east, begin at the jct. of ME 156 and ME 142 in Weld. Go north on ME 142 for 2.3 mi. Turn left on West Side Rd. At 2.7 mi., where paved West Side Rd. bears left, continue straight on gravel-surfaced Byron Rd. Reach trailhead parking for Brook Trail on the left at 6.4 mi. Continue west on the road for another 1.3 mi. to reach trailhead parking for Loop Trail on the right.

LOOP TRAIL (MBPL; AMC TUMBLEDOWN PUBLIC LANDS MAP)
Cumulative from Loop Trail trailhead on Byron Rd. (1,330 ft.) to:

Tumbledown Mtn. Trail (2,910 ft.)	1.5 mi.	1,580 ft.	1:35
Tumbledown Mtn., west peak (3,069 ft.) via Tumbledown Mtn. Trail	1.7 mi.	1,740 ft.	1:45

Loop Trail is a direct route to the west peak of Tumbledown Mtn. Ascent of this interesting trail requires considerable rock scrambling at its upper end before reaching Tumbledown Mtn. Trail high on the mountain, just west of the summit. While nontechnical, the extensive steep rock scrambling makes this route unsuitable for novices, kids, dogs, and less agile hikers.

The blue-blazed trail rises gradually to the north, crosses a brook twice, and soon passes huge Tumbledown Boulder. From here, the trail rises steeply to emerge in the open at the Great Ledges, with splendid views of the impressive 700-ft. cliffs. On the ledges, Loop Trail turns right at a large cairn. It crosses a brook and then climbs steeply up a gully. Near the top of the gully, a side trail leads to a narrow chimney-like fissure known as Fat Man's Misery. Above this is an opening in the boulders with iron rungs to aid in the ascent. The scramble from the Great Ledges cairn leads to the saddle between the craggy high peaks and to a spring (unreliable in dry weather). From this jct. at 1.5 mi., Tumbledown Mtn. Trail leads left (west) to the main summit in 0.2 mi., and right (east) to Tumbledown Pond and the jct. with Brook Trail in 0.6 mi.

BROOK TRAIL (AMC TUMBLEDOWN PUBLIC LANDS MAP)
Cumulative from Brook Trail trailhead (1,110 ft.) to:

Tumbledown Pond (2,670 ft.)	1.8 mi.	1,560 ft.	1:40
Tumbledown Mtn., west peak (3,069 ft.) via Tumbledown Mtn. Trail	2.6 mi.	2,080 ft.	2:20

MBPL This trail along Tumbledown Brook is a direct route to scenic Tumbledown Pond, tucked high into the mountain's upper reaches, where the trail connects with Tumbledown Mtn. Trail and Parker Ridge Trail.

Brook Trail climbs gradually along the east side of Tumbledown Brook at first and then veers away. Pass a huge erratic on the right. Beyond, the climbing is moderate, and at 1.1 mi., cross to the west wide of Tumbledown Brook. Above, the wide, rocky trail weaves around large boulders. The rocky footing continues as the trail crosses the brook again. The steep ascent concludes at Tumbledown Pond at the jct. of Parker Ridge Trail and Tumbledown Mtn. Trail.

LITTLE JACKSON CONNECTOR
(AMC TUMBLEDOWN PUBLIC LANDS MAP)
Cumulative from Brook Trail trailhead on Byron Rd. (1,110 ft.) to:

Parker Ridge Trail (1,210 ft.)	1.0 mi.	200 ft.	0:35
Little Jackson Trail (1,200 ft.)	1.1 mi.	200 ft.	0:40

MBPL Little Jackson Connector connects Brook Trail with Parker Ridge Trail and Little Jackson Trail. From the Brook Trail trailhead, Little Jackson Connector traverses several drainages as it heads easily northeast across the lower slopes of Tumbledown. Reach Parker Ridge Trail on the left at 1.0 mi. Little Jackson Connector crosses Parker Brook and meets Little

Jackson Trail on the left at 1.1 mi. (The wide trail straight ahead leads about 0.2 mi. to Morgan Rd.)

PARKER RIDGE TRAIL
(AMC TUMBLEDOWN PUBLIC LANDS MAP)
Cumulative from Brook Trail trailhead (1,110 ft.) to:

Parker Ridge Trail (1,210 ft.) via Little Jackson Connector	1.0 mi.	200 ft.	0:35
Tumbledown Pond (2,670 ft.)	2.8 mi.	1,660 ft.	2:15
Tumbledown Mtn., west peak (3,069 ft.) via Tumbledown Mtn. Trail	3.6 mi.	2,180 ft.	2:55

MBPL This trail, one of the oldest on the mountain, ascends to Tumbledown Pond from the southeast via Parker Ridge. Access to the start is by Little Jackson Connector at a point 1.0 mi. from the Brook Trail trailhead. Here, Little Jackson Trail continues straight ahead, while Parker Ridge Trail ascends to the left along the west side of Parker Brook. After the trail crosses a small brook and passes a huge erratic, the ascent becomes steeper. The tree canopy thins as the trail climbs over ledges, and views open up over Webb Lake to Mt. Blue. Along the airy ridgeline beyond are wonderful views of Mt. Blue, Little Jackson, Big Jackson, and the Mahoosuc Range. Follow cairns, and the west and main peaks of Tumbledown become visible. Finally, beautiful Tumbledown Pond can be seen below. Parker Ridge Trail reenters the woods and soon reaches Pond Link Trail, which enters from the right. Just beyond, Brook Trail enters from the left. Tumbledown Pond and its outlet stream, and Tumbledown Mtn. Trail, are 50 ft. ahead.

TUMBLEDOWN MTN. TRAIL
(AMC TUMBLEDOWN PUBLIC LANDS MAP)
Cumulative from Tumbledown Pond outlet (2,670 ft.) to:

Loop Trail (2,910 ft.)	0.6 mi.	360 ft.	0:30
Tumbledown Mtn., west peak (3,069 ft.)	0.8 mi.	520 ft.	0:40

MBPL Tumbledown Mtn. Trail connects Tumbledown Pond with the west peak of Tumbledown Mtn. From the outlet of Tumbledown Pond and the jct. with Brook Trail and Parker Ridge Trail, Tumbledown Mtn. Trail ascends west over mostly open ledges with wonderful views in every direction. From its high point on the narrow ridge above, the trail makes a short, steep descent into a notch, where there is a spring. Loop Trail joins from the left. From this jct., climb to the open summit of the west peak of Tumbledown, which yields great views of the Swift River valley and the summits of Old Blue Mtn. and Elephant Mtn., among many others.

POND LINK TRAIL (AMC TUMBLEDOWN PUBLIC LANDS MAP)
Cumulative from Tumbledown Pond (2,670 ft.) to:

Pond Link Trail (2,690 ft.) via Parker Ridge Trail	80 yd.	20 ft.	0:02
Little Jackson Trail (2,230 ft.)	1.1 mi.	190 ft.	0:40

MBPL This trail links Tumbledown Pond with Little Jackson Trail. From its jct. with Parker Ridge Trail, Pond Link Trail climbs to open ledges on the south shoulder of Little Jackson Mtn. It then descends to the east and, soon after crossing Parker Brook, reaches the jct. with Little Jackson Trail.

LITTLE JACKSON MTN. (3,454 FT.)
This mountain in the heart of Tumbledown PL features an extensive alpine area and fine views northeast to Jackson Mtn., east to Mt. Blue, west overlooking Tumbledown Pond and the rugged peaks of Tumbledown Mtn., and southeast to Webb Lake.

SEC 4

LITTLE JACKSON MTN. TRAIL
(AMC TUMBLEDOWN PUBLIC LANDS MAP)
Cumulative from Brook Trail trailhead on Byron Rd. (1,110 ft.) to:

Little Jackson Trail (1,200 ft.) via Little Jackson Connector	1.1 mi.	200 ft.	0:40
Pond Link Trail (2,230 ft.)	2.3 mi.	1,230 ft.	1:45
Col between Jackson Mtn. and Little Jackson Mtn. (3,130 ft.)	3.1 mi.	2,130 ft.	2:40
Little Jackson Mtn. summit (3,454 ft.)	3.7 mi.	2,455 ft.	3:05

MBPL From the Brook Trail trailhead on Byron Rd., follow Little Jackson Connector. At 1.0 mi., the trail reaches Parker Ridge Trail on the left and crosses Parker Brook to end at a jct. at 1.1 mi. Here, Little Jackson Mtn. Trail leaves sharply to the left (straight ahead, a wide path leads about 0.2 mi. to Morgan Rd.). Little Jackson Mtn. Trail follows the route of an old woods road for the first half of the climb. At 0.4 mi., the trail leaves the old road to the left and follows several switchbacks. It soon rejoins the old road and at 0.7 mi. leaves the old road to the right to follow more switchbacks. At 1.0 mi., the trail rejoins the old road and climbs at a moderate grade to reach Pond Link Trail on the left at 1.3 mi. Beyond, after a short but steep pitch, cross a small brook and then follow stepping-stones across a wet area. A gentle rising contour leads to a section of steeper, rockier terrain. Soon after the angle eases, Little Jackson Mtn. Trail breaks out into the open to reach the jct. with Jackson Mtn. Trail on the right in the col between the two mountains.

The route to Little Jackson Mtn. continues straight and then bears left and up over open ledges to a knob before dropping into a wooded ravine. Climb over bedrock to reach the summit, where several windbreaks made of rocks are visible just ahead. The 360-degree vista from this point is one of Maine's finest and includes Saddleback, Abraham, the Bigelow Range, Sugarloaf, Spaulding, Jackson, and Tumbledown.

JACKSON MTN. (3,555 FT.)

Jackson Mtn. is a rambling, heavily forested mountain with a helipad, radio repeater, solar array, and outbuilding on top. No views can be seen from the summit, but excellent views south, east, and west are possible from open ledges about halfway up.

JACKSON MTN. TRAIL (AMC TUMBLEDOWN PUBLIC LANDS MAP)
From Little Jackson Mtn. Trail in col (3,130 ft.) to:

Jackson Mtn. summit (3,555 ft.)	0.7 mi.	510 ft.	0:40

NFTM Jackson Mtn. Trail leaves from Little Jackson Mtn. Trail in the col between Little Jackson Mtn. and Jackson Mtn. The trail descends gradually over open ledges to the base of the col. In 450 ft., reach a large, pointed rock in a small opening. Turn sharply left here to enter the woods and follow a snowmobile trail. In another 200 ft., turn right off the snowmobile trail onto an unmarked footpath that leads gradually uphill through thick conifers. At 0.3 mi., reach the first of several open ledges that offer views over the col to Little Jackson Mtn. Beyond an obvious large rock next to the trail, cross a level area on the mountain's west shoulder. A moderate pitch leads up the summit cone to the clearing on top of Big Jackson Mtn.

BLUEBERRY MTN. (2,958 FT.)

This mountain is in Township 6 North of Weld, east of Jackson Mtn., Little Jackson Mtn., and Tumbledown Mtn. and north of Webb Lake. Blueberry Mtn. is part of 22,000-acre Tumbledown PL. The bare summit features interesting geological formations and excellent views in all directions.

From the jct. of ME 142 and ME 156 in Weld, drive north on ME 142. Pass West Side Rd. on the left at Weld Corner at 2.2 mi. At 3.5 mi., turn left onto gravel-surfaced Blueberry Mtn. Rd. at a sign for Blueberry Mtn. Bible Camp and Retreat Center. At 1.5 mi. from ME 142, reach the camp's main lodge and several other buildings. Park across from the main lodge.

BLUEBERRY MTN. TRAIL (USGS MADRID QUAD, MBPL MT. BLUE STATE PARK AND TUMBLEDOWN PUBLIC LANDS MAP, GAZETTEER MAP 19)
From bible camp parking lot (1,570 ft.) to:

Blueberry Mtn. summit (2,958 ft.)	1.2 mi.	1,388 ft.	1:20

MBPL Facing the main lodge, walk left through the parking lot to a corner opposite the other two buildings. Here, a path leads through a short stretch of woods to an athletic field. Cross the field to its north side, enter the woods, and follow the course of an old woods road, Blueberry Mtn. Trail, which rises steeply and crosses a logged area. Beyond, the trail leaves the old woods road for a footpath on the right and climbs at a steady, mostly steep grade for the next mile. After ascending a series of ledges (view to Webb Lake), the grade moderates and the trail passes through a section of large erratics. More steep climbing lies ahead before the grade evens out and the trail reaches the open summit at 1.2 mi. Views include the nearby peaks of Tumbledown and the Jacksons as well as the high peaks along the AT from Saddleback and Sugarloaf to the Bigelow Range.

SEC 4

RUMFORD-DIXFIELD
RUMFORD WHITECAP MTN. (2,201 FT.)

The 752-acre Rumford Whitecap Mtn. Preserve in Rumford is the signature conservation property of Mahoosuc Land Trust. The preserve includes the bald summit ridge and south slopes of Rumford Whitecap Mtn., which offer panoramic views and plenty of blueberries in season. Two maintained trails ascend the mountain from the southwest.

From the jct. of US 2 and ME 5, 0.5 mi. west of Rumford Point, go north on ME 5 toward Andover. At 2.8 mi., turn right (east) and cross the Ellis River. At 3.2 mi., turn left onto East Andover Rd. and in another 0.2 mi. reach the trailhead parking area on the left. Iles Trail begins at a red gate directly across the road. Starr Trail begins about 100 yd. north on East Andover Rd. at a gray gate.

ILES TRAIL (AMC RUMFORD WHITECAP MTN. MAP)
Cumulative from red gate on East Andover Rd. (630 ft.) to:

Black/White Trail (1,750 ft.)	1.5 mi.	1,120 ft.	1:20
Starr Trail (1,870 ft.)	1.8 mi.	1,240 ft.	1:40
Rumford Whitecap Mtn. summit (2,201 ft.)	2.3 mi.	1,570 ft.	2:00

MLT From the red gate, follow the woods road (red/orange markers) and soon reach a register box on the right. Pass through a log yard and bear left.

SEC
4

Rumford Whitecap Mtn.

Rumford, ME

Grover Rd

Isthmus Rd

P

Black Mtn Tr

Black Mtn
Ski Area

Reed Hill Rd

1000

True North

15° West

Magnetic Declination 2023

0 mile   ¼   ½   ¾   1

2000

1500

Black Mtn ▲
2354

Black White Tr

1500

1000

Whitecap Mtn ▲
2201

Iles Tr

Start Tr

1500

Boundary Tr

1000

Iles Tr

Start Tr

P

Andover Rd

5

Ridge to River Tr

Farmers Hill ▲
1708

1000

1000

Ellis River Loop

Ellis River

East Andover Rd

Climb gradually to reach Crossover Trail on the left at 0.3 mi. This connector trail (green markers) leads northwest about 0.1 mi. to cross a bridge over a stream before joining Starr Trail.

Beyond the jct., Iles Trail continues along the woods road, climbing moderately. At 0.6 mi., Boundary Trail (green markers) departs to the left; it connects to Starr Trail in 0.5 mi. Soon after the jct., Iles Trail climbs steeply via switchbacks and rock steps, contours to the east for a short distance, and then resumes climbing. Cross a semi-open area and a wide track (the old trail route to the summit, more direct but steep and eroded). Ahead, follow cairns over ledges to finally merge with the old trail route. Turn right on the wide, eroded path and climb easily to the jct. with Black/White Trail on the right at 1.5 mi. (leads 4.8 mi. to the summit of Black Mtn. and then to the base lodge of the Black Mtn. ski area). Continue to the jct. with Starr Trail (yellow markers) on the left at 1.8 mi. Staying on Iles Trail, climb gradually up the ridgeline through semi-open terrain to reach the ledges of the open summit at 2.3 mi. The spectacular 360-degree vista includes Black Mtn. to the east, the high peaks of the Mahoosuc Range to the west, the White Mountains of New Hampshire farther west, and to the south, Mt. Zircon and many other summits of the Oxford Hills.

SEC 4

STARR TRAIL (AMC RUMFORD WHITECAP MTN. MAP)
Cumulative from gray gate on East Andover Rd. (630 ft.) to:

Iles Trail jct. (1,870 ft.)	2.1 mi.	1,240 ft.	1:40
Rumford Whitecap Mtn. summit (2,201 ft.)	2.6 mi.	1,570 ft.	2:10

MLT Walk beyond the gray gate and follow the grassy tote road to a clearing. A signpost directs hikers out of the old log yard to the right. At 0.25 mi., pass a trail register on the right next to a stream. Climbing alongside the stream, at 0.35 mi., Crossover Trail (green markers) departs to the right, crosses a bridge over the stream, and proceeds to join Iles Trail in about 0.1 mi.

Starr Trail continues straight ahead on the old road and proceeds up a long hill , passing Boundary Trail (green markers) on the right at 0.7 mi. (leads 0.5 mi. to Iles Trail). At 0.8 mi., it leaves the old road to the left and proceeds on a footpath marked with yellow blazes and yellow flagging. The trail enters a large bowl at 1.0 mi. and climbs at a steady, moderate grade. It crosses a small brook and an old woods road at 1.2 mi. and then ascends through the woods beside the old road, with ledges to the right.

At 1.3 mi., reach a saddle. Signs point left to E. Andover Rd. and right to the summit. From here, climb steeply to the right through the ledges. After crossing a dip, continue the steep ascent. At 1.4 mi., bear right and up over open ledges with sweeping views that range from Mt. Abram's ski slopes and Puzzle Mtn. in the west to the Mahoosuc Range in the north. Ahead, follow cairns into the woods and proceed easily over the shoulder of the mountain. Climb ledges and slabs through the trees and then angle up and right over steep slabs. The summit of Old Speck Mtn. appears between the peaks of Puzzle Mtn. and Long Mtn. Traverse a steep slope in the open, with views to US 2 and Mt. Abram, and continue to follow cairns over slabs, mostly in the open. When the angle eases, bear right, reenter the woods, and drop slightly to the jct. with Iles Trail at 2.1 mi. The summit of Rumford Whitecap is 0.5 mi. northeast (left) via this trail.

BLACK MTN. (2,354 FT.)

Black Mtn. in Rumford, best known for the ski resort (Black Mountain of Maine) on its eastern slopes, rises just east of Rumford Whitecap. The mountain's two summits both have communications towers. Black/White Trail is a connector linking Rumford Whitecap with Black Mtn., while Black Mtn. Trail connects the top of Black Mtn. with the ski area base lodge. This strenuous route gains a little more than 1,000 ft. of elevation but loses 1,300 ft. from its high point to the ski area base. The hike is best done from Rumford Whitecap to Black Mtn. (west to east), because the start of this trail on Rumford Whitecap is easy to find, whereas negotiating the ski runs and cleared areas on Black Mtn. can be challenging on the ascent. A vehicle spot at the Black Mountain of Maine ski area base parking lot is probably a smart idea for the hike from Rumford Whitecap.

BLACK/WHITE TRAIL AND BLACK MTN. TRAIL
(AMC RUMFORD WHITECAP MTN. MAP)
Cumulative from Iles Trail on Rumford Whitecap (1,750 ft.) to:

High point on Black Mtn. at cell tower (2,290 ft.)	3.3 mi.	1,050 ft.	2:10
Black Mountain of Maine ski resort base lodge (960 ft.)	4.8 mi.	1,050 ft.	3:00

MLT From the jct. of Iles Trail at a point 1.5 mi. from East Andover Rd. and 0.8 mi. from the summit of Rumford Whitecap, Black/White Trail diverges to the right and heads northeast toward Black Mtn. The trail follows a contour below the summit dome of Rumford Whitecap and then descends via several tight switchbacks. Pass a large, split glacial erratic at

0.6 mi. and then traverse multiple drainages. The treadway is not always well defined, so follow the markers (white blazes and orange ribbons) carefully. After climbing a short, steep pitch, arrive at several rocks and trees splotched with red paint at 1.4 mi. Ignore the red-blazed trail (and one white blaze) going straight and then left uphill. Instead, turn right and proceed downhill to a small clearing, join an old woods road, and continue to descend. At 1.8 mi., reach the bottom of the valley between Rumford Whitecap and Black Mtn.

Descend rock steps to cross a stream. Reach a meadow (an emergency helicopter landing zone) at 2.0 mi. Bear right to a woods road and then bear left into the woods (signs with hiker symbol at these points). Cross a brook, go right and up, recross the brook, and then go right and up next to the drainage. Crest the ridge at 2.8 mi. Bear left and up to cross an old boundary line (orange and yellow blazes, old ax blazes). Level off and then climb higher before leveling off again and reaching a cell tower and an old building on the east peak of Black Mtn. at 3.3 mi. Pass left around the cell tower complex and continue along a gravel road. With another tower in view, bear right into the woods at the sign for Black Mtn. Lodge. Follow the well-defined trail (now called Black Mtn. Trail) through thick softwoods. Drop to a sag and then climb out to a knob. Reach a viewpoint on the left at 3.4 mi., which offers a look at the Tumbledown peaks, Mt. Blue, and the ridgeline of Bald Mtn. and Saddleback Wind.

Descend off the ridge toward the Mt. Blue view (to the northeast), passing through a logged area. Reach a cairn on a ski trail at 3.5 mi., bear left for 100 ft., and then bear right to the next cairn. Head down the skidder trail with an impressive view of the Black Mtn. base area far below. At a cairn and outlook, bear left into the woods and descend steeply along the edge of a ravine. Ahead, at a cairn next to a ski trail, bear right downhill, following the right margin of the ski trail (occasional cairns). At 3.75 mi., turn right into the woods and descend steeply over ledges. Reach the next ski trail and descend along its right edge before quickly reentering the woods. Descend the steep slope at an angle, cross another ski trail (cairns at both sides of opening; base lodge visible on left), and reenter the woods. Soon cross a brook and then descend a moderate-to-steep slope above the water. At a set of rock steps leading to an old woods road, bear left downhill. At 4.2 mi., turn right off the old road and descend the slope below. At 4.4 mi., reach a ski trail, where signs point to Black Mtn. and Rumford Whitecap Mtn. Go left to the top of the blue lift, in sight 100 yd. beyond. Bear right at the blue lift and follow it to the Black Mtn. base lodge at 4.8 mi.

SEC 4

GLASSFACE MTN. (1,916 FT.)

This mountain rises above the north bank of the Androscoggin River in Rumford Center. On the southwestern slopes, MLT owns 32-acre Glassface Mtn. Conservation Area, where Glassface Ledges Trail climbs to a high point and view overlooking the river valley.

From the jct. of US 2 and ME 232 in Rumford Point, drive east on US 2 for 3.3 mi. to the Rumford Boat Launch parking area (and trailhead parking), which is on the right immediately across from Rumford Center Meeting House and Rumford Center Cemetery.

SEC 4

GLASSFACE LEDGES TRAIL (USGS RUMFORD QUAD, MTF GLASSFACE LEDGES TRAIL MAP, GAZETTEER MAP 18)
From US 2 (610 ft.) to:

Glassface Ledges (1,280 ft.)	0.8 mi.	670 ft.	0:45

MLT Cross US 2 to the cemetery and follow the old road (path) through the center of the grounds. Beyond the cemetery, at 0.15 mi., Glassface Ledges Trail enters the woods near a white rail fence. Immediately after, bear right to meet a small brook and begin climbing. Ascend via switchbacks through the semi-open logged area. The way gets steeper above, weaving a route via more switchbacks to enter a ravine with a small brook. At 0.65 mi., cross the brook and then climb rock steps through boulders along the other side. Soon turn away from the brook and reach the end of the trail at the ledges. The view takes in Mt. Zircon, Mt. Abram, the bucolic Androscoggin River valley, and the village of Rumford Center.

MYSTERY MTN. (1,212 FT.)

This hill in Rumford Point rises steeply over the Androscoggin River valley. Ledges on its western edge offer views southwest along the river to the hills around Bethel, the ski slopes at Sunday River, the White Mountains, and south to Woodstock Hill and Greenwood Hill.

In Rumford Point at the jct. of US 2 and ME 232, follow US 2 west for 0.7 mi. Turn right on a dirt road and drive 150 ft. to a T jct. Parking is in the dirt lot to the right. Mystery Mtn. Trail begins to the left.

MYSTERY MTN. TRAIL (USGS DIXFIELD QUAD, MTF MYSTERY MTN MAP, GAZETTEER MAP 18)
From parking near US 2 (650 ft.) to:

Ledges at high point (1,160 ft.)	0.7 mi.	510 ft.	0:35

IWT Follow an old forest road for 100 ft. and then turn right on Mystery Mtn. Trail (signpost). The trail winds easily up the hillside, and at 0.3 mi., bears right to cross a skidder track and then goes up some stone steps. At

0.5 mi., reach a clifftop view on the right. Ahead, the trail winds over the back side of the hill before turning south and climbing higher along the ridge. The trail ends at a large, grassy outcropping where there is an expansive view over the river valley.

SUGARLOAF (IN DIXFIELD; 1,503 FT.)

Sugarloaf in Dixfield is conspicuous for both of its prominent and shapely summits. The mountain offers fine vistas from open ledges on its northern summit. Along Sugarloaf Trail, Bull Rock yields views over the woods and fields of the Dixfield area.

From the jct. of US 2 and ME 142 in Dixfield, drive north on ME 142 for 1.5 mi. to the entrance of Mountain View CG on the left. The campground owners allow parking on the grass in front of the obvious large mulch pile near the entrance. Please do not park on the campground road or block the ATV trail.

SEC 4

SUGARLOAF TRAIL (USGS DIXFIELD QUAD, GAZETTEER MAP 19)
Cumulative from ME 142 (490 ft.) to:

Bull Rock (900 ft.)	0.3 mi.	410 ft.	0:20
Sugarloaf north summit (1,503 ft.)	1.6 mi.	1,010 ft.	1:20

NFTM To begin, facing ME 142, cross the road, angling right to a dirt driveway (in 2022 a small shed with campfire wood for sale was on the right side of the driveway). Look for an old tote road—the trail route— just ahead and begin climbing. Beyond a bridge over a small brook, Sugarloaf Trail becomes steep and eroded. After a steady, moderate ascent on a narrow ridge, reach the lookout at Bull Rock on the right. Continue past Bull Rock on a wide, level treadway, which eventually bears left and descends gently to a T jct. at 0.5 mi. Turn left, and at the next fork, bear right to stay on the wide track. At 0.8 mi., reach a 4-way jct. and turn left. Follow the grassy old tote road (old red blazes) easily along on a contour. Cross an old log yard clearing that's becoming overgrown by alders at 1.0 mi.

At 1.3 mi., turn right on a footpath (flagging and cairn). Climb steadily, passing boulders on the right. At a level spot in the col between Sugarloaf's north and south peaks, at the remains of an old tote road in a small clearing, bear left to stay on the footpath. Follow flagging and old blazes as the slippery trail of conifer needles climbs steeply up the summit cone. Reach the open ledges on top, where the fine views include the Androscoggin River valley, the northern Oxford Hills, the Webb River valley, the Mahoosuc Range, and the White Mountain summits of Carter Dome, Mt. Washington, and others.

FAR NORTHERN FRANKLIN COUNTY
SNOW MTN. (3,967 FT.)

Snow Mtn. is in Alder Stream Township in the remote region northwest of Flagstaff Lake. An abandoned fire tower (no cab) is on the wooded summit (climb the ladder for views). The mountain and the land around it are owned by the Penobscot Indian Nation. Day use is permitted, but overnight camping is not allowed without advance permission.

From the jct. of ME 16 and ME 27 in Stratton, drive north on ME 27. At 13.0 mi., enter Alder Stream Township, and in 0.3 mi., turn left onto gravel-surfaced North Rd. Reset trip meter. At a fork at 0.3 mi., bear right. At 2.2 mi., the road to Round Mtn. Pond leaves to the left; continue straight. At a fork at 3.8 mi., bear right. At the next two forks (4.2 mi. and 4.6 mi.), stay straight. Pass a 5-mi. marker sign at 4.9 mi., and in 0.2 mi., turn left. The road climbs the hillside, and an obvious ATV track crosses at 5.5 mi; the start of Snow Mtn. Trail follows the ATV track to the left (look for several small cairns). Parking is 100 ft. ahead on the left at the end of the road (as of 2022).

SNOW MTN. TRAIL (USGS CHAIN OF PONDS AND JIM POND QUADS, GAZETTEER MAP 39)

Cumulative from parking at end of logging road (2,080 ft.) to:

Grassy ATV track, lower jct. (2,800 ft.)	1.4 mi.	720 ft.	1:05
Snow Mtn. Pond (2,804 ft.)	1.5 mi.	724 ft.	1:10
Fire Warden's Trail (2,804 ft.)	1.65 mi.	724 ft.	1:15
Grassy ATV track, upper jct. (3,060 ft.)	2.0 mi.	980 ft.	1:35
Snow Mtn. summit (3,967 ft.)	2.8 mi.	1,880 ft.	2:25

Cumulative from parking at end of logging road (2,080 ft.) to:

Grassy ATV track, lower jct. (2,800 ft.)	1.4 mi.	720 ft.	1:05
Fire Warden's Trail (3,060 ft.)	1.9 mi.	980 ft.	1:30
Snow Mtn. summit (3,967 ft.)	2.7 mi.	1,880 ft.	2:20

NFTM Follow the ATV track—Snow Mtn. Trail—into the woods, proceeding in a westerly direction. The trail climbs gradually at first and then at a moderate grade up the valley of Little Alder Stream. Cross a bridge at 0.6 mi. and a second bridge at 1.0 mi. Soon after, at a jct., leave the ATV track for a rocky and eroded treadway on the right. This jct. is marked by two boulders, two small cairns, some flagging tape, and an old signboard tacked to a tree (*Note*: This turn is easy to miss. Staying on the ATV track leads to another bridge 150 ft. beyond the jct.; should you come to the bridge, turn around and retrace your steps to find the trail jct.).

Continue on the rocky and eroded route. Ahead, a footpath leaves to the right to avoid a badly gullied section of the old trail and then rejoins it in 150 yd. At 1.4 mi., pass a cairn on a large rock and then enter a small clearing. Here, a muddy ATV track enters from the left and continues straight ahead, while a grassy ATV track leaves to the right. From this point, there are two ways to proceed: The traditional route goes straight ahead on the muddy ATV track to Snow Mtn. Pond and then up the old fire warden's trail, which involves some bushwhacking and is difficult to follow for the first 0.35 mi. The other, easier option is to turn right and follow the grassy ATV track, which intersects the old fire warden's trail partway up the mountain.

Grassy ATV track. From the clearing at 1.4 mi., turn right on the grassy ATV track. If the route has recently been used by ATVs, there should be a clear double-track to follow. The 0.5-mi. track leads northwest and gains 260 ft. of elevation as it climbs to a shallow saddle on the south ridge of Snow Mtn., where it intersects the old fire warden's trail. Turn right to hike the old fire warden's trail, which from this point to the summit (0.8 mi.) is well defined and straightforward.

**SEC
4**

Traditional route. From the clearing at 1.4 mi., the traditional route to the top of Snow Mtn. continues straight ahead on the muddy ATV track. In about 200 ft., pass (and avoid) an old trail on the right. At 1.5 mi., pass a short path on the left leading to Snow Mtn. Pond (canoes in the woods here). Continue on the muddy ATV track past the north side of the pond and, at 1.65 mi., look for a small wooden sign with an arrow on it nailed to a fir tree on the right with a small cairn at ground level; this is the start of the old fire warden's trail to the top of Snow Mtn.

The obscure trail leads slightly left over spongy ground to a downed fir tree. Turn right after the downed tree and go through grass and alder shrubs. Cross a series of blowdowns as you follow the grassy corridor. At 1.9 mi., bear right and up on a better-defined treadway. After a short, steep pitch, reach a shallow saddle at 2.0 mi., where a grassy ATV track crosses the trail route. The track from the right is the grassy ATV track alternative. Continue straight ahead and reenter the woods (entrance marked by a cairn). The old fire warden's trail is well defined and much easier to follow from this point to the summit.

Top out on a knoll at 2.1 mi., and then cross a dip and climb again. The steep, mossy trail reaches a spring at 2.3 mi. Immediately beyond, pass to the right of a cliff wall and quickly look left for a narrow, rough path up the steep slope. Climb this pitch, and at the jct. on top, turn right to continue on the better defined trail. The grade is moderate with several short, steep stretches. At 2.6 mi., the angle eases and the top of the mountain appears.

A trail from Big Island Pond enters from the left at 2.7 mi., and 0.1 mi. beyond, reach an outcropping with a view east to the Bigelows and south to the peaks around Rangeley. In another 100 ft., the ruins of the fire warden's lightning shack is on the left, and just beyond that is the old fire tower in a small clearing. Climb the tower steps to enjoy a grand panorama that takes in the high peaks of the Boundary Mountains on both sides of the international border with Canada, plus the White Mountains in New Hampshire, and Old Blue, Jackson, Tumbledown, East Kennebago, Redington, Crocker, Sugarloaf, the Bigelow Range, and much more in Maine.

KIBBY MTN. (3,656 FT.)

This remote, high mountain in Skinner Township lies in the heart of the vast forestlands northwest of Flagstaff Lake and east of the Canadian border and Chain of Ponds. A platform atop an old fire tower on the summit provides superb views of the jumble of mountain peaks in this region, as well as the many towers of the Kibby Wind Power Project.

From the jct. of ME 27 and ME 16 in Stratton, drive north on ME 27 for 16.3 mi. and turn right onto Gold Brook Rd. (signs for Kibby Wind Power Project and Weyerhaeuser Timberlands; please observe the posted land use rules, especially yielding to all logging trucks). Reset trip meter. At 2.6 mi., stay straight. Pass Series B Access Rd. on the right at 3.6 mi. Continue straight past roads on the right at 6.0 mi. and 6.6 mi. Pass Spencer Bale Rd. (Series A Access Rd.) on the right at 7.5 mi. After the 9-mi. marker, at the top of the next rise at 9.2 mi., turn right on a lesser road. A grassy parking area is on the left 0.4 mi. ahead. An old tote road, also a snowmobile trail, heads into the woods at the upper left-hand corner of the parking area; this is the starting point of the trail.

KIBBY MTN. TRAIL (USGS KIBBY MTN. QUAD, GAZETTEER MAP 39)
From parking area (2,560 ft.) to:

Kibby Mtn. summit (3,656 ft.)	2.3 mi.	1,096 ft.	1:40

NFTM Ascend gradually to the north following the old woods road. At 0.9 mi., bear right off the old woods road (flagging and a small cairn) and continue on the rising contour through a well-defined corridor of thick conifers and birch. Upon entering a small opening, the wide path turns sharply right and heads southeast. A short, moderate stretch leads to a saddle where the trail swings south past a large, mossy boulder. After a short, steep pitch, the path levels off and crosses the summit ridge. The old fire tower (1926) is in a small, rocky clearing at trail's end. The view from the observation deck is extraordinary, reaching far and wide across the wild country in every direction.

SECTION FIVE

MAHOOSUC RANGE AND GRAFTON NOTCH

Pull-Out Map
Map 6: Mahoosuc Range–Evans Notch

INTRODUCTION

This section on the Mahoosuc Range and Grafton Notch describes 22 trails on 20 mountains in the Maine portion of the Mahoosuc Range, which extends from the Maine–New Hampshire border to its northern end at the West Branch of the Ellis River in Andover. Map 6: Mahoosuc Range–Evans Notch graphically portrays nearly the entire range and all the trails on both sides of the state line. The Mahoosuc Range extends roughly 25 mi. in a southwest to northeast direction from the Androscoggin River, east of Berlin and north of Gorham and across the Maine state line to Shelburne, New Hampshire; to Old Speck Mtn. and the peaks of Baldpate Mtn. and the jumble of rugged mountains on both sides of Grafton Notch in Grafton Township, Riley Township, Andover West Surplus Township, and Newry. This rugged range, part of the White Mountains but not part of the WMNF, is bounded by the Androscoggin River and NH 16 to the west, by the Androscoggin River and US 2 to the south and east, and by East B Hill Rd. to the northeast. The AT traverses the entire Mahoosuc Range, a distance of 41 mi.

Nearly 35,000 acres of the Mahoosuc Range in Maine are protected in Grafton Notch State Park (3,191 acres) and Mahoosuc PL (31,764 acres), both owned and managed by the state of Maine. The abutting Stowe Mountain conservation easement protects an additional 3,400 acres. Nearly 10,000 acres of Mahoosuc PL are designated by the state of Maine as an ecological reserve to protect its sensitive ecosystems, including about 8,500 acres classified as subalpine forest and 269 acres classified as alpine ridge. Mahoosuc Land Trust owns 485-acre Stewart Family Preserve high on Puzzle Mtn. Inland Woods + Trails owns 1,510 acres in Bethel between its two community forest properties.

GEOGRAPHY

Among the more than two dozen mountains that compose the Mahoosuc Range are 16 summits that exceed 3,000 ft. In New Hampshire, this includes Bald Cap (3,087 ft.) and Mt. Success (3,592 ft.). In Maine, the high peaks include Mt. Carlo (3,576 ft.), Goose Eye Mtn. (3,886 ft.), Goose Eye Mtn. East Peak (3,801 ft.), Goose Eye Mtn. North Peak (3,683 ft.), Fulling Mill Mtn. (3,439 ft.), Fulling Mill Mtn. South Peak (3,401 ft.), Mahoosuc Arm (3,781 ft.), and Old Speck Mtn. (4,188 ft.) along the main Mahoosuc crest.

West of ME 26 along Grafton Loop Trail are Slide Mtn. (3,271 ft.), Sunday River Whitecap (3,368 ft.), Stowe Mtn. (2,743 ft.), and Bald Mtn. (2,097 ft.). East of ME 26 along Grafton Loop Trail are Puzzle Mtn.

(3,156 ft.), Long Mtn. (3,060 ft.), and Lightning Ledge (2,644 ft.). East of Grafton Notch is the airy shelf of Table Rock (2,431 ft.) and the west and east peaks of Baldpate Mtn. (3,694 ft. and 3,815 ft., respectively).

West of Grafton Notch are the towering cliffs of the Eyebrow (2,590 ft.) and Old Speck Mtn., which at 4,188 ft. is the highest in the Mahoosuc Range and the fifth-highest summit in Maine. The highest body of water in Maine is Speck Pond, tucked in between Old Speck Mtn. and Mahoosuc Arm (3,781 ft.) at an elevation of 3,400 ft.

Along the southern fringes of the Mahoosucs in the Androscoggin River valley are Mt. Will (1,729 ft.) in Newry, and Locke Mtn. (1,926 ft.) and Ellingwood Mtn. (1,574 ft.) in Bethel.

ROAD ACCESS

Primary access to trails in the Grafton Notch area is by ME 26 from US 2. This includes the AT and Grafton Loop Trail. For ease of travel, refer to this table for trailheads and points of interest east and west of ME 26:

SEC 5

Cumulative from jct. of ME 26 and US 2 in Newry via ME 26 north to:
Grafton Loop Trail (southern trailhead),

Stewart Family Preserve (east)	4.6 mi.
Step Falls Preserve (east)	7.8 mi.
Screw Auger Falls (west)	9.4 mi.
Mother Walker Falls (east)	10.6 mi.
Moose Cave (east)	11.3 mi.
Grafton Notch, trailhead parking and AT crossing (west)	12.1 mi.
Spruce Meadow Picnic Area (west)	13.1 mi.
North Rd. (access to Success Pond Rd. trailheads)	16.9 mi.

Access to the peaks of the Mahoosuc Range from the west is possible via Success Pond Rd., which extends the length of the range's lower western slopes. From the trailhead parking area on ME 26 in Grafton Notch at the AT crossing, drive north for 4.9 mi. Turn left on North Rd., and follow it for 4.0 mi. to a jct. with Success Pond Rd. and York Pond Rd. Bear right on Success Pond Rd., and continue south to reach the Speck Pond, Notch, Carlo Col and Goose Eye, and Success trailheads. Refer to the following summary table for detailed mileage between points.

From ME 26 via North Rd. and Success Pond Rd. to:

Speck Pond Trail trailhead	11.1 mi.
Carlo Col and Goose Eye trailhead	13.9 mi.
Success Trail trailhead	16.6 mi.
Hutchins St., Berlin, NH	22.0 mi.

Reach the AT on the north side of Baldpate Mtn. by East B Hill Rd. from the village of Andover, which in turn is reached via ME 5 from US 2 in Rumford Point. Trails in Bethel are reached via US 2.

CAMPING

There are no camping facilities in Grafton Notch State Park. In Mahoosuc PL, which includes the AT corridor, there is backcountry camping at five shelter sites: Carlo Col, Full Goose, Speck Pond, Baldface, and Frye Notch. Carlo Col, Full Goose, and Speck Pond are AMC sites. Groups of six or more persons planning to camp at AMC backcountry sites are asked to use the group notification system; find more information at outdoors.org/backcountry-campsites. A caretaker fee is charged at Speck Pond. Camping is prohibited above treeline. Below treeline, dispersed camping is allowed, but fires are not. Along the west side of Grafton Loop Trail, backpackers may tent at Bald Mtn., Sargent Brook, Slide Mtn., and Bull Run. On the east side of Grafton Loop Trail, tentsites include Stewart, Town Corner, and Lane. Along Wright Trail, there is a tentsite on Goose Eye Brook. Fires are not permitted at Stewart and Sargent Brook campsites, which are on private land. Four privately operated drive-in campgrounds are on the outskirts of the Mahoosuc Range and Grafton Notch section: two in Bethel, one in Newry, and one in Hanover.

SUGGESTED HIKES

■ Easy

The Mahoosuc Range and Grafton Notch section does not have any suggested hikes rated as easy.

■ Moderate
THE EYEBROW

LP via Eyebrow Trail and Old Speck Trail (AT)	2.2 mi.	1,060 ft.	1:40

This loop hike features some steep climbing using iron rungs, ladders, handrails, and cables to reach spectacular views of Grafton Notch from atop the 800-ft. cliff called the Eyebrow. To begin, see Eyebrow Trail, p. 247.

TABLE ROCK

	⮏	↗	◯
LP via Table Rock Trail and AT Southbound	2.4 mi.	935 ft.	1:40

A moderately steep but impressive climb leads to a prominent rock ledge overlooking Grafton Notch and an extensive slab cave system. Return via the AT for a loop hike. To begin, see Table Rock Trail, p. 248.

MT. WILL

	⮏	↗	◯
LP via Mt. Will Trail	3.1 mi.	1,090 ft.	2:30

Hike the loop over Mt. Will to the North Ledges and South Cliffs for views of the Androscoggin River valley. See Mt. Will Trail, p. 267.

LOCKE MTN.

	⮏	↗	◯
RT via Summit Ridge Trail	3.4 mi.	870 ft.	2:10

Hike to West Ledge for excellent vistas south and west over the Androscoggin River valley to the peaks of the WMNF around Evans Notch. See Summit Ridge Trail, p. 268.

ELLINGWOOD MTN.

	⮏	↗	◯
LP via Parks-Bennet Trail	2.9 mi.	810 ft.	1:50

Enjoy wonderful sights from the Prow, Porcupine Panorama, and Ellingwood Ledges on this fun loop hike through a community forest. See Parks-Bennet Trail, p. 269.

■ Strenuous
OLD SPECK MTN.

	⮏	↗	◯
RT via Old Speck Trail (AT) and Mahoosuc Trail	7.6 mi.	2,692 ft.	5:10

This moderately steep route leads to a fine panorama from the observation tower atop Old Speck, Maine's fifth-highest peak. To begin, see Old Speck Trail, p. 249.

SEC 5

BALDPATE MTN.

RT via AT Northbound	8.0 mi.	2,815 ft.	5:20

Climb to the extensive alpine area atop Baldpate Mtn.'s East Peak for outstanding scenes of the Mahoosuc Range. Bag the more wooded West Peak en route. See Baldpate Mtn. via AT Northbound, p. 250.

SPECK POND

RT via Speck Pond Trail	7.2 mi.	2,400 ft.	4:50

Hike to this pretty mountain tarn, the highest body of water in Maine, and grab the nearby open summit of Mahoosuc Arm on the way. See Speck Pond Trail, p. 251.

GOOSE EYE MTN.

RT via Wright Trail and Mahoosuc Trail (AT)	9.8 mi.	3,020 ft.	6:25

Ascend the craggy summits of Goose Eye for a bird's-eye view over the high and wild terrain of the central Mahoosucs. To begin, see Wright Trail, p. 254.

PUZZLE MTN.

LP via Grafton Loop Trail and Woodsum Spur Trail	7.6 mi.	2,570 ft.	5:00

Travel a portion of the Grafton Loop Trail to the summit ledges on Puzzle Mtn. for impressive Mahoosuc Range vistas, and then descend via scenic Woodsum Spur. To begin, see Grafton Loop Trail, Eastern Section, on p. 261.

TRAIL DESCRIPTIONS
GRAFTON NOTCH STATE PARK

This park encompasses the rugged terrain on both sides of ME 26 through Grafton Notch, from the Newry–Grafton Notch town line to about 1.5 mi. north of the height-of-land in Grafton Notch at the AT crossing. Along ME 26 are various short graded trails and paths leading to interesting natural features, including Screw Auger Falls, Mother Walker Falls, and Moose Cave. Step Falls Preserve (MLT) is just south of the park.

A large trailhead parking area with a toilet, a trail register, and an information kiosk is on the west side of ME 26 at the head of Grafton Notch, 12.1 mi. north of the jct. of ME 26 and US 2 in Newry. The AT routes to Old Speck Mtn. and Baldpate Mtn. and the trails to the Eyebrow and Table Rock leave from this point.

THE EYEBROW (2,590 FT.)

The 800-ft. cliff face known as the Eyebrow dominates the west side of Grafton Notch. The lookouts along the rim of the great cliff yield extraordinary views over the Bear River valley, which was carved into its classic U-shape by powerful glaciers eons ago. Eyebrow Trail climbs to the top of the cliff via its north side. The Eyebrow can also be reached by hiking the lower section of Old Speck Trail (AT).

SEC 5

EYEBROW TRAIL (MAP 6: B13)
From Old Speck Trail, lower jct. (1,530 ft.) to:

Old Speck Trail, upper jct. (2,500 ft.)	1.2 mi.	1,060 ft.	1:10

MBPL This trail offers a steep, challenging trek to and then along the airy lip of the Eyebrow. The route is better suited for ascent than descent.

Orange-blazed Eyebrow Trail leaves Old Speck Trail on the right, 0.1 mi. from the hiker parking area on ME 26 at the height-of-land in Grafton Notch. Pass a huge erratic on the left. Encounter a series of rock staircases as the trail climbs gradually and then moderately to the upper base of the north ridge at 0.5 mi. The next 0.1 mi. ascends steeply over rough terrain with the aid of metal rungs, handrails, and cable. Climb steep rock slabs and roots along cable handrails secured to posts and then scamper up three iron rungs. Next, cross a steep slab via a large break in the rock: use the handrails at first, then drop down using a set of rungs, and finally climb an iron ladder. The next pitch requires climbing a series of 13 iron rungs. Above, cross a small brook, with a look east toward Baldpate Mtn. Soon after, climb steeply via a long series of rock staircases. The angle of ascent eases at 0.9 mi. From here, Eyebrow Trail follows a rising contour along the rim of the cliff, passing several lookouts. After a brief descent, Eyebrow Trail rises gradually to meet Old Speck Trail. Turn right here to climb Old Speck in 2.4 mi., or turn left to descend to the hiker parking lot in 1.0 mi.

TABLE ROCK (2,431 FT.)

Table Rock Trail offers a short but steep climb to the prominent rock ledge of Table Rock on Baldpate Mtn. on the east side of Grafton Notch and affords spectacular views of Old Speck Mtn. across the notch. From the ledge, the trail continues and rejoins the AT. Table Rock Trail also features an extensive slab cave system, possibly the largest in the state.

TABLE ROCK TRAIL (MAP 6: B13)
Cumulative from ME 26 trailhead parking area (1,496 ft.) to:

Start of Table Rock Trail (1,500 ft.) via AT	0.1 mi.	25 ft.	0:05
Table Rock and jct. with upper part of loop trail (2,400 ft.)	1.0 mi.	935 ft.	1:00
Complete loop, including AT	2.4 mi.	935 ft.	1:40

MBPL From the kiosk at the hiker parking area, follow the AT northbound. Cross ME 26, and then cross a brook to reach the jct. with Table Rock Trail on the right. Table Rock Trail climbs gradually, angling across the lower slopes of the mountainside for the next 0.3 mi. The trail then turns steeply up on a rock staircase. After tackling a set of five iron rungs, scramble through boulders and over roots. Pass a slab cave at 0.7 mi. More rock steps lead steeply up to the right below a cliff wall. Reach a cave with a rectangular alcove; just beyond, a spur on the right leads 20 ft. to an outlook with views to Old Speck and the Eyebrow. Beyond, bear right below a huge overhang, and then climb rungs into an alcove of huge boulders. Bear right through an opening in the rocks (cave below on the left). Drop down a short pitch, continue across the slope, and climb over a large rock. Angle gradually back toward the top to reach a jct. From here, Table Rock is 75 ft. to the left. The extraordinary vista from the broad open rock shelf of Table Rock includes the sweep of Grafton Notch, Old Speck, the Eyebrow, Sunday River Whitecap, and Puzzle Mtn.

To descend, return to the jct. and proceed straight ahead. Descend a ladder of 7 iron rungs (handrail) and continue due north on the gradual route down to a T jct. with the AT. Turn left to follow the AT south back to the ME 26 trailhead. The mostly moderate descent passes a trail register and crosses several small brooks before reaching the highway.

MAHOOSUC PUBLIC LANDS

Mahoosuc PL essentially surrounds Grafton Notch State Park. North of the park, Mahoosuc PL encompasses the entirety of Baldpate Mtn. South of the park, the unit extends to the Maine–New Hampshire border and includes the summits of Old Speck Mtn., Mahoosuc Arm, Fulling Mill Mtn., Goose Eye Mtn., and Mt. Carlo.

OLD SPECK MTN. (4,188 FT.)

Old Speck Mtn., named for its speckled appearance caused by large areas of exposed rock and tree cover (and to distinguish it from Speckled mountains in Stoneham and Peru), dominates the western side of Grafton Notch. Old Speck is Maine's fifth-highest mountain, after Katahdin, Hamlin, Sugarloaf, and North Crocker Mtn. The open observation tower on the wooded summit offers outstanding views of Grafton Notch and the west and east peaks of Baldpate Mtn. to the north, the many summits of the Mahoosuc Range to the south, and beyond to the Carter–Moriah Range, the Wildcat peaks, and the Presidential Range.

OLD SPECK TRAIL (MAP 6: B13–C13)
Cumulative from ME 26 (1,496 ft.) to:

Eyebrow Trail, upper jct. (2,480 ft.)	1.0 mi.	984 ft.	1:05
Mahoosuc Trail (4,010 ft.)	3.5 mi.	2,514 ft.	3:05
Old Speck Mtn. summit (4,188 ft.) via Mahoosuc Trail	3.8 mi.	2,692 ft.	3:20

SEC 5

AMC This trail, part of the AT, ascends Old Speck Mtn. from a parking lot (sign: "Hiking Trails") on the west side of ME 26 at the height-of-land in Grafton Notch. From a kiosk on the north side of the lot, follow the trail leading to the left (the right-hand trail, the AT, leads north to Baldpate Mtn.). In 0.1 mi., Eyebrow Trail leaves right. Beyond, Old Speck Trail crosses a brook and soon begins to climb, following a series of switchbacks with many rock steps. At 0.5 mi., the trail zigzags steadily up the mountainside along Cascade Brook. At 0.9 mi., it crosses the brook and climbs to open ledges with a view south over the upper ridges on Old Speck. At a fork at 1.0 mi., the upper end of Eyebrow Trail enters from the right. Bear left to continue on Old Speck Trail. After more rock steps, the trail swings south to begin climbing the north ridge of the mountain. It ascends at a steady, moderate grade with several minor ups and downs and then makes the final steep ascent to the summit ridge, reaching the jct. with Mahoosuc Trail at 3.2 mi. To the right, Mahoosuc Trail descends to Speck Pond CS in 1.1 mi. Turn left to follow Mahoosuc Trail along the high, wooded ridgeline to the summit clearing atop Old Speck, where there is an observation tower (formerly a fire tower, erected in 1919).

BALDPATE MTN.: WEST PEAK (3,694 FT.), EAST PEAK (3,815 FT.)

Baldpate Mtn. rises to the east of Grafton Notch. The two prominent peaks of the mountain are the alpine summit of East Peak and the more wooded West Peak. Access to Baldpate is via the AT, which makes a complete traverse of the mountain. Table Rock is an interesting side trip to spectacular ledges high above Grafton Notch.

BALDPATE MTN. VIA AT NORTHBOUND (MAP 6: B13–B14)
Cumulative from Grafton Notch trailhead parking on ME 26 (1,450 ft.) to:

Table Rock Trail, lower jct. (1,500 ft.)	0.1 mi.	50 ft.	0:05
Table Rock Trail, upper jct. (2,100 ft.)	0.8 mi.	650 ft.	0:45
Side trail to Baldpate Lean-to (2,660 ft.)	2.3 mi.	1,210 ft.	1:45
Baldpate Mtn., West Peak (3,694 ft.)	3.1 mi.	2,170 ft.	2:40
Baldpate Mtn., East Peak (3,815 ft.) and Grafton Loop Trail	4.0 mi.	2,580 ft.	3:15
East B Hill Rd. (1,450 ft.)	10.3 mi.	3,265 ft.	6:45

MATC The AT leaves from the kiosk on the north side of the parking area on ME 26 in Grafton Notch. At a fork, the AT heads to the right and soon crosses ME 26. It runs briefly through woods and beside a marsh until, at 0.1 mi., it crosses a log footbridge over a brook. Just ahead, the AT passes Table Rock Trail, which leaves to the right. The AT rises gradually on an old woods road and passes the upper end of Table Rock Trail at 0.8 mi. It climbs steadily and then more steeply to the western knob of Baldpate Mtn., where there are views to the northwest. The AT then angles up the north side of the knob to a ridge extending toward West Peak and soon descends to a brook where, at 2.3 mi., a side trail leads south to Baldpate Lean-to.

Beyond, the AT climbs steeply to West Peak and views at 3.1 mi. It continues north to dip several hundred feet before climbing to East Peak at 4.0 mi., marked by a large cairn. The alpine summit offers extensive views of western Maine's mountain and lake country. Also at the summit, Grafton Loop Trail enters from the right (south). From here, the AT continues north for 6.3 mi. to East B Hill Rd.

BALDPATE MTN. VIA AT SOUTHBOUND FROM EAST B HILL RD. (USGS B POND AND OLD SPECK QUADS, MATC MAP 7, MAP 6: B13–B14, GAZETTEER MAP 18)
Cumulative from East B Hill Rd. (1,450 ft.) to:

Dunn Notch, West Branch of Ellis River (1,300 ft.)	0.8 mi.	−150 ft.	0:55
Frye Notch Lean-to (2,300 ft.)	4.5 mi.	1,550 ft.	3:00
Baldpate Mtn., East Peak (3,815 ft.)	6.3 mi.	3,065 ft.	4:40
Baldpate Mtn., West Peak (3,694 ft.)	7.2 mi.	3,315 ft.	5:15
Trailhead parking area on ME 26 (1,450 ft.)	10.3 mi.	3,315 ft.	6:45

MATC The AT leaves the left (south) side of East B Hill Rd. about 8 mi. west of the village of Andover. It descends from the road, crosses a small brook, and then turns south along the edge of a progressively deeper gorge cut by this brook. The AT follows the gorge for 0.5 mi. before turning west into the mouth of Dunn Notch. At 0.8 mi., the trail crosses the West Branch of the Ellis River (a large stream at this point) at the top of a double waterfall plunging 60 ft. into Dunn Notch. (Hikers can reach the bottom of the falls via an old logging road across the stream. Upstream are a small, rocky gorge and the beautiful upper falls.)

The AT crosses the old road, climbs steeply up the eastern rim of the notch, and rises moderately to the south. At 1.3 mi., the trail turns left and ascends gradually through open hardwoods along the edge of the northern arm of Surplus Mtn. At 3.0 mi., it angles right (southwest) around the nose of Surplus, climbs gently along a broad ridge, and passes near the summit. Beyond, the trail descends steeply over rough ground to reach Frye Notch Lean-to, near the head of Frye Brook, at 4.5 mi. From the lean-to, the AT climbs gradually and then more steeply, gaining about 1,300 ft. in less than 1.0 mi., to the open summit of East Peak on Baldpate Mtn. at 6.3 mi. The trail descends to a sag between the peaks and then climbs to West Peak at 7.2 mi. Beyond, the AT descends into Grafton Notch via the trail from the south, passing Baldpate Lean-to and the upper jct. and lower jct. of Table Rock Trail en route.

SEC 5

MAHOOSUC ARM (3,781 FT.)

This mountain is along the AT, between Mahoosuc Notch and Speck Pond.

SPECK POND TRAIL (MAP 6: C12–C13)
From Success Pond Rd. (1,730 ft.) to:

May Cutoff (3,765 ft.)	3.1 mi.	2,035 ft.	2:35
Speck Pond and Mahoosuc Trail (3,430 ft.)	3.6 mi.	2,035 ft.	2:50
Old Speck Mtn. summit (4,188 ft.)	5.0 mi.	3,000 ft.	4:00

AMC Speck Pond Trail ascends to Speck Pond and its campsite from Success Pond Rd. The trail begins on the west side of the Mahoosuc Range at Success Pond Rd., from a point 9.6 mi. southwest of ME 26 via North Rd. and Success Pond Rd. Parking is available on the left just before the trailhead, opposite the entrance to Speck Pond Rd.

Speck Pond Trail leaves Success Pond Rd., enters the woods, and in 100 yd. crosses Sucker Brook. In another 75 yd., the trail recrosses the brook. (*Note*: These crossings may be difficult in high water. At those times, it may be best to walk 200 yd. up Speck Pond Rd. and then bushwhack south to the trail, which runs a short distance away on the near side of the brook, parallel to the road and the brook.) Speck Pond Trail follows the north side of the brook at easy and then moderate grades for 1.4 mi., passing through brushy logged areas (follow with care). The trail then turns left, away from the brook, and heads northward across another area of recent logging, crossing several skidder roads and the top of an open brushy area. Follow markings carefully here, especially where the trail bears right at a cairn as it leaves the open area.

Speck Pond Trail swings right (east) and climbs moderately, crosses a relatively level section, and then bears left and climbs rather steeply and roughly, with four wooden ladders aiding the ascent up ledges, to the jct. at 3.1 mi. with May Cutoff (see below), which diverges right. Speck Pond Trail continues across a height-of-land, passes an outlook over the pond and to Old Speck Mtn., and then descends steeply and roughly to Speck Pond. The trail skirts the west edge of the pond, swings right at Speck Pond CS, passes left of the shelter (where a closed former section of trail is on the left), and continues 80 yd. to a new jct. with Mahoosuc Trail (p. 256), which proceeds ahead (southbound) and left (northbound, on a short relocation).

May Cutoff (AMC; Map 6: C13). This short path (0.3 mi., 50 ft. ascent, 10 min.) extends from Speck Pond Trail to Mahoosuc Trail with only minor ups and downs, ascending across a scrubby hump along the way that is probably the true summit of Mahoosuc Arm.

NOTCH TRAIL (MAP 6: C12–C13)
From parking area on Shelter Brook Rd. (1,659 ft.) to:

Mahoosuc Trail (2,460 ft.)	1.9 mi.	800 ft.	1:20

AMC Notch Trail ascends at easy grades to the southwest end of Mahoosuc Notch, providing the easiest access to that wild and beautiful place. Notch Trail begins on Shelter Brook Rd. (sign for Notch Trail), a spur that leaves Success Pond Rd. 11.1 mi. southwest of ME 26 via North Rd. and Success Pond Rd., and leads 0.3 mi. to a jct., where there is limited parking on the left. Shelter Brook Rd. turns right here (trail sign; the road ahead is blocked off) and crosses a bridge. It crosses a second bridge 0.6 mi. from Success Pond Rd. (alternate parking is available just before this bridge) and continues a short distance to where Notch Trail leaves the road on the left (trail sign); additional parking is available here.

Notch Trail ascends easily, following old logging roads along Shelter Brook, crossing to the brook's north side at 0.9 mi. and then back to the south side at 1.1 mi. The trail swings left (northeast), soon crosses the brook again, skirts to the left of an area of beaver activity, and then continues across many bog bridges up to the height-of-land, where Notch Trail meets

Mahoosuc Trail (p. 256). Turn left on it to traverse the notch. A short distance ahead along Mahoosuc Trail, the valley, which has been an ordinary one, changes sharply to a chamber formation, and the high cliffs of the notch, which have not been visible at all on Notch Trail, come into sight.

GOOSE EYE MTN. (3,886 FT.) AND
GOOSE EYE MTN., EAST PEAK (3,801 FT.)

This striking mountain in Riley Township offers excellent panoramic views from its high, rocky summit, including the Presidential Range and the surrounding peaks in the heart of the Mahoosuc Range. Goose Eye Mtn. and its subsidiary East Peak can be reached from the east via Wright and Mahoosuc trails, from the north via Notch and Mahoosuc trails, from the west via Goose Eye Trail, and from the south via Carlo Col and Mahoosuc trails.

GOOSE EYE TRAIL (MAP 6: C12–C13)
Cumulative from Success Pond Rd. (1,623 ft.) to:

Goose Eye Trail (1,660 ft.) via Carlo Col Trail	0.2 mi.	37 ft.	0:10
Goose Eye Mtn. summit (3,886 ft.)	2.9 mi.	2,263 ft.	2:35
Mahoosuc Trail (3,800 ft.)	3.0 mi.	2,263 ft.	2:40

SEC 5

AMC Goose Eye Trail ascends Goose Eye Mtn. from Carlo Col Trail (see p. 256), 0.2 mi. from Success Pond Rd., and ends at Mahoosuc Trail 0.1 mi. beyond the summit. Goose Eye Trail has easy-to-moderate grades for most of its length but then climbs very steeply, with some ledge scrambling, to the scenic summit. Follow the lower section of the trail with care through logged areas.

From the gravel logging road that Carlo Col Trail follows, Goose Eye Trail diverges left at a sign, drops down an embankment, follows a newer section of trail for 90 yd., and turns right onto the original route, an old logging road. Goose Eye Trail quickly crosses a brook, runs through a brushy and overgrown area, crosses another brook, and bears left onto a gravel road at 0.3 mi. from Carlo Col Trail. Goose Eye Trail follows this road for 0.1 mi. and then diverges right (watch carefully for sign), passing through a clear-cut where the treadway may be very obscure in tall grass. The trail swings to the right (southeast) across a wet spot at 0.6 mi. and climbs gradually through woods between logged areas, crossing an overgrown skidder road at an angle.

At 1.2 mi., Goose Eye Trail reaches the Maine–New Hampshire state line and enters a fine hardwood forest. The trail swings right (southeast) at 1.7 mi. and angles up the south side of a ridge at a moderate grade, climbs more steeply, and then eases at the crest of the ridge in dense conifers; at 2.4 mi., there is a glimpse of Goose Eye Mtn. ahead. The trail ascends moderately along the north side of the ridge and then climbs steeply, swinging left to bypass a very difficult ledge before scrambling up a somewhat less difficult ledge. Goose Eye Trail soon comes out on the open ledges below the summit, to which it makes a steep, scrambly ascent. From the summit at 2.9 mi., magnificent views spread in all directions. Goose Eye Trail then descends gradually over ledges 0.1 mi. to Mahoosuc Trail (p. 256), which turns right (southbound) and runs straight ahead at the jct. (northbound).

WRIGHT TRAIL (MBPL; MAP 6: C13)
Cumulative from parking area on Bull Branch Rd. (1,259 ft.) to:

MBPL tentsite and former loop jct. (2,302 ft.)	2.5 mi.	1,150 ft.	1:50
Mahoosuc Trail (3,630 ft.)	4.4 mi.	2,600 ft.	3:30
Goose Eye Mtn., West Peak (3,886 ft.) via Mahoosuc Trail and Goose Eye Trail	4.8 mi.	2,850 ft.	3:50

From parking area on Bull Branch Rd. (1,259 ft.) to:

Goose Eye Mtn., East Peak (3,801 ft.) via Mahoosuc Trail	4.5 mi.	2,760 ft.	3:35

MBPL This route, steep and rough in places, provides access to Goose Eye Mtn. and the Mahoosuc Range via a scenic trek from the east that begins in a place known as Ketchum, on a branch of the Sunday River (Ketchum is the original name for what is now Riley Township, where Wright Trail begins). The upper part of the trail formerly had two separate branches, but the north branch, which ascended through a small glacial cirque, was closed because of erosion and safety concerns. The south branch, which follows a craggy ridge, is the sole route up to the main ridge crest.

To reach the trailhead, leave US 2/ME 26, 2.8 mi. north of Bethel and 3.1 mi. south of Newry, and follow Sunday River Rd. to the left (northwest). At a fork at 2.2 mi., bear right (signs for covered bridge and Jordan Bowl), and at 3.3 mi., bear right again (sign for covered bridge) and continue past Artist Covered Bridge (on the left) at 3.8 mi. from US 2/ME 26. At 6.5 mi., Sunday River Rd. becomes gravel. At 7.7 mi., turn left, cross two bridges (sign for Frenchman's Hole, a popular swimming area), and then immediately turn right onto Bull Branch Rd., gravel and narrow but sound (sign for Public Reserved Land, Mahoosuc Unit). (In winter, Bull Branch Rd. is gated shortly beyond the bridges, with roadside parking available, necessitating a 1.7-mi. road walk to the trailhead). At 8.4 mi., pass a parking area for Frenchman's Hole on the left, and at 9.2 mi., cross a bridge over Goose Eye Brook. The trailhead is on the left at 9.5 mi. from

US 2/ME 26. The trail starts from a signboard with a small trail sign. Parking is available 80 yd. farther up the road on the left.

Leaving Bull Branch Rd., Wright Trail immediately splits into two branches, which rejoin in 0.5 mi. The right branch, leading ahead, is the well-trodden main route, which follows an old woods road and rises at easy-to-moderate grades.

The left and more scenic branch is narrow, sparsely marked, and lightly used, and it can be difficult to follow in places. It descends 90 yd. to Goose Eye Brook, turns right, and follows the brook's north side upstream, going out on broad ledges in the brook bed in two places and passing several cascades and pools and a 30-ft. gorge. The left branch then ascends to meet the woods road route of the right branch.

After the branches rejoin, Wright Trail follows the woods road for 0.2 mi. and then turns right onto an older road. At 0.9 mi., Wright Trail bears left off the road and descends gradually 100 yd. to Goose Eye Brook at its confluence with a tributary. Here, the trail bears right, follows the tributary for 125 yd., and then turns sharply left and crosses it. From this point, Wright Trail roughly follows the north side of Goose Eye Brook, with minor ups and downs, crossing two small tributaries, until it reaches the former loop jct. at 2.5 mi. A designated MBPL tentsite is on the right just before the jct.

SEC 5

From the former loop jct., where the north branch (closed) continued ahead across a tributary brook, Wright Trail immediately crosses Goose Eye Brook to the left and starts to climb, gradually at first and then moderately by switchbacks, with rough sections and wooden steps, to the ridge crest at 3.1 mi. At 3.4 mi., after a rough ascent, the trail reaches an open spot and then descends slightly back into the woods before resuming a steep, rough ascent on ledges to an open knob with beautiful views at 3.6 mi. Wright Trail continues along the ridge through several open areas with occasional minor descents to traverse small, muddy sags. It finally climbs moderately to Mahoosuc Trail (p. 256) in the small gap between East Peak and West Peak (main summit) of Goose Eye Mtn. at 4.4 mi. Reach West Peak by following Mahoosuc Trail to the left (southbound) for 0.3 mi. and then taking Goose Eye Trail to the right for another 0.1 mi. Craggy East Peak is reached by climbing steeply for 0.1 mi. via Mahoosuc Trail to the right (southbound).

MT. CARLO (3,576 FT.)

Mt. Carlo in Riley Township is just east of the Maine–New Hampshire border, roughly in the middle of the Mahoosuc Range. Mt. Carlo can be climbed from the west via Carlo Col Trail and from the north via either Goose Eye Trail and Mahoosuc Trail or Wright Trail and Mahoosuc Trail.

CARLO COL TRAIL (AMC; MAP 6: C12, D12–D13)
Cumulative from Success Pond Rd. (1,623 ft.) to:

Goose Eye Trail (1,660 ft.)	0.2 mi.	50 ft.	0:10
Spur path to Carlo Col CS (2,960 ft.)	2.5 mi.	1,350 ft.	1:55
Mahoosuc Trail (3,170 ft.)	2.7 mi.	1,550 ft.	2:10

AMC Carlo Col Trail ascends to Mahoosuc Trail at the small box ravine called Carlo Col and, in combination with Goose Eye Trail, makes possible a scenic loop over Mt. Carlo and Goose Eye Mtn. Carlo Col Trail leaves Success Pond Rd. on a gravel logging road (AMC trail sign and road sign for Carlo Col trailhead) that begins 13.9 mi. from ME 26 via North Rd. and Success Pond Rd., and 8.1 mi. from Hutchins St. in Berlin, New Hampshire, via Success Pond Rd. Parking for several cars is available a few yards up the road on the left.

From the parking area, Carlo Col Trail follows the road southeast, and in 0.2 mi. Goose Eye Trail (sign) diverges left down an embankment. Carlo Col Trail continues straight ahead on the road, climbing easily through a logged area. At 0.7 mi., the trail takes the left-hand road at a fork, descends on it for 0.1 mi., turns left (sign) onto a footpath into the woods, and immediately crosses the brook that flows from Carlo Col (crossing may be difficult in high water).

Carlo Col Trail ascends easily and at 1.0 mi. turns right onto a relocated section where the older route climbed left into a brushy clear-cut. The trail runs through woods between the brook and the clear-cut, swings right to cross the brook at 1.3 mi., and recrosses it in another 100 yd. The trail then skirts the edge of the clear-cut, crosses the brook again, and climbs moderately, turning right onto the original route at 1.8 mi. At 2.2 mi., the trail bears right onto a newer relocation, climbs steadily via switchbacks with many log steps, and swings left to a jct. at 2.5 mi. (Here, a spur path, the former route of Carlo Col Trail, descends left to cross a small, mossy brook—perhaps the last water for several miles—and then ascends to Carlo Col CS, about 60 yd. from the jct.) Carlo Col Trail turns right at the jct. and climbs moderately to Mahoosuc Trail (below) at Carlo Col. Mt. Carlo is 0.4 mi. to the left on Mahoosuc Trail. To the right, a fairly difficult scramble reaches a fine outlook ledge.

MAHOOSUC TRAIL
GOOSE EYE MTN., NORTH PEAK (3,683 FT.), AND FULLING MILL MTN., SOUTH PEAK (3,401 FT.)

Crossing Mahoosuc PL, Mahoosuc Trail extends across the length of the Mahoosuc Range from Gorham, New Hampshire, to the summit of Old Speck Mtn. in Maine. Beyond its jct. with Centennial Trail, Mahoosuc Trail is a link in the AT and blazed in white. Water may be scarce, particularly in dry weather. This spectacular route is among the most rugged and strenuous of its kind in the Maine and New Hampshire mountains, with numerous minor humps and deep cols, and many ledges, some of them quite steep and likely to be slippery when wet. Parts of the trail may take significantly more time than that provided by the guidebook formula, particularly for backpackers with a full pack.

Mahoosuc Notch, in particular, may require several hours to traverse. Experienced hikers regard the notch as one of the most difficult sections of the entire AT. It can be hazardous in wet or icy conditions and can remain impassable due to snow through the end of May and perhaps longer. Some alpine sections, especially the section traversing the peaks of Goose Eye Mtn., have significant weather exposure.

The entire Mahoosuc Trail is described in detail in AMC's *White Mountain Guide* (31st edition, 2022). The trail is also shown from end to end on *Maine Mountains Trail Map 6: Mahoosuc Range–Evans Notch*, included with this guide. For the purposes of this guide, detailed trail descriptions are provided for Mahoosuc Trail from Carlo Col near the Maine–New Hampshire border north to the summit of Old Speck Mtn.

SEC 5

MAHOOSUC TRAIL IN NEW HAMPSHIRE NORTHBOUND
(MAP 6: E10–E11, D11–D12)
Cumulative from Hogan Rd. parking area north of Androscoggin River in Gorham, New Hampshire (820 ft.), north to:

Mt. Hayes summit (2,573 ft.)	2.5 mi.	1,750 ft.	2:10
Centennial Trail (2,550 ft.)	2.7 mi.	1,750 ft.	2:15
Cascade Mtn. summit (2,623 ft.)	4.5 mi.	2,450 ft.	3:30
Trident Col (2,010 ft.)	5.7 mi.	2,550 ft.	4:05
Page Pond (2,220 ft.)	6.7 mi.	2,950 ft.	4:20
Wocket Ledge viewpoint (2,700 ft.)	7.3 mi.	3,450 ft.	5:20
Dream Lake, inlet brook crossing (2,620 ft.)	8.4 mi.	3,750 ft.	6:05
Austin Brook Trail (2,160 ft.)	10.5 mi.	3,950 ft.	7:15
Mt. Success summit (3,592 ft.)	13.3 mi.	5,850 ft.	9:35
Success Trail (3,170 ft.)	13.9 mi.	5,850 ft.	9:55
Carlo Col Trail at Carlo Col (3,170 ft.)	15.7 mi.	6,450 ft.	11:05

MAHOOSUC TRAIL IN MAINE NORTHBOUND
(MAP 6: D13, C13, B13)
Cumulative from Carlo Col (3,170 ft.) north to:

Mt. Carlo summit (3,576 ft.)	0.4 mi.	400 ft.	0:25
Goose Eye Trail (3,800 ft.)	1.8 mi.	1,100 ft.	1:25

Wright Trail (3,630 ft.)	2.1 mi.	1,100 ft.	1:35
Goose Eye Mtn., East Peak (3,801 ft.)	2.2 mi.	1,250 ft.	1:45
Goose Eye Mtn., North Peak (3,683 ft.)	3.4 mi.	1,550 ft.	2:30
Full Goose CS (3,008 ft.)	4.4 mi.	1,550 ft.	3:00
Notch Trail (2,460 ft.)	5.9 mi.	2,000 ft.	4:00
Foot of Mahoosuc Notch (2,150 ft.)	7.0 mi.	2,000 ft.	4:45
Mahoosuc Arm and May Cutoff (3,781 ft.)	8.6 mi.	3,700 ft.	6:15
Speck Pond CS (3,428 ft.)	9.5 mi.	3,700 ft.	6:40
Old Speck Trail (4,030 ft.)	10.6 mi.	4,550 ft.	7:35
Old Speck Mtn. summit (4,188 ft.)	10.9 mi.	4,700 ft.	7:50

MAHOOSUC TRAIL IN MAINE SOUTHBOUND
(MAP 6: B13, C13, D13)
Cumulative from Old Speck Mtn. summit (4,188 ft.) south to:

Old Speck Trail jct. (4,030 ft.)	0.3 mi.	–150 ft.	0:10
Speck Pond CS (3,428 ft.)	1.4 mi.	200 ft.	0:50
Mahoosuc Arm summit (3,781 ft.)	2.3 mi.	600 ft.	1:25
Foot of Mahoosuc Notch (2,150 ft.)	3.9 mi.	700 ft.	2:15
Notch Trail (2,460 ft.)	5.0 mi.	1,000 ft.	3:00
Full Goose CS (2,950 ft.)	6.5 mi.	1,950 ft.	4:15
Goose Eye Mtn., North Peak (3,683 ft.)	7.5 mi.	2,650 ft.	5:05
Goose Eye Mtn., East Peak (3,801 ft.)	8.7 mi.	3,050 ft.	5:55
Wright Trail (3,630 ft.)	8.8 mi.	3,050 ft.	5:55
Goose Eye Trail (3,800 ft.)	9.1 mi.	3,200 ft.	6:10
Mt. Carlo (3,576 ft.)	10.5 mi.	3,700 ft.	7:05
Carlo Col Trail at Carlo Col (3,170 ft.)	10.9 mi.	3,700 ft.	7:20

AMC From Carlo Col, 0.3 mi. east of Carlo Col Shelter and 2.6 mi. from Success Pond Rd., Mahoosuc Trail ascends steadily to the bare southwest summit of Mt. Carlo at 0.4 mi., offering views over the trees. It descends briefly and then climbs a lower knob to the northeast, crosses a mountain meadow with a fine view of Goose Eye Mtn. ahead, descends steeply over many slippery ledge slabs, and reaches a col at 1.0 mi. From the col, the trail swings left and ascends moderately by switchbacks to a southern shoulder of Goose Eye Mtn., crosses an open meadow with excellent views, and then climbs a short, steep pitch to an open, craggy knoll below the summit. The trail then passes through a sag and ascends a very steep pitch (with two sets of iron rungs and a large wooden ladder on the steepest ledges) to the narrow ridge of the main peak of Goose Eye Mtn. at 1.8 mi. (use care on this section).

At the ridgetop, Goose Eye Trail branches sharply left, reaches the open summit and spectacular views in 0.1 mi., and continues to Success Pond Rd. From the ridgetop jct., Mahoosuc Trail turns sharply right (east) here and follows the ridge crest through mixed ledges and scrub to a col at 2.1 mi., where the trail meets Wright Trail on the right (leads 1.9 mi. to a campsite and 4.4. mi. to Bull Branch Rd. in Ketchum). Mahoosuc Trail then climbs steeply for 0.1 mi. through woods and up open ledges to the bare summit of East Peak of Goose Eye Mtn. at 2.2 mi.

From East Peak, Mahoosuc Trail turns north and descends steeply, with one tricky ledge scramble; it then makes a long switchback to the east, heading downhill on plank walkways through scrub, passing the former jct. with the closed north branch of Wright Trail.

Mahoosuc Trail descends steeply again over ladders and ledges to a minor col and then rises slightly and emerges in open subalpine meadows on the broad ridge. Ahead, the trail swings left on a relocation, passes a view over a valley from the western edge of the ridge, and swings right back onto the original route in 0.1 mi. In another 0.1 mi., the trail drops to the bottom of a box ravine (possible but unreliable water), the true col between East and North peaks. It climbs steeply out of the ravine and continues mostly in the open at easy grades for another 0.4 mi., nearly to the foot of Goose Eye Mtn., North Peak. The trail ascends moderately through woods and emerges in the open on the broad summit of North Peak at 3.4 mi. Here, it swings right (east) on a relocation that bypasses the high point, turning right back onto the original route in 70 yd. Mahoosuc Trail then swings northeast down the steep slope (with excellent views), winding through several patches of scrub and dropping over several steep ledges.

At the foot of the slope, the trail enters the woods, contours along the west side of a hump, and then angles steeply down the west face of the ridge, with 2 sets of iron rungs, to the col at 4.4 mi. Ascend a ladder to Full Goose CS, on a ledgy shelf near the col; a spring is 80 yd. downhill to the right (east of the campsite). In front of the shelter, Mahoosuc Trail turns sharply left, descends a ladder, ascends steeply and then moderately, and comes into the open 0.1 mi. below the bare summit of South Peak of Fulling Mill Mtn., which is at 4.9 mi. At the broad summit ledge, Mahoosuc Trail turns sharply left and runs through a meadow. It descends northwest through woods, first gradually and then steeply, with two more sets of iron rungs and many rock steps, to the head of Mahoosuc Notch at 5.9 mi.

SEC 5

Here, Notch Trail diverges sharply left (southwest) and leads 2.2 mi. to Success Pond Rd.

From the head of Mahoosuc Notch, Mahoosuc Trail turns sharply right (northeast) and descends the length of the narrow notch along a rough treadway with numerous rock scrambles, some of which are fairly difficult. It also passes through a number of several boulder caverns, some with narrow openings where progress will be slow and where ice remains into summer. The route is blazed with white paint on the rocks. (*Caution*: Hikers should exercise great care in the notch due to numerous slippery rocks and dangerous holes. Large packs will be a particular hindrance through this section, and heavy packs will impede progress considerably. The traverse of the notch is not recommended for dogs. The notch may be impassable through early June because of snow, even with snowshoes.)

At the lower end of the notch, at 7.0 mi., Mahoosuc Trail skirts to the left of a small beaver pond. Soon after, the trail bears left and ascends, moderately but roughly at times, under the east end of Mahoosuc Mtn. along the valley that leads to Notch 2, before crossing to the north side of a brook. The trail then winds upward among rocks and ledges on the very steep wooded slope of Mahoosuc Arm on rough terrain and many slabs that may be slippery when wet. A little more than halfway up, Mahoosuc Trail passes the head of a small flume, in which there is sometimes water. Near the top of the climb, an open ledge a few yards to the right of the trail affords impressive views of Mahoosuc Notch and the Mahoosuc Range.

At 8.6 mi., a few yards past the top of the flat ledges near the summit of Mahoosuc Arm, May Cutoff diverges left and leads 0.3 mi. over the true summit to join Speck Pond Trail. Mahoosuc Trail swings right (southeast) and wanders across the semi-open summit plateau, turns left twice, climbs slightly, and then drops steeply to Speck Pond—one of the highest ponds in Maine—bordered by thick woods. The trail crosses the outlet brook and continues around the east side of the pond to a jct. a short distance east of Speck Pond CS at 9.5 mi. (In summer, there is a caretaker, and a fee is charged for overnight camping.) Here, Speck Pond Trail leads ahead 80 yd. to the shelter and continues to Success Pond Rd. in another 3.1 mi. At this jct., Mahoosuc Trail turns right (north) on a relocation and in 100 yd. turns right again to rejoin the original route.

Mahoosuc Trail turns right and climbs to the southeast end of the next hump on the ridge, passes over it, and traverses the east face of a second small hump. In the gully beyond, a few yards east of the trail, is a spring (unreliable). The trail climbs steeply up the west shoulder of Old Speck Mtn., reaching an area of open ledges with superb views, where the treadway is well defined on the crest. Near the top of the shoulder, the trail bears right, reenters the woods, descends slightly, and then ascends along the wooded crest. Shortly after Mahoosuc Trail enters Grafton Notch State Park, Old Speck Trail, which continues the AT north, diverges left toward Grafton Notch at 10.6 mi. Mahoosuc Trail continues straight ahead, ascending moderately southeast to the small summit clearing and its observation tower atop Old Speck Mtn. at 10.9 mi. Grafton Loop Trail leaves from this point and heads southeast toward Sunday River Whitecap and ME 26.

GRAFTON LOOP TRAIL

Grafton Loop Trail offers extensive hiking along a route that connects a series of scenic peaks and other natural features in the vicinity of Grafton Notch. This major trail project, completed in 2007, was a cooperative effort of AMC and other members of the Grafton Loop Trail Coalition, including MBPL, MATC, ATC, MECC, Hurricane Island Outward Bound School, several timber management companies, Sunday River Ski Resort, and private landowners. The group's goal was to develop multiday hiking opportunities that offer alternatives to heavily used sections of the AT. About 28 mi. of new trail were built on either side of Grafton Notch, which, along with an 8-mi. section of the AT between Old Speck Mtn. and Baldpate Mtn., created an impressive 36-mi. loop.

Parking for the southern trailhead (used for both eastern and western sections) is on the east side of ME 26, 4.9 mi. north of its jct. with US 2 in Newry and just north of Eddy Rd. To reach the western section trailhead (no parking), walk 0.6 mi. south on the shoulder of ME 26 to a sign for Grafton Loop Trail. The northern trailhead is on ME 26 in the Grafton Notch parking area, where the AT crosses ME 26, 12.1 mi. north of US 2.

PUZZLE MTN. (3,156 FT.), LONG MTN. (3,060 FT.), AND LIGHTNING LEDGE (2,641 FT.)

These summits lie astride the Newry–Andover town line, east of ME 26 and Grafton Notch along the eastern section of Grafton Loop Trail.

GRAFTON LOOP TRAIL, EASTERN SECTION
(MAP 6: B13–B15, C15)

Cumulative from southern trailhead on ME 26 (730 ft.) to:

Woodsum Spur Trail, lower jct. (2,500 ft.)	2.5 mi.	1,770 ft.	2:10
Puzzle Mtn. high point (3,100 ft.) and Woodsum Spur Trail, upper jct.	3.3 mi.	2,370 ft.	2:50
Stewart Tentsite spur path (2,500 ft.)	4.2 mi.	2,370 ft.	3:20

SEC 5

Town Corner Tentsite spur path (2,400 ft.)	9.0 mi.	3,770 ft.	6:25
Lane Tentsite spur path (2,000 ft.)	11.6 mi.	4,070 ft.	7:50
Baldpate Mtn., East Peak (3,790 ft.)	15.0 mi.	6,100 ft.	10:30
Grafton Notch parking area on ME 26 (1,496 ft.) via AT	18.8 mi.	6,100 ft.	12:30

MATC The eastern section of Grafton Loop Trail, completed and opened to the public in 2003, leaves ME 26 in Newry and returns to ME 26 in Grafton Notch State Park via a 4-mi. section of the AT. The trail traverses four peaks and includes three primitive campsites and an AT shelter. About half of the trail lies on private lands, with the remainder on public lands managed by MBPL as part of Mahoosuc PL and Grafton Notch State Park.

At the parking lot on ME 26, Grafton Loop Trail begins at a post with a blue blaze. The trail heads through a young forest and crosses a small brook and an overgrown logging road. It switchbacks several times on a gradual incline along parts of another old logging road, passing through a section of young spruce and white birch and then through an area thick with downed balsam fir. Grafton Loop Trail continues gradually uphill, using sections of a logging road and switchbacks. It is clearly marked with blue blazes and cairns. Avoid turning left onto smaller, unmarked paths. At about 2 mi., turn left and begin a steep climb. The trail crosses several exposed granite boulders and ledges, offering views of the Sunday River ski area, Grafton Notch, and the distant Presidential Range. The trail cuts back into the woods before climbing a steep boulder staircase with some mild rock scrambling. (*Caution*: The exposed granite can be very slippery in wet weather.)

At 2.5 mi., on the west ridge of Puzzle Mtn., reach the lower end of Woodsum Spur Trail on the right (not recommended in this direction). Continuing up the ridge, pass a large rock cairn and impressive views in all directions. The lower end of Woodsum Spur Trail enters from the right. Ahead, at 3.3 mi., Grafton Loop Trail reaches the rocky ledges near the main peak of Puzzle Mtn. Here, the upper end of Woodsum Spur Trail diverges to the right.

Descend the mountain to the north, following cairns. Grafton Loop Trail traverses rolling terrain with a few boulder scrambles and an iron ladder. Beyond, the trail descends gradually on stone steps. At 4.2 mi., it reaches the jct. with the spur path leading 300 ft. to Stewart Tentsite.

After the jct., Grafton Loop Trail makes a winding descent on switchbacks and crosses an overgrown road before leveling out as it approaches Chase Hill Brook. Take care to follow only the blue blazes in this section.

Cross Chase Hill Brook (may be difficult during times of high water). At the base of Long Mtn., the trail intersects an old road. Turn right, walk 0.25 mi., and reenter the woods at the cairn on the left side of the road. Grafton Loop Trail winds up Long Mtn., crossing, following, and leaving the woods road several times. It eventually leaves the woods road for good and continues through mature forest, following contours up a ridge on long, gradual switchbacks with occasional steep sections. As the trail gains altitude, gaps in the trees afford views of the Sunday River ski area and the summit of Mt. Washington. The trail becomes steeper; a stone staircase and wooden staircase/ladder assist with the ascent.

Near the summit of Long Mtn., a short spur path leads north to a viewpoint. Grafton Loop Trail reaches a high point on Long Mtn. and then winds easily downhill, crossing several small streams. At 9.0 mi., it reaches the 440-ft. spur to Town Corner Tentsite. Beyond spur jct., Grafton Loop crosses a snowmobile trail and a log bridge. It then descends along Wight Brook to a jct. and follows the brook through a level area, crossing the brook several times (may be difficult in high water).

At 11.6 mi., reach the jct. with a spur path leading 450 ft. to Lane Tentsite on Wight Brook. The spur continues to a lovely waterfall and pool. Beyond the spur, Grafton Loop Trail climbs steeply to reach a short spur to Lightning Ledge at 13.8 mi., where there are views of Puzzle Mtn. and the Bear River valley. Soon after, Grafton Loop Trail reaches a knob of Lightning Ledge, with a look at Baldpate Mtn.

The trail heads back into the woods and makes a short, moderate descent, with rugged rock faces to the left, back to Wight Brook, which it soon crosses. After a short ascent, the trail passes a huge glacial erratic. At 15.0 mi., it reaches the open summit of East Peak of Baldpate Mtn. and magnificent vistas of mountains and lakes in all directions. (Take care to stay on the trail to avoid disturbing the fragile alpine vegetation.) Grafton Loop Trail joins the AT on the summit for the 3.8-mi. descent to ME 26 and the Grafton Notch parking area.

WOODSUM SPUR TRAIL (MAP 6: C15)
Cumulative from Grafton Loop Trail, upper jct. (3,100 ft.) to:

Grafton Loop Trail, lower jct. (2,500 ft.)	1.8 mi.	200 ft.	1:00

MLT This loop trail on the south side of Puzzle Mtn. is part of Stewart Family Preserve, a 485-acre parcel of land protected by a conservation easement held by MLT. MLT recommends hiking this scenic trail in a clockwise direction from the upper jct.

SEC
5

The upper end of the spur leaves Grafton Loop Trail and heads east below the true summit of Puzzle Mtn. Woodsum Spur Trail passes through a wet area and then descends to a col on the southeastern ridge. A short, steep pitch climbs to the southeast peak (limited views). The trail then drops off the peak to the south and west, descending through shrub and forest with occasional open ledges. It passes through a wet area before crossing a stream. Gradually ascending as it travels westward, Woodsum Spur Trail turns sharply to the northeast and climbs briefly before descending again. It follows a contour west and then drops to rejoin Grafton Loop Trail.

BALD MTN. (2,085 FT.), STOWE MTN. (2,726 FT.), AND SUNDAY RIVER WHITECAP (3,368 FT.)

These three summits are west of ME 26 and Grafton Notch in Newry, along the western section of Grafton Loop Trail.

SEC 5

GRAFTON LOOP TRAIL, WESTERN SECTION (MAP 6: B13–C15)
Cumulative from Grafton Loop Trail, eastern section, trailhead parking area on ME 26 (730 ft.) to:

Start of Grafton Loop Trail, western section via ME 26 (730 ft.)	0.6 mi.	0 ft.	0:20
Bald Mtn. Tentsite spur (1,370 ft.)	2.2 mi.	650 ft.	1:25
High point on Bald Mtn. (2,070 ft.)	3.2 mi.	1,350 ft.	2:15
Stowe Mtn. summit (2,743 ft.)	4.5 mi.	2,250 ft.	3:25
Sargent Brook Tentsite spur (2,650 ft.)	6.0 mi.	2,500 ft.	4:15
Sunday River Whitecap summit (3,368 ft.)	7.1 mi.	3,300 ft.	5:10
Miles Notch (2,350 ft.)	8.3 mi.	3,300 ft.	5:45
Slide Mtn. Tentsite spur (2,560 ft.)	10.4 mi.	3,900 ft.	7:10
Bull Run Tentsite spur (2,870 ft.)	11.4 mi.	4,250 ft.	7:50
Old Speck Mtn. summit (4,188 ft.)	13.3 mi.	5,550 ft.	9:25
Grafton Notch (1,496 ft.) via Mahoosuc Trail and AT	17.1 mi.	5,550 ft.	11:45

AMC The western section of Grafton Loop Trail leads to spectacular views from Sunday River Whitecap (views along the rest of this section of GLT are somewhat limited). Grades are mostly easy to moderate, with a few short, steep pitches. The first 7.0 mi. of this section pass through private land (some of which is under conservation easement), where landowners have generously granted public access. Camping is allowed only at the four designated campsites, and fires are not permitted.

By agreement with the landowner, parking is prohibited at the western section trailhead. Parking at the south end of the western section of the trail is allowed only at the trailhead for the eastern section. This parking area is on the east side of ME 26, 4.9 mi. north of its jct. with US 2 at Newry and almost opposite Eddy Rd. To reach the western section trailhead, walk 0.6 mi. south on the shoulder of ME 26 to a sign for Grafton Loop Trail on the west side of the road. Mileages are given from the eastern section trailhead parking area and include the 0.6-mi. walk to the western trailhead.

From ME 26, Grafton Loop Trail passes through a gate and follows a farm road along the left edge of a field for 90 yd. It then bears left off the road (sign) and in another 125 yd. turns right to cross a snowmobile bridge over the Bear River. Marked with snowmobile trail arrows, the route crosses two fields and enters the woods, following an old road south. At 1.2 mi., the road swings left, and in another 50 yd., the trail turns right (west) off the road (sign) onto a footpath. In 20 yd., the blue-blazed trail crosses a small brook and swings right to follow it, climbing at mostly easy grades and crossing the brook three more times in the next 0.4 mi.; between the second and third crossings, the trail passes a small flume.

Grafton Loop Trail continues following the brook at moderate grades up the northeast slope of Bald Mtn., occasionally on old woods roads. It crosses the brook twice more. At 2.2 mi., just beyond the second of these crossings, a spur path leads 60 yd. left across the brook to Bald Mtn. Tentsite. At 2.4 mi., Grafton Loop Trail turns left, crosses the brook (or its dry bed) for the last time, and climbs steadily by switchbacks to the broad crest of Bald Mtn. The trail continues at easy grades across the plateau, traverses a small sag, and reaches its high point on Bald Mtn. at 3.2 mi. It then descends moderately to a flat saddle and runs nearly level to the right of a brushy logged area.

Grafton Loop Trail soon begins the ascent of Stowe Mtn., first at easy grades and then becoming steep with many rock steps as it enters spruce woods. At 4.3 mi., the trail ascends a series of wooden ladders. The grade eases as the trail crosses the flat, wooded crest of Stowe Mtn. at 4.5 mi. The trail then descends to a minor col at 4.8 mi., where it crosses a small brook and ascends briefly to the semi-open ledges on the west knob of Stowe Mtn. (limited views). Marked by cairns, Grafton Loop Trail runs across the ledges for 0.1 mi. and then reenters the woods. It follows a winding course through dense growth and then swings north and descends at mostly easy grades. The trail now traverses the southwestern slope of

SEC 5

Sunday River Whitecap through open woods, with minor ups and downs, crossing several small brooks (all unreliable).

At 6.0 mi., a spur path diverges left and leads down 0.2 mi. with a 75 ft. descent to Sargent Brook Tentsite, crossing a small brook (reliable) in 50 yd. Grafton Loop Trail heads west, turns right (north) at 6.2 mi., and ascends moderately along the western slope of Sunday River Whitecap, gaining the ridge crest in a small col at 6.7 mi. The trail follows the ridge over a hump, descends to another col, and then climbs again, emerging on open ledges at 7.0 mi. Here, AMC trail crews have used innovative construction techniques—including scree walls and raised wooden walkways—to protect the fragile alpine vegetation. Hikers are urged to stay on the defined trail and in the designated outlook areas. At 7.1 mi., just before the summit, a side path descends 25 yd. right to a designated viewing area looking east. In another 20 yd., a similar path leads 20 yd. left to a western outlook with a fine view of the northern Mahoosuc Range and the distant Presidential Range.

Grafton Loop Trail crosses the summit and descends steeply north over open ledges. It then swings more to the northeast, winding down over ledges and through patches of scrub, with excellent views of the peaks around Grafton Notch. The trail descends into a belt of woods and then in 125 yd. swings left (west) and emerges on an open shoulder. At 7.6 mi., Grafton Loop Trail enters the woods for good and descends steadily west and then southwest, through an area where some yellow blazes remain from a former unofficial trail.

The grade eases in open woods, and at 8.3 mi., Grafton Loop Trail swings left (south) on the broad floor of Miles Notch, runs nearly level for 0.1 mi., bears right (west), and ascends through partly logged areas onto the lower slope of Slide Mtn. The trail turns left (south) again and contours along the slope, with occasional rough footing, and then descends through an area of boulders to a low point at 9.1 mi. It soon swings west and ascends briefly, runs northwest at easy grades (minor ups and downs), and passes to the left of a large boulder at 9.5 mi. The trail continues at easy grades through fine hardwood forest along the base of Slide Mtn. and then rises gradually into mixed woods.

At 10.4 mi., a spur path on the right rises 110 yd. with an 80-ft. ascent to Slide Mtn. Tentsite. About 35 yd. past this jct., Grafton Loop Trail crosses a small brook (the tentsite's water source), runs west, and soon swings right and ascends through a hardwood glade. The trail then bears left and winds gradually up the east side of a valley. At 11.4 mi., a spur path leads 0.1 mi. left to Bull Run Tentsite, crossing a brook (the tentsite's water source).

Grafton Loop Trail enters conifers and climbs more steadily across the slope, gaining the crest of a southeastern spur of Old Speck Mtn. at 11.9 mi. Here, the trail swings left, ascends the ridge crest, bears left again, and rises on easy switchbacks with solid footing. At 12.2 mi., the trail climbs through a blowdown patch with restricted views south. The grade increases at 12.7 mi., and the terrain becomes rough with rocks, roots, and holes as the trail angles up the south slope of Old Speck. At 13.0 mi., an outlook offers views southeast toward Sunday River Whitecap and the Bear River valley.

Grafton Loop Trail soon swings right, and the footing improves. After a steadier climb, the trail levels, passes a trail sign, and 10 yd. farther emerges in the clearing at the summit of Old Speck Mtn. To enjoy the magnificent panorama, climb the vertical metal ladder to the observation tower platform.

From the Old Speck summit, Mahoosuc Trail leads 0.3 mi. northwest to Old Speck Trail (also the AT).

SEC 5

BETHEL
MT. WILL (1,729 FT.)

Mt. Will straddles the town lines of Bethel and Newry. A blue-blazed loop trail, maintained by IWT, ascends to two viewpoints high on the mountain. Several interpretive signs are along the lower portion of the trail. The section of trail to North Ledge goes through Bethel Town Forest, but the rest of the trail is on private land. The marked trailhead parking area is opposite the Bethel recycling center, on the west side of US 2 at a point 2.3 mi. north of the jct. of US 2 and Sunday River Rd.

MT. WILL TRAIL (MAP 6: D15)
Cumulative from ME 26 (730 ft.) to:

North Ledges (1,500 ft.)	0.9 mi.	770 ft.	0:50
Mt. Will, north summit (1,704 ft.)	1.5 mi.	1,010 ft.	1:15
South Cliffs (1,620 ft.)	2.1 mi.	1,090 ft.	1:30
Complete loop	3.1 mi.	1,090 ft.	2:30

IWT The blue-blazed trail enters the woods at a kiosk and splits in 150 ft. Go right, the recommended direction to hike the route. Ahead, cross a brook and bear left. Soon, the trail veers away from the brook and begins to contour across the mountain's lower east face. It turns steeply uphill toward mossy cliffs, makes a sharp switchback left, and then contours west. After a series of steep switchbacks past mossy cliffs, crest the ridge and reach a jct. To the right, it is 150 ft. to a lookout atop North Ledges, featuring views over the farms and fields in the Androscoggin River valley.

From the jct., continue left on the ridge and then make a slight descent to a ledge and a narrow view window. Beyond, climb the rocky ridge and, in thick spruce and fir, traverse the north summit of Mt. Will, marked by a large cairn. Descend to a sag between the north and south summits. Pass a tote road on the right with signs for Gray Memorial, which leads a short distance off-trail uphill to a memorial for Leroy and Brenda Gray, who died in a plane crash on the mountain in 1992.

Beyond, the trail contours south beneath the steep face of the south summit, on a rough path of rocks and roots. The descent moderates to reach the viewpoint at South Cliffs, which provides a look to the Androscoggin River, the Sunday River ski area, the village of Bethel, Mt. Abraham, and the White Mountains. Ahead, weave down across the mountain into a huge bowl on the east side, following switchbacks. Reach a brook and stone steps, and then walk through an area of extensive logging. Cross a brook and bear right on the wide track alongside it. Close the loop at the original trail jct. and turn right to reach the trailhead.

LOCKE MTN. (1,926 FT.)

Bethel Community Forest, purchased in 2019 by IWT, protects 978 acres on the south and west slopes of Locke Mtn., just west of the Androscoggin River. The site abuts 2,358-acre Bingham Forest, owned by the town of Bethel. In the last few years, IWT has been busy building hiking and mountain biking trails on both properties, including Summit Ridge Trail. This work-in-progress route climbs to open ledges and a high point on the southwest shoulder of Locke Mtn.; future plans call for connecting it to Sunday River Ski Resort as well as creating a loop to Bingham Cascades.

In Bethel, from the north side of the Androscoggin River at the jct. of US 2/ME 26 and North Rd., turn west onto North Rd. In 2.1 mi., turn right onto Daisy Bryant Rd. In another 0.2 mi., turn right onto Locke Mtn. Rd. Follow this gravel road 0.6 mi. to a large trailhead parking lot on the right (kiosk) at the head of a large field.

SUMMIT RIDGE TRAIL (MAP 6: D14)
Cumulative from Locke Mtn. Rd. (900 ft.) to:

Picnic Knoll (1,190 ft.)	0.8 mi.	290 ft.	0:35
West Ledge (1,540 ft.)	1.4 mi.	640 ft.	1:00
High point at trail's end (1,740 ft.)	1.7 mi.	870 ft.	1:15

IWT From the northeast corner of the parking lot, walk into the woods. At a fork in 50 ft., bear left on blue-blazed Summit Ridge Trail and pass a trail register. Ahead, turn right onto a gravel road and head straight into the woods. After crossing a grassy forest road and a small brook, begin climbing, following a stone wall, and cross another grassy forest road. Climb over a low ledge and reach a clearing on Picnic Knoll, where there are picnic tables and Adirondack chairs—and an attractive view of Barker Mtn. to the northwest. Beyond, cross Phoenix Trail and then reach the jct. with Bingham Cascades Trail on the left. Continuing straight on Summit Ridge Trail, cross another grassy track and then a wide path, Community Access Trail. Soon after, cross Summit Access Rd., angling left to climb a short rock staircase. Switchbacks lead to West Ledge, which provides an excellent view south and west over the river valley to the peaks of the WMNF around Evans Notch. Continue to climb along the edge of the ridge, crest a knob, and then reach the end of the trail (for now) and a view of Barker, Black, and Wheeler mountains.

**SEC
5**

ELLINGWOOD MTN. (1,574 FT.)

Bethel Community Forest West encompasses 532 acres that were once part of the Chadbourne Tree Farm network. The forest was purchased by IWT in 2022, but prior to that, Parks-Bennet and Red Pine Ridge trails were constructed on a subsidiary peak of Ellingwood Mtn., which rises north of the Androscoggin River west of Bethel proper and features three attractive viewpoints.

Follow the directions for Locke Mtn. above, but instead of turning right on Daisy Bryant Rd., continue another 1.6 mi. on North Rd. (a total of 3.7 mi. from US 2/ME 26) to a grassy parking area on the right.

PARKS-BENNET TRAIL (MAP 6: E14–D14)
Cumulative from North Rd. (700 ft.) to:

Red Pine Ridge Trail, lower jct. (1,030 ft.)	0.6 mi.	330 ft.	0:25
Parks-Bennet Loop (1,130 ft.)	0.8 mi.	430 ft.	0:35
Red Pine Ridge Trail, upper jct. (1,270 ft.)	2.1 mi.	810 ft.	1:25
Complete lollipop loop	2.9 mi.	810 ft.	1:50

IWT From the north end of the parking area, look for a trail sign and an old grassy road on the right; this is the route (avoid another grassy road, taped off with orange flagging tape, that leaves straight ahead from the north end of the park area). In 100 ft., Parks-Bennet Trail turns sharply left (right leads out to North Rd.). At 0.2 mi., the old road narrows. Follow a stream and then leave the old road for a path on the right and cross the stream. Turn left to climb along the east side of the stream through a ravine. At 0.6 mi., where Red Pine Ridge Trail continues straight ahead, bear left to stay on Parks-Bennet Trail to the start of the loop. From the loop jct., turn left to cross the stream and, after crossing a wide, grassy old forest road, amble up the hillside. Pass beneath the large rock face of the Prow and then wind around and up to its top. The outstanding view west ranges along the Androscoggin River to the peaks of the Carter–Moriah Range and beyond to the summits of the Presidential Range. Continue over the ridge and down to an old woods road and bear right along it. From a low point, climb via switchbacks to the cleared hilltop and a sign for Porcupine Panorama at 1.7 mi. Just ahead, join an old woods road to descend the east side of the hill; then leave the old road and cross a stream. Reach the upper jct. of Red Pine Ridge Trail on the left at 2.1 mi. Just below, pass a pretty 12-ft. cascade on the right. Close the loop and continue down and out to the trailhead.

RED PINE RIDGE TRAIL (MAP 6: D14)
Cumulative from Parks-Bennet Trail, upper jct. (1,270 ft.) to:

Parks-Bennet Trail, lower jct. (1,030 ft.)	0.5 mi.	–240 ft.	0:15

IWT This trail serves as a short, pleasant alternate descent route. From the upper section of Parks-Bennet Trail, Red Pine Ridge Trail follows a contour. At 0.2 mi., enter red pine woods and reach Ellingwood Ledges, where there are views southwest along the Androscoggin River valley to the mountains around Evans Notch and beyond, to the Carter–Moriah and Presidential ranges. Descend via switchbacks, join the route of an old woods road, and rejoin Parks-Bennet Trail, which leads back to North Rd. in 0.6 mi.

SECTION SIX

WHITE MOUNTAIN NATIONAL FOREST AND EVANS NOTCH

Pull-Out Map
Map 6: Mahoosuc Range–Evans Notch

INTRODUCTION

This section describes 34 trails on 18 mountains in the Maine section of the White Mountain National Forest in the region around Evans Notch, including the valleys of Evans Brook and Cold River that lead up to Evans Notch from the north and south, respectively. The area is bounded on the west by the New Hampshire state line from the Androscoggin River south roughly to the village of Stow, a few miles south of AMC's Cold River Camp. US 2 and the Androscoggin River form the northern boundary, from Gilead east roughly to Bethel. ME 5/35 outlines the eastern boundary from Bethel south to North Waterford. The south is bounded by ME 5 between North Waterford and Lovell, and by Kezar Lake and local roads west to Stow.

The WMNF maintains most of these trails; the remainder are cared for by AMC and the Chatham Trails Association. *Map 6: Mahoosuc Range–Evans Notch* covers the entire area, which straddles the Maine–New Hampshire state line. All the Maine trails are described in this guide. Some, but not all, of the trails entering New Hampshire to the west are mentioned, but they are not described. Hikers heading for North and South Baldface, Mt. Meader, the Wild River valley, and beyond will want to refer to AMC's *White Mountain Guide* (31st edition, 2022). CTA publishes a detailed map of its trail system in the Cold River valley.

WHITE MOUNTAIN NATIONAL FOREST

The White Mountain National Forest encompasses a diverse landscape of mountains, forests, lakes, ponds, rivers, and streams totaling 769,000 acres: 722,000 acres across central northern New Hampshire and 47,000 acres in western Maine. The Weeks Act of 1911, also known as the Organic Act, authorized the federal government to purchase private forestland for the protection of rivers and watersheds in the eastern United States. This important conservation legislation led to the establishment of the WMNF in 1918.

The WMNF is not a national park but, rather, a national forest. Whereas parks are established primarily for preservation and recreation, national forests are managed for multiple use: recreation, timber production, watershed protection, and wildlife habitat. About 45 percent of the WMNF is open to timber harvesting on a carefully controlled basis. The boundaries of the WMNF are usually marked wherever they cross roads or trails, typically by red-painted corner posts and blazes. Hunting and fishing are permitted in the WMNF under state laws; state licenses are required. Organized groups, including those sponsored by nonprofit organizations, must apply for an outfitter-guide permit if they conduct trips on WMNF land for which they charge a fee. Pets are allowed on WMNF trails; however, be sure to control your pet so it won't be a nuisance to other hikers and to clean up after your pet along the trail.

Caribou–Speckled Mtn. Wilderness

This 11,236-acre Wilderness Area east of Evans Notch, established in 1990 and managed by USFS, encompasses the peaks of Caribou, Red Rock, Butters, Durgin, Speckled, Ames, and Blueberry mountains and Spruce Hill. Twelve trails lead into the Wilderness and provide extensive opportunities to explore this mountain environment.

In accordance with USFS Wilderness policy, the trails in Caribou–Speckled Mtn. Wilderness are generally maintained to a lower standard than are non-Wilderness trails. The trails here may be rough, overgrown, or essentially unmarked with minimal signage, and considerable care may be required to follow them. Use of the Wilderness is governed by USFS Wilderness policy. Hiking groups may not exceed ten people, and no more than ten people may occupy a campsite. Motorized equipment or mechanical transport is not allowed, and there is no storing of equipment, personal property, or supplies, including geocaching and letterboxing.

WMNF Trailhead Parking Fees

Certain established WMNF trailhead parking sites have a posted fee sign indicating that hikers must display an annual or weekly WMNF Recreation Pass on their windshield or dashboard or should be prepared to purchase a daily parking pass at the trailhead. Almost all the proceeds from these passes are used for improvements in the WMNF. Annual and weekly parking passes are available at WMNF ranger offices, information centers, and other locations.

A WMNF Recreation Pass is required to park in Evans Notch at the Brickett Place Day Use Site, where a convenient self-serve day-pass station is available. Valid passes include the daily pass, annual and annual household passes, and Interagency Passes and Golden Age and Golden Access passes. Any one of these passes displayed on the parked vehicle authorizes the holder to use the site. Passes may also be purchased online.

For more information on the WMNF, forest protection areas, backcountry camping rules, parking fees and passes, and related items, visit fs.usda.gov/whitemountain.

SEC 6

GEOGRAPHY

The WMNF in Maine encompasses a jumbled mass of mountains and ridges with numerous ledges; although the peaks are not high, they offer a variety of fine walks. With the exception of a few trails off ME/NH 113, this section probably receives less hiking traffic than any comparable portion of the WMNF, allowing visitors to enjoy relative solitude on trails in an area that is quite rugged and scenic.

The highest summit in the section is East Royce Mtn. (3,114 ft.); its eastern escarpment forms the western walls of Evans Notch. On the east side of Evans Notch is the bulk of Speckled Mtn. (2,906 ft.). The second-tallest peak in the section, Speckled Mtn. is one of at least three mountains in Maine that are known by this name; its open summit ledges have exceptional views in nearly all directions. The wooded west ridge of Speckled

Mtn., which descends toward ME/NH 113, includes Ames Mtn. (2,693 ft.) and Spruce Hill (2,508 ft.). Blueberry Ridge, ending in Blueberry Mtn. (1,788 ft.), is a long, flat spur extending south from Speckled Mtn. The top of Blueberry Mtn. is mostly a large open ledge, where mature trees are slowly reclaiming what was once a burned-over summit with only sparse and stunted trees. Numerous open spaces afford excellent views, especially from the southwest ledges on Blueberry Mtn. In the valley between Blueberry Mtn. and the southwest ridge of Speckled Mtn., Bickford Brook passes the Bickford Slides, a series of beautiful flumes and waterfalls. The southeast ridge of Speckled Mtn. also bears many open ledges with fine views. A long ridge extends east from Speckled Mtn. to Miles Notch, running over Durgin Mtn. (2,410 ft.), Butters Mtn. (2,249 ft.), Red Rock Mtn. (2,143 ft.), and Miles Knob (2,190 ft.). Durgin Mtn. and Red Rock Mtn. offer interesting sights from ledges near their summits, and the south cliff of Red Rock Mtn. is one of the most impressive features of the region.

To the north of Speckled Mtn. is Caribou Mtn. (2,844 ft.), the third-highest peak in the area; its bare, ledgy summit provides grand vistas. South of Caribou Mtn. is Haystack Notch, with the cliffs of trailless Haystack Mtn. (2,218 ft.) rising on its north side. Peabody Mtn. (2,459 ft.), also trailless, is a wooded mountain that rises north of Caribou Mtn. Northeast of Caribou Mtn. is the Roost (1,371 ft.), a low mountain near Hastings, with open ledges that afford fine sights of the Wild River valley, the Evans Brook valley, and surrounding mountains. On the eastern edge of the WMNF, Albany Mtn. (1,934 ft.) has open ledges near its summit with outstanding scenery in several directions.

Deer Hill (1,364 ft.), often called Big Deer Hill, is south of Speckled Mtn. and east of Cold River. The views from the east and south ledges are excellent. Little Deer Hill (1,077 ft.), a lower hill west of Deer Hill that rises only about 600 ft. above the valley, gives attractive looks at the valley and North and South Baldface from its summit ledges. Harndon Hill (1,293 ft.), Pine Hill (1,254 ft.), and Lord Hill (1,252 ft.) rise southeast of Deer Hill, with scattered open ledges that afford interesting scenery. Several short paths in the vicinity of AMC's Cold River Camp are not covered in this guide because they are not open to the public, although some are mentioned where they intersect public trails.

ROAD ACCESS

The primary access to the western side of the WMNF and Evans Notch area is by ME/NH 113, also known as Evans Notch Rd. This scenic auto road extends from US 2 in Gilead south to US 302 in Fryeburg. It generally follows an undulating route along the Maine–New Hampshire state line, bisecting the Evans Notch region. Evans Notch Rd. provides access to three WMNF campgrounds (Basin, Cold River, and Hastings). Many trailheads are along the route, to the east and west of the road. To assist in locating these points, this mileage summary is provided:

Cumulative along ME/NH 113 southbound from US 2 in Gilead to:

The Roost, northern trailhead (east)	3.1 mi.
Wild River Rd. to Wild River CG (west)	3.3 mi.
Hastings CG (east)	3.5 mi.
The Roost, southern trailhead (east)	3.8 mi.
FR 8/Little Lary Brook Rd. to Wheeler Brook Trail (east)	3.9 mi.
Caribou/Mud Brook trailhead (east)	4.9 mi.
Haystack Notch trailhead (east)	6.3 mi.
East Royce (west) and Spruce Hill (east) trailheads	7.7 mi.
Laughing Lion trailhead (west)	8.6 mi.
Brickett Place (east) and Royce Trail (west)	10.5 mi.
Cold River CG and access road to Basin CG (west)	10.8 mi.
Mt. Meader Trail (west)	12.2 mi.
Baldfaces trailhead (east)	12.8 mi.
AMC's Cold River Camp (east)	12.9 mi.
Stow Corner	18.6 mi.
US 302 in Fryeburg	30.3 mi.

SEC 6

In winter, NH/ME 113 is not plowed between the access road to Basin Recreation Area and a gate 1.8 mi. south of US 2. Stone House Rd. (private; formerly Shell Pond Rd.) leads 1.1 mi. east from NH 113 (1.3 mi. north of AMC Rd., the entrance to AMC's Cold River Camp, and 0.9 mi. south of the road to Basin Recreation Area) to a gate and parking area; Stone House Rd. is not plowed in winter. Deer Hill Rd. (FR 9, also known as Evergreen Valley Rd. and Shell Pond Rd. within Maine) runs between NH 113 in North Chatham, New Hampshire (0.7 mi. south of AMC Rd. and 1.7 mi. north of the jct. with NH 113B), and Adams Rd. in Stoneham, Maine; Deer Hill Rd. is not plowed in winter. Other access roads are covered in individual trail descriptions.

Trails emanating from the Androscoggin River valley can be reached from US 2. Gain access to trails along the southern and eastern sides of the section from ME 5 and ME 5/35.

CAMPING

No shelters or established trailside campsites are in this section; any backcountry camping must be dispersed. The WMNF has established an array of forest protection areas (FPAs) where camping and wood or charcoal fires are prohibited throughout the year. While there are no specific FPAs along trails or around campsites in this section, the general FPA rules still apply to the roads in and around the section. No camping or wood or charcoal fires are allowed within 0.25 mi. of any trailhead, picnic and day-use site, or Wild River Rd. The WMNF operates five campgrounds in this region: at Crocker Pond just west of ME 5 in Albany Township, and at Hastings, Wild River, Cold River (in New Hampshire), and the Basin along ME/NH 113 in Evans Notch. Six privately operated campgrounds with a variety of amenities are on the outer perimeter of this section.

SUGGESTED HIKES

■ Easy
THE ROOST

RT via Roost Trail and spur path	1.2 mi.	700 ft.	0:55

A short climb from this trail's northern end leads to a spur path that descends to ledges with views of Evans Notch and the Wild River valley. See Roost Trail, p. 293.

DEER HILLS

RT to Little Deer Hill via Deer Hills Connector and Deer Hills Trail	2.2 mi.	700 ft.	1:25
LP to Little Deer and Big Deer hills via Deer Hills Connector, Deer Hills Trail, and Deer Hills Bypass	4.1 mi.	1,250 ft.	2:40

These low hills provide attractive views of the Cold River valley and North and South Baldface. Options include a shorter out-and-back trip to Little Deer Hill or a longer loop over Little Deer and Big Deer hills. To begin, see Deer Hills Trail, p.299.

CROCKER POND AND ROUND POND

RT via Albany Brook Trail	2.0 mi.	250 ft.	1:10

An easy ramble leads to a pretty pair of ponds. See Albany Brook Trail, p. 304.

■ Moderate

CARIBOU MTN. LOOP

LP via Caribou Trail and Mud Brook Trail	6.9 mi.	1,950 ft.	4:25

This loop hike leads to extensive scenery from the bare summit, with cascades along the way. To begin, see Caribou Trail, p. 278.

BLUEBERRY MTN.

LP via Shell Pond Trail, White Cairn Trail, Blueberry Ridge Trail, Lookout Loop, and Stone House Trail	4.5 mi.	1,200 ft.	2:50

A visit to Blueberry Mtn. includes many ledges with views, as well as a short side trip to beautiful Rattlesnake Pool. To begin, see Shell Pond Trail, p. 288.

ALBANY MTN.

RT via Albany Mtn. Trail and Albany Mtn. spur	3.8 mi.	1,100 ft.	2:25

This small mountain offers pleasant hiking and some pretty sights over western Maine. See Albany Mtn. Trail, p. 302.

■ Strenuous

BLUEBERRY MTN. AND SPECKLED MTN. LOOP

LP via Bickford Brook and Blueberry Ridge trails	8.6 mi.	2,500 ft.	5:35

Pairing these open summits makes for a scenic circuit. To begin, see Bickford Brook Trail, p. 282.

RED ROCK MTN.

LP via Miles Notch Trail, Red Rock Trail, and Great Brook Trail	10.3 mi.	2,900 ft.	6:35

An interesting valley-and-ridge loop for experienced hikers passes through wild, less-visited terrain, with fine views from Red Rock Mtn. To begin, see Miles Notch Trail, p. 290.

SEC
6

TRAIL DESCRIPTIONS

CARIBOU–SPECKLED MTN. WILDERNESS
CARIBOU MTN. (2,844 FT.)

The extensive open summit ledges on this mountain, in the townships of Batchelders Grant and Mason, afford superb views. Caribou Mtn. and much of the surrounding area are part of the Caribou–Speckled Mountain Wilderness. Combine Caribou Trail and Mud Brook Trail for a pleasant loop hike.

The western trailhead for Caribou Mtn., which is the start of both Caribou and Mud Brook trails, is at a parking area on the east side of ME 113, 6.0 mi. north of the WMNF Cold River CG and 4.8 mi. south of US 2. The eastern trailhead is on Bog Rd. (FR 6), which leaves the south side of US 2 4.9 mi. west of the jct. of US 2 and ME 26 in Bethel, and 5.0 mi. east of the jct. of US 2 and ME 113 in Gilead. From US 2, Bog Rd. (sign for Pooh Corner Farm) leads 2.8 mi. to a gate and parking at the end of public travel on the road.

SEC 6

CARIBOU TRAIL (MAP 6: E13–E14)
Cumulative from ME 113 (939 ft.) to:

Mud Brook Trail (2,420 ft.)	3.0 mi.	1,550 ft.	2:15
Caribou Mtn. summit (2,844 ft.) via Mud Brook Trail	3.5 mi.	1,950 ft.	2:45

Cumulative from ME 113 (939 ft.) to:

Mud Brook Trail (2,420 ft.)	3.0 mi.	1,550 ft.	2:15
Bog Rd. (874 ft.)	5.5 mi.	1,550 ft.	3:30

WMNF This route provides access (via Mud Brook Trail) to the attractive ledges of Caribou Mtn. The middle section of the trail is in the Caribou–Speckled Mtn. Wilderness. The western trailhead, which Caribou Trail shares with Mud Brook Trail, is at a parking area (restrooms) on the east side of ME 113, 5.9 mi. north of the road to Basin Recreation Area and 4.9 mi. south of US 2. This section of ME 113 is not plowed in winter. The eastern trailhead is on Bog Rd. (FR 6), which leaves the south side of US 2 1.3 mi. west of the West Bethel Post Office and 5.0 mi. east of the jct. with ME 113; a sign for Pooh Corner Farm and a road sign are at this jct. Bog Rd. leads 2.8 mi. to the trailhead, where a gate ends public travel on the road. In winter, plowed parking may be available just beyond Pooh Corner Farm, 2.0 mi. from US 2.

From the parking area off ME 113, Caribou Trail runs north, ascending slightly and then descending. It crosses Morrison Brook at 0.4 mi. (no bridge) and turns east to follow the brook, crossing it five more times and entering the Wilderness Area. The third crossing, at 2.0 mi., is at the head of Kees Falls, a 25-ft. waterfall; a side path descends steeply on the north side of the brook to a view of the falls. The trail climbs steadily and then levels off at the height-of-land as it crosses the col between Gammon Mtn. and Caribou Mtn. at 2.9 mi. Soon, Mud Brook Trail leaves right to return to ME 113 via the summit of Caribou Mtn. Caribou Trail continues ahead at the jct., descending steadily into a ravine and swinging left to cross a small brook. The trail leaves the Wilderness Area at 3.4 mi., continues down the valley of Bog Brook, and turns northeast, crossing Bog Brook at 4.3 mi. and a tributary in another 0.2 mi. Caribou Trail continues at easy grades, bears right across a brook, and at 5.2 mi., just after crossing another brook, turns left onto a logging road (FR 6). At 5.4 mi., the trail turns right at a jct. with another logging road and continues to the gate on Bog Rd. (Ascending, turn left at 0.1 mi. and bear right off the logging road at 0.3 mi.)

MUD BROOK TRAIL (MAP 6: E13–F13)
Cumulative from ME 113 (939 ft.) to:

Caribou Mtn. summit (2,844 ft.)	3.4 mi.	1,900 ft.	2:40
Caribou Trail (2,420 ft.)	3.9 mi.	1,900 ft.	2:55
Loop over Caribou Mtn. via Mud Brook Trail and Caribou Trail	6.9 mi.	1,950 ft.	4:25

SEC 6

WMNF Mud Brook Trail begins on ME 113 (this section of ME 113 is not plowed in winter) at the same parking area as Caribou Trail, 5.9 mi. north of the road to Basin Recreation Area and 4.9 mi. south of US 2. It passes over the summit of Caribou Mtn. and ends at Caribou Trail in the pass between Caribou Mtn. and Gammon Mtn. Despite the trail's ominous name, the footing on Mud Brook Trail is generally dry and solid. The eastern section of this trail is in the Caribou–Speckled Mtn. Wilderness.

From the parking area off ME 113, Mud Brook Trail runs generally south and then turns east along the north side of Mud Brook, rising gradually. The trail crosses the brook at 1.5 mi., recrosses it at 1.9 mi., and swings left (north) uphill, climbing more steeply. Mud Brook Trail crosses several smaller brooks and at 3.0 mi. comes out on a small, bare knob with excellent views east. The trail turns left into the woods and makes a short descent into a small ravine; it then turns right (north) and climbs steeply to a small, ledgy knob. It swings left across a slight depression and then emerges in the open, passing a short side path on the right leading to ledges with additional excellent views east.

Mud Brook Trail turns right and scrambles up to open ledges on the south summit knob, with pleasant scenery south and west; in reverse, the trail is hard to follow where it drops off this knob. (*Note*: In the summit area, hikers should walk only on bare rock to preserve fragile vegetation.) The trail, which is poorly marked here with small cairns and requires care to follow, runs northeast across the broad, ledgy summit, descending slightly and generally keeping to the right (southeast) side of the crest. At 3.4 mi., the trail turns left up a short scramble and then turns right (sign), with the open ledges of the north summit knob a few steps to the left. Mud Brook Trail enters the woods and descends north, passes Caribou Spring (unreliable) left at 3.6 mi., and meets Caribou Trail in the pass.

HAYSTACK NOTCH TRAIL (MAP 6: E14, F13–F14)
Cumulative from ME 113 (1,071 ft.) to:

Haystack Notch (1,810 ft.)	2.1 mi.	750 ft.	1:25
WMNF gate (920 ft.)	5.5 mi.	750 ft.	3:05

WMNF This trail, with mostly easy grades but some potentially difficult brook crossings, runs through Haystack Notch, the pass between Haystack Mtn. and the Speckled Mtn. range. The route is lightly used and in places requires care to follow. The western and eastern sections are sparsely marked with faded yellow blazes. The unmarked middle section is in the Caribou–Speckled Mtn. Wilderness. The western trailhead is on the east side of ME 113, 4.5 mi. north of the road to Basin Recreation Area and 6.3 mi. south of US 2; roadside parking is available a short distance to the north or south. This section of ME 113 is not plowed in winter.

Haystack Notch Trail's eastern trailhead is also the northern trailhead for Miles Notch Trail. To reach this trailhead, follow Flat Rd. south from US 2 opposite the West Bethel Post Office and at 3.2 mi. turn right (west) on Grover Hill Rd. Stay straight at 0.5 mi. from Flat Rd. onto Tyler Rd. (FR 5; not plowed in winter). Paving ends at 1.0 mi., where the route changes to a narrow gravel road—rough in places with a prominent hump in the middle and a rocky section at the very end that might prevent low-clearance vehicles from driving all the way to the trailhead. At 2.4 mi. the road rises steeply, bears right at a fork, descends to cross a bridge over Miles Brook, and then rises again over a small washout to a grassy clearing on the right at 2.5 mi. with a trail sign, where the road continues to the left (southwest) past a WMNF gate. Park here (alternate parking is available on the right side of Tyler Rd. in small pull-offs at 2.0 mi. and 2.4 mi.) and continue on foot up the road past the gate for 0.1 mi., where the road emerges in a large, brushy clearing, with a sign for Miles Notch Trail on the right (no sign for Haystack Notch Trail in 2021).

From the western trailhead on ME 113, Haystack Notch Trail runs generally east along the east branch of Evans Brook, crossing the branch and its south fork and then following its north fork, with three more crossings; some of the crossings are marked with small cairns. The first crossing, in particular, may be difficult in high water. The trail enters the Wilderness Area at 1.3 mi. and climbs under the cliffs of Haystack Mtn. to the broad height-of-land in Haystack Notch at 2.1 mi. For the next 2.0 mi. the trail corridor is obscure in places and requires attention to follow. Haystack Notch Trail bears right at a fork where the head of a brook (that looks like the trail) continues ahead; the trail then descends moderately through fine hardwood forest into the valley of the West Branch of the Pleasant River, where the grade becomes easy. The trail leaves the Wilderness Area at 3.4 mi. At 4.1 mi. it bears right onto an old logging road and then immediately left off it (small arrow sign on right; in reverse, bear right onto the road and then immediately left at an old double blaze on a tree and an arrow sign on the ground). At 4.4 mi., after crossing a tributary brook, Haystack Notch Trail makes the first of three crossings of the West Branch in the next 0.4 mi. (may be difficult in high water). The third crossing can be tricky even in low water due to lack of stepping-stones; the best route across is slightly upstream on the right.

Beyond the crossings, the trail rises slightly and emerges into a brushy clearing at 5.2 mi. Here, it bears left onto a small gravel road at a point where the road curves sharply (in reverse, the trail leaves this road on the right with a blaze visible just inside the woods). The trail descends along the road a short distance, turns right onto a wide and worn path through the brush, and then continues straight onto a grassy old logging road. Haystack Notch Trail follows this road east and then northeast along the north edge of the large clearing, with views south to Miles Notch. At 5.4 mi. the trail meets the northern end of Miles Notch Trail at its trail sign, 0.1 mi. southwest of the WMNF gate at Haystack Notch Trail's eastern trailhead. To reach the gate and trailhead, follow the logging road left (northeast).

In the reverse direction, from the trail sign for Miles Notch Trail in the brushy clearing, Haystack Notch Trail begins as a faint track to the right of the sign, leading to the right (west) along the north side of the clearing. Bear left at a fork 80 yd. west of the trail sign and then bear right and downhill. Cross the brushy clearing on the worn path, turn left onto the gravel road, and then bear right into the woods, 0.25 mi. from the trail sign.

SPECKLED MTN. (2,906 FT.), SPRUCE HILL (2,508 FT.), AND AMES MTN. (2,693 FT.)

Speckled Mtn. lies east of Evans Notch, in Batchelders Grant and Stoneham. It is one of at least three mountains in Maine that are known by this name. The open summit ledges have excellent views in all directions. A spring is 0.1 mi. northeast of the summit, just off Red Rock Trail. Subsidiary peaks include Spruce Hill, Ames Mtn. (trail bypasses summit), and Blueberry Mtn. (trail bypasses summit).

SPRUCE HILL TRAIL (MAP 6: F13)
Cumulative from ME 113 (1,420 ft.) to:

Spruce Hill (2,508 ft.)	1.2 mi.	1,100 ft.	1:10
Bickford Brook Trail (2,400 ft.)	1.9 mi.	1,150 ft.	1:30
Speckled Mtn. summit (2,906 ft.) via Bickford Brook Trail	3.1 mi.	1,650 ft.	2:25

WMNF, CTA This trail begins on the east side of ME 113, 3.1 mi. north of the road to Basin Recreation Area (where plowing ends in winter), 7.7 mi. south of US 2, and opposite the start of East Royce Trail (where there is parking). Spruce Hill Trail ascends to Bickford Brook Trail, and together these trails form the shortest route to the summit of Speckled Mtn. Most of Spruce Hill Trail is in the Caribou–Speckled Mtn. Wilderness. The trail ascends moderately south-southwest through woods, passing the Wilderness boundary sign at 0.6 mi., and climbs southeast to the wooded summit of Spruce Hill at 1.5 mi. The trail then descends into a sag and climbs to meet Bickford Brook Trail on the ridge crest west of Ames Mtn.

BICKFORD BROOK TRAIL (MAP 6: F12–F13)
Cumulative from ME 113 (605 ft.) to:

Blueberry Ridge Trail, lower jct. (970 ft.)	0.7 mi.	350 ft.	0:30
Spruce Hill Trail (2,400 ft.)	3.1 mi.	1,800 ft.	2:25
Blueberry Ridge Trail, upper jct. (2,585 ft.)	3.8 mi.	2,000 ft.	2:55
Speckled Mtn. summit (2,906 ft.)	4.3 mi.	2,300 ft.	3:20

CTA This trail ascends Speckled Mtn. from a parking lot at Brickett Place, a historical brick building that serves as a WMNF information center during summer (Recreation Pass required; restrooms), on the east side of ME 113, 0.3 mi. north of the road to Basin Recreation Area (where plowing on ME 113 ends in winter) and 2.8 mi. south of the parking area for East Royce Trail, near the height-of-land in Evans Notch. Although the trail offers no views until the summit, the hike is pleasant, with easy-to-moderate grades and generally solid footing. Most of the route is in the Caribou–Speckled Mtn. Wilderness.

Bickford Brook Trail enters the woods near the garage adjacent to Brickett Place. It climbs moderately and at 0.3 mi. turns right onto an old WMNF service road built for access to the former fire tower on Speckled

Mtn. The trail follows this road on a winding course generally north and soon enters the Wilderness Area. At 0.7 mi., Blueberry Ridge Trail leaves on the right (east) for the lower end of the Bickford Slides and Blueberry Mtn.; this trail rejoins Bickford Brook Trail 0.5 mi. below the summit of Speckled Mtn., affording the opportunity for a loop hike. At 1.1 mi., the upper end of Bickford Slides Loop enters on the right.

Bickford Brook Trail crosses a tributary at 1.5 mi., swings away from the main brook, and winds moderately up a southwest spur to the crest of the main west ridge of the Speckled Mtn. range, where Spruce Hill Trail enters left at 3.1 mi. Bickford Brook Trail then runs nearly level, leading east and passing north of the summit of Ames Mtn., and reaches the col between Ames Mtn. and Speckled Mtn., where Blueberry Ridge Trail rejoins right at 3.8 mi. Bickford Brook Trail continues at easy grades and then climbs steadily to the open summit of Speckled Mtn. The trail continues 30 yd. beyond the summit to a signed jct. with Red Rock Trail (straight ahead, northeast) and Cold Brook Trail (right, southeast).

COLD BROOK TRAIL (MAP 6: F13–F14)
Cumulative from Adams Rd. (485 ft.) to:

Evergreen Link Trail (1,175 ft.)	2.7 mi.	800 ft.	1:45
Speckled Mtn. summit (2,906 ft.)	4.9 mi.	2,500 ft.	3:40

WMNF This trail ascends Speckled Mtn. from the southeast and affords outstanding views from numerous open ledges in its upper section, which is in the Caribou–Speckled Mtn. Wilderness. Below the jct. with Evergreen Link Trail, Cold Brook Trail mostly follows logging roads on private land and is overgrown and poorly marked, with a confusing network of roads and snowmobile trails. Extensive recent logging has occurred on parts of this lower trail section, which may be decommissioned by USFS in the future. The trailhead for Cold Brook Trail is reached from ME 5 in North Lovell, Maine, 2.0 mi. south of the jct. with Birch Ave. near Keewaydin Lake and 8.7 mi. north of the jct. with ME 93 in Lovell. Leave ME 5 on West Stoneham Rd. Follow West Stoneham Rd. for 1.9 mi. and turn right onto Adams Rd. (Evergreen Valley Inn sign), just after the bridge over Great Brook. Continue to gravel Enid Melrose Rd. (closed to public vehicle access) on the right, 2.2 mi. from ME 5. The WMNF sign is on paved Adams Rd. (very limited parking, especially in winter). The scenic upper section of Cold Brook Trail is best approached via Evergreen Link Trail, a shorter and much more attractive alternative to the lower section of Cold Brook Trail.

SEC 6

From Adams Rd., Cold Brook Trail follows Enid Melrose Rd. to the northwest; active logging was taking place here in summer 2021. At 0.7 mi. Cold Brook Trail bears left past a gate. The next 1.0 mi. is on a road, muddy in places, that climbs and then circles at a nearly level grade to a cabin (the Duncan McIntosh House). Continue ahead on the road, taking the left fork and then the right. The trail descends to Cold Brook and crosses it at 1.9 mi. (bridged in 2021) and then crosses a logging yard, bearing right on the far side. Cold Brook Trail soon enters a site that has been extensively logged (overgrown and difficult to follow in 2021; diverging logging roads add to the difficulty). The trail climbs moderately, crosses a branch brook, and passes west of Sugarloaf Mtn. It then climbs easily past the WMNF boundary at 2.5 mi., where conditions improve, to a jct. left at 2.7 mi. with Evergreen Link Trail (sign) from Evergreen Valley.

Cold Brook Trail ascends moderately and then swings left, climbing rather steeply up the southeast side of Speckled Mtn.'s south ridge. At 3.2 mi. the yellow-blazed trail swings left where the red-blazed WMNF boundary continues ahead. In another 0.1 mi. the trail enters the Caribou–Speckled Mtn. Wilderness. The grade eases as Cold Brook Trail swings more to the north and emerges on semi-open ledges at 3.5 mi. (follow cairns and blazes carefully as the trail winds over ledges and through patches of scrub). The trail traverses an open, ledgy area with excellent views south, dips to pass a small pond on the left at 4.1 mi., and then climbs to another open, ledgy area. Above this superb viewpoint, the trail swings left across a ledgy shoulder and reenters the woods at 4.4 mi. After descending slightly, it ascends through dense conifers. At 4.9 mi., the trail emerges on semi-open ledges again (fine views east are available from a ledge 30 yd. to the right of the trail) and soon reaches a signed jct. with Red Rock Trail on the right and Bickford Brook Trail on the left; the summit of Speckled Mtn. is 30 yd. left (southwest) on Bickford Brook Trail.

EVERGREEN LINK TRAIL (MAP 6: F13)
Cumulative from upper end of gravel parking lot (660 ft.) to:

Cold Brook Trail (1,175 ft.)	1.4 mi.	650 ft.	1:00
Speckled Mtn. summit (2,906 ft.) via Cold Brook Trail	3.6 mi.	2,350 ft.	3:00

WMNF This route provides the easiest access to Speckled Mtn. via the scenic ledges on the upper section of Cold Brook Trail. Evergreen Link Trail is lightly used and is unmarked in its lower section but can be easily followed by experienced hikers. The lower 0.4 mi. is on private land. To reach the trailhead, leave ME 5 in North Lovell, Maine, 2.0 mi. south of the jct. with Birch Ave. near Keewaydin Lake and 8.7 mi. north of the jct.

with ME 93 in Lovell, on West Stoneham Rd. Follow West Stoneham Rd. northwest for 1.9 mi. Just beyond the bridge over Great Brook, turn right onto Adams Rd. (sign for Evergreen Valley) and follow it for 1.5 mi., passing the trailhead for Cold Brook Trail. Turn right onto Mountain Rd. (no sign in 2021); the trail begins as a gravel road diverging right 0.5 mi. from Adams Rd. While it may be possible to park on the rough shoulder across from the entrance to the gravel road, better parking is available in the lot of Evergreen Valley Inn, on the left 0.4 mi. from Adams Rd. (Please ask for permission at the inn office.) Distances are given from the Evergreen Valley Inn parking lot.

From the inn's parking lot, follow paved Mountain Rd. uphill on foot; where it bears left at 0.1 mi., take the gravel road straight ahead (signs: "133 Mountain Rd.," "No Motorized Vehicles") and climb steadily. At 0.4 mi., turn left onto a grassy logging road; yellow blazes soon begin. At 0.8 mi. turn right onto yellow-blazed Evergreen Link Trail proper, which starts as a woods road and coincides with a snowmobile trail (sign: "Speckled Mtn. via Cold Brook Trail"). The trail runs nearly level, bearing left off the woods road at 1.1 mi. (sign for Evergreen Link Trail) and narrowing to a footpath; it reaches Cold Brook Trail at 1.4 mi. (sign for Evergreen Link only). Turn left for the ledges and Speckled Mtn., reaching the summit in another 2.2 mi. Descending, bear right at the trail sign as Cold Brook Trail swings left and descends.

SEC 6

BLUEBERRY MTN. (1,788 FT.)

This long, outlying spur, extending southwest from Speckled Mtn. and Ames Mtn., has extensive open ledges offering fine views in all directions.

BLUEBERRY RIDGE TRAIL (MAP 6: F13)
Cumulative from Bickford Brook Trail, lower jct. (970 ft.), to:

Stone House Trail (1,780 ft.)	0.9 mi.	900 ft.	0:55
Bickford Brook Trail, upper jct. (2,585 ft.)	3.1 mi.	1,850 ft.	2:30

CTA This trail begins and ends on Bickford Brook Trail, leaving at a sign 0.7 mi. from that trail's trailhead at Brickett Place on ME 113 and rejoining 0.5 mi. below the summit of Speckled Mtn. (The upper part of Blueberry Ridge Trail may also be reached from Stone House Rd. via Stone House Trail or White Cairn Trail.) Blueberry Ridge Trail is in the Caribou–Speckled Mtn. Wilderness and is a very scenic route, with numerous views from ledges on Blueberry Mtn. and the south ridge of Speckled Mtn.

Leaving Bickford Brook Trail, Blueberry Ridge Trail descends toward Bickford Brook. At 0.1 mi., a graded spur path descends 50 yd. to the right to provide a look at the Lower Slide of the Bickford Slides from a high bank. In a short distance, the lower end of Bickford Slides Loop diverges left from the main trail, just before the latter crosses Bickford Brook. (Be careful to avoid several unofficial side paths in this area.)

Bickford Slides Loop (CTA). This 0.5-mi. side path leaves Blueberry Ridge Trail on the left just before Blueberry Ridge Trail crosses Bickford Brook, 0.1 mi. from its lower jct. with Bickford Brook Trail. About 20 yd. from its beginning, Bickford Slides Loop crosses Bickford Brook (may be difficult in high water) and ascends northeast alongside it for 0.2 mi., with three minor stream crossings. The loop climbs steeply over a low rise and descends to a jct. at 0.3 mi., where a short side path descends steeply left to a pool at the base of the Middle Slide. (The former continuation of this branching path up the steep west wall of the ravine has been abandoned.) Bickford Slides Loop now climbs on a narrow, rough treadway past the Middle and Upper slides and then drops steeply to cross the brook above the Upper Slide. Here, the loop turns sharply left and climbs easily to Bickford Brook Trail, 0.4 mi. above that trail's lower jct. with Blueberry Ridge Trail.

From the jct. with the spur path to the Lower Slide and Bickford Slides Loop, Blueberry Ridge Trail crosses Bickford Brook (may be difficult in high water) and ascends steeply southeast past a western outlook to an open area just over the crest of Blueberry Ridge, where White Cairn Trail enters right at 0.7 mi. In another 100 yd., Lookout Loop (sign) diverges right.

Lookout Loop (CTA). This 0.4-mi. path, with excellent views to the south, leaves Blueberry Ridge Trail on the right about 100 yd. after the jct. with White Cairn Trail. It runs south, nearly level, out to the south cliffs of Blueberry Mtn., swings left past several viewpoints, and then loops back to the north, skirts the true summit of Blueberry Mtn., and rejoins Blueberry Ridge Trail.

Blueberry Ridge Trail continues east from where Lookout Loop diverges, across the flat top of Blueberry Mtn., with Lookout Loop (sign) rejoining from the right just before Blueberry Ridge Trail drops over a ledge to the jct. with Stone House Trail on the right, at 0.9 mi. From the jct. with Stone House Trail, marked by signs and a large cairn, Blueberry Ridge Trail bears left, runs over a ledge, and descends gradually to a col. Here, it bears right and ascends northeast and then north up the long ridge at easy-to-moderate grades, alternating through patches of spruce woods and across ledges with fine views south and west, where the trail is marked by cairns. The best outlooks are at 1.5 mi., 1.8 mi., and 2.5 mi. After crossing a ledgy area at 2.8 mi., with the summit of Speckled Mtn. in view to the right, Blueberry Ridge Trail swings right into spruce woods, climbs slightly, and then turns right and descends to meet Bickford Brook Trail in the shallow pass at the head of the Rattlesnake Brook ravine, 0.5 mi. below the summit of Speckled Mtn.

STONE HOUSE TRAIL (MAP 6: F13)
From Stone House Rd./Shell Pond Trail (624 ft.) to:

Blueberry Ridge Trail (1,780 ft.)	1.5 mi.	1,150 ft.	1:20

CTA Stone House Trail ascends to the scenic ledges of Blueberry Mtn. from Stone House Rd. (formerly Shell Pond Rd.). The upper section of this trail is in the Caribou–Speckled Mtn. Wilderness. To reach the trailhead, leave NH 113 on the east side, 1.3 mi. north of AMC Rd. (the entrance to AMC's Cold River Camp) and 0.9 mi. south of the road to Basin Recreation Area, and follow Stone House Rd. 1.1 mi. to a padlocked steel gate, where a parking area is on the right. In winter, parking is usually available at 0.3 mi. from NH 113, at the start of Leach Link Trail. The lower section of this route, including Rattlesnake Flume and Rattlesnake Pool, is on private land, and hikers are requested to stay on the marked paths.

Walk up Stone House Rd. (which is also Shell Pond Trail here) for 0.5 mi. beyond the gate to where Stone House Trail leaves on the left (north), east of an open shed. Stone House Trail follows a logging road and approaches Rattlesnake Brook. At 0.2 mi. from Stone House Rd., the trail merges with a private road (descending, bear right at arrow) and immediately reaches the jct. with a spur path that leads right 30 yd. to a bridge overlooking Rattlesnake Flume, a small, attractive gorge. Stone House Trail soon swings right (arrow), and at 0.5 mi., just after the trail crosses a bridge over a small brook, another spur leads right 0.1 mi. to the exquisite Rattlesnake Pool, which lies at the foot of a small cascade. A short downhill scramble is required to gain access to the pool. Past the jct. with the spur path to the pool, Stone House Trail enters the WMNF and climbs moderately. At 1.2 mi. it swings left and soon bears right on a relocation (2018) that traverses to the north; it then turns southwest and makes a meandering climb to rejoin the original route at 1.5 mi. The trail ascends northwest to the top of the ridge, where it ends at Blueberry Ridge Trail, only a few steps from the top of Blueberry Mtn. The eastern jct. with Lookout Loop is 30 yd. to the left up a ledge. For Speckled Mtn., turn right (north) onto Blueberry Ridge Trail.

WHITE CAIRN TRAIL (MAP 6: F13)
From Stone House Rd./Shell Pond Trail (597 ft.) to:

Blueberry Ridge Trail (1,750 ft.)	1.4 mi.	1,150 ft.	1:15

CTA This trail, steep in places, provides access to the open ledges on Blueberry Mtn. and with Stone House Trail makes a rewarding half-day circuit. The upper section of White Cairn Trail is in the Caribou–Speckled Mtn. Wilderness. The trail begins on Stone House Rd. (formerly Shell Pond Rd.), which leaves NH 113 on the east side, 1.3 mi. north of AMC Rd. (the entrance to AMC's Cold River Camp) and 0.9 mi. south of the road to Basin Recreation Area, and runs 1.1 mi. to a padlocked steel gate, where a parking area is available on the right. In winter, parking is usually available at 0.3 mi. from NH 113, at the start of Leach Link Trail.

White Cairn Trail leaves Stone House Rd. (which is also Shell Pond Trail here) at a small clearing 0.3 mi. beyond the gate. It follows an old logging road north across a flat area and ascends moderately, entering the WMNF at 0.3 mi. from Stone House Rd. At 0.8 mi., the trail climbs steeply up a well-constructed rock staircase, turns sharply left, and begins to climb on ledges along the edge of the cliffs that are visible from the road. The grade moderates as the trail runs northwest along the crest of the cliffs, with excellent views to the south.

At 1.2 mi., White Cairn Trail passes a spring (unreliable) and then swings right (north) at easy grades; follow cairns carefully as the trail winds through ledgy areas. The trail passes another spring (unreliable) just before ending at the jct. with Blueberry Ridge Trail, 0.2 mi. west of the upper terminus of Stone House Trail. Lookout Loop, which leaves Blueberry Ridge Trail about 100 yd. east of its jct. with White Cairn Trail, provides a scenic alternate route, 0.4 mi. long, to Stone House Trail.

SHELL POND TRAIL (MAP 6: G13)
From gate on Stone House Rd. (590 ft.) to:

Deer Hill Rd. (747 ft.)	1.8 mi.	150 ft.	1:00

CTA Shell Pond Trail runs between Stone House Rd. (formerly Shell Pond Rd.), at the locked gate 1.1 mi. from NH 113, and Deer Hill Rd. (FR 9), 3.5 mi. from NH 113 (limited roadside parking nearby, not plowed in winter). Stone House Rd. (not plowed in winter) leaves NH 113 on the east side, 1.3 mi. north of AMC Rd. (the entrance to AMC's Cold River Camp) and 0.9 mi. south of the road to Basin Recreation Area. Deer Hill Rd. also leaves NH 113 on the east side, 0.7 mi. south of AMC Rd. and 1.7 mi. north of the jct. with NH 113B. The first part of Shell Pond Trail beyond the gate coincides with the extension of Stone House Rd. Much of Shell

Pond Trail is on private property, and hikers are requested to stay on the marked paths, especially in the vicinity of the Stone House. Shell Pond Trail does not come within sight of the pond itself, but Shell Pond Loop provides access to a viewpoint on the shore.

From the gate on Stone House Rd., walk east on the road. Shell Pond Loop leaves right at 0.2 mi., and in another 80 yd., White Cairn Trail leaves left. At 0.4 mi., the road emerges at the side of a large field and soon turns right onto a grassy airplane landing strip; here, at 0.5 mi., Stone House Trail diverges left, and the road ahead (not open to hikers) leads to a private house. Shell Pond Trail soon swings left and heads east across the field with views of the surrounding mountains, passing to the right of the Stone House at 0.6 mi., and soon passing to the right of another house. The trail leaves the landing strip at 0.8 mi., entering a patch of woods to the left, and follows a grassy old road through a scenic meadow. (The route is not clearly marked in this area; in the reverse direction, bear left at a fork to reach the landing strip.) Shell Pond Trail crosses a bridge over Rattlesnake Brook at 1.1 mi., passes through a wet area, and turns left off the road at 1.2 mi., where Shell Pond Loop bears right. From here, Shell Pond Trail ascends gradually to Deer Hill Rd.

SEC 6

SHELL POND LOOP (MAP 6: F13–G13)
From western jct. with Shell Pond Trail (594 ft.) to:

Eastern jct. with Shell Pond Trail (610 ft.)	1.9 mi.	200 ft.	1:05

CTA Shell Pond Loop skirts the south side of Shell Pond, making possible a pleasant loop hike in combination with Shell Pond Trail. Shell Pond Loop is almost entirely on private property; hikers are requested to stay on the marked path, which leaves the south side of Shell Pond Trail (here also the extension of Stone House Rd.) 0.2 mi. east of the gate on Stone House Rd. (formerly Shell Pond Rd.) and leads through woods near the edge of a field, making several turns marked by yellow blazes.

At 0.2 mi., Shell Pond Loop turns right onto a grassy road, crosses a bridge over Shell Pond Brook, and soon swings left (east) on a well-worn woods road. The trail traverses the slope well above the south shore of Shell Pond, with several minor ups and downs. At 1.3 mi., Shell Pond Loop turns left off the road, descends, and then meanders through the woods behind the east shore of the pond, crossing several small brooks. At 1.7 mi., a spur path leads 25 yd. left to a clearing and a bench with a fine look across the pond to North and South Baldface and Mt. Meader. Shell Pond Loop bears right here and continues at easy grades to Shell Pond Trail, 0.6 mi. west of the latter's eastern trailhead on Deer Hill Rd. and 1.2 mi. from the gate on Stone House Rd.

DURGIN MTN. (2,410 FT.), BUTTERS MTN. (2,249 FT.), RED ROCK MTN. (2,143 FT.), AND MILES KNOB (2,190 FT.)

This group of lightly visited mountains forms the long ridge extending east from Speckled Mtn. into the heart of the Caribou–Speckled Mtn. Wilderness as far as Miles Notch.

MILES NOTCH TRAIL (MAP 6: E14–F14)
Cumulative from southern trailhead (486 ft.) to:

Red Rock Trail (1,740 ft.)	3.2 mi.	1,800 ft.	2:30
WMNF gate (940 ft.)	5.5 mi.	1,800 ft.	3:40

WMNF This yellow-blazed trail runs through Miles Notch, giving access to the east end of the long ridge that culminates in Speckled Mtn. The trail is lightly used, sparsely marked, and in places requires care to follow. Future logging activity is planned on the southern 1.5 mi. To reach the trail's southern trailhead, leave ME 5 in North Lovell, Maine, 2.0 mi. south of the jct. with Birch Ave. by Keewaydin Lake and 8.7 mi. north of the jct. with ME 93 in Lovell, on West Stoneham Rd. Follow that road northwest for 1.8 mi. and then turn right onto Hut Rd. just before the bridge over Great Brook. Continue 1.5 mi. to the trailhead (sign), where parking is available on the left. In winter, the road is not plowed all the way to the trailhead, and parking is very limited. (For directions to the northern trailhead of Miles Notch Trail, see directions for the eastern trailhead of Haystack Notch Trail, p. 280.)

From the southern trailhead, Miles Notch Trail climbs north on an old logging road, soon bearing left (sign: "no ATVs") as a snowmobile trail bears right and downhill. At 0.3 mi., Miles Notch Trail bears left off the old road (arrow), climbs over a small ridge, and descends steadily northeast into the valley of Beaver Brook. At 1.2 mi., at the bottom of the descent, the trail turns left onto another old logging road and follows it 0.2 mi.; it then bears right off the road and soon crosses a branch of Beaver Brook. The trail climbs steadily, crosses Beaver Brook at 2.3 mi., and continues to ascend the east side of the valley.

Miles Notch Trail runs along the gully of a small brook and then turns left, away from the brook, and reaches Miles Notch at 2.9 mi.; on the ascent to the notch, the cliffs of Miles Knob are visible up to the left. Just north of the notch, the trail enters the Caribou–Speckled Mtn. Wilderness and descends gradually along the east side of a ravine. At 3.2 mi., Red Rock Trail leaves on the left for the summit of Speckled Mtn. Miles Notch Trail soon leaves the Wilderness Area and descends moderately, making six crossings of various branches of Miles Brook. The trail bears left onto a grassy logging road at 4.6 mi. (in the reverse direction, bear right off the road at an arrow) and swings left, down through a clearing, to cross Miles Brook at 5.0 mi. After ascending slightly across a drainage dip and past a road forking to the right, Miles Notch Trail continues on the main road into a large, brushy clearing (with a view of Caribou Mtn.), where the trail meets the eastern end of Haystack Notch Trail at a sign for Miles Notch Trail. Follow the logging road northeast for 0.1 mi. to reach the WMNF gate at the northern trailhead. (In the reverse direction, from the trail sign in the brushy clearing 0.1 mi. southwest of the WMNF gate, Miles Notch Trail begins as a grassy two-track road leading ahead [south] across the clearing.)

RED ROCK TRAIL (WMNF; MAP 6: F13–F14)
Cumulative from Miles Notch Trail (1,740 ft.) to:

Red Rock Mtn. summit (2,143 ft.)	1.2 mi.	600 ft.	0:55
Butters Mtn. summit (2,246 ft.)	2.5 mi.	900 ft.	1:40
Great Brook Trail (2,000 ft.)	3.4 mi.	1,000 ft.	2:15
Durgin Mtn. summit (2,410 ft.)	4.4 mi.	1,350 ft.	2:50
Speckled Mtn. summit (2,906 ft.)	5.6 mi.	2,050 ft.	3:45

SEC 6

WMNF This route ascends to Speckled Mtn. from Miles Notch Trail 0.3 mi. north of Miles Notch, 3.2 mi. from its southern trailhead and 2.3 mi. from its northern trailhead. Red Rock Trail traverses the long eastern ridge of the Speckled Mtn. range, affording fine views of the surrounding mountains from ledges on Red Rock Mtn. The trail is lightly used, sparsely marked, and in places requires great care to follow; hikers may encounter frequent blowdowns and overgrown sections. Due to light usage, the footing is generally solid. The entire trail is in the Caribou–Speckled Mtn. Wilderness.

Red Rock Trail leaves Miles Notch Trail, descends to cross Miles Brook in its deep ravine, and then angles up the north slope of Miles Knob and gains the ridge crest northwest of that summit. The trail descends to a col and then ascends to the east knob of Red Rock Mtn., where it passes an obscure side path that leads left 50 yd. downhill to a spectacular ledge viewpoint (potentially dangerous if wet or icy) at the top of the sheer south cliff of Red Rock Mtn. The side path leaves the trail 10 yd. east of a more obvious path that leads to a ledge with a limited view. Red Rock Trail continues to the ledgy true summit of Red Rock Mtn. at 1.2 mi., with a view to the north. A short distance beyond the summit, at a ledge with a look southwest, the trail swings right and descends over more ledges to the Red Rock–Butters col. Red Rock Trail crosses the col (avoid a beaten path leading to the right through the col) and ascends to the east knob of Butters Mtn. The trail follows the ridge, with several ups and downs, passing just south of the summit of Butters Mtn. at 2.5 mi. and then continuing to the next sag to the west. Here, at 3.4 mi., next to an open fern glade, Great Brook Trail diverges left (east) and descends steeply southeast to its trailhead on Hut Rd. Red Rock Trail swings southwest and climbs at easy-to-moderate grades, with several minor descents, through spruce woods. It reaches the summit of Durgin Mtn. (ledgy but offers no views from the trail) at 4.4 mi. Red Rock Trail descends easily to a broad col and then ascends—easily at first and then steadily, with occasional steeper pitches—generally southwest to the signed jct. with Cold Brook Trail (on the left) and Bickford Brook Trail (straight ahead); Bickford Brook Trail leads 30 yd. southwest to the open summit of Speckled Mtn. A spring (reliable) is next to the trail about 0.1 mi. east of the summit.

GREAT BROOK TRAIL (WMNF; MAP 6: F13–F14)
Cumulative from trailhead on Hut Rd. (570 ft.) to:

Red Rock Trail (2,000 ft.)	2.9 mi.	1,450 ft.	2:10
Speckled Mtn. summit (2,906 ft.) via Red Rock Trail	5.1 mi.	2,600 ft.	3:50

SEC 6

WMNF Great Brook Trail ascends to Red Rock Trail east of Speckled Mtn. The upper section of Great Brook Trail is in the Caribou–Speckled Mtn. Wilderness; this section is sparsely marked, requires care to follow, and is steep with poor footing in places. To reach the trailhead for Great Brook Trail, leave ME 5 in North Lovell, Maine, 2.0 mi. south of the jct. with Birch Ave. near Keewaydin Lake and 8.7 mi. north of the jct. with ME 93 in Lovell, on West Stoneham Rd. Follow that road northwest for 1.8 mi. Turn right onto Hut Rd. (FR 4; paved for 1.1 mi., then gravel) just before the bridge over Great Brook. Pass the trailhead for Miles Notch Trail at 1.5 mi. from West Stoneham Rd., and continue to the parking area for Great Brook Trail on the right just before a gate at 2.3 mi. In winter, the upper part of Hut Rd. is not plowed, and parking is very limited.

Great Brook Trail follows FR 4 past the gate and immediately crosses a bridge over Great Brook. In 30 yd. the trail bears right at a fork (sign: "Trail") as another road diverges left. In another 15 yd. continue straight where an older road diverges right. The trail follows the grassy road northwest, then north, and at 0.8 mi., the older road rejoins from the right. (Bear right here on the descent.)

At a fork at 1.1 mi., Great Brook Trail turns left (sign: "Trail") onto another road as the road it has been following swings right. Continuing at easy grades up the Great Brook valley, it passes a stone wall, a cellar hole, and a grave site marking the mid-1800s homestead of the Butters family on the left at 1.3 mi., just before crossing a tributary brook. The trail narrows to a footpath, passes a cascade on Great Brook, and at 1.7 mi. crosses the brook below some small cascades. Great Brook Trail climbs steadily and enters the Caribou–Speckled Mtn. Wilderness in another 0.1 mi. For the next 0.4 mi. the grade is easier, though the footing is rather rough; then the trail bears left (arrow) and climbs, steeply at times with poor footing (especially on the descent), keeping well above the brook. At the head of the valley, Great Brook Trail crosses the brook twice in a flat area and climbs a final pitch to the ridge crest, where the trail angles left to meet Red Rock Trail in the col between Butters Mtn. and Durgin Mtn.

REST OF ME 113 CORRIDOR—EVANS NOTCH
THE ROOST (1,371 FT.)

This little hill in Batchelders Grant Township offers fine views of the Wild River and Evans Brook valleys.

ROOST TRAIL (MAP 6: E13)
Cumulative from ME 113, northern trailhead (820 ft.) to:

The Roost (1,371 ft.)	0.5 mi.	550 ft.	0:30
ME 113, southern trailhead (858 ft.)	1.2 mi.	550 ft.	0:55

WMNF This route starts from two trailheads 0.7 mi. apart on the east side of ME 113. The northern trailhead (sign; parking on shoulder) is 3.1 mi. south of US 2. The southern trailhead is 0.3 mi. south of Hastings CG and 0.1 mi. north of FR 8/Little Lary Brook Rd.; parking is available north of the bridge, on the west side of the road. In winter, ME 113 is gated 1.2 mi. north of the trailhead.

Leaving the northern trailhead, Roost Trail ascends a steep bank for 90 yd., bears right (east), and ascends gradually along a wooded ridge, rejoining an older route of the trail at 0.1 mi. Roost Trail crosses a small brook at 0.3 mi. and then rises somewhat more steeply, swings right after a heavily eroded pitch, and emerges on a ledge at the summit (no views) at 0.5 mi. Here, a side path descends steeply for 0.1 mi. and 150 ft. right (southwest) through woods to spacious open ledges with attractive views, the widest of which can be obtained by descending to the lowest ridge. Roost Trail descends generally southeast from the summit at a moderate grade and crosses a small brook; then it turns right (southwest) on an old road (no sign) and follows the road past a cellar hole and a brushy area back to ME 113.

WHEELER BROOK TRAIL (MAP 6: E13)
From US 2 (690 ft.) to:

Gate on Little Lary Brook Rd./FR 8 (1,222 ft.)	3.5 mi.	1,350 ft.	2:25

SEC
6

WMNF The northern trailhead for this wooded, viewless trail is on the south side of US 2 (sign; limited roadside parking, may not be available in winter), 2.3 mi. east of the jct. of US 2 and ME 113 and 2.9 mi. west of the jct. of US 2 and Bog Rd. The southern trailhead is at a locked gate on gravel Little Lary Brook Rd. (FR 8; closed in winter), 1.6 mi. from its jct. with ME 113, which is 7.0 mi. north of the road to Basin Recreation Area and 3.8 mi. south of the jct. of US 2 and ME 113. The trail is lightly used and requires care to follow.

From US 2, Wheeler Brook Trail follows a gated, grassy logging road (FR 711) south, soon crossing an old woods road and then passing jcts. with another woods road on the right and a snowmobile trail on the left. Wheeler Brook Trail enters the WMNF at 0.3 mi., bears left on a grassy road, and follows Wheeler Brook, crossing it four times. The trail turns left (arrow) at a logging road fork at 0.9 mi., just before the third brook crossing, and rises steadily southwest to its highest point—a little more than 2,000 ft.—at the crest of the northwest ridge of Peabody Mtn. at 2.1 mi. (No trail exists to the wooded summit of Peabody Mtn.) Wheeler Brook Trail then descends generally southwest, merges onto a grassy logging road (FR 8) that comes down from the left at 3.1 mi., and reaches Little Lary Brook Rd. Turn left onto Little Lary Brook Rd. and continue about 150 yd. to a locked gate beyond the bridge over Little Lary Brook, 1.6 mi. from ME 113.

To hike the trail in the reverse (west to east) direction: Proceed along Little Lary Brook Rd. about 150 yd. from the locked gate and turn right onto FR 8 at the jct. where FR 885 continues straight ahead. The trail (arrow) leaves the left side of the road in another 0.3 mi.

EAST ROYCE MTN. (3,114 FT.) AND WEST ROYCE MTN. (3,204 FT.)

The Royces rise to the west of Evans Notch and Cold River. East Royce Mtn. is in Batchelders Grant Township, and West Royce Mtn. is in Bean's Purchase, NH.

ROYCE TRAIL (MAP 6: F12)
Cumulative from ME 113 (605 ft.) to:

Mad River Falls (900 ft.)	1.6 mi.	300 ft.	0:55
Laughing Lion Trail (2,200 ft.)	2.7 mi.	1,600 ft.	2:10
Royce Connector Trail (2,650 ft.)	2.9 mi.	2,050 ft.	2:30
Burnt Mill Brook Trail (2,610 ft.)	3.6 mi.	2,150 ft.	2:55
West Royce Mtn. summit (3,204 ft.)	4.3 mi.	2,750 ft.	3:30

AMC This yellow-blazed trail runs to the summit of West Royce Mtn. from the west side of ME 113, about 50 yd. north of the trailhead parking area (Recreation Pass required; restrooms) at Brickett Place (a seasonal WMNF information center; Recreation Pass required, restrooms) on the east side of the road. The parking area is 0.3 mi. north of the access road to Basin Recreation Area and 2.8 mi. south of the parking area for East Royce Trail near the height-of-land in Evans Notch. (In winter, plowing on ME 113 ends at the jct. with the access road.) The first two crossings of Cold River are difficult in high water. Leaving ME 113, Royce Trail follows a narrow road for about 0.3 mi., bears right where another road joins from the left, crosses Cold River, and bears off the road to the right onto a yellow-blazed footpath. The trail recrosses the river at 0.7 mi., crosses a tributary at 1.2 mi., and crosses the river a third time at 1.4 mi.

In another 100 yd. Royce Trail crosses the Mad River and then rises more steeply and passes Mad River Falls at 1.6 mi., where a side path leads left 25 yd. to a viewpoint. The trail climbs moderately up the valley, passing several cascades as it comes back near the Mad River; then it becomes rather rough and rises steeply under the imposing ledges for which East Royce Mtn. is famous. At 2.7 mi., Laughing Lion Trail enters right, and at a height-of-land at 2.9 mi., after a very steep and rough ascent, Royce Connector Trail branches right, leading to East Royce Trail for East Royce Mtn.

SEC 6

Royce Connector Trail (AMC). This 0.2-mi. trail (ascent 50 ft., rev. 100 ft., 10 min.), links Royce Trail and East Royce Trail, permitting the ascent of either summit of the Royces from either trail. From Royce Trail the connector leads east, ascends slightly, traverses some ledges (restricted views), and then descends moderately to East Royce Trail.

From the Royce Connector Trail jct., Royce Trail bears left and descends slightly, crossing a small brook, and then climbs to the brushy height-of-land between the Royces at 3.6 mi., where Burnt Mill Brook Trail to Wild River Rd. diverges right. Here, Royce Trail turns abruptly left (west) and zigzags up the steep wall of the pass with a few short scrambles, turns sharply left (southeast), and then swings toward the southwest. The trail climbs moderately up the ridge over ledges and through stunted spruce, crossing a ledge with a view east at 4.1 mi. Royce Trail passes side paths to two more outlooks on the left shortly before reaching the summit area of West Royce Mtn., where Royce Trail meets Basin Rim Trail. A short distance ahead on Basin Rim Trail, where the trail curves left, a very short, worn path diverges right to the concrete footings of the former West Royce fire tower in a ledgy clearing.

LAUGHING LION TRAIL (MAP 6: F12–F13)
From ME 113 (1,381 ft.) to:

Royce Trail (2,200 ft.)	1.1 mi.	950 ft.	1:00

CTA This yellow-blazed trail (sign) begins on the west side of ME 113 (closed in winter) 100 yd. north of a roadside picnic area, 2.2 mi. north of the road to Basin Recreation Area and 0.9 mi. south of the East Royce Trail trailhead, and ends on Royce Trail. Parking is available at a pull-off on the west side of the road, 40 yd. south of the trailhead. Laughing Lion Trail descends to and crosses Cold River (which here is a rather small brook). Then the trail ascends west to a ridge crest and follows it north, with alternating moderate and steep sections, passing two outlooks on the left looking down the valley. Laughing Lion Trail scrambles up a steep pitch where severe erosion requires the use of tree roots for ascent, swings west, and levels off just before ending at Royce Trail, 0.2 mi. south of Royce Connector Trail.

EAST ROYCE TRAIL (MAP 6: F12–F13)
Cumulative from ME 113 (1,419 ft.) to:

Royce Connector Trail (2,610 ft.)	1.0 mi.	1,200 ft.	1:05
Ledge at end of East Royce Trail (3,070 ft.)	1.3 mi.	1,650 ft.	1:30

AMC This yellow-blazed trail climbs steeply to East Royce Mtn. from a parking area on the west side of ME 113 (closed in winter), just north of the height-of-land in Evans Notch, 3.1 mi. north of the road to Basin Recreation Area and 7.7 mi. south of US 2. Leaving the parking area, East Royce Trail immediately crosses Evans Brook and ascends, soon swinging left to cross a brook on ledges at the top of a fine cascade. The trail continues up, steeply at times with rough footing, crossing several other brooks in the first 0.5 mi. At the final brook crossing at 1.0 mi., Royce Connector Trail leaves on the left, leading in 0.2 mi. to Royce Trail for West Royce Mtn.

After ascending a steep and rough section with several scrambles (use caution if wet), East Royce Trail emerges on open ledges at 1.1 mi., offering a view east to Speckled Mtn. The trail soon reaches a subsidiary summit with views to the south, turns right, and climbs to a broad, open ledge at 1.3 mi. with wide-ranging vistas, where the trail ends (sign and cairn). The most prominently seen features here are the wild cliffs of nearby West Royce Mtn. and the impressive peaks of North and South Baldface.

HARNDON HILL (1,393 FT.), LORD HILL (1,252 FT.), AND PINE HILL (1,254 FT.)
This compact group of hills just west of Horseshoe Pond in Stoneham, Stow, and Lovell can be climbed via an intricate network of three trails.

CONANT TRAIL (MAP 6: G13)
From trailhead off Deer Hill Rd. (559 ft.) for:

Complete loop over Pine Hill and Lord Hill on Conant rail	5.2 mi.	1,050 ft.	3:10

From trailhead off Deer Hill Rd. (559 ft.) for:

Loop over Lord Hill via north branch of Conant Trail and Mine Loop	4.3 mi.	850 ft.	2:35

CTA This loop hike to Pine Hill and Lord Hill is an interesting and fairly easy walk with several attractive outlooks. Much of Conant Trail, especially the south loop, is on private land. Do not confuse this trail with Conant Path, a short trail (not open to the public) near AMC's Cold River Camp. Reach Conant Trail by following Deer Hill Rd. (FR 9; not plowed in winter) from the east side of NH 113, 0.7 mi. south of AMC Rd. (the entrance to AMC's Cold River Camp) and 1.7 mi. north of the jct. with NH 113B. Turn right onto FR 9A 1.5 mi. from NH 113. Parking for a few cars is at a 4-way jct. about 100 yd. from Deer Hill Rd., where there are signs for North Barbour Rd. and Barber Rd., as well as a WMNF trail sign/hiker symbol.

SEC 6

Walk along the road that leads east (left) from the 4-way jct., soon descending to the dike across swampy Colton Brook. Beyond the dike, yellow-blazed Conant Trail continues on a gravel road to the loop jct. at 0.4 mi., where the path divides. From here, the trail is described in a counterclockwise direction. The south branch, also a snowmobile route, turns right and follows a logging road (Hemp Hill Rd.). At 0.7 mi., the trail reaches a road section that leads through an area of former beaver activity (dry in 2021). Beyond, the road climbs to a level spot at 1.0 mi. near the old Johnson cellar hole. Here, the trail turns left on a logging road and then turns left again in a few steps.

Conant Trail swings right and then left at 1.2 mi. and ascends Pine Hill, rather steeply at times, passing a ledge with a fine view west toward Eastman Mtn. and North and South Baldface at 1.4 mi. Here, the trail turns right, climbs to the west end of the summit ridge, and continues to the easternmost knob, which has a view north, at 2.0 mi. The trail swings left off the ledges and zigzags steeply down through hemlock forest. It crosses Bradley Brook at 2.3 mi. and then quickly crosses a logging road, which can be followed 0.2 mi. left (north) to Mine Loop Trail, 0.4 mi. below the mine on Lord Hill. Conant Trail then ascends moderately to an outlook over Horseshoe Pond. Here, the trail turns sharply left and climbs ledges to a jct. near the summit of Lord Hill at 3.0 mi., where Mine Loop Trail leaves on the left.

Mine Loop Trail. This 1-mi. trail is 0.1 mi. shorter than the section of Conant Trail it bypasses. Except for a critical turn, Mine Loop Trail is fairly easy to follow. From the jct. with Conant Trail near the summit of Lord Hill, Mine Loop Trail climbs briefly to the ledge at the top of the old mica mine, swings left and quickly right onto a woods road, descends for 40 yd., and turns left at 0.1 mi., where a spur path leads right 30 yd. to the mine (sign, kiosk). The trail soon swings right and at 0.3 mi. turns sharply left on a clear logging road. At 0.5 mi., it reaches a fork and turns sharply right, back onto a less-used and brushy branch road (signs). Watch carefully here; this critical turn is easily missed. (The main logging road, continuing straight at this fork, crosses Conant Trail between Pine Hill and Lord Hill in 0.2 mi. and leads south toward Kezar Lake.) Mine Loop Trail descends to a flat area and climbs easily over a shoulder. At an overgrown clearing, the trail leaves the road on the right and descends 50 yd. to rejoin Conant Trail 1.1 mi. from its trailhead (ascent 100 ft., rev. 250 ft., 35 min.).

From the Mine Loop Trail jct. near the summit of Lord Hill, Conant Trail descends, with one tricky drop over a ledge, to the jct. with Horseshoe Pond Trail on the right at 3.2 mi. Here, the trail bears left and soon turns left again through a gap in a stone wall and runs southwest at a fairly level grade, with minor ups and downs, along the south side of Harndon Hill. Conant Trail passes a cellar hole, and Mine Loop Trail rejoins on the left at 4.1 mi. At this jct., Conant Trail easily follows a logging road downhill. At 4.5 mi., the road continues straight, becomes wider (in the reverse direction, continue straight where the wider road diverges left), and bears right at a fork (in reverse, bear left at a yellow blaze and old CTA sign). It passes a cemetery on the right, reaches the loop jct., and continues straight ahead across the dike to the trailhead.

HORSESHOE POND TRAIL (MAP 6: G13)
From Deer Hill Rd. (705 ft.) to:

Conant Trail (1,115 ft.)	1.1 mi.	500 ft.	0:50

CTA This yellow-blazed trail starts from Deer Hill Rd. (FR 9; not plowed in winter), 4.7 mi. from NH 113 at a small pull-off at a curve in the road, and ends on Conant Trail, 0.2 mi. north of the ledges near the summit of Lord Hill. The former Horseshoe Pond Loop is now closed to public use, so there is no public trail access to the shore of Horseshoe Pond. Deer Hill Rd. leaves from the east side of NH 113, 0.7 mi. south of AMC Rd. (the entrance to AMC's Cold River Camp) and 1.7 mi. north of the jct. with NH 113B. From Deer Hill Rd., Horseshoe Pond Trail descends moderately for 0.1 mi. past the Stiles grave (on the right and enclosed by a stone wall; the Stiles family were early settlers of Stoneham, Maine) and then turns right onto a gravel logging road. The trail follows this road, keeping straight at a jct. in 100 yd. At 0.3 mi., the trail turns right onto a grassy road that leads up into a brushy area and ascends through a regenerating section. Horseshoe Pond Trail continues ascending moderately to the southwest through woods to Conant Trail.

LITTLE DEER HILL (1,077 FT.) AND BIG DEER HILL (1,364 FT.)

Rising southwest of Shell Pond, these low hills are crisscrossed by six interconnected trails that provide several miles of pleasant hiking near AMC's Cold River Camp.

DEER HILLS TRAIL (MAP 6: G12–G13)
Cumulative from ME 113 at Baldface Circle Trail
parking area (510 ft.) via Deer Hills Connector to:

Little Deer Hill summit (1,077 ft.)	1.1 mi.	600 ft.	0:50
Big Deer Hill summit (1,364 ft.)	1.8 mi.	1,100 ft.	1:25
Deer Hills Bypass, eastern jct. (1,025 ft.)	2.3 mi.	1,100 ft.	1:40
Deer Hill Rd. (544 ft.)	3.1 mi.	1,100 ft.	2:05

SEC 6

CTA This yellow-blazed trail ascends Little Deer Hill and Big Deer Hill, providing a relatively easy trip that offers interesting views. Deer Hills Trail runs from a jct. by Cold River, near AMC's Cold River Camp, to Deer Hill Rd. (FR 9), 1.4 mi. from NH 113, where roadside parking is limited. Deer Hill Rd. (not plowed in winter) leaves the east side of NH 113, 0.7 mi. south of AMC Rd. (the entrance to AMC's Cold River Camp) and 1.7 mi. north of the jct. with NH 113B.

Deer Hills Connector. Access to the north end of Deer Hills Trail is from the Baldface Circle Trail trailhead parking area on the east side of NH 113 (0.1 mi. north of AMC Rd.) via a yellow-blazed path called Deer Hills Connector.

Deer Hills Connector (sign) leaves the east side of the parking area, runs level for 150 yd., and then turns left down a short pitch and descends gradually on the south side of Charles Brook, in an area where the trail was eroded by Tropical Storm Irene in 2011. Deer Hills Connector passes an unmarked private path on the right at 0.3 mi. and reaches a dam on Cold River at 0.4 mi. Here, a trail from Cold River Camp enters on the right (this trail is not open to the public). At this jct., Deer Hills Trail begins; distances given include those traveled on Deer Hills Connector.

Deer Hills Trail crosses Cold River on the dam abutments. This crossing can be difficult and potentially dangerous in high water and in winter, at which times an alternate access to Deer Hills Trail should be used;

Leach Link Trail provides the best alternate access year-round. (In the reverse direction, after crossing the dam, turn right onto Deer Hills Connector at the sign "Baldface Parking Lot.") Deer Hills Trail soon passes the jct. on the left with Leach Link Trail, crosses the state line into Maine, and quickly passes the jct. on the right with Deer Hills Bypass. Deer Hills Trail continues straight ahead and climbs moderately past an outlook west; then it bears left onto ledges and reaches the open summit of Little Deer Hill at 1.1 mi., which features a fine view of North and South Baldface. Here, Frost Trail enters on the right, having ascended from Deer Hills Bypass.

Deer Hills Trail descends into a sag and then climbs to a point near the summit of Big Deer Hill at 1.8 mi. Here, the trail turns right, descends 40 yd., and turns right again, where there is a fine eastern outlook 20 yd. to the left. The trail then descends the south ridge, passing another outlook, and turns left (south) at 2.3 mi., where Deer Hills Bypass leaves on the right (northwest). Soon Deer Hills Trail turns left again and then turns right onto an old logging road at 2.5 mi. Here, a spur path (sign) follows the logging road left for 20 yd. and then turns right, descending in 0.2 mi. and 150 ft. to Deer Hill Spring, a shallow pool with air bubbles rising through a small patch of light-colored sand. Deer Hills Trail descends south from the spur path jct. for 0.5 mi. to Deer Hill Rd.

DEER HILLS BYPASS (MAP 6: G12–G13)
From western jct. with Deer Hills Trail (460 ft.) to:

Eastern jct. with Deer Hills Trail (1,025 ft.)	1.4 mi.	650 ft.	1:00

CTA This yellow-blazed trail skirts the south slopes of Little Deer and Big Deer hills, making possible various loop hikes over the summits. Deer Hills Bypass leaves Deer Hills Trail on the right (southeast) just east of the dam on Cold River and follows a level, grassy road along the river. At 0.4 mi., Deer Hills Bypass turns left off the road and soon ascends a steep ledge with a view west. The bypass trail swings left, and at 0.6 mi., Ledges Trail leaves left, and Deer Hills Bypass climbs steadily alongside a stone wall. At 0.8 mi., Frost Trail leaves left, climbing 0.15 mi. and 150 ft. to the summit of Little Deer Hill, passing a jct. on the left with Ledges Trail 70 yd. before the summit. Deer Hills Bypass descends into a shallow ravine, crosses two small brooks, and ascends again. The trail soon turns left onto a woods road, follows it for 0.1 mi., and turns left off it (both turns are marked with signs and arrows). Deer Hills Bypass then ascends easily to rejoin Deer Hills Trail on the south ridge of Big Deer Hill, 0.5 mi. below the summit.

LEDGES TRAIL (MAP 6: G12)
From Deer Hills Bypass (730 ft.) to:

Little Deer Hill summit (1,077 ft.)	0.3 mi.	350 ft.	0:20

CTA This lightly used yellow-blazed trail passes interesting ledges and a cave but is very steep and rough, dangerous in wet or icy conditions, and not recommended for descent. Ledges Trail diverges left from Deer Hills Bypass 0.6 mi. from the dam on Cold River and climbs steeply north, with several outlooks. At 0.2 mi., Ledges Trail divides: the left branch (sign: "Ledges Direct") ascends through a small cave; the slightly longer right branch (sign: "By-Pass") loops out through the woods and then swings left across an excellent outlook ledge, rejoining the left branch in roughly 140 yd. About 40 yd. above the point where these branches rejoin, Ledges Trail meets Frost Trail, a connecting path from Deer Hills Bypass. The summit of Little Deer Hill is 70 yd. to the left on Frost Trail.

LEACH LINK TRAIL (MAP 6: F12–G12)
From Stone House Rd. (545 ft.) to:

Deer Hills Trail (450 ft.)	1.2 mi.	0 ft.	0:35

SEC 6

CTA This yellow-blazed trail gives access to Little Deer Hill and Big Deer Hill from Stone House Rd. (formerly Shell Pond Rd.), which leaves NH 113 on the east side, 1.3 mi. north of AMC Rd. (the entrance to AMC's Cold River Camp) and 0.9 mi. south of the road to Basin Recreation Area. Leach Link Trail starts at a gated road on the right side of Stone House Rd. 0.3 mi. from NH 113; roadside parking is available and is usually plowed in winter. The northern section of the trail uses former Shell Pond Brook Trail.

Beyond the gate, Leach Link Trail follows a grassy road across a snowmobile bridge over Shell Pond Brook. At 0.2 mi., the trail turns right off the road (sign) and in another 50 yd. bears left and runs through hemlock woods along a bank high above the brook. Leach Link Trail then descends and at 0.5 mi. turns left where the former trail route came across the brook from the right. Leach Link Trail continues south along Cold River at easy grades and ends at Deer Hills Trail a few steps east of the dam on Cold River. To ascend Little Deer and Big Deer hills, turn left onto Deer Hills Trail.

ME 5 CORRIDOR
ALBANY MTN. (1,934 FT.)
On the eastern edge of the WMNF is a cluster of low hills, with Albany Mtn. being the highest and the only one with trails. Views from its open summit ledges are impressive in all directions.

ALBANY MTN. TRAIL (MAP 6: F14–F15)
Cumulative from FR 18 (811 ft.) to:

Albany Mtn. Spur to summit of Albany Mtn. (1,740 ft.)	1.5 mi.	950 ft.	1:15
Albany Notch (1,500 ft.)	1.9 mi.	950 ft.	1:25
Trailhead on Birch Ave. (745 ft.)	4.4 mi.	1,000 ft.	2:40

To northeast outlook on Albany Mtn. (1,910 ft.)
via Albany Mtn. Trail and Albany Mtn. Spur from:

Northern trailhead (811 ft.)	1.9 mi.	1,100 ft.	1:30
Southern trailhead (745 ft.)	3.3 mi.	1,200 ft.	2:15

WMNF This yellow-blazed trail provides access to ledges and views on Albany Mtn. from trailheads to the north and the south. Due to extensive beaver flooding north of Albany Notch, a 1.1-mi. section of Albany Notch Trail has been abandoned, and the remainder of that trail—0.6 mi. on the north end, 2.5 mi. on the south end, and a 0.4-mi. connecting path—has been combined with Albany Mtn. Trail into a single thru-route under the name of Albany Mtn. Trail, with Albany Mtn. Spur leading to the summit of Albany Mtn.

The lightly traveled southern section, partly on old, rather overgrown logging roads, is poorly marked, wet and somewhat overgrown in places, and requires care to follow. Logging activity is planned for the near future south of Albany Notch. Most use of this trail is on the northern end, which is well maintained, with many recent volunteer-built improvements, and provides the easiest access to Albany Mtn. The entire trail, except for the southernmost 1.0 mi., is marked with yellow paint blazes and in open ledge areas, small cairns.

To reach the northern trailhead, follow Flat Rd., which leads south from US 2 opposite the West Bethel Post Office and becomes FR 7 (gravel; not plowed in winter; no parking available) when it enters the WMNF at 4.5 mi. At 5.7 mi., turn right on FR 18, following signs for Crocker Pond CG. The trailhead parking lot and kiosk are on the right (sign) in another 0.6 mi. The trailhead can also be reached from ME 5, just south of Songo Pond, by turning west onto Patte Brook Rd., which becomes FR 7. At 2.8 mi., turn left onto FR 18 and follow it 0.6 mi. to the trailhead on the right. The last several miles of both of these approaches are not open to public vehicle travel in winter.

Reach the southern trailhead by leaving ME 5 at the west end of Kee-waydin Lake, 2.4 mi. west of the East Stoneham Post Office and 0.7 mi. east of the Lovell–Stoneham town line, and following Birch Ave. north. Bear right at a fork to stay on Birch Ave. at 0.4 mi. from ME 5; the trail begins at a sign at 1.0 mi., where pavement ends and the road ahead becomes gravel. The beginning of the trail (trail sign next to small white building) is in a residential area, but parking is available in a dirt clearing on the right, near the end of pavement (may be plowed in winter; may be muddy at times); parking is extremely limited beyond this point.

Leaving the northern trailhead parking lot on FR 18, Albany Mtn. Trail follows an old logging road, with a relocation up to the left. At 0.4 mi. the trail turns left on another relocation and then in 75 yd. turns right, crosses an old beaver dam, and reenters the woods. It swings left at 0.5 mi. and bears left again at 0.6 mi. toward Albany Mtn., where the abandoned section of Albany Notch Trail diverges right. Albany Mtn. Trail now ascends moderately southwest, crosses a brook at 1.0 mi., swings left, and climbs through several turns to a signed jct. at 1.5 mi., where Albany Mtn. Spur diverges left (southeast).

Albany Mtn. Spur. This spur path soon crosses a ledge with a view of the Carter-Moriah Range and Mt. Washington over the treetops. Albany Mtn. Spur winds upward at easy grades across ledges and through stands of red pine and reaches an open ledge with restricted northeast views near the summit of Albany Mtn. at 0.4 mi. from the main trail, where blazing ends. The best sights here are found by descending 50 yd. east to ledges at the edge of the ridge crest.

At the jct. with Albany Mtn. Spur, Albany Mtn. Trail immediately takes on a more primitive character and turns sharply right (west), rises slightly, and then descends moderately for 0.4 mi. to the height-of-land in Albany Notch; partway down, the trail crosses a ledge with a view west. In the notch, the trail turns sharply left (south) at a large boulder (in the reverse direction, be sure to make this right turn where the abandoned section of Albany Notch Trail continues ahead). Albany Mtn. Trail now descends moderately, with a steeper pitch just below the notch, and crosses two small brooks in quick succession. The trail then runs at easy grades until it reaches a logging road used as a snowmobile trail at 2.6 mi. and turns left onto this road. (If ascending from the south, turn sharply right off the road onto a narrow footpath leading into the woods just before the road dips to cross a small brook; in 2021 this turn was marked with surveyor's tape). In 110 yd. the trail bears right off the logging road at an easy-to-miss brushy turn (in 2021, marked with surveyor's tape), skirts the edge of a beaver swamp, and bears left onto an older logging road, following it downhill at easy grades but with wet and muddy footing.

At 3.0 mi., Albany Mtn. Trail bears right off the logging road onto another road (in reverse, watch for an arrow). The trail soon passes a WMNF gate (blazing ends) and then merges with a gravel road (FR 57) that joins from the left (very limited parking here; high-clearance vehicle required to reach this point). Albany Mtn. Trail passes several diverging roads and private driveways (in the reverse direction, stay on the main road), crosses a bridge over Meadow Brook at 3.8 mi., and climbs gradually past several private homes and camps to the southern trailhead on Birch Ave.

ALBANY BROOK TRAIL (MAP 6: F15)
From WMNF Crocker Pond CG (841 ft.) to:

Round Pond (790 ft.)	1.0 mi.	100 ft.	0:35

WMNF This short, easy yellow-blazed trail follows the shore of Crocker Pond and then leads to attractive, secluded Round Pond. In 2018, the WMNF began upgrading the first 0.2 mi. for universal accessibility. In 2021, the last 0.1 mi. of the trail was marked (blue and orange paint on trees) for a future logging operation. Albany Brook Trail begins at the turnaround at the end of FR 18, the main road at Crocker Pond CG (do not enter the actual campground), 0.9 mi. south of the northern trailhead for Albany Mtn. Trail (see that trail description on p. 302 for driving directions). The trailhead is not reachable by vehicle in winter. Leaving the west side of the turnaround, Albany Brook Trail descends to the left and follows the west shore of Crocker Pond for 0.2 mi., makes a short and moderate ascent, and then runs along the lower east slope of Albany Mtn. with minor ups and downs. It descends, crosses an old logging road at 0.9 mi. with a clearing visible on the right, and soon reaches the north end of Round Pond.

SECTION SEVEN

OXFORD HILLS AND WHITE MOUNTAIN FOOTHILLS

INTRODUCTION

This section describes 32 trails on 18 mountains in the Oxford Hills and White Mountains Foothills, which includes much of eastern, central, southern, and southwestern Oxford County.

ME 26 slices through the heart of the region, forming a rough north–south boundary between the Oxford Hills to the east and the White Mountain Foothills to the west. To the north, the Oxford Hills are bounded by US 2 and the Androscoggin River from Bethel to Canton. The county lines for Franklin County and then Androscoggin County are the eastern boundary, the Cumberland County line is the southern boundary, and, of course, ME 26 bounds the west side of the Oxford Hills. The White Mountain Foothills are outlined by ME 26 in the east and the Cumberland County line and Fryeburg town line in the south. A section of the New Hampshire border and the Maine section of the WMNF form the western boundary, while US 2 and the Androscoggin River bound the White Mountain Foothills to the north.

Many of the trails in this section are on private property and are open for public use through the generosity of various landowners, mostly land trusts. Notable exceptions include a portion of the trail on Bald Mtn. and the loop trail on Sabattus Mtn., which are on state land managed by MBPL.

GEOGRAPHY

Among the scattered lakes, ponds, streams, and rivers in the section are a series of mountains generally ranging in elevation from around 1,000 ft. to a little more than 2,200 ft. Sabattus Mtn. (1,255 ft.) is east of Kezar Lake in Center Lovell. The sweeping granite cliffs of its south face afford vistas to Pleasant Mtn., North and South Baldface, and the White Mountains. A few miles north, east of Upper Bay of Kezar Lake in North Lovell, is Heald and Bradley Ponds Reserve, a pleasant 802-acre property owned and managed by Greater Lovell Land Trust that is home to three small mountains: Whiting Hill (798 ft.), Amos Mtn. (953 ft.), and Flat Hill (884 ft.). Southeast of Sabattus Mtn. is Ladies Delight Hill (570 ft.), which rises above Lower Bay on Kezar Lake, while to the east is the scenic ridgeline (1,210 ft.) of Five Kezar Ponds Reserve.

On the west side of the pretty village of Waterford is Mt. Tire'm (1,102 ft.), which affords lovely looks over Keoka Lake. South of Keoka Lake are the popular cliffs of Hawk Mtn. (1,072 ft.). Just east of the WMNF boundary in Albany Township are Round Mtn. (1,833 ft.) and Long Mtn. (1,835 ft.); the former features an interesting rock castle near its peak and the latter yields views west to the White Mountains. In the shadow of Mt. Abram and its ski slopes, rising above the tranquil shores of South Pond in Greenwood, is Maggie's Nature Park, 86 town-owned acres where color-coded trails crisscross the slopes of Ring Hill (1,095 ft.) and Peaked Mtn. (1,250 ft.). Nearby, adjacent to North Pond, are the impressive cliff faces of Buck's Ledge (1,150 ft.), Lapham Ledge (1,090 ft.), and the fine summit of Moody Mtn. (1,430 ft.) in Buck's Ledge Community Forest. A few miles due south, the cliffs of Oversett Mtn. (1,373 ft.) look out over pristine Oversett Pond. To the southeast, still in Greenwood, is Noyes Mtn. (1,501 ft.), its trails leading to the remains of an old tourmaline mine.

Just south of Rumford and the Androscoggin River, straddling the town lines of Milton Township and Peru, is Mt. Zircon (2,245 ft.), the highest peak in the Oxford Hills, which affords wonderful scenic panoramas from its summit ledges. Straddling the town lines of Woodstock and Peru, rising steeply above Little Concord Pond and Shagg Pond, is Bald Mtn. (1,695 ft.), with its precipitous cliffs. Connected to Bald Mtn. is the craggy mountaintop of Speckled Mtn. (2,181 ft.). To the east, astride the Sumner and Peru town lines, is Black Mtn. (2,135 ft.), a broad, flat mass with five distinct summits running roughly east to west. Directly south in Paris is Crocker Hill (1,379 ft.), which hikers climb via an old carriage road. Also in Paris, the open ledges high on the north side of Singepole Mtn. (1,414 ft.) offer attractive views. Just east in Hebron is Streaked Mtn. (1,755 ft.), well known for its distinctive west face of steep granite slabs. Bear Mtn. (1,208 ft.) in Hartford, the easternmost of the Oxford Hills with a trail, looks out over Bear Pond.

SEC 7

ROAD ACCESS
Trailheads are scattered far and wide across the Oxford Hills and White Mountain Foothills. Connecting Bethel and Lovell, ME 5 is the major road at the western edge of the region and is useful for access to Sabattus Mtn., the hills of Heald and Bradley Ponds Reserve, and Ladies Delight Hill. Just east, ME 35 and ME 37 provide access to Mt. Tire'm and Hawk

Mtn. in Waterford. Five Kezar Ponds Ridge is also in Waterford off ME 35. Hikers can use ME 5/35 between Bethel and North Waterford to reach Long Mtn. and Round Mtn. ME 26 is a busy highway that slices across the Oxford Hills from the southeast at Oxford to the northwest at Bethel. From ME 26 in Locke Mills or ME 118 in Norway, use Greenwood Rd. to reach the trails at Maggie's Nature Park, Oversett Mtn., and Noyes Mtn. The trailhead for Lapham Ledge, Moody Mtn., and Buck's Ledge in Woodstock is on ME 26. From ME 26 in South Paris, use ME 177 to get to Crocker Hill, Singepole Mtn., and Streaked Mtn. Use US 2 or ME 232 to reach the Mt. Zircon trailhead along the Androscoggin River in Rumford. ME 219 offers access to trailheads for Bald Mtn., Speckled Mtn., and Black Mtn. in the Milton and Peru area. The best access to Bear Mtn. is from ME 4 in North Turner.

CAMPING

About a dozen privately operated campgrounds are in the Oxford Hills and White Mountain Foothills region.

SUGGESTED HIKES

■ Easy
WHITING HILL

LP via Whiting Hill Loop Trail and Otter Rocks Spur Trail	1.8 mi.	408 ft.	1:05

Enjoy the sights of Kezar Lake and Kearsarge North and then visit Otter Rocks on Heald Pond. To begin, see Whiting Hill Loop Trail, p. 311.

SABATTUS MTN.

LP via Sabattus Mtn. Trail	1.6 mi.	475 ft.	1:05

This interesting loop hike to the sweeping cliffs atop Sabattus Mtn. offers a grand vista from Pleasant Mtn. to the Presidential Range. See Sabattus Mtn. Trail, p. 317.

MT. TIRE'M

RT via Daniel Brown Trail	1.2 mi.	552 ft.	0:45

Hike to an overlook featuring beautiful views of Keoka Lake. See Daniel Brown Trail, p. 318.

LAPHAM LEDGE

LP via Lapham Ledge Trail and logging road	1.6 mi.	390 ft.	1:00

Enjoy several clifftop ledges looking south to Bryant Pond, Mt. Christopher, and Noyes Mtn. See Lapham Ledge Trail, p. 327.

CROCKER HILL

RT via Crocker Hill Trail	1.8 mi.	468 ft.	1:10

Follow Old Crocker Hill carriage road and then a footpath to admire an impressive scene ranging from the White Mountains and the Mahoosuc Range to the Oxford Hills. See Crocker Hill Trail, p. 333.

STREAKED MTN.

RT via Streaked Mtn. Trail	1.2 mi.	725 ft.	1:00

Hike distinctive granite slabs to enjoy the scenic panorama from Streaked Mtn.'s extensive summit ledges. See Streaked Mtn. Trail, p. 334.

■ Moderate
FIVE KEZAR PONDS RESERVE

LP via The Mountain Trail, Tom's Path, The Orange Trail, and Ron's Loop	2.9 mi.	655 ft.	1:50

Large open ledges on a pleasant ridgetop yield fine views over the pretty Five Kezar Ponds area that range from Pleasant Mtn. to Mt. Washington. To begin, see The Mountain Trail, p. 320.

LONG MTN.

LP via Long Mtn. Trail	5.5 mi.	1,130 ft.	3:20

The expansive westerly vista from Long Mtn. includes nearby Round Mtn., plus Doublehead, North and South Baldface, Speckled and Caribou mountains, East and West Royce, the Carter–Moriah Range and the Northern Presidential Range. See Long Mtn. Trail, p. 322.

SEC 7

BUCK'S LEDGE COMMUNITY FOREST

	↴↑	↗	○
LP via Lapham Ledge Trail, JnJ Backcountry Trail, and Buck's Ledge Trail	4.5 mi.	1,275 ft.	3:00

Make a grand loop through this new conservation property that visits panorama-rich Lapham Ledge, as well as Buck's Ledge and Moody Mtn. To begin, see Lapham Ledge Trail, p. 327.

OVERSETT POND AND OVERSETT MTN.

	↴↑	↗	○
LP via Sanborn River Trail, Oversett Connection, Oversett Pond Trail, and Oversett Pond Ln.	4.8 mi.	600 ft.	3:45

Explore a scenic stretch of the Sanborn River, visit pristine Oversett Pond, and enjoy superb clifftop views on Oversett Mtn. during this fine circuit hike. To begin, see Sanborn River Trail, p. 324.

NOYES MTN.

	↴↑	↗	○
LP via Noyes, Harvard, and Perham trails	2.6 mi.	861 ft.	1:45

Hike over Noyes Mtn. to the top of an old tourmaline mine for views of Pleasant Mtn., peaks along the Maine–New Hampshire border, and the White Mountains. To begin, see Noyes Trail, p. 331.

BALD MTN. AND SPECKLED MTN.

	↴↑	↗	○
RT via Bald Mtn. Trail and Speckled Mtn. Trail	5.2 mi.	1,665 ft.	3:30

Hike past Little Concord Pond to Bald Mtn.'s cliffs and then on to craggy Speckled Mtn.'s open ledges with extensive views. To begin, see Bald Mtn. Trail, p. 336.

■ Strenuous

The Oxford Hills and White Mountain Foothills section does not have any suggested hikes rated as strenuous.

TRAIL DESCRIPTIONS
HEALD AND BRADLEY PONDS RESERVE

This 802-acre conservation land in Lovell, a property of Greater Lovell Land Trust, includes more than 1 mi. of shoreline on Heald Pond and more than 0.25 mi. on Bradley Pond. A 6-mi. network of trails extends through the reserve and reaches the summits of three hills: Whiting Hill, Amos Mtn., and Flat Hill.

WHITING HILL (798 FT.)

Rising directly west of Heald Pond, this is the southernmost and lowest of the three hills in Heald and Bradley Ponds Reserve. The wooded summit offers looks over Kezar Lake to Kearsarge North and neighboring peaks in the White Mountains.

From the jct. of ME 93 and ME 5 in Lovell, drive north on ME 5 for 6.3 mi. Turn right onto Slab City Rd. and in 0.4 mi. cross a bridge and pass a boat launch and parking area on the left; in another 100 yd., trailhead parking is on the left.

WHITING HILL LOOP TRAIL (AMC HEALD AND BRADLEY PONDS RESERVE MAP, MAP 6: G14)
Cumulative from Slab City Rd. (469 ft.) to:

Westways Trail (530 ft.)	0.4 mi.	61 ft.	0:15
Whiting Hill summit (798 ft.) via Summit Spur	0.7 mi.	329 ft.	0:30
Connector to Hemlock Loop Trail (720 ft.)	0.9 mi.	329 ft.	0:35
Otter Rocks Spur Trail (550 ft.)	1.0 mi.	329 ft.	0:40
Complete loop	1.4 mi.	329 ft.	0:50

SEC 7

GLLT This trail makes a loop over Whiting Hill. The short spur to Otter Rocks on pretty Heald Pond along the east side of the mountain is a worthwhile detour.

From the trailhead parking area, walk back along Slab City Rd. toward ME 5. Immediately after the bridge, turn right on the wide trail and follow it past the remains of an old dam to a jct. and kiosk. Bear left to hike the loop clockwise. Ascend easily, following blue markers. Where Westways Trail enters from the left, continue straight on Whiting Hill Loop Trail and make a gentle ascent to Summit Spur; turn right to quickly reach the summit and a fork. Bear right at the fork to reach a granite bench in 100 ft. and a cleared view to the west; to the left, the path leads 200 ft. to another granite bench and a view through the trees to Heald Pond and the hills beyond. Return to the jct. of Whiting Hill Loop Trail and turn right to continue.

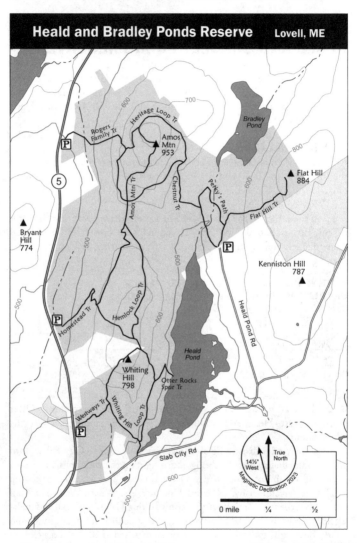

Heald and Bradley Ponds Reserve Lovell, ME

Rogers Family Tr
Heritage Loop Tr
Amos Mtn 953
Bradley Pond
Flat Hill 884
Amos Mtn Tr
Chestnut Tr
Pelky's Path
Flat Hill Tr
Bryant Hill 774
Kenniston Hill 787
Homestead Tr
Hemlock Loop Tr
Heald Pond Rd
Whiting Hill 798
Heald Pond
Otter Rocks Spur Tr
Westways Tr
Whiting Hill Loop Tr
Slab City Rd

True North
14½° West
Magnetic Declination 2023

0 mile   ¼   ½

SEC 7

Traverse the mountain to arrive at a connector trail (orange markers), which leads about 300 ft. north to Hemlock Loop Trail. Continue the descent of Whiting Hill Loop Trail to reach a T jct. Here, Otter Rocks

Spur Trail leads 0.25 mi. to Otter Rocks on the west shore of Heald Pond, a pleasant picnic and swimming spot.

From the Otter Rocks Spur Trail jct., turn right to follow level Whiting Hill Loop Trail easily out to the kiosk and then on to Slab City Rd.

Otter Rocks Spur Trail. From the jct. of Whiting Hill Loop Trail, hike the wide track north for about 0.1 mi.; then turn sharply right onto a footpath and follow it to its end at Otter Rocks on Heald Pond at 0.2 mi. The spur takes about 7 min. to hike and loses 79 ft. of elevation en route.

WESTWAYS TRAIL (AMC HEALD AND BRADLEY PONDS RESERVE MAP, MAP 6: G14)
From ME 5 (490 ft.) to:

Whiting Loop Trail (530 ft.)	0.3 mi.	40 ft.	0:10

GLLT This short trip leaves from a trailhead on ME 5 at a point 0.4 mi. north of Slab City Rd. Westways Trail provides access to Whiting Hill Loop Trail from the west. From just left of the kiosk, follow the old forest road (green markers), which soon peters out into a trail of mossy rocks. At 0.3 mi., reach a T jct. with Whiting Hill Loop Trail, which leads left 0.4 mi. to the top of Whiting Hill.

HOMESTEAD TRAIL (AMC HEALD AND BRADLEY PONDS RESERVE MAP, MAP 6: G14)
From ME 5 (470 ft.) to:

Hemlock Loop Trail (590 ft.)	0.5 mi.	120 ft.	0:20

GLLT This 0.5-mi. spur provides access to Hemlock Loop Trail from the west. From the jct. of ME 5 and Slab City Rd., drive north on ME for 0.9 mi. (passing Westways Trail trailhead at 0.4 mi.) to the trailhead for Homestead Trail. The trail starts from the east side of the parking lot, 50 ft. south of the kiosk. Follow the wide track (blue markers) into the woods. At 0.2 mi., turn left onto a footpath and, soon after, pass old foundations to the left and right of the trail. Ahead, rejoin the wide track and then turn off it again, cross a culvert, and wind upslope along old stone walls and past a foundation. After crossing a footbridge, Homestead Trail ends at Hemlock Loop Trail.

HEMLOCK LOOP TRAIL (AMC HEALD AND BRADLEY PONDS RESERVE MAP, MAP 6: G14)
Cumulative from Homestead trailhead at ME 5 (470 ft.) to:

Hemlock Loop Trail (590 ft.) via Homestead Trail	0.5 mi.	120 ft.	0:20
Amos Mtn. Trail (550 ft.)	1.0 mi.	120 ft.	0:35
Connector to Whiting Hill Loop Trail (750 ft.)	1.7 mi.	280 ft.	1:00
Complete loop via Homestead Trail	2.5 mi.	280 ft.	1:25

GLLT Hemlock Loop Trail, which makes a circuit over the north slope of Whiting Hill, is most easily reached via Homestead Trail from ME 5. Access is also provided by a connector trail from Whiting Hill Loop Trail in the south or by Amos Mtn. Trail in the north.

From the ME 5 trailhead, walk east on Homestead Trail. In 0.5 mi., turn left to follow Hemlock Loop Trail (yellow markers) clockwise. Pass above the foundations of a former homestead (sign: "McDaniel's of Amos Mtn") before joining the route of an old forest road and proceeding easily on level ground. Ahead, the trail begins a gentle descent toward the saddle between Whiting Hill and Amos Mtn. It alternates between the old road and a footpath before arriving at the jct. with Amos Mtn. Trail on the left (leads 0.5 mi. north to the top of Amos Mtn.). Hemlock Loop Trail continues to the right to reach the base of Whiting Hill's north ridge and then begins a long, straight, easy ascent along a stone wall. After walking through a gap in the wall and ascending higher, reach the ridge crest and continue on the level to meet the short connector to Whiting Hill Loop Trail on the left. Turn right to stay on Hemlock Loop Trail to traverse the shoulder of the mountain, and then make a mostly gentle but steady descent to the jct. with Homestead Trail. Bear left on Homestead Trail to return to the trailhead on ME 5.

AMOS MTN. (955 FT.)

Rising west of Bradley Pond and north of Heald Pond, this mountain is the highest and northernmost in Heald and Bradley Ponds Reserve. The most common access point to Amos Mtn. is from the west at ME 5.

From the jct. of ME 5 and Slab City Rd., drive north on ME 5 for 2.0 mi. to the trailhead for Rogers Family Trail on the right. Rogers Family Trail leaves from here and joins Heritage Loop Trail on Amos Mtn.'s west slope.

ROGERS FAMILY TRAIL (AMC HEALD AND BRADLEY PONDS RESERVE MAP, MAP 6: G14)
Cumulative from Rogers Family trailhead on ME 5 (500 ft.) to:

Heritage Loop Trail (750 ft.)	0.5 mi.	290 ft.	0:25
Amos Mtn. summit (953 ft.) via Heritage Loop Trail and Amos Mtn. Trail	0.9 mi.	495 ft.	0:35

GLLT Rogers Family Trail (blue markers) begins at the back left corner of the trailhead parking area. At an unsigned jct. in 400 ft., turn sharply right and soon cross a footbridge over a small creek. Begin climbing, and follow a rising contour and then switchbacks at a steady grade to reach the jct. with Heritage Loop Trail. To get to the summit of Amos Mtn., turn left here and follow Heritage Loop Trail and then Amos Mtn. Trail.

HERITAGE LOOP TRAIL (AMC HEALD AND BRADLEY PONDS RESERVE MAP, MAP 6: G14)

Cumulative from Rogers Family Trail (540 ft.) to:

Amos Mtn. Trail, upper jct. (900 ft.)	0.2 mi.	360 ft.	0:20
Chestnut Trail (640 ft.)	0.7 mi.	360 ft.	0:30
Amos Mtn. Trail, lower jct. (650 ft.)	1.0 mi.	460 ft.	0:45
Complete loop	1.3 mi.	630 ft.	1:00

GLLT This pleasant circuit trail connects Rogers Family Trail, Amos Mtn. Trail, and Chestnut Trail high on Amos Mtn. Heritage Loop Trail is most commonly combined with Rogers Family Trail and Amos Mtn. Trail to reach the summit of Amos Mtn.

From the jct. of Rogers Family Trail, climb steadily on Heritage Loop Trail (orange markers). Follow a contour to the left to reach El Pulpito (the Pulpit), a large erratic with a chunk of rock neatly broken out of its front side to form a seat. Views through the trees include Kearsarge North, Doublehead, North and South Baldface, Mt. Hight, Carter Dome, and more. A short distance beyond, Heritage Loop Trail reaches a grassy old carriage road and the jct. with Amos Mtn. Trail on the right (red markers; leads 0.2 mi. to the summit). To continue on Heritage Loop Trail, turn left and descend. At 0.4 mi., where the carriage road curves sharply to the left, Heritage Loop Trail continues straight on a footpath and soon swings around to the east side of Amos Mtn.

Ahead, where Chestnut Trail (blue markers) leads straight on a wide track, turn sharply right onto a narrow footpath and quickly pass an old stone foundation tucked into the hillside to the right. Follow a contour and climb gradually. Crest the mountain's south shoulder and then continue gently down, weaving between stone walls, to reach the jct. with Amos Mtn. Trail (leads left and down 0.1 mi. to Hemlock Loop Trail or 0.3 mi. right to the top of Amos Mtn.). Here, turn right and then immediately left to stay on Heritage Loop Trail. Follow a contour over the west side of the mountain to a large open ledge (sign: "SW Overlook") with views to Kezar Lake and Speckled Mtn. Close the Heritage Loop Trail at the Rogers Family Trail jct. at 1.3 mi.

SEC 7

AMOS MTN. TRAIL (AMC HEALD AND BRADLEY PONDS RESERVE MAP, MAP 6: G14)

Cumulative from Heritage Loop Trail, upper jct. (900 ft.) to:

Amos Mtn. summit (953 ft.)	0.2 mi.	55 ft.	0:10
Heritage Loop Trail, lower jct. (650 ft.)	0.5 mi.	55 ft.	0:15
Hemlock Loop Trail (550 ft.)	0.6 mi.	55 ft.	0:20

GLLT This red-blazed trail connects Heritage Loop Trail with the summit of Amos Mtn. and then descends to rejoin Heritage Loop Trail.

From the upper jct. of Heritage Loop Trail at a point 0.7 mi. from ME 5 via Rogers Family Trail and Heritage Loop Trail, turn right on Amos Mtn. Trail and follow the grassy old carriage road to the clearing on the summit, which is marked by a large cairn and a granite bench (limited views). To continue, head for a smaller cairn in sight just below and follow the path down from there to the jct. of Heritage Loop Trail. Amos Mtn. Trail continues another 0.1 mi. south to end at the jct. of Hemlock Loop Trail.

CHESTNUT TRAIL (AMC HEALD AND BRADLEY PONDS RESERVE MAP, MAP 6: G14)
Cumulative from end of Heald Pond Rd. (530 ft.) to:

Perky's Path, north end (530 ft.)	0.25 mi.	40 ft.	0:10
Heritage Loop Trail (640 ft.)	0.6 mi.	150 ft.	0:20

GLLT This trail climbs the east side of Amos. Mtn. to join Heritage Loop Trail. Follow directions below for Flat Hill to reach the trailhead at the end of Heald Pond Rd.

From the trailhead parking area, walk straight ahead on the grassy old road (blue markers). Pass Perky's Path on the right, and then bear right at a fork ahead. Chestnut Trail continues to the jct. with Heritage Loop Trail, which proceeds straight ahead up the mountain on the wide track or turns left onto a narrow footpath to cross the mountain's south slopes.

FLAT HILL (884 FT.)
This hill east of Bradley Pond and Heald Pond is the easternmost of the three hills in the reserve.

From the jct. of ME 5 and Slab City Rd., at a point 6.3 mi. north of the jct. of ME 5 and ME 93 in Lovell, turn east onto Slab City Rd. Pass the southern end of Heald Pond and, at a fork in 1.2 mi., bear left onto Heald Pond Rd. Follow this dirt road 2.0 mi. to its end at the trailhead parking area.

FLAT HILL TRAIL (AMC HEALD AND BRADLEY PONDS RESERVE MAP, MAP 6: G14)
Parking at end of Heald Pond Rd. (530 ft.) to:

Flat Hill summit (884 ft.)	0.7 mi.	355 ft.	0:30

GLLT Flat Hill Trail starts across the road from the kiosk in the parking area. Following purple dots, it soon crosses a footbridge over a small creek and then continues on an old forest road. At a fork in 0.1 mi., go right toward Flat Hill (Perky's Path is to the left) and begin a gradual ascent. In

SEC
7

a tiny clearing at 0.4 mi. Flat Hill Trail bears right (watch for a cairn and an arrow posted on a tree). After a moderate stretch, bear left at the trail arrows and continue at an easy grade onto the ridge. Flat Hill Trail ends at a small, rocky outcropping with a view west, toward the White Mountains.

LOVELL
SABATTUS MTN. (1,255 FT.)

From the top of the immense cliffs on the southwest face of Sabattus Mtn. in Lovell, hikers will enjoy extensive vistas ranging from Pleasant Mtn. to North and South Baldface on the eastern edge of the White Mountains. The trail and the protection of the mountain are provided by a joint partnership between MBPL and GLLT.

From the jct. of ME 5 and ME 93 in Lovell, drive north on ME 5 for 4.5 mi., through the village of Center Lovell, to Sabattus Mountain Rd. Reset the trip meter. Turn right onto Sabattus Mountain Rd. and continue to a fork at 1.5 mi. Bear right onto Sabattus Trail Rd. and drive 0.7 mi. on this dirt road to the trailhead parking lot (sign) on the right.

SABATTUS MTN. TRAIL (USGS NORTH WATERFORD QUAD, GLLT SABATTUS MTN. MAP, GAZETTEER MAP 10)
Cumulative from Sabattus Trail Rd. (780 ft.) to:

Sabattus Mtn. summit (1,255 ft.)	0.6 mi.	475 ft.	0:30
Tower site and side trail to cliffs (1,220 ft.)	0.9 mi.	475 ft.	0:40
Complete loop	1.6 mi.	475 ft.	1:05

SEC 7

MBPL About 200 ft. into the woods, Sabattus Mtn. Trail splits. Bear left to hike the yellow-blazed loop clockwise. The trail climbs steadily, gradually at first and then moderately, with occasional switchbacks. Reach the summit ridge and, in a small opening with a large outcropping, bear sharply right at an easy grade to pass over the wooded summit of Sabattus Mtn. Along the ridgetop, reach an outlook and a sizable outcropping of white quartzite. Pass another outlook to reach the site of the former fire tower (removed in 1962). Attached to one of the concrete stanchions is a memorial to Steven Hickey, a local young man who died while trying to save his brother after a boating accident. Just below, in the opening at the top of the cliff, is a park bench, an unusual sight on a mountaintop. The views take in numerous ponds and Pleasant Mtn. to the south and extend as far as Mt. Washington and the Presidential Range to the west. A second park bench is below.

To descend, return to the tower site and bear left. Sabattus Mtn. Trail descends easily at first and then moderately to the base of the mountain before closing the loop and returning to the parking area.

LADIES DELIGHT HILL (562 FT.)

This low, wooded hill between Middle Bay and Lower Bay on Kezar Lake in Lovell is part of Chip Stockford Reserve, 155 acres owned and managed by GLLT. Chip Stockford was a nearby resident and founding member of GLLT.

From the jct. of ME 5 and ME 93 in Lovell, drive north on ME for 2.4 mi. Turn left onto West Lovell Rd. At 1.3 mi. from ME 5, shortly after crossing a bridge over the Narrows, turn left on Ladies Delight Rd. In another 0.4 mi., reach the trailhead on the right. Parking is across the road.

BILL SAYLES TRAIL (USGS CENTER LOVELL QUAD, GLLT CHIP STOCKFORD RESERVE MAP, GAZETTEER MAP 10)
From Ladies Delight Rd. (430 ft.) to:

Complete loop via Bill Sayles Trail	1.1 mi.	150 ft.	0:35

GLLT Bill Sayles Trail makes a pleasant loop through the reserve. Entering the woods, the trail (blue diamond markers) soon reaches a kiosk. The wide path ahead passes through tall pines to reach a loop jct. at 475 ft. from the road. Continue straight to hike the loop counterclockwise. At 0.4 mi., turn sharply left to reach a jct. A spur path straight ahead leads a short distance to a granite bench with a southwesterly vista through the trees that encompasses a range of New Hampshire peaks—from Kearsarge North near Intervale to Mt. Shaw in the Ossipee Mountains. Return to the jct. and turn right to close the loop. Turn right again to reach the road.

WATERFORD
MT. TIRE'M (1,102 FT.)

Mt. Tire'm in Waterford offers an easy hike that yields views of the Long Lake region.

In the center of Waterford, just 100 ft. south of the jct. of ME 35 and ME 37, turn onto Plummer Hill Rd. and drive 0.2 mi. west. On the left, a stone wall and a plaque set into a rock mark the start of Daniel Brown Trail (often referred to as Old Squire Brown Trail). Park along the wide dirt shoulder on the left side of the road.

DANIEL BROWN TRAIL (USGS NORWAY QUAD, MTF MT. TIRE'M, GAZETTEER MAP 10)
From Plummer Hill Rd. (550 ft.) to:

Mt. Tire'm summit (1,102 ft.)	0.6 mi.	552 ft.	0:35

TOW Take the wide trail uphill into the woods, climbing steadily along a stone wall. The route is not blazed but is well defined and easy to follow. The trail runs along a contour to the southeast through large pines and hemlocks. Turning southwest along the top of the mountain's steep east face, the exposed bedrock trail reaches a large open ledge area. Keoka Lake is visible to the left; to the south are Bear Pond, Bear Mtn., Hawk Mtn., and beyond, Long Lake. The ski trails on Pleasant Mtn. can be seen to the southwest. From the outlook, follow cairns another 150 ft. to the wooded top of Mt. Tire'm.

HAWK MTN. (1,072 FT.)

This mountain in Waterford rises high above Hawk Meadow just east of Bear Pond. A favorite of local hikers, hawk watchers, and rock climbers for years, much of the mountain is now protected as Hatch Preserve at Hawk Mountain under the care of WFLT. In winter 2022, WFLT conducted a selective timber harvest on the property to generate operating revenue for future improvements at the preserve. Several of the skidder trails resulting from the operation will be developed. As of late summer 2022, Cyrus Trail and Eleazer Trail were open and passable and are described here.

In Waterford at the jct. of ME 35/37 and Mill Hill Rd. just south of Keoka Lake, turn east onto Mill Hill Rd. In 0.9 mi., turn right on Hawk Mtn. Rd. In another 0.6 mi., at the end of the pavement, turn right into the gravel trailhead parking lot.

HAWK MTN. TRAILS (USGS NORWAY QUAD, WFLT PRESERVE TRAIL – HATCH PRESERVE AT HAWK MTN., GAZETTEER MAP 10)

Cumulative from Hawk Mtn. Rd. (830 ft.) to:

Right-of-way road, lower jct. (990 ft.)	0.2 mi.	160 ft.	0:10
Eleazer Trail (1,040 ft.)	0.45 mi.	210 ft.	0:20
Hawk Mtn. summit (1,072 ft.)	0.5 mi.	242 ft.	0:22
Right-of-way road, upper jct. (1,040 ft.)	0.8 mi.	242 ft.	0:30
Overlook (960 ft.)	1.0 mi.	242 ft.	0:35
Complete lollipop loop	1.8 mi.	322 ft.	1:05

WFLT This loop hike combines Cyrus Trail, Eleazer Trail, and a right-of-way road to make a loop over Hawk Mtn. Cyrus Trail begins to the right of the trailhead kiosk. Follow the wide track, an old road. At 0.2 mi., cross a rough gravel road (this is the right-of-way road and part of the return leg of the loop). Beyond, Cyrus Trail continues a long, gradual ascent to the jct. of Eleazer Trail on the right at 0.45 mi. Continue on Cyrus Trail to a small clearing, where a cairn marks the summit of Hawk Mtn. (limited views southeast). Return to Eleazer Trail and turn left (west) to follow an old tote road. At 0.8 mi., turn left on the right-of-way road, which trends gently down, levels out, and reaches a small clearing. Continue an easy descent on bedrock to the trail's end at an overlook at 1.0 mi. The vista over Hawk Meadow and the Bear River is spectacular. Beyond are Crystal Lake, Long Lake, and the ski trails on Pleasant Mtn.

To return to the trailhead, retrace your steps on the right-of-way road to the Eleazer Trail jct. and continue to the jct. with Cyrus Trail. Turn left to follow Cyrus Trail back to the start of the hike.

FIVE KEZAR PONDS RIDGE (1,210 FT.)

This beautiful mountain ridge is part of a 314-acre conservation property in Waterford and Stoneham owned and managed by GLLT. Four trails provide about 3 mi. of hiking and views overlooking Five Kezar Ponds to the mountains beyond.

From the jct. of ME 35 and ME 118 in North Waterford, drive south on ME 35 for 0.2 mi. Turn right on Five Kezars Rd., and in another 2.0 mi., turn right on dirt Kezars Ridge Rd. At a fork in 0.6 mi., bear right on Five Kezar Ponds Rd. Trailhead parking for The Mountain Trail and Tom's Path is on the right 0.2 mi. ahead. To reach the trailhead for Ron's Loop and The Orange Trail, continue west on Five Kezar Ponds Rd. for another 0.3 mi., where a gravel drive on the right leads to a parking area.

SEC 7

THE MOUNTAIN TRAIL (USGS NORTH WATERFORD QUAD, GLLT FIVE KEZAR PONDS RESERVE MAP, MAP 6: G15, GAZETTEER MAP 10)

From Five Kezar Ponds Rd., eastern trailhead (600 ft.) to:

Tom's Path (980 ft.)	0.6 mi.	380 ft.	0:30
The Orange Trail (1,180 ft.)	0.9 mi.	580 ft.	0:45

GLLT The Mountain Trail (blue blazes) starts to the right of the parking area kiosk, climbs in a northerly direction to a wooden bench, and switchbacks up the south slope to a second bench. The jct. with Tom's Path (map post) is just ahead, on the right in a shallow saddle. The Mountain Trail continues to climb, eventually swinging west to reach the ridge crest before meeting The Orange Trail. Here, a blue-blazed spur path leads to a large open ledge and a view over Five Kezar Ponds that ranges from Pleasant Mtn. to Mt. Washington.

Tom's Path. This green-blazed 0.25-mi. spur path leaves The Mountain Trail at a point 0.6 mi. from the eastern trailhead on Five Kezar Ponds Rd. and climbs easily to a fine view over Five Kezar Ponds to Pleasant Mtn. Tom's Path gains 75 ft. of elevation en route.

THE ORANGE TRAIL (USGS NORTH WATERFORD QUAD, GLLT FIVE KEZAR PONDS RESERVE MAP, MAP 6: G15, GAZETTEER MAP 10)
Cumulative from The Mountain Trail (1,080 ft.) to:

Ron's Loop (770 ft.)	1.0 mi.	–310 ft.	0:30
Five Kezars Ponds Rd., western trailhead (600 ft.) via Ron's Loop (either leg)	1.5 mi.	–480 ft.	0:45

GLLT This route, commonly used to complete the loop over the ridge from The Mountain Trail, is described on the descent. From The Mountain Trail jct., follow The Orange Trail (orange blazes) easily along the gently rolling ridge crest. From a high point at 0.3 mi., begin a steady, moderate descent to the west into the ravine below McDaniels Hill. With a small brook on the right, descend at an easier grade, cross the brook, and continue more easily on the wide track (old woods road) on a contour. In the next ravine, leave the wide track for a path on the left, which leads to a T jct. with Ron's Loop (map post) and a footbridge over a brook. Either leg of Ron's Loop will lead to the western trailhead on Five Kezar Ponds Rd. in 0.5 mi.

RON'S LOOP (USGS NORTH WATERFORD QUAD, GLLT FIVE KEZAR PONDS RESERVE MAP, MAP 6: G15, GAZETTEER MAP 10)
GLLT This blue-blazed trail makes a wooded 1-mi. loop (both legs are 0.5 mi. in length) between the western trailhead on Five Kezar Ponds Rd. and The Orange Trail. It can be hiked on its own or used as access to or egress from The Orange Trail. The difference in elevation between the trailhead and The Orange Trail is 170 ft.

SEC 7

CROOKED RIVER HEADWATERS
In the 1970s, Bethel-area residents Mary McFadden and Larry Stifler began acquiring lands in the Oxford County towns of Albany Township, Waterford, Greenwood, and Norway with landscape-scale conservation in mind. In late 2021, a coalition of private landowners, conservation-minded organizations, and federal agencies announced the permanent protection of 12,268 acres in a conservation easement to be held and stewarded by Mahoosuc Land Trust and collectively known as the Crooked River Headwaters (although some 5,000 acres are technically in the Androscoggin River watershed). In addition to MLT, McFadden, and Stifler, partners in the project included Sebago Clean Waters, The Conservation Fund, USDA Natural Resources Conservation Service, Portland Water District, Western Foothills Land Trust, and Inland Woods + Trails. Long Mtn., Round Mtn., and Oversett Mtn. are within the bounds of the property. The trails at the three mountain locations were developed and constructed by Bruce Barrett, the longtime trail manager for McFadden and Stifler.

LONG MTN. (1,835 FT.)

This flat-topped mountain straddles the Albany Township–Greenwood town line a few miles east of the WMNF. Long Mtn. Trail climbs past a pretty waterfall to several scenic viewpoints on the mountain's west side.

From the jct. of ME 26 and ME 5/35 on the west side of Bethel, drive south on ME 5/35 for 6.6 mi. Turn left on Vernon St. and then quickly bear left at the Albany Town House. Trailhead parking is 0.9 mi. north along Vernon St. on the right.

LONG MTN. TRAIL (USGS GREENWOOD QUAD, MTF LONG MTN. TRAIL, GAZETTEER MAP 10)
Cumulative from Vernon St. (700 ft.) to:

South Ledge (1,500 ft.)	2.2 mi.	800 ft.	1:30
North Ledge (1,400 ft.)	3.7 mi.	1,030 ft.	2:20
Complete lollipop loop	5.5 mi.	1,130 ft.	3:20

MLT Long Mtn. Trail (marked by small wooden arrows) starts to the left of the parking area kiosk. In 100 ft., bear left at a jct. (Bacon Hill mountain-bike trails are to the right). Cross a footbridge over a small creek and then soon turn right along a brook. After a short stretch on an old tote road, cross the brook and turn right on a foot trail alongside it, passing small cascades and pools. Reach the Long. Mtn. Trail loop jct. at 0.9 mi. Continue straight ahead toward South Ledge to walk the loop counter-clockwise. The mossy boulders, cascades, and pools of Hidden Falls are a short distance ahead. After stepping-stones crossing a small brook, the gentle climb becomes more moderate and uses switchbacks, built rock steps, a rock staircase, and a wooden ladder to gain elevation. Reach a stone bench at 2.1 mi.; in another 0.1 mi., arrive at a side trail leading 100 ft. out to South Ledge. The expansive view westward includes nearby Round Mtn., plus the peaks of Doublehead, North and South Baldface, Speckled and Caribou mountains, East and West Royce, the Carter–Moriah Range, and the high summits of the Northern Presidential Range.

Long Mtn. Trail continues along the steep south side of the mountain, climbing gently past several more ledges with views to Round Mtn. and, beyond, to Pleasant Mtn. in Bridgton. At 2.6 mi., the trail leaves the steep edge and travels north over the mostly flat terrain of the mountaintop; it then descends west to a side trail at 3.7 mi. that leads to North Ledge, where the scenic panorama ranges from Mt. Chocorua and Kearsarge North to Mt. Washington and the Mahoosuc Range, to name just a few. From North Ledge, the trail zigzags north on an undulating route before making a steady descent to the west. After crossing a footbridge and a grassy old logging road, Long Mtn. Trail reaches the loop jct. Turn right for the final 0.8 mi. back to the trailhead.

ROUND MTN. (1,833 FT.)

The forested dome of Round Mtn. rises several miles southwest of Long Mtn. Highlights of this hike include open ledges with views to the White Mountains, and the Rock Castle, a jumble of boulders capped by a rock spire.

Follow directions for Long Mtn., but after turning off ME 5/35 onto Vernon St., turn right at the Albany Town House and drive south on Hunt's Corner Rd. for 1.2 mi. Trailhead parking is on the left.

ROUND MTN. TRAIL (USGS BETHEL AND GREENWOOD QUADS, MTF ROUND MTN., GAZETTEER MAP 10)
From Hunt's Corner Rd. (860 ft.) to:

Rock Castle Loop (1,720 ft.)	0.7 mi.	860 ft.	0:45

MLT Enter the woods on the east side of the parking area. In 200 ft., wide Round Mtn. Trail (marked by small wooden arrows) passes a trail register. At 0.2 mi., bear left onto a footpath and begin a steady, moderate ascent of the mountain's west ridge. Pass a view window west to Kearsarge North and, farther up, another to the White Mountains. Round Mtn. Trail ends at Rock Castle Loop.

SEC 7

ROCK CASTLE LOOP (USGS BETHEL AND GREENWOOD QUADS, MTF ROUND MTN., GAZETTEER MAP 10)
From Round Mtn. Trail (1,600 ft.) to:

Complete Rock Castle Loop	0.5 mi.	160 ft.	0:20

MLT This trail makes a loop high on Round Mtn. to visit an interesting rock formation known as the Rock Castle. From the end of Round Mtn. Trail at the Rock Castle Loop jct. (sign), continue straight to hike the loop counterclockwise. Climb into and out of a gully, and then climb steadily at a moderate grade toward the peak of Round Mtn. The trail avoids the wooded summit, instead traversing to the left (this is the trail's high point). Ahead, where the trail turns sharply right, step left 50 ft. to a view overlooking the Rock Castle. Beyond the side trail, Rock Castle Loop descends steadily over a moderate-to-steep pitch. Shortly before reaching the base of the ravine, step left for another look at the impressive rock pillar. Below, turn left to hike along the base of the rocks and then close the loop. Turn right to descend and return to the trailhead in another 0.7 mi.

OVERSETT MTN. (1,373 FT.)

This mountain rises nearly 500 ft. above the east shore of Oversett Pond in Greenwood. Several clifftop outlooks offer views south and west over the Sanborn River valley to Lovejoy Mtn., Peabody Mtn., and Patch Mtn., among others. Access to the pond and mountain is via a portion of Sanborn River Trail and then Oversett Connection and Oversett Mtn. Trail.

From the jct. of ME 26 and ME 219 in West Paris, drive west on ME 219 to its end at Greenwood Rd. in Greenwood City, a distance of 5.5 mi. Turn right onto Greenwood Rd. and in 0.1 mi. turn left onto Patch Mtn. Rd. At a fork 0.6 mi. ahead, with a bridge to the left, bear right on Willis Mills Rd. In another 0.1 mi., pass Oversett Pond Ln. on the right and then turn left into the trailhead parking lot.

SANBORN RIVER TRAIL (USGS GREENWOOD QUAD, GAZETTEER MAP 10)
From Willis Mills Rd. (757 ft.) to:

Oversett Connection (810 ft.)	1.1 mi.	50 ft.	0:35

MLT The Sanborn River flows east across Albany Township and Greenwood to empty into Hicks Pond. Sanborn River Trail makes a nearly 3-mi. loop along the north and south banks of the river. The 1.1-mi. section along the north bank is commonly used to reach Oversett Pond and Oversett Mtn.

From the Willis Mills Rd. trailhead, cross Willis Mills Rd. and walk along Oversett Pond Ln. for about 350 ft. to a gate. A small parking area is to the left, as is the start of Sanborn River Trail. Sanborn River Trail closely follows the pretty river. Shortly into the hike, a spur path from Willis Mills Rd. enters from the left. Ahead, cross a power-line corridor. The trail passes above a canyon of the river before rising and then falling back to river level to reach several cascades and pools. Oversett Connection is on the right at 1.1 mi.

OVERSETT CONNECTION (USGS GREENWOOD QUAD, GAZETTEER MAP 10)
From Sanborn River Trail (810 ft.) to:

Oversett Pond and Oversett Mtn. Trail (924 ft.)	0.7 mi.	150 ft.	0:25

MLT Oversett Connection links Sanborn River Trail and Oversett Pond. From Sanborn River Trail, climb gradually to the top of a narrow ridge and then follow a gently rolling route. Cross a wet depression and soon reach a grassy clearing with a firepit. Continue straight ahead to reach the southwest shore of Oversett Pond and the jct. with Oversett Pond Trail. Several old canoes are scattered about in this area. The view of the steep cliffs on Oversett Mtn. from this vantage point is impressive.

OVERSETT POND TRAIL (USGS GREENWOOD QUAD, GAZETTEER MAP 10)

Cumulative from Oversett Connection (924 ft.) to:

Trail to Oversett Pond Ln.	0.2 mi.	0 ft.	0:05
Oversett Mtn. high point (1,310 ft.)	0.8 mi.	390 ft.	0:35
Complete loop	2.0 mi.	390 ft.	1:10

MLT This trail climbs Oversett Mtn. and circumnavigates Oversett Pond. From the jct. of Oversett Connection, turn right to hike the route counterclockwise. Pass a register box and proceed on narrow Oversett Pond Trail along the pond's margin. At the southeast end, a path on the right leads to Oversett Pond Ln. and then on to Willis Mills Rd. in 1.0 mi. After swinging around the east end of the pond, Oversett Pond Trail begins a steady climb via switchbacks. Upon reaching the ridgeline, the trail angles northwest to its high point and a lookout over Oversett Pond. Continue along the top of the mountain's west face past several more viewpoints and then wind gradually down the north ridge before switchbacking back to the pond. Cross the outlet and follow the west shore with occasional views of the cliffs on Oversett Mtn. Close the loop at the jct. of Oversett Connection. To return to the trailhead, turn right to follow Oversett Connection and Sanborn River Trail to reach Willis Mills Rd. in 1.8 mi., or continue ahead on Oversett Pond Trail for 0.2 mi. and then turn right on a path leading to Oversett Pond Ln., which reaches the road in another 1.0 mi.

Oversett Pond Ln. This 1-mi. gravel lane and footpath combination connects the trailhead parking area on Willis Mills Rd. with the start of Sanborn River Trail and leads to Oversett Pond Trail at the east end of the pond. Oversett Pond Ln. may also be used for more direct but less interesting ingress to or egress from the pond and mountain. On the ascent, the route gains 114 ft.

SEC 7

GREENWOOD–WOODSTOCK

LAPHAM LEDGE (1,090 FT.), MOODY MTN. (1,430 FT.), AND BUCK'S LEDGE (1,150 FT.)

Lapham Ledge, Moody Mtn., and Buck's Ledge—the latter with an impressive granite face that is one of the area's most recognizable geographic features—are all part of Buck's Ledge Community Forest, a 946-acre property protected by a coalition of conservation interests, including the Woodstock Conservation Commission, Mahoosuc Land Trust, Forest Society of Maine, and Northern Forest Center. A network of 4.5 mi. of trails plus about 3 mi. of old logging roads (now snowmobile trails) and a gravel camp road offer various loop hike possibilities.

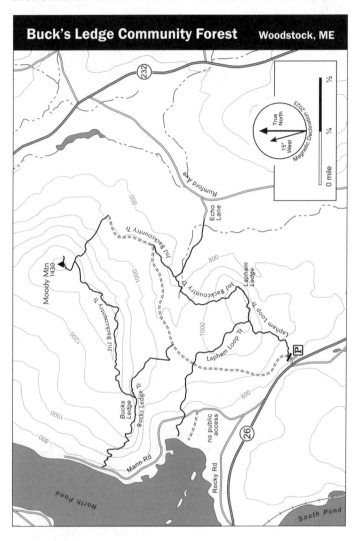

Buck's Ledge Community Forest   Woodstock, ME

SEC
7

From the post office in Bryant Pond, at the jct. of Railroad St. and North Main St. (ME 26), drive north on ME 26 for 1.4 mi. to a large trailhead parking area (sign: "Buck's Ledge Trails") on the right.

LAPHAM LEDGE TRAIL (AMC BUCK'S LEDGE COMMUNITY FOREST MAP)
Cumulative from ME 26 (790 ft.) to:

Lapham Ledge Trail (820 ft.)	33 yd.	30 ft.	0:02
Lapham Ledge Trail, north leg (1,130 ft.)	0.35 mi.	340 ft.	0:20
JnJ Backcountry Trail (1,160 ft.) via Lapham Ledge Trail	0.45 mi.	370 ft.	0:25
Lapham Ledge summit (1,180 ft.) via JnJ Backcountry Trail	0.5 mi.	390 ft.	0:30
Snowmobile Trail (960 ft.) via Lapham Ledge Trail	1.0 mi.	390 ft.	0:45
Complete loop via logging road	1.6 mi.	390 ft.	1:00

WCC This trail makes a loop over Lapham Ledge, leading to several outlook ledges and JnJ Backcountry Trail. Start on the snowmobile trail to the left of the parking area kiosk and proceed 100 ft. to a register box and the jct. of Lapham Ledge Trail (green blazes) on the right. Turn right on Lapham Ledge Trail and hike through a cutover area, pass through young woods, and then ascend past a ledge wall. Reach the ridge and bear right along it to a jct. Here, Lapham Ledge Trail descends in 0.4 mi. to a logging road that slices through the heart of the proposed forest property.

Continue easily ahead along the ridgetop. At a spur path on the right, walk 100 ft. to an overlook with a view south to Bryant Pond, Mt. Christopher, and Noyes Mtn. Return to Lapham Ledge Trail and turn right to reach the next overlook (similar views). Here, Lapham Ledge Trail ends at JnJ Backcountry Trail. The summit of Lapham Ledge is 150 ft. east on JnJ Backcountry Trail.

To continue the Lapham Ledge Trail loop, retrace your steps 0.15 mi. on Lapham Ledge Trail to Lapham Ledge Trail jct., turn right, and descend the north slope of the mountain. Reach the logging road at about 1 mi. Turn left to return to the trailhead on ME 26 in about 0.6 mi.

SEC 7

JNJ BACKCOUNTRY TRAIL (AMC BUCK'S LEDGE COMMUNITY FOREST MAP)
Cumulative from near Lapham Ledge summit (1,180 ft.) to:

Logging road (910 ft.)	0.7 mi.	130 ft.	0:25
Moody Mtn. Spur Trail (1,340 ft.)	1.3 mi.	560 ft.	0:55
Moody Mtn. summit (1,430 ft.) via Moody Mtn. Spur Trail	1.4 mi.	650 ft.	1:00
Buck's Ledge Trail (1,080 ft.)	2.2 mi.	730 ft.	1:30
Buck's Ledge (1,100 ft.)	2.25 mi.	755 ft.	1:32

WCC From Lapham Ledge Trail near the top of Lapham Ledge, red-blazed JnJ Backcountry Trail continues along the front side of the mountain and then sharply turns away to the north. The descending route follows skidder trails through a cutover area with views to Moody Mtn. At a small creek, turn sharply right along the valley floor and then turn sharply left to cross the creek. Cross a skidder trail to reach a jct., where a green-blazed trail leads straight to Woodstock Elementary School in 0.6 mi. Turn left to remain on JnJ Backcountry Trail, which follows a boundary line on a skidder trail. Ahead, turn left off the skidder trail and away from the boundary line and climb through a cutover area to reach a grassy logging road. To the left, it's 1.2 mi. back to the trailhead on ME 26 via this route. Turn right to continue on JnJ Backcountry Trail.

At 1.0 mi., leave the grassy logging road on the left. The footpath climbs a cleared corridor straight up the side of Moody Mtn. at a steady moderate grade for the next 0.3 mi. before leveling and arriving at a jct. Straight ahead it is 0.1 mi to the summit of Moody Mtn. via Moody Mtn. Spur Trail. The wooded summit has a register box but no views. However, there are excellent views of the high peaks of the Presidential Range at several points en route to the summit.

From the spur path jct., continue left toward Buck's Ledge. At 1.4 mi., leave the obvious corridor for a footpath on the left (sharp left) and continue along the ridge. From the ledges on the south side of the ridge, the trail trends gradually down toward Buck's Ledge, reaching a T jct. with Buck's Ledge Trail at 2.2 mi. To the right via Buck's Ledge Trail it is 300 ft. to Buck's Ledge and wonderful views over North Pond and South Pond to Mt. Abram and far beyond.

BUCK'S LEDGE TRAIL (AMC BUCK'S LEDGE COMMUNITY FOREST MAP)
Cumulative from ME 26 (790 ft.) to:

Lapham Ledge Trail, lower jct. (820 ft.) via logging road	33 yd.	30 ft.	0:02
Lapham Ledge Trail, upper jct. (960 ft.) via logging road	0.6 mi.	170 ft.	0:25
Buck's Ledge Trail (970 ft.) via logging road	0.7 mi.	180 ft.	0:30
JnJ Backcountry Trail (1,080 ft.)	1.15 mi.	290 ft.	0:45
Buck's Ledge (1,100 ft.)	1.2 mi.	310 ft.	0:50
Mann Rd. (700 ft.)	1.7 mi.	340 ft.	1:05
ME 26 (760 ft.) via Mann Rd.	2.8 mi.	400 ft.	1:35
Trailhead parking (790 ft.) via ME 26	3.0 mi.	430 ft.	1:40

WCC Buck's Ledge Trail begins from the logging road 0.7 mi. north of the ME 26 trailhead. Walking north on the old road, pass the lower and upper ends of Lapham Ledge Trail. In a saddle between Lapham Ledge and Buck's Ledge, turn left off the logging road onto Buck's Ledge Trail (light-blue blazes) and hike through a cutover area. The gradual ascent becomes a little steeper as the trail nears the base of Buck's Ledge. Climb below large ledge walls on rock-step switchbacks. Atop the ridge, reach a jct. with JnJ Backcountry Trail, which enters from the right. Continue easily along the ridgeline to a small log bench and an impressive vista at Buck's Ledge. Over North Pond, see Mt. Abram, Long Mtn., Speckled Mtn., Caribou Mtn., Carter Dome, Mt. Washington, and many other peaks to the west-southwest. Continue along the ledges, passing more fine outlooks, before descending steeply to Mann Rd. just above the shore of North Pond. Turn left and follow the road southeast. Reach a jct. with Rocky Rd. and then ME 26 just beyond. Walk the shoulder of ME 26 to return to the trailhead.

LOGGING ROAD (AMC BUCK'S LEDGE COMMUNITY FOREST MAP)
Cumulative from ME 26 (790 ft.) to:

Lapham Ledge Trail, lower jct. (820 ft.)	33 yd.	30 ft.	0:02
Lapham Ledge Trail, upper jct. (960 ft.)	0.6 mi.	170 ft.	0:25
Buck's Ledge Trail (970 ft.)	0.7 mi.	180 ft.	0:30
JnJ Backcountry Trail, lower jct. (910 ft.)	1.2 mi.	240 ft.	0:45
JnJ Backcountry Trail, upper jct. (900 ft.)	1.5 mi.	260 ft.	0:55

SEC 7

WCC An old logging road slices through the heart of Buck's Ledge Community Forest, allowing for loop hike opportunities. From the ME 26 trailhead, hike north on the logging road to meet the lower and upper ends of Lapham Ledge Trail, then Buck's Ledge Trail, and finally the lower jct. and upper jct. of JnJ Backcountry Trail.

RING HILL (1,095 FT.) AND PEAKED MTN. (1,250 FT.)

MLT maintains an interconnected system of color-coded trails on Ring Hill and adjacent Peaked Mtn. in Greenwood. Ring Hill is part of Maggie's Nature Park, an 86-acre woodland preserve donated to the town by Maggie Ring, a lifelong resident.

From the post office in Bryant Pond, at the jct. of Railroad St. and North Main St. (ME 26), drive north on ME 26 for 3.4 mi. to the jct. with Howe Hill Rd. (sign for Mt. Abram ski area). Turn left onto Howe Hill Rd., cross the railroad tracks, and turn left onto Greenwood Rd. Follow it for 1.4 mi. to trailhead parking on the right (sign).

RING HILL TRAIL (USGS BRYANT POND QUAD, MTF MAGGIE'S NATURE PARK MAP, GAZETTEER MAP 10)
Cumulative from Greenwood Rd. (730 ft.) to:

Ledges (1,070 ft.)	0.7 mi.	340 ft.	0:25
Complete loop	1.1 mi.	340 ft.	0:40

MLT This trail circumnavigates Ring Hill, which rises west of South Pond. Starting to the right of the kiosk at the back of the parking lot, follow orange-blazed Ring Hill Trail 50 ft. to a jct. Bear right to hike Ring Hill Trail counterclockwise. Pass purple-blazed Maggie's Path on the left; ahead at 0.2 mi., blue-blazed Abner's Path leaves right. Just beyond, pass green-blazed Mae's Path on the right. Cross the upper end of Abner's Path and head gradually uphill, switchbacking several times. At 0.6 mi., Ring Hill Trail levels off and soon reaches an open ledge with views of Mt. Abram. Cross the ledge and descend to the left. After several switchbacks, cross Abner's Path again at 0.8 mi. Abner's Path continues to the right, leading to Peaked Mtn. Trail and on to the summit of Peaked Mtn. in about 0.6 mi. Continue downhill on Ring Hill Trail. At 1.0 mi., Maggie's Path leaves left. Beyond, close the loop and reach the parking area at 1.1 mi.

ABNER'S PATH (USGS BRYANT POND QUAD, MTF MAGGIE'S NATURE PARK MAP, GAZETTEER MAP 10)
Cumulative from Greenwood Rd. (730 ft.) to:

Start of trail via Ring Hill Trail (800 ft.)	0.2 mi.	70 ft.	0:10
High point on east slope of Ring Hill (1,000 ft.)	0.5 mi.	270 ft.	0:25
Peaked Mtn. Trail (1,040 ft.)	0.8 mi.	310 ft.	0:35

MLT Abner's Path starts from Ring Hill Trail at a point 0.2 mi. north of the trailhead. From this jct., blue-blazed Abner's Path makes a rising traverse around the north slope of Ring Hill, passing Mae's Path on the left before reaching the jct. with Ring Hill Trail at 0.4 mi. Beyond, Abner's Path takes a mildly undulating route across the east slope of Ring Hill to a saddle between Ring Hill and Peaked Mtn. at 0.7 mi., where it crosses Ring Hill Trail again. Continuing on, Abner's Path ends at its jct. with Peaked Mtn. Trail at 0.8 mi.

PEAKED MTN. TRAIL (USGS BRYANT POND QUAD, MTF MAGGIE'S NATURE PARK MAP, GAZETTEER MAP 10)
Cumulative from Greenwood Rd. (730 ft.) to:

Peaked Mtn. summit (1,250 ft.) and ledges	0.9 mi.	520 ft.	0:45
Complete Peaked Mtn. loop and return to trailhead	1.8 mi.	520 ft.	1:10

MLT Peaked Mtn. Trail climbs to the summit ledges of Peaked Mtn., just south of Ring Hill. Leave the far end of the parking lot, away from the kiosk, following yellow blazes. In 100 yd., turn right off the woods road and head uphill into the woods on a footpath. Climb gradually via switchbacks to the lower jct. with red-blazed Harriet's Path on the left at 0.3 mi. Pass blue-blazed Abner's Path on the right at 0.4 mi., and the upper jct. of Harriet's Path on the left at 0.5 mi.

Arrive at a blue-painted stake at 0.5 mi. that marks the boundary of Maggie's Nature Park. Beyond, the ridge levels off. Reach a jct. with the summit loop at 0.6 mi. and continue straight ahead on the old woods road, trending easily up along the ridgeline. At 0.9 mi., turn sharply left (unmarked trail to right). The summit of Peaked Mtn. and a series of ledges with attractive views of Mt. Abram are just ahead. Beyond, leave the ledges, descend briefly, and remain on a contour before closing the loop at the jct. at 1.2 mi. Turn right and retrace your steps to the parking area, at 1.8 mi.

Harriet's Path. This 0.2-mi. path makes a loop to ledges offering views east over North Pond and South Pond and to Buck's Ledge and Lapham Ledge. The route is best hiked from its upper jct. with Peaked Mtn. Trail, which is 0.4 mi. from the trailhead on Greenwood Rd. Following red blazes, descend 0.1 mi. (losing about 100 ft. of elevation) to a spur leading 100 ft. right to the ledges. From the spur jct., continue left on a contour and then switchback down to rejoin Peaked Mtn. Trail 0.3 mi. from the trailhead.

SEC 7

NOYES MTN. (1,501 FT.)

This mountain in Greenwood is part of a 295-acre preserve owned and managed by WFLT. Three trails—Noyes, Harvard, and Perham—combine for a loop hike (marked with signs and small yellow diamonds with black arrows) that reaches the summit and an expansive viewpoint above an old tourmaline mine.

From the jct. of ME 118 and ME 117 2.0 mi. west of downtown Norway, drive west on ME 118 for 0.9 mi. Turn right onto Greenwood Rd. and travel 5.2 mi. Turn right onto Richardson Hollow Rd. and proceed 0.8 mi. to trailhead parking for Noyes Mtn. Preserve on the left.

NOYES TRAIL (USGS MT. BRYANT POND QUAD, WFLT NOYES MTN. PRESERVE TRAILS MAP, GAZETTEER MAP 10)
Cumulative from Richardson Hollow Rd. (870 ft.) to:

Harvard Trail and Perham Trail jct. (1,240 ft.)	0.6 mi.	370 ft.	0:30
Noyes Mtn. summit (1,501 ft.) via Harvard Trail	0.9 mi.	631 ft.	0:45

WFLT Proceed to the trailhead kiosk and then follow the old woods road north along the edge of a large meadow, which yields views to Streaked Mtn. and Singepole Mtn. Enter the woods at a corner of the meadow and soon reach a clearing at the jct. with Willard Trail. Turn left to continue on wide Noyes Trail and begin climbing. Level off, contour right, and then ascend rock staircases to a jct. Here, Harvard Trail leads to the right, climbs to the top of Noyes Mtn., and continues to the top of the old Harvard Mine and the upper jct. of Perham Trail in 0.7. Perham Trail leads to the left and climbs to Shavey's View at the top of the old Harvard Mine and the jct. with the upper end of Harvard Trail in 0.7 mi.

HARVARD TRAIL (USGS MT. BRYANT POND QUAD, WFLT NOYES MTN. PRESERVE TRAILS MAP, GAZETTEER MAP 10)
Cumulative from Richardson Hollow Rd. (870 ft.) to:

Harvard Trail and Perham Trail jct. (1,240 ft.)	0.6 mi.	370 ft.	0:30
Noyes Mtn. summit (1,501 ft.) via Harvard Trail	0.9 mi.	631 ft.	0:45
Shavey's View at top of old Harvard Mine (1,320 ft.) and Perham Trail	1.3 mi.	631 ft.	1:00

WFLT From the jct. of Noyes Trail and Perham Trail, Harvard Trail leads up a long series of rock staircases on an old woods road. In 500 ft., the trail leaves the old woods road for a footpath on the left. Above, crest a rocky knob and then drop into and climb out of a dip. Bear left below a ledge wall, and then angle up on a rising contour. Level off on the summit plateau and pass over the unmarked wooded summit of Noyes Mtn. Continue over the mountaintop to reach a T jct. at an old woods road. Private property is to the right; bear sharply left here and continue gradually downhill. Arrive at a grassy open ledge and cable fence line; this is Shavey's View at the top of the old Harvard Mine. Perham Trail enters from the left. The southwesterly view includes Patch Mtn., Pleasant Mtn., a jumble of peaks near the Maine–New Hampshire border, and the White Mountains beyond.

PERHAM TRAIL (USGS MT. BRYANT POND QUAD, WFLT NOYES MTN. PRESERVE TRAILS MAP, GAZETTEER MAP 10)
Cumulative from Harvard Trail (1,320 ft.) to:

Noyes Trail and Harvard Trail jct. (1,240 ft.)	0.7 mi.	230 ft.	0:30
Trailhead parking via Noyes Trail (870 ft.)	1.3 mi.	230 ft.	0:45

WFLT Perham Trail is commonly used as a descent route as part of a loop hike combined with Noyes Trail and Harvard Trail. It is therefore described on the descent. From the jct. of Harvard Trail at Shavey's View, follow Perham Trail to the left into the woods. Climb easily and follow a contour high on the south side of the mountain to reach a viewpoint called

Madison's Memory and a clear look at Pleasant Mtn. Ahead, at Ellie's Spot, the scene includes Pleasant Mtn. and Kearsarge North. Continue along the open edge before ducking back into the woods. On a long switchback to the west, pass a bench of flat rocks set into the ledge. The trail switchbacks to the east and starts to descend. Short switchbacks lead down at a moderate grade to Lynn's Lookout, where a low stone wall serves as a convenient bench. More short switchbacks below mossy cliffs and more rock steps characterize Perham Trail before it ends at the jct. of Harvard Trail and Noyes Trail. Turn right to follow Noyes Trail back to the trailhead.

PARIS–HEBRON
CROCKER HILL (1,379 FT.)

Crocker Hill in Paris is the source of the panoramic vista of the White Mountains drawn by George L. Vose, a Bowdoin College professor of engineering, in 1868. The mountain features the famous view from its west slope and views over the Oxford Hills from a point just east of the summit. Crocker Hill is part of 800 acres owned by the Makowski family. Crocker Hill Trail is maintained by New England Forestry Consultants.

From Paris Hill Rd. in Paris, just north of Paris Hill Country Club, turn east onto Lincoln St., which soon becomes Mt. Mica Rd. At 1.1 mi., turn left onto Thayer Rd. and proceed 0.7 mi. to where the road turns left. Limited parking is available along the shoulder. Do not block the green gate or the gate to the right.

SEC 7

CROCKER HILL TRAIL
(USGS WEST SUMNER QUAD, GAZETTEER MAP 11)
From Thayer Rd. (911 ft.) to:

Crocker Hill summit (1,379 ft.)	0.8 mi.	468 ft.	0:40
Log bench at trail's end (1,310 ft.)	0.9 mi.	468 ft.	0:42

NEFC Pass around the green gate and follow the old Crocker Hill carriage road. The grassy road switchbacks up to the left at 0.2 mi., to the right at 0.35 mi., and finally back to the left at 0.5 mi. At 0.6 mi., there's a cleared view to the west to Pleasant Mtn. and the White Mountains. Soon after, in an area of exposed ledge, an orange-blazed trail leaves the road to the right; turn right on this trail. A short, steep pitch leads to more moderate climbing. At a cairn above, the angle eases, and there is a view west-north-west to the Presidential and Mahoosuc ranges. Just ahead, a ledge on the left marks the summit of Crocker Hill (no sign). Continue through a break in an old stone wall and then descend slightly to a decaying log bench and a cleared vista east over the Oxford Hills.

STREAKED MTN. (1,755 FT.)

The distinctive west face of Streaked Mtn. in Hebron can be seen for miles in the Norway–South Paris area. The mountain offers a short but steep hike to the open ledges on its summit. Hebron Academy maintains the trail.

From the jct. of ME 117 and ME 119 just east of downtown South Paris, proceed east on ME 117 for 4.5 mi. to Streaked Mtn. Rd. Turn right (south) onto this road and drive another 0.5 mi., where there is parking along the side of the road. The trail starts on the left (north) side of the road, next to a brook.

STREAKED MTN. TRAIL (SGS OXFORD QUAD, MTF STREAKED MTN. TRAIL, GAZETTEER MAP 11)
From Streaked Mtn. Rd. (1,030 ft.) to:

Streaked Mtn. summit (1,755 ft.)	0.6 mi.	725 ft.	0:40

HA Start by following a brook and an old telephone line along a field bordered by a stone wall. Reach a trail sign 100 ft. into the woods. Streaked Mtn. Trail is wide but rocky and eroded. Climbing at a moderate grade, arrive at the base of bedrock slabs. Climb straight up and then angle up to the left. After a section of thick woods, the trail continues up and left. After another stretch of thick woods, go slightly right and up; then go left on a rising traverse. With several towers visible up ahead, traverse the open slabs to the telephone line, cross over a ground pipe, and turn right and up to gain the top. Pass to the right of a building to reach the old fire tower (erected in 1987; fenced-in, no access) on the summit of Streaked Mtn. ATV trails crisscross the mountaintop, which is adorned by at least nine towers and associated outbuildings. Follow ATV tracks right (east) to more ledge viewpoints.

SINGEPOLE MTN. (1,414 FT.)

Across the valley southwest of Streaked Mtn. is Singepole Mtn. in Paris. Ledges just north of the summit offer excellent views to the north, from the Mahoosuc Range to Mt. Blue.

From the jct. of ME 117 and ME 119, 0.4 mi. east of ME 26 in downtown South Paris, drive east on ME 117. Pass the west end of Brett Hill Rd. on the right at 0.6 mi. Continue on ME 117 for another 1.5 mi. to Brett Hill Rd. (its north end) and turn right. In 0.4 mi., where Brett Hill Rd. turns sharply right, continue straight ahead on dirt Durrell Hill Rd. In 0.1 mi., where Durrell Hill Rd. turns sharply left (a driveway to a house), a cable-gated old road—the trail route—continues straight ahead. Carefully turn around and park off the road in the only spot (two cars, but tight) available at the sharp corner. Do not block any of the roads.

SINGEPOLE MTN. TRAIL (USGS OXFORD QUAD, MTF SINGEPOLE TRAIL, GAZETTEER MAP 11)
From Durrell Hill Rd. roadside parking near gate (800 ft.) to:

Quarry pond (1,335 ft.)	1.2 mi.	535 ft.	0:50
Singepole Mtn. summit (1,414 ft.)	1.5 mi.	614 ft.	1:05

HA At the wire gate across the start of the trail look for a handwritten sign to the left that reads "Cornell." Proceed along the old road, which trends easily uphill. At a jct. in a small clearing at 0.25 mi., bear left. Soon after, pass several rusting vehicles on the left and then a large red barn on the right with several more rusting vehicles in the yard. Continue ahead on the old woods road. At a fork at 0.4 mi., bear right up the rocky, eroded old road. At 0.7 mi., bear right through an open area of exposed bedrock and then bear left where the track reenters the woods. Proceed easily along on the mountain's west shoulder. At a fork at 0.9 mi., stay straight and reach an interesting quarry pond on the left. Go right, around the pond, and continue up toward higher ground on exposed bedrock trail. An informal path from Hall Pond enters from the right. Beyond, pass a large cairn and reenter the woods, following the track into and out of a dip. The track bears right and then quickly left onto a narrow footpath, heading into the open again. Bear left and gradually ascend to the unmarked, open bedrock summit at 1.5 mi. The true summit offers no views, but ledges just 100 ft. to the north and slightly down provide a fine panorama that includes the Mahoosuc Range, Rumford Whitecap, Black Mtn., Streaked Mtn., Jackson Mtn., and Mt. Blue.

PERU–SUMNER–HARTFORD
BALD MTN. (1,695 FT.)
This mountain straddles the Woodstock–Peru town line near Shagg Pond. Bald Mtn. and Little Concord Pond at its western base are part of 64 acres owned by MBPL. Together with neighboring Speckled Mtn. to the east, Bald Mtn. offers an interesting mix of hiking with clifftop and summit views.

From the jct. of ME 26 and ME 219 in West Paris, go east on ME 219 for 4.9 mi. to Tuell Hill Rd. and turn left. At 6.6 mi., where Heath Rd. continues straight, turn left to continue on Tuell Hill Rd. At 7.6 mi., turn left onto Redding Rd. and follow it (road alternates between pavement and dirt) for another 3.5 mi. to Shagg Pond and a boat launch on the right (view of Bald Mtn. and Speckled Mtn. across pond). Continue another 0.5 mi. to two trailhead parking areas on the left.

SEC
7

BALD MTN. TRAIL (USGS MT. ZIRCON QUAD, MTF LITTLE CONCORD POND STATE PARK MAP, GAZETTEER MAP 11)

Cumulative from Redding Rd. (960 ft.) to:

Little Concord Pond jct. (1,110 ft.)	0.6 mi.	150 ft.	0:20
Bald Mtn. Loop (1,670 ft.)	1.2 mi.	710 ft.	0:55
Return to loop jct. via Bald Mtn. Loop	1.5 mi.	780 ft.	1:20
Speckled Mtn. summit (2,181 ft.) via Speckled Mtn. Trail	2.6 mi.	1,441 ft.	2:00

MBPL Blue-blazed Bald Mtn. Trail begins across the road from the lower parking area and follows an old woods road gradually up and over a rise. As Little Concord Pond comes into view, the trail reaches a jct. Straight ahead, a short side trail leads 150 ft. to the pond. Bald Mtn. Trail turns sharply right onto a footpath and then turns sharply right again (here, an unmaintained trail bears left to the pond), climbing over the rocks and up the slope beyond. The trail levels off near the ridge crest just south of the Bald Mtn. summit and soon reaches a jct. with Bald Mtn. Loop Trail. Turn right to follow the yellow-blazed loop, which returns to this same jct. in 0.25 mi. Bald Mtn. Loop proceeds out to and then left along open ledges that offer looks at Shagg Pond below. Ahead at the end of the ledges (view of Speckled Mtn.), bear left to return to the loop jct. at 1.5 mi. Here, turn left to return to the trailhead, or turn right to continue on Speckled Mtn. Trail to Speckled Mtn.

SPECKLED MTN. (2,181 FT.)

Speckled Mtn. lies east of Bald Mtn. in Peru. The route to Speckled Mtn. from the summit ridge of Bald Mtn. drops steeply into a col and then follows the ridge to the Speckled Mtn. summit, where there are extensive views in all directions. Speckled Mtn. can also be climbed from the north via Speckled Mtn. Pasture Trail.

SPECKLED MTN. TRAIL (USGS MT. ZIRCON QUAD, GAZETTEER MAP 11)

From Bald Mtn. Loop jct. (1,670 ft.) to:

Speckled Mtn. summit (2,181 ft.)	1.1 mi.	661 ft.	1:35

MBPL From the jct. with Bald Mtn. Loop and Bald Mtn. Trail, blue-blazed Speckled Mtn. Trail descends steeply via switchbacks to a wide notch. Cross the notch and begin climbing. At 0.3 mi., reach a stone pillar and yellow boundary line (Peru town line). Just ahead, turn sharply right to leave the boundary line. Follow cairns over bedrock trail through the conifers. Crest a knoll at 0.5 mi. and then dip down briefly to another yellow boundary line. At 0.7 mi., begin climbing steeply up the west ridge of the mountain over ledges and slabs. Reach the summit of Speckled Mtn. at 1.1 mi. The old metal pole that marked the top for years now lies on the ground. The excellent views range from Mt. Blue and Mt. Zircon to Old Speck Mtn. and Mt. Washington.

SPECKLED MTN. PASTURE TRAIL
(USGS MT. ZIRCON QUAD, GAZETTEER MAP 11)
Cumulative from Dickvale Rd. (770 ft.) to:

Logging haul road (1,250 ft.)	1.9 mi.	480 ft.	1:10
East Ridge overlook (1,940 ft.)	2.4 mi.	1,170 ft.	1:50
Speckled Mtn. summit (2,181 ft.)	3.3 mi.	1,411 ft.	2:20

NFTM Speckled Mtn. Pasture Trail offers a direct approach to the mountain instead of the route from Bald Mtn.

From ME 108 in West Peru, turn right onto Main St. Go through West Peru, staying on Main St., which becomes Dickvale Rd. in 4.3 mi. Continue on Dickvale Rd. until the pavement ends at 4.8 mi. Park on the side of the road. The route starts to the left behind a gate.

Begin at a gated, grassy road (sign on green gate: "The Searls Orchard Road") and soon reach a structure resembling a doghouse on the right. Another road joins from the left at 0.5 mi. At the 4-way jct. at 0.9 mi., continue straight over the ATV bridge, avoiding the turn to the right. Follow the old forest road/ATV trail, watching for yellow boundary blazes along the stone walls on the right. The wide and conspicuous route turns sharply right at 1.2 mi. and continues to a T intersection with a logging haul road at 1.4 mi. Turn right and proceed on the road to reach Speckled Mtn. Pasture Trail on the left at 1.9 mi. The heavily eroded treadway is marked with yellow boundary blazes and occasional orange flagging. The trail reaches ledges with views at 2.4 mi. and then reenters the woods (sign: "Caution"). After crossing ledges, the trail passes a firepit with a grill and becomes very narrow, tight, and obscure at times, following cairns and occasional flagging. Once the trail passes to the side of a false summit, the cairns and flagging lead briefly downhill on a discreet footpath. Soon the path levels out and then ascends on open rock, following cairns to the summit of Speckled Mtn. at 3.3 mi.

BLACK MTN. (2,135 FT.)
This mountain in Sumner and Peru, just east of Speckled Mtn., is a broad, flat mass with multiple summits extending roughly east to west. A trail ascends to the south summit from the Sumner side. Recent logging has

SEC 7

obliterated much of the old trail, and although marked occasionally with cairns, the ascent is still much trickier than before. Hikers attempting Black Mtn. should be experienced with navigating difficult terrain.

From the jct. of ME 26 and ME 219 in West Paris, drive 7.9 mi. east on ME 219 to Greenwoods Rd. (no street sign, sharp corner, old store [closed]). Reset trip mileage. Turn left and follow Greenwoods Rd. In 1.4 mi., bear left (Labrador Rd. on right). At 1.6 mi., turn left onto Black Mtn. Rd. Ahead at 2.3 mi., where Redding Rd. goes left, bear right to stay on Black Mtn. Rd. At 3.4 mi., pass an old gas station on the left where the road turns to dirt. At 3.7 mi., the road turns sharply left (driveway to right). Park in a grassy spot on the left 0.1 mi. ahead.

BLACK MTN. TRAIL (NFTM; USGS WORTHLEY POND QUAD, GAZETTEER MAP 11)
From Black Mtn. Rd. (800 ft.) to:

Start of trail (922 ft.)	0.2 mi.	122 ft.	0:10
Black Mtn., south summit (2,050 ft.)	1.7 mi.	1,250 ft.	1:30

Walk up the road 0.2 mi., where there is an old woods road on the right; this is the start of Black Mtn Trail. Begin new mileage. Turn right onto the grassy old woods road and pass through a barrier of four large boulders. Soon after crossing a grassy skidder track, enter a large cutover area where multiple skidder tracks converge. Continue straight across and then bear right uphill on a skidder track. Occasional small cairns mark the route. At the top of a rise in a small clearing at 0.2 mi., where a skidder track goes downhill to the left, continue straight into the woods ahead on an old jeep trail.

Multiple erosion berms cross the trail. At 0.3 mi., join a skidder track that enters from below on the left; turn right and climb. Pass a cairn in the trail at 0.4 mi.; just beyond, the trail levels off and there is a pleasant view of the upper slopes of Black Mtn. directly ahead.

At 0.6 mi., at the far end of the cutover area, continue straight ahead on a weedy, overgrown track. At about 0.7 mi. at a somewhat obscure fork, look to the right for a knee-high rock with a cairn on top; bear right here. Just beyond, cross a drainage and follow a path to a grassy skidder track at a T jct.; angle slightly left across the grassy track and then back into the woods ahead. Follow a rough, eroded path to the next skidder track. With alder shrubs on the right and a skidder track on the left going uphill, look for a trail straight into the woods ahead. At its entrance, look for a partially obscured, faded white wooden arrow on a tree on the left side of the trail and a cairn at ground level on the right. From here, follow a relatively well-defined footpath. At 0.8 mi. in a small clearing, reach a fork and bear left (cairn). At 0.9 mi. at a wide-open skidder track, bear right and up (cairn). Climb steeply and then more moderately up the right side of the eroded skidder track, marked by occasional cairns. At 1.0 mi., cross an area of exposed bedrock; continue straight ahead and up into an old cut, following the skidder track and cairns. At 1.1 mi., bear right on the skidder track and, at the top of a rise, leave the skidder track and turn left and up into the woods. (*Note*: This is an important turn! Look for a small cairn marking the turn. Behind you, there is a clear view of the wind towers on a far peak. For further reference, the elevation here is 1,770 ft.)

Locate the narrow footpath and follow it at a moderate grade through a ravine of coniferous woods (small stream below on right). At 1.25 mi., Black Mtn. Trail contours right and then continues left and up. Pass a spruce tree on the right that has a painted orange stripe on it and a cairn at its base. At 1.3 mi., cross a yellow-and-red-blazed boundary line between the towns of Sumner and Peru. Proceed easily upward through the dark green spruce woods, which give the mountain its name. At 1.45 mi., reach the bedrock summit, and at a cairn just ahead, bear right and then quickly left across the open ledges of the flat ridgetop. Look closely for several old carvings (dating to 1889) in the rock on the left, just steps from the trail. The summit ridge is crisscrossed with paths, but views are limited; Labrador Pond lies below and Streaked Mtn. is visible farther south.

SEC 7

BEAR MTN. (1,208 FT.)

This mountain in Hartford offers fine views overlooking Bear Pond and the surrounding countryside of the upper valley of the Androscoggin River.

From the jct. of ME 4 and ME 219 in North Turner, turn west onto ME 219 (Bear Pond Rd.). In 0.4 mi., turn right onto Bean St., and just 0.1 mi. ahead, turn left onto Berry Rd. Follow Berry Rd. for 2.0 mi. to the trailhead parking lot on the right.

BEAR MTN. TRAIL (NFTM; USGS BUCKFIELD QUAD, GAZETTEER MAP 11)

Cumulative from parking area (395 ft.) to:

Bear Mtn. Rd. (445 ft.)	0.3 mi.	50 ft.	0:10
Side trail to Bear Mtn., western summit (915 ft.)	1.0 mi.	520 ft.	0:45
Bear Mtn., main summit (1,208 ft.)	2.0 mi.	813 ft.	1:25

NFTM Bear Mtn. Trail (unmarked) leaves from the north end of the parking lot. Follow a skidder track easily up and then along a contour. At gravel Bear Mtn. Rd., turn right and follow the road past several houses. Ahead, the old road becomes narrower and rockier. At a fork at 0.6 mi., with a gated, grassy road on the left, bear right and up. Pass a spring on the right at 0.85 mi. and reach a side trail, an old jeep track, on the right. This unmarked trail (described below) leads 0.5 mi. to a large erratic and limited views to Bear Pond and beyond to Streaked Mtn.

Continuing straight ahead, the gradually rising road reaches a jct. at 1.2 mi., where a snowmobile trail enters from the left; stay straight. Soon after, a minor track leads left as the wide main road bends to the right. At 1.7 mi. and again at 1.8 mi., minor tracks lead left; stay straight each time. Continue to follow the old road and at 2.0 mi. make the final moderate uphill scramble to the open ledges on the summit of Bear Mtn. Four concrete stanchions of the old fire tower (erected in 1934, removed in the late 1950s) remain. The stunning vista over Little Bear Pond and Bear Pond extends south to Rattlesnake Mtn. and Streaked Mtn. and southwest to Pleasant Mtn. and the White Mountains.

Side trail to Bear Mtn., western summit. This 0.5-mi. side trail rises gradually, following an old jeep track for much of the way. Where the trail bends to the right, step across a culvert. Ahead, climb over exposed bedrock, go right through some trees, and then bear left and up into the open on an obscure track. Pass a cairn and soon reach a large erratic on the western summit. Just beyond, look for a view window to the south. The elevation gain is 205 ft.; time required is 20 min.

SEC 7

ANDROSCOGGIN RIVER VALLEY
MT. ZIRCON (2,245 FT.)

This mountain, straddling the town lines of Milton Township and Peru, rewards hikers with exceptional scenic panoramas from its craggy alpine summit, from the Presidential Range, the Mahoosuc Range, and Oxford Hills to Mt. Blue and the high peaks around Sugarloaf Mtn.

To reach Mt. Zircon from the south, from the jct. of ME 26 and ME 232 in Woodstock, go north on ME 232 for 6.8 mi. to Abbotts Mill. Turn right onto South Rumford Rd. and drive 6.4 mi. to a gated gravel road on the right, by a Rumford Water District tree farm sign. To reach the mountain from the north, from the jct. of US 2 and ME 108 in Rumford, drive west on US 2 for 0.5 mi. Turn left, cross the Androscoggin River, and follow South Rumford Rd. west for 3.2 mi. to the trailhead. Parking for several cars is available along the left side of the gravel road. Otherwise, park along South Rumford Rd. In either case, do not block the gravel road.

MT. ZIRCON TRAIL (RWD; USGS MT. ZIRCON AND RUMFORD QUADS, MTF MT. ZIRCON TRAIL MAP, GAZETTEER MAP 11)

Cumulative from South Rumford Rd. (610 ft.) to:

Old Mt. Zircon Spring Water Company springhouse (1,220 ft.)	1.5 mi.	610 ft.	1:05
Start of trail via old Zircon Rd. (1,350 ft.)	2.1 mi.	740 ft.	1:25
Mt. Zircon summit (2,245 ft.)	2.9 mi.	1,635 ft.	2:15

RWD Begin by walking south on the gravel road (old Zircon Rd.) past the locked red gate and then uphill on an easy but steady grade. The land on both sides is private property, so please keep to the road. At 1.3 mi., avoid the snowmobile trail to the left, cross a brook, and continue on the gravel road. At 1.5 mi., the springhouse of the former Mt. Zircon Spring Water Company is on the right, while below on the right is the piped Mt. Zircon Spring. In another 0.6 mi., nearly to the height-of-land, reach a footpath on the left (sign for Mt. Zircon Trail). Turn off the gravel road here and climb eastward—on a moderate grade at first—toward a saddle between Mt. Zircon and Little Mt. Zircon, at which point the trail turns south and climbs more steeply. The angle eases at 2.7 mi. Finish by ascending over the summit outcroppings to the cairn and former fire tower site atop the peak. (The 60-ft. tower, erected in 1922, was cut down in 1976 but left in place until summer 2022, when it was removed by MFS).

SEC 7

INTRODUCTION

This section describes 93 trails on 26 mountains in southwestern Maine, which includes all of York County and Cumberland County, as well as the southern part of Oxford County. The region is bordered by Casco Bay, Saco Bay, and miles of sandy beaches to the south; the Piscataqua River, the Salmon Falls River, and the state of New Hampshire to the west; an abundance of natural lakes to the north; and low hills to the east. The Saco River slices through, entering Maine at Fryeburg and emptying into the Gulf of Maine at Camp Ellis just south of Old Orchard Beach. The predominant natural feature in this part of the state is Sebago Lake; at 46 sq. mi., it is the second-largest body of water in Maine after Moosehead Lake.

The hills and mountains in this region are relatively low, rising to less than 1,000 ft. near the coast and ranging from 1,000 to 2,000 ft. farther inland. Pleasant Mtn. is the highest peak at 2,001 ft. Many of the hills and mountains are wooded all the way to the top, but others have semi-open or open summits that provide fine views of the surrounding countryside, as well as northwest to the White Mountains and east and southeast to the coast.

SEC 8

This is Maine's most populous region, and many of the trails are well traveled, although others see little use. One-third of the trails listed are on private property, and the rest are on lands protected by land trusts and public and private conservation agencies, including the state of Maine.

GEOGRAPHY

The hills of Pownal and New Gloucester are a few miles northwest of Freeport on Casco Bay. Bradbury Mtn. State Park, one of Maine's five original state parks, protects 800 acres around Bradbury Mtn. (488 ft.). Popular with hikers of all ages and abilities, Bradbury is perhaps Maine's most climbed mountain. Tryon Mtn. (396 ft.), the site of historical feldspar quarries, is connected to Bradbury by an ambitious multiagency conservation corridor that stretches west to Pineland PL. Nearby, Pisgah Hill (380 ft.) rises above the farmland along the Pownal–New Gloucester town line; it's a property of Royal River Conservation Trust. The town of Freeport owns Hedgehog Mtn. (308 ft.), an oasis of woods and trails close to the hustle and bustle of downtown. Just west of the din of the Maine Turnpike/I-95 corridor in Gray, the extensive network of trails on Libby Hill (488 ft.) offers miles of peace and quiet. The ridgeline of Rattlesnake Mtn. (1,040 ft.) in Casco offers fine views of Crescent Lake, Panther Pond, and on to the big blue waters of Sebago Lake. Pismire Mtn. (834 ft.) in Raymond, just east of Crescent Lake, is the natural focal point of Raymond Community Forest.

Douglas Mtn. (1,405 ft.) in Sebago is the highest of the four peaks of the Saddleback Hills, which rise immediately west of Sebago Lake. An old stone tower on top of Douglas rewards hikers with impressive views. Just north of Peabody Pond in South Bridgton, a preserve owned by Loon Echo Land Trust encompasses Bald Pate Mtn. (1,150 ft.), with its pitch-pine woods, pretty meadows, and granite ledges. Pleasant Mtn. (2,001 ft.), its distinctive ridgeline extending for 4 mi. across the Denmark–Bridgton town line (includes Bald Peak at 1,926 ft.), rises abruptly from the comparatively flat countryside around Moose Pond just south of US 302. Six popular hiking trails are on the slopes of Pleasant Mtn., a peak that offers attractive vistas of the White Mountains. In Fryeburg, the summit ledges on Mt. Tom (1,066 ft.), partially owned by The Nature Conservancy, provide excellent lookout points over the lovely valley of the wide and winding Saco River.

Just east of the New Hampshire state line, Jockey Cap (619 ft.) is a massive granite dome on the outskirts of Fryeburg that rises nearly 200 ft. above surrounding woods and fields, offering outstanding views for a small amount of time and effort. West of ME 113/5, the open ledges of Peary Mtn. (956 ft.) in Brownfield afford looks at the White Mountains and the mountains of western Maine. A little farther south in Brownfield, the mass of Burnt Meadow Mtn. (1,570 ft.) consists of three main summits and two lesser summits, all of nearly equal height. Deep cols separate Stone Mtn. (1,615 ft.) from the north and south peaks of Burnt Meadow Mtn. Continuing south on ME 113/5, in the village of Hiram, the extensive open ledges of Mt. Cutler (1,238 ft.) reward hikers with fine sights of nearby hills and farmlands, the Saco River valley to the south, and the White Mountains to the north. Recent preservation efforts have permanently protected Mt. Cutler and its trails. The precipitous cliffs on Bald Ledge (1,190 ft.) in Porter yield a fabulous vista eastward over Colcord Pond to the pretty hills and woods of north-central York County.

In Limerick and Limington, Sawyer Mtn. (1,226 ft.), the dominant natural feature of the Sawyer Mtn. Highlands, is part of the largest unfragmented block of undeveloped forestland in York and Cumberland counties. Knox Mtn. (824 ft.), in Newfield, and Abbott Mtn. (1,079 ft.), in Shapleigh, are amid the expansive Vernon S. Walker WMA, which spans more than 5,600 acres across the towns of Newfield, Limerick, and Shapleigh. East of the WMA, Ossipee Hill (1,066 ft.) rises high over Little Ossipee Lake, its summit ridge topped with an old wooden fire tower. The middle and north peaks of Bauneg Beg Mtn. (864 ft. and 828 ft. respectively), part of an 89-acre conservation property in North Berwick owned by Great Works Regional Land Trust, are the only major mountaintops in southern York County without a communications tower. The Mt. Agamenticus Conservation Region, a cooperative of six landowners, encompasses more than 10,000 acres of coastal woods and hills in York and South Berwick in southern York County. The central feature of these lands is the southernmost mountain in this guide, Mt. Agamenticus (693 ft.), which rises distinctively above the coastal plain. Just northeast of Mt. Agamenticus is Second Hill (558 ft.), and to the east, Third Hill (522 ft.). The mountain's geographic location makes it a rare mixing ground for a number of southern and northern plant and animal species at the limits of their ranges.

SEC 8

ROAD ACCESS

Trailheads are scattered far and wide across the three counties of southwestern Maine: Cumberland, York, and Oxford. The main travel corridor between Portland and Brunswick is I-295. From this major highway, local and state roads lead to the trails in Freeport, Pownal, and New Gloucester. The Maine Turnpike/I-95 route gets close to the trails in Gray and those in the area of Mt. Agamenticus in York. ME 11 slices across the region from Raymond and Sebago Lake to Lebanon on the New Hampshire border; this major artery provides access to many trails. US 302 and ME 113/5 are busy transportation routes that connect the urban environs of Portland to Fryeburg; these roads get visitors within striking distance of nearly half of the mountains in the area. ME 4 is an important north–south highway through central York County.

CAMPING

In addition to at least 67 privately operated campgrounds, camping is available in this region at Bradbury Mtn. State Park in Pownal and Sebago Lake State Park in Casco. Both parks provide showers, restrooms, and other amenities. No backcountry camping is available.

SUGGESTED HIKES

■ Easy
BRADBURY MTN.

| RT via Summit Trail | 0.6 mi. | 224 ft. | 0:25 |

This is the shortest and most direct route to the expansive open ledges atop Bradbury Mtn. See Summit Trail, p. 350.

SEC 8

BALD PATE MTN.

| LP via Bob Chase Scenic Loop and South Face Loop Trail | 1.4 mi. | 300 ft. | 0:50 |

Hike through pitch-pine woods to granite ledges atop Bald Pate Mtn., where there are views of Peabody Pond and Sebago Lake. To begin, see Bob Chase Scenic Loop, p. 361.

JOCKEY CAP

| LP via Jockey Cap Trail | 0.6 mi. | 195 ft. | 0:25 |

Scamper to the top of this amazing granite dome for outstanding scenery. Use the bronze profile of the surrounding mountains (a monument to the polar explorer Robert Peary) to identify all the peaks in a 360-degree arc. See Jockey Cap Trail, p. 371.

BALD LEDGE

RT via Bald Ledge Trail	1.4 mi.	320 ft.	0:50

This trip rewards hikers with a fabulous vista eastward over Colcord Pond to the pretty hills and woods of north-central York County. See Bald Ledge Trail, p. 384.

MT. AGAMENTICUS

LP via Ring Trail, Blueberry Bluff Trail, and Big A Trail	2.4 mi.	390 ft.	1:00

Climb to the grassy open summit of Mt. Agamenticus and make a circuit around the peak, enjoying the observation decks and interpretive signs along the way. To begin, see Ring Trail, p. 391.

■ **Moderate**

RATTLESNAKE MTN.

RT via Bri-Mar Trail	1.7 mi.	575 ft.	1:10

Revel in the sights of Crescent Pond, Panther Pond, and Sebago Lake from high on the ridgeline of Rattlesnake Mtn. See Bri-Mar Trail, p. 357.

DOUGLAS MTN.

LP via Eagle Scout Trail, Nature Loop, Ledges Trail, Douglas Mtn. Rd., and Ledges Rd.	2.4 mi.	405 ft.	1:25

Hike up to the old stone observation tower (1925) atop Douglas Mtn. for impressive vistas ranging from Sebago Lake to the White Mountains. To begin, see Eagle Scout Trail, p. 359.

MT. TOM

RT via West Ridge Trail	3.4 mi.	715 ft.	2:05

Hike across land owned by The Nature Conservancy to the summit ledges of Mt. Tom and a lookout over the Saco River to Pleasant Mtn. See West Ridge Trail, p. 369.

SEC 8

BURNT MEADOW MTN.

LP via Burnt Meadow Trail and Twin Brook Trail	3.3 mi.	1,130 ft.	2:15

Make a big loop over this scenic mountaintop for fine views of the Saco River valley, the White Mountains, and the surrounding hills and mountains. To begin, see Burnt Meadow Trail, p. 372.

MT. CUTLER

LP via North Trail, Ridge Walk, Northwest Trail, and Link Trail	1.7 mi.	740 ft.	1:15

This excellent loop on Mt. Cutler rewards hikers with a series of far-reaching vistas from ledges along the way. To begin, see North Trail, p. 378.

■ Strenuous
PLEASANT MTN.

RT via Southwest Ridge Trail	5.8 mi.	2,000 ft.	3:55

Pass an interesting wooden tepee on this long and scenic route to pleasant views of Moose Pond. From the main summit and fire tower, sights to the west include Fryeburg, the Saco River valley, and numerous ponds. See Southwest Ridge (MacKay Pasture) Trail, p. 366.

SEC 8

SAWYER MTN.

RT via Sherwood Libby Trail and Old Sawyer Mtn. Rd.	4.3 mi.	1,010 ft.	2:40

Get a clear look at the largest unfragmented block of undeveloped forestland in York and Cumberland counties. To begin, see Sherwood Libby Trail, p. 383.

TRAIL DESCRIPTIONS
BRADBURY MTN. STATE PARK

A network of pleasant foot trails and multiuse trails wends through the wooded 800 acres of Bradbury Mtn. State Park. The federal government acquired Bradbury Mtn. in 1939, and soon after, it became one of Maine's five original state parks, along with Sebago Lake, Aroostook, Mt. Blue,

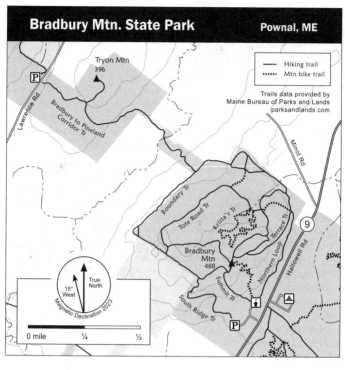

and Lake St. George. The park's campground is just north of the park entrance on the east side of ME 9.

BRADBURY MTN. (488 FT.)

The extensive open ledges on the summit of Bradbury Mtn. in namesake Bradbury Mtn. State Park yield excellent views to Casco Bay and the Portland skyline.

To reach the park, take I-95 to Exit 22 in Freeport. Drive west on ME 136/125 and immediately turn left onto Pownal Rd. Drive 4.0 mi. to Pownal Center and the jct. with ME 9 (Pownal Rd. becomes Elmwood Rd.). Turn right on ME 9 and go 0.8 mi. to the main entrance of Bradbury Mtn. State Park on the left. Past the entrance station (fee), the park road bends to the right and leads to the main trailhead parking lot, a picnic area, and pit toilets.

SUMMIT TRAIL (AMC BRADBURY MTN. STATE PARK MAP)
From main trailhead parking lot (265 ft.) to:

Bradbury Mtn. summit (488 ft.)	0.3 mi.	223 ft.	0:15

MBPL Summit Trail offers the shortest and most direct route to the top of Bradbury Mtn. It leaves the main trailhead parking lot and follows a rock-lined route through the pines of the picnic area. The white-blazed trail climbs easily through mostly hemlock woods and then ascends rock steps past a large, horizontally fractured ledge outcropping on the right. A final set of rock steps winds up and right to the large and open summit ledge, which provides broad views to the south and southeast.

NORTHERN LOOP TRAIL (AMC BRADBURY MTN. STATE PARK MAP)
From main trailhead parking lot (265 ft.) to:

Bradbury Mtn. summit (488 ft.)	1.1 mi.	224 ft.	0:40

MBPL Northern Loop Trail follows the eastern base of Bradbury Mtn. before swinging around to ascend its northeast slope. This blue-blazed trail leaves from the east end of the main trailhead parking lot, going between the pit toilets. Just past the information kiosk, cross a wide footbridge and then bear left on a spacious path. In 350 ft., Switchback Trail departs left. Continuing on Northern Loop Trail, look for remnants of an old feldspar quarry to the left. At 0.15 mi., the stone walls of an old cattle pound are on the right. Continue easily along the base of the mountain to meet Terrace Trail on the left at 0.45 mi. (map post 1). Just 20 ft. beyond this jct., Ski Trail departs left. Bear right here to stay on Northern Loop Trail. At 0.5 mi., Boundary Trail leaves to the right (map post 2); continue straight ahead on Northern Loop Trail. Reach a 4-way jct. and a bench at 0.7 mi. (map post 3). Here, white-blazed Tote Road Trail leaves right, and a short connector to Ski Trail leaves left. In another 100 ft., Ski Trail departs to the left (map post 4). Continue straight on Northern Loop Trail, which reaches the lower jct. of red-blazed Bluff Trail on the left at 0.8 mi. (map post 5). A pleasant viewpoint is 100 ft. along Bluff Trail. Northern Loop Trail turns to the right, climbing easily to the upper jct. of Bluff Trail on the left at 1.0 mi. (map post 6). Soon, Switchback Trail enters from the left (map post 7), and 10 ft. after that, Tote Road Trail enters from the right. The summit ledges atop Bradbury Mtn. are immediately beyond at 1.1 mi.

TOTE ROAD TRAIL (AMC BRADBURY MTN. STATE PARK MAP)
Cumulative from main trailhead parking lot (265 ft.) to:

Start of Tote Road Trail (365 ft.) via Northern Loop Trail	0.7 mi.	100 ft.	0:20
Bradbury Mtn. summit (488 ft.)	1.8 mi.	224 ft.	1:00

SEC 8

MBPL White-blazed Tote Road Trail diverges from Northern Loop Trail (map post 3) at a point 0.7 mi. from the main trailhead parking lot. From there, head west on a contour and quickly pass the first and second entrances to Krista's Loop, a mountain-bike trail. Crest a ridge and descend gently to a connector trail on the right at 0.2 mi. (map post 17); this short path leads north to orange-blazed Boundary Trail. Ahead on Tote Road Trail, cross a dip and then climb easily southwest around the back of Bradbury Mtn. The mostly level trail leads to a bench at 0.6 mi. Trend southeast up to a connector trail at 0.7 mi. (map post 15); this connector goes straight up a rooty pitch to join with Boundary Trail. Tote Road Trail turns sharply left at this jct. Ahead, cross a wide boardwalk and then follow the gently rolling trail to a log bench. Beyond, reach the jct. with Northern Loop Trail at 1.1 mi. The summit ledges are 200 ft. to the right.

SKI TRAIL (AMC BRADBURY MTN. STATE PARK MAP)

MBPL This short, wide route, an old downhill ski trail that sported a rope tow for a time in the 1940s, is a shortcut across a section of Northern Loop Trail. Ski Trail is 0.15 mi. long and gains 90 ft. in elevation. Ski Trail begins at map post 1 and runs to map posts 3 and 4.

TERRACE TRAIL (AMC BRADBURY MTN. STATE PARK MAP)
Cumulative from main trailhead parking lot (265 ft.) to:

Start of Terrace Trail (285 ft.) via Northern Loop Trail	0.5 mi.	20 ft.	0:15
Bradbury Mtn. summit (488 ft.) via Bluff Trail and Northern Loop Trail	1.0 mi.	224 ft.	0:35

MBPL Gray-blazed Terrace Trail leaves left from Northern Loop Trail (map post 1) at a point 0.45 mi. from the main trailhead parking lot. In 250 ft., go through a gap in an old stone wall. Slab across the east face of Bradbury Mtn. on a wide path that passes the remains of rock-walled terraces used to cultivate grapes back in the 1800s. Ahead, Terrace Trail climbs moderately to its end at the jct. of Bluff Trail (map post 8). To continue to the top of Bradbury Mtn., bear left on red-blazed Bluff Trail. Follow it to Northern Loop Trail and the summit ledges.

SEC 8

BLUFF TRAIL (AMC BRADBURY MTN. STATE PARK MAP)
Cumulative from main trailhead parking lot (265 ft.) to:

Start of Bluff Trail (425 ft.) via Northern Loop Trail	0.8 mi.	160 ft.	0:30
Bradbury Mtn. summit (488 ft.) via Northern Loop Trail	1.0 mi.	224 ft.	0:35

MBPL From Northern Loop Trail (map post 5), red-blazed Bluff Trail climbs 100 ft. to a ledge viewpoint on the left, reached by a 30-ft. spur. Beyond, after a quick, short drop, Terrace Trail enters from the left (map post 8). Bear left through a gap in a stone wall and continue to the end of Bluff Trail at its jct. with Northern Loop Trail (map post 6). Turn left to reach the summit ledges on atop Bradbury Mtn. in another 0.1 mi.

BOUNDARY TRAIL (AMC BRADBURY MTN. STATE PARK MAP)
Cumulative from main trailhead parking lot (265 ft.) to:

Start of Boundary Trail (290 ft.) via Northern Loop Trail	0.5 mi.	35 ft.	0:15
Bradbury Mtn. summit (488 ft.)	2.2 mi.	254 ft.	1:15

MBPL Follow Northern Loop Trail to the start of Boundary Trail on the right at 0.5 mi. (map post 2). Orange-blazed Boundary Trail soon reaches a stone wall and travels left along it. Ahead, the trail bears left away from the wall, crosses a wide boardwalk, and reaches a connector trail, which enters from the left (map post 9). Turn right here and soon reach a green-blazed connector trail and map post 16. Continue straight ahead to stay on Boundary Trail. After a wet area on the left, pass map post 10 and return to the stone boundary wall. Pass a gate in the wall, with a meadow just below. Beyond, where an unnamed trail continues straight, turn sharply right around a corner in the stone wall. Cross a footbridge over an intermittent stream.

At 1.2 mi. from the main trailhead parking lot, reach a jct. Here, Bradbury to Pineland Corridor Trail (sign) enters from the right, and another connector trail leaves left. Continue straight through the jct., climbing a moderate pitch along the stone wall. At 1.3 mi., pass a split log bench on the right. At 1.6 mi., a connector trail leaves left (map post 11). Just ahead, turn sharply left at the corner of two boundary walls. Pass another connector trail on the left (map post 12) and continue along the park's southern boundary. Climb a short, moderate pitch and cross three sections of boardwalk (two long, one short). Soon after another connector trail (map post 13) enters from the left, South Ridge Trail joins from the right (map post 14). Bear left to stay on Boundary Trail, and follow it easily to the top of Bradbury Mtn., 2.2 mi. from the main trailhead parking lot.

SOUTH RIDGE TRAIL (AMC BRADBURY MTN. STATE PARK MAP)
From group campsite parking lot (210 ft.) to:

Bradbury Mtn. summit (488 ft.) via Boundary Trail	0.7 mi.	279 ft.	0:30

MBPL Red-blazed South Ridge Trail starts from the far (west) end of the group campsite parking lot, 0.1 mi. from the park entrance station. In 750 ft., climb a wooden staircase with a handrail. Beyond, the ascent is moderate over sections of bedrock trail. At 0.2 mi., bear left and climb another wooden staircase. Make a rising traverse to the next staircase. At 0.3 mi., reach a jct. Here, a shortcut to the summit leaves right; continue straight ahead to the South Ridge Overlook. At a signpost, an impressive 30-ft. cliff face is in the woods to the right; to the left, a side trail leads 150 ft. to the overlook and view. From the signpost, climb rock steps up and left around the cliff face. On top, the summit shortcut trail enters from the right. South Ridge Trail continues to its end at Boundary Trail, marked by a stone wall and map post 14. Turn right here to continue 0.2 mi. to the top of Bradbury Mtn. via Boundary Trail.

FREEPORT–POWNAL– NEW GLOUCESTER–GRAY
HEDGEHOG MTN. (308 FT.)

This mountain is part of a 195-acre property owned by the town of Freeport. A 5-mi. network of trails, maintained by the town with volunteer help, is on the slopes of the mountain, the highest point in town.

From I-95, Exit 22 in Freeport, proceed west briefly on ME 136/125 to Pownal Rd. (sign for Bradbury Mtn. State Park). Turn left here and go 1.3 mi. Turn left onto Hedgehog Mtn. Rd. (signs for Town of Freeport Transfer and Recycling Facility, Hedgehog Mtn., and Town of Freeport) and proceed 0.2 mi. to trailhead parking on the left, immediately before the transfer station gate (sign, kiosk).

HEDGEHOG MTN. TRAILS (USGS YARMOUTH AND FREEPORT QUADS, TOWN OF FREEPORT–HEDGEHOG MTN. TRAILS MAP, GAZETTEER MAP 6)
Cumulative from Hedgehog Mtn. Rd. (160 ft.) to:

Hedgehog Mtn. viewpoint (220 ft.)	0.4 mi.	120 ft.	0:15
Complete loop via Hedgehog Trail, Summit Trail, and Stonewall Trail	1.2 mi.	200 ft.	0:40

TOF Hedgehog Trail begins to the right of the kiosk. Winding around the kiosk, the wide, level trail turns right to cross a footbridge and soon crosses a second footbridge. With a stone wall on the right and an informal path straight ahead, Hedgehog Trail bears sharply left to reach a T jct. Turn sharply right to continue along the base of the ledges, which are on the left. At a fork and trail sign at 0.25 mi., where Hedgehog Trail continues straight ahead, bear left, and in 30 ft., turn left onto Summit Trail, which climbs through the mossy ledges and then along a stone wall to a jct. Here, Stonewall Trail continues straight; turn left to stay on Summit Trail.

SEC
8

Climb easily along the ridge, level off, and then descend gradually to reach a granite bench and viewpoint on a bedrock outcropping at 0.4 mi. A profile display depicts the mountains in sight, from nearby Bradbury Mtn. to Pleasant Mtn. and beyond, to the high peaks of the Northern Presidential Range in the White Mountains.

Drop down off the ledge and continue through the woods over the north shoulder of the hill; then trend gradually down the south slope to a jct. at 0.7 mi. Here, Wentworth Trail and Soule Rd. are to the left, while Stonewall Trail is to the right. Turn right on Stonewall Trail and ascend along a beautiful old stone wall. Pass Foundation Trail on the left and at 0.9 mi. rejoin Summit Trail. Retrace your steps to the trailhead via Summit Trail and then Hedgehog Trail.

TRYON MTN. (396 FT.)

This low, wooded mountain in Pownal is named for the Tryon family, whose roots in the area date back to 1800. The remains of an old feldspar mining operation are on top. The mountain is reached by way of Bradbury to Pineland Corridor Trail, which connects a series of conservation lands between Bradbury Mtn. State Park and Pineland PL across the towns of Pownal, New Gloucester, Gray, and North Yarmouth.

From I-95, Exit 22 in Freeport, drive west briefly on ME 136/125 to Pownal Rd. Turn left onto Pownal Rd. and follow it for 2.4 mi. to its jct. with Verrill Rd. Here, Pownal Rd. becomes Elmwood Rd. Continue on Elmwood Rd. for 2.0 mi. to its jct. with ME 9 (convenience store on left, sign for Bradbury Mtn. State Park on right). Continue straight through the intersection (still on Elmwood Rd.) and drive an additional 2.3 mi. Turn right onto Lawrence Rd. and follow it for 0.9 mi. to trailhead parking on the left (sign, kiosk).

BRADBURY TO PINELAND CORRIDOR TRAIL
(AMC BRADBURY MTN. STATE PARK MAP)
Cumulative from Lawrence Rd. trailhead (190 ft.) to:

Tryon Mtn. side trail (360 ft.)	0.3 mi.	170 ft.	0:15
Tyron Mtn. summit area, old feldspar quarries (390 ft.)	0.5 mi.	200 ft.	0:20
Bradbury Mtn. State Park, Boundary Trail (250 ft.)	1.4 mi.	325 ft.	1:00

RRCT The trail to Tryon Mtn. begins on the opposite side of Lawrence Rd. about 100 ft. south of the parking area. Follow an old woods road gently uphill to a signed jct. Bear left here, cross a dip, and pass right of a wet area to reach another old woods road and, just ahead, a side trail to the top of Tryon Mtn. The green-blazed side trail follows an old road 0.15 mi. to the old feldspar quarries atop the mountain.

Back at the main trail, turn left (east) and soon descend to cross a stone wall. Ahead at a fork, a faint trail goes right; continue left to follow the wide main track. Descend a moderate slope of crushed rock. Where the valley narrows, turn sharply right across a low, often wet area. Turn up the other side of the valley and, ahead at a woods road, turn left to cross a footbridge over Thoit's Brook. Soon after the bridge, bear left and then right onto a footpath. Wind upslope to a stone wall marking the northwestern boundary of Bradbury Mtn. State Park. If desired, turn right here to continue on Boundary Trail to reach the summit of Bradbury Mtn. in another 1.0 mi.

PISGAH HILL (380 FT.)

This wooded ridge in New Gloucester is part of Pisgah Hill Preserve, a nearly 300-acre public landscape that protects a wide variety of wildlife habitats, mixed forests, and old quarries. A loop hike offers a clear look around the conservation property, which is owned by Royal River Conservation Trust.

From the jct. of Elmwood Rd. and ME 9 in Pownal, travel west on Elmwood Rd. for 2.4 mi. Turn left onto Allen Rd. and follow it for 0.5 mi. Turn right onto Chadsey Rd. In 0.5 mi., at the Pownal–New Gloucester town line, dirt Chadsey Rd. becomes paved Dougherty Rd. The trailhead parking lot is on the right (sign, kiosk) in another 0.4 mi.

PISGAH HILL LOOP (USGS NORTH POWNAL QUAD, RRCT PISGAH HILL PRESERVE MAP, GAZETTEER MAP 5)
From Dougherty Rd. trailhead (95 ft.) to:

Pisgah Hill summit (380 ft.)	0.6 mi.	295 ft.	0:25
Complete lollipop loop	1.3 mi.	295 ft.	0:45

SEC 8

RRCT Pass a wooden fence and hike up along the edge of the field next to the fence to enter the woods beyond. Descend to cross a metal bridge over Quarry Brook. At 0.2 mi., reach the loop jct. and go right to hike the loop counterclockwise, ascending through mixed forest. At 0.3 mi., turn sharply left in a semi-open area of ledges and boulders and climb bedrock trail through pine, oak, and juniper. Traverse a large open ledge and then drop off its back side. Proceed easily on the level for a distance before climbing higher on bedrock trail at a short, moderate pitch. Reach the wooded high point on Pisgah Hill at 0.6 mi., marked by a cairn with a rebar stake in it. Descend next to a property boundary, passing through pleasant groves of mature hemlock and pine. At 1.0 mi., a side trail leads to private land; please continue to follow RRCT trail markers. Close the loop at 1.1 mi. and turn right to return to the trailhead.

LIBBY HILL (488 FT.)

Libby Hill Forest in Gray is home to wooded Libby Hill and a pleasant network of trails on about 200 acres. Founded in 1999, the trail system was created on land donated by descendants of the Libby family and is now owned by School Administrative District 15, the town of Gray, Gray Community Endowment, and Royal River Conservation Trust. The trails are maintained by volunteers and the town of Gray. In 2022, RRCT created the new 147-acre Thayer Brook Preserve adjacent to this trail system, which provides additional hiking opportunities and another trailhead.

The trailhead for Libby Hill Forest is adjacent to Gray–New Gloucester Middle School on Libby Hill Rd. From the Maine Turnpike, Exit 63 in Gray, drive north on ME 26A for 1.5 mi. Turn left on Libby Hill Rd. and drive 0.25 mi. to trailhead parking on the right (kiosk).

LIBBY HILL LOOP (USGS GRAY QUAD, LHFT LIBBY HILL FOREST RECREATION AREA MAP, GAZETTEER MAP 5)
From Libby Hill Rd. (320 ft.) to:

Complete loop via Lynx, Moose Odyssey, Harold Libbey, and Outback trails	3.6 mi.	400 ft.	2:00

LHFT This hike combines blue-blazed Lynx Trail, white-blazed Moose Odyssey Trail, red-blazed Harold Libbey Trail, and yellow-blazed Outback Trail. From the parking area, cross to the school, and then bear right to the start of Lynx Trail, which soon merges right with Moose Odyssey Trail, which crosses a snowmobile/ATV trail. In 400 ft., Moose Odyssey Trail turns left to cross over to where Lynx Trail breaks off again. Moose Odyssey Trail climbs Libby Hill, and beyond the hill crest, descends to a jct. Here, turn left onto Harold Libbey Trail, which leads down the back of Libby Hill, passing glacial boulders and little canyons. At the next jct., Outback Trail leaves to the left and leads through the most remote portion of Libby Hill Forest. Soon reach Thayer Brook, cross a bridge over the brook, and quickly arrive at the loop jct.; bear left to hike clockwise.

Outback Trail next climbs a ridge and then descends to a marsh and a viewpoint over it. As the trail leaves the marsh area, pass the jct. with Ridge Runner Trail, which leads into Thayer Brook Preserve. Outback Trail regains the ridge and returns to the Outback loop jct. and back to Harold Libbey Trail. Bear left on Harold Libbey Trail and climb a "horseback," or esker, to pass a large boulder known as Whale Rock. Continue on to meet Lynx Trail, which enters from the right. Ahead, Harold Libbey Trail passes Ghost Trail (enters on the left) and soon meets Moose Odyssey Trail. Turn right onto Moose Odyssey Trail and at the next jct., bear left toward the summit of Libby Hill. At a long rock wall, bear right to pass through it. (To the left, it's a short walk to Secret Garden of the Woods, a perennial garden created out of the foundation of James Libby's old homestead.) Continue on Moose Odyssey Trail; then bear left on Lynx Trail to return to the trailhead.

SEBAGO LAKE AREA
RATTLESNAKE MTN. (1,040 FT.)

This mountain, in Raymond and Casco, offers fine ridge walking with views of Sebago Lake to the south and the White Mountains to the north. The mountain is privately owned by the Huntress family, which has maintained Bri-Mar Trail to the top of the mountain since 1965. The trail is named in memory of Huntress family members Brian and Marlene, who enjoyed this hike.

The trailhead in Raymond is on ME 85, 0.9 mi. south of its jct. with ME 11 in the hamlet of Webb's Mills in Raymond, or 7.1 mi. north of its jct. with US 302 in Raymond. Parking is in a small fenced-in area at the edge of a field. Please observe the rules posted on the green-and-white sign at the start of the trail. (*Note*: No dogs are allowed, and the trail is closed from April 1 to May 1 each spring.)

BRI-MAR TRAIL (USGS RAYMOND QUAD, GAZETTEER MAP 5)
From ME 85 trailhead (465 ft.) to:

Rattlesnake Mtn. main summit (1,040 ft.)	1.7 mi.	575 ft.	1:10

Huntress Family Bri-Mar Trail crosses a field and enters the forest, following a woods road for a short distance. The road forks, but both forks rejoin ahead. Soon bear right onto a foot trail and, following red markers, climb steadily up the hillside. The path levels off atop the ridge and reaches several lookouts with views south to Crescent Lake and Panther Pond. Ahead, a faint side trail marked by red dots leads right (north) 100 yd. to a small clearing with limited views through the trees to Mt. Washington and the Presidential Range. Climb over a rock knob to reach the wooded summit and the end of Bri-Mar Trail. (*Note*: An unnamed trail continues west to ledges with views to Sebago Lake and then descends the southwest side of the mountain, following blue and orange flagging, but it is obscure in places, is steep and rough, and is not recommended.)

SEC 8

DOUGLAS MTN. (1,405 FT.)

Douglas Mtn. in Sebago is the highest of the four peaks of the Saddleback Hills, which rise immediately west of Sebago Lake. The town of Sebago owns 169 acres on the mountain, where four trails offer a little more than 3 mi. of tramping. Local stewards and volunteers maintain the preserve

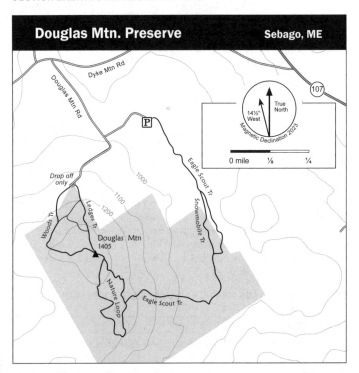

Douglas Mtn. Preserve

Sebago, ME

and its trails and charge a small fee to help support these activities. The summit features a stone observation tower built in 1925 and a large boulder with the Latin inscription *non sibi sed omnibus*, which translates to "not for one but for all." The top of Douglas Mtn. affords panoramas of the surrounding countryside, the Presidential Range, Pleasant Mtn., and the Atlantic Ocean.

From the jct. of ME 113 and ME 11/107 in East Baldwin, turn north onto ME 11/107. In 1.8 mi., ME 11 bears right. Continue on ME 107, and at 6.4 mi., reach Dyke Mtn. Rd. Turn left here (small sign: "Douglas Mtn.—1 mile"). In 1.0 mi., turn left onto Douglas Mtn. Rd., drive 0.2 mi., and turn left onto Ledges Rd. Just ahead is the parking lot for all trails (sign, kiosk).

Four trails lead to the top of Douglas Mtn. Eagle Scout Trail leaves from the parking lot and joins Nature Loop not far from the summit. To gain access to Ledges Trail and Woods Trail, walk 0.2 mi. on Ledges Rd. to Douglas Mtn. Rd. and follow it uphill for 0.2 mi. to the upper trailhead. Vehicles may drive to this point to drop off hikers, but no parking is allowed.

EAGLE SCOUT TRAIL (AMC DOUGLAS MTN. PRESERVE MAP)
Cumulative from Ledges Rd. parking lot (1,000 ft.) to:

Nature Loop (1,250 ft.)	1.3 mi.	250 ft.	0:45
Douglas Mtn. summit (1,405 ft.) via Nature Loop	1.5 mi.	405 ft.	0:55

TOS Eagle Scout Trail (orange markers) enters the woods and alternately follows a snowmobile trail/woods road and footpath, crossing several small brooks and wet areas. At the sign "To Nature Loop," Eagle Scout Trail leaves the woods road and climbs steeply to a jct. with Nature Loop (pink markers). To the right, Nature Loop leads 0.25 mi. to the summit of Douglas Mtn. and the stone tower.

NATURE LOOP (AMC DOUGLAS MTN. PRESERVE MAP)
Cumulative from Douglas Mtn. summit (1,405 ft.) to:

Eagle Scout Trail (1,250 ft.)	0.5 mi.	45 ft.	0:15
Complete loop	0.8 mi.	195 ft.	0:25

TOS From the summit tower on Douglas Mtn., head east into the woods and then turn south to reach the loop jct. of Nature Loop in 200 ft. Turn right to follow the loop counterclockwise. The pink-blazed trail descends through a hemlock grove before leveling off. Just beyond a wet area, bear sharply left, make a short climb, and then level off. (Ahead, limited views are possible from a ledge on the right.) Descend through hemlocks and then swing north to meet Eagle Scout Trail, which enters from the right at 0.5 mi. Beyond, drop easily into a shallow ravine and then climb a short, moderate-to-steep pitch to the Nature Loop jct. Continue to the Douglas Mtn. summit and tower, at 0.8 mi.

SEC 8

LEDGES TRAIL (AMC DOUGLAS MTN. PRESERVE MAP)
Cumulative from Ledges Rd. parking lot (1,000 ft.) to:

Upper trailhead and drop-off point (1,150 ft.)	0.4 mi.	200 ft.	0:15
Douglas Mtn. summit (1,405 ft.)	0.9 mi.	455 ft.	0:40

TOS This wide and eroded trail (yellow markers) is the shortest and most popular route to the summit. From the upper trailhead and drop-off point 0.4 mi. from the Ledges Rd. parking lot, proceed past two stone pillars, and follow slabs and ledges 0.5 mi. to the top of Douglas Mtn. Pass two white-blazed connector trails leading west to Woods Trail en route.

WOODS TRAIL (AMC DOUGLAS MTN. PRESERVE MAP)
Cumulative from Ledges Rd. parking lot (1,000 ft.) to:

Upper trailhead and drop-off point (1,150 ft.)	0.4 mi.	200 ft.	0:15
Douglas Mtn. summit (1,405 ft.)	1.2 mi.	455 ft.	0:45

TOS This green-blazed trail leaves the left end of the upper trailhead and drop-off point, 0.4 mi. from the Ledges Rd. parking lot. Woods Trail follows an old woods road for 300 ft. before turning left uphill. Soon, pass an old concrete tank on the left and then pass a white-blazed connector leading east to Ledges Trail. Above, bear sharply left to avoid private property. The final part of the climb trends easily up the west ridge of the mountain.

LOON ECHO LAND TRUST
PISMIRE MTN. (834 FT.)

A portion of this mountain in Raymond is in Raymond Community Forest, 356 acres of mixed woods and natural communities owned and managed by Loon Echo Land Trust. Outlooks high on the mountain offer stunning views west over Crescent Lake to Rattlesnake Mtn. and beyond, to Sebago Lake. Pismire Bluff Trail and Highlands Loop are hiking-only routes that travel over the southern slopes of Pismire Mtn. A short section of Spiller Homestead Loop, a mountain-biking and hiking trail, provides access to these routes.

From the jct. of US 302 and ME 11 in Naples, drive north on ME 11 for 7.0 mi. to Edwards Rd. Turn right onto Edwards Rd. and proceed 0.9 mi. to where it merges with Conesca Rd. Continue on Conesca Rd. for 0.7 mi. to trailhead parking on the right (sign, kiosk).

PISMIRE BLUFF TRAIL (USGS RAYMOND QUAD, LELT RAYMOND COMMUNITY FOREST TRAIL MAP, GAZETTEER MAP 5)
From Conesca Rd. trailhead (415 ft.) to:

Start of trail (460 ft.) via Spiller Homestead Loop	0.1 mi.	45 ft.	0:05
Highlands Loop (775 ft.)	0.7 mi.	360 ft.	0:30
Pismire Bluff scenic overlook (760 ft.)	0.8 mi.	360 ft.	0:35

LELT From the trailhead kiosk, head northwest on Spiller Homestead Trail (pink markers) to a jct. at 0.1 mi. Here, turn right on Pismire Bluff Trail (blue markers) and soon cross Conesca Rd. The trail heads northeast and then turns sharply southeast on a rising traverse along the base of a talus slope to reach a large set of stone steps. It climbs moderately via short switchbacks for a distance before rising more gradually to the south ridge of Pismire Mtn. At a jct. at 0.7 mi., a spur of Pismire Bluff Trail leads left

0.1 mi. to Pismire Bluff, a scenic overlook with westerly views. Also at the jct. is the start and finish of Highlands Loop, which makes a 0.7-mi. circuit on the upper south slopes of Pismire Mtn.

HIGHLANDS LOOP (USGS RAYMOND QUAD, LELT RAYMOND COMMUNITY FOREST TRAIL MAP, GAZETTEER MAP 5)
From Pismire Bluff Trail (775 ft.) to:

Complete loop	0.8 mi.	210 ft.	0:30

LELT From the jct. of the Pismire Bluff Trail spur to the scenic overlook, head north on Highlands Loop (red markers) toward the top of Pismire Mtn., trending easily along the ridge. Reach a property boundary at the base of the summit cone of Pismire (through the trees, a house is visible on the hilltop); bear right here, away from the upper face of the mountain. Highlands Loop descends easily down the back side and then heads south to join an old woods road. Bear right and, ahead, bear right again off the woods road to climb a narrow old track to the loop jct. Turn left here to return to the Conesca Rd. trailhead via Pismire Bluff Trail and Spiller Homestead Loop.

BALD PATE MTN. (1,150 FT.)
LELT established the 486-acre Bald Pate Mtn. Preserve of forests, meadows, and granite ledges in South Bridgton in 1997 to protect the land from development. The preserve's seven trails offer 7 mi. of hiking with plenty of opportunity for exploration, highlighted by a mountaintop pitch-pine forest and numerous outlooks with views of Peabody Pond and Sebago Lake.

From the jct. of US 302 and ME 107/117, 1.5 mi. south of Bridgton, turn left (west) onto ME 117. At 0.8 mi., ME 117 proceeds straight. Turn left (south) here onto ME 107. At 4.3 mi., pass Five Fields Farm on the left. Just ahead, at the top of the hill at 4.6 mi., reach a dirt drive (sign) on the left leading to the main trailhead parking (kiosk).

BOB CHASE SCENIC LOOP (AMC BALD PATE MTN. PRESERVE MAP)
Cumulative from main trailhead on ME 107 (850 ft.) to:

South Face Loop Trail (1,100 ft.)	0.6 mi.	250 ft.	0:25
Bald Pate Mtn. summit (1,150 ft.) via South Face Loop Trail	0.7 mi.	300 ft.	0:30

LELT Follow the wide, grassy track of Bob Chase Scenic Loop (blue markers) to a jct. at 0.2 mi. Here, Town Farm Brook Trail (purple markers)

SEC 8

Bald Pate Mtn. Preserve

Bridgton, ME

Five Fields Farm
XC Ski Center

107

P

Town Farm Brook Tr

Bob Chase Loop Tr

Foster Pond Lookout Tr

Foster Pond
Lookout

Moose Tr

South Face Loop Tr

1150

Bald
Pate
Mtn

Pate Tr

South Face Loop Tr

Micah Tr

Moose Cove Lodge Rd

P

Peabody
Pond

True
North

14½°
West

Magnetic Declination 2023

0 mile   ⅛   ¼   ⅜

SEC
8

enters from the left (leads 2.0 mi. north to Holt Pond Trail and to Holt Pond), and Foster Pond Lookout Trail (red markers) proceeds straight (leads 0.2 to a jct., where a spur leads 0.3 mi. east to a viewpoint over Foster Pond; to the right [south], the trail ascends easily to merge with Bob Chase Scenic Loop at 0.4 mi.).

Continuing on Bob Chase Scenic Loop, turn right (south) and climb gradually, crossing a wide track (ski trail in winter) to reach a jct. at 0.4 mi. where the trail splits. Both branches climb moderately past viewpoints to merge again at 0.6 mi. and a jct. with South Face Loop Trail (orange markers). Follow South Face Loop Trail to reach the summit at 0.7 mi., with views through the trees. A bronze plaque on the summit honors conservation supporters of Bald Pate Mtn. Several loop possibilities from this point are possible using South Face Loop Trail and Pate Trail.

FOSTER POND LOOKOUT TRAIL
(AMC BALD PATE MTN. PRESERVE MAP)
Cumulative from main trailhead on ME 107 (850 ft.) to:

Foster Pond Lookout (890 ft.) via Bob Chase Scenic Loop	0.7 mi.	100 ft.	0:25
Bald Pate Mtn. summit (1,150 ft.) via Bob Chase Scenic Loop and South Face Loop Trail	1.6 mi.	350 ft.	1:00

LELT Follow wide, grassy Bob Chase Scenic Loop (blue markers) to a jct. at 0.2 mi. Here, Town Farm Brook Trail enters from the left (leads 2.0 mi. north to Holt Pond Trail and to Holt Pond), and Foster Pond Lookout Trail (red markers) proceeds straight ahead. Bob Chase Scenic Loop turns right.

Go straight on Foster Pond Lookout Trail to the next jct. Here, a spur of Foster Pond Lookout Trail leads 0.3 mi. to Foster Pond Lookout and a view of the pond. Return to the spur jct. and turn left to climb to a jct. with the upper east section of Bob Chase Scenic Loop at a viewpoint to Peabody Pond. From here, Bob Chase Scenic Loop ascends to join South Face Loop Trail, which leads to the top of Bald Pate Mtn.

MICAH TRAIL AND PATE TRAIL (BALD PATE MTN. PRESERVE MAP)
From Moose Cove Lodge Rd. parking (650 ft.) to:

Bald Pate Mtn. summit (1,150 ft.) via Micah Trail, South Face Loop Trail, and Pate Trail	0.6 mi.	500 ft.	0:40

LELT From the main trailhead, drive south on ME 107 for 0.9 mi. Turn left onto dirt Moose Cove Lodge Rd. (sign for Camp Micah), and go 0.5 mi. to a small parking lot on the left.

SEC 8

Follow Micah Trail (white markers) to a bridge over a creek and then gradually up to the jct. with South Face Loop Trail (orange markers). Turn left on South Face Loop Trail, and in 300 ft., turn right on Pate Trail (green markers). Climb 0.2 mi. at a moderate-to-steep grade past cliffs to the Bald Pate Mtn. summit. South Face Loop Trail may be used to form a loop hike east or west from the summit back to the southern trailhead.

MICAH TRAIL AND SOUTH FACE LOOP TRAIL (AMC BALD PATE MTN. PRESERVE MAP)

Cumulative from the southern trailhead on Moose Cove Lodge Rd. (650 ft.) to:

Bald Pate Mtn. summit (1,150 ft.) via right side of South Face Loop Trail	1.0 mi.	500 ft.	0:45
Complete loop via South Face Loop Trail and Micah Trail	2.2 mi.	610 ft.	1:25

LELT From the southern trailhead on Moose Cove Lodge Rd. (see above), follow Micah Trail (white markers) to a bridge over a creek and then gradually up to a jct. with South Face Loop Trail (orange markers). To hike the loop counterclockwise, turn right on South Face Loop Trail, which leads 0.6 mi. to the top of Bald Pate Mtn., climbing the right side of the south face past a viewpoint.

From the summit, descend the mountain's west ridge on South Face Loop Trail, passing a viewpoint. At the base of the mountain, Moose Trail diverges right. (*Note*: Moose Trail is prone to ticks due to high grass and is therefore recommended as a winter trail only.) Continue easily east, pass the bottom of Pate Trail, and reach the jct. with Micah Trail. Turn right on Micah Trail to return to the southern trailhead.

PLEASANT MTN. (2,001 FT.)

This isolated mountain mass on the Denmark–Bridgton town line rises abruptly from the comparatively flat countryside around Moose Pond, its ridgeline extending 4 mi. in a generally north–south line. Pleasant Mtn. is the highest peak in southwestern Maine. LELT owns 2,064 acres on the mountain and, along with AMC, maintains the trails. TNC protects 1,400 acres on the western slopes through conservation easements, and MFS owns 20 acres on the main summit. Portions of the trail system and mountain are privately owned and are publicly available thanks to the generosity of the landowners.

The 10 mi. of hiking trails converge at the main summit, where an old fire tower has stood since 1920. The summit was once known as House

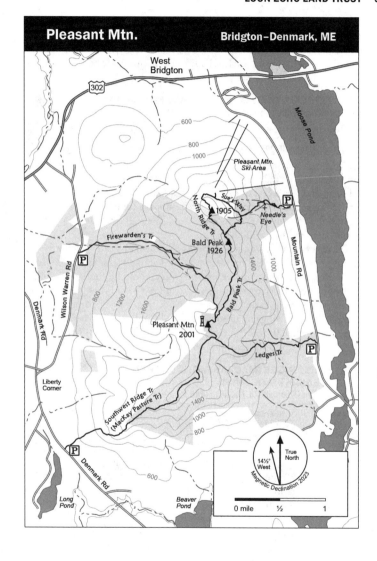

Pleasant Mtn.

Bridgton–Denmark, ME

West Bridgton

302

600

800

1000

Pleasant Mtn. Ski Area

North Ridge Tr

Sue's Way

1905

Needle's Eye

Firewarden's Tr

Bald Peak 1926

Wilson Warren Rd

P

1400

1000

Bald Peak Tr

800

1200

1600

Denmark Rd

Pleasant Mtn 2001

Moose Pond

Mountain Rd

P

P

Ledges Tr

SEC 8

Liberty Corner

Southwest Ridge Tr (MacKay Pasture Tr)

1400

1000

800

True North

14½° West

Magnetic Declination 2023

P

Denmark Rd

600

Long Pond

Beaver Pond

0 mile   ½   1

Peak because of the hotel that stood there from 1873 to 1907. Around 1860, Pleasant Mtn. was burned over, and the forests and ledges remain open enough today for outstanding views. Mt. Washington, 29 mi. to the northwest, is particularly noticeable. The Pleasant Mtn. ski area operates on the slopes of the northern peak.

FIREWARDEN'S TRAIL (AMC PLEASANT MTN. MAP)
Cumulative from Wilton Warren Rd. trailhead (470 ft.) to:

Bald Peak Trail (1,910 ft.)	2.3 mi.	1,440 ft.	1:50
Pleasant Mtn. main summit (2,001 ft.)	2.5 mi.	1,531 ft.	2:00

LELT Firewarden's Trail climbs to the main summit from the west. From US 302, at a point 2.3 mi. west of Mountain Rd. (road to the Pleasant Mtn. ski area) and 7 mi. east of Fryeburg, turn south onto Wilton Warren Rd. At 1.2 mi. south of US 302, a yellow farmhouse is on the left and a large barn is on the right. Parking is on the left. The trail starts at the right end of the parking area (sign).

The first half of Firewarden's Trail is an old woods road with few views. In recent years, this road has been used for logging and is deeply rutted in places. Several logging roads cross the path and can be confusing. Follow the red blazes to stay on the route. The trail crosses a brook several times before narrowing to a rough old jeep road with exposed bedrock much of the way. It then swings right (southeast) and climbs steadily to the summit ridge. In the final 0.2 mi., blue-blazed Bald Peak Trail comes in on the left (sign). An old storm shelter is just off the trail to the right.

SOUTHWEST RIDGE (MACKAY PASTURE) TRAIL (AMC PLEASANT MTN. MAP)
Cumulative from Denmark Rd. trailhead (448 ft.) to:

Pleasant Mtn. southwest summit (1,900 ft.)	1.7 mi.	1,452 ft.	1:35
Ledges Trail (1,810 ft.)	2.7 mi.	1,612 ft.	2:10
Pleasant Mtn. main summit (2,001 ft.) via Ledges Trail	2.9 mi.	1,803 ft.	2:20

LELT From the jct. of ME 117 and ME 160 in Denmark, take ME 160 for 0.3 mi. to the Moose Pond Dam. Turn right onto Denmark Rd. and drive 3.5 mi. to the parking area on the right, opposite the sign for Spiked Ridge Rd. (FR 78). Visitors may also approach the parking area from US 302 in East Fryeburg by following Denmark Rd. for 3.4 mi.

Southwest Ridge Trail, marked by cairns and yellow blazes, begins on private property (sign) and follows an old woods road gradually northeast, becoming steeper. At approximately 0.4 mi., the trail turns sharply right (southeast), angles across the slope, turns left, and reaches open ledges at

0.6 mi. Beyond, Southwest Ridge Trail ascends northeasterly along the mostly open ridge to an old wooden tepee at the southwestern summit (1,900 ft.) at 1.7 mi., with views over Moose Pond and Beaver Pond. The trail keeps to the ridge and then descends to a short saddle and angles across and down the hillside to a deep gully. Beyond, it ascends back to the ridge, becoming more gradual until it reaches blue-blazed Ledges Trail at 2.7 mi. (0.2 mi. from the summit).

LEDGES TRAIL (AMC PLEASANT MTN. MAP)
Cumulative from Mountain Rd. (490 ft.) to:

Overlook (1,400 ft.)	1.1 mi.	910 ft.	1:00
Southwest Ridge Trail (1,810 ft.)	1.6 mi.	1,320 ft.	1:30
Pleasant Mtn. main summit (2,001 ft.)	1.8 mi.	1,511 ft.	1:40

LELT/AMC This blue-blazed trail leaves the west side of Mountain Rd. at a point 3.3 mi. south of US 302, 1.5 mi. south of Bald Peak Trail, and 0.6 mi. north of Walker's Bridge (which separates the two sections of Moose Pond). A small parking area is on the east side of the road next to FR 54.

Ledges Trail (sign) begins by climbing a stone stairway to an information kiosk and then gradually ascending along an old woods road. At 0.5 mi., it crosses two often-dry streambeds. Continue to climb moderately for 0.6 mi., noting changes in direction as the trail traverses to the open ledges with views south and southeast. The trail follows the ledges, with the southwestern summit and a cell tower visible ahead on the left. At 1.6 mi., Southwest Ridge Trail enters on the left (sign). Ahead, Ledges Trail climbs through an area of ledges and scrub to the main summit and fire tower. Views to the west include Fryeburg, the Saco River valley, and numerous ponds.

SEC 8

BALD PEAK (1,932 FT.)
This subsidiary summit of Pleasant Mtn. is just south of Pleasant Mtn. Ski Area. Three trails cross the mountain's slopes: Bald Peak Trail, Sue's Way, and North Ridge Trail.

BALD PEAK TRAIL (AMC PLEASANT MTN. MAP)
Cumulative from Mountain Rd. (450 ft.) to:

Brook crossing and Sue's Way (1,260 ft.)	0.7 mi.	810 ft.	0:45
North Ridge Trail (1,840 ft.)	1.0 mi.	1,390 ft.	1:10
Bald Peak (1,932 ft.)	1.1 mi.	1,480 ft.	1:15
Firewarden's Trail (1,910 ft.)	2.2 mi.	1,660 ft.	1:55
Pleasant Mtn. main summit (2,001 ft.) via Firewarden's Trail	2.4 mi.	1,810 ft.	2:10

LELT Bald Peak Trail climbs the eastern side of Pleasant Mtn. to Bald Peak and then runs south along the ridge to join Firewarden's Trail just below the main summit. When combined with Ledges Trail and a 1.5-mi. walk on Mountain Rd., Bald Peak Trail forms an enjoyable circuit. Both trails follow blue blazes. (*Note:* Bald Peak Trail may have no water during dry periods.)

To reach Bald Peak Trail, follow Mountain Rd. along the western shore of Moose Pond to a point 1.8 mi. south of the road's jct. with US 302, and 1.2 mi. beyond the entrance to the Pleasant Mtn. ski area. The trailhead is on the right between utility poles 49 and 50 (sign). Limited roadside parking is available.

The trail starts westward, crosses a brook, and climbs steeply. At 0.2 mi., turn left and follow the north side of the brook. At 0.4 mi., a short but rough spur (sign) leads left to the Needle's Eye, a brook cascading through a cleft in a ledge. At 0.7 mi., just before the second of two small brooks, turn left (Sue's Way turns right; sign). Climb a steep 0.3 mi. over exposed bedrock, emerging onto ledges (cairn). Turn left and quickly reach Bald Peak (1,932 ft.) and excellent views at 1.1 mi. From Bald Peak, the trail follows the crest of the ridge, first south and then southwest over two humps, toward the main summit. At 2.2 mi., it joins Firewarden's Trail, which leads left (south) past the storm shelter to the top of Pleasant Mtn. and the fire tower.

SUE'S WAY (AMC PLEASANT MTN. MAP)
From Bald Peak Trail (1,260 ft.) to:

North Ridge Trail (1,750 ft.)	0.5 mi.	490 ft.	0:30

LELT This orange-blazed trail starts 0.7 mi. up Bald Peak Trail and leads 0.5 mi. to a jct. with North Ridge Trail (sign). At the jct., turn right and leave the woods. Go past the Pleasant Mtn. ski area summit warming hut and uphill a short distance to the top of the ski area for views to the north. Combined, Sue's Way and North Ridge Trail make an interesting loop hike. A spring is one-third along Sue's Way, and the trail is often wet in season.

NORTH RIDGE TRAIL (AMC PLEASANT MTN. MAP)
From Sue's Way (1,750 ft.) to:

Bald Peak Trail (1,840 ft.)	0.8 mi.	295 ft.	0:35

LELT This white-blazed trail begins at the jct. with Sue's Way, 100 yd. downhill (southeast) from the top of the Pleasant Mtn. ski area. North Ridge Trail heads west on the level before turning left to pass through a granite slab. The trail then circles around the northwest side of the mountain's north peak before reaching the top. Beyond, it bears right to cross an open ledge, where there are views of Bald Peak and the main summit of Pleasant Mtn. The trail then drops steeply into a col before ascending Bald Peak. Just below the top, Bald Peak Trail comes in from the left.

FRYEBURG
MT. TOM (1,066 FT.)

Mt. Tom in Fryeburg offers a pleasant walk through the woods, capped by summit ledges with rewarding views of the Saco River valley and Pleasant Mtn. Two trails offer access to the top. Much of the land on the north side of Mt. Tom is owned by the Carter family of Fryeburg, who maintain Mt. Tom Trail. The 995-acre Mt. Tom Preserve, owned by TNC, protects a sizeable chunk of the west, south, and east slopes of the mountain between Menotomy Rd. and the Saco River, as well as 3,500 ft. of frontage on that river. TNC maintains West Ridge Trail.

From the intersection of US 302 and ME 113 in Fryeburg, drive south on US 302 for 2.3 mi. Turn left (north) onto Menotomy Rd. The trailhead for West Ridge Trail is 1.1 mi. ahead at Fire Rd. 31B on the right (sign). Park as far to the right on this road as possible; do not block the road. For Mt. Tom Trail, continue on Menotomy Rd. for another 1.2 mi. to a small parking area (sign) on the right next to a large barn and field.

WEST RIDGE TRAIL (USGS FRYEBURG QUAD, MTF MT. TOM PRESERVE MAP, GAZETTEER MAP 4)
Cumulative from Menotomy Rd. (350 ft.) to:

Mt. Tom Trail (1,055 ft.)	1.6 mi.	705 ft.	1:10
Mt. Tom summit ledges (1,066 ft.)	1.7 mi.	715 ft.	1:15

SEC 8

TNC This white-blazed trail climbs Mt. Tom from the southwest. Walk 150 ft. down the fire road to the start of West Ridge Trail on the left (sign). Just into the woods are several old foundations. Pass between them, following white blazes. Ahead, cross a small stream, and soon bear right on an old woods road (sign). In another 100 ft., where the woods road crosses a bridge over a stream, bear left off the road (sign) and begin a steady ascent. At 0.9 mi., the ascent becomes steep. Follow along a lichen-covered rock wall and then climb to the left through a break in the wall. Reach the northeast ridge of Mt. Tom at 1.0 mi. A brief descent leads to an old woods road (sign). Bear left onto the old road and, a short distance ahead, bear right off the road (sign). Beyond, climb at a steady, moderate grade with several steep pitches. A rising contour leads to an outcropping and a view to the southwest. Ascend steadily along the steep, forested west face of Mt.

Tom. At 1.45 mi., climb over two rock slabs and then go up and around to gain a narrow ridge. The angle soon eases as the trail contours to reach a cairn with a painted rock at 1.6 mi. Just beyond is the jct. with Mt. Tom Trail. Bear right here to reach the top of Mt. Tom and its impressive south-facing ledges in 0.1 mi.

MT. TOM TRAIL (USGS FRYEBURG QUAD, MTF MT. TOM PRESERVE MAP, GAZETTEER MAP 4)
Cumulative from Menotomy Rd. (490 ft.) to:

West Ridge Trail (1,055 ft.)	1.1 mi.	565 ft.	0:50
Mt. Tom summit (1,066 ft.) via West Ridge Trail	1.2 mi.	575 ft.	0:55

Carter Family This old trail climbs Mt. Tom from the northwest. Mt. Tom Trail follows Old Mountain Rd. south through a field to a dirt road and the Mt. Tom Cabin (1883), owned by the Carter family. A short distance beyond the cabin, pass a house on the right. This vantage point offers lovely views to the west, including Mt. Kearsarge and other peaks of the White Mountains. The road soon turns to grass and ascends gradually to a firewood log yard. At a fork, bear left and continue easily upward through a mix of forest types, including a stand of mature hemlock. Just shy of the summit, Mt. Tom Trail merges with West Ridge Trail, which enters from the right. The south-facing ledges and summit sign are just 0.1 mi. ahead.

JOCKEY CAP (619 FT.)

This impressive granite outcropping in Fryeburg rises nearly 200 ft. above the woods and fields of the Saco River valley and offers outstanding views for a small amount of time and effort. Jockey Cap was the site of the first rope ski tow in Maine, installed in 1936. At the top, a bronze profile of the surrounding peaks is a monument to the polar explorer Robert E. Peary, who lived in Fryeburg from 1878 to 1879. The monument identifies mountaintops in a 360-degree arc, including Mt. Kearsarge, Mt. Washington, and many others.

The trailhead is on the north side of US 302 at Quinn's Jockey Cap Country Store, 1.6 mi. east of the jct. of US 302 and ME 113 (traffic light) in the center of Fryeburg. To the left of the store, two signed parking spaces are reserved for hikers. If these spaces are full, please return at another time.

(*Note*: As of 2022, Upper Saco Valley Land Trust and the town of Fryeburg were in the process of permanently protecting nearly 16 acres on Jockey Cap. When the conservation project is completed [timeline TBD], a new, larger trailhead parking area will be constructed 0.2 mi. east on US 302, and the trail network may have some changes.)

JOCKEY CAP TRAIL (USGS FRYEBURG QUAD, MTF JOCKEY CAP, GAZETTEER MAP 4)
Cumulative from US 302 at Quinn's Jockey Cap Country Store (425 ft.) to:

Jockey Cap summit (619 ft.)	0.3 mi.	195 ft.	0:15

USVLT Jockey Cap Trail begins through the gateway (kiosk on left) just north of the hiker parking spaces. At the first intersection, turn right and walk behind the Jockey Cap store and then Dollar General. Just after a trail enters sharply from the left, turn left, heading into the woods. Trending gently uphill, reach several large boulders. Just around to the right is Molly Ockett's Cave, named for Molly Ockett, an Abenaki woman who was baptized and given the name Mary Agatha. This could have been pronounced "Molly Agat" or "Molly Ockett" by Abenaki speakers, which has led to various spellings and place names.

Follow Jockey Cap Trail to the left and circle up the west side of Jockey Cap. Pass a trail on the left, and beyond, turn sharply left and soon begin climbing up the back of the dome. Emerge from the woods and cross the open summit ledges to the Peary monument. The commanding vistas range from Pleasant Mtn. and the Presidential and Carter–Moriah ranges to the peaks in the Evans Notch area.

ME 113 CORRIDOR
PEARY MTN. (956 FT.)
The open ledges of this mountain in Brownfield afford views of the White Mountains and the mountains of western Maine, including Mt. Chocorua, North and South Moat, Kearsarge, the Presidential Range, the Carter–Moriah Range, and the peaks around Evans Notch.

From the jct. of ME 160 and ME 113 in East Brownfield, proceed north on ME 113 for 2.2 mi. to Farnsworth Rd. Turn left (west) onto Farnsworth Rd. and drive 1.3 mi. to a bridge over Little Saco River. A small parking area is on the right before the bridge. It has a snowmobile trail signpost and a kiosk with maps of the snowmobile trails.

PEARY MTN. TRAIL (USGS BROWNFIELD QUAD, GAZETTEER MAP 4)
Cumulative from Farnsworth Rd. (410 ft.) to:

Saddle (830 ft.)	0.8 mi.	420 ft.	0:35
Peary Mtn. west summit (910 ft.)	0.9 mi.	500 ft.	0:40
Peary Mtn. main summit (956 ft.)	1.3 mi.	546 ft.	0:55

NFTM Peary Mtn. Trail starts on the opposite side of Farnsworth Rd. from the parking area. Follow the old woods road (snowmobile trail) past a gate

SEC
8

on the east side of the river. Just ahead, in a small clearing (old log yard), bear right. The trail heads south on the level and then climbs at a gradual grade to a saddle at 0.8 mi., in a small clearing with an old foundation and stone wall. Turn left (southeast) off the woods road and immediately left again onto another woods road. In 100 ft., turn right (cairn) onto a footpath and ascend through open woods and over ledges (following cairns) for 0.2 mi. to the south summit, which has a granite bench and outstanding views to the north and west. To reach the main summit, follow Peary Mtn. Trail 0.4 mi. northeast across open ledges and through scrub. At trail's end are views to the east and north, including Pleasant Mtn. and Pleasant Pond.

BURNT MEADOW MTN., NORTH PEAK (1,570 FT.)

This mountain mass in Brownfield consists of three main summits and two lesser summits, all of nearly equal height. Deep cols separate Stone Mtn. from the north and south peaks of Burnt Meadow Mtn. Hikers can enjoy sights of the Saco River valley, the western Maine mountains, and the White Mountains. A ski area operated on the north slope of the mountain from 1971 into the early 1980s.

From the jct. of ME 113/5 and ME 160 in East Brownfield, drive west on ME 160 through Brownfield. In 0.9 mi., bear sharply left (south) past Brownfield Community Church. Continue past Burnt Meadow Pond to trailhead parking (kiosk) on the right at 3.1 mi.

BURNT MEADOW TRAIL (AMC BURNT MEADOW MTN. MAP)
Cumulative from ME 160 (440 ft.) to:

Twin Brook Trail (770 ft.)	0.5 mi.	330 ft.	0:25
Burnt Meadow Mtn., north peak (1,570 ft.)	1.3 mi.	1,130 ft.	1:15

NFTM The blue-blazed trail climbs westerly up the slope, staying on the southern edge of the east ridge. At 0.4 mi., it passes over a small hump and drops slightly into a shallow col, reaching the jct. with yellow-blazed Twin Brook Trail at 0.5 mi. Beyond the col, Burnt Meadow Trail continues up the crest of the spur, which becomes steeper and more open, with a sharp dropoff on the left. Cairns as well as blazes mark the upper part of the route, which climbs via a series of ledges and a short scramble to reach the open summit at 1.3 mi.

TWIN BROOK TRAIL (AMC BURNT MEADOW MTN. MAP)
Cumulative from Burnt Meadow Trail (770 ft.) to:

Stone Mtn. Trail (1,150 ft.)	1.2 mi.	380 ft.	0:50
Burnt Meadow Mtn., north peak (1,570 ft.)	2.0 mi.	860 ft.	1:25

Burnt Meadow Mtn.

Brownfield, ME

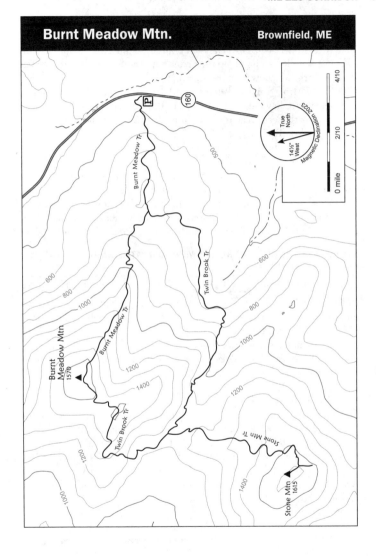

SEC
8

NFTM This yellow-blazed trail forms a loop over the summit of Burnt Meadow Mtn. when combined with Burnt Meadow Trail. Twin Brook Trail leaves Burnt Meadow Trail at a point 0.5 mi. from the trailhead on ME 160. It follows a brook up the ravine between Stone Mtn. and North Peak of Burnt Meadow Mtn. At 1.2 mi., the trail reaches a col and the jct. with Stone Mtn. Trail (leads left [south] 0.7 mi. to the 1,615-ft. summit of Stone Mtn.). Beyond, Twin Brook Trail climbs ledges on the southern flank of North Peak, reaching the summit at 2.0 mi. and the jct. with Burnt Meadow Trail.

STONE MTN. (1,615 FT.)

This mountain is the highest of the three summits of the Burnt Meadow Mtn. mass in Brownfield. Stone Mtn. Trail to the peak was constructed by AMC and volunteers from Friends of Burnt Meadow Mountains. It opened in 2010. See the descriptions for Burnt Meadow Trail and Twin Brook Trail (p. 372) for directions to the start of Stone Mtn. Trail.

STONE MTN. TRAIL (AMC BURNT MEADOW MTN. MAP)
From Twin Brook Trail (1,160 ft.) to:

Stone Mtn. summit (1,615 ft.)	0.7 mi.	455 ft.	0:35

NFTM Stone Mtn. Trail heads south from near the height-of-land between Stone Mtn. and Burnt Meadow Mtn. (North Peak) at a point 1.2 mi. from ME 160 via Burnt Meadow Trail and Twin Brook Trail. Stone Mtn. Trail ascends the north shoulder of Stone Mtn., crosses a dry brook, and then switchbacks to reach the ledges on the south flank of the mountain before continuing west to the summit at 0.7 mi.

MT. CUTLER (1,238 FT.)

The extensive open ledges of this mountain in the village of Hiram reward hikers with fine views of nearby hills and farmlands, the Saco River valley to the south, and the White Mountains to the north. The mountain is home to nearly 6 mi. of hiking on nine trails on nearly 200 acres of protected land known as Mt. Cutler Park and Conservation Area. Thanks to the determined efforts of conservation-minded Dan Hester of Hiram (who purchased the land in 2007 to save it from potential development), town officials, local residents, and many other supporters—plus a Land and Water Conservation Fund grant and assistance from TNC—ownership of the Mt. Cutler property was transferred to the town of Hiram in 2018.

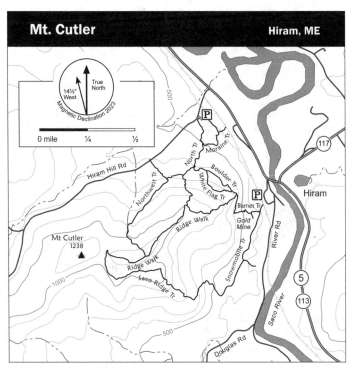

BARNES TRAIL (AMC MT. CUTLER MAP)

Cumulative from old Maine Central Railroad Depot trailhead (390 ft.) to:

Front Ledges (700 ft.) via Barnes Trail	0.4 mi.	310 ft.	0:20
Ridge Walk and White Flag Trail (700 ft.) via Barnes Trail	0.45 mi.	310 ft.	0:25

TOHCC Barnes Trail starts from the site of the old Maine Central Railroad Depot in Hiram. From the jct. of ME 113/5 and ME 117 in Hiram, cross the Saco River Bridge, turn left (south) onto River Rd., and then immediately turn right onto Mountain View Ave. Where the street turns nearest to the mountain, cross the first set of railroad tracks and park in the area between the sets of tracks. A kiosk stands here, and a trail sign is across the tracks, south of the parking area. This is the trailhead for both Barnes Trail and Snowmobile Trail. Barnes Trail, established by Dr. Lowell "Bud"

Barnes in the 1950s, is the original route to the front ledges on Mt. Cutler. Sections of this trail are very steep. It is marked by red blazes on trees and rocks and by rock cairns on ledge areas.

Cross the railroad tracks to the trail sign. Barnes Trail and Snowmobile Trail coincide up a steady grade. At about 100 yd., the path divides; Snowmobile Trail continues straight ahead, while Barnes Trail forks to the right and enters Merrill Botanical Park, a grove of large white pines. Before leaving the park, a short trail branches to the south, through an opening in a stone wall, leading to the "Gold Mine" described in some local publications. Barnes Trail dips slightly as it leaves the southwest corner of the park and crosses the (usually dry) outlet of a large vernal pool. Watch for historical dug wells in this small valley. The trail ascends quickly to enter the ravine between Mt. Cutler and the shoulder south of the mountain. Stay on the south side of the seasonal stream and steeply ascend the ravine over rough rocks. After about 100 yd. westward and upward, Barnes Trail turns sharply right and crosses a very rough boulder area (use caution). The trail passes under an overhanging ledge and makes a very steep ascent of the ledges (use extra caution here, especially when descending). At the top of this ledge, Barnes Trail turns sharply right and runs northerly to the Front Ledges overlooking the town of Hiram. Northwest of the Front Ledges, the trail turns sharply left to reach the jct. with White Flag Trail and Ridge Walk.

RIDGE WALK (AMC MT. CUTLER MAP)
Cumulative from old Maine Central Railroad Depot trailhead (390 ft.) to:

Front Ledges (700 ft.) via Barnes Trail	0.4 mi.	310 ft.	0:20
Ridge Walk and White Flag Trail (700 ft.) via Barnes Trail	0.45 mi.	310 ft.	0:25
South View Ledge (960 ft.)	0.65 mi.	570 ft.	0:40
North Trail (1,030 ft.)	0.8 mi.	640 ft.	0:45
Northwest Trail (1,170 ft.)	1.0 mi.	800 ft.	0:55
Notch/ATV trail (1,090 ft.) east of Mt. Cutler summit	1.3 mi.	800 ft.	1:05

TOHCC A continuation of Barnes Trail, Ridge Walk gradually ascends the long east–west ridge of Mt. Cutler. On the ridge are alternating outlooks with excellent views to the northwest (the Presidential Range) and to the south (the Saco River Valley to the Saco River estuary and Casco Bay). Cairns and some red blazes mark the route, although it is usually discernible without markers.

From the jct. of Barnes Trail and White Flag Trail, Ridge Walk enters a hardwood forest and ascends steadily to the west. Before entering a hemlock grove, look northeast to see Pleasant Mtn. Above the hemlocks, Ridge Walk continues a steady, moderate ascent, emerging from a small conifer grove into the open at South View Ledge and a spectacular scenic panorama. This point is not actually a summit, but it appears to be so when viewed from the town of Hiram. The ledges here are the easternmost end of a long ridge, with its west end at a notch just below the true summit of Mt. Cutler.

From South View Ledge, continue westward to North Trail, which enters from the north. Ahead at Gunsight Ledge are views to both north and south. Beyond, Ridge Walk passes the jct. with Northwest Trail, crosses a mostly wooded secondary summit (1,180 ft.), and descends to a notch traversed by an ATV trail.

SNOWMOBILE TRAIL (AMC MT. CUTLER MAP)
Cumulative from old Maine Central Railroad Depot trailhead (390 ft.) to:

Saco Ridge Trail (430 ft.)	0.5 mi.	55 ft.	0:15
Old Saco Ridge Trail (430 ft.)	0.7 mi.	55 ft.	0:20

TOHCC Snowmobile Trail starts at the same trailhead as Barnes Trail. After the initial 100 yd. uphill, where Barnes Trail forks to the right, Snowmobile Trail continues straight. It remains nearly level, passing two houses on the left (below the elevation of the trail) before descending slightly to enter open fields. Turning toward the mountain, away from the fields, the trail reenters woods, turns left, and crosses a small stream. Just beyond, Saco Ridge Trail leaves to the right at a small cairn at 0.5 mi. Continuing mostly on the level, Snowmobile Trail passes close to a steep shoulder of the mountain, where the original Saco Ridge Trail (now called Old Saco Ridge Trail) begins at 0.7 mi.

SACO RIDGE TRAIL (AMC MT. CUTLER MAP)
Cumulative from notch/ATV trail and Ridge Walk upper end (1,090 ft.) to:

Old Saco Ridge Trail (790 ft.)	0.5 mi.	60 ft.	0:15
Snowmobile Trail (430 ft.)	0.7 mi.	60 ft.	0:20
Old Maine Central Railroad Depot trailhead (390 ft.)	1.2 mi.	60 ft.	0:35

TOHCC Saco Ridge Trail is often used as a descent route and is therefore described in that direction. With Barnes Trail and Ridge Walk, Saco Ridge Trail forms a loop hike. Saco Ridge Trail (also known as South Ridge Trail) runs from the notch/ATV trail high on Mt. Cutler, at the upper end of Ridge Walk, down the most prominent southern ridge, joining Snowmobile Trail at the eastern base of the mountain. Leaving the notch, descend a short distance to the south, watching for cairns and red

**SEC
8**

blazes. The trail bears left and slabs along the south side of Mt. Cutler, gradually descending until it reaches a small notch between the bulk of the mountain and the upper part of this ridge. Saco Ridge Trail makes a short ascent to an open area with views to the east. Near the easternmost edge of this clearing, it turns sharply right (at a cairn), enters hardwoods, and descends the ridge. Several viewpoints look down to the Saco River and the neighboring farmland. Before the lowest viewpoint on Saco Ridge, reach a jct. with Old Saco Ridge Trail; steep and sometimes slippery, it is not recommended (but for an attractive view, walk 100 ft. on Old Saco Ridge Trail). The relocated Saco Ridge Trail turns north in a small clearing spotted with pines. It continues to descend northward, eventually turning right to descend eastward on an old logging road to reach Snowmobile Trail. Turn left to return to the trailhead in Hiram.

NORTH TRAIL (AMC MT. CUTLER MAP)
Cumulative from Hiram Hill Rd. (450 ft.) to:

Moraine Trail (500 ft.)	0.15 mi.	50 ft.	0:05
White Flag Trail (620 ft.)	0.3 mi.	170 ft.	0:15
Link Trail (700 ft.)	0.35 mi.	250 ft.	0:20
Ridge Walk (1,030 ft.)	0.5 mi.	580 ft.	0:35
Northwest Trail (1,170 ft.) via Ridge Walk	0.7 mi.	740 ft.	0:55
Notch/ATV trail (1,090 ft.) east of Mt. Cutler summit via Ridge Walk	1.0 mi.	740 ft.	1:05

TOHCC This blue-blazed trail ascends from the north to meet Ridge Walk high on the long eastern ridgeline of Mt. Cutler. In the town of Hiram, from the jct. of ME 113/5 and River Rd. on the west side of the bridge over the Saco River, drive north 0.6 mi. to Hiram Hill Rd. (on the left just before the concrete bridge over Red Mill Brook). Turn left onto Hiram Hill Rd., cross the railroad tracks, and continue 0.1 mi. to the trailhead parking area on the left.

North Trail begins at the entrance to the parking area. It runs parallel to the road for a short distance and then turns sharply left, passing a well house uphill from the path (this is an active and private water supply; do not approach or tamper with the well). At about 100 yd., the trail crosses a small stream next to a property corner marker (please do not disturb iron pins and flagging tape used to mark property lines). North Trail ascends at a moderate grade through hardwood forest in a southerly direction toward the mountain. At 0.15 mi., at the crest of a small ridge, white-blazed Moraine Trail enters from the left. Beyond, North Trail follows the west side of a small valley and another stream and then ascends a steep ridge notched by this brook, paralleling the brook for 150 yd. At 0.25 mi., the trail turns left, crosses the brook in a grove of large hemlocks, and ascends to the southwest, away from the water. A short distance above the brook crossing, White Flag Trail diverges to the left. After another 150 yd., North Trail reaches the foot of a steep, rocky slope, turns left, starts uphill, passes the jct. with Link Trail (connects to Northwest Trail), and ascends into dense hemlock woods. Climbing through narrow passages in thick hemlocks, North Trail emerges on sloping, open ledges with excellent views to the north and northeast. After passing through more hemlocks, the trail continues up sloping ledges to join Ridge Walk at a cairn.

WHITE FLAG TRAIL (AMC MT. CUTLER MAP)
Cumulative from Hiram Hill Rd. (450 ft.) to:

White Flag Trail (620 ft.) via North Trail	0.3 mi.	170 ft.	0:15
Barnes Trail and Ridge Walk (700 ft.)	0.55 mi.	250 ft.	0:25

TOHCC White Flag Trail forks off North Trail at 0.3 mi., a short distance above the highest brook crossing. After traversing a small ridge, the trail ascends gradually to the southeast through long-overgrown pastures. Approaching a stone wall, White Flag Trail turns sharply right, while Boulder Trail goes to the left. With the stone wall on the left, White Flag Trail ascends a steep section and then turns sharply left and slabs across gentle ledges. Boulder Trail rejoins shortly before the jct. with Barnes Trail and Ridge Walk near the Front Ledges, where there are excellent views over the town of Hiram.

Boulder Trail. This interesting alternate route parallels much of White Flag Trail at a lower contour, passing large boulders and the remains of pasture fences while climbing over several short ledges. Boulder Trail is 0.15 mi. long and gains about 40 ft. between North Trail and Barnes Trail.

MORAINE TRAIL (AMC MT. CUTLER MAP)
Cumulative from Hiram Hill Rd. (380 ft.) to:

Start of Moraine Trail via railroad tracks (380 ft.)	0.2 mi.	0 ft.	0:05
North Trail (500 ft.)	0.4 mi.	120 ft.	0:15

TOHCC From the railroad crossing on Hiram Hill Rd., walk 0.2 mi. south on the abandoned Mountain Division railroad tracks. On the right, a trail sign and white blazes mark the start of Moraine Trail. Ascending through hardwoods via two switchbacks, the trail climbs to the east end of an

SEC
8

interesting ridge (a glacial moraine), crosses a stone wall, and then follows the ridge to the jct. with North Trail.

Moraine Trail Link. This 0.1-mi. yellow-blazed connector (gains 40 ft.) links the Hiram Hill Rd. parking area with Moraine Trail partway along, avoiding the need to walk down Hiram Hill Rd. and then along the railroad tracks to the official start of the trail.

NORTHWEST TRAIL (AMC MT. CUTLER MAP)
Cumulative from Hiram Hill Rd. (600 ft.) to:

Link Trail (700 ft.)	0.15 mi.	100 ft.	0:08
Ridge Walk (1,170 ft.)	0.65 mi.	570 ft.	0:35
Notch/ATV trail (1,090 ft.) east of Mt. Cutler summit via Ridge Walk	0.95 mi.	590 ft.	0:50

TOHCC Roadside parking for Northwest Trail is available on Hiram Hill Rd. 0.3 mi. west of the main trailhead parking lot (see directions to North Trail, p. 378).

White-blazed Northwest Trail ascends with marked boundary lines on the right, crossing a small stream about halfway to the jct. with Link Trail (connects to North Trail). A short distance above that jct., Northwest Trail turns sharply right and gently ascends through a mix of hemlock and beech, with the north ledges of Mt. Cutler always to the left. Traversing a small ridge, the trail turns left to follow a fairly steep old logging road. Turning right off the old road, Northwest Trail ascends a larger ridge and then steadily rises into thick hemlocks, eventually emerging at the jct. with Ridge Walk.

SEC 8

FRANCIS SMALL HERITAGE TRUST
SAWYER MTN. (1,226 FT.)

Sawyer Mtn. is the central natural feature of the Sawyer Mtn. Highlands, a parcel of 1,472 contiguous acres spanning the town lines of Limerick and Limington. Owned and managed by Francis Small Heritage Trust, the property is part of the largest unfragmented block of undeveloped forestland in York and Cumberland counties, just 22 mi. from the major urban center of Portland. Reach Sawyer Mtn. from Limerick in the west or from Limington in the east.

More than 5 mi. of trails thread through the hilly terrain, which is home to stands of old-growth red oak, hemlock, sugar maple, and beech; miles of stone walls; and the remains of the historical Sawyer homestead. Trails are marked with small blocks of wood that have the outline of a turtle (painted yellow) carved into them; this is the mark of Captain Sandy, also known as Chief Wesumbe, of the Newichewannock Abenaki, the native people of the area.

SMITH TRAIL (USGS LIMERICK QUAD, FSHT SAWYER MTN. HIGHLANDS MAP, GAZETTEER MAP 4)
Cumulative from Sawyer Mtn. Rd. (620 ft.) to:

Old Sawyer Mtn. Rd. (950 ft.)	0.8 mi.	330 ft.	0:35
Summit side trail (1,115 ft.)	1.2 mi.	485 ft.	0:50
Sawyer Mtn. summit (1,226 ft.)	1.5 mi.	595 ft.	1:00

FSHT Smith Trail climbs Sawyer Mtn. from the Limerick side. From the post office at the jct. of ME 5 and ME 11 in the town of Limerick, drive northeast on ME 11 for 0.9 mi. Just after the boat launch and outlet dam on Sokokis Lake, turn left onto Emery Corner Rd. Follow it for 0.8 mi. to a 4-way intersection, where Quarry Rd. goes left and Pickerel Pond Rd. goes right. Proceed straight through the intersection to continue on Emery Corner Rd. In 1.2 mi., Coffin Hill Rd. diverges right; here, bear sharply left onto Sawyer Mtn. Rd. to reach Emery Corner in another 0.5 mi. Continue straight on dirt Sawyer Mtn. Rd. (paved Lombard Hill Rd. goes left and dirt Shaving Hill Rd. goes right). In 0.6 mi., Nason Corner Rd. diverges left; continue straight ahead on Sawyer Mtn. Rd. to reach the gravel trailhead parking lot on the right in another 0.3 mi. If you reach a town turnaround in sight of a red barn on a hill to the right, you've gone a little too far. (*Note*: During spring mud season, the parking lot is closed, requiring hikers to park along the roadside.)

Smith Trail leaves from the right-hand corner of the lot and proceeds uphill on a wide track. Ahead, bear left up a ridge, which climbs next to a stream in a rocky ravine. The trail soon levels off and crosses the stream. Proceeding on a contour, the path follows a jeep trail but soon bears left onto a footpath (arrow) and climbs up and left below a ridge of mossy boulders. The angle eases as Smith Trail continues through parklike woods, swinging up and right to pass a huge, ancient oak 25 ft. to the right. The trail bends gently left, easily ascends the slope, and then bears sharply left (arrow) and passes through a gap in a stone wall. Along a wide, level stretch, Smith Trail passes through two more stone walls, trends gently downhill, passes through a fourth stone wall, and soon reaches the jct. with old Sawyer Mtn. Rd. The stone foundations, cellar holes, and well of the old Sawyer family homestead (settled in 1794) are directly ahead in the woods across from the jct.

Turn right on old Sawyer Mtn. Rd. and follow this wide, eroded, and often wet road north to the height-of-land on the northwest shoulder of the mountain. Here, a side trail leaves right to follow the ridge crest for 0.3 mi. to the summit of Sawyer Mtn.

SEC 8

Visible from the ocean, the summit of Sawyer Mtn. was once the location of a whale oil light that helped guide ships into Portland Harbor in the eighteenth century. In 1884, the USGS erected a 15-ft. stone monument on the site, which was destroyed by lightning in 1913. Scattered stones from the tower still remain. From the summit sign, Smith Trail continues to a fine, flat rock in a grassy clearing, where it ends. Just below to the right is a log bench, offering views to the south and west that encompass the lowlands of York County and southern New Hampshire. On the northeast side of the summit, look out over Sebago Lake, the second-largest and deepest lake in Maine.

SUMMIT SPUR (USGS LIMERICK QUAD, FSHT SAWYER MTN. HIGHLANDS MAP, GAZETTEER MAP 4)

FSHT This short side trail connects old Sawyer Mtn. Rd. to the top of Sawyer Mtn. Hiked in that direction, Summit Spur passes the west end of Sherwood Libby Trail before ending on the summit at a bench and viewpoint, gaining about 100 ft. in elevation over its 0.3-mi. distance.

SAWYER MTN. ROAD (USGS STEEP FALLS, LIMINGTON AND LIMERICK QUADS, FSHT SAWYER MTN. HIGHLANDS MAP, GAZETTEER MAP 4)

Cumulative from ME 117 (470 ft.) to:

Summit Spur (1,115 ft.)	1.7 mi.	645 ft.	1:10
Sawyer Mtn. summit (1,226 ft.)	2.0 mi.	755 ft.	1:20

FSHT From the jct. of ME 25 and ME 117 in Limington, drive south on ME 117 for 2.5 mi. to a parking area (sign) on the right. The trailhead can also be reached by driving north on ME 117 for 2.4 mi. from the jct. of ME 117 and ME 11 in Limington.

The trail leaves the parking area and follows the right-hand branch road, old Sawyer Mtn. Rd., which is rough, rocky, and severely eroded in places. In the first 0.5 mi., pass the upper and lower legs of Veazie Trail, a loop. In the next 0.5 mi., pass a brown cabin and a red cabin, both on the right (please observe private property signs). Hall Road enters from the right at 1.0 mi., Estes Cemetery is on the right at 1.1 mi., New Skidway Rd. leaves left at 1.2 mi., and a picnic table and old foundation are on the right at 1.3 mi. The climbing soon begins in earnest, and after 0.6 mi. of rough footing, Sawyer Mtn. Road reaches Summit Spur on the left; turn here to follow this 0.3-mi. spur to the top of Sawyer Mtn.

SHERWOOD LIBBY TRAIL (USGS STEEP FALLS, LIMINGTON AND LIMERICK QUADS, FSHT SAWYER MTN. HIGHLANDS MAP, GAZETTEER MAP 4)

Cumulative from ME 117 (470 ft.) to:

Kiosk and Nature Trail, upper loop (490 ft.)	67 yd.	20 ft.	0:02
Nature Trail, lower loop (500 ft.)	0.15 mi.	30 ft.	0:05
Lower Veazie Trail (760 ft.)	0.65 mi.	290 ft.	0:30
Upper Veazie Trail (800 ft.)	0.7 mi.	330 ft.	0:32
High pasture of Ebenezer Walker (980 ft.)	1.3 mi.	510 ft.	0:50
New Skidway Rd. (825 ft.)	1.9 mi.	510 ft.	1:10
Summit Spur (1,185 ft.)	2.2 mi.	870 ft.	1:30
Sawyer Mtn. summit (1,226 ft.)	2.3 mi.	1,010 ft.	1:40

FSHT This trail leaves from the same trailhead parking area as Sawyer Mtn. Road, described above.

Take the left-hand branch road from the parking area to follow old Littlefield Pond Rd. Immediately on the left is a foundation from the 1815 Benjamin Wentworth homestead. In 200 ft., reach a small, grassy clearing with a kiosk and a jct. with Nature Trail, a 0.7-mi. loop. Soon after, pass a side trail to FSHT's Forest Carbon Project, an environmental education project designed to inform land trusts and landowners about the role of forests in carbon sequestration. The other side of Nature Loop soon enters from the right. Alternating between old forest road and footpath, the trail climbs at a moderate grade through boulders and ledges to Lower Veazie Trail and Upper Veazie Trail, both on the right. After crossing a drainage, Sherwood Libby Trail skirts a grassy area at the base of John Douglass Mtn., named for one of the first settlers in the vicinity. The trail continues to the right below towering, rocky cliffs and ascends via rock stairs to beautiful stone walls that mark the former high pasture of Ebenezer Walker, who cleared the land here in 1815. Beyond, the trail descends slightly through old fields, now grown up to forest, bounded by stone walls, and then ascends slightly to cross New Skidway Rd. Sherwood Libby Trail continues to ascend Sawyer Mtn., joining Summit Spur, which leads left (southwest) 0.15 mi. to the top and its viewpoint.

SEC 8

BALD LEDGE (1,190 FT.)

The precipitous cliffs atop this crag in Porter, not far from the New Hampshire border, reward hikers with a fabulous vista eastward over Colcord

Pond to the pretty hills and woods of north-central York County. FSHT owns 25 acres of land next to the ledges, and the Giovanella family of the nearby Bickford Pond area owns 200 acres, which includes most of Bald Ledge and its summit overlook. FSHT maintains a trail to the top from the west side.

From the jct. of Old County Rd. and ME 25/160 in Porter, drive north on Old County Rd. for 1.5 mi. Bear left onto Colcord Pond Rd. and continue 2.8 mi. to a fork. Here, Colcord Pond Rd. goes right; bear left and proceed on Dana Weeks Rd. for a very short distance; then bear right again to continue on Kennard Hill Rd. Drive 1.5 mi. up several steep hills to Danforth Ln. Turn right onto Danforth Ln. and then, at a split in the road ahead, bear right on Varney Rd. A water bar lies on this old road, so be careful. Parking is a short way down Varney Rd. at a grassy open space on the right.

BALD LEDGE TRAIL (USGS KEZAR FALLS QUAD, MTF BALD LEDGE PRESERVE, GAZETTEER MAP 4)
From Varney Rd. parking (870 ft.) to:

Bald Ledge summit outlook (1,190 ft.)	0.7 mi.	320 ft.	0:30

FSHT Walk north on Varney Rd., following the wide old road easily uphill, passing a shed on the left. At 0.3 mi., look for a red block of wood on the right with the carved outline of a turtle painted yellow; this marks the start of the foot trail to Bald Ledge. Cross the stone wall bordering the road; follow along another stone wall, and go right at a third stone wall. Pass a huge bull pine on the left, and then bear sharply left to cross a low, mossy stone wall. Proceed through woods of red and white pine. Follow the trail along the right of a large stone wall, cross another low, mossy wall, and head upslope through hemlocks to reach a jct. Here, an old trail from the Colcord Pond side enters from the left. Turn right and climb through a hemlock grove to a ledge outlook on the left (best views of Colcord Pond and the hills and woods beyond). Continue easily along the ridge to trail's end at the top of Bald Ledge and another outlook.

VERNON S. WALKER WILDLIFE MANAGEMENT AREA
KNOX MTN. (824 FT.)

This mountain in Newfield is in the northern part of the expansive Vernon S. Walker WMA, which spans 5,617 acres across the towns of Newfield, Limerick, and Shapleigh. DIFW manages the property. An unmarked trail climbs Knox Mtn. from the north.

From the jct. of ME 110 and ME 11 in Newfield, drive east on ME 11 for 2.0 mi. to an unsigned turnout on the right, directly across from the eastern end of Symmes Pond.

KNOX MTN. TRAIL (USGS LIMERICK QUAD, GAZETTEER MAP 2)
From ME 11 turnout (500 ft.) to:

Knox Mtn. summit (824 ft.)	0.8 mi.	324 ft.	0:30

NFTM From the turnout, follow the foot trail into the woods. (*Note*: The start is at an old paint-blazed boundary line; look closely because the entrance may be obscure.) Climb along a stone wall to a knoll. Descend through a cutover area, pass through a gap in a stone wall, and then cross a low, wet area. Beyond, at another stone wall, bear right and up, following the line of the wall. At 0.5 mi., go around the upper end of the stone wall to join an ATV track and continue uphill at a moderate grade, following the wide track along the north ridge. As the ridge narrows, hike over bedrock trail. At 0.7 mi., pass an obvious square-angled cut in a low ledge to the right. The tree canopy thins beyond this point. Reach the summit ledges just ahead and enjoy fine views of the surrounding Little Ossipee River valley countryside from this vantage point.

ABBOTT MTN. (1,079 FT.)

This mountain in Shapleigh is in the southeast corner of the Vernon S. Walker WMA. Managed by DIFW, the property encompasses 5,617 acres in the towns of Shapleigh, Newfield, and Limerick. An unmarked trail ascends the mountain from the south.

In the center of Shapleigh, at the intersection of ME 11 and Owl's Nest Rd., opposite a large white church, turn north on Owl's Nest Rd. and drive 3.3 mi. to the jct. of Owl's Nest Rd. and Pitts Rd. (pavement ends 0.3 mi. before this jct.). Park here on the right side of Owl's Nest Rd.

**SEC
8**

ABBOTT MTN. TRAIL (USGS MOUSAM LAKE QUAD, GAZETTEER MAP 2)
From parking at jct. of Owl's Nest Rd. and Pitts Rd. (580 ft.) to:

Abbott Mtn. summit (1,079 ft.)	1.3 mi.	499 ft.	0:55

NFTM Walk up Pitts Rd. Although this private road is drivable, the landowner requests that users visit Abbott Mtn. by "foot and hoof" only; please respect these wishes. At 0.2 mi., Pitts Rd. ends (No Parking signs). A driveway (number 43) is to the right. Walk straight ahead on the obvious old woods road (Abbott Mtn. Rd.). At a jct. at 0.4 mi., turn left to follow a wide, rocky, eroded old jeep trail. Pass an old camper trailer in the woods on the right and a small pond on the left. At 0.85 mi., where the jeep road continues straight, the trail (an ATV trail) to Abbott Mtn. turns left and ascends steeply up ledges. Climb a series of ledge steps on the eroded bedrock trail, which is crisscrossed by ATV tracks. (Stick to the most obvious route uphill.) At 1.0 mi., enter a clearing of bedrock and grass with a lone pine in the center. Go left past the pine and continue upward. A multitrunked pine is in the center of the next clearing. Behind you now are views south and west. Ahead, climb a moderate-to-steep stretch over open ledges and reach the summit rock at 1.3 mi. at an ATV roundabout. The pleasant scenery of the surrounding woodland extends west to the White Mountains. Another outlook ledge is 100 yd. north.

OSSIPEE HILL (1,066 FT.)

This hill in Waterboro Center, just west of Little Ossipee Lake, is topped by a 35-foot wooden fire tower (built in 1958) and two communications towers. Clear views northwest to the White Mountains and eastward over the Saco River valley are possible from high on the fire tower steps (the cab is locked and not open to the public).

From the jct. of US 202/ME 4 and ME 5 in East Waterboro, travel north on ME 5 for 1.8 mi. to Waterboro Center. Turn left on Old Alfred Rd., and in 150 ft., continue straight onto Ossipee Hill Rd. Just beyond, turn right onto McLucas Rd., which narrows and turns to dirt in 0.5 mi. Reach Mountain Rd. on the left at 1.7 mi. from Ossipee Hill Rd. Park on the side of McLucas Rd.

OSSIPEE HILL TRAIL (USGS WATERBORO QUAD, GAZETTEER MAP 2)
From McLucas Rd. (695 ft.) to:

Ossipee Hill fire tower (1,050 ft.)	0.9 mi.	355 ft.	0:40

NFTM Ossipee Hill Trail is also the access road to the towers. From McLucas Rd., walk south up Mountain Rd., a steady climb for the first 0.2 mi. The road then bends left and follows a contour past a silver gate and an ATV track on the right. Soon after, the road turns sharply right and climbs past an old yellow gate. After leveling off, reach an area of exposed bedrock. Descend slightly to a sag and then ascend to the end of the gravel road. Finish on the concrete track that leads past two fenced-in communications towers and ends at the base of the 1958 wooden fire tower.

BAUNEG BEG MTN. CONSERVATION AREA
BAUNEG BEG MTN.: MIDDLE PEAK (864 FT.)
AND NORTH PEAK (828 FT.)

The middle peak of this mountain in North Berwick is part of the 89-acre Bauneg Beg Mtn. Conservation Area, which is owned and managed by Great Works Regional Land Trust. The mountain's north peak is on land owned by the town of North Berwick. Bauneg Beg Mtn. (pronounced like "Bonny Beg") is the only major mountain in southern York County without a communications tower on top. Views from the summit range from the White Mountains and western Maine to the Atlantic Ocean.

From North Berwick, drive north on US 4 for 2.1 mi. Turn left onto Boyle Rd. and continue straight as it turns into Ford Quint Rd., about 5.5 mi. from US 4. Turn left onto Fox Farm Hill Rd. and proceed 0.3 mi. to the signed trailhead parking area on the left.

BAUNEG BEG TRAIL (USGS SANFORD QUAD, GWRLT BAUNEG BEG CONSERVATION AREA MAP, GAZETTEER MAP 2)
Cumulative from Fox Farm Hill Rd. (605 ft.) to:

North Peak Loop (750 ft.)	0.3 mi.	145 ft.	0:15
Ginny's Way and Linny's Way jct. (770 ft.)	0.45 mi.	165 ft.	0:20
Tom's Way (850 ft.) via Ginny's Way	0.65 mi.	245 ft.	0:27
Bauneg Beg Mtn., Middle Peak (864 ft.) via Ginny's Way	0.7 mi.	260 ft.	0:28
Bauneg Beg Mtn., Middle Peak (864 ft.) via Linny's Way	0.6 mi.	260 ft.	0:25

SEC 8

GWRLT White-blazed Bauneg Beg Trail leaves from the kiosk at the back of the parking lot. After a series of bog bridges, the path climbs gradually to the jct. of North Peak Loop, which enters from the right. Continue straight to the next jct., where Linny's Way departs right, climbing the mountain via Devil's Den (a jumble of rocks). Bear left to reach the peak via Ginny's Way.

GINNY'S WAY (USGS SANFORD QUAD, GWRLT BAUNEG BEG CONSERVATION AREA MAP, GAZETTEER MAP 2)
From Bauneg Beg Trail and Linny's Way jct. (770 ft.) to:

Tom's Way and Linny's Way jct. (850 ft.)	0.2 mi.	80 ft.	0:07
Bauneg Beg Mtn., Middle Peak (864 ft.) via Linny's Way	0.25 mi.	95 ft.	0:08

GWRLT From the 3-way jct. of Bauneg Beg Trail, Linny's Way, and Ginny's Way, bear left on orange-blazed Ginny's Way, which swings around the east side of the mountain. After a short rise, the trail bears sharply right and ascends the ridge to the jct. of Tom's Way, which descends toward Bauneg Beg Hill Rd. From this jct., continue right and up on Linny's Way 100 ft. to the north-facing summit ledges atop Middle Peak of Bauneg Beg Mtn. The view includes North Peak, part of the city of Sanford, the towers on Mt. Hope, and, on a good day, even Mt. Washington.

LINNY'S WAY (USGS SANFORD QUAD, GWRLT BAUNEG BEG CONSERVATION AREA MAP, GAZETTEER MAP 2)
From Bauneg Beg Trail and Ginny's Way jct. (770 ft.) to:

Bauneg Beg Mtn., Middle Peak (864 ft.)	0.15 mi.	95 ft.	0:08

GWRLT From the 3-way jct. of Bauneg Beg Trail, Ginny's Way, and Linny's Way, bear right on red-blazed Linny's Way. In about 250 ft., blue-blazed North Peak Loop leaves to the right. Continue left and up on Linny's Way through the boulders and ledges of Devil's Den. Atop the ridge, turn left to reach the viewpoint on Middle Peak of Bauneg Beg. Mtn. The jct. with Ginny's Way and Tom's Way is 100 ft. beyond, down to the right.

TOM'S WAY (USGS SANFORD QUAD, GWRLT BAUNEG BEG CONSERVATION AREA MAP, GAZETTEER MAP 2)
From Bauneg Beg Hill Rd. (630 ft.) to:

Ginny's Way and Linny's Way jct. (850 ft.)	0.6 mi.	220 ft.	0:25
Bauneg Beg Mtn., Middle Peak (864 ft.)	0.65 mi.	235 ft.	0:26

GWRLT This orange-blazed trail climbs Bauneg Beg Mtn. (Middle Peak) from the west at Bauneg Beg Hill Rd. To reach the Tom's Way trailhead from the Fox Farm Hill Rd. trailhead, continue north on Fox Farm Hill Rd. In 0.4 mi., turn left onto Hammond Rd. In another 0.3 mi., turn left on Bauneg Beg Hill Rd. The trailhead, a dirt pullout, is on the left 0.7 miles ahead.

From the road, Tom's Way passes through a gap in an old stone wall and then climbs gently via switchbacks over the west slope of the mountain. At the jct. of Ginny's Way and Linny's Way, continue left and up on Linny's Way to the open ledges atop Middle Peak.

NORTH PEAK LOOP (USGS SANFORD QUAD, GWRLT BAUNEG BEG CONSERVATION AREA MAP, GAZETTEER MAP 2)
From Linny's Way (780 ft.) to:

Bauneg Beg Mtn, North Peak (838 ft.)	0.3 mi.	100 ft.	0:12
Bauneg Beg Trail (750 ft.)	0.5 mi.	100 ft.	0:18

GWRLT From Linny's Way near Devil's Den, blue-blazed North Peak Loop crosses a shallow sag between Middle Peak and North Peak and then climbs via switchbacks. Ahead, after passing through a gap in a stone wall, the trail turns at a large cairn to traverse the semi-open summit area. Just before North Peak Loop turns sharply right to pass through the same stone wall again, the top of North Peak is 50 ft. off-trail to the left. On the easy descent, pass through another stone wall before reaching Bauneg Beg Trail. The Fox Farm Hill Rd. trailhead is 0.3 mi. to the left.

MT. AGAMENTICUS CONSERVATION REGION

The Mt. Agamenticus Conservation Region (MACR) encompasses more than 10,000 acres of coastal woods and hills amid an additional 30,000 acres of conservation lands in southern York County. MACR is a cooperative of six public, quasi-public, and nonprofit landowners working together for conservation, watershed protection, and recreation purposes: GWRLT, DIFW, the towns of York and South Berwick, York Land Trust, and York Water District. More than 40 mi. of trails—open year-round—are available for hiking, mountain biking, horseback riding, and ATV use. Because of its location, the mountain's environment is a rare mixing ground for variety of southern and northern plant and animal species at the limits of their ranges.

MT. AGAMENTICUS (693 FT.)

The central feature of MACR is Mt. Agamenticus, which rises distinctively above the coastal plain of southern York County. The main mountain is also known as First Hill; just northeast is Second Hill; and to the east of that, Third Hill. Mt. Agamenticus trails are open year-round, as is Mt. Agamenticus Rd. (weather permitting; the gate closes at sunset). The Learning Lodge, an environmental education center, is open on weekend afternoons from Memorial Day through mid-October.

SEC 8

From the Maine Turnpike/I-95, Exit 7 in York, follow Chases Pond Rd. west and north for 3.5 mi. Turn left onto Mountain Rd., and in 2.5 mi., reach the base of Mt. Agamenticus and the main trailhead parking lot on the right. Paved Mt. Agamenticus Rd. begins from this point, climbing 0.7 mi. to the top of the mountain and a parking lot at the summit. On the open, grassy summit are two observation decks, an old fire tower (erected in 1941; no public access), several communications towers, a barn, and the old lodge of the long-defunct Big A ski area, now the Learning Lodge. (*Note*: Major improvements are planned for the parking and facilities at the base area on Mountain Rd. and on the summit. Some of these changes may affect trailhead access points.)

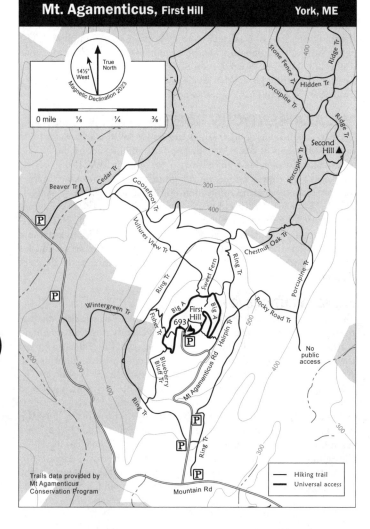

Mt. Agamenticus, First Hill   York, ME

True North

14½° West

Magnetic Declination 2023

0 mile   ⅛   ¼   ⅜

Stone Fence Tr
Ridge Tr
400
Hidden Tr
Porcupine Tr
Ridge Tr
Second Hill ▲
Beaver Tr
Cedar Tr
Goosefoot Tr
300
400
Porcupine Tr
Vultures View Tr
Chestnut Oak Tr
Ring Tr
Sweet Fern
Ring Tr
Wintergreen Tr
Big A
First Hill
Big A
Rocky Road Tr
Porcupine Tr
Fisher Tr
693
Ring Tr
No public access
500
Blueberry Bluff Tr
Mt Agamenticus Rd
Hairpin Tr
400
200
300
Ring Tr
300
400
300
Ring Tr
Trails data provided by
Mt Agamenticus
Conservation Program
Mountain Rd

SEC 8

—— Hiking trail
━━ Universal access

RING TRAIL (AMC MT. AGAMENTICUS, FIRST HILL MAP)
Cumulative from main trailhead parking on Mountain Rd. (347 ft.) to:

Ring Trail loop jct. (400 ft.)	0.1 mi.	50 ft.	0:05
Blueberry Bluff Trail (480 ft.)	0.3 mi.	130 ft.	0:15
Wintergreen Trail (500 ft.)	0.6 mi.	150 ft.	0:25
Fisher Trail (540 ft.)	0.7 mi.	190 ft.	0:30
Vultures View Trail (500 ft.)	0.9 mi.	210 ft.	0:35
Sweet Fern Trail (510 ft.)	1.0 mi.	240 ft.	0:40
Goosefoot Trail, Chestnut Oak Trail (490 ft.)	1.0 mi.	240 ft.	0:40
Witch Hazel Trail (570 ft.)	1.2 mi.	320 ft.	0:45
Rocky Road Trail, Hairpin Trail (550 ft.)	1.3 mi.	340 ft.	0:50
Complete loop	1.9 mi.	360 ft.	1:10

MACP This loop makes a circuit around Mt. Agamenticus, connecting to many of the mountain's summit trails. From the main trailhead on Mountain Rd., white-blazed Ring Trail leaves from the right rear of the parking lot and enters the woods, passing toilets, an information kiosk, and a fee station (an iron ranger, a slotted metal box for accepting the day-use fee). The trail proceeds easily north to the loop jct. at 0.1 mi. Turn left to follow Ring Trail in a clockwise direction. Just ahead, cross Mt. Agamenticus Rd. (parking) and continue following white blazes on the wide, well-used trail. At 0.3 mi., Blueberry Bluff Trail departs to the right. Ahead, crest the west shoulder of the mountain and soon reach a spur to a viewpoint on the left. At 0.6 mi., Wintergreen Trail enters from the left. Stay on Ring Trail and climb a short, moderate pitch that reaches Fisher Trail on the right at 0.7 mi. After a gentle descent, Ring Trail arrives at a clearing, an old ski lift line, and, ahead, several semi-open old ski runs. At 0.9 mi., cross Vultures View Trail.

Swinging around the north side of the mountain, reach the jct. with Sweet Fern Trail, also an old ski run, at 1.0 mi. on the right. Just ahead on the left is the base of an old T-bar lift. At the fork just beyond, Goosefoot Trail leaves at an angle to the left, while Chestnut Oak Trail departs at an angle to the right. Stay on Ring Trail, which continues to the immediate right and climbs the north shoulder via a series of switchbacks to the jct. with Witch Hazel Trail on the right at 1.2 mi. Crest the shoulder and then descend to the east side of the mountain. Arrive at a jct. at 1.3 mi. where Rocky Road Trail enters from the left, and Hairpin Trail leaves to the right. Continue to descend on Ring Trail on a narrow footpath; then climb briefly, follow an undulating route, descend on a wide treadway, and bear right onto a narrow path in a regrowth area. At 1.7 mi., a spur on the right leads 25 ft. to the auto road; bear sharply left here. Close the Ring Trail

SEC 8

loop at the jct. at 1.8 mi. Proceed straight ahead to the trailhead parking lot on Mountain Rd., which is reached in 0.1 mi.

Hairpin Trail. This short, wide, white-blazed trail extends from the jct. of Ring Trail and Rocky Road Trail to Mt. Agamenticus Rd. about 0.2 mi. before the summit parking lot, passing Summit Staircase along the way. Hairpin Trail gains 60 ft. of elevation over 0.15 mi.

Summit Staircase. This red-blazed trail is a short, direct path from Hairpin Trail to the summit lodge, crossing Big A Trail on the way. As its name implies, this moderate-to-steep route is composed of hand-set granite rocks that form a staircase to the summit. It gains 80 ft. of elevation in 375 ft.

Rocky Road. This short white-blazed path, described on the descent, extends from the jct. of Ring Trail and Hairpin Trail to Porcupine Trail. Near its end, the wide, rocky track crosses a boardwalk. Rocky Road Trail loses 140 ft. of elevation over 0.25 mi.

BIG A TRAIL (AMC MT. AGAMENTICUS, FIRST HILL MAP)
From large information kiosk near summit parking lot (693 ft.) to:

Complete Big A Trail circuit	1.0 mi.	50 ft.	0:30

MACP This universally accessible trail makes a circuit around the summit area of Mt. Agamenticus through shrubs and meadows, offering many fine viewpoints along the way. Several slight variations mark the start and finish of Big A Trail. The most straightforward start is to walk east from the large information kiosk, make a quick side trip to the summit observation deck, and then continue around the southeast side of the summit lodge. Pass Summit Staircase, which joins from the right, and then pass a rock pile (an interpretive display on the folklore of St. Aspinquid, a Micmac chief who died in 1906, and the cultural practices of native people). With views ahead to Second Hill and Third Hill, go around the old T-bar tower and snow roller (Sweet Fern Trail begins here), and then continue right around the hairpin. At 0.2 mi., Summit Staircase crosses Big A Trail.

Proceeding north along a contour, at 0.35 mi., Witch Hazel Trail departs right. At 150 ft. beyond, Sweet Fern Trail crosses Big A Trail at the remains of the old T-bar lift line. Immediately ahead, cross a footbridge. Pass a ledge outcropping to reach the jct. with Vultures View Trail, which enters from the right at 0.4 mi. Then pass the concrete base of an old lift line tower. To the left, a side trail leads to an observation deck. At the jct. and atop the deck are expansive views northwest. Continuing on, with the old fire tower (1941; cab has been removed, no access) and communications tower on the left, enter woods. At 0.6 mi., with a barn up to the left, cross Fisher Trail. Just beyond, a spur on the right leads to a bench at Big

A Overlook and to Blueberry Bluff Trail. Big A Trail winds ahead to cross a footbridge over a gully and then goes past the other side of the barn. Cross Fisher Trail again. A spur on the left just ahead goes to an overlook. The fire tower and interpretive displays at its base are to the left; toilets are to the right. At the T intersection here, go right to reach the large information kiosk and parking lot, or continue left to walk around the north side of the summit lodge.

Witch Hazel Trail. This 0.1-mi. white-blazed connector trail, which links Big A Trail to Ring Trail, is described on the descent (loss of 70 ft. in elevation). Witch Hazel Trail departs from Big A Trail on the right at 0.35 mi. from the summit lodge. The trail passes an ancient hemlock tree along its route.

BLUEBERRY BLUFF TRAIL (AMC MT. AGAMENTICUS, FIRST HILL MAP)
Cumulative from main trailhead parking on Mountain Rd. (347 ft.) to:

Start of Blueberry Bluff Trail (480 ft.)	0.3 mi.	130 ft.	0:15
Big A Trail (660 ft.)	0.5 mi.	180 ft.	0:20
Mt. Agamenticus summit (693 ft.) via Big A Trail	0.7 mi.	210 ft.	0:30

MACP Red-blazed Blueberry Bluff Trail is one of four "hiking only" trails on Mt. Agamenticus (along with Wintergreen Trail, Vultures View Trail, and Summit Staircase). The route begins from Ring Trail at a point 0.3 mi. from Mountain Rd. Blueberry Bluff Trail starts up the south ridge via several switchbacks and then climbs ledges, steps, and slabs. Following bedrock trail out of the trees, reach the Big A Overlook and a bench on the left. From this point, continue on Big A Trail, turning right just ahead to follow the loop counterclockwise up to the summit observation deck.

SEC 8

FISHER TRAIL (AMC MT. AGAMENTICUS, FIRST HILL MAP)
Cumulative from main trailhead parking on Mountain Rd. (347 ft.) to:

Start of Fisher Trail (540 ft.)	0.7 mi.	190 ft.	0:30
Big A Trail, second crossing (670 ft.)	0.9 mi.	320 ft.	0:40
Mt. Agamenticus summit (693 ft.)	1.0 mi.	340 ft.	0:45

MACP Fisher Trail starts from Ring Trail at a point 0.7 mi. from Mountain Rd. The white-blazed trail ascends easily via switchbacks, and as it breaks out into the open, the summit fire tower and communications tower are in sight. Cross Big A Trail (stone bench on left) and go around the left side of a barn. Recross Big A Trail and then walk through a grassy area and climb the stone steps to the parking lot, where Fisher Trail ends. Portable toilets are immediately to the left; a large information kiosk, the round observation deck on the summit of Mt. Agamenticus, and the Learning Lodge are straight ahead.

SWEET FERN TRAIL (AMC MT. AGAMENTICUS, FIRST HILL MAP)
Cumulative from Ring Trail (510 ft.) to:

Big A Trail, upper jct. (670 ft.)	0.2 mi.	160 ft.	0:10
Mt. Agamenticus summit (693 ft.)	0.3 mi.	181 ft.	0:15

MACP From Ring Trail, white-blazed Sweet Fern Trail climbs eroded bedrock to the old T-bar tower line and then travels directly up the mountain past three rusting towers. Cross Big A Trail and continue to follow the old lift line to the old upper T-bar lift station and old snow roller on the edge of the large summit meadow. A hairpin turn on Big A Trail is to the left; Northface Path is to the right. The Learning Lodge and summit observation deck are in sight a short distance straight ahead.

WINTERGREEN TRAIL (AMC MT. AGAMENTICUS, FIRST HILL MAP)
From Mountain Rd. (270 ft.) to:

Ring Trail (500 ft.)	0.4 mi.	230 ft.	0:20

MACP This hiker-only trail climbs the west side of Mt. Agamenticus to Ring Trail.

From the trailhead parking lot at the jct. of Mountain Rd. and Mt. Agamenticus Rd., drive west on Mountain Rd., which quickly turns to dirt. In 0.8 mi., red-blazed Wintergreen Trail starts on the right. Park just downhill on the left side of Mountain Rd.

The wide trail trends south for 0.1 mi. before swinging back to the north to follow a contour. At 0.2 mi., the trail ascends east, enters a ravine of hemlocks, and then climbs moderately on some rock steps. Wintergreen Trail ends at Ring Trail a short distance south of Fisher Trail.

CEDAR TRAIL (AMC MT. AGAMENTICUS, FIRST HILL MAP)
Cumulative from red gate on Mountain Rd. (180 ft.) to:

Goosefoot Trail (180 ft.)	0.25 mi.	0 ft.	0:08
Porcupine Trail (220 ft.)	1.1 mi.	40 ft.	0:35
Norman Mill Trail (210 ft.)	1.4 mi.	50 ft.	0:45

MACP Cedar Trail is a wide, multiuse forest road that runs along the western base of Mt. Agamenticus and Second Hill before ending at Norman Mill Trail, another wide, multiuse forest road. Use Cedar Trail to connect with Goosefoot Trail, Vultures View Trail, and Porcupine Trail.

From the main trailhead parking lot at the jct. of Mountain Rd. and Mt. Agamenticus Rd., drive west on Mountain Rd., which quickly turns to dirt. In 1.1 mi., reach a large parking lot on the right, where there is a red gate and a sign for Mt. Agamenticus WMA.

Walk by the left side of the gate on blue-blazed Cedar Trail. After a first and second jct. with Beaver Trail on the left, cross a pond outlet on a culvert. At 0.25 mi., white-blazed Goosefoot Trail leaves to the right. After a gentle climb, cross a plank bridge over a brook and pass a long stone wall on the right. White-blazed Porcupine Trail enters from the right at 1.1 mi. Ahead at 1.4 mi., Cedar Trail ends at a T jct. with Norman Mill Trail. To the right it is 0.5 mi. to Notch Trail, which connects to Stone Fence Trail and Ridge Trail on Second Hill and to Wheel Trail, which offers access to trails on Third Hill.

GOOSEFOOT TRAIL (AMC MT. AGAMENTICUS, FIRST HILL MAP)
Cumulative from red gate on Mountain Rd. AMC (180 ft.) to:

Start of Goosefoot Trail via Cedar Trail (180 ft.)	0.25 mi.	0 ft.	0:08
Ring Trail (490 ft.)	0.7 mi.	310 ft.	0:30
Mt. Agamenticus summit (693 ft.) via Ring Trail and Sweet Fern Trail	1.0 mi.	511 ft.	0:45

MACP Goosefoot Trail climbs Mt. Agamenticus from the northwest. Follow driving directions to the start of Cedar Trail on Mountain Rd.

Walk along blue-blazed Cedar Trail, an old forest road. Pass both ends of Beaver Trail on the left and then reach white-blazed Goosefoot Trail on the right at 0.25 mi. This is the base of an old ski lift line for the long-defunct Big A ski area. Turn right on Goosefoot Trail, pass the concrete stanchions of an old lift, and in 250 ft., reach a fork. Here, red-blazed Vultures View Trail goes right; bear left to continue on Goosefoot Trail and soon join a wide old forest road. Over the next 0.5 mi., the route leaves the old road (to avoid eroded sections) to follow sections of footpaths to the left and right. At 0.7 mi., Goosefoot Trail ends at the jct. of Ring Trail and Chestnut Oak Trail. Turn right on Ring Trail and then quickly turn left to follow Sweet Fern Trail to the summit of Mt. Agamenticus.

SEC 8

VULTURES VIEW TRAIL (AMC MT. AGAMENTICUS, FIRST HILL MAP)
Cumulative from Mountain Rd. (180 ft.) to:

Start of Vultures View Trail via Cedar Trail and Goosefoot Trail (180 ft.)	0.3 mi.	0 ft.	0:10
Ring Trail (500 ft.)	0.6 mi.	320 ft.	0:30
Big A Trail (640 ft.)	0.8 mi.	460 ft.	0:40
Mt. Agamenticus summit (693 ft.) via Sweet Fern Trail and Big A Trail	0.9 mi.	510 ft.	0:45

MACP Vultures View Trail, the longest "hiking only" trail on Mt. Agamenticus, climbs the mountain from the northwest. Follow driving directions to the start of Cedar Trail on Mountain Rd.

Walk along blue-blazed Cedar Trail, an old forest road. Pass both ends of Beaver Trail on the left and then reach white-blazed Goosefoot Trail on the right at 0.25 mi. This is the base of an old ski lift line for the long-defunct Big A ski area. Turn right on Goosefoot Trail, pass the concrete stanchions of an old lift, and in 250 ft., reach a fork. Here, Goosefoot Trail bears left. Bear right to continue on red-blazed Vultures View Trail and climb the wide, rocky treadway. At 0.4 mi., pass through a clearing, part of a former ski run. Just beyond, climb a rock staircase and ascend a series of smooth slabs on the wide, eroded trail. At 0.6 mi., reach the jct. of white-blazed Ring Trail. Continue straight ahead up slabs on more eroded trail and pass double metal pipes, part of an old snowmaking system. At 0.75 mi., emerge into the semi-open summit area. Climb rock steps to reach Big A Trail and then go left or right to reach the summit observation deck and lodge.

CHESTNUT OAK TRAIL (AMC MT. AGAMENTICUS, FIRST HILL MAP)
From Ring Trail and Goosefoot Trail jct. (490 ft.) to:

Porcupine Trail (380 ft.)	0.3 mi.	–110 ft.	0:09

MACP This trail is commonly used as a connector to reach the trails on Second Hill and Third Hill and therefore is described on the descent.

From the jct. of Ring Trail, Goosefoot Trail, and Chestnut Oak Trail on the north slope of Mt. Agamenticus, descend on white-blazed Chestnut Oak Trail via switchbacks. Below, follow a short boardwalk over a drainage and then follow a contour through oaks and hemlocks to end at Porcupine Trail in the sag between Mt. Agamenticus and Second Hill.

SEC 8

SECOND HILL (555 FT.)
Second Hill, in the backcountry northeast of Mt. Agamenticus, has a long north–south ridgeline of ledges and pleasant woods. The South Berwick town line is to the west, and the valley of Chicks Brook is to the east. Trails emanating on and around Mt. Agamenticus can be used to reach Second Hill.

PORCUPINE TRAIL (AMC MT. AGAMENTICUS, FIRST HILL MAP)
Cumulative from base of Rocky Road Trail (420 ft.) to:

Chestnut Oak Trail (380 ft.)	0.3 mi.	–30 ft.	0:10
Second Hill Trail, north jct. (430 ft.)	0.6 mi.	70 ft.	0:20
Stone Fence Trail (360 ft.)	0.8 mi.	70 ft.	0:25
Cedar Trail (220 ft.)	1.3 mi.	70 ft.	0:40

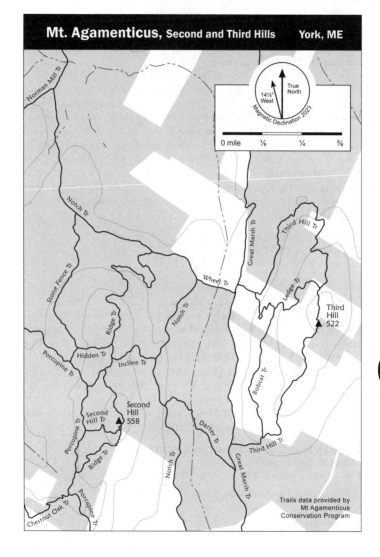

Mt. Agamenticus, Second and Third Hills   York, ME

True North

14½° West

Magnetic Declination 2023

0 mile   ⅛   ¼   ⅜

Norman Mill Tr

Notch Tr

Stone Fence Tr

Ridge Tr

Porcupine Tr

Hidden Tr

Incline Tr

Notch Tr

Wheel Tr

Great Marsh Tr

Third Hill Tr

Ledge Tr

Third Hill 522

Bobcat Tr

Second Hill Tr

Second Hill 558

Porcupine Tr

Ridge Tr

Darter Tr

Notch Tr

Third Hill Tr

Great Marsh Tr

Chestnut Oak Tr

Porcupine Tr

Trails data provided by
Mt Agamenticus
Conservation Program

SEC 8

MACP Porcupine Trail extends from the end of Old Mountain Rd. in the south to Cedar Trail on the northwest side of Second Hill. Rocky Road Trail and Chestnut Oak Trail serve as connectors to Porcupine Trail from the trails on Mt. Agamenticus.

From the base of Rocky Road Trail on the east side of Mt. Agamenticus, white-blazed Porcupine Trail heads north along a contour to cross a drainage. At 0.3 mi., Chestnut Trail enters from the left. Soon after, cross a boardwalk over a small brook and ascend slightly to the unmarked southern end of Second Hill Trail. Continue to the signed jct. of Second Hill Trail on the right at 0.6 mi., which is also marked by a large cairn. Pass an unmarked cutoff path on the right that leads to Ridge Trail. Descend gradually, cross a boardwalk over a drainage, and reach the jct. with Stone Fence Trail on the right at 0.8 mi. Ahead, walk through and along a series of stone walls on a gentle, downward-trending route to reach Cedar Trail at 1.3 mi.

SECOND HILL TRAIL (AMC MT. AGAMENTICUS, SECOND AND THIRD HILLS MAP)
Cumulative from Porcupine Trail, north jct. (430 ft.) to:

Second Hill summit (555 ft.)	0.2 mi.	125 ft.	0:10
Porcupine Trail, south jct. (380 ft.)	0.5 mi.	125 ft.	0:20

MACP Climb easily by switchbacks on wide, white-blazed Second Hill Trail at first, and then ascend a short, moderate pitch through ledge outcroppings to the ridge. An unmarked trail enters from the right (the descent leg of Second Hill Trail); turn left here, and in 50 ft., look left to see the summit sign for Second Hill on a tree (the sign faces away from the trail). To descend, return to the jct. in 50 ft. and continue straight, heading down over bedrock slabs with a view south of the lodge and towers on top of Mt. Agamenticus. Descend through ledge outcroppings and then weave over switchbacks to rejoin Porcupine Trail.

NORMAN MILL TRAIL (AMC MT. AGAMENTICUS, SECOND AND THIRD HILLS MAP)
Cumulative from red gate on Mountain Rd. (180 ft.) to:

Goosefoot Trail via Cedar Trail (180 ft.)	0.25 mi.	0 ft.	0:08
Porcupine Trail via Cedar Trail (220 ft.)	1.1 mi.	40 ft.	0:35
Norman Mill Trail via Cedar Trail (210 ft.)	1.4 mi.	50 ft.	0:45
Notch Trail (180 ft.)	1.9 mi.	70 ft.	1:00

MACP This wide, multiuse forest road extends from Pave Street Rd. to Bennett Lot Rd. A 0.5-mi. segment of orange-blazed Norman Mill Trail connects Cedar Trail to Notch Trail, which leads to the start of Stone

Fence Trail and Ridge Trail on the north side of Second Hill and to more trails to the east on Third Hill. Along Norman Mill Trail are several sections of old stone wall and a red cabin (private property).

NOTCH TRAIL (AMC MT. AGAMENTICUS, SECOND AND THIRD HILLS MAP)
Cumulative from red gate on Mountain Rd. (180 ft.) to:

Norman Mill Trail via Cedar Trail (210 ft.)	1.4 mi.	50 ft.	0:45
Notch Trail (180 ft.)	1.9 mi.	70 ft.	1:00
Stone Fence Trail (210 ft.)	2.3 mi.	100 ft.	1:10
Ridge Trail (250 ft.)	2.6 mi.	140 ft.	1:20
Wheel Trail (250 ft.)	2.8 mi.	160 ft.	1:30
Incline Trail (310 ft.)	3.1 mi.	220 ft.	1:40
Darter Trail (300 ft.)	3.3 mi.	220 ft.	1:50

MACP Notch Trail is a wide, multiuse forest road extending from Norman Mill Trail to Old Mountain Rd. The green-blazed trail provides access to Stone Fence Trail and Ridge Trail on the north side of Second Hill as well as the network of trails on Third Hill. From Norman Mill Trail, soon after crossing a brook, Notch Trail rises gently to meet Stone Fence Trail on the right. Beyond, Notch Trail climbs gently to Ridge Trail on the right. At the jct. with Wheel Trail, Notch Trail continues to the right (south) and rises to meet Incline Trail, which leaves to the right. Not far ahead, Darter Trail leaves Notch Trail to the left and descends.

Wheel Trail. This wide, yellow-blazed, 0.13-mi. multiuse trail connects Notch Trail to Great Marsh Trail at the western base of Third Hill. Hiked in that direction, the trail loses an easy 20 ft. of elevation to cross Chicks Brook and then gains it back to meet Great Marsh Trail. Third Hill Trail begins 250 ft. to the left along Great Marsh Trail.

Incline Trail. This short trail climbs the east side of Second Hill to connect Notch Trail with Ridge Trail. Hiked in that direction, the trail—steep at first but then moderate in grade—gains 130 ft. of elevation in 0.2 mi.

DARTER TRAIL (AMC MT. AGAMENTICUS, SECOND AND THIRD HILLS MAP)
From Notch Trail (300 ft.) to:

Great Marsh Trail (260 ft.)	0.4 mi.	30 ft.	0:12

MACP This trail connects Notch Trail to Great Marsh Trail between Second Hill and Third Hill. From Notch Trail, Darter Trail winds gently downslope to pass a large boulder. After crossing a wet area (Chicks

Brook), Darter Trail swings to the right around a rocky hill and ends at Great Marsh Trail. Turn left here to the southern jct. of Third Hill Trail.

STONE FENCE TRAIL (MACP; AMC MT. AGAMENTICUS, SECOND AND THIRD HILLS MAP)
Cumulative from Notch Trail (210 ft.) to:

Hidden Trail (380 ft.)	0.5 mi.	170 ft.	0:20
Porcupine Trail (360 ft.)	0.6 mi.	170 ft.	0:25

This white-blazed trail leaves from Notch Trail at a point 2.1 mi. from the red gate on Mountain Rd. via Cedar Trail and Norman Mill Trail. Stone Fence Trail climbs the north side of Second Hill, passing through and by a long series of beautiful old stone walls (some stacked as high as 4 ft.). Soon after the jct. with Hidden Trail, Stone Fence Trail terminates at Porcupine Trail.

RIDGE TRAIL (AMC MT. AGAMENTICUS, SECOND AND THIRD HILLS MAP)
Cumulative from Notch Trail (250 ft.) to:

Hidden Trail (430 ft.)	0.7 mi.	180 ft.	0:25
Incline Trail (430 ft.)	0.8 mi.	180 ft.	0:30
Second Hill summit (558 ft.)	1.0 mi.	305 ft.	0:40

MACP Ridge Trail follows a long and winding course up the north side of Second Hill from a point on Notch Trail 2.6 miles from the red gate on Mountain Rd. via Cedar Trail and Norman Mill Trail. The white-blazed trail follows several switchbacks to gain the upper ridge and then proceeds through parklike woods of pine and oak to meet Hidden Trail, which descends to the right. Just ahead, Incline Trail joins from the left. Continuing on Ridge Trail, bear left at a fork (to the right is an unmarked cutoff trail that leads about 500 ft. to Porcupine Trail), cross a short boardwalk, and climb past a long, mossy ledge. Negotiate the ledges above to reach the top of Second Hill just to the right of Ridge Trail. Second Hill Trail descends the hill to the south.

Hidden Trail. This short path, high on the north ridge of Second Hill, connects Ridge Trail to Stone Fence Trail. Hiked in that direction, the trail loses 50 ft. of elevation over 0.15 mi.

THIRD HILL (522 FT.)
This wooded peak is east of Second Hill in the backcountry northeast of Mt. Agamenticus. Chicks Brook runs along the western base of the hill, and the

Ogunquit River is to the north. Third Hill can be reached from Mt. Agamenticus and Second Hill by way of any number of trail combinations.

GREAT MARSH TRAIL (AMC MT. AGAMENTICUS, SECOND AND THIRD HILLS MAP)
Cumulative from Darter Trail (260 ft.) to:

Third Hill Trail, southern jct. (280 ft.)	0.1 mi.	20 ft.	0:03
Wheel Trail (230 ft.)	0.6 mi.	50 ft.	0:20
Third Hill Trail, northern jct. (230 ft.)	0.65 mi.	50 ft.	0:21

MACP Great Marsh Trail is a wide, multiuse forest road extending from
Old Mountain Rd. to Old County Rd. through the valley of Chicks Brook
east of Mt. Agamenticus and Second Hill and west of Third Hill. A portion
of this purple-blazed trail between Darter Trail and the northern jct. of
Third Hill Trail is described. From Darter Trail, Great Marsh Trail is bordered on each side by old stone walls. Beyond Third Hill Trail, Great Marsh
Trail descends the rocky, eroded old woods road. Ahead, Wheel Trail enters
from the left, and just beyond, Third Hill Trail leaves to the right.

THIRD HILL TRAIL (AMC MT. AGAMENTICUS, SECOND AND THIRD HILLS MAP)
Cumulative from north jct. of Great Marsh Trail and Third Hill Trail (230 ft.) to:

Ledge Trail, lower jct. (280 ft.)	0.08 mi.	50 ft.	0:02
Ledge Trail, upper jct. (490 ft.)	0.9 mi.	260 ft.	0:35
Third Hill summit (522 ft.)	1.0 mi.	292 ft.	0:40
Bobcat Trail (330 ft.)	1.5 mi.	292 ft.	0:55
Great Marsh Trail, south jct. (280 ft.)	1.6 mi.	292 ft.	1:00

SEC 8

MACP This white-blazed trail makes a north–south horseshoe traverse of
Third Hill. From Great Marsh Trail, hike east on Third Hill Trail. In 400
ft., Ledge Trail leaves to the right. Stay straight on Third Hill Trail, climb
a slope, and then contour easily north to a ledge outcropping in a small
clearing. At 0.45 mi., reach an unsigned jct. with a knee-high cairn, and
turn right to stay on Third Hill Trail. Pass another cairn and wind up the
north ridge at an easy-to-moderate grade. Hike over bedrock trail edged
with moss to reach a cairn in a semi-open area at 0.8 mi. Here, the upper
end of Ledge Trail enters from the right. Continue to climb, and then level
off and easily cross the upper ridge to reach the top of Third Hill and a 5-ft.
cairn at 0.9 mi.

Beyond the summit, trend gently down to a large open ledge and, below
that, a semi-open ridgeline. Descend on wide and then eroded treadway

over ledges to reach Bobcat Trail on the right at 1.5 mi. Third Hill Trail continues left and down to reach Great Marsh Trail in another 0.1 mi. at a point just north of Darter Trail.

LEDGE TRAIL (AMC MT. AGAMENTICUS, SECOND AND THIRD HILLS MAP)
Cumulative from Third Hill Trail, lower jct. (280 ft.) to:

Bobcat Trail, north end (370 ft.)	0.2 mi.	90 ft.	0:10
Third Hill Trail, upper jct. (490 ft.)	0.5 mi.	210 ft.	0:20
Third Hill summit (522 ft.) via Third Hill Trail	0.6 mi.	242 ft.	0:25

MACP White-blazed Ledge Trail offers a direct route up the west side of Third Hill. From the jct. of Third Hill Trail, climb through an area of ledges via a series of switchbacks to Bobcat Trail on the right at 0.2 mi. Continue the climb on Ledge Trail via switchbacks through ledges. At 0.35 mi., make an arc north over an open slab. Cross more slabs and then bear right and up toward the obvious cairns. Ascend a final ledge step to the cairn and sign at the jct. of Third Hill Trail. The top of Third Hill is 0.1 mi. right (south).

BOBCAT TRAIL (AMC MT. AGAMENTICUS, SECOND AND THIRD HILLS MAP)
Cumulative from Third Hill Trail (330 ft.) to:

Ledge Trail (370 ft.)	0.4 mi.	40 ft.	0:12
Third Hill Trail (280 ft.) via Ledge Trail	0.6 mi.	40 ft.	0:20

MACP To make a loop on Third Hill, from the jct. of Third Hill Trail and Bobcat Trail, follow narrow, white-blazed Bobcat Trail north on a contour over the lower western slope of the hill, passing ledges, outcroppings, and small cliff faces, to reach Ledge Trail at 0.4 mi. Go left down Ledge Trail on an eroded, moderate pitch at the start and then on a series of switchbacks. Join Third Hill Trail at 0.6 mi.

SECTION NINE

MIDCOAST

INTRODUCTION

This section describes 42 trails on 21 mountains in the Midcoast region, which includes the entirety of Waldo County, Knox County, Lincoln County, and Sagadahoc County. It is bounded by the counties of Cumberland, Androscoggin, Kennebec, Somerset, and Penobscot to the west and north. The Penobscot River and Penobscot Bay form the eastern boundary (the river from Winterport to Stockton Springs, and the bay from there to Spruce Head and the Muscle Ridge Islands). The sinuous coastline along the Gulf of Maine composes the southern boundary, with a series of long, fingerlike peninsulas, craggy headlands, bays and sounds, and many islands, ranging from Casco Bay to Penobscot Bay. The Androscoggin River and Kennebec River merge at Merrymeeting Bay and flow into the Atlantic Ocean east of Popham Beach. Numerous other rivers, including the Damariscotta, Sheepscot, and Georges, flow across the landscape before emptying into the ocean. Rolling hills, farmland, and lakes characterize much of the interior of the region. A mountainous belt extends from the Unity area southeast to Penobscot Bay at Camden and Rockport, near which the greatest concentration of high mountains (to a little more than 1,300 ft.) is found.

SEC 9

GEOGRAPHY

The Camden Hills are a compact and attractive complex of mountains rising above the western shore of Penobscot Bay in the towns of Lincolnville, Camden, and Rockport. These coastal summits share many characteristics with the mountains of Acadia on Mt. Desert Island a few miles to the east, including fragrant forests of spruce and fir; bold cliffs and ledges; and broad vistas of oceans, lakes, and mountains. Camden Hills State Park encompasses 6,200 acres of the scenic Camden Hills. At 1,378 ft., Mt. Megunticook is the highest peak in the Camden Hills and, with the exception of Cadillac Mtn., the highest point on the Atlantic seaboard of the United States. The great cliffs at Ocean Lookout on the southeastern ridge of Megunticook are some of the finest viewpoints anywhere along the Midcoast.

North of Mt. Megunticook are the extensive open blueberry fields atop Cameron Mtn. (809 ft.). A series of mountains continues northeast of Megunticook for several miles, including Bald Rock Mtn. (1,107 ft.) and its summit ledges overlooking Penobscot Bay; farther along are the wooded ridges of Derry Mtn. (771 ft.) and Frohock Mtn. (458 ft.). Mt. Battie (806 ft.) rises steeply just south of Mt. Megunticook. A popular auto road climbs to the Mt. Battie summit, which is adorned by a stone observation tower. Just outside the state park, near the end of the northwestern ridge of Mt. Megunticook, trails lead to Maiden Cliff (745 ft.), which overlooks Megunticook Lake. More than 30 mi. of well-maintained, blue-blazed trails crisscross the park.

Megunticook Lake and Megunticook River separate the main peaks of the Camden Hills from the mountains extending to the southwest, which include Bald Mtn. (1,273 ft.) in Camden and Ragged Mtn. (1,305 ft.) and Little Ragged Mtn. (1,230 ft.) astride the Camden–Rockport town line. The northeastern slope of Ragged Mtn. is home to the downhill ski area known as Camden Snow Bowl. Ragged Mtn. and Bald Mtn. are both the focus of conservation and trail-building efforts by Coastal Mountains Land Trust and Georges River Land Trust. Northwest of Bald and Ragged mountains in Hope rises Hatchet Mtn. (1,110 ft.), which looks out over Hobbs Pond. Just southwest of Rockport Harbor, Beech Hill (534 ft.) features open blueberry fields and a historical stone hut on its summit. Between Lincolnville and Belfast is Mt. Percival (506 ft.), in the town of Northport. Now heavily wooded, Mt. Percival once had a cleared summit and a lookout tower that offered magnificent vistas over Penobscot Bay.

Another area of hills with elevations in and around the 1,000-ft. level is about 15 mi. northwest of the Camden Hills, mostly in the town of Montville. Frye Mtn. (1,140 ft.) is the high point in the 5,240-acre Gene Letourneau (Frye Mtn.) Wildlife Management Area. Neighboring Hogback Mtn. (1,130 ft.) has a fine summit overlook. Just west is Whitten Hill (864 ft.), which is part of Sheepscot Headwaters Preserve, a property of Midcoast Conservancy. North of that is rolling Goose Ridge (916 ft.), with its high fields and lovely views. To the south, in Liberty, Haystack Mtn. (841 ft.) affords grand views over the Montville hills from its summit blueberry fields. Hills to Sea Trail extends eastward for 47 mi. through the rural countryside of Waldo County from Unity to Belfast and includes portions of trails on Whitten Hill, Hogback Mtn., and Frye Mtn.

A few miles west of Verona Island and the mouth of the Penobscot River, the summit ledges of Mt. Waldo (1,062 ft.) loom large over Frankfort. Far

SEC 9

to the southwest, on the crest of Georgetown Island between the Kennebec River and Sheepscot Bay, is Higgins Mtn. (262 ft.) and lovely woods of pitch pine, oak, and blueberry.

ROAD ACCESS

The bulk of the trails in this section are in Waldo County, from its northwestern corner to the coast at Penobscot Bay between Lincolnville and Rockport. Most of the remaining trails are near the coast in the northeastern corner of Knox County. The major highway routes leading to local roads and trailheads are ME 3 and ME 17 from east to west, and ME 220 and US 1 from south to north. Important connectors are ME 52 and ME 105 out of Camden and ME 90 out of Rockport. ME 127 from US 1 in Woolwich is the route to Georgetown Island.

CAMPING

Camping is available in the Midcoast region at Camden Hills State Park in Camden and Lake St. George State Park in Liberty. Approximately nineteen privately operated campgrounds are also available. Camden Hills State Park provides overnight camping at the Megunticook Ski Shelter in the valley between Bald Rock Mtn. and Mt. Megunticook.

SUGGESTED HIKES

■ Easy
BEECH HILL

LP via Woods Loop	2.0 mi.	294 ft.	1:00

Saunter through a sugarbush grove and then on to the open summit of Beech Hill to see the historical Beech Nut stone hut and sweeping coastal scenery. See Woods Loop, p. 431.

MT. PERCIVAL

RT via Mt. Percival Trail	0.6 mi.	181 ft.	0:25

Hike to the wooded summit of Mt. Percival and the stone base of an old rusticator's tower that once offered far-reaching views over Penobscot Bay. See Mt. Percival Trail, p. 433.

HAYSTACK MTN.

	LP via Haystack Mtn. Trail	1.3 mi.	270 ft.	0:45

From the large blueberry field on the summit of Haystack Mtn., enjoy looking over the lovely rural countryside of Montville. See Haystack Mtn. Trail, p. 441.

HIGGINS MTN.

	LP via Billie Todd Loop and Lichen Loop	0.6 mi.	130 ft.	0:20

Visit the high point on Georgetown Island on this circuit through parklike woods of pitch pine and blueberries. To begin, see Billie Todd Loop, p. 443.

■ Moderate

MT. BATTIE

	RT via Mt. Battie Trail	1.2 mi.	606 ft.	1:00

This short but steep trip to Mt. Battie's stone observation tower provides superb views of Camden Harbor and the many islands in beautiful Penobscot Bay. See Mt. Battie Trail, p. 412.

MAIDEN CLIFF

	RT via Maiden Cliff Trail and Scenic Trail	1.6 mi.	750 ft.	1:10

This fine hike makes a loop over Maiden Cliff, which features a large memorial cross and an excellent outlook over Megunticook Lake to Ragged Mtn. To begin, see Maiden Cliff Trail, p. 414.

SEC 9

BALD MTN.

	RT via Bald Mtn. Trail	2.6 mi.	625 ft.	1:35

Revel in the beautiful sights of Penobscot Bay, Ragged Mtn., and the surrounding Camden Hills from these craggy heights. See Bald Mtn. Trail, p. 430.

HATCHET MTN.

| RT via Hatchet Mtn. Trail | 1.3 mi. | 570 ft. | 0:55 |

Drink in the outstanding vista over Hobbs Pond to Bald Mtn. and Ragged Mtn. from the pretty meadow high on Hatchet Mtn. See Hatchet Mtn. Trail, p. 432.

WHITTEN HILL

| LP via Northern Headwaters Trail | 3.8 mi. | 500 ft. | 2:10 |

Stroll past old stone walls and along the headwater of the Sheepscot River on this pleasant walk over Whitten Hill. See Northern Headwaters Trail, p. 439.

MT. WALDO

| RT via North Trail | 2.0 mi. | 600 ft. | 1:20 |

Rock carvings dating to 1876 and open ledges offering looks at Swan Lake, Penobscot Bay, and the Camden Hills are the reward on this hike. See North Trail, p. 442.

■ Strenuous

MEGUNTICOOK TRAVERSE

| OW via Maiden Cliff Trail, Scenic Trail, Ridge Trail, Table-lands Trail, and Mt. Battie Trail | 5.3 mi. | 1,520 ft. | 3:35 |

This combination of trails makes for one of the finest long treks in the Camden Hills, with excellent views and plenty of great ridge walking. To begin, see Maiden Cliff Trail, p. 414.

BALD ROCK MTN.

| LP via Ski Shelter/Multi-use Trail, Bald Rock Trail, and Frohock Mtn. Trail | 3.3 mi. | 843 ft. | 2:05 |

Enjoy outstanding sights east over Penobscot Bay to Islesboro, Deer Isle, and more from the summit ledges of Bald Rock Mtn. To begin, see Ski Shelter/Multi-use Trail, p. 415.

RAGGED MTN.

↻ ↗ ○

LP via GHP (Little Ragged Section, Ridge Section)   6.1 mi.   1,240 ft.   3:00
and Round the Mtn. Trail

Tackle this fine section of Georges Highland Path, which features extensive open ledges that offer exceptional coastal scenery from the high ridgeline of Ragged Mtn. Finish via Round the Mtn. Trail. To begin, see GHP (Little Ragged Section), p. 424.

TRAIL DESCRIPTIONS
CAMDEN HILLS STATE PARK

This state park encompasses 6,200 acres of mountainous terrain on the west shore of Penobscot Bay in the towns of Camden and Lincolnville. The beautiful Camden Hills share many characteristics with the mountains of Acadia on Mt. Desert Island 30 mi. to the east, including fragrant softwood forests, bold cliffs and ledges, and far-reaching vistas of ocean, lakes, and mountains. At 1,378 ft., Mt. Megunticook is not only the highest summit in the park but also the highest mainland mountain on the Atlantic coast of the United States. The park offers more than 30 mi. of hiking on 21 blue-blazed trails, which cover—in addition to Megunticook—Mt. Battie, Bald Rock Mtn., Cameron Mtn., and several other wooded summits.

MT. BATTIE (806 FT.)

This mountain, just south of Mt. Megunticook, features one of the most popular hikes in the Camden Hills, due to both its open ledges that offer outstanding views of the coast and its proximity to the town of Camden. In 1897, a carriage road was built to the summit, and a hotel named the Summit House also was built. The hotel was torn down in 1920. A 26-ft. stone observation tower—a World War I memorial—was erected in its place the following year. The paved auto road from the east side was constructed by the Maine State Park Commission in 1965; the road leaves from the state park entrance on US 1 and climbs gradually to the top of Mt. Battie in 1.6 mi.

Follow ME 52 (Mountain St.) from its jct. with US 1 just north of downtown Camden. In 0.3 mi., turn right onto Spring St., and in another 0.1 mi., turn left onto Megunticook St. Trailhead parking is at the end of this street 0.1 mi. ahead.

SEC 9

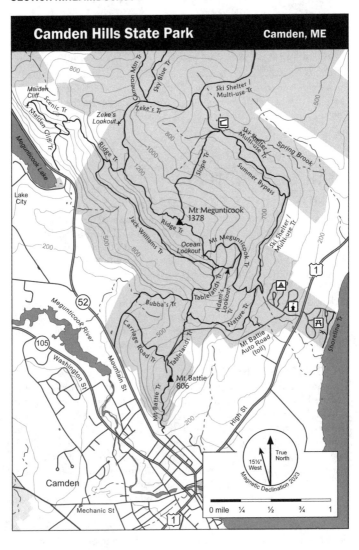

Camden Hills State Park
Camden, ME

Maiden Cliff
Scenic Tr
Maiden Cliff Tr
Megunticook Lake
Lake City
Cameron Mtn Tr
Sky Blue Tr
Zeke's Tr
Zeke's Lookout
Ridge Tr
Ski Shelter / Multi-use Tr
Spring Brook
Ski Shelter Multi-use Tr
Slope Tr
Summer Bypass
Mt Megunticook 1378
Jack Williams Tr
Ridge Tr
Ocean Lookout
Mt Megunticook Tr
Ski Shelter / Multi-use Tr
Bubba's Tr
Adam's Lookout Tr
Tablelands Tr
Nature Tr
Megunticook River
52
105
Washington St
Carriage Road Tr
Tablelands Tr
Mt Battie Tr
Mt Battie Auto Road (toll)
Shoreline Tr
Mountain St
Mt Battie 806
High St
Camden
Mechanic St
1

True North
15½° West
Magnetic Declination 2023

0 mile   ¼   ½   ¾   1

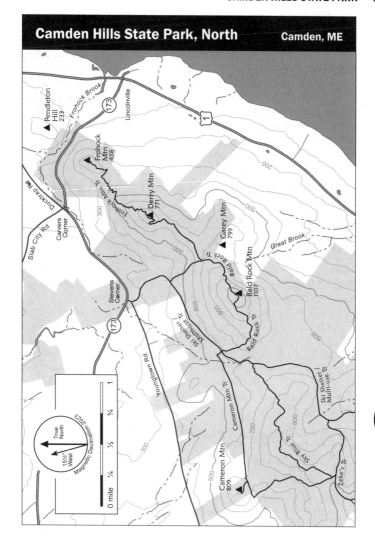

Camden Hills State Park, North Camden, ME

SEC
9

MT. BATTIE TRAIL (AMC CAMDEN HILLS STATE PARK MAP)
From Megunticook St. parking (200 ft.) to:

Mt. Battie summit (806 ft.)	0.6 mi.	606 ft.	0:35

MBPL Mt. Battie Trail rises steeply over the rocky nose of Mt. Battie from the south. It climbs steadily and then more steeply north, weaving over ledge outcroppings to a viewpoint. After a rocky gully below a rock wall, the angle moderates. Emerge onto open ledges and climb slabs along the ridgeline. Pass a huge cairn and then enter the woods. After emerging into the open once again, it's easy walking up to the stone tower on top. The expansive scene of Camden Harbor and the islands in Penobscot Bay is a Maine coast classic.

CARRIAGE ROAD TRAIL (AMC CAMDEN HILLS STATE PARK MAP)
Cumulative from ME 52 (240 ft.) to:

Bubba's Trail (207 ft.) via Carriage Road Trail	0.3 mi.	30 ft.	0:10
Tablelands Trail (740 ft.)	1.0 mi.	500 ft.	0:45
Mt. Battie summit (806 ft.)	1.2 mi.	566 ft.	0:55

MBPL Carriage Road Trail leaves the right (northeast) side of ME 52 (Mountain St.) 1.3 mi. from the jct. of US 1 and ME 52 in Camden. Look for a small wooden sign: "Old Carriage Road—Mt. Battie Rd. 1 mile." Parking is along the road. This trail climbs along the gradual western slopes of Mt. Battie via the route of an old carriage road.

From ME 52, follow Carriage Road Trail north 0.3 mi. to a jct. with Bubba's Trail, which continues straight ahead. Turn right to stay on Carriage Road Trail, which rises gently on or near the old carriage road to join Mt. Battie Auto Rd. just north of the summit parking area. Cross the road to meet Tablelands Trail at 1.0 mi., turning right onto this trail to reach the summit of Mt. Battie in another 0.2 mi.

BUBBA'S TRAIL (AMC CAMDEN HILLS STATE PARK MAP)
Cumulative from ME 52 (240 ft.) to:

Carriage Road Trail (270 ft.)	0.3 mi.	30 ft.	0:10
Tablelands Trail (630 ft.)	1.0 mi.	390 ft.	0:40
Mt. Battie summit (806 ft.) via Tablelands Trail	1.7 mi.	566 ft.	1:10
Ocean Lookout (1,140 ft.) via Tablelands Trail	1.6 mi.	900 ft.	1:15

MBPL From ME 52, follow Carriage Road Trail north to a jct., where Carriage Road Trail goes to the right. Stay straight and continue on Bubba's Trail, which climbs gradually to reach Tablelands Trail just north of the saddle between Mt. Battie and Mt. Megunticook at 1.0 mi. To the right, it is 0.7 mi. to the summit of Mt. Battie via Tablelands Trail. To the left, it is 0.6 mi. to Ocean Lookout via Tablelands Trail.

TABLELANDS TRAIL (MAP 4: B2, C1–C2)
From Mt. Battie summit (806 ft.) to:

Ocean Lookout (1,140 ft.)	1.3 mi.	570 ft.	0:55

MBPL Tablelands Trail starts from the summit of Mt. Battie near the stone tower, crosses the parking area, and descends gradually to the north. It meets Carriage Road Trail coming in from the left (west). After crossing Mt. Battie Auto Rd., Tablelands Trail passes Nature Trail on the right and then Bubba's Trail on the left. Beyond, Tablelands Trail ascends and passes Adam's Lookout Trail on the right. The route keeps to the right (east) of two lines of cliffs and swings northwest, climbing steeply to Ocean Lookout at 1.3 mi. From the expansive lookout cliffs, the views of Mt. Battie and Camden Harbor are extraordinary. The true summit of Mt. Megunticook is 0.4 mi. ahead via Ridge Trail (see p. 416).

NATURE TRAIL (AMC CAMDEN HILLS STATE PARK MAP)
Cumulative from Mt. Battie Auto Rd. hiker parking lot (260 ft.) to:

Nature Trail jct. (320 ft.)	0.1 mi.	60 ft.	0:05
Tablelands Trail (630 ft.)	0.8 mi.	413 ft.	0:35
From Mt. Battie Auto Rd. hiker parking lot (260 ft.) to:			
Mt. Megunticook Trail (420 ft.)	0.2 mi.	100 ft.	0:10

MBPL Nature Trail links the lower part of Mt. Megunticook Trail with Tablelands Trail and provides access to both Mt. Battie (via Tablelands Trail) and Mt. Megunticook (via either Mt. Megunticook Trail and Ridge Trail or Tablelands Trail and Ridge Trail).

From the Mt. Battie hiker parking lot, which is on the right 0.25 mi. up Mt. Battie Auto Rd. from the park entrance station, hike north on Nature Trail for 0.1 mi. to a T jct. To the left, Nature Trail climbs gradually west to crest a knob and then descends easily to meet Tablelands Trail in the col between Mt. Battie and Mt. Megunticook. Via Tablelands Trail, it is 0.7 mi. south to the top of Mt. Battie or 0.6 mi. north to Ocean Lookout. To the right, Nature Trail follows a rising contour to meet Mt. Megunticook Trail 0.1 mi. west of the outer edge of the campground's upper loop.

SEC 9

MAIDEN CLIFF (745 FT.)
Maiden Cliff rises abruptly above the eastern shore of Megunticook Lake. A steel cross on top stands near the spot where 12-year-old Elenora French fell to her death in 1864 in an attempt to catch her windblown hat. Maiden

Cliff Trail and Scenic Trail can be combined for a loop hike. Access to Mt. Megunticook is possible from these trails when combined with Ridge Trail or Jack Williams Trail.

The trailhead for Maiden Cliff Trail is on the northeast side of ME 52 where the road passes above Barrett's Cove on Megunticook Lake and just beyond the impressive walls of Barrett's Cove Cliff. The signed parking area is 2.8 mi. north of the jct. of ME 52 and US 1 in Camden.

MAIDEN CLIFF TRAIL (AMC CAMDEN HILLS STATE PARK MAP)
Cumulative from Maiden Cliff trailhead on ME 52 (200 ft.) to:

Scenic Trail, east jct. (480 ft.)	0.4 mi.	280 ft.	0:20
Maiden Cliff and Scenic Trail, west jct. (745 ft.)	0.8 mi.	545 ft.	0:40

MBPL Maiden Cliff Trail climbs north and then west, at first following an eroded woods road along a small brook. Cross a footbridge over the brook and proceed on the rocky trail beyond. At 0.4 mi., Scenic Trail continues ahead (north). Maiden Cliff Trail branches left (west) and climbs more steeply via switchbacks before making a mostly level run northwest to the jct. with Scenic Trail. Follow a short spur left to the top of Maiden Cliff and then scramble down a few feet for an outstanding vista over Megunticook Lake to Ragged Mtn. and the ski slopes of Camden Snow Bowl, as well as Bald Mtn.

SCENIC TRAIL (AMC CAMDEN HILLS STATE PARK MAP)
Cumulative from Maiden Cliff (745 ft.) to:

Ridge Trail (830 ft.)	0.4 mi.	205 ft.	0:20
Maiden Cliff Trail (480 ft.)	0.6 mi.	205 ft.	0:25

MBPL Scenic Trail bears right (east) from Maiden Cliff Trail just above Maiden Cliff and follows an extensive series of open knobs and ledges known as the Millerite Ledges. Occasional cairns mark the route. Views are excellent to the west over Megunticook Lake. From its high point, Scenic Trail descends to the jct. with Ridge Trail and then continues downhill to meet Maiden Cliff Trail at a point 0.4 mi. from ME 52.

MT. MEGUNTICOOK (1,378 FT.)

Mt. Megunticook, a mountain ridge extending roughly 3.5 mi. in a northwest to southeast direction between Youngtown Rd. and US 1, is the highest peak in the Camden Hills. The true summit is forested and has no view, but just to the southeast, Ocean Lookout takes in the expanse of Penobscot Bay, the town of Camden, and the nearby coastal hills. Several outlooks along Ridge Trail also offer views over Megunticook Lake. Maiden Cliff is a prominent escarpment near the northwest end of the ridge.

**SEC
9**

MT. MEGUNTICOOK TRAIL
(AMC CAMDEN HILLS STATE PARK MAP)
Cumulative from campground upper loop (310 ft.) to:

Nature Trail (420 ft.)	0.1 mi.	110 ft.	0:05
Adam's Lookout Trail (820 ft.)	0.6 mi.	510 ft.	0:30
Ocean Lookout, Tablelands Trail (1,140 ft.)	1.1 mi.	830 ft.	1:00
Mt. Megunticook summit (1,378 ft.) via Ridge Trail	1.5 mi.	1,068 ft.	1:15

MBPL Find the start of Mt. Megunticook Trail on the outer edge of the campground upper loop, a 0.5-mi. walk from the day-use parking lot across from the park entrance station. Mt. Megunticook Trail and Ski Shelter/Multi-use Trail coincide for a short stretch before Ski Shelter/Multi-use Trail breaks off to the right. Shortly after a bridge crossing, Nature Trail departs to the left. At 0.6 mi., pass Adam's Lookout Trail on the left (leads 0.3 mi. to Tablelands Trail). At 1.1 mi., Mt. Megunticook Trail reaches Ocean Lookout, where Tablelands Trail from Mt. Battie comes up from the left (south). From Ocean Lookout, follow Ridge Trail 0.4 mi. to the Mt. Megunticook summit.

ADAM'S LOOKOUT TRAIL (AMC CAMDEN HILLS STATE PARK MAP)
MBPL This 0.3-mi. trail connects Mt. Megunticook Trail and Tablelands Trail while providing an excellent lookout over Penobscot Bay to the east. It gains about 250 ft. of elevation.

SKI SHELTER/MULTI-USE TRAIL NORTHBOUND
(AMC CAMDEN HILLS STATE PARK MAP)
Cumulative from campground upper loop (310 ft.) to:

Summer Bypass Trail (530 ft.)	1.0 mi.	310 ft.	0:40
Slope Trail and Megunticook Ski Shelter (525 ft.)	2.0 mi.	360 ft.	1:10
Zeke's Trail (669 ft.)	2.4 mi.	500 ft.	1:30
Sky Blue Trail (640 ft.)	3.3 mi.	550 ft.	1:55
Bald Rock Trail and Cameron Mtn. Trail (600 ft.)	3.6 mi.	550 ft.	2:05
Frohock Mtn. Trail (400 ft.)	4.3 mi.	550 ft.	2:25
Youngtown Rd. trailhead (264 ft.)	4.8 mi.	550 ft.	2:45

SEC 9

MBPL Ski Shelter/Multi-use Trail starts at the upper campground loop. In 250 ft., Mt. Megunticook Trail diverges left while Ski Shelter/Multi-use Trail continues north. At 1.0 mi., Summer Bypass Trail leaves to the left, and Ski Shelter/Multi-use Trail continues to the right; both trails contour easily to the west and merge 0.8 mi. ahead at 1.8 mi. Beyond, cross Spring

Brook to reach the jct. with Slope Trail at 2.0 mi. To the left, Slope Trail ascends 1.0 mi. to the summit of Mt. Megunticook. Here also is the Megunticook Ski Shelter, a small cabin that can be reserved for overnight use. Continuing ahead, Ski Shelter/Multi-use Trail traverses the interior of the park, passing intersections with Zeke's Trail, Sky Blue Trail, Bald Rock Trail, Cameron Mtn. Trail, and Frohock Mtn. Trail before reaching the trailhead on Youngtown Rd.

SLOPE TRAIL (AMC CAMDEN HILLS STATE PARK MAP)
From Ski Shelter/Multi-use Trail (525 ft.) to:

Mt. Megunticook summit (1,378 ft.)	1.0 mi.	853 ft.	0:55

MBPL Slope Trail leaves Ski Shelter/Multi-use Trail 2.0 mi. north of the latter's start at the upper campground loop, opposite Megunticook Ski Shelter. Slope Trail crosses Spring Brook and climbs steeply up the northeast slope of the mountain to reach Ridge Trail at 1.0 mi. The true summit of Mt. Megunticook is 100 ft. right up Ridge Trail from this jct., in a small clearing (no views).

RIDGE TRAIL (AMC CAMDEN HILLS STATE PARK MAP)
Cumulative from Maiden Cliff trailhead on ME 52 (200 ft.) to:

Scenic Trail (480 ft.) via Maiden Cliff Trail	0.4 mi.	280 ft.	0:20
Ridge Trail via Scenic Trail (830 ft.)	0.6 mi.	630 ft.	0:30
Jack Williams Trail (900 ft.)	1.2 mi.	780 ft.	1:00
Zeke's Trail (1,180 ft.)	1.5 mi.	1,060 ft.	1:15
Mt. Megunticook summit and Slope Trail (1,378 ft.)	2.4 mi.	1,260 ft.	1:50
Ocean Lookout (1,250 ft.) and Tablelands Trail	2.8 mi.	1,260 ft.	2:00

MBPL Ridge Trail diverges from Scenic Trail 0.6 mi. from ME 52 via Maiden Cliff Trail. From Scenic Trail, Ridge Trail extends southeast along the main ridge of Mt. Megunticook, goes over the wooded summit (1,385 ft.), and proceeds to Ocean Lookout, which affords fine views of Penobscot Bay.

Follow Maiden Cliff Trail to Scenic Trail and climb steeply via switchbacks to the ridgeline and the jct. of Ridge Trail. Turning east, Ridge Trail briefly descends to traverse a couple of small brooks and then trends gradually upward past several outlooks. On a sometimes rough treadway of rocks and roots, pass Jack Williams Trail on the right. After detouring up a shallow ravine, pass Zeke's Trail entering from the left. On a level stretch ahead is a window view to Mt. Battie and its auto road and to the Megunticook River valley. After crossing a subsidiary summit (1,290 ft.), Ridge Trail descends slightly and then climbs gradually to the true summit of Mt.

Megunticook, which is wooded and marked by a large rock pile. Just beyond, Slope Trail diverges left (north). In 0.4 mi., Ridge Trail descends to meet Tablelands Trail at Ocean Lookout.

JACK WILLIAMS TRAIL (AMC CAMDEN HILLS STATE PARK MAP)
From Ridge Trail (900 ft.) to:

Tablelands Trail (1,100 ft.)	1.6 mi.	450 ft.	1:00

MBPL The mostly wooded Jack Williams Trail, , named in honor of a local trail volunteer, connects Ridge Trail and Tablelands Trail and is described in that direction from west to east. The west end of Jack Williams Trail 1.2 mi. from ME 52 is reached via Maiden Cliff Trail, Scenic Trail, and then Ridge Trail. The route is commonly used along with Ridge Trail to make a loop on Mt. Megunticook. Jack Williams Trail follows an undulating route across a shelf on the southwest slope of Mt. Megunticook, passing through some impressive stands of hardwoods before reaching its end at the jct. of Tablelands Trail.

BALD ROCK MTN. (1,107 FT.), DERRY MTN. (771 FT.), AND FROHOCK MTN. (458 FT.)

Bald Rock Mtn., which rises several miles northeast of Mt. Megunticook, is the second-highest peak in Camden Hills State Park. Its open summit ledges provide excellent views east over Penobscot Bay. Extending northeast of Bald Rock Mtn. are the wooded ridgelines and the viewless summits of Derry Mtn. and Frohock Mtn.

SKI SHELTER/MULTI-USE TRAIL SOUTHBOUND (AMC CAMDEN HILLS STATE PARK, NORTH MAP)
Cumulative from Youngtown Rd. (264 ft.) to:

Frohock Mtn. Trail (400 ft.)	0.5 mi.	140 ft.	0:20
Bald Rock Trail and Cameron Mtn. Trail jct. (600 ft.)	1.2 mi.	340 ft.	0:45
Sky Blue Trail (640 ft.)	1.5 mi.	380 ft.	1:00
Zeke's Trail (669 ft.)	2.4 mi.	430 ft.	1:25
Slope Trail (525 ft.) and Megunticook Ski Shelter	2.8 mi.	430 ft.	1:35
Mt. Megunticook Trail (310 ft.) and upper campground loop	4.8 mi.	555 ft.	2:40

SEC 9

MBPL This trail, a wide, gravel-surfaced multiuse road, serves as the approach to the mountains in the northern part of Camden Hills State Park, including Bald Rock Mtn., Cameron Mtn., Derry Mtn., and Frohock Mtn. The trail may also be used to reach several routes that climb the north side of Mt. Megunticook.

From the jct. of US 1 and ME 173 in Lincolnville, drive west on ME 173. At 2.3 mi., bear left onto Youngtown Rd. and in 200 ft. turn left into a small parking area (iron ranger, day-use fee).

In 0.5 mi. from the trailhead, reach the jct. with Frohock Mtn. Trail, which leads left (south) to meet Bald Rock Trail in 0.3 mi. and continues northeast over Derry Mtn. Frohock Mtn. Trail ends atop wooded Frohock Mtn. in 2.1 mi. Continuing on Ski Shelter/Multi-use Trail, reach the jct. of two trails at 1.2 mi. Here, Bald Rock Trail heads left (south) 0.8 mi. to the summit of Bald Rock Mtn., while Cameron Mtn. Trail leaves right and climbs 2.0 mi. to a spur that leads another 0.1 mi. to Cameron Mtn.

Ahead on Ski Shelter/Multi-use Trail, Sky Blue Trail leaves right at 1.5 mi. At 2.4 mi. from Youngtown Rd., Ski Shelter/Multi-use Trail passes Zeke's Trail on the right (leads 1.4 mi. to Ridge Trail), and at 2.8 mi., Ski Shelter/Multi-use Trail reaches a jct. with Slope Trail (leads 1.0 mi. to the true summit of Mt. Megunticook) and the Megunticook Ski Shelter (overnight shelter by reservation only). Ski Shelter/Multi-use Trail continues, swinging low around the northeast side of Mt. Megunticook to end at Mt. Megunticook Trail, just a short distance from the outer ring of the upper campground loop.

FROHOCK MTN. TRAIL (AMC CAMDEN HILLS STATE PARK, NORTH MAP)
Cumulative from Youngtown Rd. (264 ft.) to:

Frohock Mtn. Trail (400 ft.) via Ski Shelter/Multi-use Trail	0.5 mi.	140 ft.	0:15
Bald Rock Trail, east end (690 ft.)	0.8 mi.	270 ft.	0:30
Derry Mtn. (771 ft.)	1.5 mi.	400 ft.	0:55
Frohock Mtn. (454 ft.)	2.6 mi.	510 ft.	1:30

MBPL Frohock Mtn. Trail leaves from Ski Shelter/Multi-use Trail 0.5 mi. from the Youngtown Rd. trailhead. From the jct. with Ski Shelter/Multi-use Trail, turn left onto Frohock Mtn. Trail and climb southeast. In 0.3 mi., reach a jct. with Bald Rock Trail (leads 0.5 mi. to the summit of Bald Rock Mtn.). Frohock Mtn. Trail turns sharply left (northeast) and ascends easily to the wooded summit of Derry Mtn. Beyond, the trail descends gradually to a sag before a brief climb to its end atop Frohock Mtn.

BALD ROCK TRAIL (AMC CAMDEN HILLS STATE PARK, NORTH MAP)
Cumulative from Youngtown Rd. (264 ft.) to:

Bald Rock Trail, west end (600 ft.) via Ski Shelter/Multi-use Trail	1.2 mi.	340 ft.	0:45
Bald Rock Mtn. summit (1,107 ft.) and old shelters	2.0 mi.	843 ft.	1:25
Frohock Mtn. Trail (650 ft.)	2.5 mi.	843 ft.	1:40

Complete loop via Frohock Mtn. Trail and Ski Shelter/Multi-use Trail	3.3 mi.	843 ft.	2:05

MBPL Bald Rock Trail diverges left (southeast) from Ski Shelter/Multi-use Trail at a point 1.2 mi. from Youngtown Rd. Bald Rock Trail climbs easily at first and then more steeply to the open summit slabs, where there are fabulous views over Penobscot Bay to the islands beyond. Just before the summit, a short side trail leads left to a campsite and dilapidated shelter. Coming off the top of the mountain, Bald Rock Trail quickly reaches a second dilapidated shelter on the right. Beyond, the trail drops steeply and then eases, slowly curving north to meet Frohock Mtn. Trail. Straight ahead, it is 0.8 mi. to Youngtown Rd. via Frohock Mtn. Trail and Ski Shelter/Multi-use Trail; to the right it is 1.8 mi. over Derry Mtn. to the end of Frohock Mtn. Trail atop Frohock Mtn.

CAMERON MTN. (809 FT.)

In 2007, TNC acquired a 45-acre parcel that includes the wide-open summit of Cameron Mtn. The following year the land was transferred to the state of Maine and is now part of Camden Hills State Park. Commercial blueberry fields are on the summit, and hikers are asked to stay on the trail.

CAMERON MTN. TRAIL (AMC CAMDEN HILLS STATE PARK MAP)
Cumulative from Youngtown Rd. (264 ft.) to:

Cameron Mtn. Trail (600 ft.) via Ski Shelter/Multi-use Trail	1.2 mi.	340 ft.	0:45
Cameron Mtn. spur path (730 ft.)	2.2 mi.	470 ft.	1:20
Cameron Mtn. summit (809 ft.) via spur path	2.3 mi.	550 ft.	1:30
Sky Blue Trail and Zeke's Trail (980 ft.)	3.3 mi.	930 ft.	2:05

MBPL Cameron Mtn. Trail diverges right (west) from Ski Shelter/Multi-use Trail at its jct. with Bald Rock Trail, 1.2 mi. from the Youngtown Rd. trailhead. Shortly after the trails split, Cameron Mtn. Trail turns left (avoid the first left), following an old woods road. It crosses Black Brook and rises gradually past abandoned farmland, old cellar holes, and apple trees to a point just below the summit of Cameron Mtn., where a spur path leads right (north) 0.1 mi. to the cleared mountaintop.

Beyond the jct., Cameron Mtn. Trail descends for a short distance before turning left (south) and starting to climb. Where it levels off, Sky Blue Trail enters from the left, and just beyond, Cameron Mtn. Trail merges with Zeke's Trail. Zeke's Lookout is 0.3 mi. to the right, and Ridge Trail is 0.5 mi. beyond that jct. To the left, it is 0.6 mi. downhill to Ski Shelter/Multi-use Trail and then 2.4 mi. north to Youngtown Rd.

SEC 9

SKY BLUE TRAIL (AMC CAMDEN HILLS STATE PARK MAP)
From Ski Shelter/Multi-use Trail (640 ft.) to:

Cameron Mtn. Trail and Zeke's Trail (980 ft.)	1.5 mi.	445 ft.	1:00

MBPL Sky Blue Trail leaves Ski Shelter/Multi-use Trail at a point 0.3 mi. beyond the Cameron Mtn. Trail jct. and 1.5 mi. from Youngtown Rd. The trail climbs southwesterly to a ridgetop and then follows an undulating route across a series of wooded knobs before joining Cameron Mtn. Trail. Zeke's Trail is 150 ft. south of this jct.

ZEKE'S TRAIL (AMC CAMDEN HILLS STATE PARK MAP)
Cumulative from Ski Shelter/Multi-use Trail (669 ft.) to:

Cameron Mtn. Trail (980 ft.)	0.6 mi.	311 ft.	0:25
Zeke's Lookout spur path (1,120 ft.)	0.9 mi.	450 ft.	0:40
Ridge Trail (1,180 ft.)	1.4 mi.	510 ft.	0:55

MBPL Zeke's Trail diverges right (west) from Ski Shelter/Multi-use Trail at a point 2.4 mi. from the Youngtown Rd. trailhead. It ascends gradually, and at 0.6 mi., Cameron Mtn. Trail enters from the right. At 0.9 mi., a spur leads right 100 yd. to Zeke's Lookout (1,195 ft.), which offers views over the treetops to Bald Rock Mtn. and Penobscot Bay. Zeke's Trail ends at its jct. with Ridge Trail at 1.4 mi., 0.9 mi. northwest of the summit of Mt. Megunticook.

GEORGES HIGHLAND PATH AND CAMDEN SNOW BOWL

The Georges River Land Trust was established in 1987, and soon after, its founders conceived Georges Highland Path as a long-distance walking trail connecting the headwater of the St. George River in Montville to the Gulf of Maine at Port Clyde. Today, the GHP network has more than 70 mi. of blue-blazed hiking trails in 12 distinct sections throughout the watershed.

Hikers can enjoy the mountainous sections of GHP on Ragged Mtn. in Rockport and Camden, Spruce Mtn. and Mt. Pleasant in Rockport, and Frye Mtn. and Hogback Mtn. in Montville. (*Note*: Hogback is currently closed to the public.) The Hogback–Frye portion of GHP connects to the trails of Midcoast Conservancy in the northern reaches of the adjoining Sheepscot River watershed. The MCC and GRLT trails in this area are part of 47-mi. Hills to Sea Trail that connects Unity to Belfast.

SEC 9

RAGGED MTN. (1,305 FT.) AND
LITTLE RAGGED MTN. (1,230 FT.)

Ragged Mtn. straddles the town lines of Rockport and Camden. The northeast slope is home to the Camden Snow Bowl ski area. This mountain, the focus of ambitious conservation efforts by Coastal Mountains Land Trust and several private landowners, features extensive ledges and outlooks, wild blueberries, and considerable alpine-like terrain. Three trail sections of GHP—Little Ragged, Ridge, and Route 17—are on Ragged Mtn. Access to the sections is from Hope St., from ME 17 west of Mirror Lake, and from Barnestown Rd. Two trails ascend the mountain from the Camden Snow Bowl base area.

GHP (LITTLE RAGGED SECTION, RIDGE SECTION, ROUTE 17 SECTION) FROM HOPE ST. (AMC RAGGED MTN. MAP)

Cumulative from Hope St. trailhead (460 ft.) to:

Round the Mtn. Trail (450 ft.)	0.1 mi.	–10 ft.	0:03
Round the Mtn. Trail (700 ft.)	0.8 mi.	250 ft.	0:30
GHP (Little Ragged Section) from Barnestown Rd. (1,210 ft.)	1.5 mi.	750 ft.	1:10
Hosmer Brook Trail (1,150 ft.)	1.7 mi.	780 ft.	1:20
Sundown Ledge (1,260 ft.) and Red Diamond Trail	2.0 mi.	900 ft.	1:40
Ragged Mtn. summit (1,305 ft.) via Red Diamond Trail	2.15 mi.	950 ft.	1:50
Round the Mtn. Trail (450 ft.)	3.4 mi.	950 ft.	2:10
Round the Mtn. Trail (540 ft.)	4.1 mi.	1,040 ft.	2:25
ME 17 trailhead (430 ft.)	4.8 mi.	1,100 ft.	3:00

GRLT GHP (Little Ragged Section) climbs the southwest ridge of Ragged Mtn. to meet GHP and offers several pleasant viewpoints along the way. From the jct. of US 1 and ME 90 in Rockport, travel west on ME 90 for 2.7 mi. Turn right (northeast) onto ME 17 and drive 2.7 mi. to Hope St. Turn right and reach the trailhead (sign and kiosk) on the right in 0.5 mi.

The initial going is easy through old fields and young woods, across Thorndike Brook, past stone walls, and on and off old woods roads. GHP (Little Ragged Section) crosses Round the Mtn. Trail twice before climbing moderately to a scenic overlook above Grassy Pond. Ahead, the trail switchbacks and then angles across the mountainside to a jct. Here, GHP (Little Ragged Section) from Barnestown Rd. via Buzzard's Ledge enters from the left (it's 1.5 mi. to Barnestown Rd. via this trail). Continuing to the right (south) on GHP (Ridge Section), descend gradually to a sag on the ridge and then climb easily to a jct. at 1.8 mi., where Hosmer Brook Trail from

Ragged Mtn.

Camden–Rockport, ME

Gillette Rd

Round-the-Mtn Tr

Georges Highland Path

Buzzard's Ledge

Bald Mtn 1273

Bald Mtn Tr

Barnestown Rd

1000

500

500

Hosmer Brook Tr

Camden Snow Bowl

Round-the-Mtn Tr

Hope St

Ragged Mtn 1305

Hosmer Pond

Red Diamond Tr

Round-the-Mtn Tr

1000

Georges Highland Path

Grassy Pond

17

Rockland St

Mirror Lake

500

500

Georges Highland Path

Mt Pleasant St

Spruce Mtn 973

Pleasant Mtn 1058

Trails data provided by Georges River Land Trust and Coastal Mountains Land Trust

True North

15° West

Magnetic Declination 2023

0 mile   ¼   ½   ¾   1

Camden Snow Bowl enters from the left. Continuing on GHP (Ridge Section), proceed along the ridgeline, reach another sag, climb again, and then follow a contour. Ahead, bear left to avoid the obvious outcroppings, and then climb a short, steep pitch to the semi-open ledges above. Just beyond, reach a large open outcropping known as Sundown Ledge, where expansive views all the way to the White Mountains are possible. Red Diamond Trail joins GHP (Ridge Section) atop Sundown Ledge; Red Diamond Trail leads easily east for 0.15 mi. to the true summit of Ragged Mtn.

Continuing on GHP (Ridge Section), descend Sundown Ledge. The trail remains out in the open for a fair distance, crossing several ledges and knobs with attractive scenery. Climb to a cairn out on the open ledges of the west face of the mountain and enjoy a vista that includes the ocean, Spruce Mtn., and Mt. Pleasant. Descend the cliff face with the Ragged Mtn. summit towers up to the left. Turn a corner and get a wonderful look at Mirror Lake; continue in the open toward the towers. Bear left and up the rocks, and then zigzag down a short, steep pitch into a wooded ravine.

Cross a small seep and climb out of the ravine onto big, open slabs of rock with more extensive views. Follow cairns and blazes up the open slope of rocks and ledges toward the towers. Just below the towers, veer to the right and enter a grove of scrub oaks. GHP (Ridge Section) continues down the south ridge, in and out of the trees, with several more outlooks. It eventually joins an old carriage road and descends steadily toward Mirror Lake (avoiding the lake, a public water supply). Leveling off, GHP (Ridge Section) reaches a jct. with Round the Mtn. Trail, which joins from the left. The two trails coincide for 0.1 mi. before Round the Mtn. Trail diverges left. GHP continues north along the base of the mountain and bears left to traverse a brook. After crossing Round the Mtn. Trail for the final time, GHP (Route 17 Section) descends gradually, climbs easily over a knoll, and reaches the trailhead on ME 17 at 4.8 mi.

SEC 9

GHP (ROUTE 17 SECTION, RIDGE SECTION) FROM ME 17 (AMC RAGGED MTN. MAP)
Cumulative from ME 17 trailhead (430 ft.) to:

Round the Mtn. Trail (540 ft.)	0.7 mi.	180 ft.	0:00
Round the Mtn. Trail (450 ft.)	1.4 mi.	180 ft.	0:00
Sundown Ledge (1,260 ft.) and Red Diamond Trail	2.8 mi.	990 ft.	1:50
Ragged Mtn. summit (1,305 ft.) via Red Diamond Trail	2.95 mi.	1,040 ft.	2:00

GRLT GHP (Route 17 Section, Ridge Section) ascends the southwest face of Ragged Mtn. and affords views of the town of Camden and the ocean, as well as the nearby peaks of Mt. Pleasant and Spruce Mtn. From the jct.

of US 1 and ME 90 in Rockport, travel west on ME 90 for 2.7 mi. Turn right (northeast) onto ME 17. Follow ME 17 for 1.8 mi. to trailhead parking (sign and kiosk) on the right, a short distance past Mirror Lake.

GHP (Route 17 Section) enters the woods and in 0.7 mi. crosses Round the Mtn. Trail and then a small brook. Turning right, GHP (Ridge Section) contours along the base of the mountain. Round the Mtn. Trail enters from the left and after 0.1 mi. leaves straight ahead. GHP (Ridge Section) ascends steadily; Mirror Lake is visible through the trees. Reach an old carriage road and follow it easily north along the upper face of the mountain. Continue up the ridge on a foot trail, emerging on open ledges with views to the south. The trail ducks into scrub growth for a short distance before breaking into the open on ledges high on Ragged Mtn. just beneath the summit towers. From here, GHP (Ridge Section) continues down and then around the ledges of the west face of the mountain. After traversing a rugged wooded ravine, GHP climbs up and across more spectacular cliff faces and ledges. Reach Sundown Ledge at 2.8 mi., where Red Diamond Trail departs to the right to reach the summit of Ragged Mtn. in 0.15 mi. The ledges just beyond the summit offer wonderful vistas east to Mt. Megunticook.

From Sundown Ledge, it is 2.0 mi. north via GHP (Ridge Section and Little Ragged Section) to the Hope St. trailhead, and 1.9 mi. to the Barnestown Rd. trailhead.

GHP (LITTLE RAGGED SECTION) FROM BARNESTOWN RD. (AMC RAGGED MTN. MAP)
Cumulative from Barnestown Rd. trailhead (650 ft.) to:

Bald Mtn. Trail (660 ft.)	0.3 mi.	10 ft.	0:10
Round the Mtn. Trail (830 ft.)	0.8 mi.	180 ft.	0:30
GHP (Little Ragged Section) from Hope St. (1,210 ft.)	1.4 mi.	560 ft.	1:00
Hosmer Brook Trail (1,150 ft.)	1.6 mi.	590 ft.	1:10
Sundown Ledge and Red Diamond Trail (1,260 ft.)	1.9 mi.	710 ft.	1:20
Ragged Mtn. summit (1,305 ft.) via Red Diamond Trail	2.05 mi.	760 ft.	1:30

GRLT GHP (Little Ragged Section) ascends Ragged Mtn. from the northeast, offering views from Buzzard's Ledge, along the north ridge, and from the high point just below the summit.

From US 1 at a point 0.8 mi. from the center of Camden, turn northwest onto John St. At 0.8 mi. from US 1, John St. becomes Hosmer Pond Rd. Follow Hosmer Pond Rd. past the entrance to Camden Snow Bowl on the left. Beyond this point, the road is known as Barnestown Rd. Continue on

Barnestown Rd. past the intersection with Gillette Rd. on the left to the height-of-land and a trailhead parking lot on the left at 4.3 mi.

The route begins in a small field and crosses the road to a larger hayfield. Ahead at 0.3 mi., GHP bears right at the jct. with Bald Mtn. Trail and descends slightly, paralleling a brook. Below, cross the brook and begin to ascend Ragged Mtn. At 0.6 mi., cross Barnestown Rd. and ascend a short, steep pitch to a wide treadway that winds up the hill at a moderate grade. Bear right at the lip of a ravine and soon reach the jct. with Round the Mtn. Trail, which enters on the right. Continue climbing on GHP to reach Buzzard's Ledge at 1.0 mi. with views northeast to Bald Mtn. Ascend the ridge over a series of open ledges, and hike a contour around the upper east side of Little Ragged Mtn. Reach a knob beyond and descend slightly to a jct. at 1.4 mi., where GHP (Little Ragged Section) from Hope St. enters from the right. From here, it is 0.3 mi. to Hosmer Brook Trail, 0.5 mi. to Sundown Ledge and Red Diamond Trail, 0.65 mi. to the summit of Ragged Mtn. via Red Diamond Trail, and 3.3 mi. to ME 17 via GHP (Ridge Section and Route 17 Section). To continue from this point, follow the directions for GHP (Little Ragged Section and Ridge Section) from the Hope St. trailhead.

HOSMER BROOK TRAIL (AMC RAGGED MTN. MAP)
Cumulative from Camden Snow Bowl parking lot (240 ft.) to:

GHP (Ridge Section) (1,150 ft.)	1.2 mi.	910 ft.	1:05
Sundown Ledge and Red Diamond Trail (1,260 ft.)	2.1 mi.	1,030 ft.	1:35
Ragged Mtn. summit (1,305 ft.) via Red Diamond Trail	2.25 mi.	1,080 ft.	1:40
Camden Snow Bowl base area (240 ft.) via Red Diamond Trail	4.0 mi.	1,080 ft.	2:30

CMLT Hosmer Brook Trail climbs from the Camden Snow Bowl base area to the north ridge of Ragged Mtn., where it connects with GHP. From downtown Camden, travel north on US 1 for 0.8 mi. to John St. Turn right and drive 0.8 mi.; then bear left onto Mechanic St., which becomes Hosmer Pond Rd. In 2.1 mi., the entrance road for Camden Snow Bowl is on the left, just after Hosmer Pond. Park near the Camden Snow Bowl base lodge, the obvious A-frame building.

From the right side of the base lodge, walk straight up the grassy slope for about 400 ft. Two mountain bike tracks cross the slope; turn right at the second track, follow it under the triple-chairlift line, and cross a gravel access road. Cross a ski trail, and at a trail sign (Hosmer Brook Trail) ahead, bear left up another ski trail, the farthest right on the mountain. Hosmer Brook Trail zigzags up the slopes, trending in and out of the woods to either side of the wide ski trail; simply follow the obvious path straight up the slope. At 0.25 mi. from the base lodge, leave the ski trail to the right and enter the woods (sign). About 400 ft. ahead, reach an unsigned fork. A mountain bike trail diverges to the left; continue on Hosmer Brook Trail to the right.

At 0.5 mi., Hosmer Brook Trail reaches the lower loop jct. The right, more popular, fork is 0.2 mi. while the left is 0.4 mi. Both sections rejoin a short distance ahead. Take the right fork by going straight ahead. Soon cross over a stone wall, and at a rocky streambed, turn left and ascend a ravine, following switchbacks to the upper loop jct., which enters from the left. Continue straight, climbing gradually up the mountainside on switchbacks. Hosmer Brook Trail passes to the left of a large, sloping, mossy outcropping. Climb a single rock step and bear right around several huge, mossy outcroppings. Reach the jct. with GHP (Ridge Section) at 1.2 mi., on the north ridge in a semi-open area of oak and spruce. Turn left to follow GHP (Ridge Section) to Sundown Ledge and the jct. with Red Diamond Trail, which leads 0.15 mi. to the top of Ragged Mtn.

RED DIAMOND TRAIL (AMC RAGGED MTN. MAP)
Cumulative from Sundown Ledge and GHP (1,260 ft.) to:

Ragged Mtn. summit (1,305 ft.)	0.15 mi.	50 ft.	0:10
Camden Snow Bowl base area (240 ft.)	1.8 mi.	50 ft.	1:00

CMLT Red Diamond Trail is often combined with Hosmer Brook Trail and a portion of GHP to form a loop on Ragged Mtn. and is therefore described on the descent. Red Diamond Trail connects Sundown Ledge on GHP to the true summit of Ragged Mtn. and then continues through the woods and over the ski slopes of Camden Snow Bowl to its base area. The numerous outlooks en route include Bald Mtn., Mt. Megunticook, Mt. Battie, and Camden Harbor. (*Note*: This trail is not open during ski season.)

Standing on Sundown Ledge looking out, turn around to find Red Diamond Trail's entrance into the woods. Following red diamond markers, in 750 ft. reach a T jct. A side trail to the left leads 75 ft. to the summit ledges atop Ragged Mtn. and fine views to the east. Back on Red Diamond Trail, drop to a sag between the two wooded peaks of Ragged Mtn. and bear left and down past a large ledge outcropping. Descend a wide, eroded path and then bear sharply left and contour to the top of Downeast Glade. Cross the open area above the top of the triple-chairlift station, enter the woods beyond, and continue the descent. At 0.5 mi., pass the South Overlook tent platform. Continue down through the woods just south of the ski trail.

At 0.7 mi., an open-front shelter is 150 ft. to the left. Continue to follow the red diamond trail markers. Cross an open ledge with a cairn and proceed through the oak forest. Below, join with a narrow ski trail, cross a wider ski trail, and pass through Mainsail Glade. At 1.0 mi., at the next wide ski trail, make a sharp switchback right, back into the woods. Red Diamond Trail continues to switchback down through the woods on the shared mountain-bike and hiking trail. (Please do not cut switchbacks.) Cross a narrow ski trail and then reach a wide ski trail and turn left down it. Follow the right edge of the ski trail to a gravel access road just to the left of the upper station of the double-chairlift. Follow this road across the main ski slopes. At the triple-chairlift, turn right and follow the gravel access road to the base area. Cross the grassy ski slope to reach the A-frame base lodge and the end of the trail.

ROUND THE MTN. TRAIL (AMC RAGGED MTN. MAP)
Cumulative from Hosmer Pond boat launch parking (215 ft.) to:

Leave Kuller Trail (500 ft.)	1.2 mi.	285 ft.	0:45
GHP jct. (440 ft.)	2.7 mi.	455 ft.	1:35
GHP jct. (450 ft.)	2.8 mi.	465 ft.	1:40
GHP jct. (540 ft.)	3.5 mi.	605 ft.	2:05
RMT spur to Thorndike Brook trailhead (600 ft.)	4.6 mi.	805 ft.	2:40
GHP jct. (680 ft.)	4.8 mi.	885 ft.	2:50
GHP jct. (830 ft.)	6.1 mi.	1,125 ft.	3:40
Barnestown Rd. via GHP (560 ft.)	6.4 mi.	1,125 ft.	3:50

CMLT Multiuse Round the Mtn. Trail is a project of the Round the Mountain Collaboration spearheaded by CMLT, and when complete, the route will circumnavigate Ragged Mtn. Construction began in 2019, and by 2022, 6.1 mi. of the loop was complete as well as a 1-mi. spur path. RMT connects to GHP at several points, making a number of loop hikes possible.

Parking for RMT is available in the lot just before the Hosmer Pond boat launch, on the left side of the entrance road into the Camden Snow Bowl base area. Refer to Hosmer Brook Trail for driving directions.

From the boat launch parking lot, walk southwest toward the ski area. Pass the ski area parking lot on the right and bear left on a gravel road (map post and sign for Toboggan Chute). In another 50 ft., reach the start of RMT on the right (kiosk).

Follow switchbacks to a 3-way jct., with the toboggan chute below on the left. Continue straight up on the wide treadway, following RMT markers

SEC 9

(white diamonds). At 0.5 mi., turn left on Kuller Trail (coincides with RMT for 0.6 mi.) and soon enter CMLT's Ragged Mtn. Preserve. Stay on the wide path, avoiding trails diverging left or right. At 1.2 mi., Kuller Trail continues straight; turn sharply left here to remain on RMT. Just beyond is a kiosk and preserve sign. Ahead, stay on the wide path, again avoiding other trails that enter and leave RMT. After reaching the ridge crest in a saddle south of Ragged Mtn. at 2.1 mi., begin a gradual descent with one longish switchback on the way toward Mirror Lake. GHP enters from the right and quickly leaves to the right. RMT continues northwest, climbing gradually along the western base of Ragged Mtn. GHP crosses RMT at 3.5 mi. After a few switchbacks, RMT reaches a high point on the west slope of Ragged Mtn. For the next 0.7 mi., the trail follows a gently contouring route, passing through a lichen meadow in an area of exposed bedrock and then through a grove of shady hemlocks. At a T jct., a spur of RMT leads left 1.0 mi. to its Thorndike Brook trailhead on Hope St.

Follow a rising contour to a jct. with GHP and continue to climb via switchbacks to a high point on the north side of Ragged Mtn. At 5.7 mi., pass a clearing and several old buildings on the left. Just beyond is the current (2022) end of the multiuse portion of RMT. From this point, the trail continues as a footpath that winds around to the east side of the mountain to meet GHP. Turn left and descend via GHP to reach Barnestown Rd. 1.1 mi. north of the Camden Snow Bowl entrance road.

SPRUCE MTN. (973 FT.)

This mountain lies just southwest of Ragged Mtn. in Rockport. East and west summits offer views of the Camden Hills, Penobscot Bay, and beyond. The section of GHP described here heads west from Ragged Mtn. Spruce Mtn. may also be hiked from the west starting at Mt. Pleasant St. in Rockport. The Spruce Mtn. trailhead is the same as for GHP to Ragged Mtn. from ME 17.

SPRUCE MTN. TRAIL/GHP (AMC RAGGED MTN. MAP)
Cumulative from ME 17 trailhead (430 ft.) to:

Spruce Mtn. spur path	0.9 mi.	405 ft.	0:40
Spruce Mtn. high point (955 ft.) via spur path	1.3 mi.	630 ft.	1:00
Mt. Pleasant St. trailhead (500 ft.)	2.1 mi.	760 ft.	1:25

GRLT Spruce Mtn. Trail begins directly across ME 17 from the Ragged Mtn. trailhead parking lot and ascends steadily through mixed hardwoods and past old stone walls. At 0.4 mi., atop a steep rock outcropping, look for blueberry fields and views of Grassy Pond to the northwest, Ragged Mtn.

to the north, and Penobscot Bay to the east. Descend briefly, reenter the woods, and resume ascending. At 0.6, emerge on the east summit of Spruce Mtn. From here, find excellent views of Mirror Lake and Ragged Mtn. across ME 17, the islands of Penobscot Bay to the east, and Mt. Desert Island beyond.

After reentering the woods, the undulating trail trends down, crosses an old woods road, and reaches a large rock outcropping at the jct. with a 0.3-mi. spur path leading to a high point below the west summit. The spur climbs steeply before emerging on rock ledges among spruce trees but does not ascend to the wooded summit. The best observation point is from a rock outcropping below where the spur emerges. From there, enjoy excellent views of Hatchet Mtn. to the west (with Moody Mtn. peeking over its ridgeline) and of North Haven, Vinalhaven, and Mt. Desert islands to the east.

Return to the jct. with Spruce Mtn. Trail, turn left, and begin a gradual descent off the north flank of the west summit to the valley between Spruce Mtn. and Mt. Pleasant. The trail travels through a young hardwood forest and gradually flattens out in the valley as the forest becomes more mature. In the lower section, there may be wet spots that are easily crossed, and there are two bridges over streams. Shortly after crossing the second bridge, the trail begins to climb toward Mt. Pleasant. Ascend gradually at first and then more steeply, crossing under power lines and arriving at Mt. Pleasant St. in Rockport. A parking area sits on the side of the road. GHP continues on toward Mt. Pleasant across the road. Small GHP signs and blue blazes indicate the crossing.

MT. PLEASANT (1,058 FT.)

This mountain straddles the Rockport–Warren town line just southwest of Spruce Mtn.

From the jct. of US 1 and ME 90 in Rockport, travel west on ME 90 for 2.7 mi. Turn right (northeast) on ME 17, drive 0.4 mi., and turn left on Mt. Pleasant St. Follow Mt. Pleasant St., passing blueberry fields and the height-of-land between Mt. Pleasant and Spruce Mtn. before reaching the trailhead at 2.4 mi. at a wide spot in the road. Small GHP signs and blue blazes (no kiosk) mark the site.

SEC 9

MT. PLEASANT TRAIL/GHP (USGS ROCKPORT QUAD, GRLT SPRUCE MTN. AND MT. PLEASANT TRAILS, GAZETTEER MAP 14)
Cumulative from Mt. Pleasant St. trailhead (500 ft.) to:

Overlook at highest point (760 ft.)	0.8 mi.	260 ft.	0:30
Mt. Pleasant viewpoint (730 ft.)	0.9 mi.	260 ft.	0:35

GRLT This route is a continuation of the Ragged Mtn. and Spruce Mtn. section of GHP. The segment leads to an outlook with long views on the west flank of Mt. Pleasant. The trail formerly extended to a trailhead on Mt. Pleasant Rd. in Union, but that portion has been discontinued. The hike now ends at the viewpoint.

Mt. Pleasant Trail enters the woods on the west side of Mt. Pleasant St., across the street from the Spruce Mtn. section of GHP. It begins as an abandoned logging road and ascends gradually through a regenerating hardwood stand. At 0.3 mi., the trail turns sharply left and enters land protected by TNC, marked by a plaque embedded in a rock on the right side of the path. Here, Mt. Pleasant Trail begins ascending through a mature mixed forest to reach an overlook at the highest point on the trail at 0.8 mi. Descend gradually, briefly merge with a jeep trail, and quickly emerge at the upper edge of an old blueberry field, where there are views to the west. (*Note:* The hike ends here. Please respect landowners' wishes and retrace your steps to Mt. Pleasant St.)

COASTAL MOUNTAINS LAND TRUST
BALD MTN. (1,273 FT.)

This mountain in Camden is part of 537-acre Bald Mtn. Preserve, which is owned and managed by CMLT. Sights from the summit ledges of Bald Mtn. include Penobscot Bay, Ragged Mtn., and the surrounding Camden Hills. The rocky heath on the mountaintop is home to rare subalpine natural communities.

From US 1 at a point 0.8 mi. from the center of Camden, turn northwest onto John St. At 0.8 mi. from US 1, John St. becomes Hosmer Pond Rd. Follow Hosmer Pond Rd. past the entrance to Camden Snow Bowl on the left. Beyond this point, the road is known as Barnestown Rd. Continue on Barnestown Rd. past the intersection with Gillette Rd. on the left to the height-of-land and a trailhead parking lot on the left at 4.3 mi.

BALD MTN. TRAIL (AMC RAGGED MTN. MAP)
From Barnestown Rd. (670 ft.) to:

Bald Mtn. summit (1,273 ft.)	1.3 mi.	625 ft.	1:00

CMLT Bald Mtn. Trail and GHP coincide for the first 0.3 mi. The route starts in a small field and crosses the road to a larger hayfield. It then enters the woods and arrives at a jct. at 0.3 mi., where GHP continues straight ahead toward Ragged Mtn. Turn left on Bald Mtn. Trail and climb steadily on switchbacks and rock steps. Leveling off, the trail reaches a viewpoint. Beyond, scramble up a short, steep pitch to an open ledge and views of Ragged Mtn. and Buzzard's Ledge across the notch.

After an easy traverse, Bald Mtn. Trail swings back toward the mountain and ascends steeply on rocks and ledges. At the top of the climb, hike along the cliffs with views of the ocean and the peak of Bald Mtn. Bear left away from the cliffs and up to a knob. Cross a shallow col, pass beneath the summit cliffs, and reach the base of a rock staircase and ascend steeply. Above, angle upward through woods and then climb switchbacks to the huge cairn and interpretive sign on the summit at 1.2 mi. Continue a short distance south to a fine open vista.

BEECH HILL (534 FT.)

The 295 acres of Beech Hill Preserve in Rockport are owned by CMLT and managed for bird habitat and blueberries. The preserve protects the area's only bald hilltop, which offers panoramic views of Penobscot Bay and the Camden Hills. Atop the summit is Beech Nut, a beautiful, sod-roofed stone hut built in 1914. Trails climb the hill from the east and west.

SUMMIT TRAIL (USGS CAMDEN QUAD, CMLT BEECH HILL MAP, GAZETTEER MAP 14)
From Beech Hill Rd. (380 ft.) to:

Beech Hill summit (534 ft.)	0.9 mi.	154 ft.	0:30

CMLT This trail climbs Beech Hill from the west through blueberry fields and grasslands. From the jct. of US 1 and ME 90 in Rockport, travel south 0.3 mi. to Beech Hill Rd. on the right. Turn onto Beech Hill Rd. and drive 1.6 mi. to trailhead parking on the left.

Follow a footpath through young woods and then through a field along the edge of the road. At a stone gate, turn right uphill on the farm road. Please observe signs asking hikers to remain on the trail. The road angles across the hillside in the open with fine views of the surrounding landscape, the Camden Hills, and the islands of Penobscot Bay. Finish the hike at Beech Nut, the stone hut atop Beech Hill.

SEC 9

WOODS LOOP (USGS CAMDEN QUAD, CMLT BEECH HILL MAP, GAZETTEER MAP 14)
Cumulative from Rockville St. (240 ft.) to:

Beech Hill summit (534 ft.) via Upper Trail	0.9 mi.	294 ft.	0:40
Complete loop via Lower Trail	2.0 mi.	294 ft.	1:10

CMLT Woods Loop ascends Beech Hill from the east through the pleasant forest. From the jct. of US 1 and ME 90, travel south on US 1 for 2.1 mi. Turn right onto Rockville St. and follow it 0.7 mi. to trailhead parking on the right.

Walk along the wide path to a kiosk and then proceed through a sugar-bush management area. After a stone wall, reach the lower loop jct. at 0.2 mi., where Upper Trail leads left, and Lower Trail leads right. Bear left on Upper Trail to hike Woods Loop in a clockwise direction. The gently ascending Upper Trail meets the other end of Lower Trail at 0.6 mi. Continue left on Woods Loop to traverse the slope, and at a corner with a split rail fence, turn sharply right and ascend. Break out into the open at a granite bench, and then pass through a small grove of spruce to reach Beech Nut, the stone hut on top of Beech Hill. The scene to the east over Penobscot Bay, featuring the islands of North Haven and Vinalhaven, Deer Isle, and Mt. Desert Island, is breathtaking.

To descend, follow Woods Loop back to the upper jct. with Lower Trail, and hike that trail easily down the east slope past several stone walls to the lower jct. and out to the trailhead.

HATCHET MTN. (1,110 FT.)

This peak in Hope offers outstanding views over Hobbs Pond to Bald Mtn. and Ragged Mtn. and farther, to Mt. Megunticook in Camden Hills State Park. Hatchet Mtn. Preserve encompasses 27 acres on the mountain's east slope, where a trail climbs to an outlook just shy of the summit.

From US 1 and ME 105 in Camden, drive north on ME 105 for 5.1 mi. to the jct. of ME 105 and ME 235 in Hope. Turn left onto ME 105/235 and proceed another 1.3 mi. to the jct. of ME 105 and ME 235 at Hope General Store. Turn left onto ME 235 (Hatchet Mtn. Rd.) and drive 0.8 mi. to a small parking lot on the left for Hatchet Mtn. Preserve.

HATCHET MTN. TRAIL (USGS SEARSMONT QUAD, CMLT HATCHET MTN. MAP, GAZETTEER MAP 14)
From Hatchet Mtn. Rd. (ME 235) (460 ft.) to:

Hatchet Mtn. viewpoint (1,030 ft.)	0.65 mi.	570 ft.	0:35

SEC 9

CMLT From the parking lot kiosk, duck under the green gate and follow wide Hatchet Mtn. Trail on a rising contour above the road. After a switchback to the right, the trail climbs at a steady, moderate grade. Switchbacking left, the trail arrives at a fine vista on the left that looks out over Hobbs Pond to Ragged Mtn. and Bald Mtn. Ahead, the trail switchbacks right again. It narrows to a footpath and switchbacks to the left and up to contour across the slope. Crossing the upper edge of a pretty meadow, Hatchet Mtn. Trail ends at a fork halfway across the meadow, where the view north now includes Maiden Cliff, Mt. Megunticook, Bald Rock Mtn., Mt. Battie, and—across Penobscot Bay—Blue Hill Mtn. At the fork, a trail to the right climbs to the wooded top of the mountain but is on private property and should be avoided. A worn path continues across the top of the meadow but peters out at the woodline.

MT. PERCIVAL (506 FT.)

This hill in Northport rises above the west shore of Penobscot Bay. The remains of a historical lookout tower are on the wooded summit.

From the jct. of US 1 and Shore Rd. in Northport, at a point 4.9 mi. north of Lincolnville Beach, turn right onto Shore Rd. At a fork in 0.5 mi., bear left onto Upper Bluff Rd. At the next fork, 0.5 mi. ahead, bear right to stay on Upper Bluff Rd., which quickly turns to gravel. The Mt. Percival Preserve trailhead is on the left 0.6 mi. ahead. Parking is along the road on the right.

MT. PERCIVAL TRAIL (USGS ISLESBORO QUAD, CMLT MT. PERCIVAL MAP, GAZETTEER MAP 14)
From Upper Bluff Rd. (325 ft.) to:

Mt. Percival summit (506 ft.)	0.3 mi.	181 ft.	0:15

CMLT Climb the rock steps and head into the woods to the kiosk. Follow the wide path easily up the mountain's east slope to the stone base of the old tower on top, which a century ago offered far-reaching views east across Penobscot Bay. Today, thick forest blocks the view from ground level.

MONTVILLE AND KNOX
FRYE MTN. (1,140 FT.)

Frye Mtn. in Montville and Knox is in the 5,240-acre Gene Letourneau (Frye Mtn.) Wildlife Management Area, managed by DIFW. The wooded summit, formerly the site of a fire tower, is reached via a loop trail that is part of GHP and maintained by GRLT. A segment of Frye Mtn. Trail coincides with 47-mi. Hills to Sea Trail from Unity to Belfast, an ambitious project of the Hills to Sea Trail Coalition (formerly the Waldo County Trails Coalition).

From the jct. of ME 3 and ME 220 in Liberty, travel north on ME 220. Bear sharply right at Whites Corner at 3.2 mi. and reach Walker Ridge Rd. and the entrance to GLWMA on the right at 6.6 mi. Parking is available behind the DIFW maintenance building on the left.

**SEC
9**

FRYE MTN. TRAIL (USGS LIBERTY AND MORRILL QUADS, GRLT FRYE MTN. TRAIL MAP, GAZETTEER MAP 14)
Cumulative from DIFW maintenance building parking area (560 ft.) to:

Frye Mtn. Trail/Hogback Mtn. Trail jct. near ME 220 (540 ft.)	0.4 mi.	20 ft.	0:12
Frye Headwaters Trail (800 ft.)	2.7 mi.	510 ft.	1:35

Frye Mtn. summit (1,140 ft.)	4.0 mi.	1,000 ft.	2:30
Hills to Sea Trail (680 ft.)	5.1 mi.	1,250 ft.	3:10
Complete lollipop loop	11.0 mi.	1,830 ft.	6:25

GRLT To reach the start of Frye Mtn. Trail, walk behind the maintenance building and enter the woods on a snowmobile/ATV trail. Follow the well-established path for 0.3 mi. through the woods as it curves back toward ME 220. (*Note*: The start of the trail to Hogback Mtn. is reached via this same route, but Hogback Mtn. is currently closed.)

The snowmobile/ATV trail joins GHP 50 ft. before ME 220. Frye Mtn. Trail (also the route of GHP and HST) immediately turns right and begins to climb a ridge. (Hikers headed for Hogback Mtn. would turn left here and cross the road.) Traversing east, the trail passes through open woods and an old field before reaching Walker Ridge Rd. at 1.0 mi. (*Note*: This is 0.4 mi. east of the DIFW maintenance building parking area, and when the road is not closed to traffic beyond the parking area, hikers may drive to this point to start the hike.) Cross the road, reenter the woods, and quickly reach a kiosk. Ahead, cross a brook and then cross Bartlett Stream. (*Note*: A 0.5-mi. high-water path is available on the left a short distance before the stream.) Frye Mtn. Trail follows Bartlett Stream and then gradually bears away and heads south. Traverse a number of stone walls and an old road before climbing to cross a brook. Continue up a rocky ravine and reach a gravel road. (*Note*: Depending on road conditions, when the GLWMA road system is not closed to traffic, hikers may also park here.) Frye Headwaters Trail diverges to the right at this point, following the gravel road and continuing approximately 11 mi. to ME 173 in Searsmont, where the trail meets GRLT's Ridge to River Trail.

Staying on Frye Mtn. Trail, ascend to a jct. at 3.2 mi. and the start of a loop over Frye Mtn. From the jct., climb up to and across a series of ledges, passing many impressive stone walls and stone piles to reach the summit at 4.1 mi. Just beyond the summit, the trail bears right and descends quickly off the large ledge (look for a small cairn and a blue blaze). Continue easily along to the east and then descend gradually. Just before reaching the easternmost point on the loop, pass a massive oak tree. Shortly, Hills to Sea Trail departs to the left toward ME 137 in Morrill. Here, Frye Mtn. Trail continues straight ahead, swings back to the south, and contours along the southeast face of the mountain, passing through many different types and ages of forest stands and past numerous stone walls and foundations. After crossing a brook, begin to climb under a rock outcropping and watch for a ledge where there are views to the south. Continue to climb, eventually

SEC 9

reaching a ledge above the jct. where the loop began. From here, there are views to the northwest. Descend briefly, reaching the loop trail jct. at 7.8 mi. Bear left and follow the trail 3.2 mi. back to ME 220, which is at 10.9 mi.

HOGBACK MTN. (1,130 FT.)

Access to Hogback Mtn. has been closed by the landowner and is expected to remain so for the foreseeable future.

HILLS TO SEA TRAIL

Hills to Sea Trail stretches nearly 48 mi. through the hills and mountains of eastern Waldo County from Unity to Belfast through Montville, Knox, and Waldo. Opened to the public in 2016, the trail was designed and built over the course of five years by the Waldo County Trails Coalition (now the Hills to Sea Trail Coalition). More than 60 landowners have generously allowed trail access across their lands. HST also traverses more than 7,000 acres of state and private conservation land. Multiple access points, kiosks, and parking areas are along the route, which is for foot travel only. No camping is allowed. Each of HST's six sections is described individually.

HILLS TO SEA TRAIL—SECTION 1 (USGS UNITY QUAD, HSTC HILLS TO SEA TRAIL—SECTION 1, GAZETTEER MAP 22)
Cumulative from Unity (200 ft.) to:

Quaker Hill Rd.	2.8 mi.	350 ft.	1:40
Common Ground Education Center	5.7 mi.	450 ft.	3:05
Hunter Rd.	7.5 mi.	650 ft.	4:05
Clark Rd. (400 ft.)	11.8 mi.	850 ft.	6:20

HSTC The western terminus of Hills to Sea Trail is in Unity, just south of the jct. of ME 139 and US 202/ME 9. Parking is across the road at Unity Barn Raisers.

HST crosses a footbridge over Sandy Stream and heads south to the Unity College campus, crossing Quaker Hill Rd. en route. It follows a pedestrian path through the campus, crosses Loop Rd., and then travels the west margin of the soccer fields. Beyond, the trail climbs Quaker Hill, where there are expansive views from the fields, and descends to reach Quaker Hill Rd. and parking at 2.8 mi.

HST turns left to follow Quaker Hill Rd. and then turns right onto E. Mussey Rd. Leaving the road on the right, the trail crosses Mussey Brook, follows it south, passes Mussey Rd., loops north around a hilltop, and drops down to cross Sandy Stream. The stream has steep banks and may

SEC 9

require shallow wading. (If the stream is impassible due to high water, use Mussey Rd. as a cutoff route.) Beyond the crossing, the trail follows Sandy Stream south through Maine Heritage Orchard (MOFGA) and arrives at Common Ground Education Center (MOFGA) and parking on Crosby Brook Rd. at 5.7 mi.

Walk south on Crosby Brook Rd. for 0.5 mi. Turn right on Berry Rd. and follow it over Sandy Stream to meet Mussey Rd. Turn left on Mussey Rd. and follow it south to the jct. with Town Farm Rd. Continue straight through the intersection on what is now Hunter Rd. In 0.3 mi., the trail leaves Hunter Rd. and enters the woods on the left at 7.5 mi. Between Hunter Rd. and Clark Rd., HST negotiates rolling terrain with minor elevation changes. From Hunter Rd., the trail heads east to reach Sandy Stream and follows its west bank south before trending west again to cross Fly Brook (normally a stepping-stone crossing, it may be impassible in high water). Clark Rd. is south up the hill. Parking is just east on Clark Rd. at 11.8 mi.

HILLS TO SEA TRAIL—SECTION 2 (USGS UNITY QUAD, HSTC HILLS TO SEA TRAIL—SECTION 2, GAZETTEER MAP 22)
Cumulative from Clark Rd. (400 ft.) to:

Stevens Rd.	1.9 mi.	250 ft.	1:05
ME 137, Freedom	4.1 mi.	300 ft.	2:10
Freedom Pond Rd.	5.3 mi.	450 ft.	2:55
Penney Rd., Montville (650 ft.)	8.9 mi.	850 ft.	4:45

HSTC From Clark Rd., HST winds through mature forest and across undulating terrain before recrossing Clark Rd. It then winds through a cedar swamp on bog bridges to reach Stevens Rd. at 1.9 mi. For the next 0.9 mi., the trail follows Stevens Rd. north and then Weed Rd. east to a parking area. From here, the trail reenters the woods and follows Sandy Stream south for 1.0 mi. before reaching ME 137. HST turns west on ME 137 toward the town of Freedom; after 150 yd., it leaves the road and continues south.

From ME 137, it is 0.3 mi. to a spur jct. The spur leads west 0.4 mi. to Freedom General Store, where there is parking. Beyond the spur, the trail reaches Freedom Pond Rd. at 5.3 mi.

From Freedom Pond Rd., HST follows the route of Goose Ridge Trail, which is maintained by MCC. Goose Ridge Trail (see p. 440) meanders south through the mixed forest, climbing over several miles to Goose Ridge, with captivating views of farms and fields to the northeast. Beyond the high point, HST descends steeply along a pipeline corridor before reentering the woods and intersecting Penney Rd. in Montville at 8.9 mi.

HILLS TO SEA TRAIL—SECTION 3 (USGS LIBERTY QUAD, HSTC HILLS TO SEA TRAIL—SECTION 3, GAZETTEER MAP 14)
Cumulative from Penney Rd. (650 ft.) to:

Halldale Rd.	4.5 mi.	400 ft.	2:25
ME 220 (550 ft.)	8.4 mi.	900 ft.	4:40

HSTC After Penney Rd., HST follows more MCC trails through a portion of 1,100 acres of conserved land that protect the Sheepscot River headwater. From Penney Rd., Goose Ridge Trail descends to cross several branches of the Sheepscot River before joining Northern Headwaters Trail. From this point to Hemlock Hollow Trail beyond the summit of Whitten Hill, the route of HST is described as part of Northern Headwaters Trail (see p. 439). The trail follows the Sheepscot River south before climbing away toward Whitten Hill to reach the jct. with Whitten Hill Trail. From this jct., the Whitten Hill trailhead parking lot on Halldale Rd. is just 0.1 mi. east. Northern Headwaters Trail continues north along the wooded ridgeline of Whitten Hill, traveling alongside numerous fine old stone walls. Ahead, HST veers right onto Hemlock Hollow Trail and soon reaches Halldale Rd. at 4.5 mi.

Trail section closure: As of 2022, access to Hogback Mtn. has been closed by the landowner and is expected to remain so for the foreseeable future. This effectively closes the HST thru-route from Halldale Rd. to ME 220, a distance of 3.9 mi. via Hemlock Hollow Trail and GHP from Halldale Rd. and ME 220. HST hikers are asked to please respect this closure.

HILLS TO SEA TRAIL—SECTION 4 (USGS MORRILL QUAD, HSTC HILLS TO SEA TRAIL—SECTION 4, GAZETTEER MAP 14)
Cumulative from ME 220 (550 ft.) to:

SEC 9

Jeep road east of Frye Mtn.	4.9 mi.	600 ft.	2:45
Mixer Pond Rd. at ME 137 (330 ft.)	7.4 mi.	600 ft.	4:00

HSTC From ME 220, HST—now part of GHP—passes through the GLWMA (fires and camping prohibited). The trail undulates, with minor elevation gain, traversing Bartlett Stream and two gravel roads. Beyond the second gravel road, the trail ascends quickly to a jct. on the southwestern end of the Frye Mtn. ridgeline. Here, Frye Headwaters Trail enters from the right. HST/GSP continues to the left, following the ridge and coinciding with Frye Mtn. Loop to the summit of Frye Mtn. On the wooded summit, where Frye Mtn. Loop descends to the right, continue straight ahead on HST/GHP. Descend gradually over a series of ridges to the northeast. At 4.7 mi., where Frye Mtn. Loop/GHP continues to the right, stay straight on HST to reach an old jeep road at 4.9 mi., where trail exits state land.

Turn left on the jeep road and follow it north for 0.6 mi.; then turn right on a smaller dirt road, where there is seasonal parking. After 1.1 mi., leave the road for a path on the left, and in another 0.6 mi., reach ME 137 in Knox. Turn right, and in 0.2 mi., reach the Mixer Pond Rd. kiosk at 7.4 mi.

HILLS TO SEA TRAIL—SECTION 5 (USGS MORRILL AND BELFAST QUADS, HSTC HILLS TO SEA TRAIL— SECTION 5, GAZETTEER MAP 14)
Cumulative from Mixer Pond Rd. at ME 137 (330 ft.) to:

Savage Rd., Waldo	2.7 mi.	200 ft.	1:15
ME 137, Waldo County Technical Center (220 ft.)	6.5 mi.	400 ft.	3:25

HSTC From the Mixer Pond Rd. kiosk, HST follows ME 137 for 0.5 mi. and then enters the woods on the south side of the highway. A short distance into the woods, it climbs a steep 100-ft. escarpment, and in another 1.3 mi., it intersects ME 131. Now in Waldo, from this point the trail follows Savage Rd. south for 0.9 mi. to a kiosk on the left at 2.7 mi.

HST parallels the CMP utility line in the woods on the left before crossing the utility corridor, going back into the woods for 0.25 mi., and crossing a bridge over Pendleton Stream. It follows Pendleton Stream for a short distance and then roams through the woods and on a woods road for about 0.75 mi. before coming out onto gravel-surfaced Gurney Hill Rd. Follow the road to ME 137; turn right and follow the highway south for 0.4 mi.; then turn right onto Bonne Terre Rd. and proceed 0.4 mi. Ahead, leave the road on the left and enter the woods. In another 1.2 mi., reach ME 137 at 6.5 mi. Here, next to Waldo County Technical Center, is a kiosk.

HILLS TO SEA TRAIL—SECTION 6 (USGS BELFAST QUAD, HSTC HILLS TO SEA TRAIL—SECTION 6, GAZETTEER MAP 14)
Cumulative from ME 137, Waldo County Technical Center (220 ft.) to:

ME 7	2.0 mi.	50 ft.	1:00
Belfast & Moosehead Lake RR Station, Belfast (50 ft.)	4.8 mi.	150 ft.	2:30

HSTC From ME 137, HST passes a beaver pond and goes through hilly woods, turns left on a woods road for a short distance, and then reenters the woods. It passes through a recent logging cut before emerging into a field for the last short stretch to ME 7, at 2.0 mi. ME 7 has a kiosk, portable toilets, and parking.

From ME 7, HST follows a dirt road for 0.4 mi.; it then turns right into a remote, wooded stretch that features hilly terrain, mossy boulders, and a bridge across Marsh Fork. Reaching the CMP substation, the trail crosses East Waldo Rd. and proceeds through the woods to Oak Hill Rd. at the Belfast & Moosehead Lake RR Station at 4.8 mi. (kiosk and parking). This is the eastern terminus of Hills to Sea Trail. The Belfast Rail Trail continues from this point for 2.6 mi. to the public wharf on Belfast Bay at the base of Main St.

MIDCOAST CONSERVANCY LANDS
WHITTEN HILL (864 FT.)

The 410-acre Whitten Hill property in Montville is part of 1,000 acres of contiguous conservation lands in the towns of Montville and Freedom. MCC owns Whitten Hill and maintains the trails there as part of the 19-mi. Sheepscot Headwaters Trail Network.

From the jct. of ME 3 and ME 220 in Liberty, travel north on ME 220 to Whites Corner at 3.2 mi. Turn left onto Burnham Hill Rd. At 3.8 mi., bear right onto Halldale Rd., which turns to dirt at 4.7 mi. Trailhead parking is on the left at 4.8 mi.

NORTHERN HEADWATERS TRAIL (USGS LIBERTY QUAD, MCC SHEEPSCOT HEADWATERS TRAIL NETWORK MAP, GAZETTEER MAP 14)
Cumulative from Halldale Rd. (785 ft.) to:

Whitten Hill summit (864 ft.)	0.5 mi.	80 ft.	0:15
Sheepscot River (450 ft.)	1.6 mi.	80 ft.	0:50
Complete loop	3.8 mi.	500 ft.	2:10

MCC Northern Headwaters Trail climbs easily over Whitten Hill and follows a section of the headwater of the Sheepscot River, making for a pleasant and interesting woods walk. A portion of the trail coincides with 47-mi. Hills to Sea Trail from Unity to Belfast.

From the kiosk, follow the trail 100 ft. to the Whitten Hill Trail jct. To the left, Whitten Hill Trail connects to Bog Brook Trail and a series of trails south of Halldale Rd. Turn right on Whitten Hill Trail to reach the jct. of Northern Headwaters Trail in 0.1 mi. Turn right and follow blue blazes easily along the ridgetop, passing a series of stone walls on the left. Cross the unmarked and wooded summit of Whitten Hill at 0.5 mi. Hemlock Hollow Trail joins from the right at 0.8 mi. Beyond, descend easily to the west, passing a spur leading right (north) to the Northern Headwaters trailhead on Whitten Hill Rd.

SEC 9

Ahead, pass Goose Ridge Trail on the right at 1.2 mi. and soon pass Mink Run Trail, also on the right. Continue downhill on Northern Headwaters Trail to reach the east bank of the Sheepscot River at 1.6 mi. Hike south along the north side of Whitten Hill, following the course of the river, with minor ups and downs. At 2.2 mi., the trail turns away from the river and ascends gradually to reach an old woods road. It leaves the road and enters a large field with views to the south and west. At 2.9 mi., Whitten Fields Trail goes right, across the fields. Beyond the jct., reenter the woods and trend easily uphill to gain the ridge. Close the loop at the original jct. at 3.7 mi., and turn right (east) to return to the trailhead in another 0.1 mi.

GOOSE RIDGE (916 FT.)

This scenic hill in Montville is just north of Whitten Hill and features pleasant ridge walking and several open fields with views of the rural countryside. Goose Ridge is part of the MCC trail system, and the trail over the ridge coincides with 47-mi. Hills to Sea Trail from Unity to Belfast.

From the jct. of ME 3 and ME 220 in Liberty, travel north on ME 220; bear sharply right at Whites Corner at 3.2 mi. Pass Walker Ridge Rd. and the entrance to GLWMA on the right at 6.6 mi. At a jct. at 9.4 mi., where ME 220 bears right and Halldale Rd. goes left, continue straight ahead on Freedom Pond Rd. Reach the trailhead on the left at 10.5 mi. Parking is along the road.

GOOSE RIDGE TRAIL (USGS LIBERTY QUAD, MCC SHEEPSCOT HEADWATERS TRAIL NETWORK MAP, GAZETTEER MAP 14)
Cumulative from Freedom Pond Rd. (510 ft.) to:

Goose Ridge (916 ft.)	2.1 mi.	505 ft.	1:20
Penney Rd. (640 ft.)	3.6 mi.	585 ft.	2:05

MCC Follow the red-blazed trail into the woods, climbing easily. Begin a descent at 0.6 mi., pass an unsigned trail on the left, and then climb steadily. After a sharp right turn, reach a level area. Pass a sign for Spirited Horse Ranch (please stay on the trail). Bear left onto a two-wheel track, and at 1.2 mi. reach an open field with attractive views. Climb to the top of the field and reenter the woods at 1.3 mi. Hike easily along the ridge, and at a second field, bear right over a stone wall at 1.5 mi. Cross the field (views to the Camden Hills). Reenter the woods at 1.6 mi. and immediately turn right onto a woods road and proceed on level ground through a stand of young birch and maple trees. Traverse a swampy section, pass through a gap in a stone wall at 1.8 mi., and ascend to the ridgetop. At 2.1 mi., reach the high point on Goose Ridge.

Continue along the level ridge and then begin a gentle descent next to a stone wall on the left. In a semi-open area, merge with a wide track coming in from the right. Reach a signpost at 2.7 mi., bear left, and follow a grassy road. At the next signpost, bear right into the woods and climb slightly over a knob. Reach a pipeline corridor at 2.9 mi. For the next 0.4 mi., the trail alternates between the woods and the pipeline. At 3.3 mi., bear left into the woods and soon cross a wet, overgrown area with difficult footing. Emerge into a field and follow the woods line. Bear left at a corner of the field and then bear right out to Penney Rd. at 3.6 mi.

HAYSTACK MTN. (841 FT.)

This mountain in Liberty rises just east of the town and St. George Lake. Haystack Mtn. Trail, a perennial local favorite, climbs the peak from the athletic fields behind Walker Memorial School.

From ME 3 between South China and Belfast, proceed south on ME 220 for 0.8 mi. Turn left at the sign for the Vena M. Roberts Memorial Ballfield. Park in the lot behind Walker Health Center, near a basketball court.

HAYSTACK MTN. TRAIL (USGS LIBERTY QUAD, MTF HAYSTACK MTN. TRAIL [LIBERTY] MAP, GAZETTEER MAP 14)

Cumulative from Walker Health Center parking lot (570 ft.) to:

Haystack Mtn. summit (841 ft.) via spur path	0.7 mi.	270 ft.	0:30
Complete clockwise loop	1.3 mi.	270 ft.	0:45

MCC Facing the mountain, from the parking lot, angle left across to the baseball field fence and walk along behind it. Pass the bleachers, dugout, and snack stand. At a trail sign in the far corner of field, enter the woods and quickly reach a trail register. At the jct. just beyond, bear left to hike the loop in a clockwise direction. The ascent is gentle at first and then becomes more moderate. At 0.7 mi. from the parking lot, reach a spur path on the left, which heads over the summit of Haystack Mtn. and, just beyond, out of the woods and into a large blueberry field, which affords a lovely view to the north and east over the rural countryside of Montville. As of 2022, the group Friends of Haystack Mountain was actively working to purchase 63 acres on top of the mountain, including all the blueberry fields.

From the summit spur, Haystack Mtn. Trail winds down the east slope before swinging back west across rock outcroppings. The trail descends gently and crosses a footbridge before reaching the loop jct. Turn left to return to the parking lot.

SEC 9

FRANKFORT
MT. WALDO (1,062 FT.)

This attractive mountain in Frankfort is best known for the old granite quarries on its eastern side. Its many open ledges offer excellent views that include Penobscot Bay and the islands of Islesboro, North Haven, and Vinalhaven; the mountains of ANP on MDI; and Blue Hill Mtn., Tunk Mtn., and Schoodic Mtn.

From the jct. of US 1A and Loggin Rd. in Frankfort (just west of the bridge over the North Branch of the Marsh River), head south on US 1A for 0.2 mi. Turn right onto Old Belfast Rd., go beneath a railroad overpass, and at 0.4 mi., turn right onto Tyler Ln. At 0.7 mi., the road forks. Here, where Old Stage Rd. bears right, continue straight on Tyler Ln. At 2.2 mi., arrive at a dirt road and a power line on the left. Park here on either side of Tyler Ln., but do not block the dirt road.

NORTH TRAIL (USGS MT. WALDO QUAD, GAZETTEER MAP 23)
From Tyler Ln. (470 ft.) to:

Mt. Waldo summit (1,062 ft.)	1.0 mi.	600 ft.	0:50

NFTM From Tyler Ln., North Trail follows the dirt road past an old silver gate, paralleling the power line. At 0.3 mi., cross to the right, under the power line, and continue on the dirt road. The upper slopes of Mt. Waldo and its summit communications towers are visible directly ahead to the south. Reach a large meadow on the right, which soon becomes a blueberry field. At the upper left corner of the blueberry field at 0.55 mi., the road turns sharply left and proceeds on a contour above the field. At 0.65 mi., the road turns sharply left back toward the mountain and begins a steady climb over exposed granite slabs. As the trail climbs higher, expansive views open up to the north, and on a clear day, Katahdin can be seen. At 0.9 mi., the trail bears left to rejoin the power-line corridor, climbing right and up under the power line before leveling off on the approach to the rightmost tower. Where an old track bears left, step right and then walk ahead to the tower. Pass to the right of the tower to arrive at the summit of Mt. Waldo (look for a USGS marker mounted in the rock). Nearby are a number of rock carvings dating to 1876. Just beyond, the open ledges offer views west to Swan Lake and south to Penobscot Bay and the Camden Hills.

GEORGETOWN
HIGGINS MTN. (262 FT.)

This little mountain, the highest point on Georgetown Island, was burned over in the Great Georgetown Fire of 1908 and subsequent blazes. Home to pitch pines, blueberries, and the rare broom crowberry, the peak also offers treetop views east to Robinhood Cove and south to Sheepscot Bay and the Gulf of Maine. Billie Todd donated 41 acres on Higgins Mtn. to Kennebec Estuary Land Trust in 2000 after the death of her husband, Warren Todd.

From the jct. of US 1 and ME 127 in Woolwich, drive south on ME 127 for 7.6 mi. to trailhead parking on the right.

BILLIE TODD LOOP (USGS PHIPPSBURG QUAD, KELT HIGGINS MTN. MAP, GAZETTEER MAP 6)
From ME 127 (130 ft.) to:

Complete loop	0.6 mi.	120 ft.	0:20

KELT Begin Billie Todd Loop by going left, scampering up ledges and following cairns. In the semi-open terrain above, the blue-blazed trail turns sharply right and traverses the ridge to the Warren Todd memorial plaque 20 ft. before the south jct. of Lichen Loop. Continuing across the ridgetop, Billie Todd Loop passes the north jct. of Lichen Loop, crosses a stretch of boardwalk, and then descends via several short switchbacks before swinging south along the lower slopes of the mountain and returning to the trailhead.

LICHEN LOOP (USGS PHIPPSBURG QUAD, KELT HIGGINS MTN. PRESERVE MAP, GAZETTEER MAP 6)
From Billie Todd Loop, south jct. (250 ft.) to:

Complete horseshoe loop	0.6 mi.	50 ft.	0:20

SEC 9

KELT From the south jct. with Billie Todd Loop, white-blazed Lichen Loop heads northwest over the level summit area of parklike woods before dropping sharply left off the ledges. Pass through a shallow dip to reach the back edge of the KELT property, and then swing back to the east. Cross a low ledge knob to reach the north jct. of Billie Todd Loop. To the left, it is 0.4 mi. to ME 127; to the right, it is 0.2 mi. to ME 127.

SECTION TEN

ACADIA NATIONAL PARK

INTRODUCTION

This section describes 107 trails on 33 mountains in Acadia National Park on Mt. Desert Island (including several trails on a mountain in the neighboring Land & Garden Preserve), Schoodic Peninsula, and Isle au Haut.

Much, but by no means all, of ANP is on 80,000-acre Mt. Desert Island, situated east of Penobscot Bay about two-thirds of the way up Maine's coast between New Hampshire and New Brunswick, Canada. About 10 mi. south of the city of Ellsworth, Mt. Desert Island is connected to the mainland by a short bridge and causeways. Portions of Schoodic Peninsula and Isle au Haut are also preserved as part of ANP, which in its entirety encompasses 50,200 acres. The park owns 30,700 acres on Mt. Desert Island (about 38 percent of the island), 3,400 acres on Schoodic Peninsula, 2,900 acres on Isle au Haut, and 700 acres on an assortment of scattered islands; it has 12,500 acres in conservation easements.

ANP was established as Sieur de Monts National Monument in 1916. The monument became the first national park east of the Mississippi River in 1919 and was named Lafayette National Park in honor of the Marquis de Lafayette, a key French supporter of the American Revolution. The property was renamed Acadia National Park in 1929.

Of the 63 national parks, Acadia ranks 50th in size, but it is consistently one of the top 10 most visited (recent annual visitations have exceeded 4 million). The park features more than 150 mi. of hiking trails and 45 mi. of carriage roads (which connect to an additional 12 mi. of carriage roads outside the park proper) for human-powered recreation. A range of 26 granite mountain peaks extends across Mt. Desert Island from east to

SEC 10

west, and 8 of these summits exceed 1,000 ft. in elevation. Cadillac Mtn. rises to 1,529 ft., the highest point on the entire eastern seaboard of the United States. Scoured by the powerful action of glaciers eons ago, the U-shaped valleys between the mountain ridges hold forests of coniferous and deciduous trees and a multitude of streams, meadows, and peat lands that support more than 1,200 plant species; ANP's 26 pristine lakes and ponds have thriving fish populations (28 species). The park's 41 mi. of coastal shoreline feature cliffs and tidepools; beaches of sand, pebbles, and cobbles; mud flats and tidal marshes; and many other islands large and small. Rich with wildlife, ANP is home to 37 species of mammals, 11 species of amphibians, 7 species of reptiles, and more than 300 species of birds (resident and migratory). Twelve species of marine mammals are found in the ocean waters around the island, including whales, seals, dolphins, and porpoises.

Park Loop Rd. (27 mi.) and Cadillac Mtn. Rd. (3.5 mi.) visit the major scenic highlights of the park on Mt. Desert Island.

The majority of Acadia visitations occur between July and October. Visitor amenities are limited in winter months when most park buildings are closed. Pets are allowed on leashes shorter than 6 ft.

For more on outdoor recreation in ANP, see *Outdoor Adventures Acadia National Park: Your Guide to the Best Hiking, Biking, and Paddling* by Jerry and Marcy Monkman (AMC Books, 2017) and AMC's *Acadia National Park Map* (AMC Books, 2017).

ACADIA NATIONAL PARK ON MT. DESERT ISLAND
Geography

Mt. Desert Island is roughly 15 mi. across from east to west and 13 mi. long from north to south. Shaped much like a lobster claw, the island is divided into distinct east and west sides by Somes Sound, a natural fjord. Frenchman Bay is to the east of the island; Blue Hill Bay is to the west. ANP encompasses a little more than one-third of Mt. Desert Island. Many of the mountain summits, especially on the east side of the island, are relatively treeless and open and provide far-reaching ocean and mountain views.

On Mt. Desert Island's east side, just south of Bar Harbor, runs the long ridgeline of Champlain Mtn. (1,057 ft.), which trends south to encompass the Bowl, a beautiful tarn (glacial pool). The east face, or Precipice Wall, of Champlain Mtn. rises more than 900 ft. from the woods and meadows near Schooner Head. Great Head (150 ft.) is the easternmost point on the island, and Sand Beach is tucked into Newport Cove at its base. The steep pink cliffs of the Beehive (538 ft.) make it a distinctive landmark in this part of the park. The long, low ridge of Gorham Mtn. (518 ft.) flanks Ocean Dr. and peters out near Monument Cove a short distance north of Otter Cliff.

Between ME 3 and Eagle Lake is the mass of Dorr Mtn. and Cadillac Mtn. The east face of Dorr Mtn. (1,263 ft.) rises dramatically above the Tarn (a lovely but aging pond that is slowly reverting to a meadow). Kebo Mtn. (408 ft.) is a subsidiary peak on the north ridge of Dorr Mtn. A branch of Otter Creek starts on the south slopes of Dorr Mtn. A significant gorge separates Dorr Mtn. from its lofty neighbor Cadillac Mtn. (1,529 ft.). The long and mostly barren south and north ridges on Cadillac combine for a wonderful 6-mi. traverse, the longest on the island. A road winds to the top of the popular peak, which features a large parking lot; a gift shop; restrooms; and a short, universally accessible, interpretive loop trail. For several weeks each year, around the spring and fall equinoxes, the summit of Cadillac is the first spot in the United States to see the sunrise.

The bare summit of Pemetic Mtn. (1,243 ft.) is south of Eagle Lake, west of Cadillac Mtn., and east of Jordan Pond. South of Pemetic are the three peaks of the Triad (682 ft.) and Day Mtn. (584 ft.) From the extensive lawn at Jordan Pond House, visitors can enjoy the famous sight of the shapely Bubbles (North Bubble [871 ft.] and South Bubble [764 ft.] across Jordan Pond, one of the clearest in Maine). North of North Bubble are the ledges of Conners Nubble (587 ft.), which overlooks Eagle Lake.

From Jordan Pond west to ME 3/198 near Upper Hadlock Pond is a compact jumble of rugged peaks, including Sargent Mtn. (1,367 ft.). Its extensive, barren upper flanks form the second-highest summit on the island. Sargent Mtn. Pond is an attractive and secretive spot just north of the long, open ridgeline of Penobscot Mtn. (1,190 ft.). Jordan Cliffs form the steep walls of the mountain's east face above Jordan Pond. Subsidiary but very hike-worthy summits with fine views west of Sargent and Penobscot include Gilmore Peak (1,033 ft.), Bald Peak (969 ft.), Parkman Mtn. (937 ft.), and Cedar Swamp Mtn. (938 ft.). The long, wooded ridge of Norumbega Mtn. (846 ft.) forms the eastern escarpment of Somes Sound. Eliot Mtn. (458 ft.) sits in the Land & Garden Preserve between Northeast Harbor and Seal Harbor.

On the west side of Mt. Desert Island, between Somes Sound and ME 102, is flat-topped Acadia Mtn. (683 ft.). Just south, St. Sauveur Mtn. (684 ft.) rises spectacularly over Valley Cove, its 500-ft. cliffs the highest on the island. Flying Mtn. (282 ft.) looms over the Narrows at the entrance to Somes Sound. Rising precipitously above Echo Lake are Beech Cliff and

SEC 10

Canada Cliff. Beech Mtn. (843 ft.) and its summit fire tower lie just west. Long Pond is the largest water body on Mt. Desert Island, and immediately west rises the bulk of Western Mtn., which comprises two wooded peaks, Mansell Mtn. (939 ft.) and Bernard Mtn. (1,012 ft.). Great Notch and Little Notch are high and rugged defiles between these summits. The broad west ridge of Bernard Mtn. leads down to Seal Cove Pond, which is within striking distance of Blue Hill Bay.

Road Access

Mt. Desert Island is reached via ME 3 from the mainland at Trenton. ME 3 is the major highway around the east side of the island, connecting the towns of Bar Harbor and Northeast Harbor before ending at its jct. with ME 102/198 in Somesville near the head of Somes Sound. ME 233 is a major east–west connector between Bar Harbor and Somesville. ME 102 is the primary north–south route from the head of Mt. Desert Island through Southwest Harbor and on to Bass Harbor. Park Loop Rd. and Cadillac Mtn. Rd. are open from April 15 through November 30 (weather dependent). A Cadillac Vehicle Reservation is required to drive up Cadillac Mtn. from late May through late October (see Fees and Seasons below).

Park roads can be very congested during the busy summer months, so visitors are encouraged to take advantage of the free Island Explorer shuttle service that operates from late June through mid-October. Island Explorer buses run on 10 routes that serve ANP, local towns and villages, the regional airport in Trenton, and ANP on Schoodic Peninsula. These regularly scheduled buses stop at points throughout the park, including campgrounds, carriage road entrances, and many trailheads. Hikers can also flag down buses along their routes. The bus is an easy and efficient way to get around and see the park while helping to ease traffic congestion, alleviate parking problems, and reduce air pollution on the island. Buses are free, but donations are appreciated.

Hikers may also consider leaving their cars parked in Bar Harbor and hiking the village connector paths that link the town to park trails. These easy routes include Schooner Head Path, Great Meadow Loop, and Jesup Path. The ball field on Main St. in Bar Harbor has ample parking and is near these trails.

Fees and Seasons

ANP is open year-round and a park entrance pass is required at all times, regardless of how or where visitors enter. All visitors must display a valid pass on their vehicles at all park facilities.

SEC 10

Three methods allow purchase of an ANP park entrance pass:

1. Online and printed in advance from recreation.gov or the Recreation.gov mobile app.
2. At automated fee machines in the parking lot of the Hulls Cove Visitor Center on Mt. Desert Island and inside the gatehouse at the Schoodic Institute on Schoodic Peninsula.
3. In person at the fee station near the intersection of Park Loop Rd. and Schooner Head Rd. or at any of the following: Hulls Cove Visitor Center, Blackwoods CG, Seawall CG, Schoodic Woods CG, Jordan Pond Gift Shop, Acadia Regional Chamber of Commerce at Thompson Island, Bar Harbor Chamber of Commerce on Cottage St., Ellsworth Chamber of Commerce, Mt. Desert Chamber of Commerce, and Southwest Harbor/Tremont Chamber of Commerce.

For park visitors wishing to drive up Cadillac Mtn., a Cadillac Vehicle Reservation is required from late May through late October. This is in addition to the park entrance pass. Vehicle reservations for Cadillac are only sold online in advance; they cannot be purchased in the park. Go to recreation.gov or use the Recreation.gov mobile app to buy your Cadillac Vehicle Reservation. Be sure to print, fully download, or screen capture the document before your arrival because connectivity is unreliable throughout ANP. Your confirmation code must be displayed at the Cadillac Mtn. Rd. check station.

Most of Park Loop Rd. and all of Cadillac Mtn. Rd. are closed from December 1 through April 14 and at other times when conditions warrant. In winter, the section of Park Loop Rd. (Ocean Drive) from the jct. of Schooner Head Rd. to Otter Cliff Rd. is open (weather dependent). Winter visitors can also access Jordan Pond from Seal Harbor via Jordan Pond Rd. and a section of Park Loop Rd.

Thompson Island Information Center on ME 3 at the northern tip of the island is generally open from late May to early October. Hulls Cove Visitor Center at the start of Park Loop Rd. is open from Memorial Day through Indigenous Peoples' Day. Outside of these periods, information is available at the Bar Harbor Chamber of Commerce in downtown Bar Harbor. Operating hours of these facilities vary by season.

**SEC
10**

Camping

NPS operates two campgrounds on Mt. Desert Island—Blackwoods and Seawall, Schoodic Woods on Schoodic Peninsula, and Duck Harbor on Isle au Haut. No backcountry camping is allowed in any unit of ANP.

Blackwoods CG
This campground is on ME 3, about 5 mi. south of Bar Harbor. It is open from early May through mid-October and features more than 300 camp-sites for tents, campers, and RVs (up to 35 ft.). No electric or water hook-ups are available. Amenities include restrooms with cold running water, a dump station, picnic tables, fire rings, and water faucets. Showers and a small store are available a short distance from the campground during the summer season. A fee is charged throughout the camping season. Reservations are mandatory (no walk-ins) and can be made through recreation.gov.

Seawall CG
This campground, on ME 102A about 4 mi. south of Southwest Harbor, is open from late May through early October and features more than 200 campsites. Reservations are mandatory (no walk-ins) and can be made through recreation.gov. Amenities are similar to those at Blackwoods. A privately operated shower facility and store are available a short distance from the campground.

AMC's Echo Lake Camp
In Southwest Harbor just outside ANP, this waterfront camp (established in 1925) is an exceptional vacation spot amid the spectacular scenery of Acadia. Facilities include canvas-sided platform tents equipped with cots, blankets, mattresses, and pillows; a full-service dining hall; a bathhouse with hot showers; and a variety of recreational amenities.

Other Camping Options
At least seven privately operated campgrounds are on MDI and another just north on the mainland in Trenton. Lamoine State Park, in Lamoine, is also convenient to the island.

SEC 10

Trails and NPS Trail Ratings
Many of ANP's mountain summits are relatively treeless and open. Rock cairns mark the routes along these open stretches, and hikers should take care to locate the next cairn before moving ahead. Although the trails in Acadia are mostly within a short distance of roads and villages, the ter-rain is often sharp and precipitous, and hikers who stray off the marked paths may encounter rough going and dead ends at cliff edges and ravines. Visitors should be prepared for the changeable weather of the Maine

coast, which can, for example, turn quickly from bright sun to thick fog and rain.

The described trails in this section are for the most part well-marked, officially recognized, maintained paths that provide access to all the preferred summits on MDI, Schoodic Peninsula, and Isle au Haut. Most of the individual summits can be reached in comfortable half-day walks.

NPS maintains all the trails described, with the exception of those trails within Land & Garden Preserve. Trail markings include blue paint blazes, signs, and rock cairns (many of which are the traditional Bates cairns: two base stones, a mantle rock, and a pointer rock).

NPS rates trails based on these criteria:

Easy = fairly level ground

Moderate = uneven ground with some steep grades and/or gradual climbing, and footing may be difficult in places

Strenuous = steep and/or long grades, steady climbing or descending, sometimes difficult footing, difficult maneuvering

Ladder = iron rungs, ladders, handrails, and walkways placed on steep grades or difficult terrain (these trails are considered very difficult)

A 57-mi. system of fine-gravel carriage paths (45 mi. within ANP, 12 mi. outside ANP, and all closed to vehicular traffic) offers additional opportunities for pleasant walking, bicycling, horseback riding, and, in winter, cross-country skiing and snowshoeing. The trail descriptions in this section are limited primarily to mountain trails and, as such, don't cover some of the easier walks or the carriage paths; these are, however, delineated on Map 5.

For ease of traveling to ANP trailheads on the east side of MDI, the following mileages are provided, to be used in conjunction with Map 5.

From Hulls Cove Visitor Center
via Park Loop Rd. (two-way traffic) south to:

jct., ramp to ME 233	2.6 mi.
start of one-way section of Park Loop Rd.	3.1 mi.

Start of one-way Park Loop Rd. to:

Cadillac North Ridge Trail (no parking during summer/early fall)	0.3 mi.
Gorge Path	0.9 mi.
Kebo Mtn. Trail (no parking, park at Stratheden Path)	1.5 mi.
Stratheden Path	1.7 mi.
Sieur de Monts Spring access road	2.7 mi.
Champlain North Ridge Trail	3.5 mi.
Orange & Black Path crossing	4.1 mi.

Precipice Trail	4.6 mi.
park entrance station	5.4 mi.
Sand Beach	6.0 mi.
Gorham Mtn.	7.1 mi.
Otter Cliff Rd.	7.2 mi.
Hunter Brook Trail	11.6 mi.
Triad–Day Mtn. Bridge	12.6 mi.
Stanley Brook Rd., end of one-way traffic	13.4 mi.

From Hulls Cove Visitor Center
via Park Loop Rd. (two-way section) south to:

jct., ramp to ME 233	2.5 mi.
start of Kebo Brook Trail at Island Explorer bus stop	2.7 mi.
jct., start of one-way section of Park Loop Rd.	3.1 mi.
jct., Cadillac Mtn. Rd.	3.6 mi.
Bubble Pond	5.1 mi.
Bubble Rock	6.2 mi.
Jordan Pond trailhead parking area	7.7 mi.
Jordan Pond House	7.8 mi.
Stanley Brook Rd.	8.6 mi.
Seal Harbor and jct., ME 3	10.1 mi.

ACADIA NATIONAL PARK ON SCHOODIC PENINSULA

The only mainland unit of ANP is on Schoodic Peninsula, south of the town of Winter Harbor, which is east of Mt. Desert Island and the bulk of the park. Much of Schoodic Peninsula was once owned by John G. Moore, a Maine native and Wall Street financier. Moore's heirs donated the land to the Hancock County Trustees of Reservations in the 1920s, and in 1929, the spectacular 2,050-acre parcel became part of ANP. From 1935 to 2002, the US Navy operated a radio communications station on Schoodic Point. This facility is now Schoodic Education and Research Center, where the nonprofit Schoodic Institute is working to advance ecosystem science and learning for all ages through a partnership with ANP.

SEC 10

In 2015, the National Park Foundation donated 1,400 acres of land abutting the park on Schoodic Peninsula to NPS, bringing the total size of ANP at Schoodic to 3,450 acres. Before this donation, new infrastructure was privately constructed and given to the park: 4.7 mi. of hiking trails, 8.3 mi. of biking paths, Schoodic Woods CG (94 sites), a hybrid ranger station/information center, and a day-use parking area (100 spaces). More than 9 mi. of trails provide hiking enjoyment.

Geography

Flanked by Frenchman Bay to the west and the Gulf of Maine to the east, the peninsula features bold oceanfront granite cliffs and ledges, fragrant spruce and fir woods, and a craggy high point with wonderful panoramic vistas on Schoodic Head (442 ft.). Buck Cove Mtn. (224 ft.) is just to the north of Schoodic Head; farther north is Birch Harbor Mtn. (371 ft.).

Road and Water Access

From the jct. of US 1 and ME 186 in West Gouldsboro, drive south on ME 186 for 6.5 mi. to Winter Harbor. In the town, at the intersection of ME 186 and Main St., turn left onto ME 186 and travel east 0.5 mi. to Schoodic Loop Rd. Turn right onto Schoodic Loop Rd. at a sign for ANP and drive 0.9 mi. south to Schoodic Woods Campground and Information Center. The campground, information center, parking, and toilets are 0.1 mi. left on this access road.

Schoodic Loop Rd. guides visitors around the peninsula, touching most of the major scenic attractions. From ME 186 east of Winter Harbor past the Schoodic Woods complex to the picnic area at Frazer Point, Schoodic Loop Rd. allows two-way traffic. From Frazer Point to the east side of the peninsula at the head of Schoodic Harbor, the road is one-way only. Partway along, at 3.5 mi. from Frazer Point, two-way Arey Cove Rd. leads past Schoodic Education and Research Center to a magnificent outlook at the tip of Schoodic Point, perhaps the most visited spot in this unit of ANP.

An Island Explorer shuttle bus operates at Schoodic from late June through the end of August. This free service connects the ferry terminal, Winter Harbor, Schoodic Woods CG, Schoodic Point, Birch Harbor, and Prospect Harbor.

Schoodic Peninsula can also be reached by passenger ferry from the Bar Harbor Inn pier in Bar Harbor. Debarking at Schoodic Marine Center in Winter Harbor, visitors can then ride the Island Explorer bus (in season). The ferry service operates five crossings per day from Memorial Day weekend through Indigenous Peoples' Day (downeastwindjammer.com/ferries /bar-harbor-schoodic-winter-harbor; 207-288-4585).

Camping

Schoodic Woods CG, open from late May through Indigenous Peoples' Day in October, has primitive tentsites, car camping sites, RV sites with water and electricity, potable water, and toilets (no showers). Reservations are mandatory (no walk-ins) and can be made at recreation.gov.

SEC 10

ACADIA NATIONAL PARK ON ISLE AU HAUT

Isle au Haut is 5 mi. out to sea from the southern tip of Deer Isle and the town of Stonington, and 16 mi. southwest of Mt. Desert Island. The ANP unit on Isle au Haut encompasses most of the southern half of the island, some 2,700 incredibly scenic and remote acres. These lands were donated to the federal government in 1943. Isle au Haut ("High Island") was named by the French explorer Samuel de Champlain in 1604. The highest island in Penobscot Bay, it boasts a bumpy ridgeline that runs its length. Mt. Champlain, at an elevation of 540 feet, is the apex among the seven named mountains.

The island has a year-round population of 65, which grows to several hundred in summer. (*Note*: ANP limits the number of visitors to the island, and on rare occasions, visitors may be denied access. See Appendix A, p. 600, for contact information.) Outside of tourism, fishing is the economic mainstay. Amenities are few: a small general store, an ice cream stand, Maine's smallest post office, and an inn. Twelve surprisingly rugged trails offer 18 mi. of hiking, and a partially paved 12-mi. road circumnavigates the bulk of the island, offering additional walking options.

Geography

Isle au Haut features miles of rocky shoreline and pebbly beaches, craggy peaks and ridgelines, dense spruce forests, and marshes and bogs. A range of low mountains extends from north to south along the length of the 6-mi. island and includes Mt. Champlain (542 ft.), Rocky Mtn. (513 ft.), Sawyer Mtn. (495 ft.), Wentworth Mtn. (299 ft.), Jerusalem Mtn. (453 ft.), Bowditch Mtn. (425 ft.), and Duck Harbor Mtn. (311 ft.). The latter three mountains are within ANP.

Water Access

Isle au Haut is reached by a passenger ferry from Stonington on the southern tip of Deer Isle. The trip takes about 45 min. one way. The ferry, operated on a first-come-first-serve basis, runs year-round to the landing at the village of Isle au Haut. From early June through the end of the camping season in October, two of each day's ferries continue on to Isle au Haut's Duck Harbor. Contact Isle au Haut Boat Services at 207-367-5193 or visit isleauhautferryservice.com for schedule and rate information. An ANP ranger station is 0.25 mi. south of the town landing. During the summer season, a park ranger may board the ferry at the landing to answer visitors' questions en route to Duck Harbor.

SEC 10

Camping

No private campgrounds are on Isle au Haut, but there are very limited ANP facilities. Five lean-tos offer primitive camping at Duck Harbor CG from May 15 to Indigenous Peoples' Day in October. Advance reservations are required (no walk-ins) for these highly coveted spots and must be made through recreation.gov (starting on April 1 at 10 A.M. each spring). Camping is limited to one stay per year, with a three-night maximum for up to six persons. Each lean-to is equipped with a fire ring, a picnic table, and a storage locker for food and toiletries. A hand pump for water is nearby, as are several composting toilets. No trash containers are available, and campers must carry out all trash.

SUGGESTED HIKES

■ Easy
GREAT HEAD

LP via Great Head Trail	1.6 mi.	230 ft.	0:55

Explore the ruins of an old teahouse and enjoy great clifftop views over Frenchman Bay and Newport Cove on this scenic circuit. Visit nearby Sand Beach for bonus fun. See Great Head Trail, p. 473.

BUBBLE ROCK

RT via Bubbles Divide Trail and Bubbles Trail	1.4 mi.	344 ft.	0:55

Climb South Bubble to check out Bubble Rock, a 110-ton glacial erratic perched on the cliff edge, and admire the excellent scenery of Jordan Pond, Pemetic Mtn., and Penobscot Mtn. To begin, see Bubbles Divide Trail, p. 479.

JORDAN POND

LP via Jordan Pond Path	3.4 mi.	0 ft.	1:40

Trace a pleasant route all the way around the deepest body of water on Mt. Desert Island, also one of the cleanest, clearest ponds in Maine. Bonus: impressive views of Jordan Cliff and the Bubbles. See Jordan Pond Path, p. 474.

SEC 10

FLYING MTN.

⬤ 🧍 🐕 🦮 🍃 💲

LP via Flying Mtn. Trail and Valley Cove fire road	1.4 mi.	345 ft.	0:45

A short climb leads to a scenic panorama of Somes Sound, Southwest Harbor, and the islands beyond. To begin, see Flying Mtn. Trail, p. 498.

BEECH MTN.

⬤ 🧍 🐕 🦮 🍃 🗼

LP via Beech Mtn. Loop	1.1 mi.	343 ft.	0:40

Visit the fire tower atop Beech Mtn. and then drink in views of Long Pond and Western Mtn. from the ledges on the west side of Beech Mtn. See Beech Mtn. Loop Trail, p. 501.

■ Moderate

CADILLAC NORTH RIDGE—GORGE PATH

⬤ 🐕 🦮 🍃 💲

LP via Kebo Brook Trail, Gorge Path, and Cadillac North Ridge Trail	5.1 mi.	1,329 ft.	3:20

Explore the pretty gorge between Cadillac Mtn. and Dorr Mtn. and then summit Cadillac Mtn., the highest peak in ANP. Finish via the wide-open north ridge. To begin, see Kebo Brook Trail, p. 461.

CHAMPLAIN MTN.

🐕 🦮 🍃 💲

OW via Champlain North Ridge Trail, Champlain South Ridge Trail, and Bowl Trail	3.6 mi.	925 ft.	2:15

Enjoy ocean and mountain views for most of the route over Champlain Mtn. To begin, see Champlain North Ridge Trail, p. 470.

PENOBSCOT MTN. SOUTH RIDGE

⬤ 🐕 🦮 🍃 💲

RT via Asticou & Jordan Pond Path and Penobscot Mtn. Trail	5.8 mi.	1,190 ft.	3:30

Emerge from a wooded hike onto the mostly open south ridge of Penobscot Mtn. for great looks over Jordan Pond. To begin, see Asticou & Jordan Pond Path, p. 475.

BALD PEAK AND PARKMAN MTN.

🐕 📷 👟 💲   ↕️   ↗️   ⭕

LP via Hadlock Brook Trail, Bald Peak Trail, and Parkman Mtn. Trail	2.7 mi.	756 ft.	1:45

Bag these two rocky knobs while admiring scenes of Upper Hadlock Pond, Norumbega Mtn., and Sargent Mtn. To begin, see Hadlock Brook Trail, p. 487.

ACADIA MTN.

💧 🥾 🐕 📷 👟   ↕️   ↗️   ⭕

LP via Acadia Mtn. Trail and Man O' War Brook fire road	3.1 mi.	593 ft.	1:50

Enjoy dramatic views of Somes Sound and the Cranberry Isles on this pleasant loop hike. To begin, see Acadia Mtn. Trail, p. 496.

MANSELL MTN.

💧 🐕 👟 💲   ↕️   ↗️   ⭕

LP via Perpendicular Trail, Mansell Mtn. Trail, and Cold Brook Trail	2.7 mi.	874 ft.	2:45

Climb Mansell Mtn. via the more than 1,000 rock steps of Perpendicular Trail (follow the other two trails on the return) for vistas over Long Pond toward Beech Mtn. To begin, see Perpendicular Trail, p. 503.

■ Strenuous

CADILLAC MTN. SOUTH RIDGE

💧 🐕 📷 👟   ↕️   ↗️   ⭕

RT via Cadillac South Ridge Trail and Eagles Crag Trail	6.6 mi.	1,500 ft.	3:55

From ME 3, hike to Eagles Crag and the Featherbed; then revel in the sights from the long and wide-open upper south ridge to the top of Cadillac Mtn. To begin, see Cadillac South Ridge Trail, p. 460.

CHAMPLAIN MTN.—PRECIPICE FACE

🧗 🪜 👟   ↕️   ↗️   ⭕

LP via Precipice Trail, Champlain North Ridge Trail, Orange & Black Path, and Precipice Trail	3.0 mi.	1,007 ft.	2:00

Tackle the steep, exposed, and exhilarating east wall of Champlain Mtn. via iron rungs, ladders, handrails, and walkways. The rewards are

SEC 10

far-reaching views from Frenchman Bay to Cadillac Mtn. To begin, see Precipice Trail, p. 468.

SAND BEACH TO JORDAN POND

OW via Bowl Trail, Champlain South Ridge Trail, Beachcroft Path, Kane Path, Canon Brook Trail, Dorr South Ridge Trail, Cadillac–Dorr Connector, Gorge Path, Cadillac South Ridge Trail, Canon Brook Trail, Bubble & Jordan Ponds Path, and Jordan Pond Path	11.3 mi.	2,800 ft.	7:15

This lengthy traverse of the east side of Mt. Desert Island features some of ANP's best-known natural features on its route from Sand Beach to Jordan Pond. The summits of Champlain, Dorr, and Cadillac mountains are included; add a side trip to Pemetic Mtn. for more miles and fun. Spot a second vehicle at the finish or ride the Island Explorer bus in season. To begin, see Bowl Trail, p. 471.

SIX PEAKS CIRCUIT

LP via Hadlock Brook Trail, Bald Peak Trail, Parkman Mtn. Trail, Grandgent Trail, Sargent South Ridge Trail, Penobscot Mtn. Trail, Sargent South Ridge Trail, Amphitheater Trail, and Hadlock Brook Trail	5.8 mi.	1,786 ft.	3:50

Tackle six summits and enjoy extraordinary ocean, island, and mountain scenery on this rugged loop over the jumble of bare peaks between Jordan Pond and Upper Hadlock Pond, including Bald Peak, Parkman Mtn., Gilmore Peak, Sargent Mtn., Penobscot Mtn., and Cedar Swamp Mtn. Scenic bonus en route: tiny Sargent Mtn. Pond. To begin, see Hadlock Brook Trail, p. 487.

SEC 10

TRAIL DESCRIPTIONS

EASTERN MT. DESERT ISLAND: CADILLAC MTN. TO GREAT HEAD

CADILLAC MTN. (1,529 FT.)

The highest point on Mt. Desert Island, this mountain is also the highest on the eastern seaboard of the Atlantic Ocean between Newfoundland and Brazil. An automobile road, Cadillac Mtn. Rd., leads 3.5 mi. to the summit, which has a parking lot, a paved 0.4-mi. walking trail with inter-pretive displays, a small gift shop, and restrooms. The open expanse offers commanding views in all directions. Accessibility by vehicle (reservations required) makes this rocky summit the busiest in ANP. Six trails traverse the mountain's slopes.

CADILLAC NORTH RIDGE TRAIL (MAP 5: D7)
NPS rating: moderate
From Park Loop Rd. (240 ft.) to:

Cadillac Mtn. summit (1,529 ft.)	2.3 mi.	1,289 ft.	1:45

NPS The trail starts on Park Loop Rd., 0.3 mi. east of where the road becomes one-way. A pullout on the north side of the road provides very limited parking. (*Note*: During the busy summer and early fall months, hikers are not allowed to park at this trailhead but must access the start of this route from Kebo Brook Trail, which can be reached via the Island Explorer bus. See Kebo Brook Trail on p. 461 for access details.)

Begin on the south side of Park Loop Rd. and climb the north ridge of Cadillac Mtn., rising steadily through stunted softwoods onto open ledges. The trail always keeps to the east of Cadillac Mtn. Rd., although it closely approaches road switchbacks on two occasions. For much of the way, both sides of the ridge are visible. Enjoy excellent views of Bar Harbor, Eagle Lake, Egg Rock, and Dorr Mtn. as the trail proceeds over open slabs and ledges to its end on top of Cadillac Mtn., emerging onto the pavement of the summit parking lot a short distance north of the gift shop and restrooms.

GORGE PATH (MAP 5: D7)
NPS rating: moderate
Cumulative from Park Loop Rd. (220 ft.) to:

Dorr–Cadillac notch (1,050 ft.) at jct. Cadillac–Dorr Connector and A. Murray Young Path	1.4 mi.	830 ft.	1:05
Cadillac Mtn. summit (1,529 ft.)	1.9 mi.	1,309 ft.	1:35

NPS This trail ascends the scenic gorge between Cadillac Mtn. and Dorr Mtn. and provides access to both peaks. The trailhead is on Park Loop Rd., 0.9 mi. east of where it becomes one-way. Gorge Path rises moder-ately up the gorge, passing Hemlock Trail at 0.4 mi. Climbing a narrow valley next to Kebo Brook much of the time, Gorge Path finally reaches a jct. with Cadillac–Dorr Connector and A. Murray Young Path at 1.4 mi. in the deep notch between the two mountains. At this point, Gorge Path turns right (west) and climbs steeply to the summit of Cadillac Mtn., reaching it at 1.9 mi.

SEC 10

CADILLAC SOUTH RIDGE TRAIL (MAP 5: F7–E7–D7)
NPS rating: moderate
Cumulative from ME 3 (180 ft.) to:

Eagles Crag Trail, south jct. (600 ft.)	1.0 mi.	420 ft.	0:40
Eagles Crag Trail, north jct. (700 ft.)	1.2 mi.	520 ft.	0:50
Canon Brook Trail (1,000 ft.) at the Featherbed	2.4 mi.	902 ft.	1:35
Cadillac Mtn. summit (1,529 ft.)	3.3 mi.	1,432 ft.	2:20

NPS A relatively long hike for ANP, this trail starts on the north side of ME 3 100 yd. west of the entrance to Blackwoods CG. Parking is along the north shoulder of ME 3. (A level 0.7-mi. connector path also links the campground to the road and trailhead.) Cadillac South Ridge Trail climbs generally north. At 1.0 mi., a short loop trail on the right leads to Eagles Crag, with views southeast to Otter Creek and Otter Cove. The loop trail rejoins the main trail in 0.3 mi.

Ahead, Cadillac South Ridge Trail travels through a semi-open forest of pitch pines and jack pines. After leaving the woods, the trail rises gradually to cross open ledges before dropping to meet Canon Brook Trail at the Featherbed (a small tarn). Continuing a long ascent of the broad south ridge, mostly in the open with expansive views, Cadillac South Ridge Trail reaches Cadillac West Face Trail on the left. Ahead, Cadillac South Ridge Trail passes close to a switchback in Cadillac Mtn. Rd. near Blue Hill Overlook, reenters the woods, and climbs several rocky steps. The trail ends at the Cadillac Mtn. summit parking lot, adjacent to the gift shop and restrooms. The true summit of Cadillac, often overlooked, is 100 yd. before this—a large flat rock with a USGS marker on its surface 30 ft. west of the trail.

CADILLAC WEST FACE TRAIL (MAP 5: E6–E7)
NPS rating: strenuous
Cumulative from Bubble Pond parking lot (336 ft.) to:

Cadillac South Ridge Trail (1,490 ft.)	1.1 mi.	1,090 ft.	1:05
Cadillac Mtn. summit (1,529 ft.) via Cadillac South Ridge Trail	1.5 mi.	1,193 ft.	1:20

SEC 10

NPS This steep trail, the shortest route to the summit of Cadillac Mtn., is difficult anytime, but especially in wet weather, when the rock slabs can be extremely slippery. The trailhead is at the Bubble Pond parking lot on Park Loop Rd., 5.1 mi. south of Hulls Cove Visitor Center and 2.7 mi. north of Jordan Pond House. (*Note*: This very small lot is often full. Plan to arrive early or ride the Island Explorer bus.)

From the parking lot, cross a carriage road and proceed south for 100 ft. to Bubble Pond. Here, Pemetic North Ridge Trail departs right (west), while Cadillac West Face Trail leaves to the left (east). Follow Cadillac West Face Trail along the pond shore; pass a picnic table and cross the pond's outlet. Just after, leave the wide path and turn sharply right on a footpath. The trail quickly ascends on rocky treadway. Scramble over ledges, traverse steep slabs, and then climb steeply. Views of Bubble Pond and Pemetic Mtn. emerge, and, above, the vista widens to include Penobscot Mtn., Sargent Mtn., and Eagle Lake.

After more steeply sloping ledges, North Bubble and Conners Nubble are visible. A rising traverse leads to additional steep, sloping slabs—along with ocean views south to the Cranberry Isles. After the final slabs, Cadillac West Face Trail wends easily to join Cadillac South Ridge Trail. Turn left to follow Cadillac South Ridge Trail, which passes close to a switchback in Cadillac Mtn. Rd. near Blue Hill Overlook, climbs some rocky terrain through the woods, and ends at the Cadillac Mtn. summit parking lot adjacent to the gift shop and restrooms.

KEBO MTN. (408 FT.)

The northernmost mountain in ANP and the nearest to Bar Harbor, this low, twin-summited peak lies just off Park Loop Rd. at the end of the long north ridge of Dorr Mtn. Climb Kebo Mtn. on its own or extend the hike to include adjacent Dorr Mtn.

KEBO BROOK TRAIL (MAP 5: D7)
NPS rating: easy
Cumulative from Park Loop Rd. (360 ft.) at Island Explorer bus stop (North Ridge) to:

Cadillac North Ridge Trail (380 ft.)	0.1 mi.	20 ft.	0:05
Gorge Path (220 ft.)	0.5 mi.	20 ft.	0:15
Kebo Mtn. Trail (180 ft.)	0.7 mi.	50 ft.	0:20
Stratheden Path (150 ft.)	0.8 mi.	50 ft.	0:25
Great Meadow Loop at Kebo St. (100 ft.)	1.0 mi.	50 ft.	0:30

NPS This trail provides an important connection between the Island Explorer bus stop (North Ridge) on Park Loop Rd. and Great Meadow. Kebo Brook Trail links trailheads on the north side of Cadillac Mtn. and Kebo Mtn. and allows access to Cadillac North Ridge Trail, Gorge Path, Kebo Mtn. Trail, and Stratheden Path. During the busy summer and early fall months, parking is not allowed at the Cadillac North Ridge Trail trailhead on Park Loop Rd., and there is no parking on Park Loop Rd. at the start of Kebo Mtn. Trail. Limited roadside parking is available at both Gorge Path and Stratheden Path. Therefore, hikers are urged to take advantage of the Island Explorer bus (route 4 or 5) when planning to hike these trails.

SEC
10

From the bus stop, look for a trail sign to the right of the power line and follow the wide gravel path into the woods. In 0.1 mi. reach the jct. with Cadillac North Ridge Trail, which leads 50 ft. up a stone staircase to Park Loop Rd. and to the summit of Cadillac Mtn. in another 2.2 mi. Kebo Brook Trail continues, trending downhill but still parallel to Park Loop Rd. At 0.5 mi., Gorge Path leaves to the right. (Gorge Path leads 0.35 mi. to Park Loop Rd., where the path passes under the arch of a stone bridge, crosses a stream, and continues right, up steps along the bridge, and then south into the woods. From there, it is 1.8 mi. to the top of Cadillac Mtn.) Ahead on Kebo Brook Trail, cross a brook on stepping-stones, with Kebo Valley Golf Course below to the left. At 0.7 mi., Kebo Mtn. Trail departs to the right, leading 25 ft. up steps to Park Loop Rd. From there, it is 0.3 mi. to the top of Kebo Mtn. and 0.9 mi. to Dorr North Ridge Trail.

At 0.8 mi. on Kebo Brook Trail, Stratheden Path leaves to the right to reach Park Loop Rd. in 100 ft. (the trail joins Hemlock Trail in another 0.7 mi.). Kebo Brook Trail ends ahead at 1.0 mi. at its jct. with Great Meadow Loop at Kebo St.

KEBO MTN. TRAIL (MAP 5: D7)
NPS rating: easy
Cumulative from Kebo Brook Trail at Park Loop Rd. (180 ft.) to:

Kebo Mtn., north summit (408 ft.)	0.3 mi.	228 ft.	0:15
Hemlock Trail and Dorr North Ridge Trail (300 ft.)	0.9 mi.	323 ft.	0:35
Dorr Mtn. summit (1,263 ft.) via Dorr North Ridge Trail	2.0 mi.	1,286 ft.	1:40

NPS This trail leaves the south side of Park Loop Rd. 1.5 mi. after the road becomes one-way. No parking is available at the start of Kebo Mtn. Trail on Park Loop Rd. Hikers can park 0.2 mi. east at the gravel pullout for Stratheden Path and walk Kebo Brook Trail 0.1 mi. west to the start. It is also possible to hike Kebo Brook Trail (see p. 461) from the Island Explorer North Ridge bus stop, an approach of 0.7 mi.

Kebo Mtn. Trail climbs to the north summit of Kebo Mtn., drops easily into a saddle, and then climbs to the higher south summit. The trail then descends to meet Hemlock Trail and Dorr North Ridge Trail 0.9 mi. from Park Loop Rd.

SEC 10

STRATHEDEN PATH (MAP 5: D7)
NPS rating: easy
From Park Loop Rd. (150 ft.) to:

Hemlock Trail and Hemlock Rd. (70 ft.)	0.7 mi.	-100 ft.	0:20

NPS Extending from Park Loop Rd. to Hemlock Trail, this easy walk rambles along the eastern base of Kebo Mtn. Stratheden Path begins on

Park Loop Rd., 0.2 mi. east of Kebo Mtn. Trail. The path takes a fairly level route through hemlocks on its way to Hemlock Trail, which it reaches at 0.7 mi. Turn right onto Hemlock Trail to access Kebo Mtn. Trail and Dorr North Ridge Trail in 0.2 mi., or continue straight on Hemlock Rd. to reach Sieur de Monts Spring in 0.4 mi.

HEMLOCK TRAIL (MAP 5: D7)
NPS rating: easy
From Gorge Path (290 ft.) to:

Kebo Mtn. Trail (290 ft.)	0.3 mi.	20 ft.	0:09
Hemlock Road and Stratheden Path (70 ft.)	0.5 mi.	20 ft.	0:15

NPS This short trail on the lower end of the north ridge of Dorr Mtn. connects Gorge Path to Dorr North Ridge and Kebo Mtn. trails and on to Stratheden Path and Hemlock Rd. Hemlock Trail begins on Gorge Path, 1.0 mi. north of the Cadillac–Dorr notch and 0.4 mi. south of Park Loop Rd. It heads east, rising slightly to the jct. of Dorr North Ridge Trail and Kebo Mtn. Trail in 0.2 mi. Hemlock Trail then descends moderately and ends at a jct. with Stratheden Path and Hemlock Rd. (closed to vehicles) at 0.4 mi. From this jct., Sieur de Monts Spring is 0.4 mi. south via Hemlock Rd.

DORR MTN. (1,263 FT.)

This mountain, named for George B. Dorr, one of the founding fathers of ANP, lies immediately west of Sieur de Monts Spring and the Tarn. Two routes up the mountain originate from Sieur de Monts Spring, while two more begin from the Tarn near ME 3. Routes also ascend from the north and south over long ridges, and one rises from the gorge east of Cadillac Mtn. The east slope of Dorr Mtn. is particularly steep, and views from the high ridgeline on Dorr are superb. Ten trails form an extensive network for exploring this mountain from all sides.

EMERY PATH (MAP 5: D7)
NPS rating: strenuous
Cumulative from Sieur de Monts Spring (70 ft.) to:

Homans Path (420 ft.)	0.3 mi.	350 ft.	0:20
Kurt Diederich's Climb and Schiff Path (560 ft.)	0.5 mi.	490 ft.	0:30
Dorr Mtn. summit (1,263 ft.) via Schiff Path and Dorr North Ridge Trail	1.5 mi.	1,193 ft.	1:20

NPS Emery Path originates from Sieur de Monts Spring and climbs the east face of Dorr Mtn. to join Schiff Path and Homans Path. From the village green in Bar Harbor (jct. of Mt. Desert St. and Main St.), drive

SEC
10

south on ME 3 for 1.5 mi. to the Sieur de Monts Spring entrance to ANP. Turn right here and then left to reach the large Sieur de Monts Spring parking area (toilets). Wild Gardens of Acadia is on the right, and the Nature Center is just ahead.

To reach the start of Emery Path, from the patio at the Nature Center, walk the gravel path to the right of the kiosk. In just a few feet, at the entrance to Wild Gardens of Acadia, turn left and cross a footbridge. At a fork just beyond, go left for 150 ft. to a large rock inscribed "Sweet Waters of Acadia." The springhouse is ahead. From here, Emery Path follows a series of switchbacks up the northeast shoulder of Dorr Mtn. The first half of the climb features many stone steps. At 0.3 mi., Homans Path enters from the right. At 0.5 mi., Emery Path ends at a jct. with Kurt Diederich's Climb, which enters from the left, and Schiff Path, which continues on a rising traverse to meet Ladder Trail before climbing to the summit ridge of Dorr Mtn. Near the top, turn left to finish the hike on Dorr North Ridge Trail, which reaches the peak of Dorr Mtn. in 100 yd.

HOMANS PATH (MAP 5: D7)
NPS rating: strenuous
Cumulative from Hemlock Rd. (70 ft.) near Sieur de Monts Spring to:

Emery Path (420 ft.)	0.4 mi.	350 ft.	0:25
Dorr Mtn. summit (1,263 ft.) via Emery Path, Schiff Path, and Dorr North Ridge Trail	1.6 mi.	1,193 ft.	1:25

NPS Homans Path features some of the most amazing stonework of any trail in ANP. To reach the start of this trail, from the patio at the Nature Center, walk the gravel path to the right of the kiosk. In just a few feet, at the entrance to Wild Gardens of Acadia, turn left and cross a footbridge. At a fork just beyond, go right along the garden fence to intersect Jesup Path. Continue straight (right) on Jesup Path, and in 0.1 mi., turn left on Hemlock Rd. and follow it for 40 ft., where Homans Path begins on the left.

Soon after the start, Homans Path climbs rock steps and then gets steeper as it negotiates a stretch of boulders. Climb through a natural archway and follow a sidewalk-like trail across an open slope of boulders, where there are views east over Great Meadow to Schoodic Mtn. Climb steps on tight switchbacks, and just above, ascend through a narrow crevice topped by a small block of granite. Homans Path is almost entirely rock steps from here. In the woods above, it levels off and contours south to meet Emery Path at 0.4 mi. From this point, it is another 1.2 mi. to the summit of Dorr Mtn. via Emery Path, Schiff Path, and Dorr North Ridge Trail.

SCHIFF PATH (MAP 5: D7)
NPS rating: strenuous
Cumulative from jct. of Emery Path and Kurt Diederich's Climb (560 ft.) to:

Ladder Trail (800 ft.)	0.6 mi.	240 ft.	0:25
Dorr Mtn. summit (1,263 ft.) via Dorr North Ridge Trail	1.3 mi.	703 ft.	1:00

NPS This trail begins partway up the east slope of Dorr Mtn. at the jct. of Emery Path and Kurt Diederich's Climb. Schiff Path traverses above the steep east face of the mountain, ascending moderately, to reach a jct. with Ladder Trail. Here, Schiff Path turns sharply right and climbs steeply, then more moderately, to meet Dorr North Ridge Trail at 1.0 mi. Follow Dorr North Ridge Trail south 100 yd. to the summit of Dorr Mtn.

KURT DIEDERICH'S CLIMB (MAP 5: D7)
NPS rating: strenuous
Cumulative from the Tarn parking area on ME 3 (100 ft.) to:

Kurt Diederich's Climb (90 ft.) via Beachcroft Trail	0.1 mi.	–10 ft.	0:05
Emery Path and Schiff Path (560 ft.)	0.5 mi.	470 ft.	0:30

NPS Kurt Diederich's Climb takes a direct route from the north end of the Tarn to the jct. of Schiff Path and Emery Path partway up the east side of Dorr Mtn. Start at the Tarn parking area on ME 3 and proceed west via Beachcroft Trail for 0.1 mi. to the jct. with Kane Path and Jesup Path. Look for the inscription "Kurt Diederich's Climb" in the stone steps. The trail rises steeply up the steps to views and a jct. with Emery Path and Schiff Path. Follow Schiff Path to the top of Dorr Mtn. in another 1.3 mi.

KANE PATH (MAP 5: D7–E7)
NPS rating: moderate
Cumulative from north end of the Tarn (90 ft.) to:

Ladder Trail (110 ft.)	0.5 mi.	20 ft.	0:15
Canon Brook Trail (120 ft.)	0.8 mi.	30 ft.	0:25

NPS Kane Path starts at the north end of the Tarn, 0.1 mi. west of the parking area on ME 3 via Beachcroft Path. Kane Path leads south to Canon Brook Trail and links the Sieur de Monts Spring area to the southern trails of Dorr Mtn. and Cadillac Mtn. At its start, Kane Path runs south across a talus slope along the west side of the Tarn. After reaching the south end of the pond, Kane Path continues past Ladder Trail to end at Canon Brook Trail. Follow Canon Brook Trail south and then west to reach Dorr South Ridge Trail and A. Murray Young Path.

SEC 10

LADDER TRAIL (MAP 5: D7)
NPS rating: ladder
Cumulative from ME 3 (130 ft.) to:

Schiff Path (800 ft.)	0.6 mi.	670 ft.	0:40
Dorr Mtn. summit (1,263 ft.) via Schiff Path and Dorr North Ridge Trail	1.3 mi.	1,153 ft.	1:15

NPS This route leaves from ME 3 just south of the Tarn and 0.5 mi. south of the Tarn trailhead parking lot. Parking for Ladder Trail is along the west (Dorr Mtn.) side of ME 3. From ME 3, the trail soon crosses Kane Path and then steadily ascends to reach Schiff Path. Ladder Trail is steep, climbing some 1,200 stone steps and several sets of iron ladders. Turn left to finish the ascent of Dorr Mtn. via Schiff Path and Dorr North Ridge Trail.

CANON BROOK TRAIL (MAP 5: E7)
NPS rating: strenuous
Cumulative from ME 3 (180 ft.) to:

Kane Path (120 ft.)	0.2 mi.	−60 ft.	0:10
Dorr South Ridge Trail (220 ft.)	0.9 mi.	110 ft.	0:30
A. Murray Young Path (220 ft.)	1.1 mi.	120 ft.	0:35
Cadillac South Ridge Trail (1,000 ft.) at the Featherbed	2.0 mi.	900 ft.	1:15
Bubble & Jordan Ponds Path (400 ft.)	2.8 mi.	900 ft.	1:50

NPS Canon Brook Trail begins on ME 3, 0.8 mi. south of the Tarn trailhead parking area. Parking is available in a paved lot on the east side of ME 3 and in a gravel area along the west side of ME 3. Canon Brook Trail leaves from the south end of the gravel lot, descends west to cross a beaver flowage, and intersects Kane Path at 0.2 mi. Turn left (south) at the jct. and follow the beaver flowage down through the valley. After a brief, sharp rise, the trail reaches Dorr South Ridge Trail, which diverges right. Canon Brook Trail then descends to a jct. with A. Murray Young Path, which departs to the right. Here, Canon Brook Trail crosses a branch of Otter Creek and climbs gently along the north side of Canon Brook before crossing the brook and then climbing steeply past the cascades on the upper part.

The trail swings away from the brook, passes a beaver pond, and ascends to a small wetlands area known as the Featherbed. Here, it intersects Cadillac South Ridge Trail, which leads 2.3 mi. south to ME 3 near Blackwoods CG, and 1.1 mi. north to the summit of Cadillac Mtn. Ahead, Canon Brook Trail skirts the north side of the wetlands to reach a large ledge and a view to Pemetic Mtn. and the Cranberry Isles. The trail then descends steeply, first via a long series of stone steps and then with the aid of two iron rungs and four iron railings in this strenuous section, which includes a narrow rock cleft. After a footbridge across a seep and a bridge over a small stream, the angle eases. Follow the course of the stream, traverse bog bridges over the outlet of a beaver pond, and then make a short jaunt to a jct. where Canon Brook Trail ends. Bubble & Jordan Ponds Path begins here. Via this path, it is 0.4 mi. south to a carriage road (at a point 0.8 mi. south of Bubble Pond) and 1.0 mi. farther west to Park Loop Rd. near Jordan Pond.

DORR SOUTH RIDGE TRAIL (MAP 5: D7–E7)
NPS rating: moderate
Cumulative from ME 3 (180 ft.) to:

Kane Path (120 ft.) via Canon Brook Trail	0.2 mi.	−60 ft.	0:10
Dorr South Ridge Trail (220 ft.) via Canon Brook Trail	0.9 mi.	110 ft.	0:30
Dorr Mtn. summit (1,263 ft.)	2.2 mi.	1,163 ft.	1:40

NPS This route diverges right (north) from Canon Brook Trail 0.9 mi. from ME 3 at the southern end of Dorr Mtn. Dorr South Ridge Trail rises at a moderate grade over rocky ledges and through a semi-open forest of pitch pines. Enjoy frequent views of Champlain Mtn., Cadillac Mtn., and the ocean during the ascent of the long ridge. At the summit, the trail ends at the jct. with Dorr North Ridge Trail.

A. MURRAY YOUNG PATH (MAP 5: D7–E7)
NPS rating: moderate
From Canon Brook Trail (220 ft.) to:

Gorge Path and Cadillac–Dorr Connector (1,050 ft.)	1.4 mi.	830 ft.	1:05

NPS Ascending the narrow valley between Dorr Mtn. and Cadillac Mtn. from the south, A. Murray Young Path leaves Canon Brook Trail at a point 1.1 mi. west of ME 3. The path climbs gradually in close proximity to a branch of Otter Creek, crossing the creek several times on stepping-stones. Beyond, the path makes a short, steep climb into a narrow, rocky defile sandwiched between the walls of the two high peaks. North along the floor of this dramatic gorge, A. Murray Young Path ends at a jct. Here, Gorge Path arrives from the north, and Cadillac–Dorr Connector enters from the east (leads 0.2 mi. to the summit of Dorr Mtn.). Gorge Path continues to the left (west) to climb steeply to the top of Cadillac Mtn. in another 0.4 mi.

SEC 10

Cadillac-Dorr Connector (NPS; Map 5: D7). This 0.2-mi. trail starts just north of the summit of Dorr Mtn. and runs east to west, connecting Dorr

North Ridge Trail with Gorge Path at its jct. with A. Murray Young Path in the high, narrow valley between Cadillac Mtn. and Dorr Mtn. The trail loses about 200 ft. of elevation.

DORR NORTH RIDGE TRAIL (MAP 5: D7)
NPS rating: moderate
Cumulative from Kebo Mtn. Trail and Hemlock Trail (300 ft.) to:

Schiff Path and Cadillac–Dorr Connector (1,230 ft.)	1.1 mi.	930 ft.	1:00
Dorr Mtn. summit (1,263 ft.)	1.2 mi.	963 ft.	1:05

NPS Dorr North Ridge Trail offers a more gradual alternative to the summit of Dorr Mtn. than do the trails from the steeper east side. The route begins as an extension of Kebo Mtn. Trail at 0.9 mi. from Park Loop Rd. and Kebo Brook Trail. Dorr North Ridge Trail climbs the north ridge at a moderate grade, reaching the jct. with Schiff Path and Cadillac–Dorr Connector at 0.8 mi. The summit is just 100 yd. farther ahead (south), at the jct. of Dorr South Ridge Trail. Views high on the north ridge are excellent.

CHAMPLAIN MTN. (1,057 FT.)

Champlain Mtn., the easternmost major ridge on MDI, consists of the main peak of Champlain Mtn. and the subsidiary peak of Huguenot Head, just west. The Beehive and Gorham Mtn. are immediately south of Champlain Mtn. All these summits provide exceptional views. Champlain and the Beehive are very popular because of their exciting ladder trails that climb steep cliff faces overlooking Frenchman Bay. Easier trails that are better suited for children or those with a fear of heights also provide access to both peaks.

PRECIPICE TRAIL (MAP 5: D8–E8)
NPS rating: ladder
Cumulative from Park Loop Rd. (100 ft.) to:

Orange & Black Path (400 ft.)	0.5 mi.	300 ft.	0:25
Champlain Mtn. summit (1,057 ft.)	1.2 mi.	957 ft.	1:05

SEC 10

NPS Precipice Trail climbs the east wall of Champlain Mtn. in spectacular fashion, using a series of iron rungs, ladders, handrails, and walkways to guide hikers over the many exposed ledges. This route starts from the Precipice Trail parking area at the eastern base of Champlain Mtn., on Park Loop Rd., 1.9 mi. beyond the Sieur de Monts Spring entrance to ANP and 0.8 mi. before the Sand Beach entrance station.

(*Caution*: According to NPS, Precipice Trail is maintained as a nontechnical climbing route, not a hiking trail. Hikers should attempt this route only if they are in good physical condition, are wearing proper footwear, and have experience climbing near exposed cliffs and heights. Avoid Precipice Trail in inclement weather or darkness. Please stay on the trail, and do not throw or dislodge rocks, as they may strike hikers below. Precipice Trail may be closed for an undetermined amount of time each spring and summer, usually until early to mid-August, to protect nesting peregrine falcons [a Maine endangered species] from inadvertent disturbance or harassment. Violators of the closure are subject to a large fine. When Precipice Trail is closed, visitors may experience alternate ladder hikes on Beehive, Ladder [Dorr Mtn.], Beech Cliff, or Perpendicular trails.)

From the parking lot, Precipice Trail climbs steps to pass a gate and kiosk and then ascends slabs to a warning sign. Steps beyond lead to the base of Precipice Wall. The trail makes a short climb via a strenuous iron rung and then negotiates a rugged talus field of large boulders, rising northwest. After passing two cave formations, the trail makes a traverse using a long handrail. Ahead, the undulating route across the exposed face uses a series of walkways and handrails. At 0.5 mi., reach the jct. with Orange & Black Path (leads right to Champlain North Ridge Trail in 0.7 mi. and to Park Loop Rd. in 0.9 mi.).

From this jct., Precipice Trail climbs southwest, rising steeply to a point directly west of the parking area. Iron rungs, strenuous pull-ups, a rock slot, sloping ledges with a handrail, and more iron rungs up a short wall lead to a traverse left along a narrow ledge with handrails. More rungs and ladders lead ever higher over vertical ledges on the very exposed face. After the final ladders and rungs, the angle eases, and the trail climbs to the summit over gentle slopes and ledges, reaching the top of Champlain Mtn. at 1.3 mi.

ORANGE & BLACK PATH (MAP 5: D8)
NPS rating: ladder
Cumulative from Schooner Head Rd. (70 ft.) to:

Park Loop Rd. (200 ft.)	0.2 mi.	130 ft.	0:10
Spur to Champlain North Ridge Trail (400 ft.)	0.4 mi.	330 ft.	0:20
Precipice Trail (400 ft.)	1.0 mi.	380 ft.	0:40
Champlain Mtn. summit (1,057 ft.) via Precipice Trail	1.7 mi.	1,037 ft.	1:20

NPS Orange & Black Path begins from Schooner Head Rd. at a point 1.3 mi. south of the jct. with ME 3 in Bar Harbor. Parking is along the road. Start out on Schooner Head Trail; in 50 ft., Orange & Black Path diverges right. Follow this path easily uphill to Park Loop Rd. at 0.2 mi., cross the road, and proceed into the woods. Ahead, scramble over rocks and climb via stone steps to a jct. (The trail to the right leads 0.1 mi. up to a jct. with Champlain North Ridge Trail.)

Continuing left from the jct. on Orange & Black Path, traverse the face of the mountain with minor ups and downs and numerous viewpoints. Descend a crevice in the rocks on stone steps and then continue to the south. Traverse a steep section of the slope using wooden steps and an iron ladder to reach a jct. with Precipice Trail at 1.0 mi. To the right, it is 0.7 mi. to the summit of Champlain Mtn. To the left, it is 0.5 mi. down to Park Loop Rd. and the Precipice Trail parking area.

CHAMPLAIN NORTH RIDGE TRAIL (MAP 5: D8)
NPS rating: moderate
Cumulative from Park Loop Rd. (170 ft.) to:

Spur from Orange & Black Path (530 ft.)	0.5 mi.	360 ft.	0:25
Champlain Mtn. summit (1,057 ft.)	1.2mi.	887 ft.	1:05

NPS Beginning on Park Loop Rd., 0.2 mi. east of the entrance to the Bear Brook picnic area, this trail ends at the summit of Champlain Mtn., where Champlain South Ridge Trail continues on to meet Bowl Trail at the south end of the Bowl, a pretty mountain tarn.

Champlain North Ridge Trail climbs gradually from Park Loop Rd. through a mixed forest of birch, pine, and spruce on the north slope of Champlain Mtn. to a jct. To the left, a connector trail descends 0.1 mi. to Orange & Black Path. Champlain North Ridge Trail continues ahead, climbing steadily to emerge from the forest canopy, offering outstanding views of Frenchman Bay and Schoodic Peninsula on the mainland to the east. Atop the summit ridge, Beachcroft Trail enters from the right (west), and just ahead, Champlain North Ridge Trail reaches the open, rocky summit of Champlain Mtn. At the large summit cairn is the jct. with Precipice Trail and Champlain South Ridge Trail.

CHAMPLAIN SOUTH RIDGE TRAIL (MAP 5: E8)
NPS rating: moderate
Cumulative from Park Loop Rd. (70 ft.) near Sand Beach to:

Champlain South Ridge Trail (420 ft.) via Bowl Trail	0.8 mi.	350 ft.	0:35
Champlain Mtn. summit (1,057 ft.)	2.4 mi.	987 ft.	1:40

NPS This route travels from Sand Beach and the Bowl to the summit of Champlain Mtn. Champlain South Ridge Trail begins at a jct. with Bowl Trail, 0.8 mi. from Park Loop Rd. near the Sand Beach parking area. Champlain South Ridge Trail skirts the south shore of the Bowl, a small glacial tarn west of the Beehive, before ascending to the south ridge of the mountain. Ahead, the trail rises moderately before entering a semi-open forest of pitch pines. Climbing over pink granite, Champlain South Ridge Trail reaches open views on the summit of Champlain Mtn. and the jct. with Champlain North Ridge Trail and Precipice Trail.

BEACHCROFT PATH (MAP 5: D7-D8)
NPS rating: moderate
Cumulative from north end of the Tarn (90 ft.) to:

ME 3 parking area (100 ft.)	0.1 mi.	10 ft.	0:02
Champlain Mtn. summit (1,057 ft.)	1.6 mi.	987 ft.	1:20

NPS This is a convenient route from the Sieur de Monts Spring area to the summit of Champlain Mtn. via Huguenot Head. Beachcroft Path officially starts at the jct. of Jesup Path, Kurt Diederich's Climb, and Kane Path, 0.1 mi. west of ME 3 and the parking area at the north end of the Tarn. Most hikers, however, will simply start from ME 3. From the village green in Bar Harbor (jct. of Mt. Desert St. and Main St.), drive south on ME 3 for 1.6 mi. to the Tarn parking lot on the right, immediately beyond the Sieur de Monts Spring entrance to ANP.

After crossing ME 3, Beachcroft Path starts up a flight of granite steps and then heads southeast, often on more carefully placed stonework. Using switchbacks and stone steps, the trail rises across the west slope of Huguenot Head and passes just below the summit of Huguenot Head at about 0.8 mi. A brief, gradual descent into the notch between Huguenot Head and Champlain Mtn. is followed by a sharp, strenuous ascent over rocks up the northwest slope of Champlain Mtn. to the summit.

THE BEEHIVE (538 FT.)
Rising dramatically above Sand Beach and Park Loop Rd., the Beehive is one of the most popular mountains in ANP. Beehive Trail is challenging and not for hikers who may be uneasy on precipitous heights. Atop the summit cliffs, the sights of Frenchman Bay, Sand Beach, and Otter Cliff are spectacular. Bowl Trail and Beehive Trail combine for a fine loop over the Beehive.

SEC 10

BOWL TRAIL (MAP 5: E8)
NPS rating: moderate
Cumulative from Sand Beach parking area (70 ft.) to:

Beehive Trail (170 ft.)	0.2 mi.	100 ft.	0:10
Gorham Mtn. Trail, lower spur jct. (270 ft.)	0.5 mi.	200 ft.	0:20
Gorham Mtn. Trail, upper spur jct. (350 ft.)	0.6 mi.	280 ft.	0:25
The Bowl, Beehive Trail, Champlain South Ridge Trail (420 ft.)	0.8 mi.	390 ft.	0:35

NPS This hike leaves from Park Loop Rd. about 150 ft. before the entrance to the Sand Beach parking area, 0.6 mi. south of the Sand Beach entrance station. Bowl Trail is a gently sloping path that connects Sand Beach to the Bowl, a pretty mountain tarn in a wild setting. On the ascent to the Bowl, the route passes trails to the Beehive and Gorham Mtn. At the Bowl, Beehive Trail bears right and climbs over the Beehive, while Champlain South Ridge Trail bears left around the pond to Champlain Mtn.

BEEHIVE TRAIL (MAP 5: E8)
NPS rating: ladder
Cumulative from Sand Beach parking area (70 ft.) to:

Beehive Trail (170 ft.) via Bowl Trail	0.2 mi.	100 ft.	0:10
The Beehive summit (538 ft.)	0.4 mi.	468 ft.	0:25
The Bowl summit at jct. Bowl Trail and Champlain South Ridge Trail (420 ft.)	0.8 mi.	508 ft.	0:30

NPS Begin on Bowl Trail, 0.2 mi. west of Park Loop Rd., opposite the entrance to the Sand Beach parking area. At a jct., turn sharply right at the sign marked "Beehive." For 0.3 mi., the trail rises abruptly via switchbacks and climbs via iron ladders, rungs, and walkways over steep ledges to the summit of the Beehive. It continues down the northwest slope, passing a connector path leading left (south) to Bowl Trail. Ahead, Beehive Trail climbs briefly and then drops steeply to the Bowl, bearing left around the tarn to reach the jct. with Bowl Trail and Champlain South Ridge Trail.

GORHAM MTN. (518 FT.)
South of Champlain Mtn. and the Beehive, the long, low ridge of Gorham Mtn. offers fine walking and outstanding views east over Ocean Drive to Frenchman Bay and Schoodic Peninsula, and west to Cadillac Mtn. and Dorr Mtn.

GORHAM MTN. TRAIL (MAP 5: E8)
NPS rating: moderate
Cumulative from Gorham Mtn. parking area (60 ft.) to:

Cadillac Cliffs Trail, lower jct. (160 ft.)	0.3 mi.	100 ft.	0:10
Cadillac Cliffs Trail, upper jct. (300 ft.)	0.6 mi.	240 ft.	0:25
Gorham Mtn. summit (518 ft.)	1.1 mi.	458 ft.	0:50
Bowl Trail via lower spur (270 ft.)	1.5 mi.	458 ft.	1:00
Park Loop Rd. at Sand Beach (70 ft.)	1.9 mi.	458 ft.	1:15

NPS This route starts at the Gorham Mtn. parking area (also known as Monument Cove parking area) on Park Loop Rd., 1.1 mi. south of Sand

Beach. Gorham Mtn. Trail quickly reaches the jct. with Otter Cove Trail, which leads left (west) 0.4 mi. to Park Loop Rd. at the Otter Cove Causeway, crossing Otter Creek Rd. en route. Beyond, Gorham Mtn. Trail rises gently over open ledges to a jct. with Cadillac Cliffs Trail (NPS rating: strenuous) on the right at 0.3 mi. This short loop passes ancient sea cliffs and an ancient sea cave before rejoining Gorham Mtn. Trail in 0.3 mi.

Beyond the jct., Gorham Mtn. Trail continues easily over open granite ledges to where Cadillac Cliffs Trail rejoins from the right. Gorham Mtn. Trail continues north to the bare summit of Gorham Mtn. at 1.1 mi. and some of the finest scenic panoramas in ANP. Descending the north ridge, it reaches a connector trail that leaves left, offering a direct route to the Bowl, reaching the tarn in 0.3 mi. Ahead, Gorham Mtn. Trail reaches a jct. with Bowl Trail. From here, it is 0.4 mi. left to the Bowl. To the right, it is 0.2 mi. to Beehive Trail and 0.4 mi. to Park Loop Rd. near Sand Beach.

GREAT HEAD (150 FT.)

The easternmost high point on Mt. Desert Island, Great Head offers stunning vistas west over Sand Beach and Newport Cove to Champlain Mtn., the Beehive, Gorham Mtn., and Otter Point, and east across Frenchman Bay to Egg Rock Light and Schoodic Peninsula.

GREAT HEAD TRAIL (MAP 5: E8)
NPS rating: moderate
From Schooner Head Rd. parking (60 ft.) to:

Complete loop	1.6 mi.	230 ft.	0:55

NPS This scenic loop passes largely along clifftops directly above the ocean.

From the outskirts of Bar Harbor at the jct. of ME 3 and Schooner Head Rd., travel south on Schooner Head Rd. At a 4-way jct. in 2.5 mi. (left leads to Schooner Head Overlook and right leads 0.1 mi. to Park Loop Rd. at the Sand Beach entrance station), drive straight ahead another 0.4 mi. to the Great Head trailhead parking lot on the left.

Begin from the back edge of the lot, walking around the brown gate and following the wide gravel track. In 300 ft., at a jct., turn left to walk the loop clockwise. Reach a connector trail on the right that leads 0.15 mi. to the Newport Cove side of Great Head, where it rejoins Great Head Trail. Beyond the connector jct., reach the ruins of an old stone teahouse, once part of the Satterlee estate, at the apex of Great Head. Travel southwest over rocks, pass briefly through woods, and then traverse the wide-open headland. Scamper down ledges for a look south to Otter Cliff. Turn up along Newport Cove and enjoy views below to Sand Beach. The connector trail

SEC 10

mentioned previously enters from the right; continue left and down, following switchbacks over the ledges. Reach an old millstone lying flat on its side and steps with a railing on the left, marking a path that leads 200 ft. to Sand Beach. Continue to the right on the wide path to complete the loop.

EASTERN MT. DESERT ISLAND: JORDAN POND VICINITY

The Jordan Pond area is a central starting point for many interesting hikes, including Pemetic Mtn. in the east, Jordan Pond to the Bubbles in the north, and Penobscot Mtn. and Sargent Mtn. in the west. Jordan Pond, its deep, sparkling waters considered some of the cleanest in Maine, is also home to the namesake and highly popular Jordan Pond House. Known for its fine dining and scenic view of the Bubbles and Penobscot Mtn., Jordan Pond House has been serving island visitors since 1871. Hiker parking is discouraged here during the busy summer months, due to congestion. A large trailhead parking lot with a toilet is on Park Loop Rd. just 0.1 mi. north of Jordan Pond House or 7.7 mi. south of Hulls Cove Visitor Center. The Island Explorer bus is another option for reaching trails in this popular area of the park.

JORDAN POND PATH (MAP 5: E6)
NPS rating: easy
Cumulative (counterclockwise) from Jordan Pond parking area (275 ft.) to:

Bubble & Jordan Ponds Path (275 ft.)	0.4 mi.	0 ft.	0:10
Jordan Pond Carry and Bubbles Trail (275 ft.)	1.3 mi.	0 ft.	0:40
Bubbles Divide Trail (275 ft.)	1.7 mi.	0 ft.	0:50
Deer Brook Trail (275 ft.)	1.9 mi.	0 ft.	1:00
Complete circuit	3.4 mi.	0 ft.	1:40

NPS This circuit around beautiful Jordan Pond connects with six trails to the mountain summits beyond. The description provided here is for travel in a counterclockwise direction, hiking the eastern shore of Jordan Pond first. The route is fairly level, with negligible elevation gain and loss.

From the Jordan Pond trailhead parking area, follow the gravel boat launch road to the south shore of the pond, which frames the classic scene north to North and South Bubble. At the pond, turn right to start the circuit, which is also part of Jordan Pond Nature Trail for a short distance. Follow the south shore and, just after crossing an inlet on a stone causeway, reach a jct. at 0.4 mi. with Bubble & Jordan Ponds Path, which departs to the right (leads to trails on Pemetic Mtn. and the Triad).

Continue left on Jordan Pond Path, a graded, fine-gravel trail that meanders easily along the east shore of the pond, offering excellent views of

SEC 10

Penobscot Mtn. and Jordan Cliffs. At 1.3 mi., Jordan Pond Carry and Bubbles Trail diverge to the right. Winding along the northeast shore at the base of South Bubble, reach Bubbles Divide Trail, which climbs to Bubbles Gap, a high notch between North Bubble and South Bubble. Beyond, Jordan Pond Path crosses a picturesque footbridge over an inlet to reach Deer Brook Trail, which leads to trails on Penobscot Mtn. and Sargent Mtn.

Finally, Jordan Pond Path turns south along the west shore of the pond and runs under the precipitous Jordan Cliffs. At first the trail alternates between graded pathway and a footpath through shoreline boulders, but the last mile is a delightful combination of wooden boardwalks and graded gravel pathway. Views east take in the lengthy ridge of Pemetic Mtn. and the Bubbles. Jordan Pond House and its long, sloping lawn appear ahead. At the south end of the pond, merge with a carriage road and bear left to cross a bridge over Jordan Stream just south of a small dam. Beyond, follow the path along the shore and, with Jordan Pond House to the right, continue ahead to the boat launch road. Turn right here to return to the parking area.

ASTICOU & JORDAN POND PATH (MAP 5: E6 AND F5–F6)
NPS rating: easy
Cumulative from Jordan Pond House (297 ft.) to:

Spring Trail (270 ft.)	100 yd.	–30 ft.	0:05
Carriage road to start of Amphitheater Trail (160 ft.)	1.0 mi.	–130 ft.	0:30
Penobscot Mtn. Trail (140 ft.)	1.1 mi.	–140 ft.	0:35
Asticou Ridge Trail (350 ft.)	1.5 mi.	210 ft.	0:50
Sargent South Ridge Trail (260 ft.)	1.8 mi.	210 ft.	1:00
Asticou Map House (230 ft.)	2.1 mi.	210 ft.	1:10

NPS Asticou & Jordan Pond Path follows a mostly level course for much of its distance but gains some elevation to reach Asticou Ridge Trail. The path is an important link to Eliot Mtn. and to trails on the southern ridges of Penobscot, Cedar Swamp, and Sargent mountains.

Park at the Jordan Pond trailhead parking area and follow any of the short signed paths to Jordan Pond House. From the roofed terrace at the front of the facility, follow signs for the restrooms and water fountain, which are on the left (west side) of the building. On the patio adjacent to the restrooms, look for a sign on the left for Sargent Mtn., Penobscot Mtn., and Asticou trails. Asticou & Jordan Pond Path begins here.

Proceed down wide log-and-gravel steps and cross a carriage road at signpost 15. In 50 ft., where the carriage road crosses a stream, bear right onto a footpath, marked with a sign for Penobscot Mtn. and Sargent Mtn.

**SEC
10**

trails. Ahead, walk over Jordan Stream on a footbridge to reach the jct. on the right with Spring Trail, which leads uphill via rock steps to connect with Jordan Cliffs and Penobscot Mtn. trails. Asticou & Jordan Pond Path turns left here. The wide, graded path contours for a distance with minor variations in elevation. Ahead, cross a carriage road and then trend easily downhill to cross another carriage road. The start of Amphitheater Trail is 0.3 mi. north (right) via the second carriage road. Soon after, reach the jct. with Penobscot Mtn. Trail, which leaves to the right. A short distance ahead, Harbor Brook Trail departs to the left (leads 2.0 mi. south to ME 3). In another 0.5 mi., Asticou & Jordan Pond Path winds upward on a long series of stone steps to arrive at Asticou Ridge Trail, which leads 0.8 south to Eliot Mtn.

On the gradual descent beyond, Sargent South Ridge Trail departs to the right (leads 1.4 mi. to Cedar Swamp Mtn. and 2.6 mi. to Sargent Mtn.). Asticou & Jordan Pond Path ends at Asticou Map House, a small day shelter with benches and a posted map of ANP. Here also is Charles Savage Trail, which leads 0.6 mi. to Eliot Mtn. and beyond to Thuya Garden. To the left, the quiet lane adjacent to Asticou Map House leads downhill for 0.5 mi. to ME 3 at Asticou in Northeast Harbor; to the right, the lane leads 0.6 mi. to a carriage road and Brown Mtn. Gatehouse on ME 3/198. Parking is discouraged near the Map House. A small parking lot on ME 3 at Asticou is signed for visitors of Thuya Garden.

PENOBSCOT MTN. (1,190 FT.)

This mountain, the fifth highest in ANP, rises steeply west of Jordan Pond. Long and high Jordan Ridge atop the sweeping face of Jordan Cliffs offers commanding 360-degree vistas. Sandwiched between ME 3/198 and Jordan Pond, the two major trailheads, Penobscot Mtn. is part of a compact group of six peaks that are home to an intricate network of trails allowing for many fun and interesting hike combinations.

SPRING TRAIL (MAP 5: E6)
NPS rating: strenuous
Cumulative from Jordan Pond House (297 ft.) to:

Spring Trail (270 ft.) via Asticou & Jordan Pond Path	100 yd.	–27 ft.	0:05
Jordan Cliffs Trail (350 ft.)	0.3 mi.	80 ft.	0:12
Penobscot Mtn. Trail (650 ft.)	0.5 mi.	380 ft.	0:25
Penobscot Mtn. summit (1,190 ft.) via Penobscot Mtn. Trail	1.5 mi.	920 ft.	1:15

NPS Spring Trail provides the quickest access to Penobscot Mtn. from Jordan Pond House. Short but very steep in places, it should be avoided for descents, especially in wet conditions. The trail leaves from Asticou & Jordan Pond Path, 100 yd. west of Jordan Pond House.

Spring Trail extends easily west to the jct. with Jordan Cliffs Trail at 0.3 mi. Just beyond, Spring Trail crosses a carriage road and then climbs steeply, with the assistance of iron rungs and wooden handrails, boardwalks, and rock staircases, to join Penobscot Mtn. Trail at 0.5 mi., which leads 1.0 mi. along the pleasant and mostly open Jordan Ridge to the summit of Penobscot Mtn.

JORDAN CLIFFS TRAIL (MAP 5: E6)
NPS rating: ladder
Cumulative from Jordan Pond House (297 ft.) to:

Spring Trail (270 ft.) via Asticou & Jordan Pond Path	100 yd.	-27 ft.	0:05
Jordan Cliffs Trail (350 ft.)	0.3 mi.	80 ft.	0:12
Penobscot East Trail (900 ft.)	1.7 mi.	630 ft.	1:10
Deer Brook Trail (660 ft.)	2.0 mi.	630 ft.	1:20

NPS Although very rugged, Jordan Cliffs Trail is spectacular, with outstanding views over Jordan Pond to the Bubbles and Pemetic Mtn. This challenging and scenic route starts 0.3 mi. west of Jordan Pond House via Asticou & Jordan Pond Path and Spring Trail.

From Spring Trail, Jordan Cliffs Trail immediately crosses a carriage road and then rises up the east shoulder of Penobscot Mtn. in gradual pitches to reach the base of Jordan Cliffs. The trail traverses along the cliffs, via iron ladders and handrails, to a jct. with Penobscot East Trail (leads left [west] 0.4 mi. to the summit of Penobscot Mtn.). To the right, Jordan Cliffs Trail descends to join Deer Brook Trail in another 0.4 mi.

Penobscot East Trail (NPS; Map 5: E5-E6). This 0.4-mi. trail (NPS rating: moderate) climbs the upper northeast slope of Penobscot Mtn. to connect Jordan Cliffs Trail with the summit of Penobscot Mtn. Penobscot East Trail gains 290 ft.

PENOBSCOT MTN. TRAIL (MAP 5: E5-F6)
NPS rating: strenuous
Cumulative from Asticou & Jordan Pond Path (140 ft.) to:

Spring Trail (650 ft.)	1.2 mi.	510 ft.	0:50
Penobscot Mtn. summit (1,190 ft.)	2.0 mi.	1,050 ft.	1:30
Deer Brook Trail (1,050 ft.)	2.1 mi.	1,050 ft.	1:35
Sargent South Ridge Trail (1,170 ft.)	2.3 mi.	1,170 ft.	1:45

SEC 10

NPS Penobscot Mtn. Trail leaves from Asticou & Jordan Pond Path 1.0 mi. west of Jordan Pond House and heads north, climbing at an easy pace and traversing three carriage roads in its first 0.3 mi. The trail then climbs more steeply, occasionally breaking out into the open with excellent views to the south. It attains the south ridge of the mountain, known as Jordan Ridge, and the jct. with Spring Trail. Penobscot Mtn. Trail then climbs gradually over open granite ledges to the summit, where East Trail enters. Penobscot Mtn. Trail continues north, descending to a rugged notch and the jct. with Deer Brook Trail. Here, Penobscot Mtn. Trail turns left and soon reaches pretty Sargent Mtn. Pond. From the pond, the trail makes a short climb to join Sargent South Ridge Trail (leads 0.9 mi. right [north] to the top of Sargent Mtn.).

DEER BROOK TRAIL (MAP 5: E5–E6)
NPS rating: strenuous
From Jordan Pond Path (275 ft.) to:

Sargent East Cliffs Trail and Jordan Cliffs Trail (660 ft.)	0.3 mi.	385 ft.	0:20
Penobscot Mtn. Trail (1,050 ft.)	0.9 mi.	775 ft.	0:50

NPS Deer Brook Trail starts from Jordan Pond Path at the north end of Jordan Pond. The trail can be reached by hiking either east or west around the pond via Jordan Pond Path from Jordan Pond House, or by climbing over the Bubbles on Bubbles Divide Trail from the Bubble Rock parking area on Park Loop Rd. Deer Brook Trail provides access to the summits of Penobscot Mtn. and Sargent Mtn.

From Jordan Pond Path, Deer Brook Trail climbs rock steps along Deer Brook, traversing it several times below a double-arched bridge. Cross the carriage road and then climb wooden staircases and rock steps alongside Deer Brook to reach a trail jct. Here, Jordan Cliffs Trail departs left, and Sargent East Cliffs Trail leaves to the right. Ahead on Deer Brook Trail, ascend the narrow valley, traversing the brook several more times before bearing away from it. Above a set of rock steps, the angle eases, and in a notch ahead, reach the end of the trail at the jct. with Penobscot Mtn. Trail. To the right, Sargent Mtn. Pond is a 5-min. walk ahead; the open summit of Penobscot Mtn. is 0.1 mi. left.

SEC 10

NORTH BUBBLE (871 FT.), SOUTH BUBBLE (764 FT.), AND CONNERS NUBBLE (587 FT.)

The finely shaped, almost symmetrical North Bubble and South Bubble rise above the north end of Jordan Pond. Formerly covered with heavy tree growth, they were swept by fire in 1947, leaving many open views. The 110-ton glacial erratic precariously perched atop the east face of South Bubble is Bubble Rock, one of ANP's most recognized natural features. The best access is from the Bubble Rock parking area on the west side of

Park Loop Rd., 1.1 mi. south of Bubble Pond and 6.2 mi. south of Hulls Cove Visitor Center.

BUBBLES DIVIDE TRAIL (MAP 5: E6)
NPS rating: moderate
Cumulative from Bubble Rock parking area (450 ft.) to:

Jordan Pond Carry (480 ft.)	0.1 mi.	50 ft.	0:05
Bubbles Trail, lower jct. (620 ft.)	0.3 mi.	200 ft.	0:15
Bubbles Trail, upper jct. (640 ft.)	0.4 mi.	220 ft.	0:20
Jordan Pond Path (275 ft.)	0.7 mi.	220 ft.	0:30

NPS Bubbles Divide Trail bisects South and North Bubble on its way west to Jordan Pond and offers the shortest trip to the summit of either mountain. From its start, the wide and well-used trail drops a short distance to cross Jordan Pond Carry, which connects Jordan Pond with Eagle Lake. Beyond, Bubbles Divide Trail climbs toward the small notch between the Bubbles. Here, the northern section of Bubbles Trail leaves to the right (leads 0.3 mi. to North Bubble). Follow the southern section of Bubbles Trail into the notch proper, where it departs to the left to reach the top of South Bubble in 0.3 mi.; a short spur then leads to Bubble Rock.

Continuing west, at times steep and rocky, Bubbles Divide Trail descends to the north shore of Jordan Pond, ending at Jordan Pond Path. To the left, it is 0.6 mi. back to the Bubble Rock parking area via Jordan Pond Path and Jordan Pond Carry.

BUBBLES TRAIL (MAP 5: D6–E6)
NPS rating: strenuous
Cumulative from Jordan Pond Path (275 ft.) to:

South Bubble summit (764 ft.)	0.3 mi.	489 ft.	0:25
Bubbles Divide Trail (640 ft.)	0.6 mi.	489 ft.	0:35
North Bubble summit (871 ft.)	0.9 mi.	739 ft.	0:50
Conners Nubble (587 ft.)	1.8 mi.	880 ft.	1:20
Eagle Lake Trail (280 ft.)	2.3 mi.	880 ft.	1:40

SEC 10

NPS Bubbles Trail connects the north shore of Jordan Pond with Eagle Lake, taking the high route and climbing over the Bubbles and Conners Nubble. It leaves from Jordan Pond Path at a point 0.5 mi. from the Bubble Rock parking area on Park Loop Rd. via Bubbles Divide Trail and Jordan Pond Carry.

Bubbles Trail rises very steeply almost immediately, climbing via tight switchbacks over boulders and ledges. It levels off just before reaching the summit of South Bubble at 0.4 mi. Here, the vistas of Jordan Pond and beyond from the wide, open ledges below the summit are spectacular. At the summit, a short spur leads right to Bubble Rock, the large and unmistakable glacial erratic perched on the edge of the cliff face. From the summit of South Bubble, Bubbles Trail descends moderately over ledges to a notch and turns right, traveling with Bubbles Divide Trail for a short distance before turning left and climbing steeply to the summit of North Bubble. Bubbles Trail then continues north past the summit, descending at an easy pace over open ridgeline for a distance.

Beyond, the trail crosses a carriage road before making a short ascent to the open ledges on the summit of Conners Nubble, which offers excellent views of Eagle Lake and Cadillac Mtn. Bubble Trail continues north over the summit, descends into the woods, and reaches Eagle Lake Trail near the shore of Eagle Lake. From here, it is 1.8 mi. back to the Bubble Rock parking area via Eagle Lake Trail and Jordan Pond Carry.

PEMETIC MTN. (1,243 FT.)

This mountain, the fourth highest in ANP, is roughly in the center of the eastern half of Mt. Desert Island. Its long ridgeline offers some of the best scenic panoramas in ANP. Routes up the west side are short and relatively steep; routes from the north and south are more gradual and wooded.

For trails from the south, park at the Jordan Pond trailhead parking area; for trails from the north, park at Bubble Pond; and for trails from the west, park at Bubble Rock. Gain access to all parking areas via Park Loop Rd. Summer and fall crowds tend to fill these lots quickly, so plan to arrive early or to ride the Island Explorer bus.

BUBBLE & JORDAN PONDS PATH (MAP 5: E6)
NPS rating: moderate
Cumulative from Jordan Pond (275 ft.) to:

Pemetic South Ridge Trail (470 ft.)	0.5 mi.	195 ft.	0:20
Pemetic East Cliff Trail (570 ft.)	0.8 mi.	295 ft.	0:35
Carriage road (400 ft.)	1.1 mi.	295 ft.	0:40
Canon Brook Trail (400 ft.)	1.5 mi.	295 ft.	0:55

NPS This path extends from the southeast shore of Jordan Pond to the valley south of Bubble Pond, where the path meets the west end of Canon Brook Trail. Parking is at the Jordan Pond parking area. From there, follow Jordan Pond Path east for 0.4 mi. to cross an outlet and reach the jct. with Bubble & Jordan Ponds Path.

Bubble & Jordan Ponds Path leaves the pond and climbs east to cross Park Loop Rd. (limited roadside parking here). Continuing through heavy woods and by easy grades, the path ascends the valley between the Triad and Pemetic Mtn. It passes Pemetic South Ridge Trail on the left at 0.5 mi. and then turns left at a jct. with Triad Pass. Bubble & Jordan Ponds Path continues northeast to a jct. with Pemetic East Cliff Trail (left) and Triad Trail (right) at 0.8 mi. Beyond, Bubble & Jordan Ponds Path gently descends to join a carriage road at 1.1 mi., bearing left (north). Soon the path leaves the road (but parallels it through the woods to the east) and continues 0.4 mi. to merge with Canon Brook Trail (climbs steeply to the south ridge of Cadillac Mtn. at the Featherbed, 1.2 mi. south of the summit) in a low area of beaver activity.

PEMETIC SOUTH RIDGE TRAIL (MAP 5: E6)
NPS rating: strenuous
Cumulative from Bubble & Jordan Ponds Path (470 ft.) to:

Pemetic East Cliff Trail (960 ft.)	0.7 mi.	490 ft.	0:35
Pemetic Mtn. summit (1,243 ft.)	1.3 mi.	773 ft.	1:00

NPS Pemetic South Ridge Trail ascends to the summit of Pemetic Mtn. via the south ridge. The trail begins at Bubble & Jordan Ponds Path, 0.5 mi. east of its jct. with Jordan Pond Path and 0.8 mi. east of the Jordan Pond trailhead parking area. Pemetic South Ridge Trail rises steadily to a jct. with Pemetic East Cliff Trail, which enters from the right. Continuing straight ahead, Pemetic South Ridge Trail climbs over open ledges with spectacular views to reach the summit and Pemetic North Ridge Trail.

PEMETIC EAST CLIFF TRAIL (MAP 5: E6)
NPS This short but steep trail (NPS rating: strenuous) climbs from the intersection of Bubble & Jordan Ponds Path and Triad Trail to Pemetic South Ridge Trail in 0.4 mi., gaining 390 ft. and requiring about 20 min.

PEMETIC NORTH RIDGE TRAIL (MAP 5: E6)
NPS rating: strenuous
Cumulative from Bubble Pond parking area (336 ft.) to:

Pemetic Northwest Trail (1,170 ft.)	1.3 mi.	834 ft.	1:05
Pemetic Mtn. summit (1,243 ft.)	1.4 mi.	907 ft.	1:20

SEC 10

NPS This trail ascends Pemetic Mtn. from the north and offers outstanding views of Jordan Pond, the Bubbles, Sargent Mtn., and Eagle Lake. It leaves from the small Bubble Pond parking area at the north end of Bubble Pond on Park Loop Rd., 5.1 mi. south of Hulls Cove Visitor Center and 2.6 mi. north of the Jordan Pond trailhead parking area.

From the parking area, cross a carriage road and proceed south for 100 ft. to Bubble Pond. Here, Pemetic North Ridge Trail departs right (west), while Cadillac West Face Trail leaves to the left (east). Pemetic North Ridge Trail parallels the pond for a distance and then crosses a carriage road. From there, the trail climbs steadily through the forest to meet Pemetic Northwest Trail high on the mountain. Pemetic North Ridge Trail continues to the summit of Pemetic Mtn. and the jct. with Pemetic South Ridge Trail. The summit offers excellent views of the Triad, Cadillac Mtn., Jordan Pond, Penobscot Mtn., and Sargent Mtn.

PEMETIC NORTHWEST TRAIL (MAP 5: E6)
NPS rating: strenuous
Cumulative from Bubble Rock parking area (450 ft.) to:

Pemetic North Ridge Trail (1,170 ft.)	0.7 mi.	720 ft.	0:45
Pemetic Mtn. summit (1,243 ft.) via Pemetic North Ridge Trail	0.8 mi.	793 ft.	0:50

NPS This route begins at the Bubble Rock parking area on the west side of Park Loop Rd., 6.2 mi. south of Hulls Cove Visitor Center. Pemetic Northwest Trail enters the woods east of the road and climbs through thick forest cover, following a rough treadway along a rocky streambed. Log handrails then lead over steep slabs to an often wet and slippery crevice; two log ladders aid in the ascent of the defile. Beyond, the steep ascent continues on a trail of rocks, roots, and log steps. Reach the jct. with Pemetic North Ridge Trail 0.1 mi. north of the summit.

THE TRIAD (682 FT.)
The Triad is a compact group of three peaks nestled between Pemetic Mtn. and Day Mtn., just east of Jordan Pond. Hunters Brook Trail and Triad Trail crisscross its slopes.

TRIAD TRAIL (MAP 5: E6–F6)
NPS rating: moderate
Cumulative from Bubble & Jordan Ponds Path (570 ft.) to:

Hunters Brook Trail (660 ft.)	0.5 mi.	90 ft.	0:15
Day Mtn. Trail (280 ft.)	1.0 mi.	120 ft.	0:35

NPS This trail provides a route from Pemetic Mtn. to Day Mtn. via the Triad. The start of Triad Trail is best reached from the Jordan Pond trailhead parking area via a 1.1-mi. hike on Jordan Pond Path and Bubbles & Jordan Ponds Path. From the jct. of Bubbles & Jordan Ponds Path and Pemetic East Cliff Trail, Triad Trail heads south, rising moderately to cross Hunters Brook Trail in a saddle between the north and east summits before reaching the top of the Triad's east peak. From there, Triad Trail descends to end at a carriage road jct. and Triad–Day Mtn. Bridge over Park Loop Rd. The northern end of Day Mtn. Trail is here also.

TRIAD PASS (MAP 5: E6)

NPS This short link (NPS rating: easy) provides trail access from Jordan Pond to the Triad and Day Mtn. The pass begins on Bubble & Jordan Ponds Path, 0.4 mi. east of Park Loop Rd. near Jordan Pond and 0.5 mi. from the Jordan Pond trailhead parking area. Triad Pass heads southeast for 0.1 mi. to connect with Hunters Brook Trail.

HUNTERS BROOK TRAIL (MAP 5: F6–F7, E6–E7)

NPS rating: moderate
Cumulative from Park Loop Rd. (50 ft.) to:

Carriage road (350 ft.)	1.4 mi.	300 ft.	0:45
Triad Trail (650 ft.)	1.9 mi.	600 ft.	1:00
Triad Pass (550 ft.)	2.3 mi.	600 ft.	1:25
Carriage road (350 ft.)	2.9 mi.	600 ft.	1:45

NPS Hunters Brook Trail begins on Park Loop Rd., 0.1 mi. north of the ME 3 bridge over Park Loop Rd. The bridge is 0.4 mi. southwest of the entrance to Blackwoods CG via ME 3. Park on the side of ME 3 after the bridge. Scramble down the embankment to Park Loop Rd. and walk 250 ft. north to the start of the trail on the right.

The route follows the course of pretty Hunters Brook through beautiful spruce forest. At the remnants of an old road and bridge, the trail bears west away from the brook and ascends to a carriage road. Beyond, the trail climbs to meet Triad Trail just north of its east peak.

Turning right (north), Hunters Brook Trail and Triad Trail coincide for 20 ft.; then Triad Trail continues straight ahead toward Pemetic Mtn., while Hunters Brook Trail goes left and down to cross a deep ravine. The trail descends rock steps and log stairs to reach Triad Pass (a short connector leading 0.1 mi. to Bubble & Jordan Ponds Path). Hunters Brook Trail turns left and heads south (views to Wildwood Stables on the descent), ending at a carriage road at 2.9 mi., 0.3 mi. west of signpost 17 at Triad–Day Mtn. Bridge over Park Loop Rd. Follow Park Loop Rd. about 1 mi. back to the original trailhead.

SEC 10

DAY MTN. (584 FT.)

This little mountain at the southern edge of the eastern side of ANP offers sweeping views from many points on its upper slopes. Reach the top via Day Mtn. Trail and a pretty carriage road that winds its way to the summit.

DAY MTN. TRAIL (MAP 5: F6–F7)
NPS rating: moderate
Cumulative from ME 3 (250 ft.) to:

Day Mtn. summit (584 ft.)	0.8 mi.	334 ft.	0:35
Carriage road (300 ft.) and Triad Trail	1.3 mi.	334 ft.	0:50

NPS Day Mtn. Trail starts on the north side of ME 3, 1.3 mi. south of the
entrance to Blackwoods CG. A parking area is on the south side of the
road. A few feet into the woods, a side trail leads right 150 ft. to the Champlain Monument, a tribute to Samuel de Champlain, the French navigator
and explorer who visited Mt. Desert Island in 1604 and named it. Day
Mtn. Trail climbs moderately through the forest for its entire length. Periodically crossing carriage roads (six different times), it offers views of
Hunters Beach and Seal Harbor from ledges around 0.7 mi. The trail
reaches the summit at 0.8 mi. Beyond, it descends into the forest and ends
at a carriage road and Triad–Day Mtn. Bridge over ME 3. Here, Triad
Trail continues north toward the Triad and Pemetic Mtn. For a pleasant
loop, go either left or right on the carriage road to return to ME 3.

CEDAR SWAMP MTN. (938 FT.)

This scenic peak, the southernmost of a jumble of six mountains west of
Jordan Pond, is just west of Penobscot Mtn. and features a long south ridge
that divides the large and remote ravine known as the Amphitheater from
Upper and Lower Hadlock ponds. Amphitheater Trail and Sargent South
Ridge Trail cross near the Cedar Swamp Mtn. summit.

AMPHITHEATER TRAIL (MAP 5: E5 AND F5)
NPS rating: moderate
Cumulative from Harbor Brook Bridge (180 ft.) to:

Amphitheater Bridge (380 ft.)	0.7 mi.	200 ft.	0:25
Sargent South Ridge Trail at Birch Spring (850 ft.)	1.3 mi.	670 ft.	1:00
Hadlock Brook Trail (700 ft.)	1.7 mi.	670 ft.	1:10

NPS This route connects Hadlock Brook Trail to Sargent South Ridge
Trail high on Cedar Swamp Mtn. Amphitheater Trail starts 1.0 mi. west
of Jordan Pond House via Asticou & Jordan Pond Path.

From Asticou & Jordan Pond Path, proceed north on a carriage road,
which quickly crosses Penobscot Mtn. Trail. Continue on the carriage
road, paralleling Harbor Brook. In 0.2 mi., cross Harbor Brook Bridge;
Amphitheater Trail begins on the right immediately after the bridge.

Amphitheater Trail traces a route along Harbor Brook, crossing it numerous
times before and after passing under Amphitheater Bridge (the largest carriage

road bridge in the park). Beyond the bridge, the trail climbs more steeply through an area known as the Amphitheater to Birch Spring and the jct. with Sargent South Ridge Trail at 1.4 mi. To the left, it is 0.1 mi. to the top of Cedar Swamp Mtn.; to the right, it is 1.2 mi. to the summit of Sargent Mtn. via Sargent South Ridge Trail. Continuing on, Amphitheater Trail climbs briefly, skirts a wetland, and descends to end at Hadlock Brook Trail at 1.7 mi.

SARGENT SOUTH RIDGE TRAIL (MAP 5: E5)
NPS rating: moderate
Cumulative from Asticou & Jordan Pond Path (260 ft.) to:

Cedar Swamp Mtn. summit spur (920 ft.)	1.5 mi.	660 ft.	1:05
Amphitheater Trail (850 ft.) at Birch Spring	1.6 mi.	660 ft.	1:10
Penobscot Mtn. Trail (1,170 ft.)	2.2 mi.	910 ft.	1:35
Hadlock Brook Trail (1,200 ft.)	2.4 mi.	940 ft.	1:40
Maple Spring Trail (1,290 ft.)	2.6 mi.	1,030 ft.	1:50
Sargent Mtn. summit (1,367 ft.)	2.9 mi.	1,107 ft.	2:00

NPS This trail makes a long climb along the south ridge of Sargent Mtn., topping the subsidiary peak of Cedar Swamp Mtn. en route. Reach Sargent South Ridge Trail from Asticou & Jordan Pond Path by way of a 0.3-mi. hike east from the Asticou Map House or a 1.8-mi. hike west from Jordan Pond House. The trail can also be reached from Brown Mtn. Gatehouse on ME 3/198 (3.7 mi. south of its jct. with ME 233) via a 0.7-mi. walk along several carriage roads.

From Asticou & Jordan Pond Path, Sargent South Ridge Trail soon crosses a carriage road. Beyond, the trail rises moderately over the wooded ridge to reach a series of ledges on the right with views east over the expanse of the Amphitheater. Reach the spur path leading 250 ft. left to the top of Cedar Swamp Mtn., where the views range west to Western Mtn. and east to Penobscot Mtn. From the spur jct. continue steeply down to cross Amphitheater Trail at Birch Spring. Sargent South Ridge Trail then leaves the woods and rises sharply to meet Penobscot Mtn. Trail, which enters from the right. Sargent South Ridge Trail continues north over open ledges, past junctions to the left with Hadlock Brook Trail and Maple Spring Trail. Reach the wide-open summit at 2.9 mi.

SEC 10

EASTERN MT. DESERT ISLAND: HADLOCK PONDS VICINITY
SARGENT MTN. (1,367 FT.)

Sargent Mtn. is the second-highest peak on Mt. Desert Island, just 162 ft. lower than Cadillac Mtn. Rising high west of Eagle Lake, Jordan Pond, and the Bubbles, the bare granite summit of Sargent Mtn. offers sweeping 360-degree vistas. A fine network of trails leads hikers over its slopes. A small tarn, Sargent Mtn. Pond, is in the wooded col between Sargent Mtn. and neighboring Penobscot Mtn.

SARGENT EAST CLIFFS TRAIL (MAP 5: E5–E6)
NPS rating: strenuous
From Deer Brook Trail (660 ft.) to:

Sargent Mtn. summit (1,367 ft.)	0.8 mi.	707 ft.	0:45

NPS This short but steep trail connects Deer Brook Trail to the summit of Sargent Mtn. and is recommended more for ascent than descent, especially in wet weather, when the steep climb down wet rocks and ledges can be hazardous. Sargent East Cliffs Trail starts from Deer Brook at the jct. of East Trail and Deer Brook Trail, 0.3 mi. west of Jordan Pond Path at the north end of Jordan Pond. Sargent East Cliffs Trail climbs quickly up the southeast face of Sargent Mtn. with excellent views for much of its length.

GIANT SLIDE TRAIL (MAP 5: D4–D5, E6)
NPS rating: strenuous
Cumulative from ME 3/198 (50 ft.) to:

Parkman Mtn. Trail and Sargent Northwest Trail (550 ft.)	1.3 mi.	500 ft.	0:55
Grandgent Trail in notch between Parkman Mtn. and Gilmore Peak (770 ft.)	2.0 mi.	720 ft.	1:20
Maple Spring Trail (570 ft.) (CLOSED)	2.5 mi.	720 ft.	1:40

NPS This trail leaves the east side of ME 3/198, 1.0 mi. south of ME 233 (limited parking is available on both sides of the road).

Giant Slide Trail, on private land at first, climbs a gradual slope to a carriage road. It turns sharply right (south) and, following Sargent Brook, rises steeply over the tumbled boulders of Giant Slide. Hikers must negotiate several small rock passages. At 1.3 mi., Parkman Mtn. Trail diverges to the right, and Sargent Northwest Trail leaves left. Beyond the jct., Giant Slide Trail passes through a long, narrow cave in the rock and several slot passages. It eventually trends away from the brook and onto easier ground. The trail parallels and then crosses a carriage road, picks up Sargent Brook again, and runs along it on bog bridges. In a notch between Gilmore Peak and Parkman Mtn., Giant Slide Trail intersects Grandgent Trail, which goes right to Parkman Mtn. and left toward Sargent Mtn. Giant Slide Trail continues south past this jct. to meet Maple Spring Trail lower down at 2.5 mi. (*Note*: Maple Spring Trail is closed for the foreseeable future—possibly permanently—due to severe storm damage. This effectively closes Giant Slide Trail between Grandgent Trail and Maple Spring Trail.)

SARGENT NORTHWEST TRAIL (MAP 5: E5)
NPS rating: moderate
From Giant Slide Trail (550 ft.) to:

Sargent Mtn. summit (1,367 ft.)	1.1 mi.	817 ft.	1:05

NPS Sargent Northwest Trail leaves Giant Slide Trail at a point 1.3 mi. from ME 3/198. From this jct., Sargent Northwest Trail ascends east and crosses a carriage road at 0.3 mi. Ahead, it rises over slanting pitches for another 0.3 mi. before turning sharply right (south). The final stretch to the summit of Sargent Mtn. over open ledges offers spectacular views of Somes Sound, Blue Hill, the Camden Hills, and the hills around Bangor. At the top of Sargent Mtn., Sargent Northwest Trail meets Sargent South Ridge Trail and Grandgent Trail.

HADLOCK BROOK TRAIL (MAP 5: E5)
NPS rating: strenuous
Cumulative from ME 3/198 (280 ft.) to:

Parkman Mtn. Trail (270 ft.)	0.1 mi.	−10 ft.	0:04
Bald Peak Trail (260 ft.)	0.2 mi.	−20 ft.	0:08
Hadlock Ponds Trail (300 ft.)	0.3 mi.	40 ft.	0:12
Maple Spring Trail (320 ft.)	0.4 mi.	60 ft.	0:15
Amphitheater Trail (700 ft.)	1.1 mi.	440 ft.	0:45
Sargent South Ridge Trail (1,200 ft.)	1.6 mi.	940 ft.	1:15

NPS Hadlock Brook Trail provides access to Sargent Mtn. from the southwest and leads to a handful of other trails in the area of Penobscot Mtn., Cedar Swamp Mtn., and Gilmore Peak. Hadlock Brook Trail begins from the Norumbega Mtn. Trail parking area on ME 3/198, 2.7 mi. south of its jct. with ME 233.

From the east side of the road, Hadlock Brook Trail enters the woods and heads east, quickly passing Parkman Mtn. and Bald Peak trails on the left. Beyond a carriage road, Hadlock Ponds Trail enters from the south. Bearing left uphill, Hadlock Brook Trail reaches a fork. Here, Maple Spring Trail (partially closed) diverges left, while Hadlock Brook Trail heads right to follow the East Branch of Hadlock Brook through mature forest. Hadlock Brook Trail crosses a carriage road at stunning Waterfall Bridge, which frames beautiful 40-ft. Hadlock Falls. Above, the trail gets steeper, continuing to parallel the brook over rough footing, and reaches the jct. with Amphitheater Trail at 1.1 mi. Beyond, Hadlock Brook Trail climbs steeply before reaching the open terrain of the south ridge of Sargent Mtn. and Sargent South Ridge Trail at 1.6 mi. From this jct., via

**SEC
10**

Sargent South Ridge Trail, it is 0.5 mi. north to the top of Sargent Mtn. and 0.2 mi. south to Penobscot Mtn. Trail near Sargent Mtn. Pond.

MAPLE SPRING TRAIL (MAP 5: E5)
NPS rating: strenuous
Cumulative from Hadlock Brook Trail (320 ft.) to:

Giant Slide Trail (570 ft.) (PARTIALLY CLOSED)	0.4 mi.	250 ft.	0:20
Grandgent Trail (950 ft.) (CLOSED)	0.9 mi.	630 ft.	0:45
Sargent South Ridge Trail (1,290 ft.)	1.5 mi.	970 ft.	1:15
Sargent Mtn. summit (1,367 ft.) via Sargent South Ridge Trail	1.8 mi.	1,047 ft.	1:25

NPS This route climbs to the south ridge of Sargent Mtn. from the southwest, following the West Branch of Hadlock Brook for much of its length; it also provides access to Gilmore Peak via Grandgent Trail. Reach the start of Maple Spring Trail by following Hadlock Brook Trail from the Norumbega Mtn. parking area on ME 3/198 for 0.4 mi.

(*Note*: The middle section of Maple Spring Trail from Hadlock Brook Trail to Grandgent Trail between Gilmore Peak and Sargent Mtn. is closed due to severe and possibly irreparable storm damage from heavy rains on June 9, 2021. As of late 2022, it was not known if this 0.9-mi. section would ever be reopened. This closure also affects the southern section of Giant Slide Trail from its jct. with Grandgent Trail between Parkman Mtn. and Gilmore Peak to the jct. with Maple Spring Trail. Hikers are asked to please respect this closure and plan accordingly.)

From its jct. with Hadlock Brook Trail, Maple Spring Trail leads left and closely follows Hadlock Brook, traversing it several times. In high water, look for some pretty cascades and small waterfalls before and after hiking under beautiful Hemlock Bridge at a point 0.3 mi. above Hadlock Brook Trail.

[*CLOSED*: Beyond, Maple Spring Trail climbs through a small gorge before reaching Giant Slide Trail at 0.4 mi. and then Grandgent Trail at 0.9 mi. (Gilmore Peak is 0.1 mi. to the left via Grandgent Trail.)]

From the Grandgent Trail jct., Maple Spring Trail turns sharply right and climbs steeply, reaching the open south ridge and Sargent South Ridge Trail at 1.5 mi. The summit of Sargent Mtn. is 0.3 mi. to the left (north) via Sargent South Ridge Trail.

GILMORE PEAK (1,033 FT.), PARKMAN MTN. (937 FT.), AND BALD PEAK (969 FT.)

These three peaks with extensive rocky knobs as summits are among six high mountains grouped between Norumbega Mtn. and the Hadlock ponds to the west and Jordan Pond, Sargent Mtn., Penobscot Mtn., and Cedar Swamp Mtn. to the east. The panoramic vistas from each of these summits are magnificent, spanning the coastal islands just south of Mt. Desert Island, across ANP to the east and west, and north to the mainland hills nearby. Six trails are on these slopes.

PARKMAN MTN. TRAIL (MAP 5: E5)
NPS rating: moderate
Cumulative from ME 3/198 (280 ft.) to:

Parkman Mtn. Trail (270 ft.) via Hadlock Brook Trail	0.1 mi.	–10 ft.	0:04
Bald Peak Trail (890 ft.)	1.3 mi.	620 ft.	1:00
Parkman Mtn. summit (937 ft.)	1.4 mi.	667 ft.	1:10
Giant Slide Trail and Sargent North Ridge Trail (550 ft.)	2.2 mi.	667 ft.	1:25

NPS Parkman Mtn. Trail leads through woods and over a series of rocky knobs to the open summit of Parkman Mtn. The trail diverges left (north) from Hadlock Brook Trail just 0.1 mi. east of ME 3/198 and the Norumbega Mtn. parking area.

Parkman Mtn. Trail crosses carriage roads three times during the early part of the ascent, which is moderate at most. Views open up to the south, west, and east high on the south ridge. Bald Peak Trail joins from the right, and the craggy peak of Parkman Mtn. is a short distance ahead. At the Parkman Mtn. summit, Grandgent Trail leaves right (east) toward Gilmore Peak. Parkman Mtn. Trail continues north over open ledges and then through the woods, crossing a carriage road 0.5 mi. beyond the summit. The trail ends 0.3 mi. farther at the jct. of Giant Slide and Sargent Northwest trails. From here, Giant Slide Trail descends left 1.3 mi. to ME 3/198, while Sargent Northwest Trail climbs 1.1 mi. to the top of Sargent Mtn.

BALD PEAK TRAIL (MAP 5: E5)
NPS rating: moderate
Cumulative from ME 3/198 (280 ft.) to:

Parkman Mtn. Trail (270 ft.) via Hadlock Brook Trail	0.1 mi.	–10 ft.	0:04
Bald Peak Trail (260 ft.) via Hadlock Brook Trail	0.2 mi.	–20 ft.	0:08
Bald Peak summit (969 ft.)	1.0 mi.	709 ft.	0:50
Parkman Mtn. Trail (890 ft.)	1.2 mi.	709 ft.	1:00

SEC 10

NPS This direct route up Bald Peak, one of several small, rocky open mountaintops and ridges to the west of Sargent Mtn., leads quickly to outstanding views from the summit. Bald Peak Trail diverges left (north) from Hadlock Brook Trail at a point 0.2 mi. from the Norumbega Mtn. parking area on ME 3/198.

Bald Peak Trail climbs gradually at first, crosses a carriage road, and then ascends more steeply to gain the south ridge proper. Mostly in the open now, the trail finally gains the summit of this fine crag. Beyond, it makes a short but sharp drop and then a short scramble up to the jct. with Parkman Mtn. Trail just 0.1 mi. from that mountain's summit.

GRANDGENT TRAIL (MAP 5: E5)
NPS rating: strenuous
Cumulative from Parkman Mtn. summit (937 ft.) to:

Giant Slide Trail (770 ft.)	0.2 mi.	-167 ft.	0:10
Gilmore Peak summit (1,033 ft.)	0.5 mi.	263 ft.	0:25
Maple Spring Trail (950 ft.)	0.6 mi.	263 ft.	0:30
Sargent Mtn. summit (1,367 ft.)	1.1 mi.	680 ft.	0:55

NPS Grandgent Trail connects the summits of Parkman Mtn., Gilmore Peak, and Sargent Mtn. Beginning on top of Parkman Mtn., Grandgent Trail bears right along the north ridge, drops to the right into the woods, and, farther, into a deep ravine with a streamlet. Here, it intersects with Giant Slide Trail, which passes through the ravine from north to south. Continuing east, Grandgent Trail climbs steeply out of the ravine to reach the open ledges above and the broad summit of Gilmore Peak.

Grandgent Trail leaves Gilmore Peak and continues east, descending into another ravine. At the base of the ravine, the trail crosses a footbridge over a small stream before reaching the jct. with Maple Spring Trail, which enters from the right. (*Note*: In 2022, Maple Spring Trail was closed, possibly permanently, from this jct. down to Hadlock Brook Trail, a distance of 0.9 mi.) Grandgent Trail turns left here and proceeds north up the shallow valley, crossing and recrossing the stream several times. After a stretch of very rocky terrain, Grandgent Trail breaks out of the trees and follows cairns up the broad and barren upper dome of Sargent Mtn. to the large cairn on top. Here is the jct. of Sargent South Ridge Trail, Sargent Northwest Trail, and Sargent East Cliffs Trail.

SEC 10

NORUMBEGA MTN. (846 FT.)
Rising steeply from the sea-level waters of Somes Sound, shapely Norumbega Mtn. is the westernmost high mountain on the east side of Mt. Desert Island. The upper slopes may appear heavily forested, but the peak actually has a surprising number of excellent lookouts, at times east to Parkman Mtn., Bald Mtn., and the Hadlock ponds, and at other times south and west, to Somes Sound and Northeast Harbor. Three trails ascend Norumbega Mtn., and several more wend along its base.

GOAT TRAIL (MAP 5: E5)
NPS rating: strenuous
Cumulative from ME 3/198 (280 ft.) to:

Norumbega Mtn. Trail (840 ft.)	0.7 mi.	560 ft.	0:40
Norumbega Mtn. summit (846 ft.)	0.71 mi.	566 ft.	0:40

NPS Goat Trail leaves the Norumbega Mtn. parking area on the west side of ME 3/198, 2.7 mi. south of its jct. with ME 233 and 0.4 mi. north of Upper Hadlock Pond. At the start, where Lower Norumbega Trail goes left, continue straight ahead on Goat Trail and begin climbing steeply, weaving through mossy ledges on occasional rock steps and staircases. Follow a rising traverse to the right along a slab, and then scramble up a crevice. The trail eventually turns straight up to reach an outlook with views to the east. At 0.3 mi., join the north ridge and hike easily along through jack pine woods. Top out on the ridge and continue left along it with more of the same easterly views. Reach a cairn and sign marking the end of Goat Trail and the start of Norumbega Mtn. Trail. From this jct., walk 50 ft. left (east) to the true summit atop an outcropping (sign).

NORUMBEGA MTN. TRAIL (MAP 5: E5–F5)
NPS rating: moderate
Cumulative from gate on Hadlock Pond Rd. (190 ft.) to:

Norumbega Mtn. Trail (190 ft.)	0.3 mi.	0 ft.	0:10
Norumbega Trail jct. (570 ft.)	0.9 mi.	380 ft.	0:40
Norumbega Mtn. summit (846 ft.)	1.7 mi.	656 ft.	1:10

NPS Norumbega Mtn. Trail climbs the peak from the south at Lower Hadlock Pond. To reach the start, from the jct. of ME 233 and ME 3/198, drive south for 3.8 mi. Just past Brown Mtn. Gatehouse on the left, arrive at Hadlock Pond Rd. on the right. Turn left here, and park at several turnouts to either side of the road over the first 0.2 mi. from ME 3/198. No parking is allowed beyond the gate.

From the gate, walk along Hadlock Pond Rd., paralleling the pond (public water supply; no swimming). Bear right off the road at a fork and soon pass a cul-de-sac. Reach a jct. 0.2 mi. from the gate, where Reservoir Trail leaves to the left and Hadlock Ponds Trail goes straight ahead. Follow Hadlock Ponds Trail across the dam and spillway and past the pumphouse. Enjoy a pleasant view here north to Parkman Mtn., Bald Peak, Gilmore Peak, Sargent Mtn., and Cedar Swamp Mtn. At 0.3 mi., reach a jct. on the shore of the pond. Here, Hadlock Ponds Trail leads straight ahead, while Norumbega Mtn. Trail begins to the left.

SEC
10

Norumbega Mtn. Trail climbs moderately through spruce woods and then more steeply on rocks and roots. At 0.9 mi., Norumbega Trail from Northeast Harbor Golf Club enters from the left. Soon after, reach the high ridgeline of the mountain amid a fragrant forest of pines, and savor the scene of Southwest Harbor and the nearby islands, Western Mtn., Somes Sound, Flying Mtn., and St. Sauveur Mtn. Continue easily on the ridge for about 0.5 mi. to a point just south of the summit with nearly 360-degree views. Meet Goat Trail at 1.7 mi. from the start.

NORUMBEGA TRAIL (MAP 5: F5)
Cumulative from Northeast Harbor Golf Club parking lot (90 ft.) to:

Norumbega Trail (90 ft.) via Golf Club Trail	50 yd.	0 ft.	0:02
Norumbega Mtn. Trail (570 ft.)	0.7 mi.	480 ft.	0:35
Norumbega Mtn. summit (846 ft.) via Norumbega Mtn. Trail	1.5 mi.	756 ft.	1:10

NHVIS This trail climbs to the south ridge of Norumbega Mtn. from Northeast Harbor Golf Club. The Northeast Harbor Village Improvement Society maintains the lower half of the trail. From the jct. of ME 3/198 and ME 233 near the head of Somes Sound, drive south on ME 3/198 for 1.2 mi. Turn right onto Sargent Dr. and travel another 2.8 mi. to Northeast Harbor Golf Club on the left. Drive past the clubhouse and park in the lot beyond.

The hike begins at the far end of the lot (sign: "Golf Club Trail, to Tennis Club"). In 150 ft., reach a jct. Golf Club Trail continues straight ahead, but to climb Norumbega Mtn., turn left here on unsigned Norumbega Trail. Follow easily along to the left of the fairway and green on the second hole. At 0.25 mi., cut across the cart path and then go right and up. Pass an NPS boundary marker. Small cairns have marked the path to this point, but now blue blazes lead the way. A moderate but steady ascent leads to the ledges above. Wind up through the rocks and ledges to join Norumbega Mtn. Trail on the ridge crest. Turn left to continue to the top of Norumbega Mtn. in another 0.8 mi.

LOWER NORUMBEGA TRAIL (MAP 5: E5–F5)
NPS rating: moderate
Cumulative from Goat Trail (300 ft.) to:

Hadlock Ponds Trail (220 ft.)	0.9 mi.	80 ft.	0:30
Norumbega Mtn. Trail at Lower Hadlock Pond (190 ft.)	1.4 mi.	80 ft.	0:45

NPS This route connects Goat Trail, just west of the Norumbega Mtn. parking area, to Hadlock Ponds Trail near the north shore of Lower Hadlock Pond. From the Goat Trail jct., 25 ft. into the woods from the Norumbega Mtn. parking area on ME 3/198, proceed south on Lower Norumbega

Trail, which contours across the lower east face of the mountain. Soon after passing an old trail on the left (sign: "village"), begin a rising traverse on rough, rooty terrain. Traverse several streamlets before meeting Hadlock Ponds Trail at 0.9 mi. To the left, Hadlock Ponds Trail leads 0.3 mi. to ME 3/198 at the south end of Lower Hadlock Pond; to the right, Hadlock Ponds Trail continues around the pretty west side of Lower Hadlock Pond to the jct. with Norumbega Mtn. Trail in another 0.5 mi.

LAND & GARDEN PRESERVE

This lovely 1,165-acre preserve is separate from but adjacent to ANP, in Seal Harbor and Northeast Harbor on Mt. Desert Island's east side. The preserve, on land owned by the Rockefeller family for generations, includes historic Thuya Garden, Thuya Lodge, Asticou Azalea Garden, Asticou Terraces, Asticou Landing, and Abby Aldrich Rockefeller Garden. In 2015, David Rockefeller donated 1,022 acres around and including scenic Little Long Pond, bringing the preserve to its present size. Ten trails offer more than 8 mi. of hiking, much of it on Eliot Mtn. Miles of carriage roads also wind through the property.

ELIOT MTN. (458 FT.)

This wooded peak is named for Charles W. Eliot; along with George B. Dorr, he is considered one of the founding fathers of ANP. Eliot Mtn. Trail, Charles Savage Trail, and Asticou Ridge Trail all reach the wooded summit. The trails on Eliot Mtn. are some of the oldest on Mt. Desert Island.

ELIOT MTN. TRAIL (MAP 5: F5)
From ME 3 (90 ft.) to:

Eliot Mtn. summit (458 ft.)	1.0 mi.	368 ft.	0:40

LGP This trail climbs Eliot Mtn. via the south ridge. It begins on the north side of ME 3 in Northeast Harbor, 1.3 mi. east of the jct. of ME 3 and ME 198. Parking is along the road shoulder. The rooty trail soon skirts a wetlands and then gradually ascends, passing through a grove of mature spruce. At 0.7 mi., reach a jct. with The Richard Trail, which leads left (west) 0.2 mi. to the parking lot for Thuya Garden and Thuya Lodge; to the right, The Richard Trail leads to Charles Savage Trail, Harbor Brook Trail, and finally David & Neva Trail near Little Long Pond. As Eliot Mtn. Trail continues straight ahead, the angle steepens. Ledges lead into the semi-open and a large cairn at the Eliot Monument. The angle eases ahead, and Eliot Mtn. Trail soon reaches a small opening on the summit and a jct. of trails. Here, Asticou Ridge Trail departs north, while Charles Savage Trail enters from the right (east) and continues to the left (west).

SEC
10

HARBOR BROOK TRAIL (MAP 5: F5)
Cumulative from ME 3 (30 ft.) to:

The Richard Trail (60 ft.)	0.8 mi.	30 ft.	0:25
Asticou & Jordan Pond Path (110 ft.)	1.8 mi.	80 ft.	0:50

LGP This trail follows pretty Little Harbor Brook for most of its length. It begins from a gravel parking area on the north side of ME 3, 1.5 mi. east of the jct. of ME 3 and ME 198. Enter the woods in the right rear corner of the parking area. The trail quickly joins the west bank of Little Harbor Brook and heads north. In the first 0.25 mi., the route crosses and then recrosses the brook on sturdy footbridges; then it closely follows the brook to the intersection with The Richard Trail. Beyond, Harbor Brook Trail remains close to the water. At a bend in the brook to the east, Harbor Brook Trail leaves the brook and ends soon after at Asticou & Jordan Pond Path. To the right, Asticou & Jordan Pond Path leads 1.0 mi. to Jordan Pond House; to the left, the path leads 1.0 mi. to the Asticou Map House.

CHARLES SAVAGE TRAIL (MAP 5: F5)
Cumulative from The Richard Trail (270 ft.) to:

Eliot Mtn. summit (458 ft.)	0.3 mi.	188 ft.	0:15
Map House Trail (230 ft.)	0.7 mi.	188 ft.	0:25

LGP This trail is named for Charles Savage, who designed both Thuya Garden and Asticou Azalea Garden. The route extends from The Richard Trail over Eliot Mtn. to Map House Trail. From the jct. of The Richard Trail and Harbor Brook Trail, head west upslope on The Richard Trail for 0.2 mi. to a fork. Here, The Richard Trail continues left, while Charles Savage Trail diverges right.

On Charles Savage Trail, climb past low, mossy ledges. The angle soon eases on the ridge above. At 0.3 mi., reach a jct. in a small clearing on top of Eliot Mtn. Here, Asticou Ridge Trail (sign: "to Jordan Pond Trail") enters from the north, while Eliot Mtn. Trail (sign: "to Little Harbor Brook") enters from the left (south). Continue straight ahead (west) on Charles Savage Trail (sign for Map House). Soon the trail turns sharply left (sign for Asticou and Map House). It switchbacks down the west slope of Eliot Mtn., contours for a stretch, and then angles down to a jct., where a trail enters from the right (north). Walk 50 ft. to the left (west) to a gravel path, Map House Trail, at 0.7 mi. Asticou Map House is a short distance to the right; Thuya Garden and Thuya Lodge are 0.4 mi. on the left.

THE RICHARD TRAIL (MAP 5: F5–F6)
From Thuya Garden and Thuya Lodge parking lot (190 ft.) to:

Eliot Mtn. Trail (300 ft.)	0.2 mi.	110 ft.	0:10
Charles Savage Trail (270 ft.)	0.6 mi.	110 ft.	0:20
Harbor Brook Trail (60 ft.)	0.8 mi.	110 ft.	0:25
David & Neva Trail at Little Long Pond (40 ft.)	1.5 mi.	200 ft.	0:50

LGP This trail is named for Richard Rockefeller, son of David Rockefeller; Richard died in a plane crash in New York in June 2014. The Richard Trail leaves from the visitor parking lot at Thuya Garden. To reach the trailhead, from the jct. of ME 3 and ME 198 in Northeast Harbor, drive east on ME 3 for 0.8 mi. to Thuya Drive on the left. The 0.3-mi. drive ends at a cul-de-sac parking lot at Thuya Garden and Thuya Lodge.

From the parking lot, walk back along the drive 150 ft. to the start of the trail on the left. In 300 ft., a trail leaves left to the gardens; stay straight. Climb easily over ledges to the next jct., where an unmarked trail enters from the right. At 0.2 mi., The Richard Trail crosses Eliot Mtn. Trail. Continue ahead up a series of steps, over a rise, and then on a contour around the south ridge of Eliot Mtn. Pass blocky, mossy ledge faces on the way to the jct. with Charles Savage Trail. Here, bear right and down to Harbor Brook Trail. Cross a footbridge over Little Harbor Brook and swing north up the valley. Climb a pretty staircase along a mossy cliff face; soon turn sharply right and hike easily east to a carriage road. Cross the road and continue eastward to David & Neva Trail, near Little Long Pond, in another 0.3 mi. From here, it is 0.8 mi. south via David & Neva Trail to ME 3 at the south end of Little Long Pond.

ASTICOU RIDGE TRAIL (MAP 5: F5)
From Eliot Mtn. summit (458 ft.) to:

Asticou & Jordan Pond Path (350 ft.)	0.8 mi.	−108 ft.	0:25

LGP Asticou Ridge Trail begins on the summit of Eliot Mtn., at the jct. with Eliot Mtn. Trail and Charles Savage Trail. Head north on the ridge (sign: "to Jordan Pond Trail"), descend gradually, and then follow rolling terrain to a col. An open ledge on the right has views east. After a level stretch, Asticou Ridge Trail drops moderately off the north ridge, passes an ANP boundary marker, and soon reaches its end at the jct. of Asticou & Jordan Pond Path. Here, it is 1.5 mi. east to Jordan Pond House or 0.6 mi. west to the Asticou Map House.

SEC 10

WESTERN MT. DESERT ISLAND
ACADIA MTN. (683 FT.)

This mountain provides dramatic vistas of Somes Sound and the Cranberry Isles from its open summit ledges interspersed with pitch pines and scrub oaks. Combine Acadia Mtn. Trail and the Man O' War Brook fire road for a loop hike.

ACADIA MTN. TRAIL (MAP 4: E4)
NPS rating: strenuous
Cumulative from ME 102 (200 ft.) to:

Acadia Mtn. summit (683 ft.)	1.0 mi.	483 ft.	0:45
Man O' War Rd. (100 ft.), Valley Cove Trail and Valley Peak Trail	2.0 mi.	533 ft.	1:15
Complete loop via Man O' War Brook Rd.	3.1 mi.	593 ft.	1:50

NPS Parking for this trail is at the Acadia Mtn. parking area (toilet) on the west side of ME 102, 3.5 mi. south of Somesville and 3.0 mi. north of Southwest Harbor. Acadia Mtn. Trail begins on the opposite side of ME 102.

Reach a fork at 0.1 mi. and turn left (the right branch heads to St. Sauveur Mtn.). The trail descends gradually to cross Man O' War Brook Rd. and then climbs the west slope of Acadia Mtn., soon leaving the woods and reaching open ledges with frequent views. Acadia Mtn. Trail passes over the true summit and reaches the open ledges on the east summit, with views of Somes Sound. It then descends southeast and south very steeply to cross Man O' War Brook. Here, a spur leads left to the shore of the sound. Man O' War Rd. is at a jct. about 50 yd. ahead. To return to ME 102 via Man O' War Brook Rd., go right (west) at the jct. (To continue toward St. Sauveur Mtn., proceed straight to the jct. of Valley Cove Trail and Valley Peak Trail.) Follow the fire road west over gradual grades to intersect Acadia Mtn. Trail; turn left, and at the next jct., turn right to return to the parking area on ME 102.

ST. SAUVEUR MTN. (684 FT.)

This mountain overlooking Valley Cove on Somes Sound can be climbed from ME 102 in the west or from Fernald Cove Rd. in the south. Eagle Cliff (500 ft.), home to nesting peregrine falcons, forms the precipitous east face of the peak.

SEC 10

ST. SAUVEUR MTN. TRAIL (MAP 4: E4—F4)
NPS rating: moderate
Cumulative from ME 102 (200 ft.) to:

Acadia Mtn. Trail fork (260 ft.)	0.1 mi.	60 ft.	0:05
Ledge Trail (650 ft.)	0.9 mi.	450 ft.	0:40

St. Sauveur Mtn. summit (684 ft.)	1.1 mi.	485 ft.	0:50
Spur to Valley Peak Trail (670 ft.)	1.2 mi.	485 ft.	0:55
Valley Peak Trail (500 ft.)	1.5 mi.	485 ft.	1:05

NPS This easy route leads to the summit of St. Sauveur Mtn. from the northwest. Parking for this trail is the same as for Acadia Mtn. Trail. Cross ME 102 and start up the path. At 0.1 mi., Acadia Mtn. Trail leaves to the left; go right on St. Sauveur Mtn. Trail, which travels south through a softwood forest and over open slopes, rising continually to the jct. with Ledge Trail, which enters from the right. The summit of St. Sauveur Mtn. is ahead at 1.1 mi. St. Sauveur Mtn. Trail continues past the summit to a jct. Here, a spur to Valley Peak Trail leaves left, while St. Sauveur Mtn. Trail continues right, descending the south ridge of the mountain. At 1.5 mi., the trail ends at its jct. with the lower end of Valley Peak Trail. Ahead, it is 0.4 mi. to Valley Cove Rd. via Valley Peak Trail and an additional 0.1 mi. to the Flying Mtn. trailhead parking lot on Fernald Point Rd. To the left, Valley Cove Trail follows a rather strenuous route across and down to Man O' War Brook Rd., which leads 1.3 mi. via a short section of the west end of Acadia Mtn. Trail back to the trailhead on ME 102.

LEDGE TRAIL (MAP 4: F4)
NPS rating: moderate
Cumulative from ME 102 (220 ft.) to:

St. Sauveur Mtn. Trail (650 ft.)	0.6 mi.	450 ft.	0:30
St. Sauveur Mtn. summit (684 ft.)	0.8 mi.	465 ft.	0:40

NPS This hike begins at the St. Sauveur Mtn. parking area on ME 102, 0.6 mi. south of the Acadia Mtn. trailhead. Ledge Trail enters the woods and rises quickly over ledges to the jct. with St. Sauveur Trail at 0.6 mi., 0.2 mi. shy of the summit of St. Sauveur Mtn.

VALLEY PEAK TRAIL (MAP 4: E4—F4)
NPS rating: strenuous
Cumulative from Flying Mtn. trailhead (30 ft.) to:

St. Sauveur Mtn. Trail (500 ft.)	0.5 mi.	470 ft.	0:30
Acadia Mtn. Trail and Valley Cove Trail (100 ft.) at Man O' War Brook Rd.	1.8 mi.	640 ft.	1:15

NPS This trail leaves the west side of Valley Cove Rd. (no vehicle access) 0.1 mi. north of the Flying Mtn. trailhead parking area on Fernald Point Rd. Leaving the old fire road, Valley Peak Trail rises steeply northwest through shady woods on Valley Peak (the south shoulder of St. Sauveur Mtn.). At 0.5 mi., St. Sauveur Trail departs left. Stay right on Valley Peak

SEC 10

Trail to skirt the top of Eagle Cliff, with outstanding views of Valley Cove below and the mountains east of Somes Sound. At 0.9 mi., a spur path on the left leads to the summit of St. Sauveur Mtn. Valley Peak Trail continues straight, steeply descending the northeast shoulder of the mountain to end at a jct. with Acadia Mtn. Trail and Valley Cove Trail near Man O' War Brook and the east end of the Man O' War fire road at 1.8 mi. To make a loop, head south on Valley Cove Trail, which leads 1.1 mi. to Valley Cove Rd., which then leads 0.5 mi. back to the Flying Mtn. trailhead.

FLYING MTN. (282 FT.)

A short climb to the open summit of Flying Mtn. offers a pleasant panorama of Somes Sound, Southwest Harbor, and the islands to the south, including the Cranberry Isles and Greening, Sutton, Baker, and Bear islands.

FLYING MTN. TRAIL (MAP 4: F4)
NPS rating: moderate
Cumulative from Flying Mtn. trailhead (30 ft.) to:

Flying Mtn. summit (282 ft.)	0.3 mi.	250 ft.	0:15
Valley Cove Trail and Valley Cove Rd. (5 ft.)	1.0 mi.	295 ft.	0:25
Complete loop via Valley Cove Rd.	1.4 mi.	345 ft.	0:45

NPS From the jct. of ME 102 and ME 3/198 in Somesville, drive south on ME 102 for 5.4 mi. to Fernald Point Rd. in Southwest Harbor. Turn left (west) onto Fernald Point Rd. and drive 1.0 mi. to the trailhead parking lot on the left. Flying Mtn. Trail leaves the east side of the parking area and rises quickly through spruce woods, reaching the higher south summit of Flying Mtn. in 0.3 mi. It then follows the long and pleasant ridgeline of the mountain over the north summit. Just beyond, a side trail on the right leads 150 ft. to open ledges and excellent views. Descend to the shore of Valley Cove on Somes Sound. Flying Mtn. Trail follows the cove to the left to end at the jct. of Valley Cove Trail and Valley Cove Rd. at 1.0 mi. For an easy return to the parking area, follow the old fire road south for 0.5 mi.

VALLEY COVE TRAIL (MAP 4: E4—F4)
NPS rating: moderate
Cumulative from Flying Mtn. trailhead (30 ft.) to:

Valley Cove Trail (5 ft.) via Valley Cove Rd.	0.5 mi.	50 ft.	0:15
Acadia Mtn. Trail and Valley Peak Trail at Man O' War Brook Rd. (100 ft.)	1.6 mi.	250 ft.	0:50

NPS Valley Cove Trail starts on the shore of Somes Sound at Valley Cove at the end of Valley Cove Rd., 0.5 mi. from the Flying Mtn. trailhead parking area on Fernald Point Rd. From the north end of the old fire road, Valley Cove Trail leads left, while Flying Mtn. Trail goes right. Valley Cove Trail follows the shoreline under the ledge walls of Eagle Cliff high above, traversing a rock slide via a long series of rock staircases. Valley Cove Trail ends at the jct. of Acadia Mtn. Trail and Valley Peak Trail at the Man O' War Brook Rd.

BEECH MTN. (843 FT.)

This mountain rises steeply between Echo Lake and Long Pond. Its summit, adorned by the only fire tower on Mt. Desert Island, can be reached from the Beech Mtn. parking area at the end of Beech Hill Rd., from Echo Lake, or from the pumping station at the south end of Long Pond. The iron tower was erected in 1962, replacing the original wooden structure. When park staff are present, often during summer months, the fire tower platform and interior room are open for public access.

Beech Cliff and Canada Cliff, on the east side of the mountain overlooking Echo Lake, can be reached by short trails from the Beech Mtn. parking area or from the Echo Lake parking area (follow a short access road from ME 102 north of Southwest Harbor). To reach the pumping station at the south end of Long Pond, drive west on Seal Cove Rd. from its jct. with ME 198 in Southwest Harbor. At 0.6 mi., turn right onto Long Pond Rd., and proceed to the road's end at the pumping station at 1.8 mi. Parking is limited.

BEECH CLIFF TRAIL (MAP 4: E3)
NPS rating: ladder
From Echo Lake parking area (90 ft.) to:

Canada Cliff Trail (550 ft.)	0.6 mi.	460 ft.	0:30

NPS This hike offers quick but very steep access to Beech Cliff from the Echo Lake parking area at the south end of Echo Lake. From the jct. of ME 102 and ME 3/198 in Somesville, drive south on ME 102 for 4.4 mi. to the Echo Lake entrance to ANP. A large parking lot is 0.4 mi. ahead at the end of the access road.

Beech Cliff Trail begins at the north end of the parking lot and immediately passes an NPS cabin. After a stretch of moderate hiking through the woods, the trail climbs very steeply for the rest of the way via a series of stone staircases and iron ladders. It levels off at the top of Beech Cliff and the jct. with Canada Cliff Trail. Beech Cliff Loop Trail is 100 yd. to the right.

CANADA CLIFF TRAIL (MAP 4: E3—F3)
NPS rating: moderate
Cumulative from Echo Lake parking area (90 ft.) to:

Fork and spur path (400 ft.)	0.7 mi.	310 ft.	0:30
Beech Cliff Loop Trail (550 ft.)	1.3 mi.	460 ft.	0:55
From Echo Lake parking area (90 ft.) to:			
Beech Cliff parking area (500 ft.) via Canada Cliff spur path and Valley Trail	0.8 mi.	410 ft.	0:35

NPS Canada Cliff Trail starts from the south end of the Echo Lake parking area at a set of wooden stairs (diagonally opposite the Island Explorer bus stop). It runs on the level through the woods parallel to the access road and then climbs steeply via switchbacks and rock steps to a ravine. The trail climbs the left side and crosses to the right side before reaching a fork at 0.7 mi. The left branch leads 0.4 mi. to the Beech Mtn. parking area via a spur of Canada Cliff Trail and then Valley Trail.

Continuing to the right, Canada Cliff Trail contours at first and then makes a rising traverse across the east face of the mountain, with occasional outlooks. The open ledges beyond offer views to Southwest Harbor. Continue north along the ridge with minor ups and downs. After a short scramble, gain the top of the ridge and break into the open with the sight of the Beech Mtn. fire tower to the west. Arrive at a large ledge overlooking Echo Lake at 1.0 mi. Here, the views of Somes Sound, Sargent Mtn., Acadia Mtn., and St. Sauveur Mtn. are magnificent. The jct. with Beech Cliff Loop Trail is 100 yd. ahead; at that jct., Beech Cliff Loop Trail goes right for a short but very scenic 0.2-mi. loop, or left to reach the Beech Mtn. parking area in 0.2 mi.

BEECH CLIFF LOOP TRAIL (MAP 4: E3)
NPS rating: moderate
Cumulative from Beech Hill Rd. parking area (500 ft.) to:

Canada Cliff Trail (550 ft.)	0.2 mi.	50 ft.	0:10
Complete loop (500 ft.)	0.7 mi.	60 ft.	0:25

SEC 10

NPS This loop hike climbs easily to the lip of Beech Cliff from the Beech Mtn. parking area at the end of Beech Hill Rd. To reach the trailhead, follow ME 102 south through Somesville and turn right onto Pretty Marsh Rd. (first right after the fire station). Drive west on Pretty Marsh Rd. for 0.3 mi. to Beech Hill Rd. Turn left onto Beech Hill Rd. and follow it to its end at a large trailhead parking lot (toilet), 3.4 mi. from Pretty Marsh Rd.

Beech Cliff Loop Trail starts to the east, entering the woods where Beech Hill Rd. enters the parking lot. In 0.2 mi., Beech Cliff Loop Trail reaches a jct. Here, Canada Cliff Trail leads right to a jct. with Beech Cliff Trail high above Echo Lake. Turn left here and then bear right to follow the loop counterclockwise. The 0.3-mi. circuit follows the spectacular cliff edge for half of its length, with spectacular views to the east over Echo Lake.

BEECH MTN. LOOP TRAIL (MAP 4: F3)
NPS rating: moderate
Cumulative from Beech Hill Rd. parking area (500 ft.) to:

Beech Mtn. summit (843 ft.) and Beech South Ridge Trail	0.5 mi.	343 ft.	0:25
Beech West Ridge Trail (750 ft.)	0.6 mi.	343 ft.	0:30
Complete loop	1.1 mi.	343 ft.	0:45

NPS This trail leaves the northwest side of the Beech Mtn. parking area to the left of the toilet and forks in 100 yd. Turn left to hike the loop clockwise. Beech Mtn. Loop Trail ascends over ledges through semi-open woods to reach a jct. with Beech South Ridge Trail immediately below the summit fire tower. Scramble up 20 ft. to the base of the tower for fine views east. From this jct., gradually hike down to the jct. with Beech West Ridge Trail, which enters on the left. Continue right on Beech Mtn. Loop Trail, and quickly reach open ledges and extraordinary vistas over Long Pond to Mansell Mtn. and Bernard Mtn. Descend on ledges and enter the woods below. Continue to descend moderately and then swing east on a contour to close the loop near the parking area at the end of Beech Hill Rd.

VALLEY TRAIL (MAP 4: F3)
NPS rating: moderate
Cumulative from parking area at Long Pond pumping station (65 ft.) to:

Beech South Ridge Trail (400 ft.)	0.8 mi.	335 ft.	0:35
Canada Cliff Trail spur (480 ft.)	1.5 mi.	415 ft.	1:00
Beech Hill Rd. parking area (500 ft.)	1.5 mi.	435 ft.	1:05

NPS This convenient link between the pumping station at Long Pond and the Beech Hill Rd. parking area, in the notch between Beech Cliff and Beech Mtn., also provides direct access to Beech South Ridge Trail, permitting a circuit or one-way trip over Beech Mtn.

SEC 10

Valley Trail starts from the south side of the parking area (away from the pond) at the south end of Long Pond. The trail enters the woods, heading south and then east to cross a service road at a road jct. It trends easily over the lower slopes before climbing via a series of switchbacks on the south ridge of Beech Mtn. At 0.8 mi., Beech South Ridge Trail leaves left. Continuing east, Valley Trail soon swings north to make a pleasant rising traverse up the valley separating Beech Mtn. and Canada Cliff. Shortly after a spur from Canada Cliff Trail enters from the right, Valley Trail reaches the parking area at the end of Beech Hill Rd.

BEECH SOUTH RIDGE TRAIL (MAP 4: F3)
NPS rating: moderate
Cumulative from Long Pond parking area (65 ft.) to:

Beech South Ridge Trail (400 ft.) via Valley Trail	0.8 mi.	335 ft.	0:30
Beech Mtn. summit (843 ft.)	1.7 mi.	778 ft.	1:15

NPS This trail diverges left from Valley Trail at a point 0.7 mi. east of the pumping station parking area at the south end of Long Pond. Beech South Ridge Trail steadily ascends the south ridge of Beech Mtn. to the summit over a series of semi-open ledges (views to the south). The trail ends adjacent to the Beech Mtn. fire tower at the jct. with Beech Mtn. Loop Trail.

BEECH WEST RIDGE TRAIL (MAP 4: F3)
NPS rating: moderate
Cumulative from Long Pond parking area (65 ft.) to:

Beech Mtn. Loop Trail (750 ft.)	1.1 mi.	685 ft.	0:55
Beech Mtn. summit (843 ft.) via Beech Mtn. Loop Trail	1.2 mi.	778 ft.	1:00

NPS Beech West Ridge Trail starts from the east side of the parking area (away from the pumping station) at the south end of Long Pond. It enters the woods, follows the shore of Long Pond, and soon crosses a service road. In 0.4 mi., the trail leaves the pond and rises by easy grades for a short distance before steeply climbing up the west ridge of Beech Mtn. Ledges en route offer views over Long Pond to Mansell Mtn. At 1.0 mi., Beech West Ridge Trail reaches Beech Mtn. Loop Trail, which leads right 0.1 mi. to the summit of Beech Mtn. and its fire tower.

WESTERN MTN.: BERNARD MTN. (1,012 FT.) AND MANSELL MTN. (939 FT.)

Western Mtn. comprises two main peaks: Bernard Mtn. to the west and Mansell Mtn. to the east. Both summits are mostly wooded, but there are occasional view windows. Trails in this area start from three primary trailheads: at the pumping station at the south end of Long Pond, at Mill Field, and at Gilley Field.

To reach the pumping station: Follow Seal Cove Rd. west from ME 102 in Southwest Harbor. At 0.6 mi., turn right (toward the landfill) onto Long Pond Rd. The road ends at the pumping station at 1.8 mi., the starting point for Long Pond Trail, Cold Brook Trail, Valley Trail, and Beech West Ridge Trail.

To reach Mill Field and Gilley Field: Follow Seal Cove Rd. west from ME 102 in Southwest Harbor. The pavement ends at the ANP boundary at 3.9 mi. Turn right off Seal Cove Rd. at 4.6 mi. (no sign). Reset odometer. On the dirt access road, reach the jct. with Western Mtn. Rd. at 0.4 mi. (To the left, it is 1.2 mi. to the West Ledge Trail trailhead.) Turn right onto Western Mtn. Rd. and follow it to the next jct. at 1.2 mi. To reach Mill Field, turn left here and drive 0.2 mi. to the end of the road and the trailhead parking area for Sluiceway Trail and Bernard Mtn. Trail. To reach Gilley Field, turn right at the jct. and drive 0.1 mi. to the end of the road and the trailhead parking area for Gilley Trail, Mansell Mtn. Trail, and Cold Brook Trail.

LONG POND TRAIL (MAP 4: E2–F2, E3–F3)
NPS rating: easy
Cumulative from Long Pond pumping station parking area (65 ft.) to:

Perpendicular Trail (65 ft.)	0.2 mi.	0 ft.	0:05
Great Notch Trail (500 ft.)	3.0 mi.	435 ft.	1:45

NPS This pleasant footpath starts from the pumping station parking area at the south end of Long Pond. It enters the woods just beyond the pumping station and quickly reaches a jct. Here, Cold Brook Trail leaves left. Long Pond Trail continues along the west shore of the pond for 1.5 mi. and then bears west away from it to contour around the base of the north slope of Mansell Mtn. Turning south, the trail passes through a beautiful birch forest and follows Great Brook for a short distance. It then continues to a jct. with Great Notch Trail at a point 1.2 mi. east of Long Pond Fire Rd. and 0.5 mi. north of Great Notch between Mansell Mtn. and Bernard Mtn. To make a loop, continue south through the notch on Great Notch Trail; head east on Gilley Trail and then Cold Brook Trail to return to the pumping station trailhead at Long Pond in another 1.9 mi.

PERPENDICULAR TRAIL (MAP 4: F3)
NPS rating: strenuous
Cumulative from Long Pond pumping station parking area (65 ft.) to:

Perpendicular Trail (65 ft.) via Long Pond Trail	0.2 mi.	0 ft.	0:05
Mansell Mtn. summit (939 ft.)	1.2 mi.	874 ft.	1:05

NPS Perpendicular Trail ascends Mansell Mtn. from Long Pond Trail on the west shore of Long Pond. Drive to the pumping station parking area at the south end of Long Pond. From the left (west) side of the pumping station, begin walking on Long Pond Trail. In 250 ft., pass Cold Brook Trail, which departs to the left. Follow the shoreline of the pond to the start of Perpendicular Trail. This steep course on the east side of Mansell

SEC 10

Mtn. switchbacks up the scree fields and talus slopes on what some hikers refer to as the "stairway to heaven." More than 1,000 stone steps, several iron rungs, and an iron ladder mark the route. After a long, rising traverse beneath a cliff face, climb a rocky defile. At 1.0 mi., reach an outlook with superb vistas over Long Pond to the fire tower on Beech Mtn., the bulk of Sargent Mtn., Southwest Harbor, and Northeast Harbor. A short side trail leads 200 ft. to a large ledge overlook with views to Somes Sound, Sargent Mtn., and Cadillac Mtn. On the wooded summit (sign) at 1.2 mi., Perpendicular Trail meets Mansell Mtn. Trail, which ascends 0.9 mi. from Gilley Field. Just ahead on Mansell Mtn. Trail, a side trail leads right to an outlook with views west to Blue Hill and Bartlett Island.

MANSELL MTN. TRAIL (MAP 4: F3)
NPS rating: moderate
Cumulative from Gilley Field (150 ft.) to:

Razorback Trail (850 ft.)	0.9 mi.	700 ft.	0:50
Mansell Mtn. summit (939 ft.)	1.1 mi.	800 ft.	1:00

NPS This trail leaves from Gilley Field and travels up the south slope of Mansell Mtn. It ascends gradually from the trailhead to ledges that offer views of Southwest Harbor, Beech Mtn., Long Pond, and Northeast Harbor. At 0.9 mi., a short but steep 0.1-mi. spur from Razorback Trail enters from the left. From this jct., Mansell Mtn. Trail climbs to the right for the final 0.2 mi. to the wooded summit of Mansell Mtn. to meet Perpendicular Trail.

COLD BROOK TRAIL (MAP 4: F3)
NPS rating: easy
From Long Pond pumping station parking area (65 ft.) to:

Gilley Field (150 ft.)	0.4 mi.	85 ft.	0:15

NPS This pretty woods walk on a wide track is an important link between the pumping station parking area at the south end of Long Pond and Gilley Field. The trail also is a natural start or finish to a loop hike over Mansell Mtn. Begin by walking west past the pumping station to Long Pond Trail. In 100 ft., turn left and proceed on Cold Brook Trail.

GILLEY TRAIL (MAP 4: F3)
NPS rating: easy
Cumulative from Gilley Field parking area (150 ft.) to:

Razorback Trail (170 ft.)	0.1 mi.	20 ft.	0:05
Great Notch Trail (330 ft.)	0.6 mi.	180 ft.	0:23
Sluiceway Trail (330 ft.)	0.625 mi.	180 ft.	0:25

NPS This route, which starts at the Gilley Field parking area at the eastern end of Western Mtn. Rd., provides access to Mansell Mtn. and Bernard Mtn. via Razorback Trail, Great Notch Trail, and Sluiceway Trail. Gilley Trail starts next to Mansell Mtn. Trail, but instead of climbing the peak, it follows easy grades to the west, passing Razorback Trail in 0.1 mi. and then turning north and climbing moderately to its end at the jct. of Great Notch Trail. Sluiceway Trail is 250 ft. west from this jct. A short side trail halfway along Gilley Trail on the left leads 200 ft. to the Reservoir, a small dammed pond in a scenic glen.

RAZORBACK TRAIL (MAP 4: F3)
NPS rating: strenuous
Cumulative from Gilley Field (150 ft.) to:

Razorback Trail (170 ft.) via Gilley Trail	0.1 mi.	50 ft.	0:05
Mansell Mtn. spur path (830 ft.)	0.9 mi.	680 ft.	0:45
Great Notch summit (630 ft.)	1.1 mi.	680 ft.	0:55

NPS Razorback Trail diverges right from Gilley Trail at a point 0.1 mi. from the Gilley Field parking area at the east end of Western Mtn. Rd. It ascends moderately up the west side of Mansell Mtn., offering views of Great Notch and Bernard Mtn. The upper section of Razorback Trail climbs a narrow ridge of extensive open ledges (the Razorback) to reach a jct. To the right, a spur climbs steeply 0.1 mi. to Mansell Mtn. Trail, which rises an additional 0.2 mi. to the top of Mansell Mtn. Continue left on Razorback Trail, which leads down to Great Notch and the jct. with Great Notch Trail in 0.2 mi.

SLUICEWAY TRAIL (MAP 4: F2)
NPS rating: strenuous
Cumulative from Mill Field parking area (150 ft.) to:

Gilley Trail (330 ft.)	0.4 mi.	180 ft.	0:20
Bernard Mtn. Trail (850 ft.) in Little Notch	1.0 mi.	700 ft.	0:50
Bernard Mtn. summit (1,012 ft.) via Bernard Mtn. Trail	1.2 mi.	860 ft.	1:00

NPS Starting from Mill Field, Sluiceway Trail runs north 0.4 mi. to a jct. with a connector path that leads a short distance east to the jct. with Gilley Trail (Great Notch Trail is just 250 ft. farther east). From the jct., Sluiceway Trail swings northwest and climbs rather steeply up a narrow valley to meet Bernard Mtn. Trail in Little Notch. To reach the summit of Bernard Mtn., follow Bernard Mtn. Trail left (south) for 0.2 mi.

SEC 10

BERNARD MTN. TRAIL (MAP 4: F2)
NPS rating: strenuous
Cumulative from Mill Field parking area (150 ft.) to:

West Ledge Trail (900 ft.)	1.1 mi.	750 ft.	0:55
Bernard Mtn. summit (1,012 ft.)	1.6 mi.	860 ft.	1:15
Great Notch (650 ft.)	2.3 mi.	980 ft.	1:40

NPS Bernard Mtn. Trail starts at Mill Field, makes a wide and gradual arc west to the south ridge of Bernard Mtn., and swings north to meet West Ledge Trail. Here, Bernard Mtn. Trail turns right, ascending easily north over several wooded knobs to the summit. Iron posts mark an old fire tower site; just ahead is the summit sign. A short distance beyond, reach an overlook to the left and a register box. Bernard Mtn. Trail then descends steeply to Little Notch and the jct. with Sluiceway Trail. Bernard Mtn. Trail continues east, climbing over the low but rugged Knight Nubble (view to Southwest Harbor and the islands to the south) before dropping into a wet and mossy notch. Climbing out, the trail then drops steeply into Great Notch, where there is a bench and a register box. Here, Great Notch Trail leads 1.7 mi. north to Long Pond Fire Rd. and 0.5 mi. south toward Gilley Field, while Razorback Trail leads east to Mansell Mtn. in 0.5 mi.

WEST LEDGE TRAIL (MAP 4: F2)
NPS rating: strenuous
From Western Mtn. Rd. (150 ft.) to:

Bernard Mtn. Trail (900 ft.)	1.1 mi.	750 ft.	0:55

NPS West Ledge Trail connects the western end of Western Mtn. Rd. to the system of trails on Bernard Mtn. and Mansell Mtn. The vistas to the west over Seal Cove Pond to Blue Hill Bay and the islands south and west of Mt. Desert Island are spectacular. From the east, at ME 102 in Southwest Harbor, drive west on Seal Cove Rd. for 3.3 mi. (pavement ends at 1.3 mi.). Reset odometer. Turn right (north) onto Western Mtn. Rd. and pass Bald Mtn. Rd. on the left at 0.3 mi. At 0.7 mi., Western Mtn. Rd. forks. Bear left and proceed to the trailhead at 1.0 mi. Limited parking is on the left. If the few spaces are full, drive an additional 0.3 mi. to the boat launch parking area on Seal Cove Pond.

West Ledge Trail ascends moderately at first, reaching open ledges very quickly. Beyond, it begins a steady, steep climb over open granite slabs and ledges. From here, the views stretch from Bass Harbor to the Camden Hills. The angle moderates halfway along the ridge. The trail drops into a

SEC
10

shallow ravine and then ascends via steep, rocky terrain. Beyond, it crosses an open slope and climbs steeply again. From this point on, West Ledge Trail makes several forays into the woods and then back out into the open on its ascent to the jct. with Bernard Mtn. Trail, which enters from the right at 1.1 mi. From here, Bernard Mtn. Trail climbs easily to the top of the mountain in another 0.5 mi.

GREAT NOTCH TRAIL (MAP 4: F2)
NPS rating: moderate
Cumulative from Long Pond Fire Rd. (150 ft.) to:

Long Pond Trail (500 ft.)	1.2 mi.	350 ft.	0:45
Great Notch (650 ft.)	1.7 mi.	500 ft.	1:05
Gilley Trail (330 ft.)	2.2 mi.	500 ft.	1:20
Gilley Field parking area (150 ft.) via Gilley Trail	2.8 mi.	500 ft.	1:40

NPS This wooded trail is the only route providing access to Western Mtn. from the northwest. The trailhead is on Long Pond Fire Rd., about 0.1 mi. beyond the Pine Hill turnaround and parking area, at a point 1.0 mi. east of the road's jct. with ME 102 (this jct. is about 1.1 mi. south of the jct. with the road to the Pretty Marsh picnic area).

Great Notch Trail trends east and rises by easy grades to a jct. with Long Pond Trail, which enters from the left at 1.2 mi. Beyond, Great Notch Trail climbs to Great Notch at 1.7 mi., where Bernard Mtn. Trail leads right toward Bernard Mtn., and Razorback Trail leads left toward Mansell Mtn. Great Notch Trail continues through Great Notch and then on a rough treadway of rocks and roots down to Gilley Trail at 2.2 mi., where Great Notch Trail ends. Here, a connector path leads right (west) a short distance to Sluiceway Trail. Follow Gilley Trail for another 0.6 mi. to the Gilley Field parking area.

SCHOODIC PENINSULA
SCHOODIC HEAD (442 FT.)

This prominent hilltop, the highest point on Schoodic Peninsula, provides exceptional vistas east over Schoodic Harbor along the Downeast coast to Petit Manan Point and the lighthouse there, north to Winter Harbor and the mountains around Donnell Pond, and west over Frenchman Bay to the mountains on Mt. Desert Island. Five trails exist on Schoodic Head: Anvil Trail, Alder Trail, Schoodic Head Trail, East Trail, and Buck Cove Mtn. Trail. A narrow gravel road ascends nearly to the top of Schoodic Head from the west; it leaves Schoodic Loop Rd. in the area of West Pond.

SEC 10

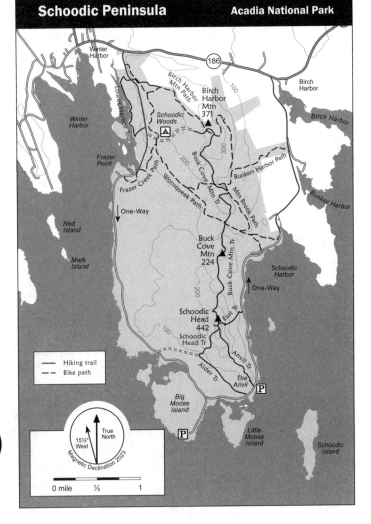

Schoodic Peninsula   Acadia National Park

Winter
Harbor

186

Birch
Harbor

Lower Harbor Tr

Winter
Harbor

Birch Harbor
Mtn Path

Schoodic
Woods

Birch
Harbor
Mtn
371

Birch Harbor

100

Frazer
Point

300

Bunkers Harbor Path

Bunker Harbor

Buck Cove Mtn Tr

200

Frazer Creek Path

Wonsqueak Path

Mtn Brook Path

One-Way

Ned
Island

Mark
Island

Buck
Cove
Mtn
224

Buck Cove Mtn Tr

Schoodic
Harbor

200

One-Way

Schoodic
Head
442

East Tr

Schoodic
Head Tr

100

Anvil Tr

Alder Tr

The
Anvil

P

—— Hiking trail
- - - Bike path

Big
Moose
Island

P

Little
Moose
Island

Schoodic
Island

SEC
10

True
North

15½°
West

Magnetic Declination 2023

0 mile   ½   1

ANVIL TRAIL (AMC SCHOODIC PENINSULA MAP)
NPS rating: moderate
Cumulative from Blueberry Hill Picnic Area (20 ft.) on Schoodic Loop Rd. to:

The Anvil (192 ft.)	0.2 mi.	172 ft.	0:10
Schoodic Head Trail (430 ft.)	1.2 mi.	472 ft.	0:50
East Trail (435 ft.)	1.25 mi.	477 ft.	0:52
Schoodic Head summit (442 ft.) via Schoodic Head Trail	1.3 mi.	484 ft.	0:54
Buck Cove Mtn. Trail (440 ft.) via Schoodic Head Trail	1.35 mi.	484 ft.	0:55

NPS This trail climbs Schoodic Head via the Anvil, a craggy ledge reached early in the hike. From the Schoodic Woods CG entrance road, drive south on Schoodic Loop Rd. for 4.2 mi. to Blueberry Hill Picnic Area on the right. The small lot provides trailhead parking for both Anvil Trail and Alder Trail. If this lot is full, proceed to a pullout 500 ft. ahead on the right side of Schoodic Loop Rd.

From Blueberry Hill Picnic Area, walk right along Schoodic Loop Rd. for 600 ft. to the start of Anvil Trail on the left. Climb a rocky defile to reach the open ledges of the Anvil. Just ahead, a short path leads 100 ft. west to a lookout with a vista of Schoodic Point and the peaks on Mt. Desert Island. Continuing on Anvil Trail, descend through rocks and on ladder steps. Look for a sharp prow on the right at the base of the descent. The trail traverses semi-open ledges, swings east along the base of Schoodic Head, and soon climbs a short, steep pitch via log and rock steps. Moderate switchbacks lead to semi-open ledges above and the jct. with Schoodic Head Trail, which enters from the left. From this point, it is 0.1 mi. to the right to the top of Schoodic Head via Schoodic Head Trail. En route, a side path on the left leads 100 yd. to a parking loop at the end of the gravel summit road. East Trail enters from the right a short distance beyond. Pass a small communications tower and reach the summit of Schoodic Head. The best scenery is just north at the unsigned jct. with Buck Cove Mtn. Trail.

ALDER TRAIL AND SCHOODIC HEAD TRAIL (AMC SCHOODIC PENINSULA MAP)
NPS rating: easy to moderate
Cumulative from Blueberry Hill Picnic Area (20 ft.) on Schoodic Loop Rd. to:

Schoodic Head Trail (70 ft.) via Alder Trail and gravel road	0.7 mi.	75 ft.	0:20
Anvil Trail (430 ft.)	1.1 mi.	430 ft.	0:45
East Trail (435 ft.)	1.15 mi.	435 ft.	0:50
Schoodic Head summit (442 ft.)	1.2 mi.	442 ft.	0:55
Buck Cove Mtn. Trail (440 ft.)	1.25 mi.	442 ft.	1:00

NPS Combine Alder Trail and Schoodic Head Trail for a pleasant trip to the top of Schoodic Head. Add Anvil Trail to the mix for a loop hike. Alder Trail departs just across Schoodic Loop Rd. from Blueberry Hill Picnic Area.

Follow the wide, grassy, mostly level path through alders and other shrubby growth to a gravel road at 0.6 mi. Go straight here on the gravel road (sign for Schoodic Head Trail). In another 0.1 mi., Schoodic Head Trail leaves the gravel road on the right and climbs at a moderate grade through spruce woods. Old metal bluebird markers can still be seen on this longtime path. Ahead, the trail becomes steeper, climbing granite staircases and wooden steps to a granite outcropping and cairn. A short path leads left to ledges and a viewpoint. Continuing on Schoodic Head Trail, cross bog bridges over a small stream in a wet area. After climbing a wooden ladder, reach sloping ledges and then the jct. with Anvil Trail on the right. From this point, it is 0.1 mi. to the left to the top of Schoodic Head. En route, a side path on the left leads 100 yd. to a parking loop at the end of the gravel summit road. East Trail enters from the right a short distance beyond. Pass a small communications tower and reach the summit of Schoodic Head. The best scenery is just north at the unsigned jct. with Buck Cove Mtn. Trail.

EAST TRAIL (AMC SCHOODIC PENINSULA MAP)
NPS rating: moderate
Cumulative from parking turnout on Schoodic Loop Rd. (50 ft.) to:

Schoodic Head Trail (435 ft.)	0.4 mi.	385 ft.	0:25
Schoodic Head summit (442 ft.) via Schoodic Head Trail	0.45 mi.	392 ft.	0:30
Buck Cove Mtn. Trail (440 ft.) via Schoodic Head Trail	0.5 mi.	392 ft.	0:35

NPS This short but steep hike scrambles up the rocky east face of Schoodic Head. From Blueberry Hill Picnic Area, drive north on Schoodic Loop Rd. for 1.0 mi. to a turnout on the right. Park here. East Trail enters the woods immediately across the road, climbing rocky outcroppings and then ascending gently across ledges to reach a small ravine. Cross the ravine and bear left. Beyond, climb steeply via switchbacks, much of the way on small, loose rocks. The angle eases at ledges with views south and east, and moderate climbing leads to the jct. with Schoodic Head Trail. From this point, it is a short distance to the right to the top of Schoodic Head via Schoodic Head Trail.

SEC 10

BUCK COVE MTN. (224 FT.) AND BIRCH HARBOR MTN. (371 FT.)

These low, mostly wooded peaks rise north of Schoodic Head and west of Schoodic Harbor. They can be reached from either Schoodic Head or Schoodic Woods CG. A popular way to make a long day hike via Buck

Cove Mtn. and Birch Harbor Mtn. is to leave a car at Schoodic Woods CG (at the information center or the trailhead parking lot 0.5 mi. beyond) and either drive a second car to Blueberry Hill Picnic Area or, in season, ride the Island Explorer bus. Then hike Anvil Trail or Alder Trail northbound to join Buck Cove Mtn. Trail near the summit of Schoodic Head. Buck Cove Mtn. Trail is therefore described from Schoodic Head north.

BUCK COVE MTN. TRAIL (AMC SCHOODIC PENINSULA MAP)
NPS rating: moderate
Cumulative from start of Buck Cove Mtn. Trail on Schoodic Head (440 ft.) to:

Buck Cove Mtn. (224 ft.)	1.0 mi.	75 ft.	0:30
Birch Mtn. high point (340 ft.)	2.8 mi.	387 ft.	1:35
Schoodic Woods CG trailhead parking (230 ft.)	3.1 mi.	387 ft.	1:45

NPS From its start, just north of the summit of Schoodic Head, follow Buck Cove Mtn. Trail down the north slope of Schoodic Head. In 0.5 mi., pass through the old (pre-2015) NPS boundary. Ahead, view windows open up to the east. Cross an old skidder trail and make a long, rising traverse to the semi-open woods on top of Buck Cove Mtn. Beyond, switchback down to traverse bog bridges over a marshy flow and then cross a bike path (Schoodic Woods CG is 1.8 mi. west on the bike path). A gentle climb leads to a ridgeline of semi-open woods with views south to Schoodic Head and east to Pigeon Hill. Descend the north side of the unnamed knoll. Soon, Buck Cove Mtn. Trail again crosses a bike path (a sign indicates that Schoodic Woods CG is 1.0 mi. west on this bike path), rounds the east side of a hill, and then climbs northwest up a narrow valley. Pass next to a cliff wall to reach easy terrain on the south slope of Birch Harbor Mtn. Cross a bike path, crest the wooded high point (340 ft.) on Birch Harbor Mtn., and soon recross the bike path. Reach the trailhead parking area at 3.1 mi. from Schoodic Head. The area is at a cul-de-sac 0.5 mi. via road or paved walkway from the Schoodic Woods CG information center, just beyond the group campsites.

ISLE AU HAUT
DUCK HARBOR TRAIL (AMC ISLE AU HAUT MAP)
NPS rating: moderate
Cumulative from park ranger station (50 ft.) near town landing to:

Bowditch Trail (80 ft.)	1.3 mi.	180 ft.	0:45
Duck Harbor and unpaved road (35 ft.)	3.5 mi.	360 ft.	1:55
Duck Harbor CG (20 ft.)	4.2 mi.	360 ft.	2:15

NPS This major north–south connector trail provides access to Duck Harbor CG and the system of trails on the southern end of Isle au Haut, plus

SEC 10

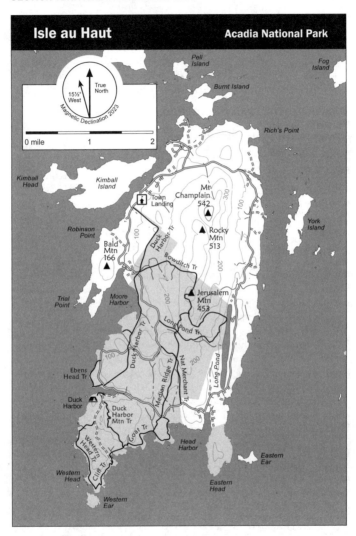

Isle au Haut

Acadia National Park

Pell Island

Fog Island

Burnt Island

True North

15½° West

Magnetic Declination 2023

0 mile 1 2

Rich's Point

Kimball Head

Kimball Island

Town Landing

Mt Champlain 542

York Island

Robinson Point

Rocky Mtn 513

Bald Mtn 166

Duck Harbor Tr

Bowditch Tr

Trial Point

Moore Harbor

Jerusalem Mtn 453

Long Pond Tr

Ebens Head Tr

Duck Harbor Tr

Median Ridge Tr

Nat Merchant Tr

Long Pond

Duck Harbor

Duck Harbor Mtn Tr

Goat Tr

Head Harbor

Eastern Ear

Western Head Tr

Cliff Tr

Western Head

Eastern Head

Western Ear

Bowditch Trail along the way. Duck Harbor Trail begins at the park ranger station on the northwest side of the island, 0.25 mi. south of the Isle au Haut town landing via a paved portion of the island's main ring road. Information, a posted map, potable water, and a toilet are available at the ranger station.

Duck Harbor Trail leaves the ranger station, heads east through the woods for 0.5 mi., and then trends southwest over several minor rocky humps. At 1.0 mi., turn left at a trail sign. Beyond, follow a footbridge over a brook and quickly reach the jct. with Bowditch Trail, which leaves to the left. Bear right to continue on Duck Harbor Trail. At 1.4 mi., walk across the unpaved road. After crossing a small brook, reach Moore Harbor and follow it closely for the next 0.3 mi. Then leave the cobble beach, cross another small brook, and pass an NPS ranger cabin in the woods uphill on the left. Follow the boardwalk to the right and then trend away from the shoreline and enter a thick stand of young spruce. At 2.5 mi., a short side path leaves right to Deep Cove; stay straight. Beyond the Deep Cove side path, traverse a brook, climb a rise, and walk across the unpaved road again. Level off and follow the ridgeline, scampering over a rocky knoll. At 3.5 mi., Duck Harbor Trail ends at the unpaved road on the north side of Duck Harbor.

To reach Duck Harbor CG, continue left (east) on the unpaved road for 0.5 mi. to Western Head Rd. Turn right onto Western Head Rd. and follow it for 0.25 mi., passing a hand-operated water pump (the water source for the campground), to a kiosk and toilet. Here, Western Head Rd. bears uphill to the left (leads to Duck Harbor Mtn. Trail and Western Head Trail and, at the road's end, to Cliff Trail and Goat Trail). Continue along the shore to the picnic tables and a kiosk adjacent to the Duck Harbor boat landing. The five shelters of Duck Harbor CG are just uphill from the water, each tucked into a mostly secluded spot.

WESTERN HEAD TRAIL (AMC ISLE AU HAUT MAP)
NPS rating: moderate
Cumulative from Western Head Rd. at Duck Harbor CG (20 ft.) to:

Western Head Trail (90 ft.)	0.5 mi.	70 ft.	0:15
Cliff Trail (35 ft.)	1.9 mi.	145 ft.	1:00

SEC 10

NPS This trail follows the western shore of Western Head and offers impressive clifftop views of Isle au Haut Bay, the Gulf of Maine, and the island of Western Ear. Combined with Cliff Trail and Western Head Rd., the trail makes a loop around Western Head.

From the kiosk and toilet near the end of the walk into Duck Harbor CG, turn uphill on Western Head Rd., a wide, grassy track. Pass a shed on the right and bear left at a fork. In 0.1 mi., Duck Harbor Mtn. Trail departs left. At 0.45 mi., Western Head Trail leaves to the right. At 0.8 mi., the trail reaches the western shore of Isle au Haut and turns south along the Gulf of Maine. The vista west includes the island of Vinalhaven and the Camden Hills. Reach a cobble beach and follow it for a stretch as Western Head Trail continues along the coast, ascending and descending between rocky headlands and cobble beaches for most of the next mile. The trail eventually jogs inland, traverses a shallow ravine, passes low cliff walls (views offshore to Western Ear), and then negotiates a dark, mossy wet area. At 1.9 mi., Western Head Trail ends at the jct. with Cliff Trail and a 0.1-mi. spur out to the gut (channel) separating Isle au Haut from the island of Western Ear. From this jct., it is 0.7 mi. north to Western Head Rd., which leads 1.1 mi. back to Duck Harbor CG.

CLIFF TRAIL (AMC ISLE AU HAUT MAP)
NPS rating: moderate
Cumulative from Western Head Trail (35 ft.) to:

Western Head Rd. (45 ft.)	0.7 mi.	120 ft.	0:25
Goat Trail (35 ft.)	0.8 mi.	120 ft.	0:30

NPS Cliff Trail connects the southern end of Western Head Trail with Western Head Rd. and Goat Trail. From its jct. with Western Head Trail near Western Ear, Cliff Trail heads north through the woods to emerge on a pocket beach. Leave the beach, pass a cliff wall, and climb over a low ridge to a rocky beach, where Eastern Head is visible to the east. Hike along the margin of the shore, alternating between the woods and the rocks. Cross a gully and make a short, steep climb out. With white cliffs in sight ahead, cross another gully and ascend a steep, rocky section. Descend wooden steps into yet another gully. At 0.7 mi., reach Western Head Rd. Turn left here, and in another 0.1 mi., reach the jct. with Goat Trail, which leaves right. Straight ahead on Western Head Rd., it is 1.0 mi. to Duck Harbor CG.

GOAT TRAIL (AMC ISLE AU HAUT MAP)
NPS rating: moderate
From Western Head Rd. (35 ft.) to:

Duck Harbor Mtn. Trail (20 ft.)	0.3 mi.	35 ft.	0:10
Median Ridge Trail, lower jct. (15 ft.)	1.2 mi.	165 ft.	0:40
Main dirt road near Median Ridge Trail, upper jct. (45 ft.)	2.0 mi.	235 ft.	1:10

SEC
10

NPS Goat Trail connects Western Head Rd. and Cliff Trail with Median Ridge Trail and the unpaved road that partially rings Isle au Haut. Goat Trail closely follows the craggy shoreline and offers stunning views of Deep Cove, Squeaker Cove, Barred Harbor, Merchant Cove, Head Harbor, and Eastern Head. From Western Head Trail, Goat Trail soon crosses a small brook and reaches Squeaker Cove and a jct. at 0.3 mi. To the right, a spur leads to a cobble beach. Duck Harbor Mtn. Trail departs to the left. Continuing straight, Goat Trail makes a short climb, drops to a small brook, and traverses exposed headland. At 0.7 mi., the trail swings inland through a swath of dead and dying spruce and fir and then through a thick understory of young spruce. Goat Trail reaches the big arc of cobble beach at Barred Harbor at 1.0 mi.; at 1.2 mi., Median Ridge Trail leaves left from the head of the large cove. Goat Trail crosses Merchant Point to reach the head of Merchant Cove at 1.7 mi. At 1.9 mi., a trail sign reads "Merchant Cove." Goat Trail heads inland from this point, and after crossing a series of bog bridges, reaches the unpaved road at 2.0 mi. Turn left and walk the unpaved road west for 200 ft. to intersect Median Ridge Trail. From this point, it is 1.1 mi. west via the unpaved road to Duck Harbor CG.

MEDIAN RIDGE TRAIL (AMC ISLE AU HAUT MAP)
NPS rating: moderate
Cumulative from Goat Trail (15 ft.) to:

Main dirt road (45 ft.)	0.3 mi.	30 ft.	0:10
Nat Merchant Trail (185 ft.)	1.3 mi.	170 ft.	0:45
Long Pond Trail (200 ft.)	1.8 mi.	295 ft.	1:05

NPS Median Ridge Trail connects Goat Trail near Merchant Cove to Long Pond Trail at a point just south of Bowditch Mtn. Median Ridge Trail departs Goat Trail and in 0.3 mi. crosses the unpaved road. From here, Median Ridge Trail climbs to a rocky ridge and then contours along the east side of the ridge through a semi-open forest of pines. After a short pitch down, the trail continues to contour across the slope, with a rocky knob up to the left. Cross a small stream, the source of Merchant Brook, at 1.2 mi. At 1.3 mi., reach a 4-way intersection with Nat Merchant Trail, which goes east and west from this point. Continuing on Median Ridge Trail, gain a ridge at 1.6 mi. and then trend easily down, passing a natural rock seat and a view to Bowditch Mtn. Make a moderate descent into a ravine and, immediately after a small stream, turn sharply right to reach the jct. with Long Pond Trail. From this jct., Long Pond Trail loops over Bowditch Mtn., drops to Long Pond, climbs back

SEC
10

to this jct., and heads east to end at the unpaved road, 2.5 mi. south of the Isle au Haut town landing.

NAT MERCHANT TRAIL (AMC ISLE AU HAUT MAP)
NPS rating: moderate
Cumulative from main dirt road (205 ft.) to:

Median Ridge Trail (185 ft.)	0.4 mi.	25 ft.	0:10
Main dirt road (55 ft.)	1.1 mi.	25 ft.	0:35

NPS Nat Merchant Trail cuts across Isle du Haut from its start on the island's unpaved road 2.9 mi. south of the Isle au Haut town landing. It intersects Median Ridge Trail and ends at the unpaved road 1.2 mi. east of the Western Head Rd. entrance to Duck Harbor CG. From its starting point, the trail climbs gently to a ridge and heads along it before trending down to intersect Median Ridge Trail at 0.4 mi. Ahead on Nat Merchant Trail, follow contours through a dark, thick stretch of young spruce. Beyond, the trail makes its way down the valley of Merchant Brook and levels out to traverse a wet area. At 1.1 mi., Nat Merchant Trail emerges on the unpaved road. Hikers can hear the ocean at Merchant Cove from this point.

JERUSALEM MTN. (505 FT.)
This wooded ridgeline rises roughly in the center of Isle au Haut, just south of ANP's northern boundary line. Bowditch Trail and Long Pond Trail are ascent routes.

BOWDITCH TRAIL (AMC ISLE AU HAUT MAP)
NPS rating: moderate
From Duck Harbor Trail (80 ft.) to:

Long Pond Trail on Bowditch Mtn. (400 ft.)	2.0 mi.	510 ft.	1:15

NPS This route connects Duck Harbor Trail and Long Pond Trail on Bowditch Mtn. Bowditch Trail diverges from Duck Harbor Trail just 300 ft. east of the unpaved road at a point 1.35 mi. south of the ANP ranger station. Bowditch Trail heads east, skirts a bog to the right, and crosses bog bridges over a marshy area. After a corridor of young spruce, the trail follows more bog bridges and then ascends the west slope of Jerusalem Mtn. At 1.0 mi., it passes a park boundary post. At a high point on the mountain, the old Bowditch Trail goes left into the bushes. The current Bowditch Trail passes another ANP boundary post at 1.2 mi. Continuing now to the south, Bowditch Trail follows the ridgeline, skirts the true summit of Jerusalem Mtn., and ends at the intersection with Long Pond Trail.

SEC 10

LONG POND TRAIL (AMC ISLE AU HAUT MAP)
NPS rating: strenuous
Cumulative from main dirt road (145 ft.) to:

Median Ridge Trail (200 ft.)	0.4 mi.	55 ft.	0:15
Bowditch Trail (400 ft.)	0.9 mi.	255 ft.	0:35
Long Pond (16 ft.)	1.9 mi.	265 ft.	1:05
Complete loop	3.5 mi.	515 ft.	2:00

NPS While Long Pond Trail is relatively easy at the start of this loop hike, the change of elevation becomes more pronounced along the way. Despite the strenuous climb of Bowditch Mtn., this trail offers attractive views of Long Pond, the largest pond on Isle au Haut, as well as access to Bowditch Trail and Median Ridge Trail. Long Pond Trail begins from the unpaved road, 2.5 mi. south of the Isle au Haut town landing. It heads east along the north edge of a cedar swamp and reaches the jct. with Median Ridge Trail (departs to the right) at 0.4 mi.

Turn left at the jct. to follow the lollipop loop of Long Pond Trail in a clockwise direction. Ascend through a parklike forest of birch and spruce. At 0.9 mi., high on Jerusalem Mtn., reach the jct. with Bowditch Trail, which enters from the left. Stay right to remain on Long Pond Trail, which drops down the east slope, levels off, and crosses to the next ridge. After a short descent, it follows the long ridge on a contour through semi-open forest. A rocky, washboard stretch of treadway leads to a footbridge over a chasm at 1.7 mi. Beyond, descend more steeply via switchbacks to reach the shore of long, narrow, and deep Long Pond at 1.9 mi. After heading south 100 ft. next to the pond, the trail climbs up and away. Cross a rocky ravine at 2.2 mi. Stone walls appear along the route at 2.4 mi. At a trail sign, old foundation stones and a well are 75 ft. to the left. In the woods at 2.7 mi., cross a field of cobblestone-sized rocks. Ahead, pass to the right of a bog, and after an easy stretch, make a short, moderate descent to the Long Pond Trail loop jct. at 3.1 mi. From this point, it is 0.4 mi. west to the main dirt road, the original trailhead.

DUCK HARBOR MTN. (309 FT.)

The long, steep, and craggy ridgeline of Duck Harbor Mtn., which links Duck Harbor CG with Goat Trail at Squeaker Cove, presents the most strenuous challenge of any of the locations on Isle au Haut. Duck Harbor Mtn. Trail can be combined with Western Head Rd. for a scenic loop hike, among several other possible combinations.

SEC 10

DUCK HARBOR MTN. TRAIL (AMC ISLE AU HAUT MAP)
NPS rating: strenuous
Cumulative from Western Head Rd. at Duck Harbor CG (20 ft.) to:

Duck Harbor Mtn. Trail (75 ft.)	0.1 mi.	55 ft.	0:05
Duck Harbor Mtn. summit (309 ft.)	0.5 mi.	289 ft.	0:25
Goat Trail (15 ft.)	1.2 mi.	365 ft.	0:50

NPS From the kiosk and toilet near the end of the walk into Duck Harbor CG, turn uphill on Western Head Rd., a wide, grassy track. Pass a shed on the right and bear left at a fork. In 0.1 mi., Duck Harbor Mtn. Trail departs left. Climb steeply over rocks to an outlook featuring Duck Harbor. At 0.2 mi., reach a rocky knob (more views). After a brief level stretch, climb a second steep pitch and scramble over more rocky knobs. At 0.4 mi., reach the top of Duck Harbor Mtn. The trail continues east along the spine of the mountain, descends a difficult rock step, climbs down another rock step, and then passes through a rock crevice. Ahead, a short pitch leads up to the first of a series of rocky knobs known as the Puddings. After several tricky rock steps, a spur on the right leads to a pinnacle and excellent views east to Eastern Head. Continue down the rocky ridge to meet Goat Trail at Squeaker Cove at 1.1 mi. To the left, Goat Trail heads north 1.7 mi. to Median Ridge Trail and the main dirt road. To the right, Goat Trail joins Western Head Rd. near Cliff Trail in 0.3 mi.

SECTION ELEVEN

DOWNEAST

In-Text Map
Donnell Pond Public Lands   547

SEC 11

INTRODUCTION

This section describes 79 trails on 40 mountains in Maine's Downeast region, which includes all of Hancock County (except for MDI and ANP) and all of neighboring Washington County in eastern Maine, a total land area of a little more than 4,000 sq mi. The southern part of the Downeast region encompasses the rugged, rocky coastline along the Gulf of Maine and many islands large and small, as well as scattered, low, craggy hills; wooded bumps; and steep headlands. Amid the extensive wild blueberry barrens that range across the central interior are several jumbles of rugged mountains with peaks reaching to elevations a little higher than 1,000 ft. The northern interior is the lowland home to many large lakes and miles of streams. A number of major rivers have their sources here and flow south to meet the Atlantic Ocean. Isolated hills with sweeping southern cliff faces dot the landscape, with the occasional mountain. One lone summit tops out at more than 1,400 ft.

GEOGRAPHY

The Downeast region extends from the Penobscot River and Penobscot Bay in the west to the Chiputneticook lakes, the St. Croix River, and Passamaquoddy Bay (on the border with New Brunswick, Canada) in the east. To the north, the Hancock and Washington county lines meet with the Aroostook and Penobscot county lines in a generally southwest to northeast direction.

The name "Downeast" broadly refers to the Maine coast from Penobscot Bay to the border of New Brunswick, Canada. The term originated in the early sailing days of New England, when ships from Boston sailed east to ports in Maine. With the prevailing winds at their sterns during this leg of the journey, the ships were sailing downwind; hence, they were said to be heading "down east." Thanks to its geography, the Downeast region has the honor of seeing first sunrise in the country at West Quoddy Head for a few weeks around the fall and spring equinoxes.

South of US 1, between Penobscot Bay in Maine and Campobello Island in New Brunswick, Canada, the Downeast coastline is characterized by a variety of wide, forested headlands or peninsulas interspersed with a series of large bays and a handful of spruce-studded islands. East of Penobscot Bay is Blue Hill Peninsula and Deer Isle, Blue Hill Bay, and Frenchman Bay. At Cape Rosier, Backwood Mtn. (286 ft.) rises out of the woods near Holbrook Island. Peeking up west of Orcutt Harbor is John B. Mtn. (251 ft.). Low, rugged Pine Hill (51 ft.) looks out over the northern tip of Little Deer Isle just south of Eggemoggin Reach. Blue Hill Mtn. (935 ft.) affords fine views over the town of Blue Hill to its namesake bay.

Beyond Schoodic Peninsula are Gouldsboro Bay and Dyer Neck, then Dyer Bay and Petit Manan Point, followed by Pigeon Hill Bay. North of Sullivan Harbor is Baker Hill (373 ft.). The craggy dome of Pigeon Hill

SEC
11

(315 ft.) offers a commanding view over Petit Manan National Wildlife Refuge. Narraguagus and Pleasant bays are south of Milbridge, Harrington, and Addison. Jonesport and Beals separate Wohoa Bay and Chandler Bay. Englishman Bay is south of Roque Bluffs. Machias Bay is the last great bay before the Bold Coast, a rugged stretch of precipitous headland leading to West Quoddy Head and its lighthouse at Lubec, the easternmost point in the United States. In isolated Lubec, Benny's Mtn. (226 ft.) overlooks Hamilton Cove; Estey Mtn. (274 ft.) looks out over the Orange River; and Klondike Mtn. (146 ft.) rises above South Bay. Mowes Mtn. (130 ft.), also in Lubec, is a hillock between Whiting Bay and Straight Bay. At Cobscook Bay State Park, tremendous ocean tides range from 12 to 26 feet, some of the greatest in the world. Attractive lookout points here include Littles Mtn. (203 ft.) and Cunningham Mtn. (161 ft.). Neighboring Bell's Mtn. (232 ft.) and Crane Mtn. (304 ft.) loom over Tide Mill Farm on Whiting Bay.

The Downeast interior between the Penobscot River and Passamaquoddy Bay is bounded by US 1 in the south and ME 9 in the north. East of Verona Island from Bucksport to ME 193, the blueberry barrens harbor several substantial freshwater lakes and ponds, as well as a jumble of low hills and mountains. Significant here is the 5,000-acre Great Pond Mtn. Wildlands, home to Great Pond Mtn. (1,009 ft.) and its massive south-facing cliffs: Mead Mtn. (662 ft.), Flying Moose Mtn. (898 ft.), Oak Hill (824 ft.), and Flag Hill (940 ft.). Just north is Bald Mtn. (1,237 ft.) in Dedham, its slopes a former ski area. South of ME 9, Blackcap Mtn. (1,026 ft.) and Woodchuck Hill (837 ft.) share a trailhead at Fitts Pond. Eagle Bluff (701 ft.) is a local crag popular with both hikers and rock climbers.

Donnell Pond PL lies between Franklin and Cherryfield; at more than 15,000 acres, it is the second-largest chunk of publicly owned land in the Downeast region. Trails climb to a small cluster of bare granite summits, including Schoodic Mtn. (1,079 ft.), Black Mtn. (1,099 ft.), Caribou Mtn. (970 ft.), and Tunk Mtn. (1,157 ft.). Donnell Pond, Tunk Lake, and the "hidden ponds" of Mud, Salmon, and Little Long, among others, are at the feet of these rugged peaks. Just east in Cherryfield is bald-topped Young Tunk Mtn. (544 ft.).

The northern reaches of the Downeast region, from ME 9 north to ME 6 and east to US 1, are dominated by vast swaths of commercial timberland and a string of large lakes. Four major rivers—Machias, Union, Narraguagus, and Pleasant—flow from these woods. Near Bangor, views of ANP abound from the great cliffs of Chick Hill (1,155 ft.) and Little Chick Hill

(914 ft.). Bald Bluff Mtn. (1,028 ft.) is the high point in Amherst Mountains Community Forest. The summits of Lead Mtn. (1,477 ft.) and Pocomoonshine Mtn. (613 ft.) are former fire tower sites. Wabassus Mtn. (843 ft.) is a wooded peak just west of Grand Lake Stream. The twin peaks of the Pineo Mountains (802 ft.) look out over the extensive waters of West Grand Lake. The long ridgeline of Passadumkeag Mtn. (1,470 ft.) in Grand Falls Township (in Penobscot County), also a former fire tower site, is now home to a windpower project.

Farther Downeast, close to Calais, is federally owned Moosehorn National Wildlife Refuge, the largest public reserve in the Downeast region, with 29,000 acres of wildlife habitat and designated wilderness. Trails lead to the site of an old fire tower atop Bald Mtn. (405 ft.) and to Magurrewock Mtn. (393 ft.), overlooking Magurrewock Marsh. Just east of Moosehorn, Devil's Head (355 ft.) rises precipitously from the banks of the St. Croix River.

ROAD ACCESS

Two major highways cross the Downeast region from west to east. US 1 winds along the coast to connect Bucksport with Calais, providing access to trails along that corridor and to peninsulas to the south. ME 9 slices through the northern interior and links Bangor with Calais, offering access to trails along that corridor and to the north. US 1A is the major route between Bangor and Ellsworth; ME 3 connects Bucksport to Ellsworth; and ME 46 connects Eddington with Bucksport. Several trailheads are along these roads. From west to east across Downeast, a number of north–south roads connect ME 9 with US 1. These include ME 180, ME 181, ME 179, ME 193, ME 192, and ME 191. ME 182 links Franklin with Cherryfield. ME 191 and ME 189 both wind eastward to far Downeast trailheads.

CAMPING

Drive-in camping, complete with restrooms and showers, is available at Cobscook Bay and Lamoine state parks. Primitive frontcountry campsites are available in the Machias River Corridor, while backcountry campers will find primitive sites at Donnell Pond and Cutler Coast public lands. Nineteen privately operated campgrounds are also available. Limited primitive walk-in camping is at Huckins Beach and Trail, part of Cobscook Shores, a Maine charitable foundation that owns and manages a system of parklands for public recreation in Lubec.

SEC
11

SUGGESTED HIKES

■ Easy

BALD MTN. (IN DEDHAM)

RT via Bald Mtn. Trail	1.0 mi.	537 ft.	1:00

Climb over bare granite slabs to ledge outlooks with beautiful views, from Phillips Lake to the mountains of Acadia. See Bald Mtn. Trail, p. 533.

JOHN B. MTN.

LP via John B. Mtn. Trail and Old School House Rd.	1.1 mi.	230 ft.	0:40

Journey through spruce woods to ledges looking out over Orcutt Harbor and Eggemoggin Reach. See John B. Mtn. Trail and Old School House Rd., p. 537.

EAGLE BLUFF

RT via Eagle Bluff Trail	1.1 mi.	340 ft.	0:50

From the top of this impressive cliff face, a favorite of local rock climbers, enjoy airy views over Cedar Swamp Pond to Lead Mtn., Chick Hill, and the peaks of Acadia. See Eagle Bluff Trail, p. 542.

BAKER HILL

LP via Baker Hill Loop Trail	1.1 mi.	235 ft.	0:40

Make a short loop on this hill to ledges offering sights of Sullivan Harbor, Frenchman Bay, and beyond to the peaks of Acadia. See Baker Hill Loop Trail, p. 556.

PIGEON HILL

SEC 11

LP via Historic Trail, Summit Loop Trail, and Silver Mine Trail	1.1 mi.	265 ft.	0:45

The summit ledges of this craggy dome offer extraordinary vistas over Dyer Bay, Pigeon Hill Bay, and far beyond along this scenic stretch of Downeast coast. To begin, see Historic Trail, p. 559.

KLONDIKE MTN.

	↴↑	↗	↻
LP via Klondike Mtn. Trail	0.7 mi.	175 ft.	0:25

This little bump in Lubec offers grand panoramas over South Bay and beyond from its bare summit. See Klondike Mtn. Trail, p. 562.

■ Moderate
GREAT POND MTN.

	↴↑	↗	↻
RT via Stuart Gross Trail	3.3 mi.	700 ft.	2:00

Visit the Great Pond Mtn. Wildlands and climb the namesake mountain to sweeping summit cliffs and broad views that take in the mountains of Acadia, Blue Hill, Penobscot Bay, and the Camden Hills. See Stuart Gross Trail, p. 528.

BLUE HILL MTN.

	↴↑	↗	↻
RT via Tower Service Trail and Hayes Trail	2.2 mi.	535 ft.	1:20

For impressive scenery featuring the village of Blue Hill, the bay beyond, and the mountain peaks of Mt. Desert Island, summit this beautiful coastal monadnock. To begin, see Tower Service Trail, p. 535.

SCHOODIC MTN.

	↴↑	↗	↻
RT via Schoodic Mtn. Trail	2.6 mi.	960 ft.	1:50

This popular mountain provides attractive views of MDI and Frenchman Bay, with a pit stop at Donnell Pond's gorgeous Schoodic Beach. See Schoodic Mtn. Trail, p. 546.

BLACK MTN.

	↴↑	↗	↻
LP via Big Chief Trail, Black Mtn. Summit Trail, and Black Mtn.–Big Chief Connector	2.6 mi.	730 ft.	1:50

Hike to Wizard Pond and continue to the pink granite ledges atop Black Mtn. To begin, see Big Chief Trail, p. 550.

TUNK MTN.

RT via Tunk Mtn. Trail	3.8 mi.	930 ft.	3:00

Pass several small ponds en route to the extensive cliffs on Tunk Mtn.'s southwestern ridgeline and pleasant views over Spring River Lake and Tunk Lake. See Tunk Mtn. Trail, p. 553.

DEVIL'S HEAD

LP via Devil's Head Trail and access road	1.7 mi.	485 ft.	1:05

Enjoy dramatic vistas of the St. Croix River and St. Croix Island—and across to New Brunswick, Canada—from this riverside bluff. To begin, see Devil's Head Trail, p. 570.

■ Strenuous
FLYING MOOSE MTN.

RT via Valley Rd., Flying Moose Tote Rd., and Flying Moose Trail	5.2 mi.	820 ft.	3:00

Top out on a sweeping cliff face for a scenic panorama ranging from the peaks of Donnell Pond PL and Branch Lake to the summits of ANP on MDI. To begin, see Flying Moose Mtn. from North Trailhead, p. 533.

CARIBOU LOOP

LP via Caribou Mtn. Trail and Caribou Loop Trail	7.7 mi.	2,130 ft.	5:10

Tackle this rugged hike through the remote backcountry of Donnell Pond PL, taking in the craggy summit ledges of Caribou Mtn. and Black Mtn. along the way. To begin, see Caribou Mtn. Trail, p. 551.

SCHOODIC CONNECTOR

OW via Schoodic Connector Trail and Schoodic Mtn. Trail	7.7 mi.	1,370 ft.	4:30

This long, interesting trek links several Frenchman Bay Conservancy properties with Donnell Pond PL, from the ledges on Baker Hill to the pink granite summit of Schoodic Mtn. To begin, see Schoodic Connector Trail, p. 556.

TRAIL DESCRIPTIONS

GREAT POND MTN. WILDLANDS AND VICINITY

The Great Pond Mtn. Wildlands in Orland and Bucksport is owned by Great Pond Mtn. Conservation Trust and managed for wildlife habitat, forestry, and low-impact recreation. The Wildlands encompass 5,000 beautiful acres of forests and streams ringed by mountain peaks across three adjacent tracts of land. Miles of old gravel roads wind through the property, remnants of logging in years past, but vehicular travel is limited to 0.9-mi. Valley Rd. Primary access is from South Trailhead on US 1/ME 3; it is open from sunrise to sunset on weekends only from mid-June through October. Outside these times, visitors must park outside the gate and enter on foot, bicycle, or horseback (or skis and snowshoes in winter). Other access points to the Wildlands include North Trailhead, Dead River Gateway, and Mountain Trailhead (to Great Pond Mtn. via Stuart Gross Trail).

A growing system of hiking trails lead to specific destinations: to Great Pond Mtn., which rises to more than 1,000 ft. in the Dead River section; and to Flag Hill, Oak Hill, Flying Moose Mtn., and Mead Mtn., in the Hothole Valley section. New trails will soon be added to Condon Hill and Hothole Mtn., with access from North Trailhead. Several mountain-bike trails are also open to hikers. The 1,100-acre area north of Mitchville CS and west of Valley Rd. is managed primarily for wildlife habitat; foot traffic is welcome in this specific area but dogs are not.

To reach South Trailhead: From downtown Ellsworth, travel west on US 1/ME 3 for 10.9 mi. From the jct. of US 1/ME 3 and ME 15 in downtown Bucksport, drive east on US 1/ME 3 for 8.4 mi. The South Trailhead parking area and gate are on the north side of the highway.

To reach North Trailhead: From South Trailhead on US 1 in Orland, drive west on US 1 for 5.4 mi. to the jct. of US 1 and Upper Falls Rd. Turn right (north) onto Upper Falls Rd. In 1.8 mi., Upper Falls Rd. becomes Mast Hill Rd. (Duck Cove Rd. enters from the left here.) In another 2.1 mi., turn right onto Bald Mtn. Rd. and drive 1.8 mi. to a fork; bear right at the fork and continue 1.1 mi. to North Trailhead (gate) on the right. Trailhead parking is just beyond, also on the right.

SEC 11

GREAT POND MTN. (1,009 FT.)

This mountain, the central natural feature of the Wildlands, is known for the sweeping granite cliffs on its southeast face, which offer broad-ranging vistas that encompass ANP, Blue Hill Mtn., Penobscot Bay, and the Camden Hills. Stuart Gross Trail is the primary hiking access route.

From US 1/ME 3 in East Orland, 1.5 mi. east of the jct. of ME 15 and US 1/ME 3 in Orland, turn north onto Hatchery Rd. (sign for Craig Brook National Fish Hatchery). At 1.4 mi., pass through the fish hatchery complex. Just beyond, cross a bridge over Craig Brook and turn right, uphill, onto Don Fish Rd. Pass Dead River Gateway (access for Hay Ledges, Picnic, and Capstone multiuse trails) on the left and continue to trailhead parking on the right at 2.4 mi. from US 1/ME 3. Stuart Gross Trail and Connector Trail (a bike/hike trail with switchbacks) start across the road at the kiosk.

STUART GROSS TRAIL (USGS ORLAND QUAD, GPMCT WILDLANDS MAP, GAZETTEER MAP 23)
Cumulative from Don Fish Rd. (330 ft.) to:

Hay Ledges Trail (460 ft.)	0.3 mi.	130 ft.	0:10
Side trail to South Overlook (950 ft.)	1.2 mi.	620 ft.	0:55
Great Pond Mtn. summit (1,009 ft.) via Summit Loop, left fork	1.5 mi.	680 ft.	1:10

GPMCT Head up the rock steps to the kiosk. Soon after, Connector Trail leaves to the left. Bear right to stay on Stuart Gross Trail (blue markers), and soon cross a wooden footbridge over a gully. Beyond, climb easily up the slope using switchbacks, pass to the left of several large boulders, and reach a jct. where Hay Ledges Trail enters from the left. To continue to Great Pond Mtn., hike straight up on Stuart Gross Trail. After passing along mossy ledges, turn right to climb up through a crevice on rock steps. Follow a rising contour on the side of the ridge and then bear left to join a wide old jeep track. Turn right to continue on Stuart Gross Trail, quickly passing Capstone Trail on the right. The ascent via the old jeep road, in places worn down to bare rock, is easy on the long, gradual west ridge.

View windows begin to open on the right (south) side of the ridge, from the Camden Hills to Blue Hill Mtn. to the peaks in ANP; Alamoosook Lake lies below. With the summit of Great Pond Mtn. visible ahead, Stuart Gross Trail reenters the woods on the left. After a gullied section, the trail climbs a wide slab past a boulder on the right. Ahead, climb another slab and then make a long traverse to the right over sloping slabs, following blue blazes on the granite. The path then trends up and left with excellent vistas to the south.

Above, at a rock cairn, a side trail departs to the east, trending down and then left 0.15 mi. to the South Overlook above impressive cliffs on the south face of the mountain. Here, the outstanding panorama includes the peaks around Donnell Pond and, closer in, Mead Mtn., Oak Hill, and Flag Hill.

To reach the true summit, from the cairn, continue left on Stuart Gross Trail and up the wide-open granite slabs. At the next cairn, the trail forks into a loop that goes over the summit. Bear left to hike Summit Loop clockwise. The trail soon reaches an open slab where views to the peaks along the AT corridor far to the north are possible on a clear day, from Borestone Mtn. all the way over the 100MW to Katahdin.

From the overlook, continue gradually up to the right and then step up and move right to traverse a ledge top. After a stretch of mossy woods, cross a slab to reach the sign atop the wooded summit of Great Pond Mtn. Just beyond, enter the woods on the right and soon close Summit Loop at the cairn marker. Turn left to return to the trailhead via Stuart Gross Trail.

ESKER TRAIL (USGS ORLAND QUAD, GPMCT WILDLANDS MAP, GAZETTEER MAP 23)
Cumulative from South Trailhead (370 ft.) to:

Esker Trail (390 ft.)	0.1 mi.	20 ft.	0:03
Drumlin Trail (400 ft.)	0.9 mi.	60 ft.	0:25
Hillside Tote Rd. (410 ft.)	1.3 mi.	100 ft.	0:40

GPMCT When the gate at South Trailhead is closed, Esker Trail offers a foot-travel access route into the Wildlands to reach Oak Hill, Flag Hill, and Mead Mtn.

From South Trailhead on US 1/ME 3, hike north on Valley Rd. for 0.1 mi. to Esker Trail on the right. Leave Valley Rd. and take Esker Trail through a cutover site. Traverse bog bridges over a wet area and follow a small glacial esker through young hardwoods. Cross a brook and then meet Drumlin Trail coming in from the left (Drumlin Trail connects to Valley Rd. in 0.3 mi.). Pass several large glacial erratics on the left before reaching a viewpoint to Great Pond Mtn. Ahead, contour across the hillside to a second viewpoint and soon reach Hillside Trail, a grassy road, at 1.2 mi. To continue to Oak Hill, turn right and follow Hillside Trail uphill for 0.4 mi. to the jct. with Oak Hill Trail.

MEAD MTN. (662 FT.)

The summit of this mountain is just outside the southwestern boundary of the Hothole Valley section of the Wildlands, but Mead Mtn. Trail climbs to ledges high on its eastern flank for a look over Hothole Valley to the hills beyond and then returns to the valley via Mitchville CS.

**SEC
11**

MEAD MTN. LOOP TRAIL (USGS ORLAND QUAD, GPMCT WILDLANDS MAP, GAZETTEER MAP 23)
Cumulative from South Trailhead (370 ft.) to:

Mead Mtn. Loop Trail (150 ft.)	1.2 mi.	20 ft.	0:35
Mead Mtn. ledge viewpoint (580 ft.)	2.4 mi.	510 ft.	1:30
Mitchville CS (120 ft.)	3.3 mi.	510 ft.	1:55
Valley Rd. (150 ft.)	3.6 mi.	540 ft.	2:05
Return to South Trailhead (370 ft.)	4.9 mi.	780 ft.	2:50

GPMCT From South Trailhead on US 1/ME 3, hike north on Valley Rd. for 1.3 mi. to Mead Mtn. Loop Trail on the left. (*Note*: If the South Trailhead gate is open, hikers can drive to a parking area at 0.9 mi. and then walk or bike from there to the start of the trail.) Follow the trail west, crossing Hopkins Meadow Brook, climbing to a clearing, and then bearing right to reach the end of the old road. Enter the woods on the left and follow blue diamond markers easily uphill. Pass three lichen-covered erratics in succession and then bear right in a small clearing. Traverse a mossy outcropping (cairn) and descend to the right, down a natural rock step, to a viewpoint on the east ledges of the mountain. The scene includes Dedham Bald Mtn., Flying Moose Mtn., and Flag and Oak hills. Mead Mtn. Loop Trail then heads downhill through some very rocky terrain, with some rough footing, past Mitchville CS on Hothole Brook and back to Valley Rd. (look for signs).

BUMP HILL TRAIL (USGS ORLAND QUAD, GPMCT WILDLANDS MAP, GAZETTEER MAP 23)
Cumulative from South Trailhead (370 ft.) to:

Hothole Brook Tote Rd. via Valley Rd. (170 ft.)	2.6 mi.	70 ft.	1:20
Bump Hill Trail (110 ft.)	3.2 mi.	110 ft.	1:40
Bump Hill boulder viewpoints (180 ft.)	3.4 mi.	190 ft.	1:50
Return to South Trailhead (370 ft.)	6.9 mi.	480 ft.	3:40

GPMCT Bump Hill Trail offers fine sights west to Mead Mtn. and Great Pond Mtn. from several boulder viewpoints, which also reveal looks at Flag Hill, the peaks of ANP, and the mountains of Donnell Pond PL.

From South Trailhead on US 1/ME 3, hike or bike north on Valley Rd. At 2.4 mi. from the gate, a few yards down a side drive, find a toilet and picnic table on the left. At 2.6 mi. from the gate, reach Hothole Brook Tote Rd. on the left (kiosk and bench). (*Note*: If the South Trailhead gate is open, hikers can drive to a parking area at 0.9 mi. and then

SEC 11

walk or bike from there to the start of the trail.) Turn left to follow Hot-hole Brook Tote Rd. west. Proceed to a bridge over Hothole Brook and on to the end of the old road in a large clearing that features a pleasant view of Great Pond Mtn.

Take wide, grassy Bump Hill Trail on the left. At an old fork, stay right. Pass to the right of a boulder, and soon the path narrows and starts to climb. Reach the loop jct. and stay left to hike the loop clockwise. Weave through rocks to a large boulder and climb on top of it for great views of Mead Mtn. and Great Pond Mtn. From the base of the boulder, continue to the right for a second viewpoint west. Walk through woods to the third boulder viewpoint. Continue to the loop jct. and turn left to return to the start of Bump Hill Trail.

OAK HILL (824 FT.)

This twin-peaked hill straddles the eastern boundary of the Wildlands, with Oak Hill West within the bounds of the preserve. Vistas from the summit take in nearby Great Pond Mtn., Craig Pond, and Flag Hill, and range north to Katahdin. Access is via Esker Trail (or Valley Rd., if desired), Hillside Tote Rd., and Oak Hill Trail. Oak Hill Trail may also be used to reach Flag Hill to the north.

OAK HILL FROM SOUTH TRAILHEAD (USGS ORLAND QUAD, GPMCT WILDLANDS MAP, GAZETTEER MAP 23)
Cumulative from South Trailhead (370 ft.) to:

Esker Trail (390 ft.) via Valley Rd.	0.1 mi.	20 ft.	0:03
Hillside Tote Rd. (410 ft.)	1.3 mi.	100 ft.	0:40
Oak Hill Trail (610 ft.)	1.7 mi.	300 ft.	1:00
Oak Hill West summit (824 ft.)	2.0 mi.	515 ft.	1:15
Flag Hill Tote Rd. (550 ft.)	2.9 mi.	515 ft.	1:40

GPMCT From South Trailhead on US 1/ME 3, walk north on Valley Rd. for 0.1 mi. to Esker Trail on the right. Leave Valley Rd. and hike Esker Trail 1.1 mi. to Hillside Tote Rd. Turn right onto Hillside Tote Rd. and ascend to the jct. of Oak Hill Trail on the right. Turn onto Oak Hill Trail and climb the slope on switchbacks to reach a grassy meadow on the semi-open summit. The trail continues north across the summit plateau on a wide track. Beyond a clearing, begin a steady descent through the woods. Cross Flag Brook and then a small meadow to reach Flag Hill Tote Rd. To ascend Flag Hill, turn right onto Flag Hill Tote Rd. and proceed 0.4 mi. to Flag Hill Trail, which climbs to the top of Flag Hill in another 0.6 mi.

SEC 11

FLAG HILL (940 FT.)

This mountain on the eastern periphery of the Wildlands lies between Oak Hill to the south and Flying Moose Mtn. to the north. Excellent views ranging from ANP to Katahdin are possible from its summit ridge. Flag Hill can be approached from either North Trailhead or South Trailhead.

FLAG HILL FROM OAK HILL (USGS BRANCH LAKE QUAD, GPMCT WILDLANDS MAP, GAZETTEER MAP 23)
Cumulative from Flag Hill Tote Rd. (550 ft.) to:

Flag Hill Trail (630 ft.)	0.4 mi.	80 ft.	0:15
Flag Hill summit (940 ft.)	1.0 mi.	390 ft.	0:40

GPMCT From South Trailhead on US 1/ME 3, follow directions to Oak Hill (via either Esker Trail or Valley Rd.), Hillside Tote Rd., and then Oak Hill Trail, which climbs to the summit of Oak Hill and descends to meet Flag Hill Tote Rd. Turn right and follow Flag Hill Tote Rd. to its end, where Flag Hill Trail goes left. Turn onto Flag Hill Trail and climb moderately to the ridge, breaking out onto bare granite slabs with views south to ANP and east to Branch Lake. Follow cairns to the open summit. Just beyond, a short loop trail leads to views north and west all the way to Bigelow Mtn., Sugarloaf, and Katahdin.

FLAG HILL FROM NORTH TRAILHEAD (USGS ORLAND AND BRANCH LAKE QUADS, GPMCT WILDLANDS MAP, GAZETTEER MAP 23)
Cumulative from North Trailhead (370 ft.) to:

Flag Hill Tote Rd. (230 ft.)	2.1 mi.	40 ft.	1:00
Flag Hill Trail (630 ft.)	3.7 mi.	440 ft.	2:05
Flag Hill summit (940 ft.)	4.3 mi.	750 ft.	2:30
Return to North Trailhead (370 ft.)	8.6 mi.	890 ft.	4:45

GPMCT From North Trailhead on Bald Mtn. Rd., follow Valley Rd. 2.1 mi. south to Flag Hill Tote Rd. Turn left onto Flag Hill Tote Rd. and proceed 1.6 mi. to Flag Hill Trail. Climb moderately to the ridge, breaking out onto bare granite slabs with views south to ANP and east to Branch Lake. Follow cairns to the open summit. Just beyond, a short loop trail leads to views north and west all the way to Bigelow Mtn., Sugarloaf, and Katahdin. Retrace your steps to return to North Trailhead.

SEC 11

FLYING MOOSE MTN. (898 FT.)

This mountain in the northeast corner of the Wildlands features outstanding vistas south and west from the sweeping cliffs on its south face. Access is easiest from North Trailhead by way of Valley Rd., Flying Moose Tote Rd., and Flying Moose Trail.

FLYING MOOSE MTN. FROM NORTH TRAILHEAD (USGS ORLAND AND BRANCH LAKE QUADS, GPMCT WILDLANDS MAP, GAZETTEER MAP 23)
Cumulative from North Trailhead (370 ft.) to:

Flying Moose Tote Rd. (210 ft.) via Valley Rd.	1.6 mi.	–160 ft.	0:50
Flying Moose Trail (580 ft.)	2.3 mi.	370 ft.	1:20
Summit cliffs on Flying Moose Mtn. (870 ft.)	2.6 mi.	660 ft.	1:40
Return to North Trailhead (370 ft.)	5.2 mi.	820 ft.	3:00

GPMCT From North Trailhead on Bald Mtn. Rd., walk south on Valley Rd. for 1.3 mi. to the jct. of Flying Moose Tote Rd. on the left. Proceed on Flying Moose Tote Rd. to the start of Flying Moose Trail 0.6 mi. ahead. On the narrow footpath, climb over granite slabs, following blue blazes on the rock. As the trail gains elevation, vistas open up, including the Camden Hills and Blue Hill Mtn. Near the top, Flying Moose Trail bears right to its end at a sweeping cliff face with a scenic panorama ranging from the peaks of Donnell Pond PL and Branch Lake to ANP and, closer in, Flag Hill. A sign nearby indicates that this is the end of the trail. Please respect the private property beyond and go no farther.

BALD MTN. (IN DEDHAM; 1,237 FT.)
This mountain in Dedham, also known as Dedham Bald Mtn., is a short hike offering pleasant scenery for the effort. From the jct. of US 1A and ME 46 in East Holden, proceed south on US 1A and in 100 ft. turn right (south) onto Upper Dedham Rd. In 2.8 mi., turn left onto Bald Mtn. Rd. (fire station on left). At 6.2 mi. from US 1A, where the road bears right, continue straight on Johnson Rd. for 100 ft. Park on ledges to the left.

BALD MTN. TRAIL (USGS GREEN LAKE QUAD, GAZETTEER MAP 23)
From Johnson Rd. (700 ft.) to:

Bald Mtn. summit (1,237 ft.)	0.5 mi.	537 ft.	0:30

NFTM Bald Mtn. Trail, an old fire tower service road, is a direct route through open fields and over bare granite ledges to the top of the peak, where there are several communications towers. From here, clear views are possible to the north and northwest, while the nearby ledges on the north side of the mountain look out over Phillips Lake. The south side offers sights of the mountains on Mt. Desert Island, Blue Hill Mtn., and the Camden Hills.

SEC 11

BLUE HILL PENINSULA: DEER ISLE
BLUE HILL MTN. (935 FT.)

This coastal monadnock rises prominently just north of the picturesque town of Blue Hill and affords excellent views of Blue Hill Bay and beyond, from the mountains of ANP on Mt. Desert Island to the Camden Hills. The town of Blue Hill and Blue Hill Heritage Trust jointly manage nearly 500 acres of conservation land on the mountain and a network of six hiking trails. Two trailheads are on Mountain Rd. on the mountain's south side.

To reach Osgood Trail trailhead: From the jct. of ME 15 and ME 172/176 in the center of Blue Hill, drive north on ME 15 (Pleasant St.) for 0.9 mi. Turn right onto Mountain Rd. and proceed 0.5 mi. to the trailhead along the road on the right.

To reach Tower Service Trail trailhead: From the Osgood Trail trailhead, continue east on Mountain Rd. for 0.5 mi. to a large gravel parking lot on the right. This trailhead can also be reached from ME 172, which is 0.4 mi. east via Mountain Rd.

Becton Trail climbs Blue Hill Mtn. from the north at Turkey Farm Rd. From the center of Blue Hill at the intersection of ME 15 and ME 172/176 (Main St.), drive east on ME 172/176. In 0.2 mi., at the Y intersection of ME 172 and ME 176, bear left uphill on ME 172. At 1.4 mi., pass Mountain Rd. (trailheads for Hayes Trail and Osgood Trail are west along this road) on the left. Continue on ME 172, and at 2.2 mi., turn left onto Turkey Farm Rd. Proceed west to the trailhead parking lot on the left at 2.9 mi.

OSGOOD TRAIL (USGS BLUE HILL QUAD, BHHT BLUE HILL MTN. MAP, GAZETTEER MAP 15)
Cumulative from Mountain Rd. (360 ft.) to:

South Face Trail (620 ft.)	0.3 mi.	260 ft.	0:15
Becton Trail (860 ft.)	0.7 mi.	500 ft.	0:35
Blue Hill Mtn. summit (935 ft.)	0.9 mi.	575 ft.	0:45

BHHT On the north side of Mountain Rd., hike the wide, well-used trail into the woods to an information kiosk. Bear right and switchback easily up the mountain, following blue blazes. The way becomes steeper as Osgood Trail climbs rock steps to a jct. with South Face Trail on the right (contours 0.25 mi. east across the south face of the mountain to connect with Hayes Trail). Continue on Osgood Trail, crossing a footbridge over a small stream. Soon after a rough section of terrain (rocks and roots), the trail breaks out onto open slabs with views to the south. Ahead, it meets Becton Trail in a small clearing. Here, Osgood Trail turns right, climbs a short section of eroded treadway, and then proceeds easily along the summit ridge to the peak in an area of extensive open ledges. The summit is unmarked, but the concrete stanchions of the old fire tower (erected in 1949, removed in 2005) remain just below (big views southward), and a communications tower is to the left. Here also is the jct. with Hayes Trail, which enters from the east.

TOWER SERVICE TRAIL (USGS BLUE HILL QUAD, BHHT BLUE HILL MTN. MAP, GAZETTEER MAP 15)
Cumulative from Mountain Rd. (400 ft.) to:

Hayes Trail, lower jct. (540 ft.)	0.3 mi.	140 ft.	0:10
Hayes Trail, upper jct. (900 ft.)	1.0 mi.	500 ft.	0:45
Blue Hill summit (935 ft.) via Hayes Trail	1.1 mi.	535 ft.	0:50

BHHT Tower Service Trail begins on the north side of Mountain Rd. at a sign for Morse Farm on Blue Hill Mtn. Follow a grassy track across a large hayfield with the impressive scene ahead of the mountain and its communications tower. At the top of the field, reach the lower jct. with Hayes Trail, which departs left up a long set of rock steps. Here also are a map post and two granite benches.

Tower Service Trail follows a narrow jeep track originally built to service the summit tower, which provides a gradual ascent. From the jct. with Hayes Trail, Tower Service Trail bears right on the jeep track, which winds up the hill. Traverse west along a contour and climb more steeply to the summit ridge to reach the upper jct. with Hayes Trail (enters from the left). Continue west on Hayes Trail, pass behind the communications tower (no trespassing), and in 0.1 mi., reach the summit and view ledges.

HAYES TRAIL (USGS BLUE HILL QUAD, BHHT BLUE HILL MTN. MAP, GAZETTEER MAP 15)
Cumulative from Mountain Rd. (400 ft.) to:

Start of trail via Tower Service Trail (540 ft.)	0.3 mi.	140 ft.	0:10
South Face Trail (650 ft.)	0.4 mi.	250 ft.	0:15
Larry's Loop, lower jct. (875 ft.)	0.5 mi.	475 ft.	0:25
Tower Service Trail, upper jct. (900 ft.)	0.6 mi.	500 ft.	0:30
Blue Hill Mtn. summit (935 ft.)	0.7 mi.	535 ft.	0:35

BHHT Hayes Trail starts from the top of the hayfield 0.3 mi. from Mountain Rd., via Tower Service Trail. Bear left and climb a long set of rock stairs to reach the jct. with South Face Trail, which heads straight across the south face of Blue Hill Mtn. to join Osgood Trail in 0.25 mi. Turn right here to continue on Hayes Trail, which climbs rocky terrain at a

SEC
11

moderate grade on switchbacks. Ahead, make a long traverse west over ledges past a rock face, and then turn uphill on a steep, rocky scramble to a shelf just below the summit communications tower. Here, at the lower jct. with Larry's Loop, are excellent views southward. From the open ledges, enter the woods beyond and negotiate a stretch of boardwalk to reach the upper jct. with Tower Service Trail, which enters from the right. Turn left to continue easily along the summit ridge on Hayes Trail. Pass a side path on the left to the fenced-in tower complex (no trespassing) and join a wide track that soon turns sharply left. Hayes Trail emerges from the woods at the upper jct. of Larry's Loop and quickly arrives at the unsigned summit of Blue Hill Mtn.

Larry's Loop. This 0.2-mi. loop leads across spectacular open ledges high on the south face of Blue Hill Mtn. From Hayes Trail, just east of the summit, descend on Larry's Loop to open ledges and grand views to the south. Turn left into the trees and follow a contour, then drop steeply into a gully, cut across the slope, and continue to more open ledges. After a wooded stretch, walk under a power line to reach another section of superb open ledges before rejoining Hayes Trail.

South Face Trail. This 0.3-mi. connector links Hayes Trail and Osgood Trail, allowing the opportunity for a loop hike over the summit and eliminating the need to walk along Mountain Rd. The trail traverses the south face of the mountain and offers excellent scenery most of the way.

BECTON TRAIL (USGS BLUE HILL QUAD, BHHT BLUE HILL MTN. MAP, GAZETTEER MAP 15)
Cumulative from Turkey Farm Rd. (360 ft.) to:

Osgood Trail (860 ft.)	2.2 mi.	500 ft.	1:20
Blue Hill Mtn. summit (935 ft.) via Osgood Trail	2.4 mi.	575 ft.	1:25

BHHT From Turkey Farm Rd., follow Becton Trail westward over bog bridges into the forest, winding gradually downhill before leveling off. Beyond the bog bridges, climb easily and then more moderately up the north slope of the mountain. A long switchback leads to views north to Great Pond Mtn. High on the west ridge, Becton Trail ends at the jct. with Osgood Trail, which continues left to reach the summit of Blue Hill Mtn.

JOHN B. MTN. (251 FT.)

SEC 11

This little hill in Brooksville lies in the heart of 38 undeveloped acres, just west of Orcutt Harbor and north of Eggemoggin Reach and East Penobscot Bay, and provides attractive views from numerous outlooks. Hikers are urged to stay on the trail to protect the fragile mountaintop ecosystem. BHHT manages the land.

From the jct. of ME 15 and ME 172/176 in Blue Hill, drive west on ME 15/172/176. In 0.75 mi., ME 172 turns south (right); go straight to remain on ME 15/176 and proceed 4.25 mi. to Grays Corner. Turn left (south) onto ME 15/175 and go 2.7 mi. to Black Corner; then turn right onto ME 175 and drive 0.6 mi. to Brooksville. At this jct. of ME 175 and ME 176, stay straight on ME 176 and travel 3.9 mi. to Breezemere Rd. on the left. Drive 0.8 mi. on Breezemere Rd. to trailhead parking on the right (sign, kiosk).

JOHN B. MTN. TRAIL AND OLD SCHOOL HOUSE RD. (USGS CAPE ROSIER QUAD, BHHT JOHN B. MTN. MAP, GAZETTEER MAP 15)
Cumulative from Breezemere Rd. (25 ft.) to:

John B. Mtn. summit via summit loop (251 ft.)	0.3 mi.	230 ft.	0:15
Complete loop	1.1 mi.	230 ft.	0:40

BHHT From the parking area, blue-blazed John B. Mtn. Trail leaves to the right and quickly goes behind a cemetery. Switchback up the hillside at a moderate grade, passing rock ledges on the left, and climb a short step next to a knotted-rope handrail. On the ridge above, pass a letterbox on the right and, immediately ahead, reach a jct. Turn left to follow the 0.2-mi. summit loop, which leads over the summit to a stone bench and several outlooks with views to Orcutt Harbor, Deer Isle, and Isle au Haut.

Returning to John B. Mtn. Trail, turn left and quickly reach another jct. Both forks descend to rejoin at the base of the mountain, but the left fork is more scenic, leading to open ledges with a log bench and views before descending, at one point over a slab with a knotted rope. The fork to the right from the jct. drops down through pleasant woods. Where the forks merge, bear left downhill past a mossy cliff face to reach an old woods road referred to as Old School House Rd. Bear left and follow Old School House Rd. along the base of the mountain, passing a large rock face (left) and a side trail leading 0.2 mi. to Long Cove (right) before returning to the trailhead.

PINE HILL (51 FT.)
Pine Hill is part of Pine Hill Preserve, a small conservation property on Little Deer Isle, protected by Island Heritage Trust. An interesting quarry is carved out of the hill's south wall.

From the jct. of ME 15 and ME 175 in Sargentville, head west on ME 15 toward Deer Isle. Cross Deer Isle–Sedgwick Bridge over Eggemoggin Reach. Soon after the bridge, reach the Deer Isle–Stonington Visitor

SEC 11

Center on the right. Turn right here (Eggemoggin Rd.), bear right at the post office, and quickly reach Blastow Cove Rd. on the left (Saunders Memorial Congregational Church on corner). Turn onto Blastow Cove Rd. and drive 0.2 mi. south to trailhead parking for Pine Hill on the right.

PINE HILL TRAIL (USGS SARGENTVILLE QUAD, IHT PINE HILL PRESERVE MAP, GAZETTEER MAP 15)
From Blastow Cove Rd. (30 ft.) to:

Pine Hill summit (51 ft.)	0.15 mi.	30 ft.	0:10

IHT Beyond the wooden gate, the trail follows grassy Old Quarry Rd. to a clearing at the base of the defunct quarry, with its scree piles and cliff face. Bear right on a path into the woods (pass a mailbox) and then scramble up the rocky edge of the quarry wall. From the top of the cliffs at trail's end are fine views over Deer Isle and Eggemoggin Reach that range from Deer Isle–Sedgwick Bridge to the peaks of ANP.

BACKWOOD MTN. (286 FT.)
This mountain is in Holbrook Island Sanctuary State Park, which occupies 1,230 acres on the north end of the Cape Rosier peninsula in Brooksville, including namesake 115-acre Holbrook Island. Two trails are on the flanks of Backwood Mtn. (also referred to locally as Bakeman Mtn.): Summit Trail and Mountain Loop.

From the center of Brooksville at the jct. of ME 175 and ME 176, proceed west on ME 176. At 4.4 mi., turn left onto Cape Rosier Rd. and continue an additional 1.7 mi. to Back Rd. and the entrance to Holbrook Island Sanctuary on the right. Turn into the park and drive 0.6 mi. to trailhead parking for Summit Trail on the left (sign). Parking for Mountain Loop Trail is 0.1 mi. farther ahead, also on the left.

SUMMIT TRAIL (USGS CAPE ROSIER QUAD, FOHIS HOLBROOK ISLAND SANCTUARY MAP, GAZETTEER MAP 15)
Cumulative from Back Rd. (160 ft.) to:

Mountain Loop Trail (150 ft.), north side	0.1 mi.	10 ft.	0:05
Backwood Mtn. summit (286 ft.)	0.5 mi.	150 ft.	0:20
Mountain Loop Trail (215 ft.), south side	0.6 mi.	150 ft.	0:25

SEC 11

MBPL This route traverses Backwood Mtn. from north to south. Following orange blazes, cross a narrow power-line corridor and walk easily to the jct. with Mountain Loop Trail. Turn left here to proceed on the coinciding trails, and at the next jct. in 150 ft., where Mountain Loop Trail goes straight ahead, turn right to continue on Summit Trail. Hike the wide trail easily through the conifers and then dip slightly before rising to the base of Backwood Mtn. amid mossy boulders. Switchback up the slope over several short, steep pitches and some rocky, eroded trail. Soon after the angle eases, turn sharply right and reach a bench on an outcropping with northwest views through the trees to several islands in Penobscot Bay and beyond to the harbor at the town of Castine. Continuing on, quickly reach the wooded summit of Backwood Mtn. Avoid the spur to the right (no views) and bear left to descend the south side of the mountain. Reach Mountain Loop Trail in 0.1 mi.

MOUNTAIN LOOP TRAIL (USGS CAPE ROSIER QUAD, FOHIS HOLBROOK ISLAND SANCTUARY MAP, GAZETTEER MAP 15)
Cumulative from Back Rd. (130 ft.) to:

Summit Trail (150 ft.), north side	0.15 mi.	25 ft.	0:05
Summit Trail (215 ft.)	0.6 mi.	95 ft.	0:20
Complete loop	1.5 mi.	150 ft.	0:50

MBPL See driving directions for Summit Trail above.

Follow the wide, orange-blazed trail into woods and soon walk under a power line. At the Mountain Loop jct., turn left. In 50 ft., Summit Trail enters from the left to merge with Mountain Loop Trail. In 150 ft., Summit Trail departs right for the top of Backwood Mtn. Continue straight ahead on the level Mountain Loop Trail along the base of the mountain. The trail eventually swings south, trends easily over the east shoulder, and then swings to the west. At 0.6 mi., a connector path leads south to Aaron Trail. Just ahead on Mountain Loop Trail, Summit Trail enters from the right. Descending, Mountain Loop Trail trends west and then south, passing below the steep, rocky slopes of the peak rising up to the right. Bearing northward again, it climbs easily over the west shoulder and then descends to reach the original loop jct. Turn left here to return to the Back Rd. trailhead.

WESTERN ME 9 CORRIDOR
BLACKCAP MTN. (1,026 FT.)

This mountain ridge, which rises steeply above Fitts Pond in East Eddington, has several communications towers on its summit. Limited views eastward over Fitts Pond to the hills beyond are possible on the steep ascent, while ledges on the summit ridge offer wider vistas. Combine Blue Trail and Blue + White Trail for a hike to the summit.

From the jct. of ME 9 and ME 46 in East Eddington, drive south on ME 46 for 0.6 mi. As an alternative, from the jct. of US 1A and ME 46 in East Holden, drive north on ME 46 for 4.4 mi. Either way, turn east onto dirt

SEC
11

Blackcap Rd. at a sign for Katahdin Area Council–Camp Roosevelt. Follow
Blackcap Rd. for 0.5 mi. and then turn left onto Camp Roosevelt Rd. Soon
pass through the wooden entrance arch of the Boy Scout camp and reach a
large open area at 1.5 mi. from ME 46. To the left is Maggie's Way, which
leads 0.2 mi. to the Peter G. Vigue Scout Center. To the right is a boat
launch on Fitts Pond. Park on the right, just before the trailhead kiosk.

The trails to Blackcap Mtn. and Woodchuck Hill emanate from Camp
Roosevelt, an 1,800-acre facility that has served as the base camp for outdoor education for the Boy Scouts of America, Katahdin Area Council,
since 1921. Visitors are asked to check in at the Vigue Scout Center to alert
camp managers of their presence on the property. For more information,
please call the scout camp at 207-866-2241.

BLUE TRAIL AND BLUE + WHITE TRAIL
(USGS CHEMO POND QUAD, GAZETTEER MAP 23)
Cumulative from Fitts Pond boat launch (320 ft.) to:

Blue + White Trail (320 ft.) via Blue Trail	0.4 mi	100 ft.	0:15
Service road on summit ridge (990 ft.), Blue + White Trail	1.1 mi.	770 ft.	0:55
Blackcap Mtn. summit (1,026 ft.)	1.7 mi.	800 ft.	1:00

KAC Blue Trail (faded blue blazes) leaves to the left of the trailhead kiosk
and quickly crosses a wooden bridge over a brook. It soon bears left and
weaves around boulders along the west shore of Fitts Pond. At 0.4 mi., reach
a signed jct. and turn right to follow Blue + White Trail, which climbs
steadily, passes between a huge rock outcropping, and then crosses an old
jeep track. The moderate ascent becomes steeper as the trail climbs straight
up over an open slab, but after entering the woods beyond, the angle eases.
A traverse to the left follows a rising contour through the spruce woods.
Pass a mossy concrete pad on the left and quickly reach a gravel service road.

Turn left along the road toward the communications towers. Just ahead,
across the bare granite on the left, is an open ledge area with a broad view
ranging from the peaks around Donnell Pond to the mountains on MDI.
Continue to the right around the towers, staying on the service road. After
the last tower, enter the woods and follow a well-defined footpath over the
ridge. The trail dips slightly into a saddle and then rises gently to the
unmarked, wooded high point on Blackcap Mtn. At a small opening with
beds of moss, bear slightly down and left. At a cairn, go left, slightly
down, and out to a large open ledge area and another expansive view to
the southeast, which now includes Burnt Pond and Mountainy Pond
below. (*Note*: Just before this viewpoint, faded blue trail blazes continue

down the mountain. Avoid this unmaintained and difficult-to-follow route; turn around here to retrace your steps back to the Fitts Pond boat launch trailhead.

WOODCHUCK HILL (837 FT.)

A lollipop loop over this mountain in East Eddington affords views over Snowshoe Pond, Fitts Pond, and Blackcap Mtn., plus looks at the peaks around Donnell Pond and on MDI. To reach the trailhead, follow the same driving directions and visitor check-in protocols as for Blackcap Mtn.

WOODCHUCK HILL TRAIL (USGS CHEMO POND QUAD, GAZETTEER MAP 23)

Cumulative from Fitts Pond boat launch parking (320 ft.) to:

Bangor Water Works Rd. (385 ft.), north crossing	0.9 mi.	150 ft.	0:30
Woodchuck Hill summit (837 ft.)	1.3 mi.	600 ft.	1:00
Bangor Water Works Rd. (412 ft.), south crossing	1.8 mi.	600 ft.	1:15
Complete loop	3.1 mi.	750 ft.	1:55

KAC From parking adjacent to the Fitts Pond boat launch, proceed past the gate and follow Camp Roosevelt Rd. east into the camp. Pass Roosevelt Lodge and Maggie's Way on the left, the Trading Post on the right, and then Starfire Field on the left. At a fork at 0.25 mi., where Council Rd. goes right, stay left on Camp Roosevelt Rd. (information kiosk and camp map at this fork). Just ahead, bear left on Tonini Rd. and pass cabins on the left and a shower house on the right. Ahead along the gravel road, pass Gary Robbins Ln. and cabins, and then Paul's Path (a road) on the left. Just after Twin Rocks cabins on the right, leave the gravel road on the left at 0.4 mi.; this turn is marked by a boulder with yellow and blue paint on it. The wide Woodchuck Hill Trail rises gently over a low ridge to cross a camp road and then descends to ledges overlooking Snowshoe Pond. Woodchuck Hill is visible beyond. The trail crosses the pond's outlet, passes a huge erratic, and arrives at Bangor Water Works Rd. (private road; gated at its entrance on ME 9 in East Eddington to the north and on the way into Little Burnt Pond to the south).

The summit loop begins here. Cross the road and enter the woods. Climb steeply past a slab cave and then negotiate a series of steep ledges using two wooden ladders. Weave up through the steep ledges, which yield views over Snowshoe Pond to Blackcap Mtn. Soon after the angle eases, reach a cairn on the wooded summit of Woodchuck Hill at 1.3 mi. An obscure path leads north from the summit (no views). To continue from the summit cairn, turn right (south) and pass a view on the left to Schoodic

SEC 11

Mtn., Black Mtn., and Tunk Mtn., as well as Catherine Mtn., which are all in the Donnell Pond area. A short distance ahead, enjoy views over Little Burnt Pond to the peaks on MDI. The moderate descent continues to a level shoulder. Ahead on the ridge, Woodchuck Hill Trail turns sharply right along the base of a concave ledge wall. At the gated Bangor Waters Works Rd. below, turn right and walk along the road back to the far end of Snowshoe Pond to close the loop at 2.3 mi. From there, retrace your steps to Camp Roosevelt and the Fitts Pond boat launch parking area.

EAGLE BLUFF (701 FT.)

The impressive south-facing granite cliffs of Eagle Bluff in Clifton have long attracted technical rock climbers; a short but highly rewarding trail to the top makes it a great spot for hikers, too. In 2014, the Clifton Climbers Alliance purchased 165 acres on Eagle Bluff to protect public access.

From the jct. of ME 9 and ME 180 in Clifton, drive south on ME 180 for 2.5 mi. to a small, unsigned trailhead parking lot on the left.

EAGLE BLUFF TRAIL (USGS CHEMO POND AND HOPKINS POND QUADS, GAZETTEER 24)
From ME 180 (360 ft.) to:

Eagle Bluff summit cliffs (700 ft.)	0.5 mi.	340 ft.	0:25

CCA Facing toward the woods and away from the road, start on Eagle Bluff Trail from the left corner of the dirt parking lot. In 75 ft., another trail from the road enters from the left. Immediately ahead is an information kiosk on the right. Beyond the kiosk, occasional pieces of orange flagging mark the trail, which climbs gradually to a fork. A well-trodden climber's path goes right; stay left to continue to Eagle Bluff. Cross an overgrown skidder trail and then climb moderately among scattered boulders. Ahead, stay straight where a narrow climber's path leaves right. As the angle eases, proceed easily along the southwest ridge. A spur leads right 40 ft. to an outlook. Just past a huge boulder on the right, climb left and up to open ledges along the top of the cliff face. Eagle Bluff offers airy views over Cedar Swamp Pond to Lead Mtn. and the peaks of ANP. To the west are several wind towers, Woodchuck Hill, and Blackcap Mtn. Eagle Bluff Trail reenters the woods and emerges at a final ledge, ending with a view north to the granite faces of Chick Hill and Little Chick Hill.

LITTLE PEAKED MTN. (A.K.A. LITTLE CHICK HILL; 914 FT.)

Little Peaked Mtn., more popularly known as Little Chick Hill, lies just west of Peaked Mtn., a.k.a. Chick Hill (see below) and features spectacular cliffs and fine views.

From the jct. of ME 9 and ME 180 in Clifton, drive east on ME 9 for 3.5 mi. Turn left (north) onto paved Chick Hill Rd. and proceed 0.7 mi. to where the pavement ends. At this point, a large dirt parking lot is on the left; to the right, a gravel road leads uphill past a telephone pole. The parking lot is the trailhead for Little Chick Hill and Chick Hill.

LITTLE PEAKED MTN. TRAIL
(USGS HOPKINS POND QUAD, GAZETTEER MAP 24)
From Chick Hill Rd. parking lot (334 ft.) to:

Little Peaked Mtn. summit (914 ft.)	0.5 mi.	580 ft.	0:30

NFTM To start up Little Chick Hill., walk back to the pavement. With the paved road to the right and the gravel road going uphill to the left, head straight into the woods on an unmarked old jeep track. In 200 ft., reach a fork and bear left. In 700 ft., the eroded old woods road narrows to a footpath. Ahead, a faint trail enters from the left; farther on, cross an overgrown skidder trail. Climbing occasionally on bedrock trail at a moderate grade, reach another faint trail on the right; stay left. Above, emerge into the open at the base of huge granite slabs. Along a short cliff wall on the right, the angle eases. With impressive cliffs on the right, ascend easily up a long granite ridge, and at the final summit outcropping, bear right into the woods. Reach a jct. with a trail entering from the left (take note of this jct. for the return hike). Turn right here to quickly finish the climb atop the south-facing cliffs with spectacular vistas east to Chick Hill and south to the mountains of Donnell Pond PL; to the southwest are Eagle Bluff, Woodchuck Hill, Blackcap Mtn., and Blue Hill Mtn.

PEAKED MTN. (A.K.A. CHICK HILL; 1,155 FT.)
Peaked Mtn., commonly called Chick Hill, straddles the Clifton–Amherst town line about 18 mi. east of Bangor. The sweeping granite cliffs on the mountain's south face can be seen from miles around and offer long views that include the peaks of ANP to the south and Katahdin in the north.

PEAKED MTN. TRAIL (USGS HOPKINS POND QUAD,
GAZETTEER MAP 24)
From Chick Hill Rd. parking lot (334 ft.) to:

Peaked Mtn. summit (1,155 ft.)	1.1 mi.	821 ft.	1:00

NFTM From the start of the trail to Little Chick Hill (see above), turn left to follow the gravel road uphill. The road turns sharply right at a height-of-land; proceed to utility pole 18 (marked in silver numbers) on the right. Just beyond, enter the woods on the right, follow an obscure jeep track for 250

SEC 11

ft., and continue on a foot trail. Climb at a moderate-to-steep grade on mossy slabs of rock to emerge into the open. Peaked Mtn. Trail then ascends slabs through an open corridor in the woods. In a small clearing, where a faint trail continues ahead and up, bear right to reach the open slabs above the south face of Chick Hill. Continue up to the left toward the communications tower, and reach the summit at the base of the former fire tower (erected in 1946, removed in 1993), where only the concrete stanchions and steel base remain. From here, admire views of Lead Mtn., the peaks of Donnell Pond PL and ANP, Blue Hill Mtn., and the hills around Lucerne. The cliff face of Fletcher Bluff is around the corner to the east.

BALD BLUFF MTN. (1,028 FT.)

Amherst Mountains Community Forest in Amherst is a 4,974-acre tract of rugged forestland encompassing six remote ponds, miles of streams, significant wetlands, and a mix of granite ledges, hills, and mountains, including Bald Bluff Mtn. The preserve is owned by MBPL and managed jointly with the town of Amherst. Bald Bluff Mtn. offers fine views of the lower Penobscot River watershed from its summit ledges.

From the jct. of ME 9 and ME 180 in Clifton, travel west on ME 9 for 8.9 mi. to a snowplow turnout on the right. Just ahead on the left is a green-and-brown MBPL sign: "Amherst Public Land." Turn left (north) off ME 9 at the sign and follow the old road (Ducktail Pond Rd.), which quickly turns to gravel. At 1.7 mi. from ME 9, reach the Partridge Pond Trail trailhead on the left. At 2.4 mi., pass Indian Camp Stream Day Use Area on the right (trailhead parking for Ducktail Pond Trail). The road bears sharply left at 2.9 mi. and again at 3.7 mi. Parking for Bald Bluff Mtn. Trail is on the right at 6.0 mi.

BALD BLUFF MTN. TRAIL (USGS THE HORSEBACK QUAD, MTF AMHERST MOUNTAINS COMMUNITY FOREST– BALD BLUFF MAP, GAZETTEER MAP 24)
Cumulative from Ducktail Pond Rd. (550 ft.) to:

Loop jct. (780 ft.)	0.3 mi.	230 ft.	0:15
Bald Bluff Mtn. summit (1,028 ft.) via south side of loop	1.1 mi.	600 ft.	0:50
Complete lollipop loop	2.1 mi.	600 ft.	1:20

MBPL From the parking area, walk back along the road for 50 ft. to the trailhead sign on the left; enter the woods here. Follow the wide Bald Bluff Mtn. Trail steadily uphill, and soon after it turns sharply right, reach the loop jct. (sign: "Overlook"). Turn right to hike the loop counterclockwise. Ascend on wide trail to wooded ledges atop a knoll, where there are views southwest toward Chick Hill and Blackcap Mtn. Contour across the slope, drop down, and then continue on a contour. After a spring, climb at a moderate grade along a rising contour. At 1.0 mi., reach large open ledges with superb views of the mountains around Donnell Pond and on MDI, plus Jellison Hill, Blue Hill, and Chick Hill. Continue up over more ledges and then bear left away from the mountain's edge. Reach the summit of Bald Bluff Mtn. in a pretty, semi-open area of moss and lichen-covered bedrock. Several boulders and small piles of rocks mark the top. Hike over the level summit, descend gradually, and reenter the thick woods. Close the loop at 1.8 mi. and continue straight out to the trailhead.

LEAD MTN. (A.K.A. HUMPBACK; 1,477 FT.)

Lead Mtn., also known as Humpback, is in T28 MD in Hancock County, just west of the Washington County line. From the jct. of ME 9 and ME 193 in T22 MD, drive east toward Beddington. In 0.5 mi., cross into Washington County. At 1.0 mi., turn left (north) at the sign for the MFS Forest Protection Division, Beddington Ranger Station. (This point is 0.1 mi. west of the bridge over the Narraguagus River on ME 9.) Reset trip meter. Proceed on CC Rd. (also called 30-00-0 Rd.), passing a snowmobile trail on the left at the MFS station. Just beyond, turn left onto a gravel road (sign for cell tower), which leads 1.7 mi. to a cul-de-sac and parking.

LEAD MTN. TRAIL (USGS LEAD MTN. QUAD, GAZETTEER MAP 24)
From parking area (695 ft.) to:

Lead Mtn. summit (1,477 ft.)	1.0 mi.	782 ft.	0:55

NFTM The hike to Lead Mtn. starts in the upper right corner of the parking area. Follow a jeep track into the woods. On a telephone pole, a yellow sign with an arrow indicates this is the way to the cell tower on top of the mountain. In 100 ft., pass around a yellow gate and proceed on the old road to a fork. Go right here, following the telephone poles, and climb on the old road, surfaced with loose gravel.

Ahead, an ATV trail leads up to the right; follow the ATV trail to the old fire warden's cabin (on the right). Soon after the cabin, the ATV trail narrows to a jeep track. Follow this easily up to a saddle. Beyond, climb steadily to the summit to find a former fire tower site, a fenced-in communications tower, and the broad summit plateau—but no views.

SEC 11

PEAKED MTN. (IN WASHINGTON COUNTY; 938 FT.)

The unmaintained trail to the old fire tower site atop Peaked Mtn. in T30 MD BPP is seriously overgrown and no longer passable.

DONNELL POND PUBLIC LANDS AND VICINITY

Donnell Pond PL encompasses 15,479 acres of woods, mountains, lakes, and ponds in the towns of Franklin and Sullivan and in T9 SD and T10 SD. Central to the preserve and popular with canoeists, boaters, and campers are namesake Donnell Pond and scenic Schoodic Beach, hemmed in by the walls of Schoodic Mtn. and Black Mtn. To the north of Black Mtn. are the backcountry wilds around Rainbow Pond and Caribou Mtn. North of ME 182, the preserve includes many of the north and east shores of pristine Tunk Lake, all the north and east shores of Spring River Lake, and a number of small, remote ponds. Rising high over this northern section is Tunk Mtn. and its great cliffs, as well as several trailless peaks. Donnell Pond PL is home to 20 mi. of hiking trails.

SCHOODIC MTN. (1,079 FT.)

This attractive mountain in T9 SD in the southwest corner of Donnell Pond PL offers fine views of Frenchman Bay and the mountains of ANP from the extensive ledges on its mostly bare granite summit. Two trails ascend the peak from the east: Schoodic Mtn. Trail and Schoodic Beach Trail. The main trailhead for Schoodic Mtn. (and Black Mtn.) is at the end of Schoodic Beach Rd.

From the jct. of US 1 and ME 3 in Ellsworth, travel 13.4 mi. east on US 1 to ME 183 in East Sullivan. Turn left (north) on ME 183 (Tunk Lake Rd.) and drive 4.3 mi. to Donnell Pond Rd. on the left (blue-and-white sign), just after crossing an old railroad bed (now Down East Sunrise Trail). Turn left here, and soon pass Black Mtn. Rd. on the right at 0.3 mi. (leads 2.0 mi. to Big Chief Trail on Black Mtn.). Stay left on Donnell Pond Rd. for an additional 1.6 mi. to its end at the Schoodic Beach parking lot, where there is an information kiosk and pit toilet.

SCHOODIC MTN. TRAIL
(AMC DONNELL POND PUBLIC LANDS MAP)
Cumulative from Schoodic Beach parking lot (250 ft.) to:

Schoodic Beach Trail (720 ft.)	0.8 mi.	470 ft.	0:35
Schoodic Mtn. summit (1,079 ft.)	1.2 mi.	830 ft.	1:05

SEC 11

MBPL This direct route to the top of Schoodic Mtn. leaves the left end of the parking lot, to the right of the pit toilet. Descend briefly and then climb, gradually at first and then steadily, passing several huge boulders with overhangs. Reach the top of a cliff and enjoy views east to Black Mtn. Beyond, Schoodic Mtn. Trail levels out and then ascends gradually to a jct. with Schoodic Beach Trail, which enters from the right (leads 0.5 mi. to

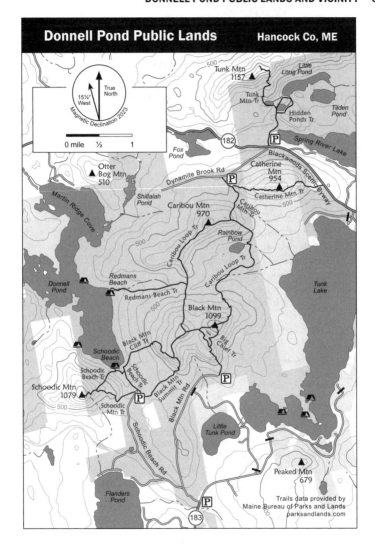

Donnell Pond Public Lands

Hancock Co, ME

True North

15½° West

Magnetic Declination 2023

0 mile   ½   1

Tunk Mtn
1157

Little
Long Pond

Tunk
Mtn Tr

Hidden
Ponds Tr

Tilden
Pond

Spring River Lake

Fox
Pond

182

Blackwoods Scenic Byway

Catherine
Mtn
954

Otter
Bog Mtn
510

Dynamite Brook Rd

Shillalah
Pond

Catherine Mtn Tr

Martin Ridge Cove

Caribou Mtn
970

Caribou Mtn Tr

500

Caribou Loop Tr

Rainbow
Pond

Caribou Loop Tr

Tunk
Lake

Redmans
Beach

Donnell
Pond

Redmans Beach Tr

500

Black Mtn
1099

Black Mtn
Cliff Tr

Big
Chief Tr

Schoodic
Beach

Schoodic
Beach Tr

Schoodic Mtn
1079

Schoodic
Beach Tr

Black Mtn
Summit Tr

Black Mtn Rd

500

Schoodic
Mtn Tr

Schoodic Beach Rd

Little
Tunk Pond

Peaked Mtn
679

Flanders
Pond

183

Trails data provided by
Maine Bureau of Parks and Lands
parksandlands.com

Schoodic Beach on Donnell Pond). For the summit of Schoodic Mtn., continue left on Schoodic Mtn. Trail. Climb moderately on bedrock trail, traverse the south side of the mountain, and finish by following cairns over extensive ledges to reach the summit towers at 1.2 mi.

SCHOODIC BEACH TRAIL
(AMC DONNELL POND PUBLIC LANDS MAP)
Cumulative from Schoodic Beach parking lot (250 ft.) to:

Schoodic Beach on Donnell Pond (120 ft.)	0.5 mi.	–130 ft.	0:15
Schoodic Mtn. Trail (720 ft.)	1.0 mi.	600 ft.	0:50
Schoodic Mtn. summit (1,079 ft.) via Schoodic Mtn. Trail	1.4 mi.	960 ft.	1:10

MBPL Begin on Schoodic Beach Trail at the far-right end of the parking lot just beyond the information kiosk. Follow this wide path 0.5 mi. to Schoodic Beach on Donnell Pond. Just before reaching the pond, arrive at a jct. on the left and a privy; this is the continuation of Schoodic Beach Trail up the mountain. Schoodic Beach, perhaps the most popular destination of visitors to Donnell Pond PL, is 250 ft. ahead and well worth a visit. Along the beach's sandy expanse are picnic tables, additional privies, individual and group campsites, and excellent swimming.

To continue on Schoodic Beach Trail up Schoodic Mtn., return from the beach and turn right at the jct. (privy) to follow an old jeep road along the base of the mountain. Turn sharply left to begin a steep ascent on rough terrain. Above, the climbing moderates on switchbacks. At the crest in a small clearing, reach the jct. with Schoodic Mtn. Trail, which enters from the left. Turn right here to follow Schoodic Mtn. Trail to the top of Schoodic Mtn. in 0.4 mi.

BLACK MTN. (1,099 FT.)

This mountain in T10 SD rises east of Donnell Pond and offers views in all directions from the open ledges atop its broad summit. Black Mtn. can be climbed from the Schoodic Beach parking lot via Black Mtn. Summit Trail or from Schoodic Beach via Black Mtn. Cliff Trail. Black Mtn. can also be reached from Caribou Mtn. in the north via Caribou Mtn. Trail and Caribou Loop Trail.

SEC 11

BLACK MTN. SUMMIT TRAIL
(AMC DONNELL POND PUBLIC LANDS MAP)
Cumulative from Schoodic Beach parking lot (250 ft.) to:

Black Mtn. Cliff Trail (940 ft.)	1.2 mi.	690 ft.	0:55
Caribou Loop Trail, west jct. (1,050 ft.)	1.8 mi.	775 ft.	1:20

Black Mtn.–Big Chief Connector to Big Chief Trail (890 ft.)	2.0 mi.	775 ft.	1:30
Black Mtn. summit (1,099 ft.) and Caribou Loop Trail, east jct.	2.3 mi.	985 ft.	1:40

MBPL From the far-right end of the Schoodic Beach parking lot (see directions to Schoodic Mtn., p. 546), follow Schoodic Beach Trail past the kiosk to a barrier and jct. Turn right on Black Mtn. Summit Trail and soon cross a small brook. Join a wide old forest road, which is often wet and muddy, and follow it in a northeasterly direction. At 0.7 mi., cross a grassy old logging road. Soon Black Mtn. Summit Trail bears sharply left toward the mountain and climbs from the base of the steep slope via rock stairs, slabs, and roots. After a rising traverse to the left, the trail swings back right and up through ledges. On the ridgetop, reach the jct. with Black Mtn. Cliff Trail on the left at 1.2 mi.

Bear right to continue on Black Mtn. Summit Trail. Proceed easily through the woods, and at 1.8 mi., reach the west jct. of Caribou Loop Trail (leads toward Redman Beach on Donnell Pond and beyond to Caribou Mtn.) near the heavily wooded western summit of Black Mtn. Continuing to the right on Black Mtn. Summit Trail, descend, steeply at times, to a notch at 2.0 mi. and a jct. with Black Mtn.–Big Chief Connector (leads 0.4 mi. over a knob to Big Chief Trail and then another 0.7 mi. down to Black Mtn. Rd.). Bear left at this jct. and soon break out onto open ledges, following cairns to reach the summit of Black Mtn. at 2.3 mi. (large cairn and sign), the east jct. of Caribou Loop Trail, and the jct. with Big Chief Trail.

BLACK MTN. CLIFF TRAIL
(AMC DONNELL POND PUBLIC LANDS MAP)
Cumulative from Black Mtn. Summit Trail (940 ft.) to:

Schoodic Beach (120 ft.)	1.2 mi.	–820 ft.	0:40
Schoodic Beach trailhead (250 ft.) via Schoodic Beach Trail	1.7 mi.	130 ft.	0:55

MBPL Black Mtn. Cliff Trail is commonly combined with Black Mtn. Summit Trail (for the ascent) to make a loop on the west side of Black Mtn. Thus Black Mtn. Cliff Trail is described here on the descent. From the jct. of Black Mtn. Summit Trail, head left to a narrow lookout with views to Schoodic Mtn. and the peaks of Acadia on MDI. Follow a contour along the top of the mountain's steep southwest slope, passing two more lookouts (similar views). Black Mtn. Cliff Trail, trending gently down at first, now begins a steep descent to the west toward Donnell Pond, crossing a small brook before the angle eases. Stepping-stones lead across another small brook. Soon after, turn sharply left along the route of an old woods road and traverse three brooks in fairly quick succession. On the level, a privy is

SEC 11

visible through the woods on the right; then a side path leads to a campsite on the right. Cross a footbridge over a gully and then bear right to cross another footbridge over a gully. Continue to Schoodic Beach at the south end of Donnell Pond (kiosk). To return to the Schoodic Beach trailhead, follow 0.5-mi. Schoodic Beach Trail.

BIG CHIEF TRAIL (AMC DONNELL POND PUBLIC LANDS MAP)
Cumulative from Black Mtn. Rd. (370 ft.) to:

Black Mtn.–Big Chief Connector (930 ft.)	0.7 mi.	560 ft.	0:35
Black Mtn. summit (1,099 ft.)	1.2 mi.	730 ft.	1:00

MBPL This route climbs to the summit of Black Mtn. via Wizard Pond. The extensive open ledges on the southeastern ridge offer excellent views east over Tunk Lake. From the jct. with Schoodic Beach Rd., drive on Black Mtn. Rd. for 2.1 mi. to a small parking area on the right. Just ahead on the left side of the road is a sign for Big Chief Trail.

Follow well-worn Big Chief Trail into the woods and ascend steadily, passing several large glacial erratics. Beyond a high cliff wall in the woods to the right, climb a short, steep pitch via several switchbacks to a viewpoint on the right; then weave through rocks as the forest cover begins to thin out. After a level open area, bear right at a large cairn, and drop down slightly to another view eastward. Follow cairns over bedrock trail to the jct. with Black Mtn.–Big Chief Connector (leads 0.4 mi. northwest to join Black Mtn. Summit Trail in the col between the east and west summits of Black Mtn.). Bear right to continue on Big Chief Trail, traversing huge, open slabs of granite, and then bear sharply right (watch for a double blaze) before dropping into a depression. Cross the outlet of Wizard Pond and climb steeply over ledges to the open summit of the east peak of Black Mtn. and the jct. with Black Mtn. Summit and Caribou Loop trails.

Black Mtn.–Big Chief Connector. This 0.4-mi. path connects Black Mtn. Summit Trail with Big Chief Trail high on Black Mtn., 0.3 mi. west of its east summit. From the jct. with Black Mtn. Summit Trail, climb a knoll via rock steps and then cross an expanse of bedrock. Beyond an overlook (sign and cairn), crest a knob, drop into a gully, and follow a series of cairns to join Big Chief Trail, 0.7 mi. from Black Mtn. Rd.

SEC 11

CARIBOU MTN. (970 FT.)
This peak in T10 SD lies to the north of Black Mtn. in the heart of the backcountry of Donnell Pond PL. From the north, reach Caribou Mtn. from Dynamite Brook Rd. via Caribou Mtn. Trail (described below); from the south, take a longer hike from Black Mtn. on Caribou Loop Trail, which makes a nearly 6-mi. loop over Caribou Mtn.

From the jct. of US 1 and ME 182 in Hancock, travel north on ME 182 (Blackwoods Scenic Byway) for 14.5 mi. to reach Dynamite Brook Rd. on the right. Look for the sign "Caribou Loop Connector Trailhead." (Trailhead parking for Tunk Mtn. trails is 100 yd. ahead to the left on ME 182.) Turn right on Dynamite Brook Rd. and drive 0.8 mi. to a small parking area on the left. Caribou Mtn. Trail starts 500 ft. farther along on the road, turning left into the woods (sign) just before a bridge.

CARIBOU MTN. TRAIL (AMC DONNELL POND PUBLIC LANDS MAP)
Cumulative from Dynamite Brook Rd. (410 ft.) to:

Catherine Mtn. Trail (530 ft.)	0.2 mi.	120 ft.	0:10
Caribou Loop Trail (850 ft.)	0.9 mi.	450 ft.	0:40

MBPL Follow the wide, blue-blazed trail gradually uphill and then ascend moderately before leveling off at a jct. Here, an informal trail diverges left to climb Catherine Mtn., while Caribou Mtn. Trail continues easily ahead to a sag between Catherine Mtn. and Caribou Mtn. Beyond, the trail rises steadily, sometimes on rough, rocky terrain, to gain the east ridge of the mountain. Pass through a cleft in the rock, crest the summit ridge, and reach a jct. with Caribou Loop Trail on an open slab. Here, the broad vista includes Tunk Lake, Black Mtn., and Schoodic Mtn. To the right on Caribou Loop Trail are more lookouts, as well as the wooded summit of Caribou Mtn.; to the left, Caribou Loop Trail descends to Rainbow Pond before climbing to the east peak of Black Mtn.

CARIBOU LOOP TRAIL (AMC DONNELL POND PUBLIC LANDS MAP)
Cumulative from Caribou Mtn. Trail (850 ft.) to:

Redman Beach Trail (450 ft.)	1.7 mi.	200 ft.	0:30
Black Mtn. Summit Trail, west jct. (1,050 ft.)	2.6 mi.	840 ft.	1:40
Black Mtn., east summit (1,099 ft.)	3.1 mi.	1,050 ft.	2:05
Rainbow Pond outlet (320 ft.)	5.1 mi.	1,150 ft.	3:10
Caribou Mtn. Trail (850 ft.)	5.9 mi.	1,680 ft.	3:50

MBPL Blue-blazed Caribou Loop Trail is described in a counterclockwise direction from the jct. of Caribou Mtn. Trail, 0.9 mi. from Dynamite Brook Rd. Much of this route lies within 1,940-acre Donnell Pond Ecological Reserve, designated for the protection and study of the rare natural areas and plants found here. Please stay on the trail to minimize damage to plants and soils.

From the jct., turn right and contour across the south face of Caribou Mtn., alternating between wooded patches and open ledges. Vistas south and east toward the coast are extraordinary. At 0.4 mi., pass over the

SEC 11

unmarked wooded summit of Caribou Mtn. and then trend gently down along a contour to a low point on the ridge. Beyond, emerge onto open slabs for a grand view of Black Mtn. and Schoodic Mtn before turning sharply left and descending. Scamper down a short rock staircase, move along the base of a ledge wall, pass a shallow slab cave, and then walk under a ledge roof. After going up and over several ledges, Caribou Loop Trail reaches the jct. with Redman Beach Trail, which leads 1.4 mi. to the east shore of Donnell Pond. Shortly after the jct., begin climbing Black Mtn. at a steady, moderate grade. Pass a large, fern-covered erratic on the ascent through the tall spruce woods. Soon after the angle eases, Caribou Loop Trail reaches a jct. with Black Mtn. Summit Trail; the two trails coincide for the next 0.5 mi. to the east summit of Black Mtn.

At the jct., turn left to start down toward the col between the west and east peaks of Black Mtn. At 2.8 mi., pass Black Mtn.–Big Chief Connector on the right. Just ahead, rock-hop across a wet area in the low point between the peaks. Soon the trail climbs over semi-open slabs and then into the open on the spectacular pink granite summit ledges. Reach the east summit of Black Mtn. at 3.1 mi. and the jct. of Big Chief Trail. The scenic panorama from this vantage point—ranging from Acadia to Katahdin on a clear day—is one of the finest of any mountaintop along the Maine coast.

To continue on Caribou Loop Trail, follow cairns to the east, descending the open ledges with views of Tunk Lake. At 3.3 mi., enter the trees and soon turn sharply left (an old trail goes straight). Wind down the slope, stepping between boulders and meandering below mossy cliffs. (Parts of the treadway may be indistinct at times; watch carefully for old blue blazes to stay on track.) Travel over several knolls, walk by a large erratic, and reach a stream, following along its bank. Then cross the stream and soon cross another stream as the trail makes a wide arc around a wetland. Climb up and over a low rise, passing a huge erratic. At 5.1 mi., traverse the outlet of Rainbow Pond and soon begin climbing the east side of Caribou Mtn. The trail turns sharply right at a large, square-shaped erratic with a blue blaze on it. Beyond, weave through mossy boulders, climbing steadily to reach the jct. with Caribou Mtn. Trail and close the loop. Turn right into the woods to descend 0.9 mi. to Dynamite Brook Rd.

TUNK MTN. (1,157 FT.)

This mountain in T10 SD offers superb views to the south and east from its extensive summit ledges. A loop trail offers access to several remote ponds at its eastern base.

To reach the Tunk Mtn. trailhead, follow directions for Caribou Mtn. Trail. Continue east on ME 182 from the jct. with Dynamite Brook Rd.

for 100 yd. to trailhead parking on the left for Tunk Mtn. and Hidden Ponds trails. A vault toilet and an information kiosk are provided here. Much of Tunk Mtn. Trail (and Hidden Ponds Trail) lies within 4,274-acre Spring Lake Ecological Reserve, designated for the protection and study of the rare natural areas and plants found here. Please stay on the trail to minimize damage to plants and soils.

TUNK MTN. TRAIL (AMC DONNELL POND PUBLIC LANDS MAP)
Cumulative from ME 182 (250 ft.) to:

Hidden Ponds Trail, lower jct. (310 ft.)	0.6 mi.	110 ft.	0:20
Hidden Ponds Trail, upper jct. at Salmon Pond (300 ft.)	0.7 mi.	110 ft.	0:25
High point on Tunk Mtn. (1,120 ft.)	1.8 mi.	930 ft.	1:25
End of trail at viewpoint to north (1,080 ft.)	1.9 mi.	930 ft.	1:30

MBPL Tunk Mtn. Trail begins to the right of the kiosk, descends wooden steps, and enters the woods. The wide and well-worn trail, an old woods road, leads past an informal trail on the left. Follow blue blazes to the jct. with Hidden Ponds Trail on the right. (This 0.9-mi. trail makes a loop around Salmon Pond, rejoining Tunk Mtn. Trail 0.1 mi. north.) Ahead, reach Salmon Pond and the upper jct. of Hidden Ponds Trail. Bear left to climb a rise and then drop down to Mud Pond. Hike along the pond and cross its inlet on the west shore. Soon after, leave Mud Pond and begin climbing steeply over a winding staircase of rock steps. Ascend at a moderate grade via switchbacks to cross a semi-open area with views south.

Enter thick woods at a cairn and traverse east across the mountain. Then climb easily to a spur on the right, which leads 100 yd. to a series of huge, sloping ledges and impressive views south to the Gulf of Maine, Catherine Mtn., Caribou Mtn., Spring River Lake, and Mud and Salmon ponds below. After a long switchback and a stretch of moderate-to-steep climbing, ascend three steel rungs attached to the rock. The view south expands as the trail gains elevation and now includes Black Mtn., Schoodic Mtn., and Tunk Lake. At a sign for Monument Vista, a spur path leads 200 ft. down to the right to another excellent outlook and a plaque honoring the family of Harold Pierce, who donated the land on Tunk Mtn. to the state of Maine in 1994. Continuing on Tunk Mtn. Trail, climb slabs to emerge on the summit ledges. Follow blazes and cairns from this point to the ridge crest on the northeast shoulder of Tunk Mtn. Here, the trail—now on TNC's 9,000-acre Spring River Preserve—avoids the true summit, crosses the ridge, drops into a gully, and ends atop a sweeping granite slab with outstanding views to the north—including Katahdin on a clear day.

SEC 11

HIDDEN PONDS TRAIL (AMC DONNELL POND PUBLIC LANDS MAP)
Cumulative from Tunk Mtn. Trail, upper jct. (300 ft.) to:

Spur to Salmon Pond (310 ft.)	0.1 mi.	10 ft.	0:05
Little Long Pond (230 ft.)	0.3 mi.	30 ft.	0:10
Salmon Pond (290 ft.)	0.7 mi.	150 ft.	0:25
Tunk Mtn. Trail, lower jct. (310 ft.)	0.9 mi.	150 ft.	0:30

MBPL This short, blue-blazed loop trail, which diverges from Tunk Mtn. Trail to visit two remote ponds, Salmon Pond and Little Long Pond, makes for an interesting detour on the descent from Tunk Mtn. The loop is described from its upper jct. with Tunk Mtn. Trail, 0.7 mi. from ME 182. Hidden Ponds Trail follows the north shore of Salmon Pond to a spur on the right, which leads 75 ft. to the pond's shore. Beyond, Hidden Ponds Trail bears away from Salmon Pond and soon joins the course of a stream leading to Little Long Pond. An informal trail leads along that pond's south shore, but Hidden Ponds Trail turns sharply uphill to the right. After a huge erratic, traverse mossy ledges to a second view of Little Long Pond. Finally, bear away from the pond and hike south, contouring across the hillside to Salmon Pond, where there are views of Tunk Mtn. Ahead at a T jct., an informal trail leads left; turn right to continue through the woods above Salmon Pond to rejoin Tunk Mtn. Trail. Turn left to reach the trailhead on ME 182 in 0.6 mi.

CATHERINE MTN. (954 FT.)

This mountain in T10 SD lies east of Caribou Mtn., just outside the boundary of Donnell PL. Catherine Mtn. is commonly hiked from west to east, beginning from Caribou Mtn. Trail, 0.2 mi. from that trail's start at Dynamite Brook Rd., and ending on ME 182 1.1 mi. east of Dynamite Brook Rd. Sweeping cliffs on the south side of the mountain offer excellent views southward over Tunk Lake to the coast.

CATHERINE MTN. TRAIL
(AMC DONNELL POND PUBLIC LANDS MAP)
From Caribou Mtn. Trail (530 ft.) to:

Catherine Mtn. high point (920 ft.)	0.9 mi.	390 ft.	0:40
ME 182	1.6 mi.	420 ft.	1:00

NFTM From the jct. of Caribou Mtn. Trail, Catherine Mtn. Trail climbs at a steady grade up the west ridge and crosses an orange-blazed property boundary; shortly after, a spur on the right leads to a view of Black Mtn. Occasional cairns mark the route of Catherine Mtn. Trail across areas of granite slab. At 0.5 mi., enjoy another look south to the peaks of Black Mtn. and to Schoodic Mtn. The next viewpoint, not far along, also takes in Tunk Lake and Caribou Mtn. Follow a contour along the ridge to a large open slab and a low cairn, where the trail splits; turn sharply left here to remain on the Catherine Mtn. Trail. Ascend to a granite bench partially enclosed by sharp stones. Bear sharply right here and follow blue blazes and cairns into the woods. At 0.9 mi., climb easily to a knob with a squarish stone. Beyond, descend over rocks to arrive at a jct., where a blue-blazed side trail on the left leads 300 ft. to an excellent view to Spring River Lake and Tunk Mtn. Continue steadily down the east ridge on Catherine Mtn. Trail. After the angle eases, the trail crosses another orange property boundary and joins an old jeep track. Follow this out to a grassy clearing and parking along ME 182.

YOUNG TUNK MTN. (544 FT.)

This bald-topped hill rises just west of the Narraguagus River in Cherryfield. A favorite of locals and blueberry pickers for years, the informal path formerly known as Sprague's Falls Trail was greatly improved by Savage Bloomer, a Narraguagus High School student, for his Eagle Scout service project in 2015. (The mountain is on property owned by Bloomer's family.)

From the jct. of US 1 and ME 182 in Cherryfield, drive west on ME 182 toward Franklin. In 1.9 mi., turn right on Sprague Falls Rd. In another 2.0 mi., there is a grassy parking spot on the left; this is the start of Young Tunk Trail (sign).

YOUNG TUNK TRAIL (USGS SCHOODIC LAKE QUAD, GAZETTEER MAP 25)
From Sprague's Falls Rd. (120 ft.) to:

Young Tunk Mtn. summit (544 ft.)	0.7 mi.	424 ft.	0:35

Savage Bloomer Follow Young Tunk Trail in a southwesterly direction, climbing gradually. After crossing a bridge over a small stream, the trail swings to the northwest and then back to the southwest. Follow bog bridges across a wet area and continue the ascent through mixed woods. The final part of the hike rises at a gradual but steady grade up the mountain's north slope. After a sharp left turn, Young Tunk Trail quickly turns right to climb an enormous granite outcropping, which yields sights of Tunk, Catherine, Caribou, and Lead mountains, among others. Continue to the next outcropping and the summit of Young Tunk Mtn., where there are views through the trees to the peaks of ANP on MDI.

SEC
11

FRENCHMAN BAY CONSERVANCY
BAKER HILL (373 FT.)

The 58-acre Lower Baker Hill Preserve, managed by FBC, protects the scenic southern slopes of Baker Hill in Sullivan. About 1.5 mi. of trails loop through the property, leading to ledges with views over Sullivan Harbor to Frenchman Bay and beyond, to the peaks of ANP on MDI. Combine Baker Hill Loop Trail and Boundary Trail for a circuit hike.

From the jct. of US 1 and ME 200 in Sullivan, travel east on US 1 for 1.5 mi. Turn left (north) onto Punkinville Rd. and go 0.2 mi. to trailhead parking on the left (sign).

BAKER HILL LOOP TRAIL AND BOUNDARY TRAIL
(USGS SULLIVAN QUAD, FBC BAKER HILL PRESERVE MAP,
GAZETTEER MAP 24)
Cumulative from Punkinville Rd. (160 ft.) to:

Baker Hill overlook (373 ft.)	0.5 mi.	215 ft.	0:20
Boundary Trail (350 ft.)	0.6 mi.	215 ft.	0:25
Cleft Rock Trail (270 ft.)	0.8 mi.	215 ft.	0:30
Close of loop at T jct. (190 ft.)	1.1 mi.	235 ft.	0:40

FBC Marked by small blue triangles, Baker Hill Loop Trail leaves left of the parking area kiosk and quickly reaches a T jct. Turn left to hike the loop clockwise. Just beyond the jct., a side trail leads to trailhead parking for the Schoodic Connector Trail; bear sharply right here. At the next fork, stay left to climb the outer loop for the best scenery. Views west are limited at first but open up along the upper cliff edge. After a short connector trail enters from the right, Baker Hill Loop Trail crosses an open slab with excellent views. Once over the wooded summit of Baker Hill, the trail trends mildly down to reach the jct. with Boundary Trail and Baker Hill Trail (leads north into Long Ledges Preserve). Turn right (east) on Boundary Trail and follow red blazes along the property line between the two preserves. At the next jct., bear right on the eastern leg of Baker Hill Loop Trail, climb through a shallow ravine, and then make a moderate descent to the base of Baker Hill. At the original T jct., turn left to return to the trailhead.

SCHOODIC CONNECTOR TRAIL (USGS SULLIVAN QUAD,
MTF SCHOODIC CONNECTOR TRAIL, GAZETTEER MAP 24)
Cumulative from SCT trailhead on Punkinville Rd. (160 ft.) to:

Baker Hill Trail (350 ft.) via Baker Hill Loop Trail (west leg)	0.5 mi.	190 ft.	0:15
West Loop Trail (290 ft.)	0.8 mi.	190 ft.	0:25

SCT (290 ft.)	1.3 mi.	230 ft.	0:40
Spur to parking on Schoodic Bog Rd. (270 ft.)	3.6 mi.	380 ft.	2:00
Down East Sunrise Trail (190 ft.)	4.8 mi.	480 ft.	2:40
Schoodic Mtn. summit (1,079 ft.)	6.5 mi.	1,370 ft.	3:50
Schoodic Beach parking lot (250 ft.)	7.7 mi.	1,370 ft.	4:30

FBC Schoodic Connector Trail links a series of foot trails between Punkinville Rd. near US 1 in Sullivan and the top of Schoodic Mtn. in Donnell Pond PL, making the 6.5-mi. route one of the longest hikes in the Downeast region. The conservation lands across which the trail extends were assembled between 2005 and 2015 by FBC and include Baker Hill, Long Ledges, Long Ledges II, Dutchman, and Schoodic Bog preserves. Beyond Schoodic Bog Preserve, SCT crosses state-owned, multiuse Down East Sunrise Trail before climbing Schoodic Mtn. on privately owned land.

SCT is most commonly traveled from south to north, saving the climb up Schoodic Mtn. for last. The southern trailhead for SCT is at Baker Hill Preserve. From the jct. of US 1 and ME 200 in Sullivan, travel east on US 1 for 1.5 mi. Turn left (north) onto Punkinville Rd. and go 0.2 mi. to trailhead parking on the left (sign).

To begin the SCT route, enter the woods and reach a T jct. in 300 ft. Turn left to follow Baker Hill Loop Trail (blue triangles) to the cliffs above, where there are pleasant views west and south. At 0.5 mi., on the north side of Baker Hill, reach a jct. with Boundary Trail on the right. Stay on Baker Hill Loop Trail straight ahead into Long Ledges Preserve. At the next jct. at 0.8 mi., bear left on West Loop Trail and follow it over ledges through semi-open forest.

At 1.3 mi., reach the jct. with SCT. Turn left on SCT and climb to a ridgetop west of Long Pond. Cross the boundary line of Long Ledges II Preserve and enjoy glimpses of Long Pond below on the right through the trees. Continue along the ridge past a few erratics and then descend. After a grove of mature spruce and pine, cross a footbridge over Long Pond Brook to enter Dutchman Preserve. Climb the hillside immediately beyond at a moderate grade and traverse the west slope of Long Pond Hill. Eventually, SCT makes an arc around a red maple swamp before crossing a gravel road. Just ahead, bear left on the same gravel road and follow it east. At the next trail sign, turn left off the gravel road to reach a boundary line for Schoodic Bog Preserve. At 3.6 mi., arrive at a jct. To the left, SCT continues; to the right, a spur leads 0.25 mi. to a trailhead parking lot on Schoodic Bog Rd. (To use this alternate parking area, follow driving directions for SCT trailhead parking on Punkinville Rd. Continue on Punkinville Rd. for another 2.0 mi. Turn left on Punkin Ledge Rd. and follow it

SEC 11

for 0.8 mi. to Schoodic Bog Rd. Turn left onto this road to reach the trailhead in another 0.1 mi.)

Continue north on SCT and soon reach a bench on the right with a view of Schoodic Mtn. Shortly after, turn left on a gravel road, where views open up to the right over Schoodic Bog. A beaver flowage blocks the road, necessitating a jog left into the woods on a footpath. Cross Johnny's Brook and rejoin the gravel road. At 4.8 mi., cross Down East Sunrise Trail and enter private property. Follow blue flagging along a jeep trail to a T jct.; turn right here on another jeep trail, which leads east along the base of Schoodic Mtn. Go straight at the next jct. and traverse a power-line corridor. At a cairn on the left (watch for this), leave the jeep trail and follow a footpath as it angles up the slope. The path soon joins an eroded ATV trail and turns left, uphill. Follow the rough, rocky trail until the angle eases at an open ledge of bedrock. Soon after, crest the west ridge of Schoodic Mtn. and turn right (east). Take the bedrock trail into the open and then follow cairns and orange flagging. Attractive sights abound: the hills around Bangor, Blue Hill Mtn., the Camden Hills, the mountains of ANP, Frenchman Bay, Schoodic Bog, and Flanders Pond.

Reach the summit of Schoodic Mtn. and its fenced-in communications tower at 6.5 mi. Impressive views here include Chick Hill, Lead Mtn., Donnell Pond, Tunk Mtn., Caribou Mtn., Catherine Mtn., the twin peaks and cliffs of Black Mtn., Pigeon Hill, and Schoodic Head. Also at the summit is the jct. with Schoodic Mtn. Trail, which leads to the Schoodic Beach parking lot in 1.2 mi. (Alternatively, it is 1.4 mi. to the Schoodic Beach parking lot via Schoodic Beach on Donnell Pond using the Schoodic Mtn. and Schoodic Beach trails.)

To spot a car at the Schoodic Beach parking lot in Donnell Pond PL, follow driving directions for Schoodic Mtn.

TUCKER MTN. (410 FT.)

This trail has been decommissioned by FBC due to unsafe parking access.

DOWNEAST COASTAL CONSERVANCY
PIGEON HILL (315 FT.)

Pigeon Hill in Steuben, the highest point along the coast in Washington County, is part of Pigeon Hill Preserve, a stunning 170-acre property protected by DCC. A network of five trails traces the eastern and southern slopes of the hill. The summit ledges of Pigeon Hill offer extraordinary scenic panoramas over Dyer and Pigeon Hill bays west to Blue Hill Mtn. and MDI, south to the lighthouse on Petit Manan Point and the islands of the Greater Pleasant Bay archipelago, and north to the peaks of Donnell Pond PL. Historic Trail is the traditional route to the peak, but hikers can also combine Silver Mine and Summit Loop trails to reach the top. Ledge Woods Trail offers a leisurely descent route.

From the jct. of US 1 and ME 186 (West Bay Rd.) in Gouldsboro, drive east on US 1 for 10.8 mi. to Steuben. Here, turn right (south) onto Pigeon Hill Rd. and drive 4.6 mi. to Pigeon Hill Preserve and trailhead parking on the right (sign), opposite an old cemetery.

HISTORIC TRAIL (USGS PETIT MANAN POINT QUAD, DCC PIGEON HILL PRESERVE MAP, GAZETTEER MAP 17)
Cumulative from Pigeon Hill Rd. (50 ft.) to:

Silver Mine Trail (80 ft.)	100 ft.	30 ft.	0:01
Summit Loop Trail and Silver Mine Trail (220 ft.)	0.3 mi.	170 ft.	0:15
Pigeon Hill summit (315 ft.)	0.4 mi.	265 ft.	0:20

DCC Enter the woods at the trailhead kiosk and proceed 100 ft. to a map stand at a jct., where yellow-blazed Silver Mine Trail departs to the right. Stay left to follow blue-blazed Historic Trail. Pass the interpretive signs ("Jack Pine Woodlands" and "Big Maple") before reaching the upper jct. with Silver Mine Trail, which enters from the right, and Summit Loop Trail, which leaves to the left. Continue straight ahead on Historic Trail and climb to ledges with views south and east. Above, the vista widens at a rock bench. Continue in the open to the summit, where a sign notes how Pigeon Hill played an important role in the Eastern Oblique Arc survey triangulation of the eastern United States from New Orleans, Louisiana, to Calais, Maine, between 1833 and 1898.

SILVER MINE TRAIL AND SUMMIT LOOP TRAIL (USGS PETIT MANAN POINT QUAD, DCC PIGEON HILL PRESERVE MAP, GAZETTEER MAP 17)
Cumulative from Pigeon Hill Rd. (50 ft.) to:

Historic Trail (80 ft.)	100 ft.	30 ft.	0:01
Historic Trail and Summit Loop Trail (220 ft.)	0.4 mi.	170 ft.	0:15
Ledge Woods Trail, lower jct. (200 ft.)	0.5 mi.	170 ft.	0:20
Ledge Woods Trail, upper jct. (270 ft.)	0.6 mi.	240 ft.	0:30
Pigeon Hill summit (315 ft.) via Summit Loop Trail	0.7 mi.	285 ft.	0:35

SEC 11

DCC Silver Mine Trail and Summit Loop Trail, both blazed in yellow, can be combined for an ascent of Pigeon Hill. At a jct. 100 ft. from the trailhead, turn right on Silver Mine Trail and ascend to an overlook on the right. Ahead, pass through semi-open forest to reach a granite bench with views south and east. Soon after, look for the tailings from an old silver mine and the interpretive sign "Silver Mine." Silver Mine Trail then bears left past cliffs and a talus slope to a jct. with Historic Trail, which turns right and goes directly to the top of Pigeon Hill. From the jct., continue straight ahead on Summit Loop Trail to contour around the east and then south side of the hill, passing the lower and upper jct. with Ledge Woods Trail. Above, views open up west to Mt. Desert Island and north to Schoodic Mtn. and Black Mtn. The summit is just ahead.

LEDGE WOODS TRAIL (USGS PETIT MANAN POINT QUAD, DCC PIGEON HILL PRESERVE MAP, GAZETTEER MAP 17)

Cumulative from Pigeon Hill summit (315 ft.) to:

Start of Ledge Woods Trail (270 ft.) via Summit Loop Trail	0.1 mi.	−45 ft.	0:03
Glacial Erratic Spur (140 ft.)	0.6 mi.	−175 ft.	0:15
Summit Loop Trail (200 ft.)	0.7 mi.	100 ft.	0:25
Pigeon Hill Rd. (50 ft.) via Summit Loop and Silver Mine trails	1.2 mi.	100 ft.	0:40
Pigeon Hill Rd. (50 ft.) via Summit Loop and Historic trails	1.1 mi.	100 ft.	0:35

DCC Ledge Woods Trail is described here as a descent route from the summit of Pigeon Hill. Depart the top of the hill via Summit Loop Trail, descending open ledges to reach the jct. with Ledge Woods Trail in the semi-open woods below. Turn right onto red-blazed Ledge Woods Trail and continue to descend the southern slope of the hill to the jct. with Glacial Erratic Spur, a white-blazed trail leading 0.2 mi. to the so-called Lonely Boulder, a huge erratic in the woods that is well worth a visit. Beyond the spur, Ledge Woods Trail drops to a 100-ft. contour before climbing back to end at a jct. with Summit Loop Trail. To the right, it is about 0.5 mi. to the base of Pigeon Hill via Summit Loop Trail and either Historic Trail or Silver Mine Trail.

ESTEY MTN. (274 FT.)

This wooded bump of a mountain in Whiting rises above Roaring Lake in the Orange River Conservation Area, a preserve owned and managed by DCC that protects 700 acres and 9 mi. of shoreline along the Orange River. Estey Mtn. Trail climbs to the west-facing ledges on top, where pleasant views over the lakes and woods of rural Whiting are possible. Access to the trail is by canoe or kayak only, a paddling trip of 1.3 mi. each way. A hand-carry boat launch at Reynolds Marsh Overlook on US 1 is the closest access point.

From the jct. of ME 189 and US 1 in Whiting, drive south on US 1 for 2.6 mi. to the overlook parking lot on the right. Walk a path 100 yd. to the water and the put-in on Orange River Water Trail.

From the launch, paddle to the left and then swing around to the right, and push through the thick marsh growth to the main channel. Head north to the first beaver lodge and follow the river bend to the left. As the marsh opens up, there are more bends, but the channel is better defined. The low mountain visible to the north is Estey Mtn., but it is not a straight line to get there. After a second beaver lodge and a dock with a railing on the left, paddle to the right, and soon after, bear left around an island of cedar trees. A large area of open water is now to the right (north-northeast). Continue paddling to the left along the Orange River channel. Rounding the point on the right, look for a small gray sign (no writing) on a tree and a picnic table in the woods (a grove of large white spruce); take out here.

ESTEY MTN. TRAIL (USGS WHITING QUAD, DCC ORANGE RIVER CONSERVATION AREA MAP, GAZETTEER MAP 26)
Cumulative from Orange River takeout (75 ft.) to:

Estey Mtn. summit (274 ft.)	0.8 mi.	200 ft.	0:30

DCC Estey Mtn. Trail (blue blazes and small brown-and-white hiker sign) heads northeast from the picnic table. Beyond a wet area, the trail rises gently through the conifers. Soon after a sharp left turn, reach an old gravel road. Bear right onto the old road, which forks in 50 ft. Bear left to continue on the grassy/gravelly road, which begins to climb. Estey Mtn. Trail levels off amid a forest floor of delicate lichens and mosses; please stay on the trail to avoid damaging the flora. At the summit, continue ahead and down to the open ledges to take in the scenery.

KLONDIKE MTN. (146 FT.)
Owned and managed by DCC, 46-acre Klondike Mtn. Preserve in Lubec is home to the namesake mountain as well as some 3,600 feet of saltwater shorefront on South Bay. Summit views from Klondike Mtn. range nearly 360 degrees and include Fowler's Mill Pond and the old mill pond dam, plus South Bay.

From the jct. of US 1 and ME 189 in Whiting, proceed east on ME 189 for 8.9 mi. Turn left (north) onto North Lubec Rd. and drive 1.1 mi. to a grassy trailhead parking lot on the left (sign). Here also are an arboretum, an interpretive sign and map, picnic tables, and a park bench.

SEC 11

KLONDIKE MTN. TRAIL (USGS WEST LUBEC QUAD, DCC KLONDIKE MTN. PRESERVE MAP, GAZETTEER MAP 27)
Cumulative from North Lubec Rd. (100 ft.) to:

Fowler's Mill Pond Trail (45 ft.)	0.3 mi.	30 ft.	0:10
Klondike Mtn. north summit (146 ft.)	0.5 mi.	125 ft.	0:20
Complete lollipop loop	0.7 mi.	175 ft.	0:25

DCC The trail leads through the arboretum into the pretty meadow (formerly a cow pasture) and passes right of an old orchard. Enter the woods and walk the wide path downhill to another old pasture. Follow blue diamond markers to a fork in Klondike Mtn. Trail. Continue straight ahead along the woods line, enter the woods, and soon reach a jct. with Fowler's Mill Pond Trail on the left. Turn right here and quickly come to a spur on the left leading to an overlook. Then follow switchbacks up the short but steep slope to emerge on the mostly open south summit of Klondike Mtn. Beyond, drop into a shallow dip, where an alternate (easier) descent goes to the right. Scramble up to an overlook and a bench on the north summit. From the top, drop down a short, rocky pitch. After the alternate descent trail joins from the right, continue down at a moderate grade, level off, and then go along a rocky spine. Close the loop in the meadow and turn left to return to the trailhead.

LUBEC
BENNY'S MTN. (226 FT.)

Maine Coast Heritage Trust owns and manages Hamilton Cove Preserve in Lubec. This rugged 1,225-acre property encompasses 1.5 mi. of cobble beaches, steep cliffs, and rocky promontories on the Gulf of Maine. Although Benny's Mtn. is inland, it offers far-reaching views, ranging from Carrying Place Cove and the town of Lubec to Grand Manan Island in Canada. (The mountain is shown as Porcupine Hill on some maps.)

From the jct. of ME 189 and South Lubec Rd., 1.2 mi. west of downtown Lubec (sign for Quoddy Head State Park), drive south on South Lubec Rd. for 2.7 mi. to a fork. Here, turn right onto Boot Cove Rd. and proceed 2.5 mi. to trailhead parking for Hamilton Cove Preserve on the left.

BENNY'S MTN. TRAIL (USGS WEST LUBEC QUAD, MCHT HAMILTON COVE PRESERVE MAP, GAZETTEER MAP 27)
Cumulative from Boot Cove Rd. (50 ft.) to:

Benny's Mtn. summit (226 ft.) via loop	1.1 mi.	175 ft.	0:40

MCHT Benny's Mtn. Trail is an in-and-out route with a lollipop loop around the summit. From the parking area, walk east 250 ft. to an information kiosk in a small meadow (posted map). Here, Main Trail leaves left, the trail to the beach at Hamilton Cove goes straight, and Meadow Trail and Benny's Mtn. Trail head to the right. In 75 ft., Meadow Trail breaks off left, while Benny's Mtn. Trail continues right to cross Boot Cove Rd. The wide, grassy trail traverses an alder grassland and multiple sections of bog bridging, bears sharply left at a signpost, climbs stone steps to a low ridge, and then crosses a bridge over a small stream. A gentle ascent leads to the base of the wooded, rocky knob of Benny's Mtn. and the summit loop jct. Go straight to walk the loop clockwise. Climb around and up the final knob on rocky steps to several pleasant outlooks. Descend via rock steps through large boulders to close the loop, and then turn left to return to the trailhead.

MOWES MTN. (130 FT.)

This wooded hump is part of Race Point Park, one of 16 parklands in Lubec and Whiting owned and managed by Cobscook Shores, a family-funded Maine charitable foundation that provides public access to miles of undeveloped beaches, bluffs, coves, and islands for hiking, biking, paddling, and other nonmotorized recreational activities.

From the jct. of ME 189 and Crow's Neck Rd. in Lubec, 5.3 mi. west of downtown and 500 ft. west of the jct. of ME 191 and ME 189, turn north onto Crow's Neck Rd. and follow it for 5.8 mi. to its end at Race Point Park and trailhead parking.

MOWES MTN. TRAIL (USGS WHITING AND WEST LUBEC QUADS, COB RACE POINT MAP, GAZETTEER MAP 27)
Cumulative from Crow's Neck Rd. (60 ft.) to:

Mowes Mtn. Trail (40 ft.) via Maple Canopy Trail	0.2 mi.	30 ft.	0:05
Mowes Mtn. summit (130 ft.)	0.4 mi.	90 ft.	0:15

COB Mowes Mtn. Trail is accessed via Maple Canopy Trail. From the kiosk, walk right, across the parking lot. Maple Canopy Trail leaves to the right, immediately after the toilet. Follow the trail over a rise, and then cross a stone wall to reach the jct. with Mowes Mtn. Trail. Turn right on wide Mowes Mtn. Trail and climb easily to the ridge crest. The unmarked ledge outcropping ahead, known as Mowes Overlook, is the summit, which offers a view through the trees to Raft Cove and up Denny's Bay.

COBSCOOK BAY STATE PARK AND VICINITY

SEC 11

Cobscook Bay State Park, which occupies 888 acres on Whiting Bay in Edmunds Township, was carved out of Moosehorn National Wildlife Refuge in 1964 and remains part of the federal refuge by virtue of a long-term, no-cost lease. Tides at Cobscook Bay average 24 ft. and can be as high as

28 ft. when the meteorological conditions are just right. The nutrient-rich waters support a wide variety of sea creatures and birds, making wildlife watching here a popular activity. In addition, camping, hiking, sea kayaking, and boating are available. Two short hiking trails lead to park high points at Littles Mtn. and Cunningham Mtn.

LITTLES MTN. (203 FT.)

A 65-foot steel fire tower, erected in 1963, adorns this wooded bump in the northern section of the park. The tower is closed to the public, and there is no access to the ladder rungs. The summit offers limited views east to Whiting Bay.

From the jct. of US 1 and ME 198 in Whiting, drive north for 4.2 mi. Turn right (east) onto South Edmunds Rd. and proceed 0.5 mi. to Burnt Cove Rd. on the right and the entrance to Cobscook Bay State Park. The entrance station is 0.1 mi. ahead on this road. Trailhead parking for both Littles Mtn. and Cunningham Mtn. is to the right (west), in front of a kiosk. A toilet is nearby.

LITTLES MTN. TRAIL (USGS WHITING QUAD, MBPL COBSCOOK BAY STATE PARK GUIDE & MAP, GAZETTEER MAP 27)
Cumulative from state park entrance station (90 ft.) to:

South Edmunds Rd. (90 ft.)	0.1 mi.	0 ft.	0:03
Littles Mtn. summit (203 ft.)	0.25 mi.	115 ft.	0:12

MBPL Littles Mtn. Trail starts directly across the road from the parking area on the opposite side of the entrance station. Walk through the woods and soon cross South Edmunds Rd. Watch for the sign "Firetower Trail– 0.2 to top." Follow the wide old road on a short but steep and rocky 0.2-mi. climb to the summit tower.

CUNNINGHAM MTN. (161 FT.)

The ledges on this mountaintop on the western side of Cobscook State Park offer fine views to Burnt Cove, Broad Cove, and Whiting Bay, as well as the fire tower atop Littles Mtn. Refer to Littles Mtn. Trail for directions to trailhead parking.

NATURE TRAIL (USGS WHITING QUAD, MBPL COBSCOOK BAY STATE PARK GUIDE & MAP, GAZETTEER MAP 27)
Cumulative from park entrance station (90 ft.) to:

Cunningham Mtn. summit (161 ft.)	0.9 mi.	150 ft.	0:30
Complete loop via Burnt Cove Rd.	1.4 mi.	150 ft.	0:45

MBPL Nature Trail leaves to the left of the kiosk at the entrance station, heading gently downhill to Burnt Cove Brook and the remains of a log bridge. Bear left and soon pass a big white pine. The trail then follows the brook, sometimes above it and other times beside it. Beyond a ravine, cross a plank bridge next to a tidal flat on Burnt Cove and quickly reach a jct. Bear left (the trail straight ahead leads 0.3 mi. along Burnt Cove to the state park campground) to climb on eroded trail through cedars.

At the jct. (sign: "Scenic Overlook"), turn right onto the summit spur path. Scramble on rocky and sometimes steep terrain to reach the summit and an overlook a few steps to the right. Beyond, descend stone stairs to reach a second overlook on large open ledges. To continue, retrace your steps to the jct. and the main part of Nature Trail, and then turn right to reach Burnt Cove Rd. and the trail's end. From here, it is 0.4 mi. north via this park road back to the entrance station and trailhead.

BELL'S MTN. (232 FT.) AND CRANE MTN. (304 FT.)

These two low mountains in Edmunds Township are close to each other on lands that are part of Tide Mill Farm. A conservation easement on the 1,523-acre active saltwater farm held by DIFW protects the farm's ecology while ensuring public access to non-farmstead portions of the property. Both mountains offer short, easy loop hikes.

From the jct. of US 1 and ME 189 in Whiting, drive north on US 1 for 2.5 mi. Turn left (west) on Bell Mtn. Rd. and drive 0.3 mi. to a grassy semicircular parking area on the left (sign).

BELL'S MTN. TRAIL (USGS WHITING QUAD, GAZETTEER MAP 27)
Cumulative from Bell's Mtn. parking area (100 ft.) to:

Bell's Mtn. summit (232 ft.)	0.3 mi.	130 ft.	0:15
Complete loop	0.7 mi.	130 ft.	0:25

DIFW Avoid the wide, grassy road entering the woods to the left of the trailhead sign. Look farther left, toward the mountain, for the signed opening in the woods on the southeastern edge of the parking area.

Enter the woods and immediately bear left at the loop jct. to ascend the mountain in a clockwise direction. The white-blazed trail climbs rock steps and weaves between rocks, making a rising traverse on the mountain's eastern slope (limited view windows). Cresting the ridge of the heavily forested peak, proceed easily to the summit ledges and a partially obscured view over Tide Mill Farm below and farther to Whiting Bay. Descend a fractured cliff face and then contour along the western side of the peak to close the loop.

SEC
11

CRANE MTN. TRAIL (USGS WHITING QUAD, GAZETTEER MAP 27)
Cumulative from Crane Mtn. parking area (210 ft.) to:

Crane Mtn. summit (304 ft.)	0.3 mi.	95 ft.	0:10
Complete loop	0.7 mi.	125 ft.	0:25

DIFW Follow directions to Bell Mtn. and continue on Bell Mtn. Rd. for an additional 0.7 mi. Bear right to quickly reach a dead end and a grassy parking area (sign). To hike Crane Mtn. Trail in a clockwise direction, take the trail to the left of the parking area sign. Climb through thick spruce and fir on the west side of the mountain to reach an outlook on the left; just ahead, a large open ledge offers views north to the wetlands along Crane Mill Brook. Walk easily through mature spruce, circling around the peak to the south. Make a descending traverse, bear west around the mountain, and negotiate a mossy ledge to complete the loop a few yards east of the parking area sign.

MOOSEHORN NATIONAL WILDLIFE REFUGE
Moosehorn National Wildlife Refuge is the easternmost such refuge in the US, part of a vast federal system designed to protect wildlife and its habitats while providing wildlife-related education and recreation opportunities. Established in 1937, the refuge is an important stop for migratory birds on the Atlantic Flyway. MNWR comprises two geographic units: 20,192 acres in Baring Plantation (the Baring Division) and 8,872 acres in nearby Edmunds (Edmunds Division). One-third of the refuge is designated wilderness and is part of the National Wilderness Preservation System. Trails lead to Magurrewock Mtn. and Bald Mtn.

BALD MTN. (IN BARING PLANTATION; 405 FT.)
This Bald Mtn., one of 18 so-named in Maine, is in the Baring Division of MNWR.

From US 1/ME 9, at a point 0.5 mi. west of International Ave. Bridge on the outskirts of downtown Calais, and 2.0 mi. east of the jct. of US 1/ME 9 and ME 191, turn south onto Charlotte Rd. Drive 2.4 mi. to Headquarters Rd. on the right and a sign for MNWR; turn here. From the refuge entrance, proceed west on Headquarters Rd. In 0.3 mi., the one-way road to the right leads to the refuge headquarters and visitor center. Continue straight ahead to reach trailhead parking (left) and restrooms (right) in another 0.2 mi. The main foot trail into the refuge (a gravel road at this point) starts to the left of the flagpole at a sign for Headquarters Rd. Trail.

HEADQUARTERS RD., WILDERNESS TRAIL, AND
TOWER TRAIL (USGS MEDDYBEMPS LAKE EAST QUAD,
USFWS MNWR BARING DIVISION MAP, GAZETTEER MAP 36)
Cumulative from trailhead parking (215 ft.) to:

Wilderness Trail (180 ft.)	0.8 mi.	−35 ft.	0:25
Tower Trail (273 ft.)	1.9 mi.	140 ft.	1:00
Bald Mtn. summit (405 ft.)	2.5 mi.	300 ft.	1:20

MNWR From the trailhead parking area, walk west on Headquarters Rd., one of many refuge road "trails" that are closed to all but official vehicles. Pass Barn Meadow Rd. on the right and then Mile Bridge Rd. on the left. Ahead, where Two Mile Rd. leads sharply left, continue straight on Headquarters Rd. to Mullen Meadow and enter a federally designated wilderness area. Just past the wetlands of Mullen Meadow on the right, Headquarters Rd. reaches a jct. with Conic Trail and Wilderness Trail. Bear left to continue on Wilderness Trail, which narrows to a footpath marked with blue blazes.

Following the route of an old road, Wilderness Trail traverses the Bertrand E. Smith Natural Area, 160 acres set aside in the late 1940s to preserve a representative sample of old-growth white pine. Soon, reach a jct. with Tower Trail on the left. Hike white-blazed Tower Trail east, at a moderate and then more gradual grade, to the wooded summit of Bald Mtn. Here are the downed remains of the old 100-ft. wooden fire tower (erected in 1937). Although there are no views, the concrete stanchions, bolts, cables, and other detritus from the fire tower and fire warden's camp make for interesting exploration.

MAGURREWOCK MTN. (393 FT.)
This low mountain in Calais is just inside the northern boundary of MNWR, Baring Division. The trailhead is on Icehouse Rd. on the south side of US 1/ME 9, 2.8 mi. east of the jct. of US 1/ME 9 and ME 191, and 0.7 mi. west of International Ave. Bridge to Canada on the outskirts of downtown Calais. Park outside the gate on the shoulder of US 1.

MAGURREWOCK MTN. TRAIL
(USGS CALAIS QUAD, GAZETTEER MAP 36)
From US 1 at Icehouse Rd. (70 ft.) to:

Magurrewock Mtn., south summit (393 ft.)	1.0 mi.	320 ft.	0:40

MNWR From the information kiosk, follow Icehouse Rd. (part of the East Coast Greenway, a 3,000-mi. multiuse recreation trail from Calais, Maine, to Key West, Florida), with Middle Magurrewock Marsh on the right. At

0.4 mi. from US 1, the unsigned Magurrewock Mtn. Trail leaves Icehouse Rd. on the left. (At this jct., look for two small signs: "MNWR Auto Tour Route 4.1 mi." and "Mature Forest.") Turn left to follow the wide, grassy jeep track—the trail—on an easy grade, trending east before swinging back west to reach the wooded summit at 1.0 mi., where there are three small communications towers. A path in front of the leftmost (westernmost) tower leads 50 ft. to ledges and a narrow view west over Magurrewock Marsh to the St. Croix River and into New Brunswick, Canada.

DOWNEAST LAKES AREA
WABASSUS MTN. (843 FT.)

This mountain in T43 MD BPP in Washington County is in Downeast Lakes Community Forest, a 55,578-acre parcel of conservation land protected by Downeast Lakes Land Trust.

From the jct. of ME 9 and ME 193 in Beddington, drive east on ME 9 for 14.6 mi. to Machias River Rd. on the left, marked by a blue-and-white MBPL sign. Turn here to enter state-owned Machias River Corridor PL. Drive north on Machias River Rd. (also referred to and sometimes signed as CCC Rd.). At 8.7 mi. from ME 9, turn right to cross a bridge over the Machias River. Immediately after the bridge, turn left to continue north on Little River Rd. At 13.0 mi., pass a DLLT sign on the right. At 15.5 mi., turn left onto a road signed "60-00-0" and "Reggie's Way." At 17.6 mi., the road forks; bear right onto Wabassus Mtn. Rd. At 18.3 mi. from ME 9, reach small, grassy trailhead parking area on the left (no sign).

WABASSUS MTN. TRAIL (USGS GRAND LAKE STREAM QUAD, DLLT DLCF VISITOR'S GUIDE, GAZETTEER MAP 35)
Cumulative from Wabassus Mtn. Rd. (360 ft.) to:

Wabassus Mtn. summit (843 ft.)	0.75 mi.	483 ft.	0:40
Complete summit loop	0.9 mi.	523 ft.	0:45

DLLT From the parking area, walk ahead on Wabassus Mtn. Rd. for 200 ft. The trail (signed) begins on the right just before a stream/culvert. In 50 ft., pass a trail register. Follow blue-and-silver trail markers through a hemlock grove along the course of the stream. Ahead, bear right to cross a short footbridge over the stream. (Faded yellow blazes also mark the lightly used trail.) Climb to a saddle and then bear right up the southeast ridge to reach the jct. with the summit loop. Bear left to follow the short loop clockwise. The wooded summit is marked by a rock with a yellow blaze in a small clearing. Limited views appear through the trees and ahead along the loop. Close the loop and descend left to the trailhead.

PINEO MTN., WEST PEAK (802 FT.)

Pineo Peaks Trail, completed in 2022, is the newest in the DLLT system. The trail explores the peaks of Pineo Mountain that rise above the northeast shore of West Grand Lake, a remote section of the vast DLCF that's entirely within an ecological reserve.

At a point on Grand Lake Stream Rd. 5.5 mi. west of its jct. with US 1 in Indian Township and 4.6 mi. east of the village of Grand Lake Stream, turn north onto Amazon Rd. Drive 8.0 mi. and then turn left on Pineo Point Rd. In 1.6 mi., reach trailhead parking and two trail access points.

PINEO PEAKS TRAIL (USGS OXBROOK LAKES QUAD, DLLT DLCF VISITOR'S GUIDE, GAZETTEER MAP 35)
Cumulative from Pineo Point Rd. (348 ft.) to:

Complete loop	0.8 mi.	350 ft.	0:35

DLLT At the two trail access points, the trail on the left is Pineo Peaks Trail. (The trail on the right leads along the shore of West Grand Lake and reaches Princeton Island CS in 1.6 mi.) Pineo Peaks Trail, easy at first, climbs steadily up the west side of the mountain, winding through mixed hardwood forest. Atop the ridge look for partial views over West Grand Lake. Near the top of the west peak of Pineo Mtn., a short lollipop loop leads to interesting geological features, including granite ledges, small crevasses, caves, and rockfalls.

POCOMOONSHINE MTN. (613 FT.)

This mountain in Princeton, rising nearly 500 ft. above Pocomoonshine Lake, is the former site of an MFS fire tower.

From US 1, 2.3 mi. south of Princeton and 10.5 mi. north of the jct. of US 1 and ME 9 in Baileyville, turn southwest onto South Princeton Rd. Drive 0.9 mi. and then turn right onto Pokey Rd. (unsigned). Follow this gravel road (parallels the power line for much of the way) for 4.0 mi. to a high point on the south side of Pocomoonshine Mtn. and the start of a narrow gravel road, the former MFS fire tower road. Park on the shoulder of the gravel road.

POCOMOONSHINE MTN. TRAIL (USGS PRINCETON QUAD, GAZETTEER MAP 36)
From parking along Pokey Rd. (248 ft.) to:

Pocomoonshine Mtn. summit (613 ft.)	0.6 mi.	365 ft.	0:30

SEC 11

NFTM At the start, the trail route follows the old MFS road across the power-line clearing and uphill into the woods. Stay right (straight) at a fork. Above, the gravel road levels off. At 0.4 mi., look for an old jeep track on the left and climb it to the ridge crest. Farther along, look left into the thick woods to see the concrete stanchions of the old fire tower (removed in the 1970s). To reach the true summit, continue on the jeep track for 250 ft. through two wet depressions. A rusty tow sled sits in the small summit clearing (no views).

CALAIS
DEVIL'S HEAD (355 FT.)

Devil's Head Conservation Area, a 315-acre property owned and managed by the city of Calais, preserves the dramatic granite headland known as Devil's Head, as well as cobble beaches and upland forests on the US side of the international St. Croix River estuary. Devil's Head Trail makes a horseshoe loop over this escarpment on the St. Croix River, offering several views into New Brunswick, Canada. Devil's Head is a variant of "D'Orville's Head," which refers to Sieur d'Orville, an early settler on nearby St. Croix Island, which was established in 1604 as the first French colony in North America.

In the center of downtown Calais, from the jct. of US 1 and ME 9, at the turn for Ferry Point International Bridge to New Brunswick, Canada, drive south on US 1 for 6.2 mi. to a prominent green-and-gold sign on the left for Devil's Head Conservation Area. An information kiosk and a privy are on the edge of the large parking lot. Continue through the lot on the gravel access road and drive 0.3 mi. to the start of Devil's Head Trail on the right. Parking is 100 ft. beyond on the left. Another privy is just past the trail start.

DEVIL'S HEAD TRAIL (USGS DEVIL'S HEAD QUAD, MTF DEVIL'S HEAD CONSERVATION AREA MAP, GAZETTEER MAP 37)
Cumulative from access road, western trailhead (120 ft.) to:

Devil's Head summit (355 ft.)	0.8 mi.	235 ft.	0:30
Eastern trailhead near St. Croix River (50 ft.)	1.3 mi.	235 ft.	0:45
Return to western trailhead via access road	1.7 mi.	485 ft.	1:05

CC Ascend gradually to the northwest ridge. After a switchback, follow a contour along the west side of the hill and then bear left and climb to the southeast ridge. Turn left to climb rock steps along a cleared corridor to reach a bench and a look south to the St. Croix River and St. Croix Island. Beyond, top out on the wooded summit of Devil's Head (bench on the right and a view over the river to New Brunswick). Descend several short, moderate pitches, and then complete the descent to the access road via switchbacks. Turn right to reach the lower parking lot. A privy is on the left; an interpretive sign is on the right and describes some of the area's fascinating history. Stone steps lead from the sign 150 ft. to the shore of the St. Croix River and a dramatic vista downriver past Devil's Head to St. Croix Island. To return to the western trailhead, follow the access road west for 0.4 mi.

GRAND FALLS TOWNSHIP
PASSADUMKEAG MTN. (1,470 FT.)

Passadumkeag Mtn., in Grand Falls Township in Penobscot County (just over the Hancock County line), rises well above the relatively level countryside and extends in a gradual east–west arc for about 5 mi. The mountain is the site of a 13-turbine windpower project. The approach is from the west.

From the jct. of US 2 and Greenfield Rd. in Costigan, proceed east on Greenfield Rd. The road turns to a good dirt road at 11.7 mi. and passes under a major power line that begins to follow the north (left) side of the road at 13.0 mi. Greenfield Rd. goes through an open gate at 13.9 mi., and at 18.1 mi., the power line leaves the north (left) side of the road at a locked gate on a side road that travels underneath the power line. Park in any of the areas off Greenfield Rd. near the gate.

PASSADUMKEAG MTN. TRAIL (NFTM; USGS SAPONAC QUAD, GAZETTEER MAP 34)
From gate on Greenfield Rd. (428 ft.) to:

Passadumkeag Mtn. summit (1,470 ft.)	2.1 mi.	1,040 ft.	1:30

NFTM From the locked gate, follow the side road toward Passadumkeag Mtn., which is visible ahead. At 1.25 mi., pass the old fire warden's camp and a tiny pond on the right. Continue to the next jct. at 1.6 mi., and take the road to the left (the road to the right goes to a wind turbine tower) to a cabin on the left side of the road at 1.9 mi. The old fire tower (1919), once on top of the mountain, now rests on its side behind the cabin. For a 180-degree vista from the summit ridge, ranging from Katahdin west to Mt. Washington and south to the peaks of ANP, continue on the road, passing a tower on the right and then another on the left, where the road surface becomes grass. Proceed to a clearing just before the wind turbine tower at 2.1 mi.

SEC 11

SECTION TWELVE
AROOSTOOK COUNTY

INTRODUCTION

This section describes 26 trails on 16 mountains in the sprawling 6,830-square-mi. expanse of Aroostook County, Maine's largest county— an area larger than Connecticut and Rhode Island combined. Often called the "Crown of Maine" for its geographic sweep across the northern part of the state, the county stretches 120 mi. from north to south between the town of Madawaska and Molunkus Township, and 104 mi. from east to west between T11 R17 WELS and Easton. The county is bounded on the west by the Canadian province of Quebec and on the north and east by New Brunswick, Canada. The St. Francis River and St. John River form part of the northern boundary. To the south are the counties of Somerset, Piscataquis, Penobscot, and Washington.

GEOGRAPHY

Aroostook County is known for its wealth of forestland, lakes, ponds, rivers, hills, and mountains. The county is 89 percent forested, and much of this is commercial timberland. Extensive farmland lies along the US 1 corridor in the east near the Canadian border and upward into the St. John River valley. The Fish River, Allagash River, and St. John River flow northward through Aroostook, and the northern portion of the famous 92-mile-long Allagash Wilderness Waterway is here. Long Lake, Square Lake, Cross Lake, Eagle Lake, and Scopan Lake are in the northeast. Just south of those lakes, the Aroostook River flows northeast into Canada.

The mountains of Aroostook County are widely scattered and often remote, many requiring considerable driving distance over gravel logging roads to reach. They range in elevation from around 1,000 ft. to around 2,000 ft. Peaked Mtn. rises to 2,270 ft. in T10 R8 WELS; it is Aroostook County's highest peak but is trailless.

A number of mountains are near US 1 in the eastern region of Aroostook County. The hills west of Bridgewater include Number Nine Mtn. (1,648 ft.). In the town of Mars Hill, close to the international border at New Brunswick, Canada, is perhaps the county's best-known mountain, Mars Hill (1,741 ft.), which rises prominently from the level land around its base. Just south of the city of Presque Isle is Aroostook State Park, Maine's oldest, where twin-peaked Quaggy Jo Mtn. (the south peak is 1,220 ft. while the north peak is 1,140 ft.) looms over Echo Lake. Popular Quaggy Jo may be the most climbed mountain in the county.

West of Presque Isle, Scopan Mtn. (1,480 ft.) rises east of Scopan Lake amid the 16,700 acres of Scopan PL. Northwest of Scopan is the craggy bump of Haystack Mtn. (1,150 ft.). Hedgehog Mtn. (1,581 ft.) is hemmed between ME 11 and St. Froid Lake. Continuing west, Deboullie PL occupies the entire unorganized township of T13 R12 WELS. Rising from the rugged terrain dotted by pristine ponds are Deboullie Mtn. (1,975 ft.), Black Mtn. (1,909 ft.), Whitman Mtn. (1,815 ft.), and Gardner Mtn. (1,843 ft.). The famed 92-mile-long AWW slices through the vast forestland of west-central Aroostook County and extends far south into Piscataquis County, close to the northern end of Baxter State Park. Two mountains are in the wild and scenic Allagash River corridor: Round Pond Mtn. (1,509 ft.) in Aroostook and Allagash Mtn. (1,813 ft.) in Piscataquis. West of the town of Ashland and just north of the Piscataquis County line are Round Mtn. (2,155 ft.) and Horseshoe Mtn. (2,084 ft.). In northern Piscataquis County, just east of where the Aroostook County and Penobscot County lines meet, lies Norway Bluff (2,284 ft.). Because the best access to Norway Bluff is from Ashland in Aroostook County, it is included in this section.

Half of the Aroostook County mountains lie within the boundary of North Maine Woods, a large block of forestland, most of which is privately owned and cooperatively managed for renewable forest resources while providing outdoor recreational opportunities for the public. Visitors must register at an entry checkpoint and pay camping and day-use fees (cash or check only) to enter the area. See p. xxv for information on access to the lands managed by NMW.

The International Appalachian Trail threads its way across Aroostook County on its way from KAWW through New Brunswick, Quebec, Prince Edward Island, and Nova Scotia to its North American terminus at Crow Head in Newfoundland, a total distance of nearly 1,600 mi. The IAT enters Aroostook north of Patten and leaves the US northeast of Mars Hill. The section of the IAT leading to the summit of Mars Hill is described in this section of the guide.

ROAD ACCESS

Trailheads are scattered far and wide across the great expanse of Aroostook County. I-95 is the primary highway access to the county from the south. From I-95, ME 11 connects Sherman Station to Fort Kent. From the terminus of I-95 in Houlton, US 1 heads north along the eastern margin of the county, parallel to the Canadian border as far as Van Buren. ME 163 is a major connector between Presque Isle and Ashland. ME 11 at Ashland and ME 163 at St. Francis are two of a number of jumping-off points for entry into NMW, where travel to remote trailheads is over long distances on active gravel logging roads.

CAMPING

Aroostook State Park features drive-in campsites, showers, and restrooms as well as a backcountry shelter on Quaggy Jo Mtn. Deboullie PL has primitive campsites, most of them drive-in, but a few are in the backcountry with access by an extensive trail system. Many NMW-authorized campsites are dispersed throughout Aroostook County, not including those with access from the St. John River. A handful of state campsites are available on the water approaches to Round Pond Mtn. and Allagash Mtn. in the AWW. Several primitive water-access campsites are in Scopan PL. Seven privately operated campgrounds lie in eastern Aroostook County.

SUGGESTED HIKES

■ Easy
HAYSTACK MTN.

		↕	↗	↻
RT via Cpl. Dustin J. Libby Summit Trail		0.5 mi.	255 ft.	0:30

Make this short but steep climb for broad views ranging across the vast forestlands of Aroostook County as far as Katahdin. A memorial bench on top makes a great spot for a break. See Cpl. Dustin J. Libby Summit Trail, p. 582.

HEDGEHOG MTN.

		↕	↗	↻
RT via Hedgehog Mtn. Trail		1.2 mi.	521 ft.	1:10

Hike to the open ledges on this summit for a panorama that includes Portage Lake, the Fish River, St. Froid Lake, the rugged peaks of Deboullie PL, and Katahdin. See Hedgehog Mtn. Trail, p. 583.

CRATER POND

		↕	↗	↻
RT via Crater Trail and access road		3.5 mi.	325 ft.	1:55

Circle pretty Crater Pond and enjoy the scenery from several craggy lookouts on this pleasant ridge walk. To begin, see Crater Trail, p. 590.

■ Moderate

QUAGGY JO MTN.

LP via South Peak Trail, Ridge Trail, and North Peak Trail	2.0 mi.	825 ft.	1:30

Travel a scenic loop over twin summits for views across Echo Lake and to the hills and farmland beyond. To begin, see South Peak Trail, p. 578.

MARS HILL

RT via IAT	2.4 mi.	1,110 ft.	2:20

Hike a section of the IAT for extensive vistas southwest to Katahdin and east into Canada, as well as a close-up look at Maine's first wind-power project. See IAT Northbound to Mars Hill, p. 579.

SCOPAN MTN.

RT via Scopan Mtn. Trail	3.8 mi.	660 ft.	2:15

This enjoyable loop hike reaches two lookouts with attractive views—first to the east and then to the west—over the vast, forested landscape of eastern Aroostook County. See Scopan Mtn. Trail, p. 581.

DEBOULLIE POND

LP via Deboullie Loop Trail	5.7 mi.	340 ft.	3:00

Make a wonderful loop around this large, lovely pond for great sights of Deboullie Mtn. and Black Mtn., passing ice caves and a small beach along the way. See Deboullie Loop Trail, p. 587.

ALLAGASH MTN.

RT via Allagash Mtn. Trail	3.8 mi.	832 ft.	2:40

From the summit's renovated fire tower, drink in outstanding views of über-scenic Allagash Lake, the Allagash River region, and far beyond. See Allagash Mtn. Trail, p. 596.

■ Strenuous
DEBOULLIE MTN. AND BLACK MTN.

LP via Black Mtn. Trail, Tower Trail, and Deboullie Loop Trail	5.8 mi.	1,300 ft.	3:30

Hike the premier summits in this wild and remote region. Enjoy a handful of craggy outlooks and an old fire tower on Deboullie Mtn. and then circle back along pristine Deboullie Pond. To begin, see Black Mtn. Trail, p. 586.

GARDNER MTN. AND GARDNER POND

LP via Gardner Loop Trail	9.3 mi.	1,750 ft.	5:35

Explore the bumpy ridgeline of Gardner Mtn. and loop around the clear waters of Gardner Pond for a look at the talus slopes and cliff faces on the mountain's north side. See Gardner Loop Trail, p. 591.

TRAIL DESCRIPTIONS
AROOSTOOK STATE PARK

This park, just south of Presque Isle proper, was established in 1938 on 100 acres of land donated by local citizens as Maine's first state park. Subsequent donations have increased the size of the property to its present 900 acres, which encompass the surprisingly rugged peaks of Quaggy Jo Mtn. and much of the west shore of Echo Lake. The park offers year-round recreation, including hiking, swimming, boating, picnicking, cross-country skiing, and snowshoeing. Camping is available at 30 drive-in sites (restrooms, showers, potable water).

From a point on US 1 that is 4 mi. south of Presque Isle and 10.7 mi. north of Mars Hill, turn west onto Spragueville Rd. (sign for state park). At 1.0 mi. from US 1, turn left onto State Park Rd. and proceed to the park entrance station (fee). The day-use parking area is a short distance beyond, on the left just above Echo Lake.

QUAGGY JO MTN. (SOUTH PEAK 1,220 FT., NORTH PEAK 1,140 FT.)

This mountain rises abruptly west of Echo Lake and is the central natural feature of Aroostook State Park. Quaggy Jo is a version of its Wabanaki name, *QuaQuaJo*, which translates to "twin-peaked." A four-trail network

SEC 12

on the mountain offers 3.25 mi. of hiking. If visitors plan to hike the entire 3-mi. loop over Quaggy Jo Mtn. (including South Peak Trail, Ridge Trail, and North Peak Trail), park officials highly recommend doing so in a clockwise direction, starting with South Peak Trail.

SOUTH PEAK TRAIL (USGS ECHO LAKE QUAD, MBPL AROOSTOOK STATE PARK: HIKING AND CROSS-COUNTRY SKI TRAILS MAP, GAZETTEER MAP 65)
From campground at site 18 (645 ft.) to:

Quaggy Jo Mtn., South Peak (1,220 ft.)	0.4 mi.	575 ft.	0:30

MBPL South Peak Trail starts from the campground at site 18 (sign); from the day-use parking lot, walk west on the park road through the campground to the outer edge of the lower loop. The trail starts out on a cross-country ski trail, following blue blazes. In 350 ft., Notch Trail departs to the right (leads 0.25 mi. to the Quaggy Jo ridgeline north of and below South Peak). At 0.1 mi., begin a steep ascent. At 0.2 mi., scramble on slabby rock up the left side of a rock face. At 0.3 mi., negotiate a wide and steep path of loose rock, and soon after, weave up a rock face (views back to Echo Lake). At 0.4 mi., Ridge Trail leaves to the right. Communications towers are visible ahead. Continue easily up, pass to the right of the towers, and reach the summit sign ("South Peak") 100 ft. beyond the Ridge Trail jct. Bear right and drop down a side path to the lookout platform for a wonderful view to the west, as well as to Quaggy Jo's North Peak and the city of Presque Isle.

Notch Trail. This short connector trail extends from near the start of South Peak Trail to a notch north of and below South Peak and gains 235 ft. of elevation. At 350 ft., begin climbing rock steps through a ravine. Ahead, cross two footbridges over an intermittent stream. At 0.25 mi., join Ridge Trail.

RIDGE TRAIL (USGS ECHO LAKE QUAD, MBPL AROOSTOOK STATE PARK: HIKING AND CROSS-COUNTRY SKI TRAILS MAP, GAZETTEER MAP 65)
From South Peak Trail (1,200 ft.) to:

Quaggy Jo Mtn., North Peak (1,140 ft.)	1.0 mi.	250 ft.	0:40

MBPL Ridge Trail heads north from the jct. with South Peak Trail just below the top of South Peak. Descend moderately at first along the north ridge of South Peak and then more steeply over a short pitch of loose rocks. The path levels out at 0.2 mi. and reaches the jct. with Notch Trail on the right at 0.3 mi. Continuing on Ridge Trail, climb at an easy grade to join a grassy jeep track at a signpost at 0.6 mi.; go right to stay on Ridge Trail.

Proceed easily on the wide track to an Adirondack-style shelter and picnic table on the right at 0.75 mi. This vantage point on the ridge offers a view east over Echo Lake and south to Mars Hill. From the shelter, descend easily, and then ascend on the wide track to reach the jct. with North Peak Trail, which enters from the right at 0.95 mi. Continue straight ahead on Ridge Trail, pass a viewpoint on the left, and arrive at the top of North Peak at 1.0 mi., where there is a view of Echo Lake and Presque Isle.

NORTH PEAK TRAIL (USGS ECHO LAKE QUAD, MBPL AROOSTOOK STATE PARK: HIKING AND CROSS-COUNTRY SKI TRAILS MAP, GAZETTEER MAP 65)
From Ridge Trail (1,125 ft.) to:

Campground near playground (585 ft.)	0.6 mi.	−540 ft.	0:20

MBPL From the jct. with Ridge Trail just below the top of North Peak, descend easily at first and then steeply. At 0.25 mi., the grade eases. Soon after, cross a cross-country ski trail at an angle; then follow a series of boardwalks. At 0.4 mi., QuaQuaJo Nature Trail on the left leads 200 ft. to the day-use parking area above Echo Lake. Break here to end the hike, or continue on a long, easy contour to end at the campground just above the playground.

US 1 CORRIDOR
MARS HILL (1,741 FT.)
This monadnock rises abruptly in the eastern section of the namesake town of Mars Hill, in an almost-level area of farms and woodland. The mountain extends in a north–south direction for about 3 mi. and parallels the Canadian border, just to the east. It is the site of the first large-scale windpower project in New England, with 28 turbines lining the long ridgetop.

To reach the trailhead from the jct. of US 1A and US 1 in Mars Hill, take US 1A north for 0.3 mi. Turn right (east) onto Boynton Rd., and go 1.3 mi. to a T intersection. Turn right onto East Blaine Rd., and soon after, turn left onto Graves Rd., which leads to the Bigrock Mtn. ski area. Park in the gravel parking lot near the base lodge.

IAT NORTHBOUND TO MARS HILL (USGS MARS HILL QUAD, IAT/SIA INTERNATIONAL APPALACHIAN TRAIL: MAINE SECTION MAP, GAZETTEER MAP 59)
From Bigrock Mtn. ski area parking lot (630 ft.) to:

IAT jct. atop ridge (1,550 ft.)	0.9 mi.	920 ft.	0:55
Mars Hill south summit (1,741 ft.) via IAT and multiuse trail	1.2 mi.	1,110 ft.	1:10

SEC 12

IAT The route is marked with light-blue blazes and blue-and-white IAT markers. From the right (south) side of the base lodge, walk right (south) past the Space Shuttle—a surface carpet lift—to the Apollo Triple Chair. Climb Outer Orbit ski trail to the upper station of the chairlift, and then proceed past the lift line and station and across the clearing to Hooch, a ski trail that rises steeply up the mountain. At this point, look to the left (north) for an IAT trail marker and an opening in the woods that indicates the first in a series of four switchbacks. The switchbacks are all marked and help reduce the steepness of the ski trail while giving hikers more of a backcountry feel during the ascent, because each switchback enters and exits on the ski trail. Follow Hooch for short segments while progressing to each subsequent switchback. After the final switchback, proceed on the Hooch to a footpath on the right (east) side of the ski trail. This path intersects with a gravel multiuse trail near the base of one of the wind towers.

Follow the multiuse trail to the right (south) to reach the summit of Mars Hill, a shelter (the IAT Mars Hill Lean-to), picnic tables, and a privy. From the summit clearing just beyond, views extend across forests and farmland in all directions, ranging as far southwest as Katahdin and east into New Brunswick, Canada, across the St. John River valley. (*Note*: From the jct. with the multiuse trail, the IAT continues northbound along the ridgeline of Mars Hill toward Fort Fairfield and the Canadian border, a distance of 5.1 miles.)

NUMBER NINE MTN. (1,648 FT.)

This peak is west of Bridgewater in a small group of mountains clustered around Number Nine Lake. In Bridgewater, from the jct. of US 1 and Bootfoot Rd., turn west onto Bootfoot Rd. (paved) and continue for 3.1 mi. to a T intersection. Turn right onto the unmarked gravel road (Number Nine Lake Rd.). Pass Whitney Brook Rd. on the right at 4.5 mi. At 11.4 mi., bear left at the fork and go uphill to reach the Number Nine Lake parking lot and boat launch site at 12.1 mi. (*Note*: Number Nine Lake Rd. follows a power line for about the first 10 mi. Where the power line leaves the road on the left at 11.4 mi., proceed directly to Number Nine Lake.) No camping is allowed in the area of the boat launch (posted sign).

NUMBER NINE MTN. TRAIL (USGS NUMBER NINE LAKE QUAD, GAZETTEER MAP 59)

From parking area and boat launch (1,100 ft.) to:

Number Nine Mtn. summit (1,648 ft.)	1.5 mi.	548 ft.	1:00

NFTM From the boat launch and parking area, follow a camp road across a bridge over the outlet stream and south along the east side of the lake. At

0.4 mi., pass a gravel road on the left. At 0.5 mi., Number Nine Mtn. Trail departs on a left fork through a yellow gate and starts climbing on what appears to be a gravel road at the start but is paved. At 1.1 mi., pass through a second yellow gate. The trail extends to a communications tower and small building owned by Fraser Company. The actual summit is a short distance beyond the tower and has some open ledges with views. (*Note*: A 350-megawatt wind farm with as many as 119 turbines is proposed for the mountains around Number Nine Lake. As of 2022, it was not known how this project, if approved, will affect access to Number Nine Mtn. and the route of this trail.)

ME 163 CORRIDOR
SCOPAN MTN. (1,480 FT.)

This long, bumpy ridge in T11 R4 WELS between Presque Isle and Ashland rises east of Scopan Lake amid 16,700-acre Scopan PL.

From the jct. of US 1 and State St. in downtown Presque Isle, turn west onto State St. and drive across the bridge over Presque Isle Stream to ME 163 in 0.2 mi. Turn left onto ME 163 and drive west for 7.1 mi. to West Chapman Rd. in Mapleton. Reset trip meter. Turn south onto West Chapman Rd. and drive 6.9 mi. to a fork (road turns to gravel at 6.0 mi.). Stay right at the fork, and at 8.8 mi., turn right (small sign). At the next fork at 9.1 mi., stay right, and at 10.7 mi. from ME 163, turn left into the trailhead parking lot (kiosk, pit toilet).

SCOPAN MTN. TRAIL (USGS SCOPAN LAKE EAST QUAD, MTF SCOPAN MTN. TRAIL, GAZETTEER MAP 58)
Cumulative from trailhead parking (785 ft.) to:

Scopan Mtn. summit ridge (1,410 ft.) and first viewpoint	2.0 mi.	625 ft.	1:20
Complete loop	3.8 mi.	660 ft.	2:15

MBPL Scopan Mtn. Trail makes a circuit over the northern portion of the mountain from the base of its eastern slope. The blue-blazed trail leaves to the left of the trailhead kiosk and proceeds north on the level to a fork at 0.1 mi. To follow the loop counterclockwise as described, go right at the fork. Ahead, traverse a wet section on several sets of bog bridges and then trend west and begin climbing. At 1.0 mi., the trail joins an old forest road. Follow the wide track up a shallow ravine. Reach a level shelf and then veer left and up to a winding rock staircase. Traverse north across the mountainside on an undulating route, passing a low, mossy rock wall on the left at 1.6 mi. At 1.9 mi., after a moderate pitch via a rock staircase, arrive at a view window to the east. A short, steep pitch via a couple of switchbacks

SEC 12

leads to the summit ridge, which has a log bench and a view east over Alder Lake to Quaggy Jo Mtn. and Presque Isle.

Swing around the wooded summit and start down the ridge. At several large, bucked-up logs at 2.25 mi., look for Peaked Mtn. and a jumble of hills to the southwest. Continue the descent, cross an old forest road in a saddle, and amble easily along the rolling ridge to a knob on the east side of the mountain at 2.9 mi. Begin a steady descent and then contour southwest into a ravine. Pass below a mossy cliff face before angling down the slope to the mountain's base. Close the loop and turn right to return to the trailhead.

HAYSTACK MTN. (1,250 FT.)

Haystack Mtn., an extinct volcano, is on the north side of ME 163 in Castle Hill, east of Ashland and west of Presque Isle. MBPL owns and manages the 215-acre property surrounding the mountain. In 2011, the summit trail was named in honor of Dustin J. Libby of Castle Hill, a US Marine corporal who was killed in action in Iraq in 2006. The town of Castle Hill maintains the trail.

From the jct. of ME 11 and ME 163 in Ashland, drive 9.3 mi. east on ME 163. Alternatively, from the jct. of US 1 and State St. in downtown Presque Isle, turn west onto State St. and drive across the bridge over Presque Isle Stream to ME 163 in 0.2 mi. Turn left on ME 163 and drive west for 11.0 mi. A short gravel driveway provides access to the trailhead, a well-marked parking lot, and a picnic area at a height-of-land on the north side of ME 163. No water or toilets are available, and camping and overnight parking are not allowed.

CPL. DUSTIN J. LIBBY SUMMIT TRAIL (USGS MAPLETON QUAD, MTF HAYSTACK MTN. TRAIL: CASTLE HILL, GAZETTEER MAP 64)
From ME 163 parking lot (995 ft.) to:

Haystack Mtn. summit (1,250 ft.)	0.25 mi.	255 ft.	0:15

TCH The trail starts to the left of the information kiosk at the north end of the parking lot. Well graded at the start, it becomes rougher as it climbs moderately and then steeply to an unmarked jct. at the base of the open ledges on the upper mountain. Here, the trail bears left and rises. (*Note*: To the right, a rocky scramble up a gully leads to an exposed ledge face that hikers must scale to reach the summit. MBPL does not recommend this route, even though it is shown on MBPL's map as part of a Haystack Mtn. loop.) Beyond, Libby Summit Trail ascends on more rugged terrain and then makes a short climb over ledges before swinging around to the top.

The grassy, rocky summit offers a scenic panorama that includes Katahdin to the southwest, Mapleton farmland to the south and east, Scopan

Mtn. and Scopan Lake immediately to the south, Quaggy Jo Mtn. and Mars Hill to the south-southeast, and Round Mtn. in the heart of NMW to the west. The bench dedicated to Corporal Libby is a fine spot for a break.

ME 11 CORRIDOR
HEDGEHOG MTN. (1,581 FT.)

Hedgehog Mtn. in T15 R6 WELS rises just west of St. Froid Lake. The trailhead is on the west side of ME 11, 3.5 mi. south of Winterville and 12.9 mi. north of Portage (jct. of ME 11 and West St.). Parking is available at a well-marked highway rest area, where there are picnic shelters, a spring, and a vault toilet, but no camping or overnight parking. A trail to the top of the mountain is maintained by Hedgehog Mtn. Land Trust.

HEDGEHOG MTN. TRAIL (USGS WINTERVILLE QUAD, MTF HEDGEHOG MTN. TRAIL: WINTERVILLE, GAZETTEER MAP 63)
From picnic area and parking on ME 11 (1,060 ft.) to:

Hedgehog Mtn. summit (1,581 ft.)	0.6 mi.	521 ft.	0:35

HMLT Hedgehog Mtn. Trail leaves from the southwest corner of the picnic area. Look right, into the woods, for a small blue sign with a white arrow posted to a tree. Walk to the arrow and then bear left up the now-obvious trail. The moss-covered concrete spring will be immediately on your left. The trail soon passes between the old fire warden's cabin and a white building. Then it climbs steadily up the south ridge to a picnic table on the summit, where there was once a fire tower (erected in 1914, removed in 1978). From the open ledges are fine views of Portage Lake, the Fish River, and St. Froid Lake to the south and west. Deboullie Mtn. and Black Mtn. are visible to the west. Katahdin can be seen far to the south.

OAK HILL (1,096 FT.)

The path to the Oak Hill fire tower is heavily overgrown and no longer usable.

DEBOULLIE PUBLIC LANDS

In T15 R9 WELS, in the vast forestland south of St. Francis and northwest of Portage, Deboullie PL is one of the most remote properties in the Maine public lands system. Deboullie is an adaptation of the French word *déboulier*, which translates to "tumble down," a reference to the many rock slides, or talus fields, in the area. The 21,871 acres encompassed by Deboullie PL include 17 scenic ponds and a cluster of low, rugged mountains. Deboullie Mtn. is the highest of the group at 1,975 ft., with a fire tower on top that offers expansive views. Neighboring Black Mtn. is nearly as high (1,909 ft.). Incorporated in Deboullie PL is a 6,903-acre ecological reserve

SEC 12

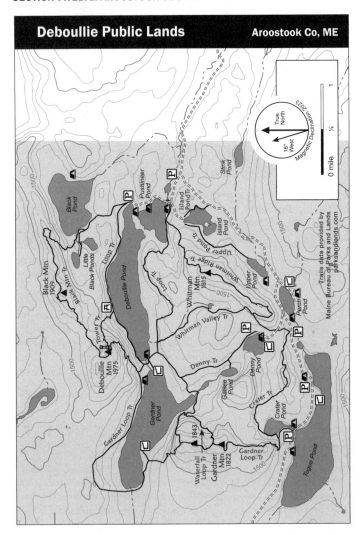

Deboullie Public Lands
Aroostook Co, ME

Trails data provided by Maine Bureau of Parks and Lands. parksandlands.com

that protects the shorelines of 11 remote ponds. A 30-mi. network of blue-blazed hiking trails extends across the rugged backcountry. Remote campsites are on Deboullie Pond and Gardner Pond. Frontcountry campsites are on or near Pushineer Pond, Deboullie Pond, Togue Pond, Crater Pond, Denny Pond, Upper Pond, and Perch Pond. All campsites are primitive and include only a fire ring, picnic table, and privy.

Access from the north at St. Francis: From the jct. of US 1 and ME 161 in Fort Kent, drive west on ME 161 for 17 mi. to the tiny village of St. Francis (town office and post office). From there, drive an additional 6.0 mi. to Chamberlain's Market on the left at the jct. of ME 161 and St. Francis Rd. Reset trip meter. Turn left (south) onto unsigned St. Francis Rd., and at a fork in 0.3 mi. stay straight. At 0.4 mi., reach NMW's St. Francis Checkpoint, where visitors must register and pay a day-use fee (and camping fee, if applicable) to enter (cash or check only). At 7.0 mi., Hewes Brook Rd. joins from the left; continue straight. Cross a bridge at 7.3 mi. Gardner Brook Rd. enters from the left at 8.2 mi.; continue straight. At 8.7 mi. from ME 161, turn left onto an unsigned gravel road (small signs for Deboullie PL and Red River Camps).

Enter Deboullie PL just ahead at 8.9 mi. (blue-and-white sign). Stay straight at all jcts. At 15.2 mi., on the left is the Togue Pond trailhead and parking for Gardner Loop Trail and Crater Trail. On the left at 16.5 mi. is the Whitman Mtn. trailhead (east end of Crater Trail, Whitman Ridge Trail, and access to Whitman Valley Trail). Denny Pond Rd. leaves to the left at 16.7 mi. (access to Denny Pond Trail is 0.5 mi. north on this road). At 17.1 mi., a road to Perch Pond goes right; bear left here, and reach a T intersection at 18.9 mi. Here, T15 R9/Red River Rd. enters from the right (access route from Portage). Turn left, and in another 0.2 mi., bear right at a fork (left goes to southeast end of Deboullie Loop Trail and on to Red River Camps). Drive 0.8 mi., passing the outlet of Pushineer Pond, the Deboullie East campsites, and a boat launch and parking site to arrive at the hiker parking area at the end of the road.

Access from the southeast at Portage: From the jct. of ME 11 and West Rd. (opposite Coffin's General Store and the Portage post office and next to Dean's Motor Lodge and Restaurant), turn left (west) on West Rd. and drive along the south end of Portage Lake. Just beyond the lake, at 1.0 mi., turn left onto Rocky Brook Rd. and drive through an active commercial woodyard (Maine Wood Company). At the next jct., at 1.8 mi., stay straight. At 5.3 mi., reach NMW's Fish River Checkpoint, where visitors must register and pay a day-use fee (and camping fee, if applicable) to enter (cash or check only). At 7.1 mi., leave Rocky Brook Rd. and turn right onto Hewes Brook Rd. Cross a one-lane bridge over the Fish River at 10.4 mi. At 12.4 mi., a road on the left leads to Fish River Lake; continue straight on Hewes Brook Rd. At 19.9 mi., just after crossing the Red River, leave Hewes Brook Rd. and turn left onto T15 R9/Red River Camps Rd. At 27.4

SEC 12

mi., enter Deboullie PL (blue-and-white sign). To the right, it is 1.0 mi. to the trailhead at the end of the road (just beyond the Deboullie Pond boat launch and parking area and the Deboullie East campsites).

DEBOULLIE MTN. (1,975 FT.) AND BLACK MTN. (1,909 FT.)

Deboullie Mtn. rises steeply above the western end of Deboullie Pond. Visitors can enjoy a fine look at the prominent peak and tower from the eastern end of the pond, and they can reach the peak via Deboullie Loop Trail and Tower Trail or via Black Mtn. Trail. The 48-ft. fire tower on the summit affords excellent views that extend south to Katahdin, southeast to Haystack Mtn., and southwest to Horseshoe Mtn.

Black Mtn. is just northeast of Deboullie Mtn., connected by a long ridge. The approach to the wooded peak via Black Mtn. Trail passes Little Black Ponds and Black Pond and features numerous outlooks with clear views to the south and north. Continue over Deboullie Mtn. and return to the trailhead via the north shore of Deboullie Pond for a fine loop hike.

BLACK MTN. TRAIL (AMC DEBOULLIE PUBLIC LANDS MAP)
Cumulative from Deboullie Pond hiker parking area at end of road (1,150 ft.) to:

Little Black Ponds Trail (1,290 ft.)	0.6 mi.	150 ft.	0:25
Black Mtn. summit (1,909 ft.)	2.3 mi.	850 ft.	1:35
Deboullie Mtn. summit and fire tower (1,975 ft.)	3.7 mi.	1,250 ft.	2:30
Gardner Pond Trail (1,240 ft.)	4.4 mi.	1,250 ft.	2:50

MBPL Black Mtn. Trail connects the east and west ends of Deboullie Pond via an ascent over the long, undulating ridgelines of Black Mtn. and Deboullie Mtn. At the hiker parking area at the end of the road a short distance beyond the Deboullie Pond boat launch and the Deboullie East campsites, look for a sign for Deboullie Mtn. Trail, Black Ponds, and Deboullie Tower. Deboullie Loop Trail enters the woods on the left; follow this to quickly connect to Black Mtn. Trail.

At a jct. in 0.1 mi. (sign), Black Mtn. Trail goes right, while Deboullie Loop Trail goes straight ahead; turn right to continue on Black Mtn. Trail, which proceeds easily north on an old jeep track. Climb a rocky stretch and then descend to a jct. Black Pond is through the woods to the right. Here, Little Black Ponds Trail extends 0.5 mi. west to the two Little Black Ponds.

From the jct., Black Mtn. Trail soon passes a side path on the right that leads 50 ft. to Black Pond. Black Mtn. Trail then swings around the west side of the pond before climbing in earnest via rock steps. The ascent is steady at a moderate-to-steep grade. At a shallow notch at 1.2 mi., the trail bears right to gain a shelf above and then drops to Black Mtn. Overlook, which offers fine vistas south over Black Pond. Beyond, climb a short, steep pitch and then descend to a shelf and follow a route west across the ridgeline of Black Mtn. At 1.7 mi., reach Four Ponds Overlook immediately to the left. From here, Deboullie, Black, Pushineer, and Island ponds are all visible. At 2.2 mi., climb rock steps to reach the wooded high point on Black Mtn.

Ahead, descend the western ridge to Fifth Pelletier Brook Lake Overlook on the right at 2.4 mi. After a contour, regain the ridge and then descend toward Deboullie Mtn. Pass an unsigned outlook to the north at 2.8 mi. and make a moderate descent before traveling easily along the ridge. Reach a saddle at the base of Deboullie and join an old jeep track up and west for a short stretch. On foot trail again, circle around the rugged upper rocks of Deboullie. At 3.6 mi., a view on the right looks out over Gardner Pond to the Gardner Mtn. rock slide. At 3.7 mi., reach the summit of Deboullie Mtn. and its 48-foot fire tower (erected in 1929; a new cab was installed in 2020). Here also is a picnic table, the old fire warden's cabin, a privy, and another outbuilding. To the south, Tower Trail leaves to the left side of the clearing.

To continue on Black Mtn. Trail from the top of Deboullie Mtn., looking south, return to the right edge of the clearing where the path entered. Turn left onto an unsigned trail, and soon begin a very steep descent on a narrow path down the south side of the mountain. At 3.9 mi., the angle eases, and at 4.0 mi., reach the base of a talus slope and proceed along its base. Turn away from the slope at 4.2 mi. and begin a mostly steady descent to reach a T jct. with Gardner Loop Trail at 4.4 mi. To the right, this trail leads west around Gardner Pond. To the left, Gardner Pond Trail connects with Deboullie Loop Trail near the western end of Deboullie Pond.

DEBOULLIE LOOP TRAIL (AMC DEBOULLIE PUBLIC LANDS MAP)
Cumulative from Deboullie Pond hiker parking area at end of road (1,140 ft.) to:

Tower Trail (1,140 ft.)	1.4 mi.	50 ft.	0:40
Gardner Loop Trail (1,140 ft.)	2.2 mi.	50 ft.	1:10
Whitman Valley Trail (1,180 ft.)	2.7 mi.	90 ft.	1:25
Whitman Ridge Trail (1,150 ft.)	4.7 mi.	340 ft.	2:30
Access road to Red River Camps (1,180 ft.)	4.9 mi.	340 ft.	2:35
Complete loop via access roads	5.7 mi.	340 ft.	3:00

MBPL At the trailhead parking lot at the end of the road a short distance beyond the Deboullie Pond boat launch and the Deboullie East campsites, look for a sign for Deboullie Mtn. Trail, Black Ponds, and Deboullie Tower. Deboullie Loop Trail enters the woods on the left. At a jct. in 0.1 mi. (sign), Black Mtn. Trail goes right, while Deboullie Loop Trail goes straight ahead.

SEC 12

Continue on Deboullie Loop Trail through the woods away from Deboullie Pond, and then return toward the shore. At 0.5 mi., a side path on the left leads 40 ft. to the pond. Soon after, pass a sign on the right: "Ice Caves." (In the narrow, shaded rock crevices here, ice and snow can remain year-round.) At 1.2 mi., reach a talus slope. Cross the slope above the pond and enjoy views ahead to the Deboullie Mtn. fire tower and Gardner Mtn. Reenter the woods and reach the jct. with Tower Trail on the right at 1.4 mi. (picnic table on the left).

From the jct., Deboullie Loop Trail stays fairly close to the pond. At 2.0 mi., walk through a section of large, mossy boulders, and at 2.2 mi. arrive at an unsigned jct. To the right, Gardner Loop Trail heads west to meet the west end of Black Mtn. Trail and then continues around Gardner Pond. To the left, Deboullie Loop Trail and Gardner Loop Trail coincide for the next 0.3 mi. Turn left and soon cross the outlet of Gardner Pond. Just beyond, reach Gardner Portage Trail; this 0.1-mi. path connects Deboullie Pond and Gardner Pond. From the jct., Deboullie Pond and the Deboullie West campsites are 100 ft. left (east); Gardner Pond and Gardner East Shelter are 0.1 mi. to the right (west).

From the jct., continue ahead on Deboullie Loop Trail, following an old woods road. Ahead, bear left onto a footpath, and reach another old road at a jct. at 2.5 mi. Here, Gardner Loop Trail turns right, while Deboullie Loop Trail heads left. Go left on Deboullie Loop Trail. In another 0.2 mi., Whitman Valley Trail departs on the right. After this jct., Deboullie Loop Trail crosses a stream and follows an old woods road. At 3.0 mi., the trail diverges right off the old road and bears left along the base of a large, mossy cliff wall. Climb the left side of the wall via steps, iron rungs, and roots; then make a rising traverse across the slope. Reach a high point and follow a contour, now high above Deboullie Pond. Descend steeply off the ridge and follow a contour again.

At 3.8 mi., arrive at a bench next to a boulder with a view to the north across Deboullie Pond to the talus slope on Black Mtn. Thread through mossy boulders, make a long descent to Pushineer Pond, cross a streamlet, and reach the pond's south shore at 4.5 mi. Follow the shore east to the jct. with Whitman Ridge Trail, which enters from the right at 4.7 mi. From here, follow the old woods road out to the access road that leads to Red River Camps, where Deboullie Loop Trail ends at 4.9 mi.

To return to the Deboullie Pond trailhead, turn left and walk downhill to a privy on the left. Enter the woods at the privy and go steeply downhill to join the access road near Pushineer South CS. Walk north along the road, which crosses the outlet of Pushineer Pond. Pass four campsites and two boat launches en route to the Deboullie Pond trailhead at the end of the road, 0.5 mi. ahead.

TOWER TRAIL (AMC DEBOULLIE PUBLIC LANDS MAP)
Cumulative from Deboullie Pond hiker parking area at end of road (1,140 ft.) to:

Tower Trail (1,140 ft.) via Deboullie Loop Trail	1.4 mi.	50 ft.	0:40
Deboullie Mtn. summit and fire tower (1,975 ft.)	2.1 mi.	885 ft.	1:30

MBPL Tower Trail climbs from the north shore of Deboullie Pond to the summit fire tower on Deboullie Mtn. It leaves from Deboullie Loop Trail at a point 1.4 mi. west of the Deboullie Pond trailhead.

From Deboullie Pond, Tower Trail ascends a rock staircase, crosses a footbridge, and climbs more rock steps. The grade is moderate all the way to the ridge, which is gained at 0.4 mi. Walk easily west and then make a steep, rocky climb, winding up the slope on switchbacks. At the base of another rock staircase, a view window yields a look to the northeast. Just above, the angle eases, and the trail climbs the final rock staircase to the summit fire tower in a small clearing atop Deboullie Mtn.

WHITMAN MTN. (1,810 FT.)
In the southeast corner of Deboullie PL, the wooded ridge of Whitman Mtn. extends from Perch Pond northeast to Pushineer Pond. Several outlooks on the mountain offer views of Deboullie Pond, Deboullie Mtn., and Black Mtn. Whitman Ridge Trail traverses the ridge. Combine Whitman Ridge Trail with Whitman Valley Trail and a section of Deboullie Loop Trail for a loop hike.

WHITMAN RIDGE TRAIL (AMC DEBOULLIE PUBLIC LANDS MAP)
Cumulative from Whitman Mtn. trailhead (1,250 ft.) to:

Whitman Valley Trail (1,500 ft.)	0.5 mi.	250 ft.	0:20
Whitman Mtn. summit (1,815 ft.)	1.8 mi.	555 ft.	1:10
Deboullie Loop Trail (1,150 ft.)	2.7 mi.	555 ft.	1:40

MBPL From the Whitman Mtn. trailhead on the Deboullie access road, Whitman Ridge Trail heads north and in 0.2 mi. crosses Denny Pond Rd. The trail follows an old woods road that ascends easily up to a jct. at 0.5 mi. Here, Whitman Valley Trail goes straight, while Whitman Ridge Trail continues to the right, up rock steps. After a short, moderate climb, the trail turns right onto another old woods road. In another 0.1 mi., it bears left off the road onto a footpath. At 0.75 mi., make a moderate climb up rock stairs and then head south along the edge of the ridge. Reach Perch

SEC 12

Pond Overlook and a bench on the right at 0.8 mi. Crest the ridge of Whitman Mtn. at 1.0 mi. in a small open area.

Follow the undulating ridge northeast, traversing the wooded high point on Whitman Mtn. at 1.8 mi., where a bench offers a view west to the talus slope of Gardner Mtn. above Gardner Pond. Descend beyond the bench. At 2.2 mi., a vantage point on the left looks north to Deboullie Mtn., its tower, and Black Mtn. Descend steep switchbacks to another bench (similar views). Continue the descent of Whitman Mtn. and reach the jct. with Deboullie Loop Trail at 2.7 mi. To the left, Deboullie Loop Trail leads 2.0 mi. to Whitman Valley Trail, a good option for a loop hike. To the right, Deboullie Loop Trail leads 0.2 mi. to its end at the access road to Red River Camps.

WHITMAN VALLEY TRAIL (AMC DEBOULLIE PUBLIC LANDS MAP)
From Deboullie Loop Trail (1,180 ft.) to:

Whitman Ridge Trail (1,500 ft.)	1.5 mi.	320 ft.	0:55

MBPL Whitman Valley Trail extends from Deboullie Loop Trail near the west end of Deboullie Pond south to Whitman Ridge Trail, 0.5 mi. north of the Whitman Mtn. trailhead on the Deboullie access road. From Deboullie Loop Trail, follow Whitman Valley Trail south on an easy grade along a brook. At 0.4 mi., bear right away from the brook and soon pass a swampy area on the left. At 0.8 mi., with a beaver bog on the left, swing away (west) to the base of a mossy cliff face. Hike along the cliff base, sometimes under overhanging rock, for the next 0.3 mi. Eventually, trend away from the cliff to join an old woods road. Turn right and head gradually downhill to the jct. of Whitman Ridge Trail at 1.5 mi. The Whitman Mtn. trailhead on the Deboullie access road is 0.5 mi. straight ahead.

CRATER TRAIL (AMC DEBOULLIE PUBLIC LANDS MAP)
Cumulative from Whitman Mtn. trailhead (1,250 ft.) to:

High point on ridge (1,578 ft.)	0.5 mi.	325 ft.	0:25
Gardner Loop Trail (1,240 ft.)	1.7 mi.	325 ft.	1:00
Togue Pond trailhead (1,200 ft.)	2.0 mi.	325 ft.	1:10

MBPL Crater Trail climbs west to several craggy outlooks before circling pretty Crater Pond. The trail begins as a wide, grassy path at the Whitman Mtn. trailhead and enters the woods at a point 25 ft. left of the kiosk and Whitman Ridge Trail. On the level at first, Crater Trail climbs gradually, then moderately, and then steeply on switchbacks to the ridge above, which features a view north to Denny Pond, the cliffs around Denny Pond and Galilee Pond, and the Deboullie Mtn. fire tower. Descend to a notch, and then ascend via two log staircases to a bench at 0.5 mi. (view south to Togue Pond). Climb to the apex of the ridge and descend to a saddle. Follow the undulating ridge and descend a short, steep pitch. Cross a streamlet, climb up and left along the base of a great cliff face, cross another small stream, and walk beneath a mossy cliff wall. At 1.6 mi., the trail travels below a huge vertical cliff wall. Reach Crater Pond and thread through the mossy boulders along the west shore. Impressive cliffs and talus fields are visible up to the right. Soon bear right, away from the pond, to reach Gardner Loop Trail at 1.9 mi. Turn left to reach the Togue Pond trailhead on the Deboullie access road in another 0.3 mi.

GARDNER MTN. (SOUTH PEAK 1,822 FT., NORTH PEAK 1,843 FT.)

The wooded south–north ridge of this mountain extends from Togue Pond to Gardner Pond in the south-central section of Deboullie PL. Rugged cliffs and talus slopes characterize the peak's north side, which faces wild and scenic Gardner Pond. Gardner Loop Trail makes a circuit over the mountain and around the pond.

GARDNER LOOP TRAIL (AMC DEBOULLIE PUBLIC LANDS MAP)
Cumulative from Togue Pond trailhead (1,200 ft.) to:

Gardner Mtn., south peak (1,822 ft.)	1.4 mi.	625 ft.	1:00
Gardner Mtn., north peak (1,843 ft.)	1.8 mi.	750 ft.	1:20
Side trail to Gardner Point Shelter on Gardner Pond (1,135 ft.)	2.6 mi.	750 ft.	1:40
Deboullie Loop Trail (1,140 ft.)	5.4 mi.	1,000 ft.	3:15
Complete loop (via south fork of Waterfall Loop Trail on Gardner Mtn.)	8.9 mi.	1,650 ft.	5:20

From Togue Pond trailhead (1,200 ft.) to:

Complete loop (via north fork of Waterfall Loop Trail on Gardner Mtn.)	9.3 mi.	1,750 ft.	5:35

MBPL From the Togue Pond trailhead on the Deboullie access road, follow an old woods road north. At 0.15 mi., turn left off the road onto a foot trail. At 0.25 mi., Crater Trail departs to the right. Stay left on Gardner Loop Trail and ascend gradually to the base of Gardner Mtn. The steep climbing begins at 0.4 mi. as the trail switchbacks up the slope, eventually passing to the right of a rock wall. The angle eases, and the trail arrives at a view on the right at 0.6 mi. that looks east over Crater Pond. Continue to a bench and a view that includes Togue Pond as well as Crater Pond. Climb ahead; then descend a steep slope. Proceed at an easy-to-moderate grade up the

SEC 12

ridge, hike very briefly on an old woods road, and then turn left to go beneath a mossy cliff face. Wind up the west side of the peak to reach the wooded south summit of Gardner Mtn. at 1.4 mi. Descend the north side to reach the jct. with the south fork of Waterfall Loop Trail, which enters from the right at 1.5 mi. Traverse the saddle separating the two peaks and climb to the wooded north summit of Gardner Mtn., reaching it at 1.8 mi. Cross the ridgeline to the next jct. at 2.0 mi., where the north fork of Waterfall Loop Trail enters from the right. Bear left here to continue on Gardner Loop Trail in a clockwise direction.

Make a moderate descent off the north side of the mountain. From a shelf partway down, enjoy a look at Gardner Pond below. Reach the base of the mountain and a jct. at 2.6 mi., where a spur on the right leads 0.15 mi. to Gardner Point Shelter on Gardner Pond, which provides an excellent view of the Gardner Mtn. rock slide.

From the shelter jct., the trail soon reaches the shore of Gardner Pond and a huge grove of old-growth cedars. It crosses a small stream on the west side of the pond, bears left away from the pond, and crosses a footbridge. It then returns to the pond and turns left to traverse an earthen berm through a cedar swamp. After the swamp, the trail makes a moderate-to-steep ascent away from Gardner Pond to a high point on the north side of the pond at 3.8 mi. Ahead, follow an undulating route across the steep slope of the hillside before descending a rock staircase. Skirt a beaver pond and continue down to the north shore of Gardner Pond. Gardner Loop Trail then climbs a mossy gully of rocks to reach an unmarked jct., where a side path on the right leads 500 ft. to Gardner North CS on Gardner Pond. Just beyond this jct., a side path on the left leads 150 ft. to views south over Gardner Pond to the impressive cliffs and talus slopes on the north face of Gardner Mtn.

At 5.3 mi., Black Mtn. Trail from the top of Deboullie Mtn. enters from the left. In another 0.1 mi., Gardner Loop Trail merges with Deboullie Loop Trail, which enters from the left. The two trails coincide for the next 0.3 mi., crossing Gardner Portage Trail just ahead (this canoe carry trail connects Gardner Pond and Deboullie Pond). At a jct. at 5.7 mi., Deboullie Loop Trail follows the old tote road to the left (east). Turn right to continue on Gardner Loop Trail, which heads southwest, alternately following the old tote road and a parallel path in the woods to the left. At 6.1 mi., Denny Trail departs to the left. Turn right to stay on Gardner Loop Trail; cross a tote road and enter the woods. Ahead, alternate between the old tote road and a path in the woods to the right. Descend toward an arm of Gardner Pond. Cross an inlet and then turn north along the west side of the pond to reach a jct. at 6.8 mi.

From this jct., the forks to the left and right form Waterfall Loop Trail (as noted on the MBPL map). Turn left uphill to climb past a seasonal waterfall to reach Gardner Loop Trail in a saddle between the two summits of Gardner Mtn. in 0.6 mi.; then head south to return to the Togue Pond trailhead in another 1.5 mi. Alternatively from this jct., turn right and descend steeply to Gardner Pond. The trail then climbs steeply away from the pond for 0.5 mi. to the jct. with Gardner Loop Trail just north of the north summit of Gardner Mtn. at a point 1.9 mi. from the Togue Pond trailhead.

WATERFALL LOOP TRAIL (AMC DEBOULLIE PUBLIC LANDS MAP)
From Gardner Loop Trail on the east side of Gardner Mtn. (1,240 ft.) to:

Gardner Loop Trail on north side of Gardner Mtn., north peak via north fork (1,810 ft.)	0.6 mi.	640 ft.	0:40

From Gardner Loop Trail on the east side of Gardner Mtn. (1,240 ft.) to:

Gardner Loop Trail on south side of Gardner Mtn., north peak via south fork (1,700 ft.)	0.5 mi.	460 ft.	0:30

MBPL *North fork*: From the jct. with Gardner Loop Trail on the east side of Gardner Mtn., the north fork of Waterfall Loop Trail descends steeply to Gardner Pond and then rises steeply to a viewpoint overlooking the pond. The steep climb continues to the next viewpoint, which looks out over the pond to Deboullie Mtn. and its summit fire tower. A short distance beyond, the angle eases, and the trail leads across the level north side of the north summit of Gardner Mtn. to join Gardner Loop Trail.

South fork: From the jct. with Gardner Loop Trail on the east side of Gardner Mtn., the south fork of Waterfall Loop Trail climbs up to and across the base of a seasonal waterfall. The steep climbing continues, with several short ups and downs, on the narrow trail. Cross a small stream, and after a stretch of easier walking, ascend through a ravine beneath cliff walls. Switchback up through mossy ledges and soon reach a jct. with Gardner Loop Trail in a saddle between the two summits of Gardner Mtn.

DENNY TRAIL (AMC DEBOULLIE PUBLIC LANDS MAP)
From Gardner Loop Trail (1,220 ft.) to:

Denny Pond trailhead (1,280 ft.)	1.1 mi.	80 ft.	0:35

MBPL Denny Trail leaves from Gardner Loop Trail at a point 0.4 mi. west of its jct. with Deboullie Loop Trail and 0.7 mi. from the jct. with Gardner Portage Trail, which connects Deboullie Pond and Gardner Pond. Denny Trail follows an old woods road on a contour through a narrow valley. At 0.7 mi., a side path to the right leads to Galilee Pond, set in a wild amphitheater of impressive cliffs. Reach Denny Pond at 1.0 mi. The end of the

SEC 12

trail is just ahead at a campsite at 1.1 mi. From here, it is 0.5 mi. south via Denny Pond Rd. to the Deboullie access road.

ALLAGASH WILDERNESS WATERWAY

The AWW is a magnificent 92-mile corridor of lakes, ponds, rivers, and streams meandering northward through the heart of Maine's vast industrial forestland from Telos Lake in Piscataquis County to the town of Allagash in Aroostook County, where the Allagash River joins the St. John River. The Maine legislature established the AWW in 1966 to preserve, protect, and enhance the wilderness character of the Allagash River region. The waterway received enhanced protection in 1970 when the US Dept. of the Interior designated the AWW as the first state-administered component of the National Wild and Scenic River system. A paddling excursion along the AWW is the canoe trip of a lifetime and a Maine classic. Some 80 primitive campsites are along the route. Vehicular access to the AWW is over long distances on gravel logging roads. Two mountains with hiking trails rise amid the beauty of the AWW: Round Pond Mtn. and Allagash Mtn.

ROUND POND MTN. (1,519 FT.)

From the fire tower atop Round Pond Mtn., hikers are treated to outstanding vistas of the surrounding wild country along the upper portion of the AWW in western Aroostook County. The trailhead for Round Pond Mtn. is on the eastern shore of Round Pond in 20,000-acre Round Pond PL in T13 R12 WELS. Access to the trailhead is only by canoe or kayak, so Round Pond Mtn. is most often climbed by paddlers on the Allagash River, but day hikers can certainly enjoy the adventure as well. The nearest canoe access site is on Blanchet Rd. on the north side of Henderson Brook Bridge; designated parking for river users is just south of the bridge.

Access from the east at Ashland: From ME 11 on the west side of the Aroostook River in Ashland, turn left on Garfield Rd. In 0.5 mi., bear right on American Realty Rd., which quickly turns to gravel and soon passes through a woodyard. Proceed 5.5 mi. to NMW's Six Mile Checkpoint, where visitors must register and pay a day-use fee (and camping fee, if applicable) to enter (cash or check only). Immediately after the checkpoint, bear right to continue on American Realty Rd. Follow the road for 37.0 mi. and then turn right (north) onto Blanchet Rd. Proceed on Blanchet Rd. for 16.3 mi. to canoe access parking on the right. Henderson Brook Bridge is 0.1 mi. ahead; the canoe access site is on the far side of the bridge on the left. (For alternate travel routes to Henderson Brook Bridge, consult the *Maine Atlas and Gazetteer* and NMW's *Map of North Maine Woods*.)

From the canoe access site, paddle down the Allagash River to Round Pond and then head northeast across the pond to Tower Trail CS (sign), a distance of 2.4 mi. For hikers wishing to camp at Round Pond, there are five other sites in addition to Tower Trail: Round Pond Rips, Squirrel Pocket, Back Channel, Inlet, and Outlet. Paddlers and campers in the AWW are subject to the special rules governing this Wilderness river corridor (see maine.gov/allagash).

ROUND POND MTN. TRAIL (USGS ROUND POND AND FIVE FINGER BROOK QUADS, MBPL ALLAGASH WILDERNESS WATERWAY GUIDE & MAP, NMW MAP OF MAINE NORTH WOODS, GAZETTEER MAP 62)
From Tower Trail CS and trailhead on Round Pond (782 ft.) to:

Round Pond Mtn. summit (1,509 ft.)	2.4 mi.	730 ft.	1:35

MBPL Round Pond Mtn. Trail leaves from the back of Tower Trail CS. The footpath, unmarked but well defined, ascends gradually east before turning north, crossing two grassy old logging roads in the first 1.2 mi. Cross a small brook at 1.7 mi. and then a sturdy gravel logging road at 2.2 mi. Just beyond is the moderate but short final ascent to the large clearing on the summit. Climb the fire tower (erected in 1946; new cab installed in 2020) for extraordinary vistas over the woods and waters of the AWW, the vast forestlands beyond, and mountain peaks from Deboullie in the north to Katahdin in the south. Closer in, Round Pond dominates the southwesterly view.

ALLAGASH MTN. (1,770 FT.)
Allagash Mtn. rises prominently above the southwest shore of 4,210-acre Allagash Lake in T7 R14 WELS in northern Piscataquis County. The lake is part of the AWW system and is the headwater for the Allagash River. No direct vehicle access exists to Allagash Lake. Access by canoe or kayak is possible from the upper part of Allagash Stream or from Johnson Pond west of the lake. Access by foot is from the south via Carry Trail (a portion of which is a gated road) and Allagash Mtn. Trail.

Access from the south at Abol Bridge: From Abol Bridge over the West Branch of the Penobscot River, about 18 mi. northwest of Millinocket, drive west on Golden Rd. for 9.3 mi. Turn right (north) onto Telos Rd. and cross a bridge over the West Branch of the Penobscot River. Begin new mileage count. Follow Telos Rd. for 14.4 mi. to NMW's Telos Checkpoint, where visitors must register and pay a day-use fee (and camping fee, if applicable) to enter (cash or check only). Continue on Telos Rd., enter Telos PL at 20.9 mi., and reach a T jct. at 22.9 mi. (Chamberlain Bridge, a short distance to the right, is worth investigating). Turn left onto Guy Allen Rd. (also referred to as Umbazooksus Rd.). At 29.3 mi., turn right (north) on Grande Marche Rd. (also referred to as Trans Canada Rd.). At 39.3 mi., turn left on Ledge Rd. From here, follow signs for Loon Lodge, avoiding Old Ledge Rd. on the right at 41.7 mi. Pass the entrance to Loon Lodge on the left at 46.9 mi. Just beyond, at 47.2 mi., Round Pond CS is on the left and Allagash Mtn. Rd. is on the right. Turn right onto Allagash Mtn. Rd. and drive 2.1 mi. to a small parking area on the right just before a locked yellow gate at 49.3 mi. (For alternate travel routes to Allagash Lake, consult the *Maine Atlas and Gazetteer* and NMW's *Map of North Maine Woods*.)

ALLAGASH MTN. TRAIL (USGS ALLAGASH LAKE QUAD, MBPL ALLAGASH WILDERNESS WATERWAY GUIDE & MAP, NMW MAP OF NORTH MAINE WOODS, GAZETTEER MAP 55)
Cumulative from parking at yellow gate on Allagash Mtn. Rd. (1,090 ft.) to:

Start of Allagash Mtn. Trail (1,090 ft.)	0.8 mi.	90 ft.	0:25
Allagash Lake Ranger Station (1,038 ft.)	1.2 mi.	100 ft.	0:35
Allagash Mtn. summit (1,770 ft.)	1.9 mi.	832 ft.	1:20

MBPL Walk under the yellow gate and continue north along the gravel road. At 0.6 mi., the road narrows to a grassy tote road that enters the woods. At 0.8 mi., reach a fork. To the right, Carry Trail leads 0.4 mi. to Carry Trail CS on the south shore of Allagash Lake. Bear left to continue on Allagash Mtn. Trail, which leads to Allagash Lake Ranger Station on the lake's southwestern shore. Walk in front of the ranger station to reenter the woods and begin climbing up the eastern slope of Allagash Mtn. In typical fire warden trail style, the steady grade is moderate to steep. Scramble up the summit rock to emerge onto the open ledges around the fire tower (erected in 1924; new cab installed in 2020). The 360-degree vista from the tower, one of the finest of any mountaintop in Maine, stretches far out across the forested wildlands of northwestern Maine and includes Chamberlain Lake, Eagle Lake, and Churchill Lake to the east; the upper St. John River watershed to the west; and the upper Penobscot River watershed to the south. Mt. Chase, Katahdin, Traveler, Jo-Mary, and White Cap are particular mountain highlights.

NORTH MAINE WOODS
ROUND MTN. (2,155 FT.)
Round Mtn. is in T11 R8 WELS, about two miles southeast of Rowe Lake. Round Mtn. Pond lies at the foot of the mountain's northeast slope. Round Mtn. is the northernmost of three adjacent peaks—Round, Middle,

and Peaked—that extend in a northeast to southwest range. Peaked Mtn. (2,260 ft.) is the highest of the three but has no trail to its summit.

Access from the east at Ashland: From ME 11 on the west side of the Aroostook River in Ashland, turn left onto Garfield Rd. In 0.5 mi., bear right onto American Realty Rd., which quickly turns to gravel and soon passes through a woodyard. Proceed 5.5 mi. to NMW's Six Mile Checkpoint, where visitors must register and pay a day-use fee (and camping fee, if applicable) to enter (cash or check only). Immediately after the checkpoint, bear right to continue on American Realty Rd. Follow the road for 18.8 mi. to Rowe Lake Rd. on the left. Turn onto Rowe Lake Rd. and begin new mileage count. At a fork at 0.8 mi., bear right. At a triangle jct. at 1.9 mi., bear right. At a jct. at 2.4 mi., turn left. At 3.4 mi., where JD Dr. continues straight ahead, bear left. Turn right off Rowe Lake Rd. at 5.1 mi., and at 6.3 mi. from American Realty Rd., reach Round Mtn. Lodge (private camp) and the trailhead for Round Mtn. Out of consideration for the camp owners' privacy, please park along the road out of sight of the lodge.

ROUND MTN. TRAIL (USGS ROUND MTN. QUAD, NMW MAP OF NORTH MAINE WOODS, GAZETTEER MAP 63)
From Round Mtn. Lodge (1,313 ft.) to:

Round Mtn. summit (2,155 ft.)	0.6 mi.	842 ft.	0:45

NFTM Round Mtn. Lodge, a private camp, is the site of the former fire warden's cabin, which has since been incorporated into one of the two buildings. Round Mtn. Trail, the route of the old fire warden's trail, leaves from the back left corner of the camp lot near the covered spring. In the woods, colored flagging tape on trees marks the sometimes indistinct treadway of the trail, which climbs at a steady moderate-to-steep grade up the west slope of Round Mtn. (*Note*: Hikers will encounter blowdowns.) The trail ends at the old fire tower (erected in 1918; no cab) in a small clearing. A ruined outbuilding is nearby on the clearing's edge. The ladder of the fire tower offers an excellent scenic panorama of Katahdin to the south-southwest, Mt. Chase to the south-southeast, Horseshoe Mtn. to the west, Haystack Mtn. to the east, and Deboullie Mtn. to the north.

HORSESHOE (A.K.A. ROCKY BROOK) MTN. (2,084 FT.)
This mountain in T11 R10 WELS is part of the Rocky Brook Mountains, which rise just to the north of the Aroostook County–Piscataquis County line and east of the Musquacook chain of lakes. The extensive 360-degree vistas from the steps of the summit fire tower range north to Deboullie Mtn. and south to Katahdin. (*Caution*: The treadway of Horseshoe Mtn. Trail is not well defined, and although marked occasionally with bits of

SEC 12

colored flagging tape, the route should be attempted only by experienced hikers well versed in navigating over rough terrain using a map and compass or GPS.)

Access from the east at Ashland: From ME 11 on the west side of the Aroostook River in Ashland, turn left onto Garfield Rd. In 0.5 mi., bear right onto American Realty Rd., which quickly turns to gravel and soon passes through a woodyard. Proceed 5.5 mi. to NMW's Six Mile Checkpoint, where visitors must register and pay a day-use fee (and camping fee, if applicable) to enter (cash or check only). Immediately after the checkpoint, bear right to continue on American Realty Rd. Follow the road for 26.5 mi. to the unsigned *second* entrance to Mink Marsh Rd. on the left (the first entrance to Mink Marsh Rd. 0.2 mi. before is rough and not recommended). At 1.2 mi. from American Realty Rd., Mink Marsh Rd. curves sharply to the left and an old tote road (the trail) diverges to the right. Park at this jct., but do not block either road.

HORSESHOE MTN. TRAIL (USGS MOOSELEUK LAKE AND FIFTH MUSQUACOOK LAKE QUADS, NMW MAP OF NORTH MAINE WOODS, GAZETTEER MAP 62)
From Mink Marsh Rd. (1,268 ft.) to:

Horseshoe Mtn. summit (2,084 ft.)	1.5 mi.	816 ft.	1:15

NFTM The trail, an old woods road becoming overgrown with shrubs and trees, leads southwest. At 0.3 mi., a still-used tote road (tire tracks are visible) goes uphill to the right; continue straight ahead into thicker brush. After a small brook flows under the old road, climb gradually. At 0.6 mi., walk through a small clearing. Soon after, Horseshoe Mtn. and its summit fire tower are visible directly ahead. Push through young alder growth, and at 0.9 mi., another brook goes under the old road. Soon after, reach a shrubby clearing with a view of the mountain and a track on the right that leads uphill; avoid the track on the right and continue straight ahead for about 300 ft. to where a small intermittent stream flows across the old road. Look right for a small cairn on the ground and flagging tape on a tree. This is the start of the old fire warden's trail to the top of Horseshoe Mtn.

The route follows the drainage in a northwesterly direction and then bears west-southwest to avoid the rocky terrain and steep cliffs above before climbing directly and steeply to a sag at about 1,950 ft. on the south shoulder of the mountain. Portions of the old treadway may be visible on the lower part of the ascent. On the upper part of the climb to the sag, sections of black telephone cable may be seen as well. (When fire towers were still used for spotting fires, watchers used telephones to communicate their observations.) Colored flagging tape occasionally marks the route. In the sag, the trail turns to the north as it heads for the top; the treadway becomes more distinct and is somewhat easier to follow, although frequent blowdowns may hinder progress. The trail emerges from the woods into the summit clearing, where the fire tower (erected in 1951; no cab) and a small outbuilding stand.

NORWAY BLUFF (2,284 FT.)
Norway Bluff rises north of Munsungan Lake astride the boundary line of T9 R9 WELS and T8 R9 WELS. A radio communications facility occupies the summit, which features expansive views that include Katahdin and Traveler Mtn. in BSP. The old (1914) fire tower on top was removed and relocated to Ashland Logging Museum in 2012.

Access from the east at Ashland: From ME 11 on the west side of the Aroostook River in Ashland, turn left onto Garfield Rd. In 0.5 mi. bear right on American Realty Rd., which quickly turns to gravel and soon passes through a woodyard. Proceed 5.5 mi. to NMW's Six Mile Checkpoint, where visitors must register and pay a day-use fee (and camping fee, if applicable) to enter (cash or check only). Just beyond the checkpoint, bear left onto Pinkham Rd. At 23.2 mi. from Six Mile Checkpoint, soon after crossing Mooseleuk Stream, reach a 4-way intersection. Here, turn right on Pell and Pell Rd. (denoted as Pelletier Rd. in the *Gazetteer*) and drive 8.7 mi. to a side road (small sign for Norway Bluff) on the left. Turn onto the side road and continue 4.1 mi. to a small gravel pit on the left where there is parking.

NORWAY BLUFF TRAIL (USGS MOOSELEUK QUAD, NMW MAP OF NORTH MAINE WOODS, GAZETTEER MAP 57)
From gravel pit parking area (1,606 ft.) to:

Norway Bluff summit (2,284 ft.)	0.9 mi.	678 ft.	0:50

NFTM Facing the ridgeline of Norway Bluff, look for a cairn marking the start of the trail on a gravel bank just above the road. The trail, an old ATV track, enters the woods on the upper right edge of the gravel pit. Marked occasionally with colored flagging tape, Norway Bluff Trail climbs at a mostly steady, moderate grade over the northwest slope of the mountain to a fork, where a sign on the right states: "No Motorized Vehicles Beyond This Point." Bear right here (straight ahead, the trail leads a short distance to a radio repeater and the base of an old fire-tower-like structure; very limited views) and proceed southwesterly along the ridge on the grassy track; then scramble up the summit knob to reach the communications tower, solar array, and helipad on top. The far-reaching views to the east, south, and west are outstanding. Please heed the warning signs and do not disturb any of the equipment.

SEC 12

APPENDIX A

HELPFUL INFORMATION AND CONTACTS

Organization	Office	Phone number
Appalachian Mountain Club (AMC)	Main Office	617-523-0636 (membership, headquarters)
	Contact Service Center	603-466-2727 (reservations)
AMC Cold River Camp		603-694-3291
AMC Echo Lake Camp	Camp Managers	207-244-3747
AMC Four Thousand Footer Club		
AMC Maine Chapter		
AMC Maine Woods Initiative		207-695-3085
Acadia National Park		207-288-3338
Allagash Wilderness Waterway	Bureau of Parks and Lands, Northern Parks Region Office	207-941-4014
Appalachian Trail Conservancy (ATC)	Headquarters and Visitor Center	304-535-6331
ATC New England Regional Office		802-281-5894
Baxter State Park	Headquarters	207-723-5140 (info and reservations)
Bethel Conservation Commission c/o Town of Bethel		207-824-2669
Blue Hill Heritage Trust		207-374-5118
Camden Snow Bowl		207-236-3438
Camp Roosevelt, Boy Scouts of America Katahdin Area Council		207-866-2241
Chatham Trails Association		

Address or location	Website, email
10 City Square, Boston, MA 02129	outdoors.org, AMCmembership@outdoors.org AMClodging@outdoors.org
32 AMC Rd., N. Chatham, NH 03813	amccoldrivercamp.org
P.O. Box 219, Mt. Desert, ME 04660	amcecholakecamp.org, ELCmanagers@outdoors.org
P.O. Box 444, Exeter, NH 03833	amc4000footer.org, savage@amc4000footer.org
	amcmaine.org
166 Moosehead Lake Rd., Greenville, ME 04441	outdoors.org/destinations/maine, AMClodging@outdoors.org
P.O. Box 177, Bar Harbor, ME 04609	nps.gov/acad
106 Hogan Rd., Bangor, ME 04401	parksandlands.com
P.O. Box 807, 799 Washington St. Harpers Ferry, WV 25425	appalachiantrail.org, info@appalachiantrail.org
P.O. Box 649, Hartford, VT 05047	appalachiantrail.org
64 Balsam Dr., Millinocket, ME 04462	baxterstatepark.org
P.O. Box 1660, 19 Main St., Bethel, ME 04217	bethelmaine.org, info@bethelmaine.org
P.O. Box 222, 157 Hinckley Ridge Rd., Blue Hill, ME 04614	bluehillheritagetrust.org, info@bluehillheritagetrust.org
P.O. Box 1207, 20 Barnestown Rd., Camden, ME 04843	camdensnowbowl.com, info@camdensnowbowl.com
45 Camp Roosevelt Rd., Eddington, ME 04428	katahdinareabsa.org /CampRoosevelt
	chathamtrails.org

Organization	Office	Phone number
City of Calais		207-454-2521 x10
Clifton Climbers Alliance		
Coastal Mountains Land Trust		207-236-7091
Cobscook Shores		207-400-0015
Downeast Coastal Conservancy		207-255-4500
Downeast Lakes Land Trust		207-796-2100
Forest Society of Maine	Main Office	207-945-9200
Francis Small Heritage Trust		207-221-0853
Freeport Conservation Trust		207-865-3985 ext. 212
Frenchman Bay Conservancy		207-422-2328
Friends of Holbrook Island Sanctuary		207-326-4012
Garmin		207-846-7000
Georges River Land Trust		207-594-5166
Great Pond Mountain Conservation Trust		207-469-6929
Great Works Regional Land Trust		207-646-3604
Greater Lovell Land Trust		207-925-1056
Hebron Academy	Outdoor Education Program	207-966-2100
Hedgehog Mtn. Land Trust		
High Peaks Alliance		207-491-2750

Address or location	Website, email
P.O. Box 413, Calais, ME 04619	calaismaine.org, asstmanager@calaismaine.org
P.O. Box 1876, Bangor, ME 04401	cliftonclimbersalliance.org, info@cliftonclimbersalliance.org
101 Mt. Battie St., Camden, ME 04893	coastalmountains.org, info@coastalmountains.org
65 N. Lubec Rd., Lubec, ME 04652	cobscookshores.org, admin@cobscookshores.org
P.O. Box 760, 6 Colonial Way (Suite 3), Machias, ME 04654	downeastcoastalconservancy.org, info@downeastcoastalconservancy.org
4 Water St., Grand Lake Stream, ME 04668	downeastlakes.org, info@downeastlakes.org
115 Franklin St., 3rd Floor, Bangor, ME 04401	fsmaine.org, info@fsmaine.org
P.O. Box 414, Limerick, ME 04048	fsht.org
P.O. Box 433, 57 Depot St., Freeport, ME 04032	freeportconservationtrust.org
P.O. Box 150, 71 Tidal Falls Rd., Hancock, ME 04640	frenchmanbay.org, info@frenchmanbay.org
P.O. Box 244, 172 Indian Bar Rd., Brooksville, ME 04617	friendsofholbrookisland.org, friendofholbrookisland@gmail.com
2 DeLorme Dr., Suite A, Yarmouth, ME 04096	garmin.com/en-US/
8 North Main St., Suite 200, Rockland, ME 04841	georgesriver.org
P.O. Box 266, 77 Main St. (Heyward Bldg.), Orland, ME 04472	greatpondtrust.org, info@greatpondtrust.org
Mail: P.O. Box 151, South Berwick, ME 03908; Physical: 610 Main St., Ogunquit, ME 03907	gwrlt.org, info@gwrlt.org
P.O. Box 225, 208 Main St., Lovell, ME 04051	gllt.org, info@gllt.org
P.O. Box 309, 339 Paris Rd., Hebron, ME 04238	hebronacademy.org
P.O. Box 250, Eagle Lake, ME 04788	
P.O. Box 987, Farmington, ME 04938	highpeaksalliance.org

Organization	Office	Phone number
Hills to Sea Trail Coalition		
Inland Woods + Trails		207-200-8240
Island Heritage Trust		207-348-2455
Katahdin Woods and Waters National Monument		207-456-6001
Kennebec Estuary Land Trust		207-442-8400
Kennebec Land Trust		207-377-2848
Lake George Regional Park		207-474-1292
Land & Garden Preserve		207-276-3727
Leave No Trace Center for Outdoor Ethics		800-332-4100
Libby Hill Forest c/o Gray Community Endowment		207-657-2173
Loon Echo Land Trust		207-647-4352
Mahoosuc Land Trust		207-824-3806
Maine Appalachian Trail Club		
Maine Appalachian Trail Land Trust		207-808-2073
Maine Audubon	Gilsland Farm Audubon Center	207-781-2330
Maine Bureau of Parks and Lands	Headquarters	207-287-3821
Maine Campground Owners Association		207-782-5874
Maine Chapter of the IAT		
Maine Coast Heritage Trust	Main Office	207-729-7366

Address or location	Website, email
P.O. Box 381, Unity, ME 04988	hillstosea.org, info@hillstosea.org
14 Main St. (#1 and #7), Bethel, ME 04217	woodsandtrails.org; info@woodsandtrails.org
P.O. Box 42, 420 Sunset Rd., Deer Isle, ME 04627	islandheritagetrust.org
P.O. Box 446, Patten, ME 04765	nps.gov/kaww
P.O. Box 1128, 92 Front St., Bath, ME 04530	kennebecestuary.org, info@kennebecestuary.org
P.O. Box 261, 331 Main St., Winthrop, ME 04364	tklt.org
P.O. Box 896, Skowhegan, ME 04976	lakegeorgepark.org, infolgrp@gmail.com
P.O. Box 208, Seal Harbor, ME 04675	gardenpreserve.org, info@gardenpreserve.org
1000 North St., P.O. Box 997, Boulder, CO 80306	lnt.org, info@lnt.org
P.O. Box 1376, Gray, ME 04039	libbyhill.org, libbyhilltrails@gmail.com
8 Depot St., Suite 4, Bridgton, ME 04009	lelt.org, info@lelt.org
P.O. Box 981, 162 North Rd., Bethel, ME 04217	mahoosuc.org, info@mahoosuc.org
P.O. Box 7564, Portland, ME 04112	matc.org, info@matc.org
P.O. Box 761, Portland, ME 04104	matlt.org, srucker@matlt.org
20 Gilsland Farm Rd., Falmouth, ME 04105	maineaudubon.org, info@maineaudubon.org
22 State House Station, 18 Elkins Ln. (Harlow Bldg), Augusta, ME 04333	parksandlands.com
229 Center St., Unit 5, Auburn, ME 04210	campmaine.com
P.O. Box 320, Dresden, ME 04342	maineiat.org, coordinator@maineiat.org
1 Bowdoin Mill Island, Suite 201, Topsham, ME 04086	mcht.org, info@mcht.org

Organization	Office	Phone number
Maine Dept. of Inland Fisheries and Wildlife	Headquarters	207-287-8000
MFS Campfire Permits: Forest Protection Offices	Northern Region Headquarters, Ashland	207-435-7963
	Southern Region Headquarters, Augusta	207-624-3700
	Central Region Headquarters, Old Town	207-827-1800
	State Office	207-287-4990
Maine Huts & Trails		207-265-2400
Maine Land Trust Network	c/o Maine Coast Heritage Trust	207-729-7366
Maine Outdoor Adventure Club		
Maine State Park Campground Reservations Service		800-332-1501 (in Maine)
		207-624-9950 (outside Maine)
Maine State Police	Emergency	911
	24-hr. Regional Communications Center (RCC), Augusta	207-624-7076
	24-hr. RCC, Bangor	207-973-3700
	24-hr. RCC, Houlton	207-532-5400
Maine Trail Finder	c/o Center for Community GIS	
McPherson Timberlands/ Wilderness Realty		207-947-6970
Midcoast Conservancy		207-389-5150
Moosehorn National Wildlife Refuge		207-454-7161

Address or location	Website, email
41 State House Station, 353 Water St., Augusta, ME 04333	maine.gov/ifw, info.ifw@maine.gov maine.gov/dacf/mfs
496C Main St., Kingfield, ME 04947	mainehuts.org, info@mainehuts.org
1 Bowdoin Mill Island, Suite 201, Topsham, ME 04086	mltn.org
P.O. Box 11251, Portland, ME 04104	moac.org, info@moac.org
	maine.gov/dacf/parks/camping /reservations
	campground.reservations@maine .gov
	maine.gov/dps/msp
	mainetrailfinder.com
1182 Odlin Rd., Hermon, ME 04401	wildernessrealty.com
P.O. Box 439, 290 Route 1, Edgecomb, ME 04556	midcoastconservancy.org, info@midcoastconservancy.org
103 Headquarters Rd., Suite 1, Baring, ME 04694	fws.gov/refuge/moosehorn, fw5rw_mhnwr@fws.gov

Organization	Office	Phone number
Mt. Agamenticus Conservation Program		207-361-1102
The Nature Conservancy	Maine Field Office	207-729-5182
North Maine Woods	Main Office	207-435-6213
Northeast Harbor Village Improvement Society		
Penobscot Nation		207-817-7349 (tribal office)
Rangeley Lakes Heritage Trust		207-864-7311
Recreation.gov		877-444-6777 (reservations)
Royal River Conservation Trust		207-847-9399
Rumford Water District		207-364-8531
7 Lakes Alliance		207-495-6039
Spencer Pond Camps		207-745-1599
Sugarloaf	Marketing Director	800-843-5623
Town of Carrabassett Valley		207-235-2645 or 207-235-2646
Town of Castle Hill		207-764-3754
Town of Freeport		207-865-4743
Town of Hiram	Conservation Committee	207-625-4663
Town of Leeds		207-524-5171
Town of Sebago		207-787-2457
Town of Waterford		207-583-4403
Trails for Rangeley Area Coalition		

Address or location	Website, email
86 York St., York, ME 03909	agamenticus.org
14 Maine St., Suite 401, Brunswick, ME 04011	nature.org, naturemaine@tnc.org
P.O. Box 425, 92 Main St., Ashland, ME 04732	northmainewoods.org
P.O. Box 722, Northeast Harbor, ME 04662	
	penobscotnation.org
2424 Main St., Rangeley, ME 04970	rlht.org, info@rlht.org
	recreation.gov
P.O. Box 90, 52 North Rd., Yarmouth, ME 04096	rrct.org, info@rrct.org
25 Spruce St., Rumford, ME 04276	rumfordwaterdistrict.org
P.O. Box 250, 137 Main St., Belgrade Lakes, ME 04918	7lakesalliance.org; info@7lakesalliance.org
806 Spencer Pond Rd., Beaver Cove, ME 04441	spencerpond.com, coyoteridgeguide@gmail.com
5092 Sugarloaf Access Rd., Carrabassett Valley, ME 04947	sugarloaf.com, info@sugarloaf.com
1001 Carriage Rd., Carrabassett Valley, ME 04947	carrabassettvalley.org
P.O. Box 500, 103 Pulcifur Rd., Mapleton, ME 04757	mapleton.me/town-information /castle-hill
30 Main St., Freeport, ME 04032	freeportmaine.com
16 Nasons Way, Hiram, ME 04041	townofhiram.org/mt-cutler
P.O. Box 206, 8 Community Dr., Leeds, ME 04263	townofleeds.com, townofleeds@fairpoint.net
406 Bridgton Rd. (Route 107), Sebago, ME 04029	townofsebago.org
366 Valley Rd., Waterford, ME 04088	waterfordme.org
	facebook.com/ TrailsforRangeleyAreaCoalition, rangeleytrac@gmail.com

Organization	Office	Phone number
United States Geological Survey	Headquarters	888-392-8545
Upper Saco Valley Land Trust		603-662-0008
Western Foothills Land Trust		207-739-2124
White Mountain National Forest	Headquarters	603-536-6100
	Androscoggin Ranger District	603-466-2713
	Saco Ranger District	603-447-5448
Woodstock Conservation Commission		207-744-7667

Address or location	Website, email
12201 Sunrise Valley Dr., Reston, VA 20192	usgs.gov, usgsstore@usgs.gov
P.O. Box 2233, 111 Main St., Conway, NH 03818	usvlt.org, info@usvlt.org
P.O. Box 107, 445 Main St., Norway, ME 04268	wfltmaine.org
71 White Mountain Dr., Campton, NH 03223	fs.usda.gov/whitemountain
300 Glen Rd., Gorham, NH 03581	
33 Kancamagus Highway, Conway, NH 03818	
P.O. Box 317, 26 Monk Ave., Bryant Pond, ME 04219	woodstockmaine.org

APPENDIX B

NEW ENGLAND 4,000-FOOTERS

AMC's Four Thousand Footer Club was formed in 1957 to bring together hikers who had traveled to some of the less frequently visited sections of the White Mountains. The Four Thousand Footer Committee recognizes three lists of peaks: the White Mountain 4,000-footers, the New England 4,000-footers, and the New England Hundred Highest. Applicants for the White Mountain Four Thousand Footer Club must climb all 48 peaks in New Hampshire. To qualify for membership, a hiker must climb on foot to and from each summit on the list. The official lists of the 4,000-footers in New Hampshire, Maine, and Vermont are included at the end of this appendix. Criteria for mountains on the official list are (1) each peak must be 4,000 ft. high, and (2) each peak must rise 200 ft. above the low point of its connecting ridge with a higher neighbor. All 67 4,000-footers are reached by well-defined trails, although the paths to Owl's Head and Mt. Redington, as well as some short spur paths to other summits, are not officially maintained. Applicants for the New England Four Thousand Footer Club must also climb the 14 peaks in Maine and the 5 in Vermont. Separate awards are given to those who climb all peaks on a list in winter; to qualify as a winter ascent, the hike must not begin before the hour and minute of the beginning of winter (winter solstice) or end after the hour and minute of the end of winter (spring equinox).

If you are interested in becoming a member of one or more of the clubs, please visit amc4000footer.org or send a self-addressed, stamped envelope to the Four Thousand Footer Committee, Appalachian Mountain Club, P.O. Box 444, Exeter, NH 03833. An information packet, including application forms, will be sent to you. If you are interested in the New England Four Thousand Footer Club or the New England Hundred Highest Club, please specify this in your letter, as these lists are not routinely included in the basic information packet. After climbing each peak, please record the date of the ascent, your companions, if any, and other remarks.

On the following lists, two elevations are given in feet for each peak: the elevation from the recent LiDAR survey as interpreted by AMC cartographer Larry Garland and the elevation obtained from the 7.5 minute USGS maps, some of which are metric, requiring conversion from meters to feet. When no exact elevation is given on the USGS map, the elevation has been estimated by adding half the contour interval to the highest contour shown on the map; elevations so obtained are marked with an asterisk on the list.

4,000-FOOTERS IN NEW HAMPSHIRE

Mountain	Elevation (LiDAR)	Elevation (7½' USGS quad)	Date Climbed
1. Washington	6,288	6,288	
2. Adams	5,797	5,774	
3. Jefferson	5,713	5,712	
4. Monroe	5,369	5,384*	
5. Madison	5,363	5,367	
6. Lafayette	5,242	5,260*	
7. Lincoln	5,080	5,089	
8. South Twin	4,899	4,902	
9. Carter Dome	4,840	4,832	
10. Moosilauke	4,800	4,802	
11. Eisenhower	4,763	4,780*	
12. North Twin	4,759	4,761	
13. Bond	4,696	4,698	
14. Carrigain	4,680	4,700*	
15. Middle Carter	4,624	4,610*	
16. West Bond	4,518	4,540*	
17. Garfield	4,501	4,500*	
18. Liberty	4,457	4,459	
19. South Carter	4,445	4,430*	
20. Wildcat	4,399	4,422	
21. Hancock	4,398	4,420*	
22. South Kinsman	4,356	4,358	
23. Flume	4,329	4,328	
24. Osceola	4,328	4,340*	
25. Field	4,325	4,340*	
26. Pierce (Clinton)	4,313	4,310	
27. Willey	4,299	4,285	
28. North Kinsman	4,274	4,293	
29. Zealand	4,264	4,260*	
30. Bondcliff	4,263	4,265	

Mountain	Elevation		Date Climbed
	(LiDAR)	**($7\frac{1}{2}'$ USGS quad)**	
31. South Hancock	4,257	4,319	
32. Cabot	4,161	4,170*	
33. East Osceola	4,161	4,156	
34. North Tripyramid	4,160	4,180*	
35. Middle Tripyramid	4,135	4,140	
36. Cannon	4,083	4,100*	
37. Passaconaway	4,079	4,043	
38. Hale	4,067	4,054	
39. Wildcat D	4,060	4,050*	
40. Jackson	4,052	4,052	
41. Tom	4,048	4,051	
42. Moriah	4,047	4,049	
43. Galehead	4,029	4,024	
44. Owl's Head	4,029	4,025	
45. Whiteface	4,018	4,020*	
46. Waumbek	4,011	4,006	
47. Isolation	4,004	4,004	
48. Tecumseh	3,995**	4,003	

4,000-FOOTERS IN MAINE

Mountain	Elevation		Date Climbed
	(LiDAR)	**($7\frac{1}{2}'$ USGS quad)**	
1. Katahdin, Baxter Peak	5,267	5,268	
2. Katahdin, Hamlin Peak	4,752	4,756	
3. Sugarloaf	4,238	4,250*	
4. Crocker	4,228	4,228	
5. Old Speck	4,188	4,170*	
6. North Brother	4,143	4,151	
7. Bigelow, West Peak	4,134	4,145	

Mountain	Elevation		Date Climbed
	(LiDAR)	($7\frac{1}{2}'$ USGS quad)	
8. Saddleback	4,122	4,120	
9. Bigelow, Avery Peak	4,082	4,090*	
10. Abraham	4,050	4,050*	
11. South Crocker	4,048	4,050*	
12. Saddleback, The Horn	4,024	4,041	
13. Spaulding	4,011	4,010*	
14. Redington	4,002	4,010*	

4,000-FOOTERS IN VERMONT

Mountain	Elevation		Date Climbed
	(LiDAR)	($7\frac{1}{2}'$ USGS quad)	
1. Mansfield	4,396	4,393	
2. Killington	4,230	4,235	
3. Camel's Hump	4,078	4,083	
4. Ellen	4,083	4,083	
5. Abraham	4,013	4,006	

*No exact elevation is given on the USGS map; therefore, elevation has been estimated by adding half the contour interval to the highest contour shown on the map.

**The LiDAR survey gives Mt. Tecumseh an elevation of 3,995 ft. and reveals that neither South Hancock nor Mt. Lincoln has the requisite 200 ft. rise from its col with a higher neighbor. A more traditional GPS-based measurement performed in 2019 by the Young Surveyor's Group of the New Hampshire Land Surveyors Association gave Mt. Tecumseh an elevation of 3,997 ft. Mt. Guyot has been raised to qualifying status because the LiDAR survey indicates that it has at least a 200-ft. rise from all three of its surrounding cols. However, in 2021, the AMC Four Thousand Footer Committee made the decision to retain the current list of 48 New Hampshire peaks with no changes for the foreseeable future, at least until new USGS maps are published.

INDEX

Trail names in **bold type** indicate a detailed description found in the text.

Where multiple page references appear, bold numbering indicates the main entry or entries for the trail.

[Bracketed information] indicates which of the six maps displays the features and where, by map section letter and number.

ABOUT THE AUTHOR

Carey Michael Kish has led countless hiking, backpacking, and white-water-rafting trips in Maine. He is a registered Maine Guide and a former president and founding member of the Maine Outdoor Adventure Club. He is the author of *AMC's Best Day Hikes Along the Maine Coast* as well as *Beer Hiking New England* and is the founder and editor-in-chief of Maine Geographic, which explores the best of Maine and Mainers, from adventure and travel to beer, nature, history, culture, and more at mainegeographic.com.

ABOUT AMC IN MAINE

The Appalachian Mountain Club's Maine Chapter was founded in 1956 as the Portland chapter. Today, the chapter has more than 5,300 members and is active throughout the state of Maine. It advocates strong conservation efforts within Maine and offers its members a full range of programs and activities, including hiking, cross-country skiing, and outdoor leadership classes.

You can learn more about this chapter by visiting outdoors.org /community/chapters. To view a list of AMC activities in Maine and other parts of the Northeast, visit activities.outdoors.org.

AMC BOOKS UPDATES

AMC Books strives to keep our guidebooks as up-to-date as possible to help you plan safe and enjoyable adventures. If we learn after publishing a book that relevant trails have been relocated or that route or contact information has changed, we will post the updated information online. Before you hit the trail, visit outdoors.org/books-and-maps and click the link in the Book Updates section near the bottom of the page. While hiking, if you notice discrepancies with the trip descriptions or maps, or if you find any other errors in this book, please let us know by submitting them to amcbookupdates@outdoors.org or to Books Editor, c/o AMC, 10 City Square, Boston, MA 02129. We will verify all submissions and post key updates each month. AMC Books is dedicated to being a recognized leader in outdoor publishing. Thank you for your participation.